RELIGIOUS ENLIGHTENMENT IN THE EIGHTEENTH-CENTURY NORDIC COUNTRIES

LUND UNIVERSITY PRESS

Religious Enlightenment in the eighteenth-century Nordic countries

Reason and orthodoxy

EDITED BY
JOHANNES LJUNGBERG AND
ERIK SIDENVALL

Lund University Press

Copyright © Lund University Press 2023

While copyright in the volume as a whole is vested in Lund University Press, copyright in individual chapters belongs to their respective authors.

Lund University Press
The Joint Faculties of Humanities and Theology

LUND
UNIVERSITY
PRESS

P.O. Box 192
SE-221 00 LUND
Sweden
http://lunduniversitypress.lu.se

Lund University Press books are published in collaboration with Manchester University Press.

British Library Cataloguing-in-Publication Data
A catalogue record for this book is available from the British Library

ISBN 978-91-987404-00 hardback
ISBN 978-91-987404-24 open access

First published 2023

An electronic version of this book is also available under a Creative Commons (CC-BY-NC-ND) licence, which permits non-commercial use, distribution and reproduction provided the author(s) and Lund University Press are fully cited and no modifications or adaptations are made. Details of the licence can be viewed at https://creativecommons.org/licenses/by-nc-nd/4.0/

The publisher has no responsibility for the persistence or accuracy of URLs for any external or third-party internet websites referred to in this book, and does not guarantee that any content on such websites is, or will remain, accurate or appropriate.

Lund University Press gratefully acknowledges publication assistance from the Thora Ohlsson Foundation (Thora Ohlssons stifelse)

Typeset
by Cheshire Typesetting Ltd, Cuddington, Cheshire
Printed in Great Britain
by TJ Books Ltd, Padstow

Contents

List of figures *page* vii
Notes on contributors ix
Acknowledgements xiii
List of abbreviations xv
Map displaying the Nordic monarchies xvii

Reason and orthodoxy in the Nordic countries: an introduction
Johannes Ljungberg and Erik Sidenvall 1

Part I: Enlightenment in rural societies

1 The rural spectator: clergy as agents of Enlightenment in eighteenth-century Norway
   Arne Bugge Amundsen 33

2 Promoting individualism under the guise of uniformity: a bishop's instructions in late eighteenth-century Sweden
   Erik Sidenvall 54

3 Tuomas Ragvaldinpoika: the Finnish self-taught and disabled man as a writer of ephemeral literature
   Tuija Laine 79

4 Applications of the three-estate doctrine: Swedish local sermons and the social order, 1790–1820
   Joonas Tammela 99

Part II: Dealing with the Catholic past (and present)

5 In the midst of thick and wretched darkness: enlightened orthodoxy and the heritage of the medieval Church
   Terese Zachrisson 129

6 A problematic legacy: negotiating the medieval past in
Danish eighteenth-century church interiors
Martin Wangsgaard Jürgensen 155

7 Saints and Enlightenment: St Erik of Sweden in
eighteenth-century Swedish history-writing
Henrik Ågren 191

8 A history of its own? The Catholic era as presented in
Norwegian history-writing during the eighteenth century
Rolv Nøtvik Jakobsen 211

9 Gustav III, Enlightenment and religion: ecumenical
visions and Catholicizing strategies
Yvonne Maria Werner 230

Part III: Milestones of Enlightenment challenged

10 Melancholy diagnostics: on pietist introspection and
forensic psychiatry *in statu nascendi*
Tine Reeh and Ralf Hemmingsen 263

11 Changing practices of censorship: the Faculty of
Theology at the University of Copenhagen, 1738–1770
Jesper Jakobsen and Lars Cyril Nørgaard 287

12 Sabbath crimes in a city of Enlightenment: religious and
commercial (dis)order in eighteenth-century Altona
Johannes Ljungberg 312

13 A commercial alliance between agents of Enlightenment:
Struensee's statecraft and the Moravian Brethren
Christina Petterson 341

14 New medical knowledge in the parish: mass vaccinations
in rural Finland, 1802–1825
Esko M. Laine 364

Epilogue: the piety of Enlightenment – much more than
rationalism
Anders Jarlert 394

Index 411

Figures

Map displaying the Nordic monarchies, 1719–1809		page xvii
5.1	Sketch of a sculpture of St Olaf, from Carl Linnaeus' *Skånska resa*, 1751. Photo: The National Library of Sweden.	130
5.2	Remnants of a Marian tabernacle shrine from Norra Fågelås parish church, early fifteenth century. Photo: Lennart Karlsson, Swedish Historical Museum.	141
6.1	Interior of the church of Bellinge on the island of Funen. Medieval and post-medieval furnishings and decorations side by side. Photo: Arnold Mikkelsen.	160
6.2	Krogstrup Church on Zealand with the sacristy and chapel attached to the chancel. Photo: National Museum of Denmark.	162
6.3	St Dionysius from Ejsing Church in western Jutland, c. 1500. Photo: Arnold Mikkelsen.	165
6.4	Plaque from 1671 above the figure of St Dionysius in Ejsing Church, western Jutland. Photo: Arnold Mikkelsen.	166
6.5	The retable from c. 1500 in Hald Church in eastern Jutland. Photo: National Museum of Denmark.	169
6.6	The altarpiece in Borbjerg Church, western Jutland. Photo: Arnold Mikkelsen.	170
6.7	One of the painted angels from around 1750–1775 in Greve Church. Photo: National Museum of Denmark.	174
6.8	Altar decoration in Magleby Church on Zealand, painted c. 1750–1775. Photo: author's own.	175
6.9	The retable from 1756 in Maria Magdalene Church in eastern Jutland. Photo: Kristian Hude (1908).	176
6.10	The cleansed, white interior of Melby Church with the pulpit from c. 1820, altarpiece from 1916 and pews from 1927. Photo: Arnold Mikkelsen.	183

6.11 The interior of Vonsild Church in Jutland. Photo: National Museum of Denmark. 185
9.1 King Gustav III guided by Pope Pius VI in the Vatican sculpture gallery, painted by Bénigne Gagneraux. Photo: National Museum of Sweden. 237
9.2 King Gustav III attending Christmas mass in St. Peter's Cathedral, painted by Louis Jean Desprez. Photo: National Museum of Sweden. 238
12.1 Sketch of Altona listing the minority churches among the noteworthy buildings of the town. From C. G. Dilleben, *Geometrischer Grundriss von der Stadt Altona*, in *Frederik den Femtes Atlas*, vol. 29, repr. 76, 1745. Photo: The Royal Library in Copenhagen. 320
12.2 Copper engraving of Altona listing the minority churches among the noteworthy buildings of the town, from C. Praetorius, *Grund-Riss der Stadt Altona*, 1780. Photo: The Royal Library in Copenhagen. 321

Contributors

Henrik Ågren is a Professor of History at Uppsala University, Sweden. Among his different areas of research, a key focus is early modern Swedish social and cultural history. Within this field, his English-language publications include 'Causes of change in early modern Swedish history writing: a medieval saint king viewed by Reformation and Enlightenment era historians', *Storia della Storiografia*, 72 (2013), and 'Gustav Vasa and the Erikmas in Uppsala: a question of the source for political symbolic value', in Steffen Hope and others (eds), *Life and Cult of Cnut the Holy: The First Royal Saint of Denmark* (Odense: Syddansk Universitetsforlag, 2019).

Arne Bugge Amundsen is Professor of Cultural History at the University of Oslo. Recent publications include 'The Nordic Zion: the coronation of Christian III, King of Denmark–Norway, in 1537' and 'Christiania – Jerusalem or Babel? Conflicts on religious topography in seventeenth-century Norway', both in Eivor Andersen Oftestad and Joar Haga (eds), *Tracing the Jerusalem Code* (Berlin and Boston: De Gruyter, 2021). See also 'The Middle Ages in the construction of nineteenth-century Norway', in Jürg Glauser and others (eds), *Myth, Magic, and Memory in Early Scandinavian Narrative Culture* (Turnhout: Brepols, 2021).

Ralf Hemmingsen is an Emeritus Professor of Psychiatry at the University of Copenhagen, where he served as Vice-Chancellor between 2005 and 2017. His recent contributions to the field of history include 'Common sense, no magic: a case study of female child murderers in the eighteenth century', *Sjuttonhundratal: Nordic Journal for Eighteenth-Century Studies*, 15 (2018), and 'Var hun from eller sindssyg?', *Kirkehistoriske Samlinger* (2019).

Jesper Jakobsen is a post-doctoral researcher at the Centre for Privacy Studies, University of Copenhagen, and the division for Book History, Lund University. Recent publications include 'Commercial newspaper and public shame pole: exposure of individuals in the Copenhagen gazette "Adresseavisen" 1759–73', in Sari Nauman and Helle Vogt (eds), *Private/Public in Eighteenth-Century Scandinavia* (London: Bloomsbury, 2022).

Rolv Nøtvik Jakobsen holds a doctorate in theology from the University of Oslo and is an independent scholar based in Norway. His recent works include *Gunnerus og nordisk vitenskapshistorie* (Oslo: Scandinavian Academic Press, 2015) and 'Toleration, anti-Catholicism and Protestantism: Ludvig Holberg and the eighteenth century politics of religious toleration', in Silvert Angel and others (eds), *Were We Ever Protestants? Essays in Honour of Tarald Rasmussen* (Berlin: De Gruyter, 2019).

Anders Jarlert is a Senior Professor of Church History at Lund University, Sweden. Recent studies include the edited volume *Spiritual and Ecclesiastical Biographies: Research, Results, and Reading* (Stockholm: Kungliga Vitterhets- historie- och antikvitetsakademien, 2017) and 'De-sacralisation and new "Sacralisation" of religious buildings', *Kirchliche Zeitgeschichte*, 31 (2018).

Martin Wangsgaard Jürgensen holds a doctorate in theology and is an editor at the ongoing multi-volume publication project *Danmarks Kirker* ('The churches of Denmark'), published by the National Museum of Denmark. He recently published *Ritual and Art Across the Danish Reformation: Changing Interiors of Village Churches, 1450–1600* (Turnhout: Brepols, 2018). He is currently working on a volume about the role played by the cult of saints in Denmark from the Middle Ages to the present day.

Esko M. Laine is an Associate Professor in Church History at the University of Helsinki and at the University of Eastern Finland. Recent publications include 'Pietism as a way to self in early modern Finland', in Otfried Czaika and Wolfgang Undorf (eds), *Schwedische Buchgeschichte: Zeitalter der Reformation und Konfessionalisierung* (Göttingen: Vandenhoeck & Ruprecht, 2021).

Tuija Laine is an Associate Professor in Church and Book History at the University of Helsinki and at the University of Eastern Finland.

Her most recent publications include 'Literacy, schooling and the role of common people in the educational field in Finland in the eighteenth century', in Merethe Roos and others (eds), *Exploring Textbooks and Cultural Change in Nordic Education 1536–2020* (Leiden: Brill, 2021) and 'Motivation to read? Reading among the upper class children in Finland during the 17th and 18th centuries', *Knygotyra*, 76 (2021).

Johannes Ljungberg is a post-doctoral researcher at the Centre for Privacy Studies, University of Copenhagen. His most recent publications include the volume *Tracing Private Conversations: Talking in Everyday Life*, co-edited together with Natacha Klein Käfer (London: Palgrave Macmillan, forthcoming in 2023), and 'Talking in private – and keeping it private: protecting conversations from exposure in Swedish Pietism investigations, 1721–29', in Sari Nauman and Helle Vogt (eds), *Private/Public in Eighteenth-Century Scandinavia* (London: Bloomsbury, 2022).

Lars Cyril Nørgaard is a Senior Lecturer in Church History at the University of Copenhagen. He recently published 'Copie ou Création? Les petits livres secrets de Madame de Maintenon', in Mathieu da Vinha and Nathalie Grande (eds), *Toute la cour était étonnée: Madame de Maintenon ou l'ambition politique au féminin, actes du colloque* (Rennes: Presses Universitaires de Rennes, 2022). Together with Michaël Green and Mette Birkedal Bruun, he is the editor of *Early Modern Privacy: Sources and Approaches* (Leiden: Brill, 2021).

Christina Petterson holds a PhD in Cultural Studies from Macquarie University, Australia. She is an independent scholar specializing in the role of Christianity in social change. Recent publications include *The Moravian Brethren in a Time of Transition: A Socio-Economic Analysis of a Religious Community in Eighteenth Century Saxony* (Leiden: Brill, 2021) and the anthology (co-edited together with Felicity Jensz) *Legacies of David Cranz's 'Historie von Grönland' (1765): Christianities in the Trans-Atlantic World* (London: Palgrave Macmillan, 2021).

Tine Reeh is an Associate Professor in Church History at the University of Copenhagen. She is co-editor of *Crossroads of Heritage and Religion: Legacy and Sustainability of World-Heritage-Site Moravian Christiansfeld* (New York: Berghahn,

2022). She wrote her forthcoming monograph *Unintended Secularization? Theological Agents in the Abolition of Mosaic Law in Western Scandinavia* as the holder of one of the prestigious Carlsberg Monograph Fellowships.

Erik Sidenvall is Adjunct Professor of Church History, Lund University, Sweden. In addition to early modern history, his main area of research is twentieth-century European religious history. His recent contributions include 'Local contexts of interpreting a Cold War relationship: Pommersche Landeskirche and Växjö Diocese, 1975–1989', *Kirchliche Zeitgeschichte* 33 (2021), and 'Förnuftskritik och teologiskt motiverad sakkritik: ett bidrag till förståelsen av frihetstidens historieskrivning', *Historisk Tidskrift*, 133 (2019).

Joonas Tammela is a PhD candidate in History at the University of Jyväskylä, Finland. He has published articles on the uses of sermons as historical sources.

Yvonne Maria Werner is a Senior Professor of History at Lund University, Sweden. Her recent works include 'Concepts, ideas, and practices of masculinity in Catholicism and Protestantism around 1900', in Daniel Gerster and Michael Krüggeler (eds), *God's Own Gender? Masculinities in World Religions* (Würzburg: Ergon-Verlag, 2018), and 'Gender and religion', in Toyin Falola and Mohammed Bashir Salau (eds), *Handbook of Religious Culture in Nineteenth-Century Europe* (Berlin: De Gruyter, 2022).

Terese Zachrisson is a post-doctoral researcher at the University of Gothenburg. Her English publications include 'Visiting holy wells in seventeenth-century Sweden: the case of St. Ingemo's Well in Dala', in Celeste Ray (ed.), *Sacred Waters: A Cross-Cultural Compendium of Hallowed Springs and Holy Wells* (Abingdon: Routledge, 2020) and 'The saint in the woods: semi-domestic shrines in rural Sweden, c. 1500–1800', in Salvador Ryan (ed.), *Domestic Devotions in Medieval and Early Modern Europe* (Basel: MDPI, 2019).

Acknowledgements

This volume was conceived under the ominous cloud of a global pandemic. In April 2020 we had planned to gather a select group of scholars working on various aspects of Nordic eighteenth-century religion in Farfa outside Rome, Italy, to create a joint inventory of perspectives and resources. As organizers, we were not at first greatly concerned by the news of a virus gradually spreading from China. When we became aware of the tragic and sudden spread of the disease in northern Italy, we began to realize that our anticipated meeting of minds was in serious jeopardy. In the end, of course, we were forced to cancel the entire event.

After a digital conversation among the intended participants of the meeting, we decided to make a joint effort to produce an edited volume which would explore the theme of 'Enlightenment and Lutheran confessional culture' in the Nordic countries. The comparatively mild COVID-19 restrictions in Sweden allowed some of us to gather in Ystad in the far south of the country in early October 2020, a meeting generously sponsored by Riksbankens Jubileumsfond (the Bank of Sweden Tercentenary Foundation). Other contributors were present digitally. This get-together was subsequently followed by additional digital seminars organized among the group of contributors.

As editors, we would like to express our gratitude to all those who have contributed chapters to this book. Without their continued enthusiasm for this project, our work would have been much more difficult. Working together with a group of colleagues who have always prioritized responding to our various suggestions, emails and comments made the entire process of producing a complete typescript into an enjoyable experience. In addition, we have greatly benefited from the insightful comments offered by Professor Pasi Ihalainen at the University of Jyväskylä, Finland. We would also like to thank the two anonymous peer reviewers commissioned by

Lund University Press for their generous and constructive comments on the typescript.

We are deeply indebted to the editorial committee of Lund University Press for their willingness to include this volume in their prestigious line of publishing. Throughout the entire process, the Lund University Press director, Professor Marianne Thormählen, has been more than generous with her time, offering both advice and perceptive remarks. The care and professionalism of the people at Manchester University Press, especially Alun Richards, have turned the last legs of this journey into an enjoyable experience. The editors and publisher are also extremely grateful to Joe Haining of Blenheim Editorial for superb copy-editing conducted with great patience and unflappable cheerfulness.

Johannes Ljungberg and Erik Sidenvall
Editors
Copenhagen and Lund, June 2023

Abbreviations

GSA	Göteborgs stifts arkiv, Gothenburg (Gothenburg Diocesan Archive)
KB	Kungliga biblioteket, Stockholm (The Royal Library, Stockholm)
KFBA	Kaarle Fr. Berghin arkisto (Kaarle Fr. Berghin's Archive)
KH	Kansallisarkisto, Helsinki (The Finnish National Archive, Helsinki)
KHä	Kansallisarkisto, Hämeenlinna (The Finnish National Archive, Hämeenlinna)
KJ	Kansallisarkisto, Joensuu (The Finnish National Archive, Joensuu)
KJy	Kansallisarkisto, Jyväskylä (The Finnish National Archive, Jyväskylä)
KM	Kansallisarkisto, Mikkeli (The Finnish National Archive, Mikkeli)
KO	Kansallisarkisto, Oulu (The Finnish National Archive, Oulu)
KT	Kansallisarkisto, Turku (The Finnish National Archive, Turku)
KV	Kansallisarkisto, Vaasa (The Finnish National Archive, Vaasa)
LSH	Landesarchiv Schleswig-Holstein, Schleswig (Schleswig-Holstein County Archive)
MSA	Malmö stadsarkiv, Malmö (Malmö City Archive)
NQJP	Nils Quiding Jönssons predikosamling (Nils Quiding Jönsson's collection of sermons)
ONS	Olof Nordenströms samling (Olof Nordenström's collection)
RG	Riksarkivet, Gothenburg (The Swedish National Archive, Gothenburg)

RÖ	Riksarkivet, Östersund (The Swedish National Archive, Östersund)
RV	Riksarkivet, Vadstena (The Swedish National Archive, Vadstena)
SAr	Statens arkiver, Copenhagen (The Danish National Archives)
SKHS	Suomen kirkkohistoriallisen seuran arkisto (Archive of the Finnish Church History Society)
TTA	Turun tuomiokapitulin arkisto (Turku Diocesan Chapter Archive)
UUB	Uppsala universitetsbibliotek (Uppsala University Library)

Map displaying the Nordic monarchies, 1719–1809

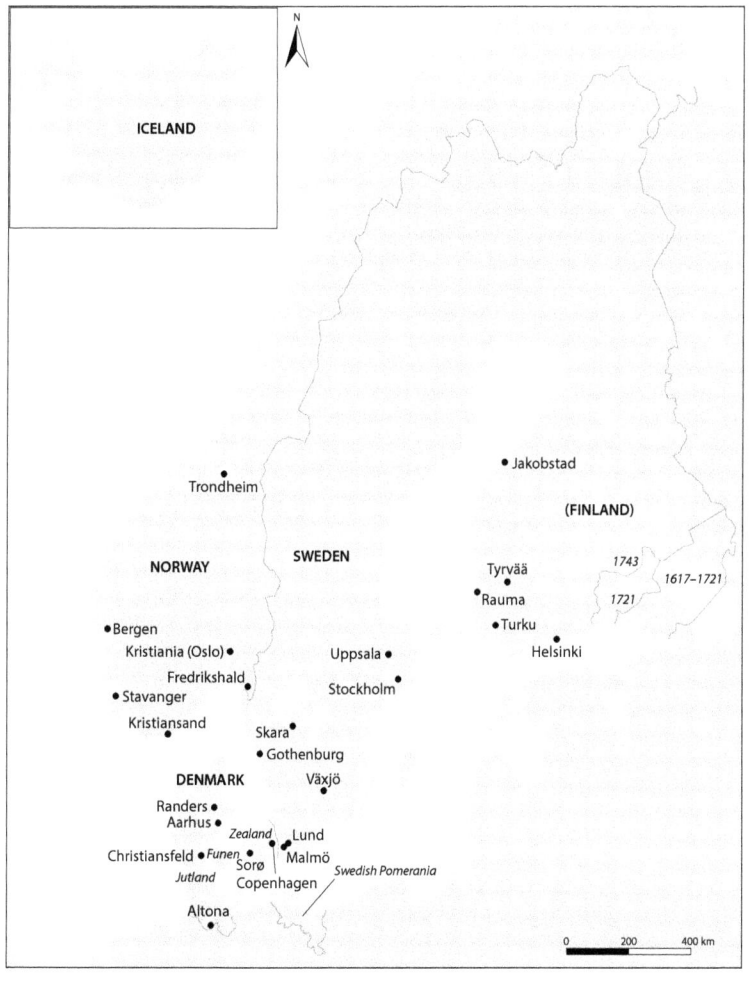

Reason and orthodoxy in the Nordic countries: an introduction

Johannes Ljungberg and Erik Sidenvall

No volume dealing with religion in eighteenth-century Europe can avoid commenting on the relationship between Enlightenment and religion. Until the early 1990s, most scholars tended to take an antagonistic relationship between the two for granted. The Enlightenment, with its emphasis on empirical knowledge, reason, freedom and utility, the cradle of modern society, has customarily been portrayed as being in radical opposition to religion as such, and especially the powerful religious institutions upholding an *ancien régime*. Voltaire's (1694–1778) famous exhortation *Écrasez l'infâme!* has often been quoted in order to illustrate the attitude towards religion that was evinced by all leading proponents of Enlightenment.

Since around 2000, this simplistic view has increasingly been called into question.[1] A 'religious turn' in Enlightenment studies is now well under way. This revision within the field of eighteenth-century historiography rests on a reconsideration of at least two conceptual propositions that have previously been taken for granted. First, should 'Enlightenment' be understood in the singular and with a capital 'E'? We need only think of Peter Gay's famous statement that 'there were many philosophers in the eighteenth century, but there was only one Enlightenment'.[2] Yet after the appearance of various volumes produced by, for example, Roy Porter, J. G. A. Pocock and Mikuláš Teich, such a view now seems increasingly

---

1 For an authoritative guide to Enlightenment historiography, see John Robertson, *The Case for the Enlightenment – Scotland and Naples, 1680–1760* (Cambridge: Cambridge University Press, 2007), pp. 1–44.
2 Peter Gay, *The Enlightenment: An Interpretation*, I: *The Rise of Modern Paganism* (New York: Norton, 1966), p. 3.

dated.[3] Instead of imagining a unified movement sweeping across Europe and North America, with varying degrees of success, most contemporary research has tended to emphasize the local character of the Enlightenment. Hence, the number of Enlightenments has rapidly multiplied. There were Scottish, Swiss, Austrian, American and numerous other Enlightenments, all with a unique 'dialect'. 'Enlightenment' was thus a transnational phenomenon with a steady flow of core texts, practices and techniques that travelled across geographical borders. However, national preoccupations and ambitions, as well as diverse political and intellectual cultures, added local flavours to the omnipresent concepts 'reason' and 'scientific enquiry'. Secondly, the French Enlightenment, once seen as the given point of reference, has increasingly been identified as a 'special case'. In other words, the French radical, sceptical and profoundly anti-clerical Enlightenment that once occupied the centre stage has been provincialized. Advanced French voices are no longer regarded as providing the template of the Enlightenment, the standard by which all other expressions of Enlightenment are eventually to be measured. Such a historiographical move does not only relate to our understanding of the centres and peripheries of eighteenth-century Europe; it has also had a profound impact on our understanding of the relationship between Enlightenment and religion. Once French Enlightenment, with its opposition to organized religion, has been pushed aside, this shift creates room for a renewed and constructive scholarly engagement with theology as a vehicle of Enlightenment, and with the churches (and various religious groups) as instruments of reform. Consequently, eighteenth-century religion has become 'increasingly central to historians' understanding of the way in which eighteenth-century society functioned', to borrow the words of John Gascoigne.[4]

---

3 Roy Porter and Mikuláš Teich (eds), *The Enlightenment in National Context* (Cambridge: Cambridge University Press, 1981); J. G. A. Pocock, *Barbarism and Religion*, 6 vols (Cambridge: Cambridge University Press, 1999–2015); J. G. A. Pocock, 'Historiography and enlightenment: a view of their history', *Modern Intellectual History*, 5:1 (2008), 83–96. See also Richard Butterwick, Simon Davies and Gabriel Sánchez Espinosa (eds), *Peripheries of the Enlightenment* (Oxford: Voltaire Foundation, 2008).
4 John Gascoigne, 'Anglican Latitudinarianism, rational dissent and political radicalism in the late eighteenth century', in Knud Haakonssen (ed.), *Enlightenment and Religion: Rational Dissent in Eighteenth-Century Britain* (Cambridge: Cambridge University Press, 1996), p. 219.

Introduction: reason and orthodoxy

Since the 1990s, studies dealing with the intricate relationship between religion and Enlightenment have proliferated.[5] When attempting to pinpoint the nature of national/local Enlightenments, religion has frequently been put forward as contributing to their distinctive flairs. As Jonathan Sheehan has remarked, 'religion was the dominant qualification of the *kind* of Enlightenment peculiar to distinct geographical areas'.[6] Presbyterianism directed the course of Enlightenment in Scotland,[7] reform Catholicism

---

5 For a particularly rich multi-authored volume gathering many of the experts in the field, see William J. Bulman and Robert G. Ingram (eds), *God in the Enlightenment* (Oxford: Oxford University Press, 2016). See also Thomas Ahnert, *The Moral Culture of the Scottish Enlightenment* (New Haven, CT: Yale University Press, 2013); Thomas Ahnert, *Religion and the Origins of the German Enlightenment: Faith and the Reform of Learning in the Thought of Christian Thomasius* (Rochester, NY: University of Rochester Press, 2006); Nigel Aston, *Christianity and Revolutionary Europe, 1750–1830* (Cambridge: Cambridge University Press, 2003); S. J. Barnett, *Enlightenment and Religion: The Myths of Modernity* (Manchester: Manchester University Press, 2003); David A. Bell, *The Cult of the Nation in France: Inventing Nationalism, 1680–1800* (Cambridge, MA: Harvard University Press, 2001); Johannes van den Berg (ed.), *Religious Currents and Crosscurrents: Essays on Early Modern Protestantism and the Protestant Enlightenment* (Leiden: Brill, 1999); Albrecht Beutel and Martha Nooke (eds), *Religion und Aufklärung* (Tübingen: Mohr Siebeck, 2016); Michael Brown, *The Irish Enlightenment* (Cambridge, MA: Harvard University Press, 2016); Jefferey D. Burson, 'Reflections on the pluralization of Enlightenment and the notion of theological Enlightenment as process', *French History*, 26:4 (2012), 524–37; David Sorkin, *A Wise, Enlightened and Reliable Piety: The Religious Enlightenment in Central and Western Europe 1689–1789* (Southampton: University of Southampton, 2002); David Sorkin, *Moses Mendelssohn and the Religious Enlightenment* (Berkeley, CA: University of California Press, 1996). Dale K. Van Kley, *The Religious Origins of the French Revolution: From Calvin to the Civil Constitution, 1560–1791* (New Haven, CT: Yale University Press, 1996); Nathaniel Wolloch (ed.), 'New perspectives on the Mediterranean Enlightenment', *European Legacy* 25:7/8 (2020). An early discussion of the religious antecedents of the Enlightenment in France is presented in Robert Mauzi, *L'idée du bonheur dans la littérature et la pensée françaises au XVIIIe siècle* (Geneva and Paris: Albin Michel, 1979).
6 Jonathan Sheehan, 'Enlightenment, religion, and the enigma of secularization: a review essay', *American Historical Review*, 108:4 (2003), 1066–80 (1066). This is probably the reason why various manifestations of Protestant Enlightenment are treated as separate phenomena; see, for example, Ritchie Robertson, *The Enlightenment: The Pursuit of Happiness, 1680–1790* (London: Allen Lane, 2020), pp. 157–82.
7 Ahnert, *The Moral Culture*.

in Austria,⁸ and in the Nordic countries there was, hardly surprisingly, a Lutheran Enlightenment.⁹ There is no shortage of examples.

Specialist historians of various kinds have pushed these insights even further. Advocacy of many of the features that we tend to associate with the Enlightenment – such as novel educational ideals and a more egalitarian social order – were in fact already to be found among reforming religious groups, for example Jansenists and Pietists, in the late seventeenth century.¹⁰ Indeed, several scholars have found the cornerstones of the French anti-clerical Enlightenment hidden within radical expressions of

---

8 David Sorkin, *The Religious Enlightenment: Protestants, Jews, and Catholics from London to Vienna* (Princeton, NJ: Princeton University Press, 2008). For Catholic Enlightenment, see Jürgen Overhoff and Andreas Oberdorf (eds), *Katholische Aufklärung in Europa und Nordamerika* (Göttingen: Wallstein, 2019); Ulrich L. Lehner, *The Catholic Enlightenment: The Forgotten History of a Global Movement* (New York: Oxford University Press, 2016); Ulrich L. Lehner, *Enlightened Monks: The German Benedictines, 1740–1803* (Oxford: Oxford University Press, 2011); Michael Printy and Ulrich Lehner (eds), *Companion to the Catholic Enlightenment in Europe* (Leiden: Brill, 2012).
9 Joachim Whaley, 'The Protestant Enlightenment in Germany', in Porter and Teich, *The Enlightenment in National Context*, pp. 106–18; Nina Witozek, 'Fugitives from utopia: the Scandinavian Enlightenment reconsidered', in Bo Stråth and Øystein Sørensen (eds), *The Cultural Construction of Norden* (Oslo: Scandinavian University Press, 1997), pp. 72–90; Thomas Bredsdorff, *Den brogende oplysning: Om følelsernes fornuft og fornuftens følelse i 1700-tallets nordiske litteratur* (Copenhagen: Gyldendal, 2003).
10 David Bebbington, *Evangelicalism in Modern Britain: A History from the 1730s to the 1980s* (London: Routledge, 1989); Richard Gawthrop, *Pietism and the Making of Eighteenth Century Prussia* (Cambridge: Cambridge University Press, 1993); D. Bruce Hindmarsh, *The Spirit of Early Evangelicalism: True Religion in a Modern World* (New York: Oxford University Press, 2017); Anders Jarlert, 'Evangelical Germany', in Anders Jarlert (ed.), *Piety and Modernity*, The Dynamics of Religious Reform in Northern Europe 1780–1920, 3 (Leuven: Leuven University Press, 2012), pp. 225–54; W. R. Ward, *Early Evangelicalism: A Global Intellectual History, 1670–1789* (Cambridge: Cambridge University Press, 2006). See also the essays included in Fred van Lieburg (ed.), *Confessionalism and Pietism: Religious Reform in Early Modern Europe* (Mainz: von Zabern, 2006); James E. Bradley and Dale K. Van Kley (eds), *Religion and Politics in Enlightenment Europe* (Notre Dame, IN: University of Notre Dame Press, 2001).

Introduction: reason and orthodoxy

seventeenth-century religion.[11] Some have ventured even further along this path, unearthing the roots of secular ideals from within the world of early modern European Christian theology itself.[12] Others have revisited the (perhaps less contentious) site of scholarly criticism. To these researchers, new ideals of philology and textual criticism did not come from radicalized Christian phalanxes; they arose out of the operational modes and priorities of confessional orthodoxies.[13] As Demitri Levitin has remarked: 'Paradoxically, it could be the case that what we treat as "enlightenment" in the study of the history of religion in fact emerged far earlier than we thought, and stemmed from confessionalization, and the scholarly opportunities that it offered.'[14]

In sum, the relationship between Enlightenment and religion has been turned topsy-turvy since the 1990s. Bearing this in mind, it

---

11 Barnett, *Enlightenment and Religion*; S. J. Barnett, *Idol Temples and Crafty Priests: The Origins of Enlightenment Anticlericalism* (New York: Palgrave Macmillan, 1999); J. A. I. Champion, *The Pillars of Priestcraft Shaken: The Church of England and its Enemies, 1660–1730* (Cambridge: Cambridge University Press, 1992); Knud Haakonssen (ed.), *Enlightenment and Religion: Rational Dissent in Eighteenth-Century Britain* (Cambridge: Cambridge University Press, 1996).

12 Alyssa Sepinwall, *The Abbé Grégoire and the French Revolution: The Making of Modern Universalism* (Berkeley, CA: University of California Press, 2005); Jonathan Sheehan, *The Enlightenment Bible: Translation, Scholarship, Culture* (Princeton, NJ: Princeton University Press, 2005); Adam Sutcliffe, *Judaism and Enlightenment* (Cambridge: Cambridge University Press, 2003); Anton M. Matytsin and Dan Edelstein (eds), *Let There Be Enlightenment: The Religious and Mystical Sources of Rationality* (Baltimore, MD: Johns Hopkins University Press, 2018); Kaius Sinnemäki and others (eds), *On the Legacy of Lutheranism in Finland: Societal Perspectives* (Helsinki: Finnish Literature Society, 2019); Bo Kristian Holm and Nina Javette Koefoed (eds), *Pligt og omsorg: Velfærdsstatens lutherske rødder* (Copenhagen: Gad, 2021).

13 Arnoud Visser, *Reading Augustine in the Reformation: The Flexibility of Intellectual Authority in Europe, 1520–1620* (Oxford: Oxford University Press, 2011); Demitri Levitin, 'From sacred history to the history of religion: Paganism, Judaism, and Christianity in European historiography from Reformation to "Enlightenment"', *Historical Journal*, 55:4 (2012), 1117–60; Hilmar M. Pabel, 'Sixteenth-century Catholic criticism of Erasmus' edition of St Jerome', *Reformation and Renaissance Review*, 6 (2004), 231–62; Jean-Louis Quantin, 'Reason and reasonableness in French ecclesiastical scholarship', *Huntington Library Quarterly*, 74 (2011), 401–36; Erik Sidenvall, 'Förnuftets och teologins kritik: ett bidrag till förståelsen av frihetstidens historieskrivning', *Historisk tidskrift*, 139:2 (2019), 223–50.

14 Levitin, 'From sacred history', 1160.

comes as no surprise that the need for Enlightenment as an analytical category has been called into question. The disappearance of the once-self-evident opposition between Enlightenment and religion has left a profound mark on the very concept of 'Enlightenment'. What becomes of the concept and its explicatory capacity, if antagonism towards revealed religion and religious institutions is to a considerable extent removed? Some have even taken the nominalist route and proposed that the Enlightenment is, in reality, a figment of our own imagination. In historical research, there is no need for such a concept to explain what was happening during a 'long' eighteenth century.[15]

Historians dealing with the Nordic countries during the eighteenth century have been slow to introduce the concept of 'religious Enlightenment'.[16] The limited employment of this concept is best understood in relation to the character of early modern Nordic societies. Recent works on the political and religious history of this European region have tended to emphasize the continued hegemonic strength of Lutheran confessional cultures throughout the 1700s, rather than underlining the impact of fundamentally changing trends associated with that which we call Enlightenment.[17] Early modern

---

15 Stated perhaps most poignantly in J. C. D. Clark, *English Society, 1660–1832: Religion, Ideology and Politics during the Ancien Regime*, 2nd edn (Cambridge: Cambridge University Press, 2000; first edn 1985), p. 9.
16 For some notable exceptions accessible to an international readership, see Arne Bugge Amundsen, 'Miracles and accommodation: between old and new belief in Norway 1780–1820', in Tuija Hovi and Anne Puuronen (eds), *Traditions of Belief in Everyday Life* (Åbo: Åbo akademi, 2000), pp. 97–112; Tine Reeh, 'Cross trade and innovations: judicial consequences of German historical exegesis and pietistic individualism in Denmark', in Stefanie Stockhorst and Søren Peter Hansen (eds), *Deutsch-dänische Kulturbeziehungen* (Göttingen: Vandenhoeck & Ruprecht, 2019), pp. 41–53; Tine Reeh, 'Historical and critical studies of Church and Christianity: the missing link of Enlightenment in Denmark–Norway?', in Beutel and Nooke, *Religion und Aufklärung*, pp. 219–26. For an evaluation of the potential of an application of this concept to the Nordic countries, see Eva Krause Jørgensen, 'Den nordiske oplysning og 1700-tallet i et konfessionskulturelt perspektiv', *Sjuttonhundratal*, 15 (2018), 138–44.
17 Pasi Ihalainen, 'The Enlightenment sermon: towards practical religion and a sacred national community', in Joris van Eijnatten (ed.), *Preaching, Sermon and Cultural Change in the Long Eighteenth Century* (Leiden: Brill, 2009), pp. 219–60; Pasi Ihalainen, *Protestant Nations Redefined: Changing Perceptions of National Identity in the Rhetoric of the English, Dutch and Swedish Public Churches, 1685–1772* (Leiden: Brill, 2005);

Introduction: reason and orthodoxy

Nordic countries can be singled out from the rest of Europe by their almost completely mono-confessional Lutheran character. The process of Lutheran confessionalization had been particularly successful and far-reaching in the kingdom of Denmark–Norway and within the Swedish realm. In legal matters, these nations were modelled after the Ten Commandments and the Lutheran teaching of the Christian *fundamenta* (see below). Yet, on closer scrutiny, there are clear signs that new ideals of reason, rationalism and reform were establishing a foothold from the late seventeenth century onwards. For example, historians have noted the reception of natural law and contract theories, respectively,[18] the emergence of new forms of historical criticism,[19] and the advance of a polite taste when it came to dealing with the material remains of past centuries.[20] The ways in which Pietism – most clearly in Denmark–Norway during the era of so-called 'state Pietism' (see below) – brought a

---

Michael Bregnsbo, *Samfundsorden og statsmagt set fra prædikestolen: Danske præsters deltagelse i den offentlige opinionsdannelse vedrørende samfundsordenen og statsmakten 1750–1848, belyst ved trykte prædikener: en politisk-idéhistorisk undersøgelse* (Copenhagen: Museum Tusculanum, 1997); Erik Bodensten, *Politikens drivfjäder: Frihetstidens partiberättelser och den moralpolitiska logiken* (Lund: Lund University, 2016); Johannes Ljungberg, *Toleransens gränser: Religionspolitiska dilemman i det tidiga 1700-talets Sverige och Europa* (Lund: Lund University, 2017).

18 Sören Koch, 'Natural law and the struggle with Pietism in eighteenth-century Denmark–Norway: Ludvig Holberg (1684–1751)', in Kjell Å. Modéer and Helle Vogt (eds), *Law and the Christian Tradition in Scandinavia: The Writings of Great Nordic Jurists* (Abingdon: Routledge, 2021), pp. 163–79; Kari Saastamoinen, 'Liberty and natural rights in Pufendorf's natural law theory', in Virpi Mäkinen and Petter Korkman (eds), *Transformations in Medieval and Early-Modern Rights Discourse* (Dordrecht: Springer, 2006), pp. 225–56.

19 Henrik Ågren, *Erik den helige – landsfader eller beläte? En rikspatrons öde i svensk historieskrivning från reformationen till och med upplysningen* (Lund: Sekel, 2012); Knud Haakonssen and Sebastian Olden-Jørgensen (eds), *Ludvig Holberg (1684–1754): Learning and Literature in the Nordic Enlightenment* (Abingdon: Routledge, 2017); Brian Kjær Olesen, 'Monarchism, Religion, and Moral Philosophy: Ludvig Holberg and the Early Northern Enlightenment' (unpublished doctoral thesis, European University Institute, 2016).

20 Mia Münster-Swendsen and others (eds), *Ora Pro Nobis: Space, Place and the Practice of Saints' Cults in Medieval and Early-Modern Scandinavia and Beyond* (Odense: University Press of Southern Denmark, 2019); Terese Zachrisson, *Mellan fromhet och vidskepelse: Materialitet och religiositet i det efterreformatoriska Sverige* (Gothenburg: University of Gothenburg, Department of Historical Studies, 2017).

new sense of individualized religiosity has been frequently commented upon, although the correlations between such expressions and Enlightenment have not always been explored. As the eighteenth century progressed, the signs of an advance on the part of more pronounced forms of enlightened Christianity were increasingly obvious. The advanced, rational Lutheran theology, espoused by such ecclesiastics as Danish court preacher Christian Bastholm (1740–1819) and Swedish bishop Jacob Axelsson Lindblom (1746–1819), marks the apogee of the influence of German Enlightenment theology in the European North.[21] Such tendencies have been well researched; but these studies neither venture beyond the intellectual world of clerical elites, nor have they explored the intertwined and often harmonious coexistence of Enlightenment ideas and still-tangible elements of confessional society.

Recent historiographical revisions provide a serviceable starting point from which to introduce the theme of this volume. The book offers a novel perspective on the introduction of Enlightenment ideas and practices in the Nordic countries (inspired by Alasdair MacIntyre); we understand an 'Enlightenment practice' to be 'any coherent form of socially established cooperative human activity' that we can identify as being informed by notions of, above all, rationality.[22] Drawing on research into 'religious Enlightenment' in other parts of Europe, the contributors discuss the ways in which traditional Lutheran so-called confessional cultures merged with novel ideas during the 'long' eighteenth century (this volume covers the period c. 1680–1820, with most chapters focusing on the late 1700s). It is the overall contention of this book that confessional culture had a profound impact on the reception and understanding of the symbolic world of Enlightenment.[23] Several contributions

---

21 Henrique Laitenberger, 'Protestant Enlightenment(s)? The Origins and Dissemination of Enlightenment Theology in Anglicanism, German Lutheranism, and Swedish Lutheranism' (unpublished doctoral thesis, University of Oxford, 2021), pp. 228–78; Michael Neiiendam, *Christian Bastholm: studier over oplysningens teologi og kirke* (Copenhagen: Gad, 1922). For German *Aufklärungstheologie*, see, for example, Albrecht Beutel, *Aufklärung in Deutschland – Die Kirche in ihrer Geschichte* (Göttingen: Vandenhoeck & Ruprecht, 2006).

22 Alasdair C. MacIntyre, *After Virtue: A Study in Moral Theory* (Notre Dame, IN: University of Notre Dame Press, 1981), p. 184.

23 We are profoundly indebted to Jacob Christensson's masterly dissertation from 1996 for providing the inspiration for the conceptual framework

Introduction: reason and orthodoxy

also demonstrate how the introduction of Enlightenment ideals invigorated some of the long-standing reforming concerns of Lutheran ecclesiastics and public officials.

Our approach could be compared to Jonathan Israel's distinction between different intellectual currents within eighteenth-century Europe: radical Enlightenment, moderate Enlightenment and anti-Enlightenment. Israel's second category comprises those who publicly defended the position of the absolute state, the established Church and the social hierarchies of the *ancien régime* while privately supporting and promoting Enlightenment ideas.[24] The chapters in this volume will, to a considerable extent, speak about agents, institutions and practices that might, with Israel's terminology, be described as 'moderate'. However, instead of measuring Enlightenment by the extent and level of support for ideal-typical Enlightenment ideas, the focus here is placed on different examples of coexistence and intertwinement between the confessional society and concepts and practices related to Enlightenment. Thus, the chapters in this volume still speak about Enlightenment; but on a number of occasions it is Enlightenment lacking the definite article. In most cases, the discussion is devoid of references to the intellectual terrain of Voltaire, d'Alembert (1717–1783) and Diderot (1713–1784). Instead, it targets a more everyday world in which reason, usefulness, individualism and empiricism informed new practices and policies.[25]

Contributors to this volume explore the merging of confessional culture and Enlightenment through the lens of novel practices and institutions. Focal points include practices of reform, implementation of policy and the impact of scholarly/scientific novelties. Implicitly, this leads us to challenge narratives that privilege the rise of a philosophical radicalism as an overarching (albeit implicit) explicatory cause of reform.[26] Instead, this book emphasizes the importance of

---

outlined here. See Jakob Christensson, *Lyckoriket: Studier i svensk upplysning* (Stockholm: Atlantis, 1996).
24 Jonathan I. Israel, *The Enlightenment that Failed: Ideas, Revolution, and Democratic Defeat, 1748–1830* (Oxford: Oxford University Press, 2019), pp. 27–33.
25 This approach is inspired by Whaley's description of the German Enlightenment as a practical reform movement; see Whaley, 'The Protestant Enlightenment in Germany'.
26 Compare Sheehan, *Enlightenment Bible*, pp. xi–xii. Discussed in Helmut Zedelmaier and Martin Mulsow (eds), *Die Praktiken der Gelehrsamkeit in der Frühen Neuzeit* (Tübingen: M. Niemeyer, 2001).

intermediaries of various kinds navigating environments that seem to us to be filled with contradictory currents and concepts. To a considerable extent, the success of Enlightenment in the European North presupposed altered attitudes and practices on the part of these people.

Numerous historians testify to the difficulty of combining insights from intellectual history with a from-below perspective when studying the 'the age of Enlightenment'.[27] This is partly owing to the scarcity and inaccessibility of sources, but also to the more conceptual problem of pinpointing the relationship between the world of ideas and the everyday world of eighteenth-century government officials, clergy and ordinary men and women. Instead of offering a philosophical, somewhat speculative, definition of the ways in which this relationship should be understood, our ambition is more modest: we are simply pointing at the importance of practices and institutions as sites of human interaction to be explored empirically by the present-day historian.

Enlightenment in the Nordic countries

In order to understand the introduction of Enlightenment in the Nordic countries, some turning points should be identified. In the case of the Swedish realm, the formation of the Royal Swedish Academy of Science in 1739, which assembled and fostered internationally recognized scientists such as the physicist Anders Celsius (1701–1744), the chemist Countess Eva Ekeblad de la Gardie (1724–1786) and, most prominently, the botanist Carl Linnaeus (1707–1778), needs to be mentioned.[28] The scientific endeavours of the Royal Academy and its members were generally perceived as being in harmony with the general drift of Lutheran theology, and they were to some extent inspired by the so-called 'physico-theology' of Christian Wolff (1679–1754), professor of philosophy in Halle and Marburg.[29] Particular attention

---

27 For a recent work which successfully combines the two perspectives, see Jeremy L. Caradonna, *The Enlightenment in Practice: Academic Prize Contests and Intellectual Culture in France, 1670–1794* (Ithaca, NY: Cornell University Press, 2012). A standard work on the social history of the Enlightenment (which includes sections on Scandinavia) is Thomas Munck, *The Enlightenment: A Comparative Social History 1721–1794* (London: Arnold, 2000). See also Roger Chartier, *Les Origines culturelles de la Révolution française* (Paris: Seuil, 1990).

28 This was soon followed by the Society of Sciences in Copenhagen (1742) and the Royal Norwegian Society of Sciences in Trondheim (1760).

29 Lars Magnusson, 'On happiness: welfare in cameralist discourse in the seventeenth and eighteenth centuries', in Ere Nokkala and Nicholas B. Miller

Introduction: reason and orthodoxy

has to be given to the effects of scientific journeys, especially those of Linnaeus' many disciples to various locations that were exotic at the time.[30] With the creation of *Tabellverket* (The Table Office) in 1749, the Swedish realm established a remarkably diligent system for collecting medical data and population statistics of various kinds. This new institution not only implemented scientific novelties and paved the way for early forms of national censuses but also, as an unintended effect, made the local clergy into a new kind of intermediary who supplied central government agencies with countless sets of local statistics.[31] Another example of large-scale eighteenth-century scientific endeavour can be found in the various measures taken to investigate the conditions (geography, agriculture, antiquities and natural resources) of remote rural areas. In 1743, the central administration in Copenhagen instructed public officials in Norway to provide information about local conditions in the entire country. In 1770, similar measures were taken to procure more comprehensive knowledge of Iceland.[32] Such initiatives, including the various surveys conducted by the Swedish Table Office, were motivated by a mercantilist desire to measure natural resources and, if possible, increase both production and population. Ambitions to promote trade and prosperity within the population at large were greatly aided by long periods of peace around the Baltic Sea, saving both personal and material resources.[33]

(eds), *Cameralism and Enlightenment: Happiness, Governance and Reform in Transnational Perspective* (New York: Routledge, 2019), pp. 23–46 (pp. 31–32); Hans-Martin Bachmann, *Die naturrechtliche Staatslehre Christian Wolffs* (Berlin: Duncker und Humblot, 1977).

30 See the contributions in Hanna Hodacs, Kenneth Nyberg and Stéphane Van Damme (eds), *Linnaeus, Natural History and the Circulation of Knowledge* (Oxford: Voltaire Foundation, 2018); Gunnar Broberg, *Mannen som ordnade naturen* (Stockholm: Natur & Kultur, 2019); Göran Rydén, 'The Enlightenment in practice: Swedish travellers and knowledge about metal trades', *Sjuttonhundratal*, 10 (2013), 63–86.

31 Peter Sköld, 'The birth of population statistics in Sweden', *The History of the Family*, 9:1 (2004), pp. 5–21; Karin Johannisson, *Det mätbara samhället: Statistik och samhällsdröm i 1700-talets Europa* (Stockholm: Norstedt, 1988). See also Chapter 14.

32 Kristin Røgeberg, Margit Løyland and Gerd Mordt (eds), *Norge i 1743: Innberetninger som svar på 43 spørsmål fra Danske Kanselli*, 5 vols (Oslo: Solum, 2003–2008); Ingi Sigurdsson, 'The publication of educational works for the people of Iceland and their reception, c. 1770–1830', *Sjuttonhundratal*, 5 (2008), 99–124 (101).

33 Lars Magnusson, 'Comparing cameralisms: the case of Sweden and Prussia', in Marten Seppel and Keith Tribe (eds), *Cameralism in Practice: State*

The honing of mercantilist principles had considerable influence on the treatment of religious outsiders. In the Swedish realm, freedom of religion for Calvinists was introduced in 1741, after having previously been granted only to heavily restricted collectives of craftsmen.[34] Mercantilism motivated the introduction of freedom of religion in the free towns of Altona (1664), Fredericia (1682), Fredrikstad (1682) and Kristiansand (1686) within the Danish realm. In 1771, Moravians were invited to establish the town of Christiansfeld. This was to become a successful free-trade town.[35] Throughout the eighteenth century, collisions between confession-orientated and mercantilist rationales can be observed. This is evident in, for example, the struggles over the abolishment of holy days and in contemporary measures to increase (or regulate) Sabbath observance.[36]

A considerable amount of research dealing with Enlightenment in Denmark–Norway has focused on the author, historian and playwright Ludvig Holberg (1684–1754).[37] In addition to his extensive publications in the fields of history and natural law, Holberg appealed to a wider public with his many essays and comedies. At the end of his life, Holberg transformed the ancient Sorø Academy, located eighty kilometres west of Copenhagen, into a hotspot of Enlightenment teaching inspired by the French *philosophes*, in particular Montesquieu (1689–1755). The academy's illustrious teachers, such as Jens Schielderup Sneedorff (1724–1764), Johann Bernhard Basedow

---

Administration and Economy in Early Modern Europe (Cambridge: Boydell & Brewer, 2017), pp. 17–38; Göran Rydén, 'Balancing the divine and the private: the practices of *Hushållning* in eighteenth-century Sweden', in Seppel and Tribe, *Cameralism in Practice*, pp. 179–202; Bård Frydenlund, 'Political practices among merchants in Denmark and Norway in the period of absolutism', in Pasi Ihalainen and others (eds), *Scandinavia in the Age of Revolution: Nordic Political Cultures, 1740–1820* (Farnham: Ashgate, 2012), pp. 241–54; Patrik Winton, 'The politics of commerce in Sweden, 1730–1770', in Ihalainen and others, *Scandinavia in the Age of Revolution*, pp. 217–28.

34 For example, French craftsmen worked at Stockholm Castle; see Linda Hinners, *De fransöske handtwerkarne vid Stockholms slott 1693–1713: Yrkesroller, organisation, arbetsprocesser* (Stockholm: Stockholm University, 2012).

35 See chapters 12 and 13.

36 Göran Malmstedt, 'In defence of holy days: the peasantry's opposition to the reduction of holy days in early modern Sweden', *Cultural History*, 3:2 (2014), 103–25. See also chapters 11, 12 and 13.

37 Haakonssen and Olden-Jørgensen, *Ludvig Holberg*; Olesen, 'Monarchism, religion, and moral philosophy'.

Introduction: reason and orthodoxy   13

(1724–1790) and Tyge Rothe (1731–1795), combined this line of teaching with loyal support for the absolute monarchy and its centralizing efforts to map and reform the country, a blend that has been labelled 'the Sorø Enlightenment'.[38] The absence of equivalent key figures and centres of Enlightenment within the Swedish realm has triggered the suggestion that Sweden was only sporadically influenced by Enlightenment ideas prior to the concluding decades of the eighteenth century, and then rather in the context of Romanticism, most notably represented by the poet and radical writer Thomas Thorild (1759–1808).[39] However, this understanding of the Swedish situation depends heavily on the argument that any Enlightenment worthy of the name should propagate the same tenets, and foster the same antagonisms, as the French Enlightenment.[40] Yet, from the 1730s onwards, books and new periodicals increased their readership significantly. One of the most prevalent figures active within this new literary milieu, the Royal Librarian and historical writer Olof von Dalin (1708–1763), started the periodical *Swänska Argus*, with inspiration from the British *Spectator*, in 1732. His magisterial work of national history, *Svea Rikes historia* (1747–1761), is stylistically inspired by the French Enlightenment. In much of his literary oeuvre, we find a critique – often witty – of Church and clergy (although he took care not to attack the Lutheran, or the Christian, faith as such).[41] However, most printed books were still of a religious character. As the century progressed, there was an increased interest in pietist literature.[42] Pietism also inspired various reforms aimed at an increase in overall readership levels. The Danish poor laws of 1708, which provided deprived children with the right to receive a free education, were by and large the result of pietist initiatives. A pietist understanding of the role of conversion inspired

---

38 Carl Henrik Koch, *Dansk oplysningsfilosofi* (Copenhagen: Gyldendal, 2003), pp. 257–71; Helle Vogt, 'Den juridiske undervisning på det andet ridderlige akademi i Sorø', *Tidsskrift for Rettsvitenskap*, 120:4 (2007), 579–613.
39 For a further discussion of Thorild as an agent of Enlightenment, see Israel, *The Enlightenment that Failed*.
40 Tore Frängsmyr, 'The Enlightenment in Sweden', in Porter and Teich, *The Enlightenment in National Context*, pp. 164–75.
41 Ingemar Carlsson, *Olof von Dalin: samhällsdebattör, historiker, språkförnyare* (Varberg: CAL-förl., 1997); Tilda Maria Forselius, *God dag, min läsare! Bland berättare, brevskrivare, boktryckare och andra bidragsgivare i tidig svensk veckopress 1730–1773* (Lund: Ellerström, 2015).
42 Ove Nordstrandh, *Den äldre svenska pietismens litteratur* (Stockholm: Svenska kyrkans diakonistyrelse, 1951).

the confirmation liturgy that was introduced in the Danish and Norwegian Church in 1736. This act was preceded by lessons in reading for every child. This reform was followed in 1739 by the formation of a compulsory schooling system in all Danish and Norwegian parishes (although ambitions were not always fulfilled, and in many cases reading skills were taught in comparatively informal ways).[43] In Sweden, confirmation was not introduced until 1811 and mandatory rural schools in 1842. However, the Swedish Church Law of 1686 already stipulated that everyone should be able to recite and comprehend fundamental parts of the Lutheran creed in order to be admitted to communion. Literacy in the Nordic countries increased to the extent that the vast majority of the population, both men and women, were able to read (but not write) by the mid-eighteenth century.[44]

The various measures that triggered this increase in reading ability tend to be understood as expressions of Lutheran confessional culture. Arguably, they were primarily aimed at forming pious subjects. Unintentionally, they also contributed to the formation of a reading public at large, and thus to the dramatic expansion of the book market in the 1750s.[45] This development takes us to a unique aspect of the Enlightenment in the Nordic countries: the ground-breaking Press Acts of 1766 (Sweden) and 1770 (Denmark–Norway). The two key agents behind the 1766 Act came from the Finnish part of

---

43 Charlotte Appel, 'Printed in books, imprinted on minds: catechisms and religious reading in Denmark during the seventeenth and early eighteenth centuries', in Charlotte Appel and Morten Fink-Jensen (eds), *Religious Reading in the Lutheran North: Studies in Early Modern Scandinavian Book Culture* (Newcastle: Cambridge Scholars Publishing, 2011), pp. 70–87; Ingrid Markussen, *Til Skaberens Ære, Statens Tjeneste og Vor Egen Nytte: Pietistiske og kameralistiske idéer bag framvæksten af en offentlig skole i landdistriktene i 1700-tallet* (Odense: Odense Universitetsforlag, 1995); Nina Javette Koefoed, 'The Lutheran household as a part of Danish confessional culture', in Bo Kristian Holm and Nina Javette Koefoed (eds), *Lutheran Theology and the Shaping of Society: The Danish Monarchy as Example* (Göttingen: Vandenhoeck & Ruprecht, 2018), pp. 321–40.
44 Egil Johansson, 'The history of literacy in Sweden', Educational Reports Umeå, 12 (1977), repr. in Harvey J. Graff and others (eds), *Understanding Literacy in its Historical Contexts: Socio-Cultural History and the Legacy of Egil Johansson* (Lund: Nordic Academic Press, 2009), pp. 29–57; Charlotte Appel and Morten Fink-Jensen, 'Introduction: books, literacy and religious reading in the Lutheran North', in Appel and Fink-Jensen, *Religious Reading in the Lutheran North*, pp. 1–15.
45 Appel, 'Printed in books'.

Introduction: reason and orthodoxy

the Swedish realm: Peter Forsskål (1732–1763), a botanist and the son of a clergyman, who wrote the pamphlet on civil liberty in 1759 that first triggered the debate; and Anders Chydenius (1729–1803), a country pastor who eagerly advocated the proposition in the Swedish *Riksdag* (parliament, or diet). The Press Act abolished the censor's office, permitted open debate on political issues and proclaimed an unusual principle of unrestricted public access to state documents (which is still in force in both Finland and in Sweden). However, the Act prohibited criticism directed against the monarch and the Lutheran faith. From now on, the publisher was to be held responsible for the contents of works he had made available to the public.[46] None of these restrictions were included in the even more radical, albeit short-lived, Danish Press Act of 1770. It was issued by Johann Friedrich Struensee (1737–1772), counsellor to the autocratic King Christian VII (r. 1766–1808). The Danish Press Act was famously praised by Voltaire. However, it was restricted by Struensee himself as early as 1771 (after the opportunity to deliver criticism anonymously had, hardly surprisingly, backfired). The earlier practices concerning censorship were not restored, though.[47] According to Jonathan Israel, these two Press Acts mark the apogee of Scandinavian Enlightenment. With these Acts, traditional social hierarchies were transformed to a greater extent than in any other Western country.[48]

Interestingly, the Nordic Press Acts were issued by the two different types of government that established the respective frameworks of the two Nordic states of the eighteenth century. While Denmark–Norway had been governed by an absolute sovereign

---

46 Jonas Nordin and John Christian Laursen, 'Northern declarations of freedom of the press: the relative importance of philosophical ideas and of local politics', *Journal of the History of Ideas*, 81:2 (2020), 217–37; Ere Nokkala, 'World's first freedom of writing and of the press ordinance as history of political thought', in Ulla Carlsson and David Goldberg (eds), *The Legacy of Peter Forsskål: 250 Years of Freedom of Expression* (Gothenburg: Nordicom, 2017), pp. 39–52; Johan Hirschfeldt, 'Freedom of speech, expression and information in Sweden: a legacy from 1766', in Carlsson and Goldberg, *The Legacy of Peter Forsskål*, pp. 53–70.
47 Henrik Horstbøll, Ulrik Langen and Frederik Stjernfelt, *Grov Konfækt: Tre vilde år med trykkefrihed 1770–73*, 2 vols (Copenhagen: Gyldendal, 2020); Michael Bregnsbo, 'Struensee and the political culture of absolutism', in Ihalainen and others, *Scandinavia in the Age of Revolution*, pp. 55–66. See also chapter 11.
48 Israel, *The Enlightenment that Failed*, pp. 757–62.

since 1660, declared in the King's Code of 1665, the Swedish realm abolished autocracy in 1719 and became a constitutional monarchy. That event marked the beginning of what contemporaries were already referring to as the 'Age of Liberty' (1719–1772). This was a period when the Council of the Realm held ultimate executive power, and the *Riksdag* constituted the primary arena for political debate and decision-making at the national level. In the *Riksdag*, the peasantry had its own corporation and a vote of equal value to those of each of the other three Estates – the nobility, the clergy and the burghers – although they were carefully kept out of discussions in the Privy Council in matters relating to foreign policy.[49] In Denmark–Norway, there were no assemblies of Estates or any other institution which involved inhabitants in political decision-making. In particular, the role of the peasantry was circumscribed. From 1733, male peasants were even forbidden to move without the express permission of the landlord or of the king.[50] Members of the nobility did not enjoy any privileged access to public office, even though we can find several examples indicating that local groups did not lack opportunities to influence an autocratic ruler.[51] Conditions were very different in the Norwegian part of the realm, where farms owned by the nobility were few and local societies were marked by what has famously been labelled 'peasant communalism'.[52] The different types of government in Sweden and in Denmark–Norway, respectively, had some effect on policies in matters of religion. In accordance with his own personal convictions, the Danish king Christian VI (r. 1730–1746) developed what has been described as state Pietism, with Moravians and other radical groups sent out on missions in the Danish colonial world.[53] By contrast, Sweden took a particularly harsh stand against all kinds

---

49 Jonas Nordin, 'The monarchy in the Swedish Age of Liberty (1719–1772)', in Ihalainen and others, *Scandinavia in the Age of Revolution*, pp. 29–40.
50 Palle Ove Christensen, 'Culture and contrasts in a northern European village: lifestyles among manorial peasants in 18th-century Denmark', *Journal of Social History*, 29:2 (1995), 275–94.
51 Yrjo Blomstedt (ed.), *Administrasjon i Norden på 1700-talet* (Oslo: Universitetsforlaget, 1985).
52 Steinar Imsen, *Norsk bondekommunalisme, fra Magnus Lagabøte till Kristian Kvart*, 2 vols (Flataasen: Tapir, 1990–1994).
53 See the contributions in Tine Reeh (ed.), *Religiøs oplysning: Studier over kirke og kristendom i 1700-tallets Danmark-Norge* (Odense: Syddansk Universitetsforlag, 2018); Bredsdorff, *Den brogede oplysning*.

Introduction: reason and orthodoxy 17

of Lutheran dissent during its Age of Liberty, perceiving Pietists as a threat against the unity of the confessional state. The Conventicle Act of 1726 limited religious meetings to family prayers, attended only by members of the household, and compelled the local clergy to perform regular examinations in households to ensure that their members possessed an adequate degree of knowledge of the Lutheran catechism. Moreover, a decree of 1735 allowed local pastors to actively interrogate parishioners suspected of silently holding radical pietist views.[54] After the *coup d'état* by Gustav III (r. 1771–1792) in 1772, which restored much of the former royal executive powers, a regulation for Jewish worship became operational in 1781, and Roman Catholics were granted the freedom to worship (on condition that they were foreign subjects) in 1782. These reforms came in the name of Enlightenment and tolerance. In Denmark–Norway, Crown Prince Frederik's *coup d'état* in 1784 was followed by an intensified discussion on civil liberties, which resulted in some substantial concessions to the peasantry, most of whom became landowners as a result. Although this reform has been described as a peaceful and consensus-orientated path towards increasing liberties, freedom of religion was not introduced until the 1840s. Instead, these reforms were to a considerable extent motivated by the intent to foster good Christian citizens.[55]

Compared to other parts of Europe, the specific setting for Enlightenment ideas and practices that materialized in the Nordic countries was marked by two specific characteristics: the rural character of these countries, and their two hundred years of almost undisturbed mono-confessional Lutheranism. Taking the continued

---

54 Johannes Ljungberg, 'Threatening piety: perceptions and interpretations of pietist activities during the early phase of Sweden's Age of Liberty, 1719–1726', *Pietismus und Neuzeit*, 45 (2021), 27–47; Ljungberg, *Toleransens gränser*.
55 Michael Bregnsbo, 'The Danish way: freedom and absolutism. Political theory and identity in the Danish state ca. 1784–1800', in Knud Haakonssen and Henrik Horstbøll (eds), *Northern Antiquities and National Identities: Perceptions of Denmark and the North in the Eighteenth Century* (Copenhagen: Det Kongelige Danske Videnskabernes Selskab, 2008), pp. 277–87; Thomas Munck, 'Absolute monarchy in later eighteenth-century Denmark: centralized reform, public expectations, and the Copenhagen press', *Historical Journal*, 41:1 (1998), 201–24; Eva Krause Jørgensen, 'The feud of the Jutlandic proprietors: protesting reform and facing the public in late eighteenth-century Denmark', *Eighteenth-Century Studies*, 52:4 (2019), 411–29.

importance of confessional culture into account, these two characteristics are placed at the centre of the first two sections of this volume, while a third section is dedicated to challenging some of the established points of reference for Enlightenment in the Nordic countries.

Enlightenment in rural societies

The Nordic countries of the eighteenth century were largely rural: 90 per cent of the inhabitants of the Swedish realm lived in rural areas, and so did about 85 per cent of the inhabitants of Denmark–Norway.[56] Moreover, the urban population was concentrated in Copenhagen, Stockholm and Bergen; there were few towns that exceeded five thousand inhabitants. Consequently, the first section of the book focuses on agents and pastoral practices in rural societies.

The first two contributions offer detailed overviews of the geographical and institutional frameworks of the two Nordic states. Arne Bugge Amundsen introduces the concept of 'pastoral Enlightenment' in the first chapter. He explores the ways in which Enlightenment was introduced in rural Norway through the lens of three eighteenth-century pastors. This concept returns in the following chapter, written by Erik Sidenvall, which is a study of how a bureaucratic model of oversight could be turned into a vehicle of individualizing religious practices in late eighteenth-century Sweden. The literary output of the Finnish disabled and self-taught writer Tuomas Ragvaldinpoika (1724–1804) is explored in the next chapter of this section. Tuija Laine offers a close reading of his various works. This chapter offers a unique view of how old and new ideals blended in a rural voice placed very much at the margins of society. In the final chapter of this section, written by Joonas Tammela, the religio-political messages conveyed from rural Swedish pulpits are placed at the centre of attention. This chapter argues for the continued strength of a traditional, Lutheran orthodox definition of the social order, but also for its adaptability at a time when new ways of life increasingly came to influence local societies. Taken together, these contributions reveal some of the long-standing continuities of rural Nordic societies; but they also show how clerical intermediaries negotiated Enlightenment ideals and explored the ambiguities of Lutheran orthodoxy in an endeavour to promote reform.

---

56 See chapters 1 and 2.

Dealing with the Catholic past (and present)

In various ways, agents of Enlightenment in the European North were driven to comment on the countries' Catholic, medieval past. In spite of two centuries of Lutheran hegemony, there had been moments when the Lutheran confession was threatened. For Sweden, this was primarily during the short reign of Sigismund Vasa as king of both Sweden and Poland (r. 1592–1599) before he was defeated by his uncle Duke Charles, later Charles IX (r. 1604–1611), who also reinforced the Lutheran confession of the state in alliance with the Church at the Uppsala Synod of 1593. Religious minorities had also been present and visible in both Denmark–Norway and Sweden with Finland, the Russian Orthodox minority in eastern Finland forming a noteworthy example. In addition to that, freedom of worship had been granted to skilled craftsmen of Reformed and Catholic faiths, inhabitants of certain free towns and foreign subjects associated with the embassies established in both Stockholm and Copenhagen during the second half of the seventeenth century. As mentioned above, judging from what caused stricter confessional legislation in the early eighteenth century, (Lutheran) Pietists emerged as embodying the most tangible 'threat' to the Lutheran Church in Sweden. This might be seen as a 'light' crisis of pluralism when compared to the historical experiences of other early modern states, but these were nevertheless events that triggered a militant confessional response.

The most fundamental opponent was, however, the Papal Church. A counter-identity built around the notion of 'the Other' in the shape of the Papal Church was forged as early as the sixteenth century; but interestingly enough, the Reformed, Calvinist churches were also frequently dressed in enemy colours. The Lutheran Reformation differed from other stances evinced by Protestant Christianity. For example, this difference is evident in its attitude to religious images. During the eighteenth century, a willingness to do away with 'superstitious' uses of remaining images intermingled with a renewed interest in antiquities and a re-evaluation of what might be described as historical narratives.

In this section, the contributors demonstrate various ways of dealing with the pre-Lutheran past. The first two chapters, written by Terese Zachrisson and Martin Wangsgaard Jürgensen, approach the theme from the vantage point of material culture. To a considerable extent, the material remnants of the medieval Church were preserved in the parish churches of both Denmark–Norway and Sweden. Just as historians became increasingly hostile towards the Middle Ages during the eighteenth century, numerous leading clerics and aristocratic patrons felt a growing discomfort at the still-existing material remains of the Papal Church. Paradoxically, these chapters also reveal how new ideals could contribute to the preservation of remnants of bygone times. The two ensuing chapters focus on historiographical interpretations of the nations' medieval, Catholic past. Whereas previous generations of historians had been relatively tolerant towards some of the expressions of medieval Christendom, the chapters written by Henrik Ågren and Rolv Nøtvik Jakobsen reveal how an emphasis on common-sense rationality led to increasingly hostile views of the 'Catholic past'. As is shown in Nøtvik Jacobsen's contribution, Norwegian historical writing eschewed the Middle Ages in pursuit of a pre-Christian past in which it found the nucleus of proto-national sentiment. In the final chapter of this section Yvonne Maria Werner explores not a relationship to historic Catholicism but the attraction of Sweden's Gustav III to contemporary Roman Catholic liturgical practices. This chapter reveals how a longing for aesthetic pleasure and liturgical splendour could be combined with a relatively advanced, 'enlightened' reform agenda.

Milestones of Enlightenment challenged

The final section of the book challenges some of the hitherto taken-for-granted points of reference for Enlightenment in the Nordic countries. The implementation of natural law, the abolition of censorship, mitigations of confessional legislation and mass vaccination campaigns have generally been understood as the outcomes and expressions of Enlightenment. That notion is questioned by the five chapters included in this section. In different ways, the writers reveal how changes that we tend to associate with the Enlightenment were intertwined with changing practices and rationales within Lutheran confessional culture.

The section begins with a chapter, co-authored by Tine Reeh and Ralf Hemmingsen, on so-called 'melancholic murders' in Denmark. Instead of discussing how novel legislation was inspired by natural law, the writers direct our attention to how jurisprudence was increasingly influenced by a pietist anthropology. In the ensuing contribution by Jesper Jakobsen and Lars Cyril Nørgaard, the received view of the Press Act of 1770 in Denmark–Norway as a radical break with previous practices is challenged. By examining the

Introduction: reason and orthodoxy

institutional practices of censorship at the Faculty of Theology at the University of Copenhagen in the mid-eighteenth century, this chapter reveals how several rationales, both confessional and commercial, transformed the practice of censorship long before 1770. Johannes Ljungberg's chapter demonstrates how the implementation of the Danish Sabbath ordinance, a reform introduced by the confessional state, was invigorated by the implementation of police regulations in the eighteenth century. Taking the extreme example of Altona, the first free town of the Danish realm, the chapter demonstrates how Sabbath legislation caused tension between two Enlightenment values: commercial interest and tolerance of religious pluralism. The following contribution, written by Christina Petterson, also dwells on the borderland between religious and commercial rationales, offering a close analysis of the state initiative to invite Moravians to build and settle in the Danish town of Christiansfeld. Medical themes return in the final chapter in this section; in his contribution to this volume, Esko Laine provides a detailed account of the implementation of vaccination policies as they were performed by pastors in rural Finland.

The people of eighteenth-century Nordic societies used the terms 'enlightened' and 'enlightenment' in ways that could simultaneously be associated with a pious Lutheranism, with rational reform and with a clandestine esoterism. By way of a conceptual analysis, Anders Jarlert's epilogue explores the tensions that arose from these different uses, thereby adding further dimensions to the theme of the book.

In sum, this volume deals with several well-rehearsed themes of Enlightenment studies. Scientific novelties, realized policies, reading and printing practices are all themes that return in this book; but here they are understood in relation to various modes and rationales of confessional culture. Furthermore, all the contributions to the present volume deal with ideas related to three 'R's: reason, rationalism and reform. But the eighteenth century encountered here is not only a story of oppositions. Reason is not necessarily seen as replacing religious belief; nor is rationalism viewed as opposed to rationales occurring within religious policies or institutions. Evidence of reform may in some cases be interpreted as expressions of Enlightenment; but there is also a recurring echo of previous religious reforms and measures promoting renewal, not least in relation to the historical experience of the Lutheran Reformation. Therefore, we have chosen to place the notion of 'religious Enlightenment' at the core of this book, whose various chapters all proceed from this fundamental conception in their explorations of ideas and practices that were embedded in a landscape shaped by both reason and orthodoxy.

Bibliography

Ågren, Henrik, *Erik den helige – landsfader eller beläte? En rikspatrons öde i svensk historieskrivning från reformationen till och med upplysningen* (Lund: Sekel, 2012).

Ahnert, Thomas, *The Moral Culture of the Scottish Enlightenment* (New Haven, CT: Yale University Press, 2015).

——, *Religion and the Origins of the German Enlightenment: Faith and the Reform of Learning in the Thought of Christian Thomasius* (Rochester, NY: University of Rochester Press, 2006).

Amundsen, Arne Bugge, 'Miracles and accommodation: between old and new belief in Norway 1780–1820', in Tuija Hovi and Anne Puuronen (eds), *Traditions of Belief in Everyday Life* (Åbo: Åbo akademi, 2000), pp. 97–112.

Appel, Charlotte, 'Printed in books, imprinted on minds: catechisms and religious reading in Denmark during the seventeenth and early eighteenth centuries', in Charlotte Appel and Morten Fink-Jensen (eds), *Religious Reading in the Lutheran North: Studies in Early Modern Scandinavian Book Culture* (Newcastle: Cambridge Scholars Publishing, 2011), pp. 70–87.

Appel, Charlotte and Morten Fink-Jensen, 'Introduction: books, literacy and religious reading in the Lutheran North', in Charlotte Appel and Morten Fink-Jensen (eds), *Religious Reading in the Lutheran North: Studies in Early Modern Scandinavian Book Culture* (Newcastle: Cambridge Scholars Publishing, 2011), pp. 1–14.

Aston, Nigel, *Christianity and Revolutionary Europe, 1750–1830* (Cambridge: Cambridge University Press, 2003).

Bachmann, Hans-Martin, *Die naturrechtliche Staatslehre Christian Wolffs* (Berlin: Duncker und Humblot, 1977).

Barnett, S. J., *Enlightenment and Religion: The Myths of Modernity* (Manchester: Manchester University Press, 2003).

——, *Idol Temples and Crafty Priests: The Origins of Enlightenment Anticlericalism* (New York: Palgrave Macmillan, 1999).

Bebbington, David, *Evangelicalism in Modern Britain: A History from the 1730s to the 1980s* (London: Routledge, 1989).

Bell, David A., *The Cult of the Nation in France: Inventing Nationalism, 1680–1800* (Cambridge, MA: Harvard University Press, 2001).

Berg, Johannes van den (ed.), *Religious Currents and Crosscurrents: Essays on Early Modern Protestantism and the Protestant Enlightenment* (Leiden: Brill, 1999).

Beutel, Albrecht, *Aufklärung in Deutschland – Die Kirche in ihrer Geschichte* (Göttingen: Vandenhoeck & Ruprecht, 2006).

Beutel, Albrecht and Martha Nooke (eds), *Religion und Aufklärung* (Tübingen: Mohr Siebeck, 2016).
Blomstedt, Yrjo (ed.), *Administrasjon i Norden på 1700-talet* (Oslo: Universitetsforlaget, 1985).
Bodensten, Erik, *Politikens drivfjäder: Frihetstidens partiberättelser och den moralpolitiska logiken* (Lund: Lund University, 2016).
Bradley, James E. and Dale K. Van Kley (eds), *Religion and Politics in Enlightenment Europe* (Notre Dame, IN: University of Notre Dame Press, 2001).
Bredsdorff, Thomas, *Den brogende oplysning: Om følelsernes fornuft og fornuftens følelse i 1700-tallets nordiske litteratur* (Copenhagen: Gyldendal, 2003).
Bregnsbo, Michael, *Samfundsorden og statsmagt set fra prædikestolen: danske præsters deltagelse i den offentlige opinionsdannelse vedrørende samfundsordenen og statsmakten 1750–1848, belyst ved trykte prædikener: en politisk-idéhistorisk undersøgelse* (Copenhagen: Museum Tusculanum, 1997).
——, 'Struensee and the political culture of absolutism', in Pasi Ihalainen and others (eds), *Scandinavia in the Age of Revolution: Nordic Political Cultures, 1740–1820* (Farnham: Ashgate, 2012), pp. 55–66.
——, 'The Danish way: freedom and absolutism. Political theory and identity in the Danish state ca. 1784–1800', in Knud Haakonssen and Henrik Horstbøll (eds), *Northern Antiquities and National Identities: Perceptions of Denmark and the North in the Eighteenth Century* (Copenhagen: Det Kongelige Danske Videnskabernes Selskab, 2008), pp. 277–87.
Broberg, Gunnar, *Mannen som ordnade naturen* (Stockholm: Natur & Kultur, 2019).
Brown, Michael, *The Irish Enlightenment* (Cambridge, MA: Harvard University Press, 2016).
Bulman, William J. and Robert G. Ingram (eds), *God in the Enlightenment* (Oxford: Oxford University Press, 2016).
Burson, Jefferey D., 'Reflections on the pluralization of Enlightenment and the notion of theological Enlightenment as process', *French History*, 26:4 (2012), 524–37.
Butterwick, Richard, Simon Davies and Gabriel Sánchez Espinosa (eds), *Peripheries of the Enlightenment* (Oxford: Voltaire Foundation, 2008).
Caradonna, Jeremy L., *The Enlightenment in Practice: Academic Prize Contests and Intellectual Culture in France, 1670–1794* (Ithaca, NY: Cornell University Press, 2012).
Carlsson, Ingemar, *Olof von Dalin: samhällsdebattör, historiker, språkförnyare* (Varberg: CAL-förl., 1997).
Champion, J. A. I., *The Pillars of Priestcraft Shaken: The Church of England and its Enemies, 1660–1730* (Cambridge: Cambridge University Press, 1992).

Chartier, Roger, *Les Origines culturelles de la Révolution française* (Paris: Seuil, 1990).
Christensson, Jakob, *Lyckoriket: Studier i svensk upplysning* (Stockholm: Atlantis, 1996).
Christensen, Palle Ove, 'Culture and contrasts in a northern European village: lifestyles among manorial peasants in 18th-century Denmark', *Journal of Social History*, 29:2 (1995), 275–94.
Clark, J. C. D., *English Society, 1660–1832: Religion, Ideology and Politics during the Ancien Régime*, 2nd edn (Cambridge: Cambridge University Press, 2000; first edn 1985).
Forselius, Tilda Maria, *God dag, min läsare! Bland berättare, brevskrivare, boktryckare och andra bidragsgivare i tidig svensk veckopress 1730–1773* (Lund: Ellerström, 2015).
Frängsmyr, Tore, 'The Enlightenment in Sweden', in Roy S. Porter and Mikuláš Teich (eds), *The Enlightenment in National Context* (Cambridge: Cambridge University Press, 1981), pp. 164–75.
Frydenlund, Bård, 'Political practices among merchants in Denmark and Norway in the period of absolutism', in Pasi Ihalainen and others (eds), *Scandinavia in the Age of Revolution: Nordic Political Cultures, 1740–1820* (Farnham: Ashgate, 2012), pp. 241–54.
Gascoigne, John, 'Anglican Latitudinarianism, rational dissent and political radicalism in the late eighteenth century', in Knud Haakonssen (ed.), *Enlightenment and Religion: Rational Dissent in Eighteenth-Century Britain* (Cambridge: Cambridge University Press, 1996), pp. 219–40.
Gawthrop, Richard, *Pietism and the Making of Eighteenth Century Prussia* (Cambridge: Cambridge University Press, 1993).
Gay, Peter, *The Enlightenment: An Interpretation*, I: *The Rise of Modem Paganism* (New York: Norton, 1966).
Haakonssen, Knud (ed.), *Enlightenment and Religion: Rational Dissent in Eighteenth-Century Britain* (Cambridge: Cambridge University Press, 1996).
Haakonssen, Knud and Sebastian Olden-Jørgensen (eds), *Ludvig Holberg (1684–1754): Learning and Literature in the Nordic Enlightenment* (Abingdon: Routledge, 2017).
Hindmarsh, D. Bruce, *The Spirit of Early Evangelicalism: True Religion in a Modern World* (New York: Oxford University Press, 2017).
Hinners, Linda, *De fransöske handtwerkarne vid Stockholms slott 1693–1713: Yrkesroller, organisation, arbetsprocesser* (Stockholm: Stockholm University, 2012).
Hirschfeldt, Johan, 'Freedom of speech, expression and information in Sweden: a legacy from 1766', in Ulla Carlsson and David Goldberg (eds), *The Legacy of Peter Forsskål: 250 Years of Freedom of Expression* (Gothenburg: Nordicom, 2017), pp. 53–70.
Hodacs, Hanna, Kenneth Nyberg and Stéphane Van Damme (eds), *Linnaeus, Natural History and the Circulation of Knowledge* (Oxford: Voltaire Foundation, 2018).

Holm, Bo Kristian and Nina Javette Koefoed (eds), *Pligt og omsorg – velfærdsstatens lutherske rødder* (Copenhagen: Gad, 2021).
Horstbøll, Henrik, Ulrik Langen and Frederik Stjernfelt, *Grov Konfækt: Tre vilde år med trykkefrihed 1770–73*, 2 vols (Copenhagen: Gyldendal, 2020).
Ihalainen, Pasi, 'The Enlightenment sermon: towards practical religion and a sacred national community', in Joris van Eijnatten (ed.), *Preaching, Sermon and Cultural Change in the Long Eighteenth Century* (Leiden: Brill, 2009), pp. 219–60.
——, *Protestant Nations Redefined: Changing Perceptions of National Identity in the Rhetoric of the English, Dutch and Swedish Public Churches, 1685–1772* (Leiden: Brill, 2005).
Imsen, Steinar, *Norsk bondekommunalisme, fra Magnus Lagabøte till Kristian Kvart*, 2 vols (Flataasen: Tapir, 1990–1994).
Israel, Jonathan I., *The Enlightenment that Failed: Ideas, Revolution, and Democratic Defeat, 1748–1830* (Oxford: Oxford University Press, 2019).
Jarlert, Anders, 'Evangelical Germany', in Anders Jarlert (ed.), *Piety and Modernity*, The Dynamics of Religious Reform in Northern Europe 1780–1920, 3 (Leuven: Leuven University Press, 2012), pp. 225–54.
Johannisson, Karin, *Det mätbara samhället: Statistik och samhällsdröm i 1700-talets Europa* (Stockholm: Norstedt, 1988).
Johansson, Egil, 'The history of literacy in Sweden', *Educational Reports Umeå*, 12 (1977), repr. in Harvey J. Graff and others (eds), *Understanding Literacy in its Historical Contexts: Socio-Cultural History and the Legacy of Egil Johansson* (Lund: Nordic Academic Press, 2009), pp. 28–59.
Jørgensen, Eva Krause, 'Den nordiske oplysning og 1700-tallet i et konfessionskulturelt perspektiv', *Sjuttonhundratal*, 15 (2018), 138–44.
——, 'The feud of the Jutlandic proprietors: protesting reform and facing the public in late eighteenth-century Denmark', *Eighteenth-Century Studies*, 52:4 (2019), 411–29.
Koch, Carl Henrik, *Dansk oplysningsfilosofi* (Copenhagen: Gyldendal, 2003).
Koch, Sören, 'Natural law and the struggle with Pietism in eighteenth-century Denmark–Norway: Ludvig Holberg (1684–1751)', in Kjell Å. Modéer and Helle Vogt (eds), *Law and the Christian Tradition in Scandinavia: The Writings of Great Nordic Jurists* (Abingdon: Routledge, 2021), pp. 163–79.
Koefoed, Nina Javette, 'The Lutheran household as a part of Danish confessional culture', in Bo Kristian Holm and Nina Javette Koefoed (eds), *Lutheran Theology and the Shaping of Society: The Danish Monarchy as Example* (Göttingen: Vandenhoeck & Ruprecht, 2018), pp. 321–40.
Laitenberger, Henrique, 'Protestant Enlightenment(s)? The Origins and Dissemination of Enlightenment Theology in Anglicanism, German Lutheranism, and Swedish Lutheranism' (unpublished doctoral thesis, University of Oxford, 2021).

Lehner, Ulrich L., *The Catholic Enlightenment: The Forgotten History of a Global Movement* (New York: Oxford University Press, 2016).

——, *Enlightened Monks: The German Benedictines, 1740–1803* (Oxford: Oxford University Press, 2011).

Levitin, Demitri, 'From sacred history to the history of religion: Paganism, Judaism, and Christianity in European historiography from Reformation to "Enlightenment"', *Historical Journal*, 55:4 (2012), 1117–60.

Lieburg, Fred van (ed.), *Confessionalism and Pietism: Religious Reform in Early Modern Europe* (Mainz: von Zabern, 2006).

Ljungberg, Johannes, 'Threatening piety: perceptions and interpretations of Pietist activities during the early phase of Sweden's Age of Liberty, 1719–1726', *Pietismus und Neuzeit*, 45 (2021), 27–47.

——, *Toleransens gränser: Religionspolitiska dilemman i det tidiga 1700-talets Sverige och Europa* (Lund: Lund University, 2017).

MacIntyre, Alasdair C., *After Virtue: A Study in Moral Theory* (Notre Dame, IN: University of Notre Dame Press, 1981).

Magnusson, Lars, 'Comparing cameralisms: the case of Sweden and Prussia', in Marten Seppel and Keith Tribe (eds), *Cameralism in Practice: State Administration and Economy in Early Modern Europe* (Cambridge: Boydell & Brewer, 2017), pp. 17–38.

——, 'On happiness: welfare in cameralist discourse in the seventeenth and eighteenth centuries', in Ere Nokkala and Nicholas B. Miller (eds), *Cameralism and Enlightenment: Happiness, Governance and Reform in Transnational Perspective* (New York: Routledge, 2019), pp. 23–46.

Malmstedt, Göran, 'In defence of holy days: the peasantry's opposition to the reduction of holy days in early modern Sweden', *Cultural History*, 3:2 (2014), 103–25.

Markussen, Ingrid, *Til Skaberens Ære, Statens Tjeneste og Vor Egen Nytte: Pietistiske og kameralistiske idéer bag framvæksten af en offentlig skole i landdistrikterne i 1700-tallet* (Odense: Odense Universitetsforlag, 1995).

Matytsin, Anton M. and Dan Edelstein (eds), *Let There Be Enlightenment: The Religious and Mystical Sources of Rationality* (Baltimore, MD: Johns Hopkins University Press, 2018).

Mauzi, Robert, *L'idée du bonheur dans la littérature et la pensée françaises au XVIIIe siècle* (Geneva and Paris: Albin Michel, 1979).

Munck, Thomas, 'Absolute monarchy in later eighteenth-century Denmark: centralized reform, public expectations, and the Copenhagen press', *Historical Journal*, 41:1 (1998), 201–24.

——, *The Enlightenment: A Comparative Social History 1721–1794* (London: Arnold, 2000).

Münster-Swendsen, Mia and others (eds), *Ora Pro Nobis: Space, Place and the Practice of Saints' Cults in Medieval and Early-Modern Scandinavia and Beyond* (Odense: University Press of Southern Denmark, 2019).

Neiiendam, Michael, *Christian Bastholm: studier over oplysningens teologi og kirke* (Copenhagen: Gad, 1922).

Nokkala, Ere, 'World's first freedom of writing and of the press ordinance as history of political thought', in Ulla Carlsson and David Goldberg (eds), *The Legacy of Peter Forsskål: 250 Years of Freedom of Expression* (Gothenburg: Nordicom, 2017), pp. 39–52.

Nordin, Jonas, 'The monarchy in the Swedish Age of Liberty (1719–1772)', in Pasi Ihalainen and others (eds), *Scandinavia in the Age of Revolution: Nordic Political Cultures, 1740–1820* (Farnham: Ashgate, 2012), pp. 29–40.

Nordin, Jonas and John Christian Laursen, 'Northern declarations of freedom of the press: the relative importance of philosophical ideas and of local politics', *Journal of the History of Ideas*, 81:2 (2020), 217–37.

Nordstrandh, Ove, *Den äldre svenska pietismens litteratur* (Stockholm: Svenska kyrkans diakonistyrelse, 1951).

Olesen, Brian Kjær, 'Monarchism, Religion, and Moral Philosophy: Ludvig Holberg and the Early Northern Enlightenment' (unpublished doctoral thesis, European University Institute, 2016).

Overhoff, Jürgen and Andreas Oberdorf (eds), *Katholische Aufklärung in Europa und Nordamerika* (Göttingen: Wallstein, 2019).

Pabel, Hilmar M., 'Sixteenth-century Catholic criticism of Erasmus' edition of St Jerome', *Reformation and Renaissance Review*, 6 (2004), 231–62.

Pocock, J. G. A., *Barbarism and Religion*, 6 vols (Cambridge: Cambridge University Press, 1999–2015).

——, 'Historiography and enlightenment: a view of their history', *Modern Intellectual History*, 5:1 (2008), 83–96.

Printy, Michael and Ulrich Lehner (eds), *Companion to the Catholic Enlightenment in Europe* (Leiden: Brill, 2012).

Quantin, Jean-Louis, 'Reason and reasonableness in French ecclesiastical scholarship', *Huntington Library Quarterly*, 74 (2011), 401–36.

Reeh, Tine, 'Cross trade and innovations: judicial consequences of German historical exegesis and pietistic individualism in Denmark', in Stefanie Stockhorst and Søren Peter Hansen (eds), *Deutsch-dänische Kulturbeziehungen* (Göttingen: Vandenhoeck & Ruprecht, 2019), pp. 41–53.

——, 'Historical and critical studies of Church and Christianity: the missing link of Enlightenment in Denmark–Norway?', in Albrecht Beutel and Martha Nooke (eds), *Religion und Aufklärung* (Tübingen: Mohr Siebeck, 2016), pp. 219–26.

—— (ed.), *Religiøs oplysning: Studier over kirke og kristendom i 1700-tallets Danmark-Norge* (Odense: Syddansk Universitetsforlag, 2018).

Robertson, John, *The Case for the Enlightenment – Scotland and Naples, 1680–1760* (Cambridge: Cambridge University Press, 2007).

Robertson, Ritchie, *The Enlightenment: The Pursuit of Happiness, 1680–1790* (London: Allen Lane, 2020).

Røgeberg, Kristin, Margit Løyland and Gerd Mordt (eds), *Norge i 1743: Innberetninger som svar på 43 spørsmål fra Danske Kanselli*, 5 vols (Oslo: Solum, 2003–2008).

Rydén, Göran, 'Balancing the divine and the private: the practices of Hushållning in eighteenth-century Sweden', in Marten Seppel and Keith Tribe (eds), *Cameralism in Practice: State Administration and Economy in Early Modern Europe* (Cambridge: Boydell & Brewer, 2017), pp. 179–202.

———, 'The Enlightenment in practice: Swedish travellers and knowledge about metal trades', *Sjuttonhundratal*, 10 (2013), 63–86.

Saastamoinen, Kari, 'Liberty and natural rights in Pufendorf's natural law theory', in Virpi Mäkinen and Petter Korkman (eds), *Transformations in Medieval and Early-Modern Rights Discourse* (Dordrecht: Springer, 2006), pp. 225–56.

Sepinwall, Alyssa, *The Abbé Grégoire and the French Revolution: The Making of Modern Universalism* (Berkeley, CA: University of California Press, 2005).

Sheehan, Jonathan, *The Enlightenment Bible: Translation, Scholarship, Culture* (Princeton, NJ: Princeton University Press, 2005).

———, 'Enlightenment, religion, and the enigma of secularization: a review essay', *American Historical Review*, 108:4 (2003), 1066–80.

Sidenvall, Erik, 'Förnuftets och teologins kritik: ett bidrag till förståelsen av frihetstidens historieskrivning', *Historisk tidskrift*, 139:2 (2019), 223–50.

Sigurdsson, Ingi, 'The publication of educational works for the people of Iceland and their reception, c. 1770–1830', *Sjuttonhundratal*, 5 (2008), 99–124.

Sinnemäki, Kaius and others (eds), *On the Legacy of Lutheranism in Finland: Societal Perspectives* (Helsinki: Finnish Literature Society, 2019).

Sköld, Peter, 'The birth of population statistics in Sweden', *The History of the Family*, 9:1 (2004), 5–21.

Sorkin, David, *Moses Mendelssohn and the Religious Enlightenment* (Berkeley, CA: University of California Press, 1996).

———, *The Religious Enlightenment: Protestants, Jews, and Catholics from London to Vienna* (Princeton, NJ: Princeton University Press, 2008).

———, *A Wise, Enlightened and Reliable Piety: The Religious Enlightenment in Central and Western Europe 1689–1789* (Southampton: University of Southampton, 2002).

Sutcliffe, Adam, *Judaism and Enlightenment* (Cambridge: Cambridge University Press, 2003).

Van Kley, Dale K., *The Religious Origins of the French Revolution: From Calvin to the Civil Constitution, 1560–1791* (New Haven, CT: Yale University Press, 1996).

Visser, Arnoud, *Reading Augustine in the Reformation: The Flexibility of Intellectual Authority in Europe, 1520–1620* (Oxford: Oxford University Press, 2011).

Vogt, Helle, 'Den juridiske undervisning på det andet ridderlige akademi i Sorø', *Tidsskrift for Rettsvitenskap*, 120:4 (2007), 579–613.

Ward, W. R., *Early Evangelicalism: A Global Intellectual History, 1670–1789* (Cambridge: Cambridge University Press, 2006).

Whaley, Joachim, 'The Protestant Enlightenment in Germany', in Roy Porter and Mikuláš Teich (eds), *The Enlightenment in National Context* (Cambridge: Cambridge University Press, 1981), pp. 106–18.

Winton, Patrik, 'The politics of commerce in Sweden, 1730–1770', in Pasi Ihalainen and others (eds), *Scandinavia in the Age of Revolution: Nordic Political Cultures, 1740–1820* (Farnham: Ashgate, 2012), pp. 217–28.

Witoszek, Nina, 'Fugitives from utopia: the Scandinavian Enlightenment reconsidered', in Bo Stråth and Øystein Sørensen (eds), *The Cultural Construction of Norden* (Oslo: Scandinavian University Press, 1997), pp. 72–90.

Wolloch, Nathaniel (ed.), 'New perspectives on the Mediterranean Enlightenment', *European Legacy*, 25:7/8 (2020).

Zachrisson, Terese, *Mellan fromhet och vidskepelse: Materialitet och religiositet i det efterreformatoriska Sverige* (Gothenburg: University of Gothenburg, Department of Historical Studies, 2017).

Zedelmaier, Helmut and Martin Mulsow (eds), *Die Praktiken der Gelehrsamkeit in der Frühen Neuzeit* (Tübingen: M. Niemeyer, 2001).

Part I
Enlightenment in rural societies

1
The rural spectator: clergy as agents of Enlightenment in eighteenth-century Norway

Arne Bugge Amundsen

With few urban centres and a scattered peasant population, eighteenth-century Norway was not easily administered or controlled by the strictly centralized twin monarchy of Denmark–Norway. The most central apparatus for communicating with the population was actually the Lutheran clergy. Being a pastor in the Norwegian countryside was quite different from holding a pastor's office in an urban context: the challenges were different, the tasks more extensive, the congregations less motivated for change and contact with colleagues was limited. This chapter raises the following question: how did a rural pastor in Norway consider his duties, and what means did he have at his disposal to spread Enlightenment to his congregation? In the search for the characteristics of 'pastoral Enlightenment' in Norway, three representatives of the clergy from the latter part of the eighteenth century will serve as examples.

The chapter is divided into three parts. The first part discusses whether the Norwegian eighteenth-century clergy had distinctive features – not necessarily in respect of theological thinking, but when it came to structural and structuring conditions for pastoral activities. The second part addresses issues related to ideals and instruments for the dissemination of new theological ideas. The third and final section is an analysis of three pastors who illustrate the Norwegian 'pastoral Enlightenment' in different ways (see also Sidenvall's chapter in this volume for alternative uses of this concept).

Eighteenth-century Norwegian church history has not received much attention, nor has it been pursued systematically. There are several reasons for this. As Norway had been in a union with Denmark since the late Middle Ages, and then formed a kind of vassal state from the sixteenth century onwards, research has focused on periods when major changes took place. Consequently, the sixteenth century and the Reformation have come in for a great deal of attention. The same is true of the nineteenth century, when Norway gained a more independent status and its own institutions after 1814. The period 1660–1814 was characterized by the absolutist and strongly centralized Danish-Norwegian Lutheran Church, with the king as its supreme head and the Danish Chancellery in Copenhagen as the most important executive bureaucratic institution. To distinguish Danish from Norwegian in this period is both difficult and historically problematic, even though national church historians have largely done just that. The transnational perspectives have been few and scattered.

Background

When examining the context of the Norwegian theological Enlightenment, it is relevant to compare the geography and demography of Denmark and Norway. The majority of the population of sixteenth-century Denmark–Norway lived in agricultural areas; and in most cases, parish borders remained unchanged during the Reformation and in the ensuing centuries. Slowly, however, demography changed. The population increased, as did the number of towns. Norway had approximately 440,000 inhabitants in the 1660s and 883,000 in 1801. In 1801, 8 per cent of the country's population lived in urban areas.[1] Denmark had a population of approximately 600,000 in 1536 and 929,000 in 1801. The urban population in 1801 was 21 per cent.[2] By comparison, in 1570 Sweden had approximately 900,000 inhabitants and in 1800, 2,347,000. In 1800, about 10 per cent of the population lived in urban areas.[3]

These figures show that Denmark and Norway developed differently with regard to demographics during the eighteenth century. Denmark was – unlike Norway – to a large degree characterized by urban culture and small market-town communities with

---

1 Statistisk sentralbyrå, 'Historisk statistikk: 3.1 Hjemmehørende folkemengde', www.ssb.no/a/histstat/tabeller/3-1.html [accessed 10 September 2020].
2 Charlotte Appel and Carsten Porskrog Rasmussen, 'Reformation og magtstat, 1523–1660', https://danmarkshistorien.dk/perioder/reformation-og-magtstat-1523-1660 [accessed 3 February 2023]; *Befolkningsforholdene i Danmark i det 19. Aarhundrede* (Copenhagen: Bianco Luno, 1905), pp. 10, 14.
3 Gustaf Sundbärg, *Sveriges land och folk* (Stockholm: P. A. Norstedt, 1901), pp. 90, 97.

complex institutions. The connection is quite simple: in the highly centralized Danish-Norwegian state, Norway lacked important institutions such as universities and political decision-making bodies, and at the same time had a population that was spread across large geographical areas.

In 1801, the urban structure in Denmark was also different to that of Norway. At that time, 11 per cent of the population lived in the capital, Copenhagen (101,000), while 10 per cent (93,000) resided in provincial market towns, which were as many as eighty-eight in number. The size of these towns could vary from a few hundred inhabitants to four or five thousand.[4] In 1801, Norway had twenty-three market towns; in addition, there were seventeen so-called staple ports, with limited rights in trade and economy. The largest provincial centres in Norway were the diocesan cities – Bergen, Kristiania, Trondheim and Kristiansand, with 18,100, 9,200, 8,800 and 2,223 inhabitants, respectively. The other towns were smaller, and in some cases considerably smaller.

Norway only had four dioceses, while the geographically much smaller Denmark had six. The two largest Norwegian dioceses – Kristiania and Trondheim – were very extensive, but they differed in respect of demographic structures.[5] The market towns and staple ports were unevenly distributed between the dioceses: ten towns and seven staple ports were located in the Diocese of Kristiania, and with the exception of the mining town of Kongsberg, they were all located on both sides of the Kristiania fjord. Six towns and ten staple ports were located along the coast in the Diocese of Kristiansand. The Diocese of Bergen had only one – the city of Bergen, which was very dominant. The Diocese of Trondheim had six market towns, but apart from the diocesan city of Trondheim they were small, especially in northern Norway. The dioceses were also different demographically: the dioceses of Kristiania and Kristiansand, covering eastern and southern Norway, had about 466,000 inhabitants, or 53 per cent of the country's population,

---

4 Astrid Schriver, 'Danmarks befolkningsudvikling 1769–2015', https://danmarkshistorien.dk/leksikon-og-kilder/vis/materiale/danmarks-befolkningsudvikling/ [accessed 10 September 2020]. See also Christian Wichmann Matthiessen, *Danske byers folketal 1801–1981*, Statistiske undersøgelser nr. 42 (Copenhagen: Danmarks Statistik, 1985).
5 The present capital of Norway, Oslo, was named Christiania (from 1877 Kristiania) between 1624 and 1924.

while the geographically much larger Diocese of Trondheim had about 181,000, or only 20 per cent of the population.[6]

Some important conclusions can be drawn from these observations: Norway had few urban centres. Located along the coast, they were particularly important along the coastline from Fredrikshald in the east to Stavanger in the west, and situated in the dioceses of Kristiania and Kristiansand. Compared with Denmark, Norway was mainly composed of rural parishes. The educated reading public in Norway was presumably smaller than the one in Denmark, and most of the Norwegian clergy had an agrarian and pre-industrial society as their main cultural context.

Another important difference between Denmark and Norway must also be pointed out, namely the forms of governance. After the introduction of absolute monarchy in 1660, a number of large aristocratic estates were established in Denmark (1671) – counties and baronies – with far-reaching authority within economy, jurisdiction and, not least, Church organization. This new noble elite held its estates at the king's pleasure, but in practice they controlled the estates on behalf of the king. *Ius patronatus* and *ius vocandi* were among the privileges of these estates. This implied that control of churches and clergy over large parts of Denmark resided with the landowners. In Norway, this was not the case; after 1671, only two counties and one barony were established. The counties were situated west of the Kristiania fjord, while the barony was centrally located in the Diocese of Bergen. This meant that the traditional structure of the Lutheran Church, with an appointed pastor reporting to and communicating directly with the central government through the Church structure (parish pastors, deans and bishops) remained intact in most of Norway.[7]

A possible hypothesis is that the Norwegian clergy – especially in the rural parishes – were relatively more independent than their colleagues in Denmark. This hypothesis derives from the observation

---

6 Thorsnæs, Geir, 'Norge (bosettingsmønster)', https://snl.no/Norge_-_bosettingsm%C3%B8nster [accessed 10 September 2020]; *Folketeljinga 1801* (Oslo: Statistisk Sentralbyrå, 1980).

7 Carsten Porskrog Rasmussen, 'Manors and states: the distribution and structure of private manors in early modern Scandinavia and their relation to state policies', *Scandinavian Economic History Review*, 66 (2018), 1–18; Arne Bugge Amundsen, 'Reformation, manors and nobility in Norway 1500–1821', in Jonathan Finch and others (eds), *Estate Landscapes in Northern Europe* (Aarhus: Aarhus University Press, 2019), pp. 233–70.

that the Norwegian pastors were not subject to the preferences of a noble landlord, and that many of them were located in geographically large parishes far from the diocesan cities. This meant that the possibilities of controlling them were fewer than in Denmark and in the Danish-Norwegian towns and cities. In addition, Norway – despite a few attempts[8] – lacked the important Danish arena of the *landemode*, an annual assembly of canons or a synod. When it came to control, deliberation and communication within the clergy, this synod had been crucial in Denmark since the Reformation, as it functioned as a regular meeting place for the diocesan clergy. At the *landemode*, the ecclesiastical superiors presented their demands and expectations, as well as new laws and regulations. The clergy could also participate in discussions about ecclesiastical affairs and share opinions and experiences between them.[9] The fact that the Norwegian clergy lacked such a central forum implied that they were partly left to their own judgement, or had to await formal visits by the dean or bishop to have their practice evaluated.

It should be added that within the Danish-Norwegian clergy there was a basic cultural and theological community. The kingdom had one university and one faculty of theology. All future pastors had to go through the same education and the same test of skills and aptitudes. The liturgy and – with minor modifications[10] – the Church Law was identical in both countries. Many Danish-born men served as pastors in Norway for shorter or longer periods. In addition, Norwegian-born pastors, though perhaps fewer, held offices in Denmark.[11] To some degree, too, Danish- and Norwegian-born bishops in the eighteenth century circulated between the two countries.[12] There are indications that the introduction of the absolute monarchy made this circulation of clergy in Norway possible, whereas

---

8 A. V. Heffermehl, *Geistlige Møder i Norge: Et Bidrag til den norske Kirkes Historie efter Reformationen til 1814* (Kristiania: Alb. Cammermeyer, 1890).
9 Erik Alstrup and Poul Erik Olsen (eds), *Dansk kulturhistorisk opslagsværk*, 2 vols (Copenhagen: Dansk historisk Fællesforening, 1991), I, pp. 545–46.
10 In 1607 a separate Norwegian Church Law was introduced by King Christian IV (1577–1648), but the differences between the Norwegian and the Danish church laws were minor, contrary to what the Norwegian bishops had recommended.
11 This has, however, never been investigated systematically.
12 Compare Karsten Hermansen, *Kirken, kongen og enevælden: En undersøgelse af det danske bispeembede 1660–1746* (Odense: Syddansk Universitetsforlag, 2005).

the control of the aristocratic landlords in central parts of Denmark made such circulation more difficult.

Generally speaking, this leaves the impression that the pastoral conditions in eighteenth-century Norway differed from those in Denmark in many ways. In order to understand 'Enlightenment' in these countries, such differences must be taken into account. Some researchers have described these differences by claiming that 'Enlightenment' in Norway was mainly a 'pastoral Enlightenment', thus pointing out that in most local communities the parish pastor was the most central representative of the king and the main mediator of political, cultural and theological change.[13] 'Enlightenment' in the sense of motivating and enhancing changes in thinking, attitudes and practice was an important dimension of eighteenth-century clerical practice, regardless of theological observance. The Norwegian clergy had few competitors in this respect.

Arenas

A central part of the Lutheran pastoral ideal was the clergy's being visible to the congregation. The pastor was not to perform rituals in secret or only for a small group of people, but be publicly available to all. In order to be able to perform his work, the pastor therefore needed a number of arenas and instruments.

The most central arenas were, of course, the church building, including the rectory, the family of the pastor and the pastor's economy. In urban parishes, the pastors rented or bought their own house, had no farm of their own, were dependent on a monetary economy and lived relatively secluded from their congregation. In the countryside, however, the situation was very different.

The pastor was a preacher on a number of occasions, at ordinary or occasional services and rituals. The sermons combined predictability – based on biblical texts, catechetical texts and rhetorical conventions – with variation and innovation. New sermon ideals introduced in the latter part of the 1700s placed greater emphasis on body language, persuasive gestures and voice, focusing on 'moving' the audience in order to motivate a change of thinking and behaviour.[14] The degree to which this actually had an impact on the average

---

13 See J. Peter Burgess (ed.), *Den norske pastorale opplysning: Nye perspektiver på norsk nasjonsbygging på 1800-tallet* (Oslo: Abstrakt, 2003).
14 Olav Hagesæther, *Norsk preken fra Reformasjonen til omlag 1820* (Oslo, Bergen, Tromsø: Universitetsforlaget, 1973), pp. 133–42.

Norwegian countryside pastor is difficult to determine, but the point is that the new homiletic ideal was designed to promote change. This new ideal had its roots in pietistic thinking, not least as expressed in the pastoral theology of professor and bishop Erik Pontoppidan (1698–1764).[15] It was developed further by rationalist Enlightenment theologians such as Christian Bastholm, *confessionarius* to the royal court in Copenhagen.[16]

The rectory was centrally located in the local community and frequently close to the parish church. It was often a large farm constructed according to local standards. Through various laws and regulations, the parishioners had a number of duties related to its maintenance. The rectory was thus integrated into the local agricultural economy; and its maintenance affected not only the pastor but also a large number of servants, tenants, farmers, service providers and general observers. Far from being a private enterprise, the administration and keeping of a rectory was a visible public issue and hence an important instrument for promoting change in agricultural technology, economy and mentality.[17]

The pastor's family was also a central part of the clergy's field of practice. The Lutheran ideal of the Christian household had its optimization in the family of the pastor. The pastor, the pastor's wife, children and servants were all part of this optimization. The unmarried clergyman – if such occurred – was an anomaly in Lutheran culture. Through their visibility, their behaviour and their practice, the pastor's family as a whole was a realization of the Lutheran ideal,[18] in spite of a significant potential for conflict in this visibility.[19] This picture also included exposure of the clergy's expertise in writing, reading, medicine and obstetrics, agricultural economics, social care and legislation.[20]

---

15 Erik Pontoppidan, *Collegium Pastorale Practicum* (Copenhagen: Det Kongelige Waysenhuus, 1757).
16 Christian Bastholm, *Den Geistlige Talekonst, tilligemed en Bedømmelse over en af Saurins Tale* (Copenhagen: Gyldendal, 1775).
17 Arne Bugge Amundsen, 'Poteter og snusfornuft? Opplysningstidens prester og prestegårder', *Prest og prestegard: Maihaugen Årbok 1999* (1999), 52–65.
18 Arne Bugge Amundsen, '"Byen som ligger på fjellet": Presten som kulturbærer i gammel tid', *Tidsskrift for kirke, religion og samfunn*, 3 (1990), 67–81.
19 Arne Bugge Amundsen, 'Embetsmann, lensmann, bonde', *Varden: Tidsskrift utgitt av Onsøy Historielag 1992* (1992), 27–35.
20 Reimund Kvideland, 'Prestefolket som lækjarar', *Prest og prestegard: Maihaugen Årbok 1999* (1999), 67–79.

The pastor's remuneration was also – *mutatis mutandis* – an arena for the display of theological ideals. In a rural parish, this was part of a complex system with many variations. The main source was, of course, the income from the rectory. The pastor was a farmer. In addition came the tithe of the agrarian production of the parish, offerings and fees at church holidays and ritual celebrations. By charging a fee for a funeral sermon, the pastor could enter into a dialogue with his parishioners about the memory of the deceased, focusing on cultural and religious ideals and standards: what was a good Christian, an honest farmer and a law-abiding subject of the king?[21]

The sermon, the rectory, the pastor's family and remuneration constituted a public arena, creating opportunities for influence and negotiation between pastor and congregation. This arena primarily had references to the parish, where the pastor actually met people and dealt with them directly. If a pastor wanted to address a wider public, there were a few possibilities. The most important were to report and communicate through the clerical bureaucracy or to engage in publishing activities. Reporting through the bureaucracy was in many ways a closed system: as a civil servant, the pastor acted in solidarity with the government; but he could also position himself and influence decisions. Publishing, on the other hand, meant appealing to a general public whose reaction was less predictable; but at the same time, it entailed a potential for 'improvement' and increased 'Enlightenment' among readers. These readers did not represent physical quantities but a more abstract, indirect reality.

The bureaucratic public sphere was mainly focused on liturgy, legislation, education and charity. Since the 1680s, the Danish-Norwegian church government had explored the clergy's views on shortcomings and desired changes.[22] This had few results until the end of the eighteenth century, when the Danish Chancellery wanted legitimization for planned changes in the liturgy. Discussion of liturgical changes became a virtually explosive literary genre in Denmark–Norway in the 1780s, with a large number of authors

---

21 Arne Bugge Amundsen, 'Prestesekken som aldri ble full... Folkelige reaksjoner på sportler som del av prestens inntekt i efterreformatorisk tid', *Tidsskrift for Teologi og Kirke*, 58 (1987), 253–71.
22 Helge Fæhn (ed.), *Betenkninger fra geistligheten i Norge om Kirkeordinansen 1607 og 2. bok av Norske Lov 1687* (Oslo: Norsk historisk kjeldeskriftinstitutt, 1985).

from both countries contributing booklets and proposals that either defended the status quo or called for radical reorientation.[23]

On a more general basis, the Danish-Norwegian bureaucracy used the clergy's assessment of local conditions to inform the government and improve the quality of political and economic decisions. For example, a large number of Norwegian officials, including many pastors, answered the Danish Chancellery's questions from 1743 about local and regional history, antiques, culture and natural resources.[24]

The printing presses of Norway were regulated by censorship until 1814.[25] However, this did not prevent the emergence of a literary public sphere which also encompassed ecclesiastical and religious issues. The clergy in Norway also contributed; they prioritized having their publications printed in Copenhagen, which had by far the largest number of publishers and printing houses and thus afforded their publications the greatest possible distribution and attention. However, Bergen, Trondheim and Kristiania had printing presses and publishers in the eighteenth century, and they were used as well.[26] These printing houses had a regional impact, though they were still subject to censorship. In cases where publications were not sent to Copenhagen, they were produced in a closer relationship between author, censor and readers than could be expected in the Danish-Norwegian capital.

The observations so far are that the eighteenth-century Norwegian clergy were increasingly used to inform about, and evaluate, various aspects of culture and society. The censorship imposed limits on how freely they could express themselves; but the central authorities

---

23 Helge Fæhn, *Ritualspørsmålet i Norge 1785–1813: En liturgisk og kirkehistorisk undersøkelse med særlig henblikk på geistlighetens stilling til tidens reformplaner* (Oslo: Land og Kirke, 1956); Arne Bugge Amundsen, 'Hvem eier ritualene? Et essay om 1780-årenes liturgidebatt', in Malan Marnersdóttir, Jens Cramer and Anfinnur Johansen (eds), *Eyðvinur: Heiðursrit til Eyðun Andreassen* (Tórshavn: Føroya Fróðskaparfelag, 2005), pp. 100–7.
24 Kristin Røgeberg, Margit Løyland and Gerd Mordt (eds), *Norge i 1743: Innberetninger som svar på 43 spørsmål fra Danske Kanselli*, 5 vols (Oslo: Solum, 2003–2008).
25 Øystein Rian, *Sensuren i Danmark-Norge: Vilkårene for offentlige ytringer 1536–1814* (Oslo: Universitetsforlaget, 2014). For a more detailed account about the censorship in Denmark–Norway, see the contribution by Jakobsen and Nørgaard in this volume.
26 Gunnar Jacobsen, *Norske boktrykkere og trykkerier gjennom fire århundrer 1640–1940* (Oslo: Den norske boktrykkerforening, 1983).

also increasingly emphasized that clerical officials should contribute to change in the cultural and ecclesiastical area. A number of media and arenas were thus available to the clergy. The Lutheran ideal of the pastor's visibility helped make the clergy a particularly useful instrument for communicating needs for improvement and change in relation to a wide range of topics, from medicine and farming to ethics, politics and theology.[27] In a local context, the rural clergy – in a completely different way from the urban clergy and other civil servants – were in possession of a number of arenas and media that could be used for 'Enlightenment'. In the literary public sphere the possibilities were fewer, but they were more far-reaching.

Messages

Then, of course, comes the big question: what is Enlightenment – *was ist Aufklärung*? With pastoral practice as a point of departure, it is possible to downplay the philosophical and theological differences within the eighteenth-century Norwegian clergy. Instead, the variety of opportunities and endeavours will be demonstrated by an analysis of three clergymen who were variously concerned with creating change by imparting new knowledge and new practice, using arenas accessible to them. Despite their different cultural and theological backgrounds, they had forms of 'Enlightenment categories' in common.[28] Herman Ruge (1706–1764), Hans Strøm (1726–1797) and Peder Hansen (1746–1810) covered three generations of clergymen and the entire latter half of the eighteenth century.

---

27 Compare Øystein Lydik Idsø Viken, *Frygte Gud og ære Kongen: Preikestolen som politisk instrument i Noreg 1720–1814* (Oslo: University of Oslo, 2014); Michael Bregnsbo, *Samfundsorden og statsmagt set fra prædikestolen: danske præsters deltagelse i den offentlige opinionsdannelse vedrørende samfundsorden og statsmagt 1750–1848, belyst ved trykte prædikener: en politisk-idéhistorisk undersøgelse* (Copenhagen: Museum Tusculanum, 1997).

28 Several candidates could be relevant here, for example Jacob Nicolai Wilse (1736–1801), rector of Spydeberg and Eidsberg. See Tore Stubberud, *Jacob Nicolai Wilse: En opplysningsmann* (Rakkestad: Valdisholm, 2016); Harald Bakke, *Jacob Nicolaj Wilse: En kulturhelt* (Kristiania: Mallingske bogtrykkeri, 1912). Other examples include Johan Ernst Gunnerus (1718–1773) and Gerhard Schønning (1722–1780); see Arne Bugge Amundsen, 'Pastoralt kulturminnevern: Gerhard Schøning, Jacob Neumann og Magnus Brostrup Landstad', *Fortidsminneforeningen: Årbok 2019*, 173 (2019), 9–26. Compare the general overview found in Ludvig Selmer, *Oplysningsmenn i den norske kirke* (Bergen: Lunde, 1923).

Herman Ruge (1706–1764): critical reader and provider of books

Herman Ruge was the son of a pastor who served in Nesodden parish outside Kristiania. He became a student in 1724. In the years 1737–1763 he was the pastor of Slidre parish in Valdres. He then took up a position in Eidanger, but died soon after arriving there. In his own time, Ruge was known as a learned, active clergyman, with extensive knowledge of theology, philosophy, history, topography, medicine and science. He practised as a physician, recommended his congregation to grow potatoes as a remedy against famine and worked to improve agriculture and forestry in Valdres. As a student, he had had the celebrated professor and author Ludvig Holberg as a private tutor. Ruge declared his dependence on Christian Wolff's and Holberg's attempts to reconcile natural science with theology and religion. Little is known about Ruge's relationship with his congregation in Valdres. Local tradition, however, has retained the memory of his combative and critical encounters with farmers who were, in his opinion, self-willed and uninformed.[29]

Though none of his sermons have been preserved, in 1754 he published a book in Copenhagen in which he presented *Fornuftige Tanker over adskillige Curieuse Materier, udi XI. Breve afhandlede til gode Venner* (['Rational thoughts on several curious matters, in eleven letters written for friends']).[30] At first glance, the issues discussed in these letters are surprising: most of the topics relate to (local) folklore and folk beliefs – about changelings, ghosts, supernatural beings, Christmas traditions and the bear's winter den. Ruge also addressed topics such as the punishments of hell, the banishment of sinners, promiscuity and the forbidden tree in Paradise. He attempted to place supernatural beings in a scientific context, but without rejecting their real existence; according to him, there were natural explanations for the existence of these creatures. His aim was to 'enlighten', but also to explain existing phenomena and locate the contemporary popular culture in its proper scientific context. Ruge is thus far from Erik Pontoppidan with his total rejection of popular traditions such as paganism and papism.

---

29 Compare Kristen Valkner, 'Ruge, Herman', *Norsk biografisk leksikon*, 19 vols (Oslo: Aschehoug, 1923–1983), XII (1954), pp. 17–20.
30 Herman Ruge, *Fornuftige Tanker over adskillige Curieuse Materier, udi XI. Breve afhandlede til gode Venner, Hvorhos følger et ey tilforn trykt Klage-Vers over den Høy-Salige Dronning Lovises Død* (Copenhagen: Berlingske Arvingers Bogtrykkerie, 1754).

On this basis, one might have thought that Ruge would have been unequivocally in favour of the popular religious culture, but that is not the case; instead, he wanted to explain that culture to the reading public and disconnect it from 'the common man's fabulous imagination'.[31] The 'Enlightenment' that Ruge pursued in the local public arena was critical, and it was aimed at changing practices and attitudes, for instance in agriculture, nutrition and medicine. His local recognition is indicated by the rumour that he was a keeper of secret magical books, so-called 'black books'. This probably expresses more of a respect for Ruge's special connection to supernatural powers than a willingness to listen to his actual message, in writing or speech.

This ambivalence is not part of Ruge's role as an author addressing the national public. He gave the content of his book a discursive touch by shaping it as letters to 'friends'. Through the dedication to Erik Pontoppidan, who had served his last year as Bishop of Bergen in 1754 and was on his way back to Copenhagen as the university's Vice-Chancellor, Ruge sought to address the learned public. It is obvious that Ruge would rather have seen himself in the position of a professor than as a clergyman banished to a remote parish vocation. He used his book as an imperfectly concealed application for such a career change. To be noticed in even higher circles, he also included in the book a mourning poem about the late and very popular Danish-Norwegian queen Louise (1724–1751).

Not even this book from 1754 yielded any immediate benefit for Ruge. It would be almost ten years before he was awarded an office in an urban area, and he never received a university position. In Norwegian intellectual history, he has often been sidelined as one of the 'forgotten'. This does not do him justice. He is an interesting and early example of a rural pastor using his possibilities to act as an agent of change in a local context and to address a literate public with observations based on his pastoral practice.

Hans Strøm (1726–1797): indefatigable writer and rural spectator

Hans Strøm was born in Norway into a widely branched family of pastors. He became a student in 1743 and a theology graduate

---

31 Arne Bugge Amundsen, 'Med overtroen gjennom historien: Noen linjer i folkloristisk faghistorie 1730–1930', in Siv Bente Grongstad and others (eds), *Hinsides: Folkloristiske perspektiver på det overnaturlige* (Oslo: Spartacus, 1999), pp. 13–49 (pp. 14–17, 20).

two years later. In 1750, he became chaplain to his father's successor as parish pastor in Borgund. Strøm was appointed parish pastor in Volda in 1764, a position he exchanged for Eker parish near Kristiania in 1779.[32]

For posterity, Strøm has often been highlighted as a prominent zoologist and natural scientist. However, he was primarily – in line with Herman Ruge – a Wolffian theologian who saw God's will and plan in nature and in natural phenomena. With Wolffianism as a background, 'Enlightenment' became important for Strøm as well. His many articles on natural phenomena gained a national and international readership; but as a clergyman, he related to several dynamic public arenas different from those of natural science.

In the 1760s, Strøm published a two-volume topographical description of Sunnmøre, which quickly became a model for similar works in Denmark–Norway.[33] His potential readership was national, but much of the knowledge presented in the book was gained by observing and talking to local people during his fourteen years as a chaplain. Though the topography of Sunnmøre was a scholarly work according to the standards of the time, it was also built on pastoral practice.

Another printed work was his two-volume magazine *Tilskueren paa Landet* ('The rural spectator'), published in Copenhagen in 1775.[34] Here Strøm acts as an observer who comments and interacts with his contemporaries. In the preface, he stresses his conviction that not only urban readers but also readers living in the countryside could find useful arguments and thoughts in his writings. Therefore, he wrote so that 'common people' could be acquainted with what might 'improve the human sense and heart'.[35] From the towns and cities, increased Enlightenment and knowledge would come, Strøm believed, and all 'savagery and senselessness' would eventually disappear.[36] In his journal, he addressed not only scientific topics but also psychological, ethical, agricultural-economic, political and folkloristic ones. The appeal to 'common people' was explicit; but

---

32 See Hjalmar Christensen, 'Hans Strøm', *Edda* XI (1919), 208–29; Arne Apelseth, *Hans Strøm (1726–1797): Ein kommentert bibliografi* (Volda: Høgskulen i Volda, 1995).
33 Hans Strøm, *Physisk og Oeconomisk Beskrivelse over Fogderiet Søndmøer*, 2 vols (Sorø, 1762–1766).
34 Hans Strøm, *Tilskueren paa Landet*, 2 vols (Copenhagen: H. C. Sander, 1775).
35 'Meenige Mand'; 'forbedre den menneskelige Forstand og Hierte'.
36 'Vildskab og Sandsesløshed'.

as the magazine was published in Copenhagen, the readership seemed far away from his local congregation or the regional 'spectators' in Sunnmøre. The 'common people' became an imaginary reader, a rhetorical figure who had limited connections with Strøm's pastoral practice in Volda parish.

Strøm took up office in Eker in 1779, thus moving to a very different part of Norway. Here, too, he was active as a preacher; and in the 1790s, he published a collection of sermons intended as a 'devotional exercise for the common people'.[37] Though the book was printed in Copenhagen, it was dedicated to his local congregation. In these sermons, Strøm appeared as a conservative, Lutheran preacher, bound to the current liturgical texts. However, he added a chapter with 'instructions for the common people on how to know God by his deeds in nature',[38] referring to his 'Rural Spectator' magazine published twenty years earlier. In this chapter, Strøm explained how traditional church preaching was the explanation of God's creation. This collection of sermons from the 1790s can be interpreted as a summary of Strøm's 'Enlightenment'. Those who were enlightened among his parishioners in Eker should learn both from nature and from theology: 'not all peasants (as Luther has said) are geese just because they are grey'.[39]

With less success, Strøm had attempted the genre of 'nature sermons', following contemporary German conventions, in the 1780s. He realized that in meetings with common people, the pastor had to 'push on with the most necessary information and repeat it a hundred times'. One could not, then, aspire to achieve the stylistic level of, for instance, Christian Bastholm. Such fashionable and elevated styles disagreed with the taste of the common people: 'fashionable new words and expressions do not fit in with the concepts and ways of speaking used among common people'.[40]

Strøm's 1790 collection of sermons summarized his life-long work for 'Enlightenment'. Both pastors and congregations were in need of a widened understanding of God's creation and an improved

---

37 'Andagtsøvelse for Almuen', in Hans Strøm, *Prædikener over alle Søn- og Festdages Evangelier til Andagtsøvelse for Almuen* (Copenhagen: Gyldendal, 1792).
38 'Anviisning for Almuen til at kiende Gud af hans Gierninger i Naturen'.
39 'ikke alle Bønder (som Luther har sagt) ere Giæs, fordi de ere graae'.
40 'drive paa med det mest fornødne og hundrede Gange at gjentage det'; 'de nyemoedens Ord og Talemaader [ere] ikke passende til deres Begreb og Mund-Art'; Hagesæther, *Norsk preken fra Reformasjonen*, pp. 278–88 (quotations found on pp. 279, 282).

utilization of nature. The divine voice, expressed through the local pastor's mouth, still had to adhere to traditional patterns. 'Enlightenment', then, had two faces: one was traditional, the other experimental and forward-orientated.

Peder Hansen (1746–1810): fighter against superstition

Peder Hansen was born in Copenhagen. His father was a craftsman and his mother a wet-nurse. Fortunately for him, she was chosen to breastfeed the future King Christian VII. Thanks to this connection to the court and his obvious talents, Hansen made a remarkable career. He graduated with a theological degree 'with distinction' in 1768, and then received a royal scholarship to study abroad. In Halle and Jena, he encountered modern, Bible-critical theology. In 1780 he became an extraordinary professor of theology, and in 1793 was awarded a doctorate in theology in Halle. In 1771, Hansen became resident chaplain at Elsinore's castle and garrison congregation, and in the following year he was appointed to preach to the scandalized and arrested Danish-Norwegian queen Caroline Mathilde (1751–1775) at Kronborg castle. In 1775, he became pastor in Skanderborg, in 1779 in Ringsted and in 1787 in Copenhagen. In 1799, he was appointed Bishop of Kristiansand and in 1804 Bishop of Funen.[41]

Hansen was originally influenced by Christian Wolff's thinking. In a collection of sermons published in the 1780s, he expressed himself in a rather conservative manner. In the 1790s, however, he became influenced by more radical German theology. In 1795, he published a book on the 'gravity' of Lutheran clergy, in which he discusses pastoral dignity squeezed between modern thinking and conservative values. He also dealt with this issue in 1803, when he claimed that the pastor was an ordinary civil servant in the service of the state who worked for Enlightenment, refinement and 'happiness' (*lyksalighed*) among the king's subjects. Authorship and clerical practice show Hansen's ideological development, but they also demonstrate the complexity that many clergymen grappled with at the time, adapting ('accommodating') to their listeners' knowledge and cultural level.

Peder Hansen's foremost interest as a bishop was educational work. His explicit goal was to replace widespread prejudice and

---

41 Arne Bugge Amundsen, 'Hansen, Peder', *Norsk biografisk leksikon*, 10 vols (Oslo: Kunnskapsforlaget, 1999–2005), IV (2001), pp. 79–80.

superstition with rational moral and religious concepts. Hansen started by reforming the schools in the city of Kristiansand. After visitations in his diocese, he concluded that there was an urgent need for school reform. The remedy was to provide better training for schoolteachers and to motivate common people to read. Between 1799 and 1802, Hansen himself held annual courses for schoolteachers, and he submitted several proposals for improving education and conditions for teachers. Interest in reading was to be supported by local associations 'for enlightenment and the dissemination of good conduct',[42] where members were given access to books and exposed to favourable influences through pastors. Hansen's school and reading programme included both modern religious literature and a wide range of 'useful' topics. He also organized his own synods, where new theology and new ideals for practical church life were discussed according to his instructions.

Hansen's way of thinking is also displayed in his work on liturgy. He wanted to simplify worship, hymn singing and clerical dress according to the demands of the new age. In his opinion, the modern, 'enlightened' *Evangelisk-Christelig Psalmebog* ('Evangelical-Christian hymn book') from 1798 should be imposed on all parishes, and the clergy were encouraged to choose sermon texts on a free basis and not feel obliged to adhere to the prescribed sequence of the liturgical year. Hansen wanted to reduce or simplify the old liturgical forms, for instance allowing the pastor to perform the service from the pulpit, wearing an everyday robe. In addition, Hansen launched his own draft of a new baptism and communion liturgy. He began his short episcopate in Norway by distributing a letter to the clergy in which he warned against fanatical and irrational religiosity. In particular, he referred to the pietistic revival movement inspired by the commoner Hans Nielsen Hauge (1771–1824) as an obvious danger to Church and state. His last official act in Norway was in the spring of 1804, reporting on this movement, which seriously set the Danish Chancellery in motion to stop its leader. A comprehensive expression of Hansen's efforts as a bishop in Kristiansand is the two-volume *Archiv for Skolevæsenets og Oplysnings Udbredelse i Christiansands Stift* ('Archive for the increase of school education and enlightenment in the Diocese of Christiansand', 1800–1803). In this publication the bishop published his reform proposals, presented school arrangements, submitted messages from the clergy

---

42 'til Oplysning og gode Sæders Udbredelse'.

and offered information about topography, history and 'the superstition of the common people'.⁴³

Peder Hansen had important networks in the Danish-Norwegian capital of Copenhagen, and he demonstrated an ability to promote his own career. Addressing a national reading public with messages directed towards the bureaucratic church establishment became his most important instrument for appearing as an advocate of 'Enlightenment'. Theologically, Hansen was radical. However, his major problem as Bishop of Kristiansand may have been that he did not understand Norwegian conditions, and that he was too eager to show his superiors in Copenhagen that he was a man of action, reason and progress. As a bishop, Hansen had limited access to the local public, and the 'Enlightenment' he presented and represented had limited significance in the local and regional context.

Conclusion

The Norwegian eighteenth-century Enlightenment had many arenas, instruments, spokesmen and lines of argument. Though 'pastoral Enlightenment' was dominant in Norway, where the clergy was central in a state administration of the king's subjects, options for control, deliberation and communication were limited. A mainstream idea in the latter part of the century was that religion and mentality ought to be developed according to new standards and ideals, and not just defended as something from the past or unchangeable. Sharing this perspective, Pietists acted along the same lines as advocates of enlightened progress: the present was a problem, change was the solution, and action and strategy had the future as their horizon. 'Enlightenment' was about a desire for improvement and change, but this desire could be justified by various theological positions.

In a country like Norway, the clergy had to balance between different public spheres and arenas. A pastor of a rural congregation had to understand his parishioners, but he must also criticize and correct them. In this endeavour, the pastor had limited options. The Norwegian farmers were not serfs; they were not bound by stakes, but had an independent perception of the local religious context and their own rights to negotiate with their pastor. They owed him

---

43 'Almuens Overtroe'. See also Peder Hansen, *Archiv for Skolevæsenets og Oplysnings Udbredelse i Christiansands Stift*, 2 vols (Copenhagen: J. Breinholm, 1800–1803).

services, but he was dependent on them. The enlightened pastor's solution to this dilemma was accommodation, adaptation to the local public. Herman Ruge was an example of this dual position: he acted locally and argued nationally, but may not have succeeded either way. In his local parish, he was only remembered as a pastor with magic power.

During the 1790s, having experienced a brutal and offensive public in Copenhagen, Peder Hansen evolved a vision of 'Enlightenment' influenced by a new-found respect for the clergy. Whether that enabled him to interpret the cultural context of the many rural parishes in the Diocese of Kristiansand is an open question. However, there are many indications that he, with his Danish urban background, was not able to achieve balance between the various public arenas in his diocese.

Hans Strøm arguably succeeded better than Ruge and Hansen when it came to defining a 'Norwegian voice' in the absolutist double monarchy. Strøm had intimate knowledge of Norway; his background was a Norwegian, orthodox-pietistic clerical family; and he was able to interpret the contemporary need to combine tradition with renewal. There were novel traits in Strøm's 'Enlightenment', but it was simultaneously rooted in local traditionalism. He balanced between local and national public arenas, and he tried – with the authority of his clerical office – to understand the 'commoners' in all their complexity.

In the enlightened public arenas, between the local and the national, Hans Strøm – and many clergymen with him – ended up as 'rural spectators'. They sought to understand and interpret their congregations; and they communicated and negotiated with them while simultaneously addressing a national literate audience. Balancing this cultural and theological ambiguity, these clergymen demonstrate the complexity of the 'Enlightenment' in the European North. It was, in the words of the Danish literary historian Thomas Bredsdorff, a 'variegated Enlightenment'.[44]

---

44 Thomas Bredsdorff, *Den brogede oplysning: Om følelsernes fornuft og fornuftens følelse i 1700-tallets nordiske litteratur* (Copenhagen: Gyldendal, 2003).

Bibliography

Digital sources

Appel, Charlotte and Carsten Porskrog Rasmussen, 'Reformation og magtstat, 1523–1660', https://danmarkshistorien.dk/perioder/reformation-og-magtstat-1523-1660 [accessed 3 February 2023].

Schriver, Astrid, 'Danmarks befolkningsudvikling 1769–2015', https://danmarkshistorien.dk/leksikon-og-kilder/vis/materiale/danmarks-befolkningsudvikling/ [accessed 10 September 2020].

Statistisk sentralbyrå, 'Historisk statistikk: 3.1 Hjemmehørende folkemengde', www.ssb.no/a/histstat/tabeller/3-1.html [accessed 10 September 2020].

Thorsnæs, Geir, 'Norge (bosettingsmønster)', https://snl.no/Norge_-_bosettingsm%C3%B8nster [accessed 10 September 2020].

Printed sources and literature

Alstrup, Erik and Poul Erik Olsen (eds), *Dansk kulturhistorisk opslagsværk*, 2 vols (Copenhagen: Dansk historisk Fællesforening, 1991).

Amundsen, Arne Bugge, '"Byen som ligger på fjellet": Presten som kulturbærer i gammel tid', *Tidsskrift for kirke, religion og samfunn*, 3 (1990), 67–81.

——, 'Embetsmann, lensmann, bonde', *Varden: Tidsskrift utgitt av Onsøy Historielag 1992* (1992), 27–35.

——, 'Hansen, Peder', *Norsk biografisk leksikon*, 10 vols (Oslo: Kunnskapsforlaget, 1999–2005), IV (2001), pp. 79–80.

——, 'Hvem eier ritualene? Et essay om 1780-årenes liturgidebatt', in Malan Marnersdóttir, Jens Cramer and Anfinnur Johansen (eds), *Eyðvinur: Heiðursrit til Eyðun Andreassen* (Tórshavn: Føroya Fróðskaparfelag, 2005), pp. 100–7.

——, 'Med overtroen gjennom historien: Noen linjer i folkloristisk faghistorie 1730–1930', in Siv Bente Grongstad and others (eds), *Hinsides: Folkloristiske perspektiver på det overnaturlige* (Oslo: Spartacus, 1999), pp. 13–49.

——, 'Pastoralt kulturminnevern: Gerhard Schøning, Jacob Neumann og Magnus Brostrup Landstad', *Fortidsminneforeningen: Årbok 2019*, 173 (2019), 9–26.

——, 'Poteter og snusfornuft? Opplysningstidens prester og prestegårder', *Prest og prestegard: Maihaugen Årbok 1999* (1999), 52–65.

——, 'Prestesekken som aldri ble full … Folkelige reaksjoner på sportler som del av prestens inntekt i efterreformatorisk tid', *Tidsskrift for Teologi og Kirke*, 58 (1987), 253–71.

——, 'Reformation, manors and nobility in Norway 1500–1821', in Jonathan Finch and others (eds), *Estate Landscapes in Northern Europe* (Aarhus: Aarhus University Press, 2019), pp. 233–70.

Apelseth, Arne, *Hans Strøm (1726–1797): Ein kommentert bibliografi* (Volda: Høgskulen i Volda, 1995).
Bakke, Harald, *Jacob Nicolaj Wilse: En kulturhelt* (Kristiania: Mallingske bogtrykkeri, 1912).
Bastholm, Christian, *Den Geistlige Talekonst, tilligemed en Bedømmelse over en af Saurins Tale* (Copenhagen: Gyldendal, 1775).
Befolkningsforholdene i Danmark i det 19. Aarhundrede (Copenhagen: Bianco Luno, 1905).
Bredsdorff, Thomas, *Den brogede oplysning: Om følelsernes fornuft og fornuftens følelse i 1700-tallets nordiske litteratur* (Copenhagen: Gyldendal, 2003).
Bregnsbo, Michael, *Samfundsorden og statsmagt set fra prædikestolen: danske præsters deltagelse i den offentlige opinionsdannelse vedrørende samfundsorden og statsmagt 1750–1848, belyst ved trykte prædikener: en politiskidéhistorisk undersøgelse* (Copenhagen: Museum Tusculanum, 1997).
Burgess, J. Peter (ed.), *Den norske pastorale opplysning: Nye perspektiver på norsk nasjonsbygging på 1800-tallet* (Oslo: Abstrakt, 2003).
Christensen, Hjalmar, 'Hans Strøm', *Edda* XI (1919), 208–29.
Fæhn, Helge (ed.), *Betenkninger fra geistligheten i Norge om Kirkeordinansen 1607 og 2. bok av Norske Lov 1687* (Oslo: Norsk historisk kjeldeskriftinstitutt, 1985).
———, *Ritualspørsmålet i Norge 1785–1813: En liturgisk og kirkehistorisk undersøkelse med særlig henblikk på geistlighetens stilling til tidens reformplaner* (Oslo: Land og Kirke, 1956).
Folketeljinga 1801 (Oslo: Statistisk Sentralbyrå, 1980).
Hagesæther, Olav, *Norsk preken fra Reformasjonen til omlag 1820* (Oslo, Bergen, Tromsø: Universitetsforlaget, 1973).
Hansen, Peder, *Archiv for Skolevæsenets og Oplysnings Udbredelse i Christiansands Stift*, 2 vols (Copenhagen: J. Breinholm, 1800–1803).
Heffermehl, A. V., *Geistlige Møder i Norge: Et Bidrag til den norske Kirkes Historie efter Reformationen til 1814* (Kristiania: Alb. Cammermeyer, 1890).
Hermansen, Karsten, *Kirken, kongen og enevælden: En undersøgelse af det danske bispeembede 1660–1746* (Odense: Syddansk Universitetsforlag, 2005).
Jacobsen, Gunnar, *Norske boktrykkere og trykkerier gjennom fire århundrer 1640–1940* (Oslo: Den norske boktrykkerforening, 1983).
Kvideland, Reimund, 'Prestefolket som lækjarar', *Prest og prestegard: Maihaugen Årbok 1999* (1999), 67–79.
Matthiessen, Christian Wichmann, *Danske byers folketal 1801–1981*, Statistiske undersøgelser nr. 42 (Copenhagen: Danmarks Statistik, 1985).
Pontoppidan, Erik, *Collegium Pastorale Practicum* (Copenhagen: Det Kongelige Waysenhuus, 1757).
Rasmussen, Carsten Porskrog, 'Manors and states: the distribution and structure of private manors in early modern Scandinavia and their

relation to state policies', *Scandinavian Economic History Review*, 66 (2018), 1–18.
Rian, Øystein, *Sensuren i Danmark-Norge: Vilkårene for offentlige ytringer 1536–1814* (Oslo: Universitetsforlaget, 2014).
Røgeberg, Kristin, Margit Løyland and Gerd Mordt (eds), *Norge i 1743: Innberetninger som svar på 43 spørsmål fra Danske Kanselli*, 5 vols (Oslo: Solum, 2003–2008).
Ruge, Herman, *Fornuftige Tanker over adskillige Curieuse Materier, udi XI. Breve afhandlede til gode Venner, Hvorhos følger et ey tilforn trykt Klage-Vers over den Høy-Salige Dronning Lovises Død* (Copenhagen: Berlingske Arvingers Bogtrykkerie, 1754).
Selmer, Ludvig, *Oplysningsmenn i den norske kirke* (Bergen: Lunde, 1923).
Strøm, Hans, *Physisk og Oeconomisk Beskrivelse over Fogderiet Søndmøer*, 2 vols (Sorø, 1762–1766).
——, *Prædikener over alle Søn- og Festdages Evangelier til Andagtsøvelse for Almuen* (Copenhagen: Gyldendal, 1792).
——, *Tilskueren paa Landet*, 2 vols (Copenhagen: H. C. Sander, 1775).
Stubberud, Tore, *Jacob Nicolai Wilse: En opplysningsmann* (Rakkestad: Valdisholm, 2016).
Sundbärg, Gustaf, *Sveriges land och folk* (Stockholm: P. A. Norstedt, 1901).
Valkner, Kristen, 'Ruge, Herman', *Norsk biografisk leksikon*, 19 vols (Oslo: Aschehoug, 1923–1983), XII (1954), pp. 17–20.
Viken, Øystein Lydik Idsø, *Frygte Gud og ære Kongen: Preikestolen som politisk instrument i Noreg 1720–1814* (Oslo: University of Oslo, 2014).

2
Promoting individualism under the guise of uniformity: a bishop's instructions in late eighteenth-century Sweden

Erik Sidenvall

In eighteenth-century Europe, reformers of church practices often had to contend with inflexible systems of ecclesiastical law or with church ordinances (whatever form they took) formed during previous centuries. In spite of the zeal for improvement that characterized the age, reform of ecclesiastical statutes was often a slow, gradual and many times a haphazard process.[1] In the Nordic countries, canon law was abolished as part of the Lutheran Reformation. In Denmark–Norway, the Lutheran *Kirkeordinansen* (Church Ordinance) gained royal sanction as early as 1537–1539. By 1571 a similar set of statutes was in place in the Swedish realm. Although less ambitious in scope, these sets of ecclesiastical statutes aimed at replacing canon law as the legal framework of the nationalized churches together with Lutheran confessional documents. As a result of the process of seventeenth-century confessionalization, however, ecclesiastical statutes came to be included in national law. This occurred with the Danish Code of 1683, and in Sweden the Church Law of 1686 had a similar effect.

---

1 For a general overview, see Antonio Padoa Schioppa, *A History of Law in Europe: From the Early Middle Ages to the Twentieth Century* (Cambridge: Cambridge University Press, 2017). For studies focusing on particular parts of Europe, see for example Richard Burgess Barlow, *Citizenship and Conscience: A Study in the Theory and Practice of Religious Toleration in England during the Eighteenth Century* (Philadelphia, PA: University of Pennsylvania Press, 1962); Joris van Eijnatten, *Liberty and Concord in the United Provinces: Religious Toleration and the Public in the Eighteenth-Century Netherlands* (Leiden: Brill, 2003); Ulrich L. Lehner, *The Catholic Enlightenment: The Forgotten History of a Global Movement* (New York: Oxford University Press, 2016), Chapter 2; and Michael J. Sauter, *Visions of the Enlightenment: The Edict on Religion of 1788 and the Politics of the Public Sphere in Eighteenth-Century Prussia* (Leiden: Brill, 2009).

In the European North, generally speaking, much of the statutory framework regulating local church life was hence rooted in the ideals of Lutheran orthodoxy. As a consequence, most ecclesiastical reformers – of whom there were many in the Nordic countries during the eighteenth century, not least the Danish-Norwegian bishop Erik Pontoppidan – had to learn to be loyal to, or to operate from within, rather inflexible systems of regulations. This did not mean that change was impossible or out of reach for those who sincerely believed that traditional religious habits should be transformed. On the one hand, church authorities – however much they embraced a reforming agenda and a rationalizing theology – were forced to promote ecclesiastical dictates rooted in an age with a different spiritual ambiance; on the other hand, we may say that proponents of what we call the Enlightenment found ways to work from within the machinery of traditional religious cultures (here represented by church laws and ordinances) in order to enforce and propagate the new. As Jeremy Gregory has remarked, '[i]f the procedures were old-fashioned, it did not mean that there was no room for manœuvre, and if major changes cannot be found in the legislative structures of the Church, they may nevertheless be found in its local history'.[2] This occurred at a time when many European rulers, Sweden's Gustav III being only one example among many, tried to promote Enlightenment by way of 'top-down' dictates and a centralized state apparatus. Throughout Europe, local persons of ecclesiastical authority could therefore easily find official sanctioning for their frequently inventive ways of promoting change.[3]

---

2 Jeremy Gregory, *Restoration, Reformation and Reform, 1660–1828: Archbishops of Canterbury and Their Diocese* (Oxford: Oxford University Press, 2000), p. 8. See also D. W. Hayton, 'Parliament and the established church: reform and reaction', in D. W. Hayton, James Kelly and John Bergin (eds), *The Eighteenth-Century Composite State* (London: Palgrave Macmillan, 2010), pp. 78–106.

3 Lehner, *The Catholic Enlightenment*, pp. 33–40; Raquel Poy Castro, 'Regeneración educativa y cultural de la España moderna: reformas monárquicas en educación y el papel de los obispos de la ilustración en el siglo XVIII', *Cuadernos Dieciochistas*, 10 (2011), 185–217; M. I. Florutau, 'Regional Enlightenment in Transylvania: the educational reforms of Bishop Petru Pavel Aron, their influences and effects on the Uniate society in Transylvania in the Age of Enlightenment', *Slovo*, 27:1 (2015), 9–33. For the Swedish situation, see Börje Harnesk and Marja

Even though the new often lived under the guise of the old, or in its close proximity, this feature of eighteenth-century reform has received surprisingly little scholarly attention. The present chapter approaches this issue by way of a micro study. By studying how the late eighteenth-century Swedish bishop Olof Wallquist (1755–1800) introduced novel ideas by way of legal commentary, and exploited a top-down system of ecclesiastical management in his diocese, this chapter picks up on the cue offered by Gregory. Analysing Wallquist's systematic methods of promoting change, as well as the ways in which local rectors responded to their superior's initiatives, produces a case study of how individualizing practices could be introduced within intractable, and largely collectivistic, legal and social frameworks. The outcome is another perspective on 'pastoral Enlightenment'.

A changing social landscape

Before we take a closer look at Bishop Wallquist and his reforming measures, the scene needs to be set by means of some basic information about the cultural and social/demographic conditions in Sweden during the long eighteenth century. In terms of geography, the realm then known as Sweden was of considerably larger proportions than today. Historically speaking, much of today's Finland was an integral part of the Swedish kingdom. Duties and privileges were extended in equal measure to the inhabitants of both the western and the eastern part of the kingdom. Finland and Sweden, for example, both took part in the Swedish parliament, the *Riksdag*. As a result of a series of unsuccessful wars during the 1740s, parts of the eastern border region were lost to Russia; it was, however, not until 1809 that Sweden was forced to cede the eastern part of the realm to the Tsar. During the period covered by this volume, a few coastal cities and regions in today's Germany were under Swedish governance, too (unlike Finland, though, they did not form part of Sweden proper). Following the Peace of Nystad (1721), they consisted of the town of Wismar in Mecklenburg and so-called Swedish Pomerania.

Taussi Sjöberg (eds), *Mellan makten och menigheten: ämbetsmän i det tidigmoderna Sverige* (Stockholm: Institutet för rättshistorisk forskning, 2001); Peter Nordström, *Reformer och rationalisering: Kung, råd och förvaltning under tidig gustaviansk tid, 1772–1778* (Uppsala: Almqvist & Wiksell International, 1991).

In terms of population, numbers rose steadily from the 1740s onwards. In 1800, today's Sweden had about 2,347,000 inhabitants;[4] in what is now Finland, the population figure for the same year amounted to approximately 833,000.[5] In terms of the ratio between urban and rural populations, Sweden was, just like Norway, markedly less urbanized than Denmark. About 10 per cent of the population lived in towns and cities, a figure that remained fairly constant throughout the period covered by this volume. In the 1730s, the smallest of these densely populated places, Falsterbo in southernmost Sweden, had just a little over 100 inhabitants, whereas the largest, Stockholm, had about 57,000 during the same decade.[6] In Finland, twenty-four towns were scattered along the Baltic coast in the south. Turku (Åbo in Swedish), the largest of these, boasted approximately 5,700 inhabitants in 1749.[7] The largest of the cities grew significantly during the eighteenth century. By 1800, Stockholm had a population of 75,500. Still, most regional centres (most of which were also cathedral cities) only had a population of 1,000–2,000 in the early 1800s.[8]

All in all, eighteenth-century Sweden consisted of fourteen dioceses. Two of these – Turku and Porvoo – were located in what is now Finland. Within the different dioceses, the traditional, medieval, structure of parishes remained intact throughout the period. Especially in the easternmost regions of the realm and in the far north, the dioceses (but also the parishes) were of considerable geographical proportions, which made proper episcopal supervision a more than troublesome charge. Both parochial visitations and regular clergy conferences (*prästmöte*) were powerful control instruments placed in the bishop's hands by the Church Law.

Contrary to what was the case in most other European nations at the time, local landowners (a majority of whom were commoners) had a considerable influence on local church life. Direct aristocratic patronage was relatively uncommon (save in the southernmost, and previously Danish, Province of Scania). In most parishes, the power

---

4 *Historisk statistik för Sverige, [Population 1720–1967]*, 2nd edn (Örebro: Statistiska centralbyrån, 1969), I, p. 47.
5 Petri Karonen, *Pohjoinen suurvalta: Ruotsi ja Suomi 1521–1809* (Helsinki: Werner Söderström, 2008), p. 37.
6 http://ortshistoria.se/befolkning/1730t [accessed 29 October 2021].
7 Karonen, *Pohjoinen suurvalta*, p. 40.
8 Stads- och kommunhistoriska institutet, 'Alla svenska städer: befolkning', http://ortshistoria.se/befolkning/1800 [accessed 6 February 2023].

to elect the pastor rested either with the local community or with the diocesan chapter. In comparison with Denmark–Norway, this gave a distinctive flair to early modern Swedish church life.

Apart from those who belonged to a thinly dispersed nobility, most men who entered the clergy and the civil service had received their basic intellectual training at the cathedral schools located at the diocesan centres of the realm. For those aiming for the Church, and for a considerable proportion of other prospective office holders at the Stockholm-based centres of national administration, a degree from one of the four universities of the nation – Uppsala (1477), Åbo [Turku] Royal Academy (1640) in today's Finland, Greifswald in Pomerania (Swedish from 1648) and Lund (1666) in the Province of Scania – increasingly became a prerequisite. Though mostly traditionally orientated, these universities, most of which were poorly endowed, became channels of new philosophical ideals and new techniques of scientific enquiry (see also the introduction to this volume).

Church Law and eighteenth-century religious life

Most scholars of early modern church life in Sweden regard the Church Law as the apogee of Lutheran orthodoxy. In many ways it was the culmination of the so-called 'confessionalization' of Swedish society, seemingly marking the end of much clerical endeavour to bring about a unified Lutheran nation.[9] Yet the passing of the Church Law was also the terminus of a long religio-political struggle for power in which the devout, and absolute, King Charles XI (r. 1672–1697) had finally gained the upper hand. The Church Law of 1686, which was to a considerable extent a product of the King's closest advisers, aimed at creating uniform ecclesiastical practices within the Swedish domains.[10] Hitherto, the statutes (of which the most important was the Church Ordinance of 1571) regulating national church life had given ample scope to the evolution of varying observances within the different dioceses.

---

9 For this term, see Heinz Schilling, *Religion, Political Culture and the Emergence of Early Modern Society: Essays in German and Dutch History* (Leiden: Brill, 1992), pp. 205–45.
10 See Göran Inger, 'Kyrkolagstiftningen under 1600-talet', in Ingun Montgomery (ed.), *Sveriges kyrkohistoria*, IV: *Enhetskyrkans tid* (Stockholm: Verbum, 2002), pp. 204–13; Sven Kjöllerström, *Kyrkolagsproblemet i Sverige 1571–1682* (Stockholm: Svenska kyrkans diakonistyrelses bokförlag, 1944).

Seventeenth-century bishops, vested in both political and religious power, created ordinances and practices that were to be observed throughout their respective dioceses. As a consequence, medieval 'diocesan particularity' endured within the Lutheran Church. With the ratification of a national Church Law, the hope was that this state of things was to come to an end.

With this new set of statutes in place, the emphasis on the need for national unity in all matters ecclesiastical was more strongly felt. There were to be no discrepancies among the parishes in terms of services, the obligations of the clergy and the religious duties of parishioners. Even though the passing of a Church Law was a deed at first regretted by a significant proportion of the Church leadership, its main objective (to enforce a national religious uniformity) was to be shared by leading ecclesiastics throughout the eighteenth century.[11]

The ambition to create homogeneity in a hitherto heterogeneous Church resulted in the regulation of minute details in church life and practice. Even in respect of particulars, the clergy – bound by oath to uphold and abide by the king's law – had to be sensitive to the intentions and precise regulations found in the statutes. It goes without saying that the law passed in 1686 could be seen both as a codification of the church practices that had evolved within Swedish domains since the late sixteenth century (in many cases the Church Law was an attempt to create a national benchmark among varying practices) and as a 'project' to be realized in the future. Throughout the eighteenth century (and beyond), the correct application of the Church Law was an issue that was to trouble both ecclesiastics and the leading men of the realm. It should be noted that in 1760, Sven Wilskman (1716–1797), at the time a schoolmaster at the cathedral school of Skara, edited *Swea rikes ecclesiastique wärk*, an encyclopaedia-like volume containing abstracts from the Church Law and additional – both later and earlier – statutes and royal proclamations.[12] This work, very much in line with the contemporary vogue for exhaustive knowledge and for publishing tomes of collected documents, came to be extensively used in diocesan chapters and thereby contributed to consistency in diocesan decision-making.

---

11 Inger, 'Kyrkolagstiftningen under 1600-talet'.
12 See Sven Wilskman, *Swea rikes ecclesiastique wärk, i alphabetisk ordning sammandragit, utur lag och förordningar, privilegier och resolutioner, samt andra handlingar; af Sven Wilskman* (Skara, 1760). A new and revised edition appeared in 1781–1782.

As is often the case, the ambition to create sameness results in new uncertainties; a void appears which is filled with regulation, interpretation and commentary. The need to explain and augment the Church Law was a theme that kept recurring throughout the eighteenth century. As the century progressed, it became evident that the Church Law had not managed to create a standard in all matters of church life, even though that had been the lawgiver's ambition. The spread and acceptance of new modes of thought and conduct caused new conflicts to which the legal edifice was ill suited. The issue of how the new ideas, tastes and manners that came with Enlightenment and Pietism might be combined with the Church Law of 1686 was a challenge, as well as an opportunity, for most of those who desired the reform of religion.[13]

It was the duty of bishops and diocesan chapters to monitor the observance of the Church Law among the clergy, and their subordinates were of course obliged to adhere to it. Through a variety of means – such as circular letters, charges and local visitations – bishop and chapter tried to ensure that the applicable statutes were followed and interpreted in the correct manner. In those cases where detailed measures and procedures were not to be found in the Church Law, or explained in later statutes, the bishops often saw it as their duty to issue instructions on proper conduct. Such episcopal directives were to be followed by the diocesan clergy. Regional homogeneity was often regarded as a first step towards national uniformity. As this chapter argues, there was more than a degree of ambivalence in the struggle to standardize religious practices during the final decades of the eighteenth century. A language of uniformity could be used to justify and enforce the most rigid Lutheran orthodoxy; at the same time, though, it could be used by those wishing to introduce novel ideas into the body of national religion.

An enlightened bishop and his diocese

Olof Wallquist was appointed to the See of Växjö after a phenomenally rapid ecclesiastical career that was eventually to launch him into the higher echelons of national political life. After having

---

13 Urban Claesson has argued that the Church Law could be used to promote the more practical forms of Christianity that came with Pietism; see Urban Claesson, *Kris och kristnande: Olof Ekmans kamp för kristendomens återupprättande vid Stora Kopparberget 1689–1713: pietism, program och praktik* (Gothenburg: Makadam, 2015), pp. 132–33.

graduated from Uppsala University in 1779, he had served as chaplain to various members of the royal household from 1780. As a royal favourite, he was appointed to the lucrative living of Alseda (in the north-eastern part of the Diocese of Växjö) in 1783. However, Wallquist did not relocate until the autumn of 1785. Following the death of the increasingly incapacitated bishop Olof Osander (1700–1787) in June 1787, Wallquist was appointed his successor at the age of thirty-two. Wallquist was decidedly a man of enlightened tastes. A practical man, he favoured usefulness and delighted in the progress of human society. In coming years, he was to become a reputed scholar of ecclesiastical law. As a preacher, he advocated simplicity and biblical commentary over the heavy scholasticism associated with Lutheran orthodoxy. Legalism and the slow but steady reform of traditional customs were to mark his episcopacy. He was on amicable terms with Jacob Axelsson Lindblom, perhaps the most consistent and learned representative of Enlightenment among the contemporary clerical elite. Lindblom was made Bishop of Linköping the year before Wallquist's appointment to the See of Växjö.[14]

Wallquist knew little about the diocese that was now entrusted to his care. It consisted of the rural inland of much of the Province of Småland in southern Sweden; the coastal region of the county formed the Diocese of Kalmar. All in all, the Diocese of Växjö comprised ninety-one benefices. Only three cities were to be found within the diocese – Växjö (the cathedral city), Jönköping and Gränna. These cities were of very modest proportions. The number of inhabitants found in the most sizeable rural parishes (such as Urshult and Rydaholm) almost equalled that of the largest city parish, Jönköping, which in the early 1800s consisted of just over 2,500 parishioners. As in most other parts of rural Sweden, the population had been growing slowly but steadily since the early 1700s.[15]

---

14 For a general introduction to Wallquist, see Tage Linder, *Biskop Olof Wallquists politiska verksamhet till och med riksdagen 1789* (Stockholm: Almqvist & Wiksell, 1960). The best brief introduction to Wallquist's theological profile is found in Bertil Rehnberg, *Prästeståndet och religionsdebatten 1786–1800* (Uppsala: Almqvist & Wiksell, 1966), pp. 283–94. See also Josef Rosengren, *Om Olof Wallqvist såsom biskop och eforus* (Lund: Gleerups, 1901).

15 Statistical information regarding the diocese can be obtained from M. E. Forssander, *Wexiö stifts-matrikel* (Växjö, 1810). See also *Historisk statistik*, I, p. 49.

Only a few months after his appointment, Wallquist issued a questionnaire to the rectors of the diocese. It consisted of no less than twenty-three questions to which he wanted accurate and instantaneous responses.[16] These questions were constructed with the aim of ensuring full adherence to the applicable statutes. Teaching activities, parish poor relief and the maintenance of ecclesiastical records were topics covered by the young bishop's questions. Even issues that might seem insignificant today, such as the time of the early Christmas Day morning service, were mentioned in this dispatch.

Wallquist was not the first bishop to use questionnaires as a means of gaining a general view of the state of the parishes.[17] In the latter half of the eighteenth century, bishops were far from the only persons of authority who distributed surveys of various kinds to be answered by local clergy. This was a manifestation of the inclination of contemporaneous Swedish government officials and private scholars alike to collect empirical evidence as a means of getting to grips with the problems of the day and suggesting future measures of reform.[18]

Wallquist was to prove an able ecclesiastical administrator. He obviously had a talent for twisting bureaucratic procedures into

---

16 Both the questionnaire and the rectors' answers were published in the twentieth century; see Hilding Pleijel (ed.), *Gustavianskt kyrkoliv i Växjö stift: Prästerskapets svar på biskop Wallquists promemoria 12 nov. 1787. Utgivna med introduktion och register av Hilding Pleijel* (Växjö: Växjö stiftshistoriska sällskap, 1981).

17 Lars Hagberg, *Jacob Serenius' kyrkliga insats: kyrkopolitik, kristendomsförsvar, undervisningsfrågor* (Stockholm: Svenska kyrkans diakonistyrelses bokförlag, 1952), pp. 218–20. See also Archbishop von Troil's questionnaire published in Fredric Öhrströmer (ed.), *Ecclesiastike samlingar, utgifne af Fredric Öhrströmer*, 3 vols (Strängnäs: Nordström, 1806–1813), I (1806), pp. 135–7.

18 Maria Adolfsson, 'Fäderneslandets känning', in Jakob Christensson (ed.), *Signums svenska kulturhistoria: Frihetstiden* (Lund: Signum, 2006), pp. 325–43; see also Mattias Legnér, *Fäderneslandets rätta beskrivning: mötet mellan antikvarisk forskning och ekonomisk nyttokult i 1700-talets Sverige* (Helsinki: Svenska litteratursällskapet i Finland, 2004). It is interesting to note that similar uses of science were found within European colonial administration as well; see John Gascoigne, *Science in the Service of Empire: Joseph Banks, the British State and the Uses of Science in the Age of Revolution* (Cambridge: Cambridge University Press, 1998; rep. 2010); James E. McClellan, III, and François Regourd, 'The colonial machine: French science and colonization in the ancien régime', *Osiris*, 15 (2000), 31–50.

effective means of monitoring and influencing his subordinates. As we are about to see, the composition of this questionnaire was but a first step towards a 'streamlining' of ecclesiastical supervision brought about by the young bishop. Submitted answers to the questionnaire became a point of departure for interviews conducted during episcopal visitations; subsequently, gathered reports and protocols from the visitations formed the basis for a coming episcopal charge issued at the next clerical synod. A bureaucratic rationalism was to be an integral part of Wallquist's episcopacy.

Towards the end of the letter attached to the questionnaire, Wallquist stated: 'In the execution of and compliance with the law a public official has his only, but most reliable, defence.'[19] In spite of this declaration, Wallquist did not only try to enforce strict adherence to the Church Law, he also forcefully boosted practices that were not to be found within the legislative framework in this dispatch. We might say that he was using his mandate as an interpreter of relevant statutes to give sanction to new manners and customs in local religious life. In this way, Wallquist could skilfully manoeuvre the statutory framework in order to promote Enlightenment among the populace.

The most important among the reforming measures found in the young bishop's questionnaire of 1787 was the instruction he gave for a solemn rite to be performed at the terminus of the catechetical instruction of the parish youth (an act of, as was the term gradually gaining acceptance in eighteenth-century Sweden, confirmation). The Church Law had not stipulated in what manner the catechetical instruction of the young was to be concluded. It only prescribed that the younger members of the congregation could not be admitted to Holy Communion without sufficient knowledge of the fundamentals of the Christian creed as mediated by central Lutheran catechetical works.[20] Over the course of the eighteenth century, the

---

19 'I Lagarnes efterföljd och verkställande har en Ämbetsman sit enda, men mycket säkra försvar'; Pleijel, *Gustavianskt kyrkoliv*, p. 46.
20 *Kyrkio-lag och ordning, som then stormächtigste konung och herre, herr Carl then elofte, Sweriges, Göthes och Wändes konung, &c. åhr 1686. hafwer låtit författa, och åhr 1687. af trycket utgå och publicera. Jemte ther til hörige stadgar* (Stockholm, 1687), Chapter 2, Section 10. See also Einar Lilja, *Den svenska katekestraditionen mellan Svebilius och Lindblom: en bibliografisk och kyrkohistorisk studie* (Stockholm: Svenska kyrkans diakonistyrelses bokförlag, 1947); Daniel Lindmark, *'Sann kristendom och medborgerlig dygd': Studier i den svenska katekesundervisningens historia* (Umeå: Arbetsenheten för religionsvetenskap, 1993).

need for a proper rite by which the young were to be given access to Holy Communion asserted itself. Public examination in the company of the entire congregation was a custom that spread gradually, and without much controversy, over the course of the eighteenth century. Whether this practice was to be accompanied by a solemn liturgical rite was a more contentious issue, though. Within the Danish realm, such a rite had been introduced during the era of 'state Pietism', as early as 1736. Conservative-minded Lutherans feared that such a ceremony, which to them threatened to cloud the meaning of baptism, seemed to be nothing but an expression of a pietistical orientation.[21] When Wallquist wrote these instructions, however, those objections had by and large evaporated.[22] During the *Riksdag* of 1769–1770, the Clerical Estate had taken measures to introduce a liturgical rite of confirmation.[23] This suggestion was repeated during the *Riksdag* of 1778–1779.[24] Still, these advances were not to receive any official sanctioning before the early nineteenth century.[25]

In other words, the rite recommended by Wallquist (the fact that he mentioned that its 'universal acceptance' would 'delight him' indicates that it was not a mere proposal[26]) in his questionnaire is far from unique. His liturgical instructions are worth citing in full. According to Wallquist's recommendations, those who have passed the pastor's final catechetical examination are to be

> called to an additional examination before the congregation on a Sunday morning, after this has been duly announced. Then the most important sections of the catechetical instruction shall be surveyed. Thereafter follows confession and the catechumens take Holy Communion alone, among themselves, on the same day. After the

---

21 Ingmar Brohed, *Offentligt förhör och konfirmation i Sverige under 1700-talet: En case study rörande utvecklingen i Lunds stift* (Lund: Liber/Gleerup, 1977), pp. 162–72. For the introduction of the confirmation ritual in Denmark, see P. G. Lindhardt, *Konfirmationens historie i Danmark* (Copenhagen: Lohse, 1936), and Niels Reeh, *Secularization Revisited – Teaching of Religion and the State of Denmark* (Cham: Springer, 2016), pp. 81–98.
22 But see opinions expressed at the 1793 Reformation jubilee; Rehnberg, *Prästeståndet och religionsdebatten*, p. 172.
23 Carl-E. Normann (ed.), *Cleri comitialis circulär, 1723–1772* (Stockholm: Svenska kyrkans diakonistyrelses bokförlag, 1952), pp. 389–90.
24 Stefan Lundhem (ed.), *Prästeståndets riksdagsprotokoll, XXIV: 1778–1779* (Stockholm: Norstedt, 1990), pp. 193–97.
25 Brohed, *Offentligt förhör och konfirmation*, pp. 107–9.
26 Pleijel, *Gustavianskt kyrkoliv*, p. 42.

sermon, when the Communion Prayer is to be read, the preacher summons the congregation to pray for this delightful plantation.[27]
The ways in which this rite collided with the traditional customs of a rural majority are easily missed. Wallquist mentions explicitly that the young catechumens will take Holy Communion among themselves (in the Swedish original: *Communicera samma dag ensame*). To put it differently, Wallquist supported an 'individualization' of communion; the young who had just been granted access to the Eucharist by passing an examination (both in the rectory and, after that, publicly in the presence of the congregation) were to receive the sacrament on their own, and not together with their parents and certain other members of their household, as was the traditional custom (one I will hereafter refer to as 'household communion').[28] It should be noted that the practice of household communion was actually implied in the Church Law.[29] The exact origin of the practice the bishop now wanted to introduce remains unclear. We know that Wallquist was far from the first bishop to issue such recommendations. In 1758 Engelbert Halenius (1700–1767), Bishop of Skara 1753–1767, had endorsed such a practice during his visitations, and a few years later the powerful and conservative Bishop of

---

27 'De, som då finnas skicklige, kallas til ytterligare examen inför Församlingen en Söndags morgon efter derom förut skedd kungörelse. Då genomgås de angelägnaste och viktigaste Christendoms-Stycken. Därefter Skriftas Catechumeni och Communicera samma dag ensame. Efter Predikan, när Communion-Bönen skall läsas, anmanar Predikanten Församlingen at bedja GUD för denna vackra plantering'; Pleijel, *Gustavianskt kyrkoliv*, p. 42. It should, however, be noted that Wallquist, unlike several other leading ecclesiastics working for reform, opposed the revision of the church's liturgy. His resistance seems to have been motivated by his deep-seated loyalty to the king. See Rehnberg, *Prästeståndet och religionsdebatten*, pp. 101, 161–2.
28 Organizing communion in the frequently minuscule parish churches would often raise practical issues. One of them involved securing some kind of order among large groups of communicants. The available literature (which is relatively old) reveals the existence of local customs and variations. Yet the pattern of household communion seems to have prevailed in most parts (and on most occasions) until the nineteenth century. See Karl Herbert Johansson, *Kyrkobruk och gudstjänstliv under 1700-talet* (Stockholm: Svenska kyrkans diakonistyrelses bokförlag, 1938), pp. 102–12; Ernst Enochsson, *Den kyrkliga seden med särskild hänsyn till Västerås stift* (Stockholm: Svenska kyrkans diakonistyrelses bokförlag, 1949), pp. 48–64 (p. 57). See also Göran Malmstedt, *Bondetro och kyrkoro: Religiös mentalitet i stormaktstidens Sverige* (Lund: Nordic Academic Press, 2002; repr. 2020), pp. 134–43.
29 *Kyrkio-lag*, Chapter 8, Section 2.

Strängnäs, Jacob Serenius (1700–1776), had issued similar instructions to his area deans.[30] In fact, the rite suggested at the *Riksdag* of 1769–1770 had as its finale the communion of the recently confirmed (but it left the exact manner in which the rite was to be performed undefined).

Given that the introduction of such a novel practice went against the largely collectivistic nature (above all in a rural context) of early modern Sweden, one might easily connect it to rising pietist and/or Enlightenment sentiment and frames of mind. The individualizing drift of both aforementioned 'movements' is well known; but it should also be borne in mind that leading adherents of Lutheran orthodoxy had had their qualms vis-à-vis the ingrained collectivism of much of the population.[31] There was more than a degree of ambivalence in their attitude. On the one hand, traditionally orientated ecclesiastics were always suspicious of attitudes that could be associated with what they saw as an *ex opere operato* way of understanding communion (in other words, that the rite in itself, without repentance and belief, was a religiously effective act). Such attitudes reeked of Catholicism (as they understood it, that is). On the other hand, such acts could be understood as perfectly natural representations of the pious community. They were reflections of the prescribed social order according to which the household was the fundamental component of the Lutheran ecclesiastical edifice.[32]

---

30 Brohed, *Offentligt förhör och konfirmation*, pp. 58, 119–20. The practice appears to have been recommended in the Diocese of Västerås in the 1760s; see Enochsson, *Den kyrkliga*, p. 85.
31 Bishops had previously expressed their disapproval of collectivistic communion practices. Early modern Swedish visitations records abound with such statements; see, for example, Riksarkivet, Gothenburg (RG), Odensåker kyrkoarkiv [parish archive] KI:1 (containing transcripts from a visitation in 1747); RG, Norra vings kyrkoarkiv KI:1 (containing transcripts from a visitation in 1746). (I am indebted to Terese Zachrisson for these references.) However, the practice of household communion itself was not censured. See also, for example, Olle Larsson, *Biskopen visiterar: den kyrkliga överhetens möte med lokalsamhället 1650–1760* (Växjö: Växjö stiftshistoriska sällskap, 1999), p. 178.
32 See, for example, Kajsa Weber, *Undersåten som förstod: den svenska reformatoriska samtalsordningen och den tidigmoderna integrationsprocessen* (Skellefteå: Artos, 2013). For an older, and still much debated, study, see Hilding Pleijel, *Hustavlans värld: Kyrkligt folkliv i äldre tiders Sverige* (Stockholm: Verbum, 1970). See also Tammela's contribution to this volume. For the Danish-Norwegian situation, see Michael Bregnsbo, *Samfundsorden og statsmagt set fra prædikestolen: danske præsters deltagelse i den offentlige*

It is evident that a majority among the local clergy, and indeed a significant number among the bishops, had been prepared not only to tolerate but to endorse collectivistic habits. Of course, most parish clergy realized the need to come to a *modus vivendi* with their parishioners; if reforms were needed, you had to tread carefully in order not to upset the religious instincts of the people at large – this was part of the rural ecclesiastical 'political culture'. However, a change began in the latter half of the eighteenth century. Whereas an older breed of Lutheran orthodox clergy had been relatively tolerant towards the vestiges of traditional religion, new generations – touched by Enlightenment and/or pietist ideas, tastes and practices – were not equally patient. For the new to gain ground, traces of the old had to be removed.[33]

The following sections take a closer look at how the rectors of the diocese responded to this set of instructions in their written replies to the bishop. Did they notice the ways in which Wallquist's suggested rite ran against the customs, and backbone reflexes, of a majority among their parishioners? What impact did the bishop's instructions have?

Opposition and compliance: the rectors' responses

Judging from the communications the rectors sent to their bishop in response to his questionnaire, liturgical usage was already being employed in the diocese, albeit only in a limited number of parishes. Of the all in all fourteen responses indicating that such a practice was already in place, two came from benefices where Wallquist had already managed to intervene to promote change.[34] The remaining twelve included the city parish of Jönköping. In terms of geography, these benefices were fairly well distributed across the diocese.

---

opinionsdannelse vedrørende samfundsorden og statsmagt 1750–1848, belyst ved trykte prædikener: en politisk-idéhistorisk undersøgelse (Copenhagen: Museum Tusculanum, 1997), pp. 99–124; Nina Javette Koefoed, 'The Lutheran household as part of Danish confessional culture', in Bo Kristian Holm and Nina Javette Koefoed (eds), *Lutheran Theology and the Shaping of Society: The Danish Monarchy as Example* (Göttingen: Vandenhoeck & Ruprecht, 2017), pp. 321–40 (pp. 327–31).

33 See Zachrisson's contribution to this volume. For a revisionist interpretation of Danish peasant social traditionalism, see Peter Henningsen, 'Den rationelle bonde: en historisk-antropologisk analyse af traditionalismen i dansk bondekultur', *Historisk Tidsskrift*, 100 (2000), 329–81.
34 The benefices of Alseda and Rydaholm.

In other words, novel practices were neither restricted to, nor did they emanate from, any particular regions within the diocese. The only observable pattern is that most rectors who tended to affirm that the bishop's instructions were already in place were those that had been recently appointed to their livings.[35] Two out of three had been beneficed during the 1780s. This by no means amounts to suggesting that it was among the younger clergy that such habits spread (only the best-connected among the clergy could expect to be appointed to a benefice before the age of forty), but perhaps that such alterations were more easily carried out when the rector was new in post.

A majority among the rectors testified to the continued strength of household communion. According to the acting vicar of Skatelöv's parish, Per Abraham Bursie (1758–1840):

> Those that proved sufficiently adept in the final examination are called to another, public, examination before the congregation on Palm Sunday after the conclusion of the service. Thereafter they followed their parents to the most precious Sacrament.[36]

Lars Rosengren (1723–1807), a blacksmith's son who in his late fifties had managed to secure the living of Ölmstad in the northernmost part of the diocese, had even devised a somewhat unusual ritual to be used in his parish. It included prayers and communion not only for the young catechumens but also for their parents. Before the rest of the congregation, they were summoned to the altar to receive communion together.[37]

It is also noticeable that not every rector who had introduced the custom of a liturgical confirmation (often with apparent similarities with the confirmation rite introduced in Denmark in 1736) had included a separate communion for the young. The learned rector of Visingsö's benefice, Johannes Almqvist (1731–1816), who many believed would have been appointed bishop in 1787 instead of Wallquist, mentions that upon confirmation, young people had hitherto been granted liberty to register for Holy Communion

---

35 These were the benefices of Barkeryd, Bolmsö, Dädesjö, Fryele, Järsnäs, Lekaryd, Nottebäck, Skärstad, Slätthög and Tofteryd.
36 'hvarefter de skickelige befundne blifvit kallade til offäntlig examen inför församlingen på palmsöndagen efter gudstjenstens slut, hvarpå de följt sine föräldrar til den högvärdiga nattvarden'; Pleijel, *Gustavianskt kyrkoliv*, p. 67. The Swedish term *nådårspredikant* is here translated as 'acting vicar'.
37 Pleijel, *Gustavianskt kyrkoliv*, p. 364.

Promoting individualism

'whenever they wished'.[38] With the bishop's instructions in place, however, this was to change. In the future, declared Almqvist, the act of communion was to be an integral part of confirmation. It was the clergy's backbone reflex, and their bounden duty, to adhere to the decree of their superiors. Acting vicar of Kulltorp Carl Rosenblad (1755–1810), eager to please his superior, mentioned that he had already announced this alteration from the pulpit.[39] Others declared an even greater enthusiasm when reading the new bishop's instruction, recognizing in his edict the establishment of a rite of confirmation and an evolution of ideals they had cherished themselves. Jonas Johan Lagergren (1759–1833), at that time acting vicar of Svarttorp's benefice, affirmed: 'what greater satisfaction than to demonstrate one's serene obedience in matters that surely promote God's glory and must appear edifying and moving to both young and old hearts'.[40] Interestingly enough, quite a few of these rectors mentioned that an act of confirmation would elicit pious emotions on the part of the congregation; they might add that such acts would provide ample opportunities to instruct the entire congregation in 'practical Christianity'. Yet in some answers we can sense more than a bit of hesitation as to the feasibility of such a reform in local parish life. Carl Lundh (1729–1796), rector of Fröderyd's benefice, declared, somewhat waveringly, his willingness to follow 'what the Most Reverend Bishop had benevolently decreed, zealous for the glory of God and the true prosperity of the young, I will as far as possible, through the grace of God, observe'.[41]

In spite of the natural inclination of the clergy, there were a few that protested against the bishop's instructions. The rector of Moheda benefice, Magnus Stålhös (1734–1790), for instance, objected on the grounds that such a novelty would be unworkable in large and populous parishes. He also mentioned that a departure from household communion would go against the religious instincts of both young and old: 'On such a tender occasion the child wishes to accompany its father and mother, and the father and mother

---

38 'när de häldst ville'; Pleijel, *Gustavianskt kyrkoliv*, p. 357.
39 Pleijel, *Gustavianskt kyrkoliv*, p. 301.
40 'och hvilken glädje skal nu blifva större än at få visa sig i högsta lydig i saker, som så säkert befordrar Guds ära och måste finnas uppbyggeliga och rörande för ett ungt och äldre hjerta'; Pleijel, *Gustavianskt kyrkoliv*, p. 222.
41 'Det ... som Högvördiga Herr Biskopen hög-gunstigt och af nit för Guds ähra och ungdomens sandskyldiga välfärd behagat förordna, skal, genom Guds nåd, i giörligaste måtto efterlefvas'; Pleijel, *Gustavianskt kyrkoliv*, p. 323.

desire to have their offspring in joy ... by their side on Good Friday or on Easter Sunday.'[42] On similar grounds, Nils Alin (1732–1784) – rector of Järstorp on the outskirts of Jönköping and a man, unlike Stålhös, inclined to express Enlightenment sentiment – remonstrated against a departure from the habit of household communion. When the young were to receive communion together with their parents for the first time, this was an act that elicited 'much pious stirring' among those involved. Even though Alin declared his willingness to adhere to the bishop's 'method' (the standard term used in eighteenth-century Swedish) in every other respect, he was apparently reluctant to abandon this custom, even at his bishop's bidding.[43]

As we have seen, the rectors' responses to the bishop's instructions were varied. As mediators they had to find a way to abide by the instructions of their superior; and yet, simultaneously, they needed to maintain the confidence of their parishioners. Historical research has revealed that the Swedish parish council (*sockenstämman*) provided an arena for debate on certain customs related to the liturgical life of the parish church. It was far from the humdrum gathering where landholding farmers, under the auspices of their rector and local gentry, were only to decide on matters related to the fabric of the local church or the upkeep of the rectory.[44] Interestingly enough, Wallquist cautions the

---

42 'Barnet önskar vid så ömt tillfälle följa fader och moder och fader och moder åstundar uti glädje ... vid thess sida och thet långfredagen eller påskedagen'; Pleijl, *Gustavianskt kyrkoliv*, p. 72. A comparison could be made with the situation in Germany. Wolfgang Kaschuba, among others, has noted a popular, hidden and ambiguous resistance towards bureaucratized measures of reform in the 1700s; see Wolfgang Kaschuba, *Volkskultur zwischen feudaler und bürgerlicher Gesellschaft: zur Geschichte eines Begriffs und seiner gesellschaftlichen Wirklichkeit* (Frankfurt am Main: Campus, 1988), p. 102.
43 'mycken andackts rörelse'; Pleijl, *Gustavianskt kyrkoliv*, p. 241.
44 Peter Aronsson, *Bönder gör politik: Det lokala självstyret som social arena i tre Smålandssocknar, 1680–1850* (Lund: Lund University Press, 1992); Carin Bergström, *Lantprästen: prästens funktion i det agrara samhället 1720–1800: Oland-Frösåkers kontrakt av ärkestiftet* (Stockholm: Nordiska museet, 1991); Karl Herbert Johansson, *Svensk sockensjälvstyrelse: 1686–1862: studier särskilt med hänsyn till Linköpings stift* (Lund: Gleerups, 1937). For the radically different Danish situation, see Carsten Porskrog Rasmussen, 'Manors and states: the distribution and structure of private manors in early modern Scandinavia and their relation to state policies', *Scandinavian Economic History Review*, 66 (2018), 1–18.

Promoting individualism

rectors in his questionnaire not to let matters regulated by Church Law (and, implicitly, by ecclesiastical authorities) be subjects of debate on parish councils.[45] Some rectors were, understandably, reluctant to enforce reform because they feared opposition among their flock (or, perhaps, because they were themselves tied to the customs of old). Others greeted Wallquist's instructions with enthusiasm. Measures suggested by Wallquist were lauded as they were deemed to result in religious uplift among the populace at large.

Wallquist's questionnaire and its aftermath

What happened after the rectors had sent their replies to their bishop? Can we establish that Wallquist's questionnaire actually resulted in changes in local church practices regarding the instruction of the parish youth? The only way to ascertain this is to consult the preserved church records. Even though eighteenth-century Swedish clergymen were diligent keepers of records on their flocks, there are limits to the usefulness of the documents they compiled. Preserved communion records (of which there are many) were composed in such a manner that they do not reveal the introduction of individualizing communion practices. These records allow us to see which households took communion on a given Sunday, but not the exact order in which the members of a household received the sacrament. Even though the parish youth who had recently passed their examinations may have received communion independently, their kin may have followed them just a few minutes later during the same service.

Alternative sources that may be consulted are the books of announcements (*pålysningsböcker*) kept for each church. In these records, the preacher mostly noted messages orally presented to the congregation regarding coming services or more general changes concerning the liturgical life. It seems probable that the changes suggested by the bishop would have been announced in due time to the entire congregation and therefore noted in these books. The only problem is that the information recorded in these volumes was understood to be of an ephemeral character; very few of them have survived to the present day. For the years 1787 and 1788, only two such volumes are preserved for the Diocese of Växjö. It is interesting

---

45 Pleijel, *Gustavianskt kyrkoliv*, p. 46.

to note that both these books (for the parishes of Åseda and Moheda, where, as we have seen, the recalcitrant Magnus Stålhös was rector) contain notes revealing that the rector announced the alteration initiated by Wallquist to their flock in good time before Easter.[46] That the separate communion of the catechumens was explicitly mentioned in both parishes indicates that this was a controversial measure which should be imbued with the authority of official dictate.

Local changes can also be observed if we take a closer look at visitation records. During the summer months of 1788, Wallquist embarked on an extensive tour of the southern parts of the diocese. Within two months, no less than eighteen parishes were inspected by the energetic bishop with entourage. The preserved and detailed minutes reveal that Wallquist used both the questionnaire and the submitted answers as templates for interviews conducted with the local rector. Here, Wallquist once more emerges as a systematic and rational bureaucrat bent on using his authority to secure the full obedience of his subordinates. In almost every case, the local clergyman affirmed that the bishop's recommended changes had been followed meticulously. Whether this was in fact the case is, of course, a completely different matter. On one occasion, in the small parish of Hallaryd, the minutes reveal that the bishop decided to address the issue of an altered communion ritual in the presence of the entire congregation.[47] The reasons for this decision remain unclear, but it is likely that the bishop's choice was motivated by acts of resistance on the part of the local community.

The questionnaire of 1787 made a final appearance at the diocesan synod of clergy of 1793. According to the printed transcripts of this gathering (that the proceedings were printed for the benefit of a reading public was in itself a novelty at this time), the bishop frequently used both visitation transcripts and his dispatch of 1787 to remind the assembled clergy of their obligations. When it came to instruction of the parish youth, the bishop was emphatic in his insistence that this was a prime duty of all parish clergy. Instructions given in the questionnaire were to be followed to the last detail. In the mind of the bishop, such fidelity was not without its compensations: 'the Teacher reaps benefits in his office, love and reverence

---

46 Riksarkivet, Vadstena (RV), Moheda kyrkoarkiv, Pålysningsböcker PI:1–2; RV, Åseda kyrkoarkiv, Pålysningsböcker PI:2.
47 RV, Växjö domkapitels arkiv, Visitationshandlingar, FIII:3–6.

from all his listeners'.⁴⁸ In the end, to a late eighteenth-century ecclesiastic the fulfilment of one's duty was not only to be rewarded in the world to come.

Conclusion

'Gradual reforms for sensible reasons, obedience and fidelity to the Code and those in positions of authority, proper benevolence and fellowship to all, in particular to the common people with whom my brethren in office must live, [these] I struggled to impart.'⁴⁹ In this manner Wallquist summarized his efforts during the 1793 clergy synod in a letter to the pastor of his home parish in central Sweden. Indeed, it could be seen as an idealized summary of how this gifted eighteenth-century ecclesiastic understood his episcopacy.

When considering the wider theme of this volume, what could be learnt from the ways in which Wallquist contrived to instigate religious change within a solidified statutory framework, and from the ways in which the rectors responded to the wishes of their bishop? This chapter seems to point in the direction of a – far from surprising – 'received view' of the Enlightenment in a Nordic (and indeed a European) rural setting. New ideas were launched by a high-ranking member of a clerical elite, negotiated by (clerical) intermediaries and resisted by the people at large. Wallquist was far from being the only high-ranking proponent of Enlightenment who used a position of authority to promote change.

Yet on closer inspection the encounter between Wallquist, the rectors and the parishioners – whose voices are only heard here as mediated by local clerics – reveal some intriguing features.

The episcopal duty to interpret the Church Law and to establish uniformity in religious customs within the diocese was used by Wallquist to enforce a new practice which went against the deep-seated collectivism of a rural majority. In Wallquist's hands,

---

48 'Läraren får hugnad i sit Embete, kärlek och wördnad af alla sina Åhörare'; *Handlingar, angående prästmötet i Wexiö* (Växjö, 1793), pp. 31–2.
49 'Reformer sagta och med förstånd, lydnad och trohet åt Lag och Öfverhet, rätt välvilja och förbindelse til alla, särdeles til Allmogen, med hvilken mine Embets Bröder måst lefva, har jag velat insinuera'; Lunds universitetsbiblioteks arkiv, Olof Wallquists samling [collection], Olof Wallquist to Eric Waller, 10 January 1794.

the language of uniformity became a means not only to secure the religious ethos of confessional Lutheran culture, but to pursue an individualizing practice and train of thought. In other words, at a micro-level we have seen how Wallquist employed the rationale of confessional culture to promote Enlightenment in a rural setting. This testifies to a process of gradual, microscopic dislocations in which key elements of a previous social order were overtaken step by step by different standards of behaviour.

The urge to improve the people at large was actually not a feature novel to the eighteenth century, nor did it arrive with the Enlightenment. On the contrary, Lutheran confessional culture was imbued with notions of reform. The people were to live in conformity with certain religious and social standards. To a clerical elite, they (as a collective) were always seen as wanting. Especially during the first half of the eighteenth century, when it was widely believed that Moravianism and early Pietism were threatening the religious unity of the nation, the need to reform and elevate the laity was strongly felt among elites. Wallquist stood in a long line of bishops who aimed to improve the people. Changes that must have been seen as novelties in the eyes of ordinary people had occurred long before the advent of Enlightenment. Wallquist's directives offer an example of how the struggle for what was considered the religious improvement of the populace gained new connotations. For the rectors, as well as their parishioners, his measures were but the latest expression of imposed change that had to be negotiated and interpreted in the local arena.

The changes brought by the Enlightenment were innovations in the rural milieu, yet the struggle for reform was in itself far from a new thing in late eighteenth-century Sweden. If we attempt to see the changes imposed by Bishop Wallquist from the vantage point of the eighteenth-century rural Swedish milieu, we may even ask ourselves: was the Enlightenment such a 'big deal' after all? It brought innovation that followed other innovations and measures of reform (although the latter were bearers of a different theological and philosophical stance). To put it another way, when the Enlightenment did become a 'big deal' – when conflict arose upon the introduction of new practices – was this due to an intrinsic 'quality' in the alterations implemented, or to a failure to establish a new point of convergence in local society?

Bibliography

Archival sources

Gothenburg

Riksarkivet, Gothenburg (RG)
Norra vings kyrkoarkiv [parish archive] KI:1
Odensåker kyrkoarkiv KI:1

Lund, Sweden

Lunds universitetsbiblioteks arkiv
Olof Wallquists samling [collection]

Vadstena, Sweden

Riksarkivet, Vadstena (RV)
Åseda kyrkoarkiv PI:2
Moheda kyrkoarkiv PI:1–2
Växjö domkapitels arkiv FIII:3–6

Digital sources

Stads- och kommunhistoriska institutet, 'Alla svenska städer: befolkning', http://ortshistoria.se/befolkning/1730t [accessed 6 February 2023].
Stads- och kommunhistoriska institutet, 'Alla svenska städer: befolkning', http://ortshistoria.se/befolkning/1800 [accessed 6 February 2023].

Printed sources and literature

Adolfsson, Maria, 'Fäderneslandets känning', in Jakob Christensson (ed.), *Signums svenska kulturhistoria: Frihetstiden* (Lund: Signum, 2006), pp. 325–43.
Aronsson, Peter, *Bönder gör politik: Det lokala självstyret som social arena i tre Smålandssocknar, 1680–1850* (Lund: Lund University Press, 1992).
Barlow, Richard Burgess, *Citizenship and Conscience: A Study in the Theory and Practice of Religious Toleration in England during the Eighteenth Century* (Philadelphia, PA: University of Pennsylvania Press, 1962).
Bergström, Carin, *Lantprästen: prästens funktion i det agrara samhället 1720–1800: Oland-Frösåkers kontrakt av ärkestiftet* (Stockholm: Nordiska museet, 1991).
Bregnsbo, Michael, *Samfundsorden og statsmagt set fra prædikestolen: danske præsters deltagelse i den offentlige opinionsdannelse vedrørende*

samfundsorden og statsmagt 1750–1848, belyst ved trykte prædikener: en politisk-idéhistorisk undersøgelse (Copenhagen: Museum Tusculanum, 1997).

Brohed, Ingmar, *Offentligt förhör och konfirmation i Sverige under 1700-talet: En case study rörande utvecklingen i Lunds stift* (Lund: Liber/Gleerup, 1977).

Castro, Raquel Poy, 'Regeneración educativa y cultural de la España moderna: reformas monárquicas en educación y el papel de los obispos de la ilustración en el siglo XVIII', *Cuadernos Dieciochistas*, 10 (2011), 185–217.

Claesson, Urban, *Kris och kristnande: Olof Ekmans kamp för kristendomens återupprättande vid Stora Kopparberget 1689–1713: pietism, program och praktik* (Gothenburg: Makadam, 2015).

Eijnatten, Joris van, *Liberty and Concord in the United Provinces: Religious Toleration and the Public in the Eighteenth-Century Netherlands* (Leiden: Brill, 2003).

Enochsson, Ernst, *Den kyrkliga seden med särskild hänsyn till Västerås stift* (Stockholm: Svenska kyrkans diakonistyrelses bokförlag, 1949).

Florutau, M. I., 'Regional Enlightenment in Transylvania: the educational reforms of Bishop Petru Pavel Aron, their influences and effects on the Uniate society in Transylvania in the Age of Enlightenment', *Slovo*, 27:1 (2015), 9–33.

Forssander, M. E., *Wexiö stifts-matrikel* (Växjö, 1810).

Gascoigne, John, *Science in the Service of Empire: Joseph Banks, the British State and the Uses of Science in the Age of Revolution* (Cambridge: Cambridge University Press, 1998; repr. 2010).

Gregory, Jeremy, *Restoration, Reformation and Reform, 1660–1828: Archbishops of Canterbury and Their Diocese* (Oxford: Oxford University Press, 2000).

Hagberg, Lars, *Jacob Serenius' kyrkliga insats: kyrkopolitik, kristendomsförsvar, undervisningsfrågor* (Stockholm: Svenska kyrkans diakonistyrelses bokförlag, 1952).

Handlingar, angående prästmötet i Wexiö (Växjö, 1793).

Harnesk, Börje and Marja Taussi Sjöberg (eds), *Mellan makten och menigheten: ämbetsmän i det tidigmoderna Sverige* (Stockholm: Institutet för rättshistorisk forskning, 2001).

Hayton, D. W., 'Parliament and the established church: reform and reaction', in D. W. Hayton, James Kelly and John Bergin (eds), *The Eighteenth-Century Composite State* (London: Palgrave Macmillan, 2010), pp. 78–106.

Henningsen, Peter, 'Den rationelle bonde: en historisk-antropologisk analyse af traditionalismen i dansk bondekultur', *Historisk Tidsskrift*, 100 (2000), 329–81.

Historisk statistik för Sverige [Population 1720–1967], 2nd edn (Örebro: Statistiska centralbyrån, 1969).

Inger, Göran, 'Kyrkolagstiftningen under 1600-talet', in Ingun Montgomery (ed.), *Sveriges kyrkohistoria*, IV: *Enhetskyrkans tid* (Stockholm: Verbum, 2002), pp. 204–13.

Johansson, Karl Herbert, *Kyrkobruk och gudstjänstliv under 1700-talet* (Stockholm: Svenska kyrkans diakonistyrelses bokförlag, 1938).

——, *Svensk sockensjälvstyrelse: 1686–1862: studier särskilt med hänsyn till Linköpings stift* (Lund: Gleerups, 1937).

Karonen, Petri, *Pohjoinen suurvalta: Ruotsi ja Suomi 1521–1809* (Helsinki: Werner Söderström, 2008).

Kaschuba, Wolfgang, *Volkskultur zwischen feudaler und bürgerlicher Gesellschaft: zur Geschichte eines Begriffs und seiner gesellschaftlichen Wirklichkeit* (Frankfurt am Main: Campus, 1988).

Kjöllerström, Sven, *Kyrkolagsproblemet i Sverige 1571–1682* (Stockholm: Svenska kyrkans diakonistyrelses bokförlag, 1944).

Koefoed, Nina Javette, 'The Lutheran household as part of Danish confessional culture', in Bo Kristian Holm and Nina Javette Koefoed (eds), *Lutheran Theology and the Shaping of Society: The Danish Monarchy as Example* (Göttingen: Vandenhoeck & Ruprecht, 2017), pp. 321–40.

Kyrkio-lag och ordning, som then stormächtigste konung och herre, herr Carl then elofte, Sweriges, Göthes och Wändes konung, &c. åhr 1686. hafwer låtit författa, och åhr 1687. af trycket utgå och publicera. Jemte ther til hörige stadgar (Stockholm, 1687).

Larsson, Olle, *Biskopen visiterar: den kyrkliga överhetens möte med lokalsamhället 1650–1760* (Växjö: Växjö stiftshistoriska sällskap, 1999).

Legnér, Mattias, *Fäderneslandets rätta beskrivning: mötet mellan antikvarisk forskning och ekonomisk nyttokult i 1700-talets Sverige* (Helsinki: Svenska litteratursällskapet i Finland, 2004).

Lehner, Ulrich L., *The Catholic Enlightenment: The Forgotten History of a Global Movement* (New York: Oxford University Press, 2016).

Lilja, Einar, *Den svenska katekestraditionen mellan Svebilius och Lindblom: en bibliografisk och kyrkohistorisk studie* (Stockholm: Svenska kyrkans diakonistyrelses bokförlag, 1947).

Linder, Tage, *Biskop Olof Wallquists politiska verksamhet till och med riksdagen 1789* (Stockholm: Almqvist & Wiksell, 1960).

Lindhardt, P. G., *Konfirmationens historie i Danmark* (Copenhagen: Lohse, 1936).

Lindmark, Daniel, *'Sann kristendom och medborgerlig dygd': Studier i den svenska katekesundervisningens historia* (Umeå: Arbetsenheten för religionsvetenskap, 1993).

Lundhem, Stefan (ed.), *Prästeståndets riksdagsprotokoll*, XXIV: *1778–1779* (Stockholm: Norstedt, 1990).

Malmstedt, Göran, *Bondetro och kyrkoro: Religiös mentalitet i stormaktstidens Sverige* (Lund: Nordic Academic Press, 2002; repr. 2020).

McClellan, James E., III, and François Regourd, 'The colonial machine: French science and colonization in the ancien regime', *Osiris*, 15 (2000), 31–50.
Nordström, Peter, *Reformer och rationalisering: Kung, råd och förvaltning under tidig gustaviansk tid, 1772–1778* (Uppsala: Almqvist & Wiksell International, 1991).
Normann, Carl-E. (ed.), *Cleri comitialis circulär, 1723–1772* (Stockholm: Svenska kyrkans diakonistyrelses bokförlag, 1952).
Öhrströmer, Fredric (ed.), *Ecclesiastike samlingar, utgifne af Fredric Öhrströmer*, 3 vols (Strängnäs: Nordström, 1806–1813), I (1806).
Pleijel, Hilding (ed.), *Gustavianskt kyrkoliv i Växjö stift: Prästerskapets svar på biskop Wallquists promemoria 12 nov. 1787. Utgivna med introduktion och register av Hilding Pleijel* (Växjö: Växjö stiftshistoriska sällskap, 1981).
——, *Hustavlans värld: Kyrkligt folkliv i äldre tiders Sverige* (Stockholm: Verbum, 1970).
Rasmussen, Carsten Porskrog, 'Manors and states: the distribution and structure of private manors in early modern Scandinavia and their relation to state policies', *Scandinavian Economic History Review*, 66 (2018), 1–18.
Reeh, Niels, *Secularization Revisited – Teaching of Religion and the State of Denmark* (Cham: Springer, 2016).
Rehnberg, Bertil, *Prästeståndet och religionsdebatten 1786–1800* (Uppsala: Almqvist & Wiksell, 1966).
Rosengren, Josef, *Om Olof Wallqvist såsom biskop och eforus* (Lund: Gleerups, 1901).
Sauter, Michael J., *Visions of the Enlightenment: The Edict on Religion of 1788 and the Politics of the Public Sphere in Eighteenth-Century Prussia* (Leiden: Brill, 2009).
Schilling, Heinz, *Religion, Political Culture and the Emergence of Early Modern Society: Essays in German and Dutch History* (Leiden: Brill, 1992).
Schioppa, Antonio Padoa, *A History of Law in Europe: From the Early Middle Ages to the Twentieth Century* (Cambridge: Cambridge University Press, 2017).
Weber, Kajsa, *Undersåten som förstod: den svenska reformatoriska samtalsordningen och den tidigmoderna integrationsprocessen* (Skellefteå: Artos, 2013).
Wilskman, Sven, *Swea rikes ecclesiastique wärk, i alphabetisk ordning sammandragit, utur lag och förordningar, privilegier och resolutioner, samt andra handlingar; af Sven Wilskman* (Skara, 1760).

3
Tuomas Ragvaldinpoika: the Finnish self-taught and disabled man as a writer of ephemeral literature

Tuija Laine

The Lutheran Church had underlined the importance of being able to read ever since the Reformation, but it did not put any emphasis on the writing skills of the common person. According to the Church Law of 1686, being able to read the catechism was necessary for attending the Eucharist, obtaining permission to marry and being suitable for the task of godparent. Therefore, the ability of the common people to read and understand the catechism was tested annually by the clergy. It was the duty of parents to teach their children to read, as there were still no schools for the children of the common people. Only those parents who themselves had poor reading skills could receive assistance from the Church in order to have their children taught. In the beginning, people 'read' by heart, although the ability to understand the texts as well was emphasized by the Bishop of Turku Johannes Gezelius the elder (1615–1690) in the last decades of the seventeenth century. For most peasants and other common people in the seventeenth and eighteenth centuries, this was enough, and they did not feel any need to seek out more education.[1]

From the seventeenth century onwards, there were nevertheless some peasants and craftsmen who were more interested than others in writing as well. They usually had the task, alongside their real work, of acting as scribes among the common people. For instance, they helped others to write letters or compile estate-inventory deeds.

---

1 Esko M. Laine and Tuija Laine, 'Kirkollinen kansanopetus', in Jussi Hanska and Kirsi Vainio (eds), *Huoneentaulun maailma: Kasvatus ja koulutus Suomessa keskiajalta 1860-luvulle* (Helsinki: Suomalaisen Kirjallisuuden Seura, 2010), pp. 258–306 (p. 265); Tuija Laine, *Aapisen ja katekismuksen tavaamisesta itsenäiseen lukemiseen: Rahvaan lukukulttuurin kehitys varhaismodernina aikana* (Helsinki: Suomalaisen Kirjallisuuden Seura, 2017), pp. 37–9, 45.

Because they were literate, they may also have taught children to read. Towards the end of the eighteenth century, the number of people with such ability gradually increased, although it was only during the next century that writing skills spread among the common people to any significant extent.[2]

In the last decades of the eighteenth century, even the common people were touched by the ideas of the Enlightenment. In many cases this happened through enlightened clergy, but it also took place directly through literature disseminated by the literate peasants and craftsmen. There were several educational projects among the clergy with the aim of establishing schools and improving the intellectual education of the common people. The best-known was the work of the society *Pro Fide et Christianismo*, which published religious literature and founded schools. It had several members among the Finnish clergy. The chief purpose of the society was 'to promote the growth of real Christianity'. For the Swedish clergy, the Enlightenment meant the spreading of true Christianity and education for the common people. This stance partly originated in fear of the new international Enlightenment, which questioned the truths of Christianity.[3]

This chapter introduces one of the best-known Finnish self-taught men from the eighteenth century, the poet Tuomas Ragvaldinpoika, who had an active role in the writing of various texts. The chapter addresses the following questions: what kind of texts were they? For what purpose were they written? And what was their position in the public Enlightenment project outlined above?

---

2 Arja Rantanen, *Pennförare i periferin: Österbottniska sockenskrivare 1721–1868* (Åbo/Turku: Åbo akademis förlag, 2014); Kirsi Keravuori, '*Rakkat poikaiset!' Simon ja Wilhelmina Janssonin perhekirjeet egodokumentteina (1858–1887)* (Turku: Turun yliopisto, 2015), p. 23; Laine, *Aapisen*, pp. 166–7.

3 Minna Ahokas, 'Pro fide et christianismon kristillinen valistustoiminta 1770-luvulta 1800-luvun alkuun', in Esko M. Laine and Minna Ahokas (eds), *Hyödyllisen tiedon piirit: Tutkimuksia papistosta, rahvaasta ja tiedon rakentumisesta 1700-luvulla* (Helsinki: Suomalaisen Kirjallisuuden Seura, 2018), pp. 84–142; Minna Ahokas and Päivi Räisänen-Schröder, 'Papisto ja hyödyllinen tieto 1700-luvun Ruotsissa', in Laine and Ahokas, *Hyödyllisen tiedon piirit*, pp. 7–44.

Tuomas Ragvaldinpoika – self-taught hymn writer

Tuomas Ragvaldinpoika was the son of the peasant Ragvald Hannunpoika from Tyrvää in western Finland. He was born physically disabled, with a congenital harelip and a cleft palate. In addition, at the age of twenty-two, he suffered some misfortune which left him with a stiffened knee. These conditions made it impossible for him to work in a normal way. He was married three times and had nine children, only two of whom reached adulthood. Ragvaldinpoika and his family lived mostly on poor relief, which they received from the Church. People with disabilities were exhorted to work as far as they could; but at the end of the nineteenth century, people with disabilities were still the largest group living on poor relief.[4]

According to the church examination registers of Tyrvää, Tuomas Ragvaldinpoika was a good reader, and so were his sister and their parents. Reading was his means of escape. As a disfigured, disabled man, he was able to teach children and received permission to do so. All members of the workforce were important to the Swedish realm (which included today's Finland) as the economy was starting to prosper, even people with disabilities. The literacy of Tuomas Ragvaldinpoika represented active reading, which was also a sign of modernity. His own family was a testimony to the social importance of literacy, his father's reading ability having earned respect among his peers in the community. Even more than reading and teaching, Ragvaldinpoika devoted himself to literary work. He wrote and published 148 hymns in 53 publications, all occasional publications or ephemeral literature of different kinds. There were collections of hymns, poetry for funerals and marriages, congratulations and edifying texts with moral warnings.[5]

---

4 Pekka Raittila, *Tuomas Ragvaldinpoika* (Vammala: Tyrvään seudun Museo- ja Kotiseutuyhdistys, 1949), pp. 11, 15–16, 30–1; Simo Vehmas, *Vammaisuus: Johdatus historiaan, teoriaan ja etiikkaan* (Helsinki: Gaudeamus, 2005), p. 49; Esko M. Laine, 'Tuomas Ragvaldinpoika (1724–1804)', in *Suomen kansallisbiografia*, 10 vols (Helsinki: Suomalaisen Kirjallisuuden Seura, 2003–2007), X (2007), pp. 52–4; Esko M. Laine, 'Tuomas Ragvaldinpoika ja hyödyllisen tiedon rajat ja piirit 1700-luvun suomalaisessa sääty-yhteiskunnassa', in Laine and Ahokas, *Hyödyllisen tiedon piirit*, pp. 45–83 (pp. 56–7).
5 Pehr Kalm, *Enfaldiga tankar om nyttan och nödvändigheten för en präst, at äga insikt i Medicine, med wederbörandes samtycke, under ... H. Pehr Kalms inseende ... Öfwerlämnade af Samuel Lithovius, Isacs son, Österbotninge* (Åbo/Turku, 1762), p. A2; Raittila, *Tuomas Ragvaldinpoika*,

The French sociologist Pierre Bourdieu has written about the three forms of cultural capital which people use in order to achieve success in society: embodied, objectified and institutionalized. The last-mentioned form refers to education, for example formal degrees, while objectified cultural capital refers to such things as pictures, books and musical instruments. Embodied cultural capital means physical appearance and the skills required to behave naturally in various cultural contexts. This is the most demanding form of cultural capital.[6] Since Tuomas Ragvaldinpoika did not have any formal education, he could not compete at all in this respect. As regards physical capital, he had even less chance to compete and gain success, being a disabled man. The only way for him to win respect was by displaying his literary talents; consequently, his writing was very important to him on a personal level. He did not have much in material terms (economic capital), nor was he very successful in terms of social capital; but he possessed intangible assets, and ideas about how to use them.

Much research has been done into the multi-faceted cognitive preconditions for writing. It has been established that writing calls for skills in composing, reviewing, goal-setting, planning and organizing. A capacity for self-reflection and imagination is a significant requirement. Writing is, of course, an even more demanding skill than reading; but the possession of both skills makes a person a more independent individual in the modern sense.[7]

The writings of Tuomas Ragvaldinpoika may be roughly divided into three groups: hymns and hymn collections; autobiographical texts; and poetry for funerals, marriages and other special occasions. All the texts evince a strong, even profound, religious spirit. They also display a pietistic and Moravian dimension, although they clearly represent ecclesiasticism.[8] The ensuing pages examine his

---

pp. 15, 88–96; Pierre Bourdieu, 'The forms of capital', in John Richardson (ed.), *Handbook of Theory and Research for the Sociology of Education* (New York: Greenwood Press, 1986), pp. 241–58; Daniel Lindmark, *Läs- och skrivkunnigheten före folkskolan: Historisk läskunnighetsforskning i nordiskt och internationellt perspektiv* (Umeå: Forskningsarkivet, 1990), pp. 5–7; Laine, 'Tuomas Ragvaldinpoika ja hyödyllisen', pp. 54, 58, 61.

6 Bourdieu, 'The forms of capital', p. 243.
7 Lindmark, *Läs- och skrivkunnigheten*, pp. 14–15.
8 Raittila, *Tuomas Ragvaldinpoika*, pp. 52–64; Laine, 'Tuomas Ragvaldinpoika ja hyödyllisen', p. 62.

autobiographical texts, as well as some of his warning texts and hymns and verses for funerals and weddings.⁹

Hymns as ego documents

Letters, autobiographies, diaries as well as memoirs have been called 'ego documents' in historical research. The term was coined by Jacques Presser and further developed by Rudolf Dekker. In an ego document, a person describes his or her own life in the first person. The question of the constructive nature of ego documents came in for special attention in 1990s Germany. Not only do such genres as letters or diaries contain autobiographical material; broadsheets and other ephemera do so as well. In Sweden, for example, plenty of broadsheets are preserved that refer to blind people, where they describe their life and destiny. Dekker does not mention hymns as ego documents but does refer to Presser's definition of that category. Presser categorized 'all written sources, in which we meet a man more clearly, more personally than in other sources, and who thus becomes us instead of a "nameless human" – whatever that might be – a distinctive ego'.[10] Hymns where Tuomas Ragvaldinpoika described his own life in the manner defined by Presser may also be called ego documents, even though he wrote them in the form of poems or hymns, not as prose. As ego documents, these hymns also tell us about the norms and traditions of writing, or they create new ones, suitable for the enlightened world.

The first published text by Tuomas Ragvaldinpoika was a collection of three short hymns about himself written in Turku in 1759, when he was recovering at the mineral spring of Kupittaa. In those hymns, he describes his life of illness and misfortune since birth. The congenital harelip was a visible mark on his face. Because of the cleft palate, it was impossible to nurse him, so his parents were compelled to feed him cow's milk. When he was two and a half years old, his

---

9 The wedding poem he wrote about his own wedding (*Yxikertainen hää-weisu*, 1765) has not been digitized and was unfortunately not accessible at the time of writing due to the COVID-19 situation.
10 Arianne Baggerman and Rudolf Dekker, 'Jacques Presser, egodocuments and the personal turn in historiography', *European Journal of Life Writing*, 7 (2018), 90–110 (90–1); Keravuori, *'Rakkat poikaiset!'*, pp. 11, 14, 20; Karin Strand, '"Let me tell you my life in a song": on autobiography and begging in broadsheet ballads of the blind', *European Journal of Life Writing*, 7 (2018), 34–52 (36).

father died. At the age of twenty-two he was further disabled in consequence of influenza, and in the next year his mother died. Ragvaldinpoika experienced many more serious illnesses and ailments. He interpreted all these health issues as the consequence of (original) sin. In the early modern era, sickness and suffering were regarded as a permanent aspect of human existence. At the end of the collection, Ragvaldinpoika mentions useful medicinal plants; but according to him, the reason for the plants' healing power lies in God, because God created them and it was God who imparted knowledge of their properties to wise men and doctors. As an example of a good doctor, he mentioned Johan Haartman (1725–1787), the first Finnish professor of medicine and author of the first Finnish *Home Doctor*.[11] A similar emphasis can be seen in the *Hyödyllinen huwitus luomisten töistä* ('Useful book on creation'), a devotional book and scientific account of nature in the same package, written by the minister of Sotkamo, Johan Frosterus. Both Haartman and Frosterus considered natural knowledge to be subordinate to religious or divine knowledge. Physico-theology, which underlined the connection between nature and religion, was a well-known and frequently followed trend at the Åbo [Turku] Royal Academy in the eighteenth century, the most profound influence coming from the British scholar William Derham (1657–1735) and the German Christian Wolff.[12]

In the Åbo [Turku] Royal Academy, modern Enlightenment science was accepted so long as it did not lead to atheism, materialism, indifferentism or deism. German Enlightenment philosophers – such as Leibniz, Wolff and Thomasius – were viewed as remarkable, and the Wolffian idea of harmony and balance between faith and reason played an important role in the first half of the eighteenth century.

---

11 Tuomas Ragvaldinpoika, *Sen wirhen, ja ristin alla hamast lapsudesta ja nuorudesta, rasitetun weisu, Sanct. Hendrikin lähten terweyden nautitzemisen alla, wuonna 1759, parannuxen wuotella maatesa, elämänsä perään ajatellesa ja Jumalan johdattamista tutkistellesa, Turun caupungisa, cocoonpandu Thomas Rawaldin pojalda, Tyrwän pidäjästä ja Lauculan kylästä* (Turusa, 1760); Gary B. Ferngren, *Medicine and Religion: A Historical Introduction* (Baltimore, MD: Johns Hopkins University Press, 2014), p. 151; Yrjö Kotivuori, 'Ylioppilasmatrikkeli 1640–1852: Johan Haartman' (University of Helsinki, 2005), https://ylioppilasmatrikkeli.helsinki.fi/henkilo.php?id=6683 [accessed 3 May 2020].
12 Seppo J. Salminen, *Den finländska teologin under frihetstiden* (Helsinki: Finska kyrkohistoriska samfundet, 1994), pp. 87–9; Päivi Räisänen-Schröder, 'Johan Frosterus ja hyödyllinen tieto luomakunnasta', in Laine and Ahokas, *Hyödyllisen tiedon piirit*, pp. 143–83 (p. 145).

The idea was to lead people to happiness in both temporal and eternal life. The new tendencies of natural theology – such as physico-theology – were symbols of this harmony. However, these Wolffian ideas also encountered resistance, not least from Pietism. Later in the eighteenth century, rationalism especially gained ground in the Åbo [Turku] Royal Academy.[13]

The next ego document by Tuomas Ragvaldinpoika describes the surgery on his harelip in Turku in 1763. Surgery of this kind was still quite rare at the time. As in other countries during the Enlightenment, the role of priests as healers and doctors at the local level was highlighted in Finland, a country in which there were few properly trained medical practitioners. Harelip surgery was a highly exacting task, and in this case was performed by the city doctor of Turku, Gerhard Odenadt. The operation fixed the harelip, but it did not help with the patient's speech. The opportunity to have his harelip remedied was very important for Ragvaldinpoika, however, as he seems to have suffered grievously – mentally as well – from his physical disabilities. In folklore, there were stories about changelings; even Martin Luther had regarded children with mental disabilities as changelings sent by Satan.[14] We do not know whether Ragvaldinpoika or his parents heard similar characterizations. It is possible, however, because both his outward appearance and his speech probably made an unpleasant, even frightening, impression on those he met for the first time. His ego documents repeatedly refer to his disabilities, especially to the harelip, which was a conspicuous feature on his face.

Ragvaldinpoika was nevertheless uncertain whether it was right to change the face that God had created. His world view with regard to his disabilities seems to have resided on the border between old and new. In the broadsheets of the eighteenth and early nineteenth centuries, disabilities were usually explained as trials sent by God and as living examples of God's power and mercy. As was pointed out above, Ragvaldinpoika saw his disabilities and suffering as a consequence of his (original) sin, a common interpretation in Lutheran orthodoxy. However, he tried to find help to improve the situation,

---

13 Salminen, *Den finländska teologin*, pp. 89–90, 139–42.
14 Ragvaldinpoika, *Sen wirhen, ja ristin alla*, pp. 2–3; Kalm, *Enfaldiga tankar*; Raittila, *Tuomas Ragvaldinpoika*, pp. 19–20; Vehmas, *Vammaisuus*, p. 49; Claes G. Olsson, *Omsorg och kontroll: En handikappshistorisk studie 1750–1930. Föreställningar och levnadsförhållanden* (Umeå: Umeå University, 2010), pp. 35–9; Ferngren, *Medicine and Religion*, pp. 160–4.

like many others at that time who suffered from diseases that were difficult or impossible to cure. He did not think that disabilities were an eternal destiny or an example of God's power, although God had created him with them. He did wonder if it would be proper to cure them; but in the end, and on the advice of a counsellor, he was convinced that the operation would not be a sin. According to natural theology, sin and eternal damnation were to be put aside. Instead, God wanted a man to be happy. The Enlightenment also raised the question of people's perfectibility, and some indeed tried to cure themselves of various disabilities.[15] Because of his harelip, Ragvaldinpoika was not happy or perfect; on the contrary, he felt he was to be pitied. He did not express his ideas in such straightforward terms, but it is possible that the ideas of happiness in natural theology and the general ambition to remedy his disabilities played a part when he developed the courage to undergo the operation.

Although the surgery was frightening and extremely painful, Ragvaldinpoika was very pleased to find a doctor ready to undertake it. After the successful operation, he thanked God for all the help he had received. It was God who had cured him and God had done so through the doctor, whom Tuomas called 'the doctor of nature'.[16] Here, too, the Enlightenment emphasis on nature surfaced, as in his first ego document from 1760.

The description of the operation is quite vivid, even dramatic. During the operation, Ragvaldinpoika meditated on the sufferings of Christ and compared his pains with them. When the doctor made

---

15 Ragvaldinpoika, *Sen wirhen, ja ristin alla*, n.p.; Tuomas Ragvaldinpoika, *Christillinen jälkimuisto cosca poicainen nuorucainen Adrian Näppius pitkällisen cowan cuoleman taistelemuxen ja campauxen cautta ... hywästi jätti... wuonna 1763* (Prändätty Turusa, [1763]), pp. 1–2; Matti Klinge, 'Luonnonteologia ja luonnonoikeus', in *Kuninkaallinen Turun akatemia 1640–1808: Helsingin yliopisto 164–1990 Ensimmäinen osa* (Helsinki: Otava, 1987), pp. 668–78 (p. 669); Romel W. Mackelprang and Richard O. Salsgiver, 'People with disabilities and social work: historical and contemporary issues', *Social Work*, 41:1 (1996), 7–14 (8); Johann Anders Steiger, *Medizinische Theologie: Christus medicus und theologia medicinalis bei Martin Luther und im Luthertum der Barockzeit. Mit Edition dreier Quellentexte*, Studies in the history of Christian traditions, 121 (Leiden: Brill, 2005), pp. 51–2; Olsson, *Omsorg och kontroll*, p. 54; Ferngren, *Medicine and Religion*, pp. 151–2, 164; Strand, '"Let me tell you my life in a song"', 38.
16 Ragvaldinpoika, *Christillinen jälkimuisto*, pp. 1–2; Ferngren, *Medicine and Religion*, p. 139.

an incision in his lip, he thought about the wounds of Christ, and during the sewing of the wound he thought about the lance that pierced the side of Christ. This helped him to withstand the pain.[17] The theme of the Passion of Christ had been common and popular in devotional literature ever since the Middle Ages. The genre was a common one in Finland too. The Finnish reformer Mikael Agricola (1507–1557) issued the Passion of Christ (*Se meiden Herran Jesuxen Christuxen pina, ylösnousemus ja taiwasen astumus, niste neliest evangelisterist coghottu*) in 1549, which was later published in two further editions (1616 and 1620). Similar works had also appeared in several *Manuale Finnonicum* publications in the seventeenth century. In 1690, Matthias Salamnius (*c.* 1650–1690) had even written a long poem on the sufferings of Christ. According to the Church Law of 1686, the Passion was supposed to be read in churches regularly during Lent.[18] It is very likely that these texts were familiar to Ragvaldinpoika. However, he further developed the synoptic account of the Passion, adding his own experiences to it as a parallel to the sufferings of Christ. The active role of the author through a comparison of this kind was something new, a special product of the Enlightenment.

The ego documents of Tuomas Ragvaldinpoika also include the funeral hymn published in 1792 about his son, who died in the 1780s war with Russia. It does not tell us as much about Tuomas himself as about the son, but it describes the feelings of a grieving father. It actually consists of five separate hymns, the fourth of which is a song of praise to God, who led the author through so many difficult trials. That section has an even more personal touch than the other four pieces in the publication. The fifth part is a fictional hymn from the perspective of the dead son, in which he comforts the family and reminds them of the importance of knowing Christ.[19] Ragvaldinpoika clothed his greatest sorrows in religious ideas and sought comfort directly from God. The funeral hymn is

---

17 Ragvaldinpoika, *Christillinen jälkimuisto*.
18 Lahja-Irene Hellemaa, Anja Jussila and Martti Parvio (eds), *Kircko-Laki Ja Ordningi 1686: Näköispainos ja uudelleen ladottu laitos vuoden 1686 kirkkolain suomennoksesta* (Helsinki: Suomalaisen Kirjallisuuden Seura, 1986), Chapter 2, Section 8; Tuija Laine and Rita Nyqvist (eds), *Suomen kansallisbibliografia, 1488–1700* (Helsinki: Suomalaisen Kirjallisuuden Seura and Helsingin yliopiston kirjasto, 1996), numbers 166–8, 2538–47, 3309.
19 Tuomas Ragvaldinpoika, *Yhdeldä murheliselda ja surulliselda isäldä Thomas Ragwaldin pojalda, hänen omasta pojastansa sydämen haikkeudella Johan*

also important as a conveyor of consolation to the surviving members of the family.

After his son's death, Ragvaldinpoika seemed to wonder a great deal about the young man's fate. His funeral hymn expresses his anxiety about the state of his son's soul. He was told that before his death his son had listened to a sermon, confessed his sins and participated in the Eucharist. Ragvaldinpoika very much wished him to have turned to God at the moment of death. According to both the Church and old Finnish peasant culture, a death that took place suddenly and unexpectedly was a bad death. A good death was one which the deceased was prepared for, as well as other people. It has also been called a 'tamed death'.[20] Church prayers included wishes to avoid an unexpected death; it was important to repent before death, but a sudden death made that impossible.[21] This is why his son's last moments were so important to Tuomas Ragvaldinpoika: it was a question of his son's salvation. The farewell to the son describes the deepest wishes of the father as he tried to convince himself of the good life his son had in heaven.

Hymns for public occasions

Tuomas Ragvaldinpoika wrote and published nineteen funeral hymns, nine marriage hymns, five congratulatory hymns addressed to the royal family, three other congratulatory hymns addressed to different people and seven hymns for various occasions. Most of the funeral hymns were written for dead clergymen.[22] All the hymns have a very strong religious emphasis, with the religiosity somewhere between Lutheran orthodoxy and Pietism. Although there are many hymns for specific people, they provide very little

---

Lindström, *Wollentöristä. Sen elämän ja kuoleman ylitze, yxi raskas jälkimuisto, omasille. Joka Jumalan jo ijankaikkisen näkemisen ja saldimisen jälken sota tiellä pikaisesti taphdui tosin niiden puhetten jälken tehty jotka siinä läsnä ja sapuilla oliwat. Paljo puutuwaisesti kirjoitettu ja wiidesä osasa Lojman pitäjäsä ja Hirwikosken kyläsä kokonpandu wuonna 1791* (Turusa, 1792).

20 Philippe Ariès, *Western Attitudes toward Death: From the Middle Ages to the Present*, trans. Patricia M. Ranum (Baltimore: Johns Hopkins University Press, 1974), pp. 1–26, 55–108.
21 Ragvaldinpoika, *Yhdeldä murhelliselda*; Kaarina Koski, *Kuoleman voimat: Kirkonväki suomalaisessa uskomusperinteessä* (Helsinki: Suomalaisen Kirjallisuuden Seura, 2011), pp. 90–2.
22 Raittila, *Tuomas Ragvaldinpoika*, pp. 88–96.

personal information about them. The hymns are mostly reminders about the importance of Christian life, penitence, the meaning of grace and ways to obtain it. Conversion features in several of them. There are no Enlightenment features in these texts, rather folk beliefs. As noted above with the compositions for his own son, some of the funeral hymns contain fictional texts from the perspective of the deceased in which they bid farewell to their family and relatives, often mentioning them one by one. The first hymn of this kind was published in 1764, a hymn to Maria Azell, widow of the merchant Mikko Nordström.[23] These are exhortations to stay with Christ, but are also intended to comfort for those still on earth.

Funeral poems in the early modern period usually consisted of three separate parts. The *lamentation* bewailed the power of death and expressed grief for the dead person. The *laudation* extolled the deceased's fame and achievements. The third part, the *consolation*, was supposed to comfort friends and relatives. This comfort might, as noted, be fictionally dispensed by the dead person themselves. This tripartite structure, a tradition which originated in the literature of Antiquity, was recommended in manuals of rhetoric and poetics.[24] Ragvaldinpoika's funeral poems may to some extent have derived from the dream that he had after the death of his mother. In the dream he stood by his mother's grave, looking down into it. There he saw a small boy like an angel with his mother. He asked them to come out of the grave, but his mother told him that she felt well there. At that moment, Ragvaldinpoika woke up and saw them no more.[25] Relationships between the living and the dead were much more complicated at that time than they are today. There were common beliefs – folk beliefs, in particular – about dead people appearing to the living in order to convey messages or warnings.[26] In dreaming about his dead mother, Ragvaldinpoika was linked to the beliefs of his time about dead people as messengers from beyond the grave. The small boy-like angel in the grave of his mother may

---

23 Raittila, *Tuomas Ragvaldinpoika*, pp. 42, 89.
24 Raija Sarasti-Wilenius, 'Latinankielinen promootio-, hää- ja hautarunous Suomessa', in Tuija Laine (ed.), *Vanhimman suomalaisen kirjallisuuden käsikirja* (Helsinki: Suomalaisen Kirjallisuuden Seura, 1997), pp. 224–39 (pp. 234, 236).
25 Ragvaldinpoika, *Sen wirhen, ja ristin alla*, pp. 3^v–4^r.
26 Koski, *Kuoleman voimat*, p. 88.

evoke the angel at the tomb of Christ, a biblical parallel similar to those in the hymn Ragvaldinpoika wrote about his surgery.

Using the Bible as a source

The previous section mentioned several ways of using the Bible that Tuomas Ragvaldinpoika applied in the occasional literature he wrote. In his ego documents, he mostly used parallels between the Passion of Christ and his own personal life. In his other poems and hymns, the Bible likewise had a prominent role, with frequent references to biblical events or texts. The suffering of Christ and the wedding at Cana are perhaps the most frequently cited events in his hymns. The latter is not only used in the wedding hymns; it occurs in other hymns as well. Similarly, Ragvaldinpoika referred to the suffering of Christ in many different hymns, even in a wedding poem to Jacob Mennander and his bride Maria Catharina Sjöstedt in 1784. According to him, the two most remarkable 'weddings' were the wedding at Cana and the death of Christ at Golgotha, where Christ as a 'groom' gave himself for the salvation of the whole world.[27] Ragvaldinpoika did not question the miracles of the Bible in any way.

Ragvaldinpoika rarely specified the biblical passages or verses he referred to, although there are some funeral poems where biblical verses are mentioned in the footnotes. When he did provide explicit references to biblical passages, there would be a connection of some kind between the Bible and the destinies of the dead people the funeral poems were written for. For example, the funeral poem for Adrian Näppius, son of the furrier Carl Gustaf Näppius, begins with the story of the centurion whose son died and was raised from the dead by Jesus. While Adrian Näppius did not arise from the dead, the grief of a bereaved father was the same in Finland in the 1760s as during Jesus' time. Similarly, the funeral hymn to the minister of Loimaa, Gustaf Haartman, compares Haartman to several biblical characters who died as suddenly as Haartman did. In oratory, expressions of this kind are called *exempla*. The exempla are based on texts that are thought to be already known to readers; in these

---

27 Tuomas Ragvaldinpoika, *Christillinen ja sydämmellinen häitten onnen-toiwotus Wesilahden pitäjäsä ja Anjan rustholisa sille … Marian kirkon seurakunnan halulliselle opettajalle herralle apulaiselle herr Jacob Mennanderille yljälle; niin myös sille neitzy Maria Catharina Sjöstedtille morsiamelle;* … (Turusa, 1785).

instances, the familiar text is the Bible, and therefore brief references are sufficient.[28] The biblical verses or stories are not the main object, but an aid to handling the situation when someone has died, making it more comprehensible. At the same time, those parallels bring history to life, as a reminder that similar events have happened before, in the time of the Bible.

Ragvaldinpoika referred to both the Old and New Testaments. The collection of biblical verses and stories proves that he had a good knowledge of the entire Bible and was able to draw on it in quite a creative way when writing his own occasional literature. Not only the Bible but also many forms of rhetorical writing were familiar to Ragvaldinpoika. It is not known whether he learnt them from textbooks or from other authors, or solely by imitating earlier funeral poems and other occasional literature, which must have been available in the Turku region.

Broadsheets and hymns as commercial articles

We do not know what gave Tuomas Ragvaldinpoika the idea of writing and publishing his texts. Pekka Raittila has considered this question and found some external stimuli for his activity. There had been literary projects in Tyrvää even before Ragvaldinpoika, but he probably found a greater enthusiasm for writing and publishing in Turku, where he most probably moved in the 1750s. Turku offered much better opportunities for publishing, and there was a group of people with the same religious sentiments as himself. This friendly group took care of him, offering him both a religious home and material support.[29]

Generally speaking, occasional poetry, hymns and verses for funerals and weddings were written specifically for these events at the time, and they were printed in small editions. But at least some of them had more far-reaching goals: to serve the public after the actual event in prayers and devotion. Autobiographical texts, for example *Lebensläufe* in the Moravian tradition, were not only used at funerals; they were read at religious meetings in order to arouse

---

28 Ragvaldinpoika, *Christillinen jälkimuisto*; Stina Hansson, *Svensk bröllopsdiktning under 1600- och 1700-talen: Renässansrepertoarernas framväxt, blomstring och tillbakagång* (Gothenburg: University of Gothenburg, 2011), p. 25.

29 Raittila, *Tuomas Ragvaldinpoika*, pp. 20–2; Laine, 'Tuomas Ragvaldinpoika ja hyödyllisen', p. 59.

devotion and present examples of the religious life of the deceased. Most hymns and verses by Tuomas Ragvaldinpoika were written from this point of view. In this respect, these writings of his belong to the genre of broadsheets or ephemeral songs, which were usually printed cheaply on poor-quality paper and sold at markets. As well as broadsheets, these poems were written as hymns, naming a suitable tune to which they could be sung. In appearance, they resemble broadsheets more than traditional occasional literature.[30] There is no information about the sale of these publications, but several features invite conclusions based on the commercial nature of the publications.

All the traditional parts (lamentation, laudation and consolation) are present in the poetry of Tuomas Ragvaldinpoika. The personal parts concerning the subjects of the poems are quite restricted, even in the funeral poetry written for well-known citizens, for example local clergymen. Only the broadsheets about Ragvaldinpoika himself and his own son were written from a more personal perspective. The other texts are strikingly devotional, admonitory, moral and edifying in their nature. This feature was noted in 1862 by Julius Krohn in his dissertation on Finnish poetry during the Swedish era.[31] Other evidence of the commercial importance of these publications is the number of editions printed, which Raittila has ascertained. He shows that from 1763 there was more than one (first) edition of several publications, mostly of broadsheets and funeral hymns and verses. The first editions were quite often printed at least one year after the deceased person's death, which indicates that they were more apt to be used as memoirs or devotional literature than at funerals. The funeral hymns to the furrier's son Adrian Näppius, Michel Holma and the clergyman Abraham Wanochius, Master of Arts, appeared in four editions; the hymn to the minister of Piikkiö,

---

30 Hansson, *Svensk bröllopsdiktning*, p. 32; Anna Nilsson, *Lyckans betydelse: Sekularisering, sensibilisering och individualisering i svenska skillingtryck 1750–1850* (Höör: Agerings, 2012), pp. 33–5; Esko M. Laine, '"Herkkinä kasvun vuosinani kannoin huolta autuudestani": Suomalaissyntyisten herrnhutilaisten 1700-luvun hengelliset autobiografiat (Lebensläufe) kirkkohistoriallisena tutkimuskohteena', in Hanna-Maija Ketola and others (eds), *Suurmiehistä rahvaannaisiin: Yksilö ja yhteisö kristinuskon historiassa* (Helsinki: Suomen kirkkohistoriallinen seura, 2014), pp. 289–318 (pp. 293–302); Strand, '"Let me tell you my life in a song"', 36.
31 Julius Krohn, *Suomenkielinen runous ruotsinvallan aikana ynnä kuvaelmia suomalaisuuden historiasta*, dosentinväitöskirja (Helsinki, 1862), p. 179.

David Henric Deutsch, in five editions; and the hymn to Anna Rogel, who was famous for preaching in her dreams, in a total of eight editions. The new editions were mostly published in the nineteenth century, but some appeared as late as the beginning of the twentieth century. Only the funeral hymn to David Henric Deutsch states the price of the publication on the last page: 'six *öre* in silver'. Besides the funeral hymns, the short collections of hymns were popular and printed in several editions. Ragvaldinpoika was not very keen on selling his own life story – there are two editions of the hymns about his own life (1760 and 1771), and the hymn about his surgery was only printed once. It is also possible that these ego documents were not as commercially appealing to other people as the funeral poems. The latter were even more devotional and exhortative, closer to the genre of devotional literature. In Sweden, autobiographical ephemera about blind people and those with other disabilities were written and sold from the late seventeenth to the mid-twentieth centuries as their authors sought to earn a living.[32] This does not seem to have been a motive impelling Ragvaldinpoika to publish his autobiographical hymns, although he published and sold his other writings with pleasure. However, it was in his autobiographical texts that Enlightenment features appeared most clearly. The other poems and hymns are more traditional by nature.

The most widespread publication by Tuomas Ragvaldinpoika was the hymn lamenting a maid from Paimio, Helena Jacobintytär, who was convicted of infanticide and hanged. According to the title page, the condemned maid herself had asked Ragvaldinpoika to write it as a warning to worldly people. No other evidence about the role of the maid in this publication is available, so we do not know whether this statement was merely a sales trick. Nevertheless, the person concerned was a real Finnish woman from Paimio, not a fictional character. Broadsheets before the 1850s were mostly moral and exhortatory by nature, like this one as well as other broadsheets and hymns by Ragvaldinpoika. Altogether thirty editions of this broadsheet were printed between 1764 and 1903. Some years saw the publication of several editions, for example as many as five in 1764. Most editions were printed in the nineteenth century.[33]

---

32 Raittila, *Tuomas Ragvaldinpoika*, pp. 62–3, 88–96; Strand, '"Let me tell you my life in a song"', 35, 38.

33 Paimio, Suomen sukuhistoriallinen yhdistys ry., Syntyneet – vihityt – kuolleet 1728–1766, JK257 (1764, 163); Tuomas Ragvaldinpoika, *Murhellinen*

At that time, the popularity and dissemination of broadsheets was already greater than during the previous century.

Despite the large number of editions of various broadsheets and hymns, the publications were not advertised in the Turku newspapers. They were probably sold at the fair, like other broadsheets.

Conclusion

In his writings, Tuomas Ragvaldinpoika trod a fine line between the ideas of Lutheran orthodoxy and of the Enlightenment. His autobiographical texts represent a comparatively new world view; but the commercial texts written for other people's funerals and weddings adhered to traditional lines, reflecting features of Lutheran orthodoxy, Pietism and folk belief. From the Enlightenment, Ragvaldinpoika especially adopted conceptions about medicine and doctors. Trying to heal congenital disabilities is no sin, according to him. These things were dear to his heart for personal reasons, in that he himself suffered from various disabilities. The Enlightenment ideas in medicine brought more hope and help in his circumstances than the old world view of Lutheran orthodoxy. For Ragvaldinpoika, these new ideas did not carry any theological significance. On the other hand, in respect of the more dogmatic questions he did not have any such personal need to assume a considered position in relation to enlightened ideas, highlighting the meaning of reason, for instance. Conversion is needed for salvation, and apostasy was one of the reasons for war, he said.

Although Tuomas Ragvaldinpoika wrote about himself, he was either not very interested in selling his own life story or did not have enough buyers for it. His moral, admonitory and devotional poems were printed in a larger number of editions than the stories of his own experiences. Then as now, a murder story would be a best-seller, and the tale of the hanged infanticide sold exceptionally well. Ragvaldinpoika was at least partly capable of earning his

---

ero-wirsi, koska piika Paimion pitäjästä ja Lowen kylästä, Helena Jacobin tytär, joka lapsens murhan tähden, Paimion kirkon nummella, parhan nuorudens ijän kukoistuxen ajalla mestattin, sinä 16. p. heinä kuusa wuonna 1764... (Vasa, 1764); Raittila, *Tuomas Ragvaldinpoika*, p. 93; Anneli Asplund, *Balladeja ja arkkiveisuja: Suomalaisia kertomalauluja*, Suomalaisen Kirjallisuuden Seuran toimituksia, 563 (Helsinki: Suomalaisen Kirjallisuuden Seura, 1994), p. 613.

living through literary work, writing and selling his own texts. That was quite an achievement for a self-taught, disabled man in the eighteenth century, and it affords us an indication of the effect of folk Enlightenment.

Bibliography

Archival sources

Paimio, Finland

Suomen sukuhistoriallinen yhdistys ry.
  Syntyneet – vihityt – kuolleet 1728–1766 (JK257)

Digital sources

Kotivuori, Yrjö, 'Ylioppilasmatrikkeli 1640–1852: Johan Haartman' (University of Helsinki, 2005), https://ylioppilasmatrikkeli.helsinki.fi/henkilo.php?id=6683 [accessed 3 May 2020].

Printed sources and literature

Ahokas, Minna, 'Pro fide et christianismon kristillinen valistustoiminta 1770-luvulta 1800-luvun alkuun', in Esko M. Laine and Minna Ahokas (eds), *Hyödyllisen tiedon piirit: Tutkimuksia papistosta, rahvaasta ja tiedon rakentumisesta 1700-luvulla* (Helsinki: Suomalaisen Kirjallisuuden Seura, 2018), pp. 84–142.
Ahokas, Minna and Päivi Räisänen-Schröder, 'Papisto ja hyödyllinen tieto 1700-luvun Ruotsissa', in Esko M. Laine and Minna Ahokas (eds), *Hyödyllisen tiedon piirit: Tutkimuksia papistosta, rahvaasta ja tiedon rakentumisesta 1700-luvulla* (Helsinki: Suomalaisen Kirjallisuuden Seura, 2018), pp. 7–44.
Ariès, Philippe, *Western Attitudes toward Death: From the Middle Ages to the Present*, trans. Patricia M. Ranum (Baltimore: Johns Hopkins University Press, 1974).
Asplund, Anneli, *Balladeja ja arkkiveisuja. Suomalaisia kertomalauluja*, Suomalaisen Kirjallisuuden Seuran toimituksia, 563 (Helsinki: Suomalaisen Kirjallisuuden Seura, 1994).
Baggerman, Arianne and Rudolf Dekker, 'Jacques Presser, egodocuments and the personal turn in historiography', *European Journal of Life Writing*, 7 (2018), 90–110.
Bourdieu, Pierre, 'The forms of capital', in John Richardson (ed.), *Handbook of Theory and Research for the Sociology of Education* (New York: Greenwood Press, 1986), pp. 241–58.

Ferngren, Gary B., *Medicine and Religion: A Historical Introduction* (Baltimore, MD: Johns Hopkins University Press, 2014).

Hansson, Stina, *Svensk bröllopsdiktning under 1600- och 1700-talen: Renässansrepertoarernas framväxt, blomstring och tillbakagång* (Gothenburg: University of Gothenburg, 2011).

Hellemaa, Lahja-Irene, Anja Jussila and Martti Parvio (eds), *Kircko-Laki Ja Ordningi 1686: Näköispainos ja uudelleen ladottu laitos vuoden 1686 kirkkolain suomennoksesta* (Helsinki: Suomalaisen Kirjallisuuden Seura, 1986).

Kalm, Pehr, *Enfaldiga tankar om nyttan och nödvändigheten för en präst, at äga insikt i Medicine, med wederbörandes samtycke, under ... H. Pehr Kalms inseende ... Öfwerlämnade af Samuel Lithovius, Isacs son, Österbotninge* (Åbo/Turku, 1762).

Keravuori, Kirsi, *'Rakkat poikaiset!' Simon ja Wilhelmina Janssonin perhekirjeet egodokumentteina (1858–1887)* (Turku: Turun yliopisto, 2015).

Klinge, Matti, 'Luonnonteologia ja luonnonoikeus', in *Kuninkaallinen Turun akatemia 1640–1808: Helsingin yliopisto 164–1990 Ensimmäinen osa* (Helsinki: Otava, 1987), pp. 668–78.

Koski, Kaarina, *Kuoleman voimat: Kirkonväki suomalaisessa uskomusperinteessä* (Helsinki: Suomalaisen Kirjallisuuden Seura, 2011).

Krohn, Julius, *Suomenkielinen runous ruotsinvallan aikana ynnä kuvaelmia suomalaisuuden historiasta*, dosentinväitöskirja (Helsinki, 1862).

Laine, Esko M., '"Herkkinä kasvun vuosinani kannoin huolta autuudestani": Suomalaissyntyisten herrnhutilaisten 1700-luvun hengelliset autobiografiat (Lebensläufe) kirkkohistoriallisena tutkimuskohteena', in Hanna-Maija Ketola and others (eds), *Suurmiehistä rahvaannaisiin: Yksilö ja yhteisö kristinuskon historiassa* (Helsinki: Suomen kirkkohistoriallinen seura, 2014), pp. 289–318.

———, 'Tuomas Ragvaldinpoika (1724–1804)', in *Suomen kansallisbiografia*, 10 vols (Helsinki: Suomalaisen Kirjallisuuden Seura, 2003–2007), X (2007), pp. 52–4.

———, 'Tuomas Ragvaldinpoika ja hyödyllisen tiedon rajat ja piirit 1700-luvun suomalaisessa sääty-yhteiskunnassa', in Esko M. Laine and Minna Ahokas (eds), *Hyödyllisen tiedon piirit: Tutkimuksia papistosta, rahvaasta ja tiedon rakentumisesta 1700-luvulla* (Helsinki: Suomalaisen Kirjallisuuden Seura, 2018), pp. 45–83.

Laine, Esko M. and Tuija Laine, 'Kirkollinen kansanopetus', in Jussi Hanska and Kirsi Vainio (eds), *Huoneentaulun maailma: Kasvatus ja koulutus Suomessa keskiajalta 1860-luvulle* (Helsinki: Suomalaisen Kirjallisuuden Seura, 2010), pp. 258–306.

Laine, Tuija, *Aapisen ja katekismuksen tavaamisesta itsenäiseen lukemiseen: Rahvaan lukukulttuurin kehitys varhaismodernina aikana* (Helsinki: Suomalaisen Kirjallisuuden Seura, 2017).

Laine, Tuija and Rita Nyqvist (eds), *Suomen kansallisbibliografia, 1488–1700* (Helsinki: Suomalaisen Kirjallisuuden Seura and Helsingin yliopiston kirjasto, 1996).

Lindmark, Daniel, *Läs- och skrivkunnigheten före folkskolan: Historisk läskunnighetsforskning i nordiskt och internationellt perspektiv* (Umeå: Forskningsarkivet, 1990).
Mackelprang, Romel W. and Richard O. Salsgiver, 'People with disabilities and social work: historical and contemporary issues', *Social Work*, 41:1 (1996), 7–14.
Nilsson, Anna, *Lyckans betydelse: Sekularisering, sensibilisering och individualisering i svenska skillingtryck 1750–1850* (Höör: Agerings, 2012).
Olsson, Claes G., *Omsorg och kontroll: En handikappshistorisk studie 1750–1930. Föreställningar och levnadsförhållanden* (Umeå: Umeå University, 2010).
Räisänen-Schröder, Päivi, 'Johan Frosterus ja hyödyllinen tieto luomakunnasta', in Esko M. Laine and Minna Ahokas (eds), *Hyödyllisen tiedon piirit: Tutkimuksia papistosta, rahvaasta ja tiedon rakentumisesta 1700-luvulla* (Helsinki: Suomalaisen Kirjallisuuden Seura, 2018), pp. 143–83.
Ragvaldinpoika, Tuomas, *Christillinen jälkimuisto cosca poicainen nuorucainen Adrian Näppius pitkällisen cowan cuoleman taistelemuxen ja campauxen cautta ... hywästi jätti ... wuonna 1763* (Prändätty Turusa, [1763]).
——, *Christillinen ja sydämmellinen häitten onnen-toiwotus Wesilahden pitäjäsä ja Anjan rusthollisa sille ... Marian kirkon seurakunnan halulliselle opettajalle herralle apulaiselle herr Jacob Mennanderille yljälle; niin myös sille neitzy Maria Catharina Sjöstedtille morsiamelle; ...* (Turusa, 1785).
——, *Murhellinen ero-wirsi, koska piika Paimion pitäjästä ja Lowen kylästä, Helena Jacobin tytär, joka lapsensa murhan tähden, Paimion kirkon nummella, parhan nuorudens ijän kukoistuxen ajalla mestattin, sinä 16. p. heinä kuusa wuonna 1764 ...* (Vasa, 1764).
——, *Sen wirhen, ja ristin alla hamast lapsudesta ja nuorudesta, rasitetun weisu, Sanct. Hendrikin lähten terweyden nautitzemisen alla, wuonna 1759, parannuxen wuotella maatesa, elämänsä perään ajatellesa ja Jumalan johdattamista tutkistellesa, Turun caupungisa, cocoonpandu Thomas Rawaldin pojalda, Tyrwän pidäjästä ja Lauculan kylästä* (Turusa, 1760).
——, *Yhdeldä murhelliseldä ja surulliselda isäldä Thomas Ragwaldin pojalda, hänen omasta pojastansa sydämen haikkeudella Johan Lindström, Wollentöristä. Sen elämän ja kuoleman ylitze, yxi raskas jälki-muisto, omasille. Joka Jumalan jo ijankaikkisen näkemisen ja saldimisen jälken sota tiellä pikaisesti taphdui tosin niiden puhetten jälken tehty jotka siinä läsnä ja sapuilla oliwat. Paljo puutuwaisesti kirjoitettu ja wiidesä osasa Lojman pitäjäsä ja Hirwikosken kyläsä kokonpandu wuonna 1791* (Turusa, 1792).
Raittila, Pekka, *Tuomas Ragvaldinpoika* (Vammala: Tyrvään seudun Museo- ja Kotiseutuyhdistys, 1949).
Rantanen, Arja, *Pennförare i periferin: Österbottniska sockenskrivare 1721–1868* (Åbo/Turku: Åbo akademis förlag, 2014).

Salminen, Seppo J., *Den finländska teologin under frihetstiden* (Helsinki: Finska kyrkohistoriska samfundet, 1994).

Sarasti-Wilenius, Raija, 'Latinankielinen promootio-, hää- ja hautarunous Suomessa', in Tuija Laine (ed.), *Vanhimman suomalaisen kirjallisuuden käsikirja* (Helsinki: Suomalaisen Kirjallisuuden Seura, 1997), pp. 224–39.

Steiger, Johann Anselm, *Medizinische Theologie: Christus medicus und theologia medicinalis bei Martin Luther und im Luthertum der Barockzeit. Mit Edition dreier Quellentexte*, Studies in the history of Christian traditions, 121 (Leiden: Brill, 2005).

Strand, Karin, '"Let me tell you my life in a song": on autobiography and begging in broadsheet ballads of the blind', *European Journal of Life Writing*, 7 (2018), 34–52.

Vehmas, Simo, *Vammaisuus: Johdatus historiaan, teoriaan ja etiikkaan* (Helsinki: Gaudeamus, 2005).

4
Applications of the three-estate doctrine: Swedish local sermons and the social order, 1790–1820

Joonas Tammela

Historiography has emphasized the significance of the Age of Revolution as a critical period for the shifts – caused by the different forms of Enlightenment – in ideas concerning the structure of society, as well as the rights and duties of the individual.[1] These phenomena were also prominent in the macro-level Swedish political discourses that took place in many forums. For example, among the political elite there appeared – increasingly from the latter half of the eighteenth century, and especially after the events of 1809 when Sweden was forced to secede Finland to Russia – descriptions of the state that proceeded from the perspectives of individuals. This gradual shift meant that societal rights and responsibilities belonged to individuals instead of to the political Estates. This trend challenged the older ideal of society which was based on the ideals of stability and collectivism.[2] On the basis of studies of the debates about patriotism in the newspapers, it has likewise been argued that there was an active discursive struggle about the level of corporatism in Swedish society after the events of 1809.[3] Indeed, those events are seen as a watershed in political discourses about the structure of society and the political role of the people in both Sweden and Finland.

---

1 I refer to the period between the late eighteenth century and the early nineteenth century as the Age of Revolution owing to the events and many changes at various levels in societies, with greater or lesser intersections for the Enlightenment; see Pasi Ihalainen and Karin Sennefelt, 'General introduction', in Pasi Ihalainen and others (eds), *Scandinavia in the Age of Revolution: Nordic Political Cultures, 1749–1820* (Farnham: Ashgate, 2011), pp. 1–13.
2 Martin Melkersson, *Staten, ordningen och friheten: En studie av den styrande elitens syn på statens roll mellan stormaktstiden och 1800-talet* (Uppsala: Uppsala University, 1997), pp. 213–19, 223–24.
3 Henrik Edgren, *Publicitet för medborgsmannavett: Det nationellt svenska i Stockholmstidningar 1810–1831* (Uppsala: Uppsala University, 2005), pp. 310–12.

The use of concepts at the *Riksdag* indicates that Sweden took a step towards recognizing the individual civil liberties of the people while Finland emphasized the more conservative privileges of the Estate corporations.[4]

The changing perceptions of the structure of society have also been regarded as influencing the expressions of traditional Lutheran views on the body politic. The Lutheran interpretation of the doctrine of the three estates viewed the structure of the worldly society from the perspective of Christian teaching.[5] The three-estate doctrine outlined the relationship of obedience between the people in different spheres of societal coexistence and human life. The system consisted of clergymen and listeners (*Ecclesia*), authorities and subjects (*Politia*), and fathers and children (*Oeconomia*). Each of these estates had a function to maintain religious practice in society. The notion of the three estates was a core doctrine of the official early modern Lutheran formulations of society. During the seventeenth and eighteenth centuries, the system was presented in the Lutheran Household Code (*hustavla/huoneentaulu*) in the official catechisms.[6] Catechisms were a key tool for teaching the Christian doctrines and the basics of literacy. They were, in principle, among the most crucial texts for the common horizon of understanding in the eighteenth century, both for the educated clergymen and for the non-educated masses. Every member of society was made to at least try to internalize the doctrines of the catechism by reading and listening.[7]

---

4 Pasi Ihalainen and Anders Sundin, 'Continuity and change in the language of politics at the Swedish Diet, 1769–1810', in Pasi Ihalainen and others (eds), *Scandinavia in the Age of Revolution: Nordic Political Cultures, 1740–1820* (Farnham: Ashgate, 2011), pp. 169–92 (pp. 169–70, 192).

5 For clarity's sake, 'Estates' (with a capital 'E') refers to the representatives gathering at the Swedish *Riksdag*, whereas 'estates' is used for the relationship between *Ecclesia*, *Politia* and *Oeconomia* in Lutheran social teaching.

6 Hilding Pleijel, *Hustavlans värld: Kyrkligt folkliv i äldre tiders Sverige* (Stockholm: Verbum, 1970), pp. 32–44.

7 See, for example, Esko M. Laine and Tuija Laine, 'Kirkollinen kansanopetus', in Jussi Hanska and Kirsi Vainio-Korhonen (eds), *Huoneentaulun maailma: Kasvatus ja koulutus Suomessa keskiajalta 1860-luvulle* (Helsinki: Suomalaisen Kirjallisuuden Seura, 2010), pp. 258–306 (pp. 259–61, 285–6); Egil Johansson, 'Den kyrkliga lästraditionen i Sverige – en konturteckning', in Mauno Jokipii and Ilkka Nummela (eds), *Läskunnighet och folkbildning före folkskoleväsendet*, XVIII: *Nordiska historikermötet i Jyväskylä 1981*.

In the Swedish realm, the three-estate doctrine was not the same as the four political Estates with their particular societal privileges. Every member of society – regardless of his or her status in the political Estates – formed part of all three estates. This doctrinal system merely reflected the patriarchal obedience between the different parts of the established hierarchies. Still, when speaking about the three-estate doctrine there was no separation between the spheres of state and religion as such. There were various styles to reconcile the structuring of society rooted in Lutheran doctrine and the political Estates in theological and political discussions. Therefore, the increasing critique of the division between the political Estates and their privileges during the eighteenth century and the beginning of the nineteenth also affected the discursive strategies for legitimizing the three-estate system.[8]

Even in early studies, the change of society has been seen as a cohesive force in reducing the role of the three-estate system in the official Lutheran teaching material in the early nineteenth century. In the Swedish catechism reform in 1809, the structure of the Household Code no longer relied so much on the three estates. Instead, the new strategy appeared to attach importance to the more general patriarchal relations. It has been suggested that the doctrine of the three estates was not regarded as being up to date, as society had changed a great deal during the eighteenth century and the influence of natural law had overtaken the hierarchical construction of the worldly society.[9] In the Finnish part of the realm, the older

---

Mötesrapport (Jyväskylä: University of Jyväskylä, 1981), pp. 193–224; Tuija Laine, *Aapisen ja katekismuksen tavaamisesta itsenäiseen lukemiseen: Rahvaan lukukulttuurin kehitys varhaismodernina aikana* (Helsinki: Suomalaisen Kirjallisuuden Seura, 2017).

8 Carola Nordbäck, *Lycksalighetens källa: Kontextuella närläsningar av Anders Chydenius budordspredikningar 1781–82* (Turku: Åbo Akademi, 2009), pp. 209–11; Carl-E. Normann (ed.), *Cleri comitialis cirkulär 1723–1772* (Stockholm: Svenska kyrkans diakonistyrelse, 1952), pp. 22–4, 28–34; Pleijel, *Hustavlans värld*, pp. 40–1; Sten Carlsson, *Ståndssamhälle och ståndspersoner 1700–1865: Studier rörande det svenska ståndssamhällets upplösning* (Lund: Gleerup, 1949), pp. 247–69. On the conflicts regarding divisions between the political Estates, see also Kaarlo Wirilander, *Herrskapsfolk: Ståndspersoner i Finland 1721–1870*, trans. Eva Stenius (Stockholm: Nordiska museet, 1982 [1974]).

9 See, for example, Pleijel, *Hustavlans värld*, pp. 44–50. See also Daniel Lindmark, *Uppfostran, undervisning, upplysning: Linjer i svensk folkundervisning före folkskolan* (Umeå: Umeå University, 1995), pp. 24–5, 161–4,

form of catechism remained even after 1809 as an official version. During the eighteenth century, however, the use of alternative forms of catechisms was constantly increasing.[10]

Despite these reforms, studies by Daniel Lindmark and Joachim Östlund have argued that at the turn of the nineteenth century, the importance of patriarchal relations – adhering to the structure of the three-estate doctrine – was in fact momentarily strengthened, both in the local control of literacy skills and in the rhetoric of the authorities.[11] Having studied Swedish Church protocols, Lindmark suggests that the changing perceptions and the strengthening of the three-estate system should not necessarily be read as a paradoxical act from the clergy's viewpoint. Still, he points out that there were variations in teaching strategies between the dioceses at the turn of the nineteenth century, and that these variations call for further research.[12] It seems that the Age of Revolution marked – in principle – a time of change even for the official Lutheran definitions concerning the order of society. Therefore, it would be relevant to study how these shifts in macro-level political discourses and ideas of the Swedish realm affected Lutheran teaching about the structures of society *in practice*.

Several studies have argued that Lutheran teaching on the three estates had a huge impact during the early modern era. Swedish church historian Hilding Pleijel in particular is known for his studies on the role of the three-estate system in Swedish Lutheranism. He has described the three estates as a fundamental part of the teaching on Christian doctrine – in which sermons played an important

---

191; Jakob Christensson, *Lyckoriket: Studier i svensk upplysning* (Stockholm: Atlantis, 1996), pp. 371, 387. It has been argued that three-estate doctrine as such was less frequently used even in Danish sermons during the 1810s, see Michael Bregnsbo, *Samfundsorden og statsmagt set fra prædikestolen: danske præsters deltagelse i den offentlige opinionsdannelse vedrørende samfundsordenen og statsmagten 1750–1848, belyst ved trykte prædikener: en politisk-idéhistorisk undersøgelse* (Copenhagen: Museum Tusculanum, 1997), pp. 118–19.

10 Laine, *Aapisen ja katekismuksen*, pp. 121–36; Laine and Laine, 'Kirkollinen kansanopetus', pp. 274–5.

11 Lindmark, *Uppfostran, undervisning, upplysning*, pp. 159, 182–92, 211–14; Joachim Östlund, *Lyckolandet: Maktens legitimering i officiell retorik från stormaktstid till demokratins genombrott* (Lund: Sekel, 2007), pp. 172, 206.

12 Lindmark, *Uppfostran, undervisning, upplysning*, pp. 184–5, 213–14.

part – during the seventeenth and eighteenth centuries by the ecclesiastical authorities.[13]

Sermons as an instrument in local political cultures

This chapter asks how relations between the members of society emerged in sermon manuscripts written by local clergymen in the Swedish realm from 1790 to 1820.[14] Since the 1990s, a growing number of scholars have studied the early modern sermon as a source for broad intellectual changes in European societies.[15] Not least in Scandinavia, a wide range of historians have studied the role of sermons in the dissemination of political values, ideals and opinions in the eighteenth century.[16] However, research on sermons has mainly focused on printed materials, for example the state sermons held at the *Riksdag* and the model sermons.[17] Ordinary Sunday sermons held weekly in local parishes are strikingly absent in studies evaluating continuity and change in the political preaching of the late eighteenth and early nineteenth centuries. Still, it has been pointed out that local clergymen generally explained the issues of their time on the basis of the circumstances in their local

---

13 Pleijel, *Hustavlans värld*, pp. 23, 36–40. Pleijel's interpretations of the three-estate doctrine as a strong basis for the early modern folk mentalities and the thinking of the masses have subsequently been criticized and reconsidered; see, for example, Peter Aronsson, 'Hustavlans värld: folklig mentalitet eller överhetens utopi?', in Christer Ahlberger and Göran Malmstedt (eds), *Västsvensk fromhet* (Gothenburg: University of Gothenburg, 1993), pp. 11–42 (pp. 11–14, 35–6).
14 Lindmark's observation concerning the small number of studies on the teaching practices of the three-estate doctrine is valid even today; see Lindmark, *Uppfostran, undervisning, upplysning*, p. 152.
15 See, for example, Keith A. Francis and William Gibson (eds), *The Oxford Handbook of the British Sermon* (Oxford: Oxford University Press, 2012); Peter McCullough and others (eds), *The Oxford Handbook of the Early Modern Sermon* (Oxford: Oxford University Press, 2011).
16 See, for instance, Bregnsbo, *Samfundsorden og statsmagt*; Pasi Ihalainen, *Protestant Nations Redefined: Changing Perceptions of National Identity in the Rhetoric of the English, Dutch and Swedish Public Churches, 1685–1772* (Leiden: Brill, 2005); Øystein Lydik Idsø Viken, *Frygte Gud og ære Kongen: Preikestolen som politisk instrument i Noreg 1720–1814* (Oslo: University of Oslo, 2014).
17 On these sermon genres, see Ihalainen, *Protestant*, pp. 70–3, 79–84; Nordbäck, *Lycksalighetens källa*, pp. 25–7.

communities.[18] This would imply that local sermons are not to be considered as mere 'photocopies' of the printed sermon material. Nor should they be understood as direct manifestations of the edicts and declarations issued by the secular and ecclesiastical authorities.

The study presented in this chapter is based on handwritten sermon manuscripts from six clergymen representing seven different parishes in the Swedish realm, and later Sweden and Finland, between 1790 and 1820. There were clear differences between the parishes regarding both local circumstances and geographical location. In Sweden proper, I study the sermons of Anders Hasselgren (1772–1832) in Offerdal, Nils Quiding Jönsson (1773–1824) in Caroli parish in Malmö and Anders Widberg (1752–1825), who served first in the poorhouse of Gothenburg and later in Okome. In Finland, the sermons are those by Karl Fredrik Bergh (1763–1844) in Suonenjoki, Lars Mathesius (1760–1830) in Jakobstad and Erik Levan (1746–1837) in Rauma. The language of the sermons was Swedish in five parishes, and in two parishes the main preaching language was Finnish.[19] The analysis concentrates especially on the national Intercession Days and on pericopes of the liturgical year that invited explanations of social relations.[20]

These manuscripts are rather unusual sources. For a long time, they have been preserved in clerical families. To begin with, not all clergymen wrote down their sermons. Furthermore, old manuscripts were not always kept. It is therefore pure chance that has determined

---

18 See, for example, Edvard Leufvén, *Upplysningstidens predikan*, I: *Frihetstiden* (Stockholm: Svenska kyrkans diakonistyrelse, 1926), p. 90. For parallel arguments on the local varieties in recent Norwegian studies, see Viken, *Frygte Gud og ære Kongen*, pp. 25, 97–8, 430; Thomas Ewen Daltveit Slettebø, *In Memory of Divine Providence: A Study of Centennial Commemoration in Eighteenth-Century Denmark–Norway (1717–1760)* (Bergen: University of Bergen, 2016), pp. 11, 189, 476.

19 On the studied clergymen, parishes and sermon material, see Joonas Tammela, 'Yhteiskunnan rakentuminen ruotsalaisen ja suomalaisen paikallispapiston saarnoissa noin 1790–1820' (thesis, forthcoming in 2023).

20 One should not forget the relevance of the prayer-day declarations issued by worldly authorities that specified the overall themes of sermons; see, for example, Östlund, *Lyckolandet*. On the other hand, it seems that the prayer-day sermons of local clergymen were even more individually written than ordinary Sunday sermons if viewed from the use of collections of sermons; see Niklas Antonsson and Joonas Tammela, 'Postillor och predikanten: en undersökning av Erik Levans (1746–1837) användning av predikolitteratur', *Historisk Tidskrift för Finland*, 106:2 (2021), 215–48 (243).

Applications of the three-estate doctrine

which clergymen's manuscripts have survived. The preserved sermon material in Swedish and Finnish archives is mainly from the mid-eighteenth century onwards. One explanation for this time limit might be the spread of the synthetic sermon structure among Swedish clergymen during the eighteenth century.[21] It was common to re-use old manuscripts – even ones that were decades old – many times over the years.[22] During the late eighteenth century, most of the older manuscripts of predecessors were perhaps no longer usable. Even the manuscripts that form part of my study represent the synthetic structure of sermons, though there are sometimes slight differences in the outlines of sermons. Handling styles and viewpoints regarding the gospel text of the day varied.[23]

In the present chapter, the sermons are studied as speech acts performed in temporal, intellectual and social contexts pertaining to the late eighteenth and early nineteenth century in local communities.[24] Since the early twentieth century, the concept of 'the Swedish Enlightenment sermon' has been used somewhat flexibly, from the loose interpretation of various kinds of German homiletic influences on the overall structure of the sermon to the strict interpretation that there were no clear forms of Enlightenment sermons in eighteenth-century Sweden.[25] My intention is not to define 'the level of Enlightenment' for local sermons. Instead, I use the Enlightenment concept as an analytical tool; here it constitutes a designation for currents within the Age of Revolution with a potential for broad political, social and intellectual shifts. Indeed, recent

---

21 Nordbäck, *Lycksalighetens källa*, p. 142.
22 In this chapter, references to the manuscripts also contain information regarding their later uses. If, for instance, a manuscript was used in 1796 and re-used in 1804 and 1817, the reference will be in the form 1796/1804/1817. See also Antonsson and Tammela, 'Postillor och predikanten', 247.
23 Tammela, 'Yhteiskunnan rakentuminen ruotsalaisen'. The corpus of this study is based on the roughly nine thousand sermon manuscripts gathered and inventoried by the writer in different Swedish and Finnish official archives.
24 See, for instance, Quentin Skinner, *Visions of Politics*, I: *Regarding Method* (Cambridge: Cambridge University Press, 2002), pp. 82–7, 107–11, 132–4.
25 On older and more recent interpretations of the Enlightenment sermon in Scandinavia, and more broadly in Western Europe, see, for instance, Pasi Ihalainen, 'The Enlightenment sermon: towards practical religion and a sacred national community', in Joris van Eijnatten (ed.), *Preaching, Sermon and Cultural Change in the Long Eighteenth Century* (Leiden: Brill, 2009), pp. 219–60.

studies have argued that the Nordic eighteenth-century sermon had many intersections with the overall shifts in society;[26] likewise, political identities had an overall impact on sermons during the late eighteenth and early nineteenth centuries. Therefore, the temporal relationship between 'the Enlightenment' and 'the local sermon', as I understand it, amounts to their having been simultaneous phenomena. The clergy took a stand on the different currents of the Age of Revolution in one way or another.

From the 1980s onwards, Swedish and Finnish studies have paid increasing attention to the central role of clergymen in early modern local political cultures. The roles of local clergymen as channels of communication, as leaders of local governments and as intermediaries between locals and the different levels of secular and ecclesiastical governments have been emphasized. My perspective on the *implemented policies* at the local level is based on the interpretation, put forward by Peter Aronsson, that local policy-making was highly dependent on the socio-economic circumstances of local communities. This means that clergymen had to apply their interests according to local conditions in order to achieve their goals.[27] Therefore, I regard sermons as a part of the process of political activity conducted by local clergymen, and also as a form of interaction between clergymen and their local communities. The way clergymen applied the structures of the societal order in their proclamations was not mechanical political propaganda by the state, but a strategy of negotiation between the clerical authorities and their audience.[28]

---

26 See for example Nordbäck, *Lycksalighetens källa*, pp. 315–16; Michael Bregnsbo and Pasi Ihalainen, 'Gradual reconsiderations of Lutheran conceptions of politics', in Pasi Ihalainen and others (eds), *Scandinavia in the Age of Revolution: Nordic Political Cultures, 1749–1820* (Farnham: Ashgate, 2011), pp. 107–19 (p. 119); Viken, *Frygte Gud og ære Kongen*, pp. 442–3.

27 Peter Aronsson, *Bönder gör politik: Det lokala självstyret som social arena i tre smålandssocknar, 1680–1850* (Lund: Lund University Press, 1992), pp. 300–5, 309–10. For studies about the role of clergymen in eighteenth-century local political cultures, see also, for example, Martin Linde, *I fädrens spår? Bönder och överhet i Dalarna under 1700-talet* (Hedemora: Gidlund, 2009); Ella Viitaniemi, *Yksimielisyydestä yhteiseen sopimiseen: Paikallisyhteisön poliittinen kulttuuri ja Kokemäen kivikirkon rakennusprosessi 1730–1786* (Tampere: University of Tampere, 2016).

28 About the simplistic interpretations of clergymen as one-eyed political tools of the government, see Laine and Laine, 'Kirkollinen kansanopetus', p. 300.

Social relations in the local sermon

The Lutheran Household Code was widely used in the sermons studied for this chapter. To be sure, the three-estate doctrine was often only implicitly described in the local sermons, as the explicitly societal themes were not always the main purpose of the sermons – not even on national Intercession Days. Still, it was not uncommon for clergymen to describe the three-estates system clearly to their audiences at the turn of the nineteenth century. For example, in a sermon held in 1798, Bergh pointed to the wholeness of society as well as the distinct hierarchical orders when he blessed the inhabitants of the realm by saying, 'God bless both the authorities and the subjects, clergymen and listeners, men and women, parents and children, old and young people, God bless every subject in this parish as well as in the whole of Sweden and Finland.'[29] In turn, Widberg illustrated the duty to perform good deeds in 1803 by telling his listeners about the orders of ruler, clergyman, parent and master, and the obedience owed to them by their respective subordinates.[30] Outlining the structures of society, this exhortation clearly reflects the role of the three-estate system. Parallel examples can be found in the output of other clergymen.

Despite the reconsiderations of the official function of the three-estate doctrine that took place in Sweden at the turn of the nineteenth century, it is easy to observe that these doubts about the relevance of the three-estate system did not have any further implications for the use of the system in local sermons. In varying forms, the three-estate system was frequently used in sermon materials throughout the period from the 1790s to the end of the 1810s in order to outline the structure of society. In 1811, for example, Jönsson warned every order of society about arrogance and voluptuousness. Parents had to fulfil their duties concerning their children, household and work. Jönsson analysed how the authorities, the men of manual labour and the members of the clergy each had to work diligently on their own tasks – instead of succumbing to the various kinds of temptations that were associated with the

---

29 Helsinki, Kansallisarkisto (KH), Kaarle Fr. Berghin arkisto (KFBA), v.1: Concio Sacra Die poenit: 4ta, 1798.
30 Riksarkivet, Gothenburg (RG), Göteborgs Stifts arkiv – predikosamlingar mm (GSA), v.52: 3. Store Bönedagen, 1803.

different estates.³¹ Correspondingly, Mathesius urged his listeners in 1818 to pray separately for the authorities, the clergy and parents to be able to fulfil their respective tasks for the good of the coexistence of human beings.³²

Members of society had their own positions and tasks, all of which served the good of the whole. The turbulent Age of Revolution did not invalidate the relevance of the doctrine of the three estates in sermon material, as has been suggested – drawing on different materials – by Lindmark. In line with the interpretations of Lindmark and Östlund, one may ask whether it might have been more important to point to conventional societal ideals during times of change in political cultures. With the material I have used, there is no possibility of making comparisons regarding the relative significance of the three-estate system over a long time period. It is, nevertheless, reasonable to suggest that the nature of sermons as expressions of conservative political theory, as well as the role of the clergy as defenders of the prevailing social order, laid emphasis on conventional ways of describing the basic structures of society.³³ The external pressure to redefine the very contents of sermons only took effect gradually and over a much longer period of time.

Conventional use of Lutheran political language was much to the fore when local clergymen explained the social order to their listeners during the Age of Revolution. But another essential feature was that local clergymen formulated models of official Lutheran conceptions of the social order depending on their audience and local circumstances. They adapted their proclamations and addressed them directly to their parishioners. Local circumstances had effects on the expressions of societal structures in each parish that I have studied. This can be traced even in socio-economically homogeneous local communities. The parish of Suonenjoki in Eastern Finland is an example of a very agrarian local community. Effectively, it consisted solely of a variety of peasants with minor social and economic differences. With no persons belonging

---

31 Malmö stadsarkiv (MSA), Nils Quiding Jönssons predikosamling (NQJP), H.M.P. 2: S: eft 3tondedagen, 1811/1819. On the hierarchy within the household in eighteenth-century Norwegian sermons, compare Viken, *Frygte Gud og ære Kongen*, pp. 340–2.
32 KH, Suomen kirkkohistoriallisen seuran arkisto (SKHS), C v.96a: Högmässan 4:de Böndagen, 1818. On the continuity of the three-estate doctrine through the re-use of local sermons, see RG, GSA v.53: Michaëlis dag 1800/1814/1815/1824.
33 See Bregnsbo and Ihalainen, 'Gradual reconsiderations', p. 107.

to the higher orders – besides the vice pastor Bergh – and no significant towns nearby, social or professional diversity was slight indeed. Any differences between members of the local community mainly consisted in their different positions inside households.[34]

This state of things had effects on society as a whole, as described by Bergh. In 1796, he stressed the Christian way of life. This meant that everyone had to live, in compliance with Lutheran teaching, within the framework of their own earthly vocation (Swedish *kallelse*, Finnish *kutsumus*) in society.[35] Bergh emphasized the three estates by analysing the tasks of authorities, priests, parents and elderly people – and, on the other hand, the tasks of subjects and churchgoers. In addition to this, he formulated the structure of the social orders by emphasizing the sinfulness of every higher and lower member of society, which meant 'the Estate of the Authorities and the Estate of the Peasants'.[36] This is an illustrative example of how the roles of different Estates and professions were actually softened and instead traditional patriarchal relations were seen as having greater relevance. The duties of listeners in the sphere of an agrarian community, as subjects of the ruler and as members of peasant households, were emphasized.

A socio-economically homogeneous local community did not mean that the varying professions and tasks in society were always excluded from sermons. The parish of Offerdal in northern Sweden was, just like the parish of Suonenjoki, an agrarian community almost entirely made up of moderately subsisting peasant households. The locals engaged in different forms of agriculture in fields and forests.[37] Adjunct pastor Hasselgren nevertheless illustrated the social diversity inside the community by explaining the structure of the

---

34 Jari Ropponen, *Suonenjoen historia: Pitäjien takamaasta mansikkakaupungiksi* (Suonenjoki: Suonenjoen kaupunki, 1993), pp. 126–9, 137. See also Kaarlo Wirilander, *Savon historia*, III: *Savo kaskisavujen kautena. 1721–1870* (Kuopio: Savon säätiö, 1960), pp. 78–87, 94–112. On the vaccination practices employed by Bergh in Suonenjoki parish, see the chapter by Esko M. Laine in this volume.

35 On the connection between the three estates and the Lutheran idea of vocations, see for example Bregnsbo, *Samfundsorden og statsmagt*, pp. 104–5.

36 KH, KFBA, v.1: Concio Sacra Die poenit: 2da, 1796; Bergh quoted Matthew 5:16 and Philippians 2:15.

37 Holger Wichman, 'Befolkning och bebyggelse', in Holger Wichman (ed.), *Jämtlands och Härjedalens historia*, IV: *1720–1880* (Stockholm: P. A. Norstedt & Söner, 1962), pp. 63–99 (pp. 73–7); Sven Olofsson, *Till ömsesidig nytta: Entreprenörer, framgång och sociala relationer i centrala Jämtland ca 1810–1850* (Uppsala: Uppsala University, 2011), pp. 61, 88, 113.

body politic (*samhällskropp*) and the importance of diligent work by even the most insignificant, lowly and poor member of the community for the common good. Hasselgren analysed the different tasks and orders within society by stressing, on a general level, three categories: the officials (*ämbetsmän*), the townspeople and the farmers.[38]

But the area of Offerdal had a special feature that significantly coloured everyday life in the area. It was the lively trading route which ran between the Province of Jämtland and the relatively nearby, and large, trading centres of Trondheim and Levanger in Norway. The locals were therefore in close contact with diversified trading markets.[39] This aspect was emphasized in sermons delivered in Offerdal, for example when Hasselgren stressed the significance of the work and virtue of an individual for the common good of society – a phenomenon characteristic of Swedish sermons in the late eighteenth century.[40] Hasselgren warned his audience that lack of a common good caused a society to suffer. Among other varieties of unworthy conduct, such as reluctance to pay taxes, a state of emergency would arise in the nation if the subjects were extortionists in the trading of goods. Conversely, God bestowed well-being on the people if they themselves took care of the common good. In his sermon, Hasselgren also legitimized the idea of societal duties by telling his listeners that giving for the common good did not mean that a subject would suffer scarcity himself. God gave the people what he saw they needed in their earthly life.[41] Owing to the lively trading markets and relatively moderate living standards among the inhabitants of the parish, the sermon was directed at the listeners. The functions of society were formulated so as to be applicable to the everyday lives of locals.

---

38 Riksarkivet, Östersund (RÖ), Olof Nordenströms samling (ONS), v.3: 23. S. e. Tref, 1799/1803. And vice versa, the agricultural professions were not necessarily invisible in urban parishes; compare RG, GSA v.52: 4. Store Bönedag, 1794.
39 Holger Wichman, 'Handeln', in Wichman, *Jämtlands och Härjedalens historia*, IV, pp. 197–237 (pp. 213–18); Olofsson, *Till ömsesidig nytta*, pp. 73–88. On the more limited trading business in Suonenjoki, compare Ropponen, *Suonenjoen historia*, pp. 130, 135–7.
40 Bregnsbo and Ihalainen, 'Gradual reconsiderations', pp. 116–17; Ihalainen, *Protestant*, pp. 484, 596; Nordbäck, *Lycksalighetens källa*, pp. 77, 101.
41 RÖ, ONS, v.3: 23. S. e. Tref, 1799/1803.

The doctrine of the three estates and social diversity

Proclamations concerning social structures were not identical in every parish, which means that the social nuances of parishioners had an effect on the discourses presented in sermons. The phenomenon may be analysed especially by studying urban parishes, where there was at least a degree of diversity on the part of Estates and professions. For instance, the marine towns of Jakobstad and Rauma were connected to the Baltic Sea trade. The trading business of Jakobstad especially, closely connected to the lively Ostrobothnian markets, increased throughout the late eighteenth century, full staple rights permitting even more comprehensive foreign trade. In Rauma the rather limited maritime trade also increased during the late eighteenth century, albeit more moderately. In Jakobstad the marine traffic, together with the limited small industry and the tradesmen and craftsmen of a small town, did make for socio-economic diversity in the parish, even though most of the locals engaged in various forms of agriculture and labouring occupations. By way of comparison, the local community of Rauma – besides embodying a large peasant population with relatively limited means – consisted of the occupations and vocations of a rather small maritime town.[42]

Even so, it emerges from the sermon material that such local diversities were much more clearly outlined by the chaplain Mathesius in Jakobstad. In his New Year sermon in 1792, Mathesius hoped that 'not only the nobleman and the child of fortune in his palace but also the poor man in his humble hut' could give praise to God for their adequate living conditions. Mathesius reminded his listeners of the honest fear of God, and of their responsibility to advance the common good. He also emphasized, in parallel with the eighteenth-century Swedish tendency to describe the nation as a collective economic actor, that 'the collective fear of God is like a flood which gives bliss and wealth to the land with the help of trades and skills, as well as many other earthly blessings from God'. Mathesius also

---

42 Alma Söderhjelm, *Jakobstads historia*, II: *Andra perioden – daningens tid 1721–1808* (Helsinki: Akademiska Bokhandeln, 1909), pp. 213–35, 249–65; Pentti Virrankoski, *Pohjanlahden ja Suomenselän kansaa: Kahdeksan vuosisataa Keski-Pohjanmaan historiaa* (Kokkola: Keski-Pohjanmaa-säätiö, 1997), pp. 95–104; Ulla Koskinen and others (eds), *Uudistuva maakunta: Satakunnan historia*, VI: *1750–1869* (Pori: Satakunnan museo, 2014), pp. 166–9, 427–9.

uttered itemized blessings both for the different groups listed in the Household Code and for the different orders of society.[43] Elsewhere, Mathesius similarly warned his listeners about negligence in their lives as Christians, reminding them of the requirement to be diligent in one's own occupation and tasks, whether socially significant or not. Therefore, everyone in every order – rulers, judges, soldiers, clergymen, merchants, craftsmen and peasants – had to work conscientiously.[44] The wide social spectrum is a notable feature on the part of the society in question.

In the sermons of Pastor Levan in Rauma, social diversities were less prominent; he placed greater emphasis on more general patriarchal relations and differences in wealth.[45] For example, in 1802 Levan emphasized the idea of hierarchies as 'the lottery of life' in general terms only. God determined the different external circumstances of human beings. One was placed as a king and one as a servant, one was rich and the other poor, and a man had nothing to say about this.[46] In Levan's sermons, the diversity in occupations caused by the maritime trade was occasionally outlined, alongside agriculture, when he spoke about the vital Providence of God in fulfilling the everyday tasks of a man.[47] Levan pointed out that people had set positions in society. Even if local circumstances had a considerable impact on the wording of the sermons, not all clergymen placed so much explicit emphasis on the structures of worldly society in their sermons. Levan's sermons also remind us not to make too sharp social divisions between the early modern towns and rural areas.

To return to the sermons of Mathesius, the evident differences between the occupations within society did not mean that Mathesius sought to break up the model of the three estates. In 1793 he

---

43 KH, SKHS, C v.96a: Nyårs Dagen, 1792. On Sweden as a collective economic actor in eighteenth-century state sermons, see Ihalainen, *Protestant*, p. 596.
44 KH, SKHS, C v.96a: 4:de Sönd: efter Påsk, 1796/1804/1817. On interpretations of continuities in discourses on the diligent work in Swedish Lutheran political cultures, see Christensson, *Lyckoriket*, pp. 378–9.
45 Both Bregnsbo and Viken have viewed the Danish-Norwegian discourses of wealth differences in society as an application of the three-estate system; see Bregnsbo, *Samfundsorden og statsmagt*, pp. 125–41; Viken, *Frygte Gud og ære Kongen*, pp. 301–5.
46 KH, SKHS, C v.86: Novi anni, 1802; Levan quoted Proverbs 16:33 and Jeremiah 10:23.
47 KH, SKHS, C v.86: Öfver 4. Böned. Otesangs Texten, 1791; KH, SKHS C v.86: Novi anni, 1802.

explained the context of the gospel text for the day to his listeners. The Epistle to the Colossians 'provided guidance for the sections [*classer*] of people who belonged to the Household Hierarchy [*hushållsstånd*]'. Mathesius emphasized the way of life that led to temporal and eternal bliss, which required that 'people should obey God's orders in general matters of Christian life, but also in private matters, the nature of which would vary from one estate to another in worldly society'. This meant that 'the king and the subject, the clergyman and his listener, the parent and child, the master and servant, they all draw from the Word of God those special instructions by which they must live'. Mathesius explained that if the people obeyed the commandments of God in general and private matters, the blessing of God would flourish – in both towns and countryside – in the form of peace, health, good harvests and trade with a good profit. Everyone would enjoy the worldly blessings and there would be no poverty.[48] According to Mathesius, it was the duty of every person to live according to the demands of their own respective worldly calling. Only then would the realm flourish. Even though Mathesius drew more attention to occupational varieties than, for example, Bergh in Suonenjoki, the three-estate doctrine was at least an equally important basis for life as a member of society.

The parish of Caroli in Malmö consisted of citizens of an urban area. In Caroli, the social diversity of the parishioners was somewhat wider than in most of the other parishes mentioned in this study, with persons from all walks of life. At the turn of the nineteenth century, Malmö was among the largest cities in the realm. Trading connections with the rest of Sweden and abroad were lively, albeit not on as large a scale as in Gothenburg.[49] The townscape was also coloured – besides people from the lower orders – by different kinds of officials, as well as by the various bourgeois professions.[50] The context of the sermons delivered in Malmö was an urban one,

---

48 KH, SKHS, C v.96a: Högmässan 2:dra Bönedagen, 1793; Mathesius referred to Colossians 4:2. On the varying societal uses of 'sections' in Danish sermons, see Bregnsbo, *Samfundsorden og statsmagt*, pp. 133–41.
49 On trading business in Jönsson's sermons, see, for example, MSA, NQJP: H:M:Pr. 4: Bönedagen, 1814.
50 Olle Helander, 'Stadens historia 1719–1820', in Oscar Bjurling (ed.), *Malmö stads historia*, II (Malmö: Malmö stad, 1977), pp. 351–537. For more recent interpretations regarding the relations and dynamics between the different social groups in Malmö, see also Lars Edgren, *Stadens sociala ordning: Stånd och klass i Malmö under sjuttonhundratalet* (Lund: Lund University, 2021).

and the differences between listeners in respect of social status were evident. Indeed, the sermons of Pastor Nils Quiding Jönsson frequently and clearly emphasized the diversity that characterized the social structure of his audience.

In 1810, for example, Jönsson stressed the idea of different vocations, or callings, for the members of society. He stated that 'the king, the officials of the administration with their different spheres of operation, the judges, the clergymen, the soldiers, the burghers, the farmers, the crofters and the day-labourers all have their own vocations in worldly society'. In some vocations there were wider and in some narrower possibilities to advance the common good, and the work of some was not as prominent as the work of others in society as a whole. But 'even the most insignificant person on his small plot of land [was] still an irreplaceable link in the great chain of producing the common good that was built by the Almighty'. The duties of some required more perseverance, skills and talents than those of others. However, God looked only at how faithfully everyone had fulfilled their own duties and their God-given vocation.[51] Despite the diversity of occupations, Jönsson frequently emphasized the interconnectedness that characterized the functions of the different estates. He thus ascribed importance to the Household Code. The Easter sermon that he used many times during his time in Malmö is a good example of this phenomenon.[52] Social diversity was expressed in such a way that every occupation, and each of the estates, was closely connected to the totality of society and the common good.

Conflicts concerning the privileges of the different Estates and occupations were common at the macro-level of political discourses during the early nineteenth century. They were also expressed in local sermons delivered by Jönsson. He often treated these conflicts in terms of the nature of vocations. For example, Jönsson emphasized that a man from the lower orders should not be envious of a man belonging to the higher orders. A man from the lower orders often yearned for 'the might and honour' of the man from the higher orders, being dissatisfied with the limited opportunities afforded by

---

51 MSA, NQJP: H.M.P. 2. S. eft: Påsk, 1810/1822. The responsibility of both high and low members of society for the well-being of that society was frequently brought up during the eighteenth and nineteenth centuries; see the examples from Denmark in Bregnsbo, *Samfundsorden og statsmagt*, pp. 129–31.
52 MSA, NQJP: Annandag Påsk, 1804/1806/1808/1815.

Applications of the three-estate doctrine

his own calling in society. Poor men and labourers often coveted 'the abundance, comfort and possibilities of the rich to enjoy life'. Jönsson argued that this kind of yearning was wrong. The all-wise God had created both the rich and the poor to live together. It was natural that some constantly had to work hard in their respective occupational sphere, while others had the possibility to rest and enjoy themselves at leisure. Jönsson therefore urged his listeners to be content with their lot in the world, regardless of whether it entailed material abundance or scarcity.[53] Jönsson legitimized the prevailing social structures in his sermons by emphasizing the differences with regard to the external conditions of human beings as being the work of God. People of lower orders were thus required to focus on the duties pertaining to their restricted forms of work and accept their more modest livelihood.

Jönsson also handled the conflicts that arose from social diversity by emphasizing virtuous behaviour in different kinds of occupation. For example, he reminded people from the higher orders of their responsibilities.[54] Jönsson stated that the social hierarchy did not erase the duty to love everyone. A man was not allowed to be proud of his high social status and reputation. Beauty, wealth and nobility (*höghet*) were only temporary. A wealthy person 'should not avoid ... contacts with the poor, workmen or day-labourers, because they possessed less in the way of worldly goods than he'. The social position of a person from the higher orders allowed his good deeds to gain better and wider visibility than the deeds of an insignificant person; but the latter might still be a much more virtuous human being. Indeed, Jönsson said that 'there is often more virtue and merit beneath the frieze shirt or rags of the beggar than beneath the ribbons and stars of honour'. In spite of that, Jönsson emphasized the reciprocal obligations of the higher and lower orders in their coexistence.[55] With such speeches, Jönsson reminded persons from the higher orders that they must behave virtuously instead of simply

---

53 MSA, NQJP: H.M.P. 2. S. eft: Påsk, 1810/1822; Jönsson quoted Philemon 4:12. On the church as a meeting place for the different orders of society in Malmö, see Edgren, *Stadens*, pp. 136–40.
54 On a parallel phenomenon in Norwegian sermons at the turn of the nineteenth century, compare Viken, *Frygte Gud og ære Kongen*, pp. 301–3.
55 MSA, NQJP: Afts: p: 3. S. eft Trettonded, 1806/1808. On external badges of honour for people of the higher orders, see also MSA NQJP: H.M.P. 26. p. Tr, 1807/1816. For a parallel discourse in Danish sermons, compare Bregnsbo, *Samfundsorden og statsmagt*, pp. 145–6.

relying on their position in society, stressing that external signs of honour should not eliminate interaction between the higher and lower orders.[56] But that did not reduce the role played by patriarchal relations in the interaction between the different estates.

Anders Widberg and the changing contexts of local sermons

The sermons of Anders Widberg provide an interesting perspective on the nuances of local preaching about structures in society. During the period covered in this chapter, Widberg served in two parishes which were rather different with regard to the socio-economic circumstances of the local communities and of parishioners. From 1789 to 1798 his audience consisted of the members of the poorhouse of Gothenburg, whose social standards were obviously relatively low. At the start of the nineteenth century, Gothenburg was the second-biggest city of the realm. The large-scale maritime trade was an important part of city life, besides the many different urban occupations in the context of a large eighteenth-century Nordic town or city. This made for a lively social townscape, with plenty of social diversity.[57] The poorhouse was, therefore, not a cross-section of the average inhabitants of the city, even though socio-historical studies have suggested that the low-income proportion of the population was quite large in Gothenburg.[58]

As one might have expected, Widberg frequently emphasized the theme of material wealth when talking about the different circumstances in which people found themselves. He pointed out how both rich and poor were equally significant in the eyes of God.[59] Sometimes Widberg even paid direct attention to the special character of the poorhouse parish in his sermons. In 1793 he declared that every member of society, 'from the lowest inhabitant of the poorhouse to the highest official', was obliged to live according to Christian virtues,

---

56 On the external symbolic value of honour in eighteenth-century political culture, see also Martin Tunefalk, *Äreminnen: Personmedaljer och social status i Sverige cirka 1650–1900* (Lund: Nordic Academic Press, 2015), pp. 35–6, 141–5, 278–81.
57 Bertil Andersson, *Göteborgs historia*, II: *Näringsliv och samhällsutveckling. Från fästningsstad till handelsstad 1619–1820* (Stockholm: Nerenius & Santérus, 1996), pp. 143–5, 362–3, 390–4. It is nevertheless noteworthy that people in Gothenburg used to attend services in other churches than their own; see Andersson, *Göteborgs historia*, p. 128.
58 Andersson, *Göteborgs historia*, pp. 341–7.
59 See, for example RG, GSA, v.52: 3: Store Bönedag, 1794.

thereby promoting the common good by living in harmony, unity and neighbourly love. Besides this general Christian behaviour, they had to promote the common weal in their worldly pursuits according to their particular orders and occupations. Widberg stated that because the inmates of the poorhouse were 'neither of benefit nor harm to the common affairs', he would not bother to present a detailed analysis of how all members of society should advance the good of the realm by fulfilling the responsibilities of their respective worldly vocations.[60] The socio-economic circumstances of parishioners did not release them from the obligation to work for the common good in general ways by living according to the virtues of Christian coexistence. Even so, their position in the body politic was somewhat indefinable. This sermon forms a concrete illustration of the fact that the functions of the hierarchical society were not always easy to apply in a manner that would fit the social realities of the local community.

In 1798 Anders Widberg left his position as preacher at the poorhouse in Gothenburg in order to serve as pastor of the agrarian parish of Okome. The local context for his sermons changed radically as a result of the move. Okome was a peasant-dominated community in south-western Sweden, with rather slight differences when it came to the occupations of parishioners. The Okome area was relatively wooded and was therefore not among the most profitable and developed agricultural communities in south-western Sweden. The socio-economic circumstances of locals were fairly homogeneous.[61] When compared to the poorhouse of Gothenburg, the audience in Okome had a much more clearly defined place in the structure of society; and when addressing them, Widberg was notably explicit about relations and mutual duties within the household as well as within the agrarian local community. For example, in 1801 he emphasized the reciprocal duties of the clergyman and his listeners, parents and children and the master and mistress of the house in relation to their servants. He even stated that 'the people of the

---

60 RG, GSA, v.52: 1. Store Bönedag, 1793. For expressions of harmony in national-prayer-day declarations, see Östlund, *Lyckolandet*, p. 76.
61 Pablo Wiking-Faria, *Freden, friköpen och järnplogarna: Drivkrafter och förändringsprocesser under den agrara revolutionen i Halland 1700–1900* (Gothenburg: University of Gothenburg, 2009), pp. 51–61, 319–22; Carl Malmström, 'Landskapsbildens förändringar i Halland under de senaste 300 åren', in Jerker Rosén and others (eds), *Hallands historia*, II: *Från freden i Brömsebro till våra dagar* (Halmstad: Hallands läns landsting, 1959), pp. 589–616 (pp. 595–605).

higher and lower orders, rich and poor, men and women, farmhand and maid, as well as the learned and the simple-minded' were equally responsible for their actions.[62] As we can see, the application of the three-estates system was much more straightforward in the social circumstances of a standard agrarian community.

In Okome, Widberg more frequently emphasized – and targeted – the conventional theme of misuse of wealth. In 1814, however, he named pride and arrogance as sins common to all kinds of people. They were the sins 'not only of rich, learned and prominent people, but also of disadvantaged, simple-minded and poor people'. Even if the poor did not have much opportunity to display great external splendour, they could still 'swell with inner pride' and demonstrate their splendour in minor things. Widberg went on to say that this kind of sin was not only characteristic of towns but also of the countryside, and that a disadvantaged person might be even more arrogant than a member of the higher orders of society.[63] Widberg pointed out that not even members of the peasant population were safe from the temptations of swaggering and boasting, although they were far from prosperous. The obligation to be frugal and reasonable was a virtue that should be shared by everyone, regardless of rank in the community.

Moreover, the sermons delivered by Widberg demonstrate that alongside the strong continuities, the post-1809 changes in the political system had at least some effects on local sermons. Earlier studies have demonstrated that during the Gustavian era, even in state sermons, the political role of the subjects was described as being quite passive.[64] These kinds of expressions were also familiar in local sermons, as these merely emphasized that the ultimate duty of a subject was to obey. All kinds of political decision-making or legislative work were outside the sphere of an individual subject.

---

62 RG, GSA, v.52: 2. St: Bönedagen, 1801.
63 RG, GSA, v.52: 1. Store Bönedagen, 1814. For the general discourses on luxury and pride in the sermons that Widberg delivered in Gothenburg, compare, for example, RG, GSA, v.52: 4. Store Bönedag, 1794. Compare Nordbäck, *Lycksalighetens källa*, p. 233.
64 Bregnsbo and Ihalainen, 'Gradual reconsiderations', p. 112. In Denmark–Norway, the idea of the political participation of subjects was constantly seen as unprofitable in sermons during the late eighteenth century and the first half of the nineteenth century, even if the discourses on the duties of authorities and citizens were not stable; see Bregnsbo and Ihalainen, 'Gradual reconsiderations', pp. 111, 114–15, 117–19; Viken, *Frygte Gud og ære Kongen*, pp. 439–43.

Subjects should not even consider whether the laws were good or bad. There was no doubt that those tasks belonged to the authorities.[65]

In studies of state sermons, however, it has been argued that the societal changes in Sweden in 1809 had a clear effect on discourses during the 1810s. Citizens were described as being increasingly active in political participation. In Finland the traditionally restrained language of politically passive subjects under the Russian emperor remained after 1809. In the national prayer-day declarations, there were no signs of any conspicuous changes in discourse during the 1810s.[66] The study of Finnish local sermons indicates that the subjects, both before and after the events of 1809, were regarded as politically passive and faithful in fulfilling the orders of the authorities, with no expressions of popular sovereignty in any sense. In Sweden, too, expressions of that kind were extremely rare in local sermons. Nevertheless, during the 1810s there are hints of a reconsidered role for the country's subjects, a phenomenon that mirrors the overall discursive shift of the early nineteenth century.

Widberg continually emphasized the idea of unquestioning obedience of orders given by the authorities.[67] Besides, the 1810s saw him begin to emphasize the political activity of a subject. In 1816, in fact, Widberg used worldly freedom as a point of comparison in relation to the spiritual freedom of a man. Widberg explained to his listeners that it was an enormous God-given worldly blessing that the people were not subjugated under foreign rule but 'under their own authorities, whose reign was not based on their own will and desire but afforded space for the public to participate in the decisions of important councils and in the making of beneficial laws'. According to Widberg, it meant that 'every inhabitant of the land distributed in the different Estates, had the possibility to think about what should be done and permitted, and to undertake a thorough and confidential consideration before the matter came under the executive power of the authorities'. By contrast, it was an enormous misfortune and a matter for lamentation if the people had to be 'under the slavery imposed by a foreign ruler and forced

---

65 KH, SKHS C v. 96a: Nyårs Dagen, 1792; RÖ, ONS v.3: 23. S. e. Tref, 1799/1803.
66 Bregnsbo and Ihalainen, 'Gradual reconsiderations', pp. 115–17; Östlund, *Lyckolandet*, pp. 177–8.
67 Compare RG, GSA, v.49: 23. Sönd: eft: Trinit, 1799/1811.

to obey the laws and habits of foreign rule, and to do everything they were told to do, whether it was for good or for ruin'.[68]

This sermon accentuates the changing attitudes to popular sovereignty and the functions of the state.[69] Instead of passivity, the political activity of subjects in society was expressed very clearly. Society was nevertheless corporate, as can be seen in the strong emphasis on the political Estates.[70] Widberg's sermon cannot be said to have promoted the increasing trend towards individualism and the decreasing function of the state as such; local sermons were merely following the overall changes in societal values. Even so, Widberg's statements do reflect how the changes in political cultures that took place during the Age of Revolution also affected the proclamations made by local clergymen.

Conclusion

This study of sermons delivered in seven different kinds of local parishes in the Swedish realm at the end of the eighteenth century and the beginning of the nineteenth century demonstrates the impact of and the remarkable continuity in discourses defending the idea of a corporate state system. Everyone was declared to have their own fixed position in the structure of society. This order was described as having been set by God. Instead of the individual benefit, the common good was seen as the fundamental idea for maintaining obedience.[71] The early modern ideas of a stable and hierarchical society – based on doctrines that were especially clearly presented in the Lutheran Household Code – permeated the sermons given by local clergymen in different parts of the realm and in different kinds of local communities. A good example of continuity is also the re-use of the same manuscripts many times over the years. For example, Mathesius and Widberg used manuscripts they had written at the turn of the nineteenth century – manuscripts that dealt with the social order – over twenty years later.

---

68 RG, GSA, v.53: Joh: Döpar: Dag, 1816.
69 It is reasonable to argue that the observable shifts in the language of sermons reflect the overall change in political language that had already happened earlier in other political forums; see Ihalainen, *Protestant*, pp. 12–14.
70 The role of the Estates was also legitimized in contemporary state sermons; see Bregnsbo and Ihalainen, 'Gradual reconsiderations', p. 116.
71 On the individual benefit, compare the ideas expressed in the sermons of Anders Chydenius; see Nordbäck, *Lycksalighetens källa*, p. 210.

Applications of the three-estate doctrine

Explicit references to the three estates were frequent when the social order was formulated in local sermons during the late eighteenth and early nineteenth centuries. In several sermons, however, we can see that at the same time the argumentation merely invoked general patriarchal relations in society. This absence of specifications reflects how either hierarchical or patriarchal relations in society were widely emphasized at the same time, with no need to highlight just one of them. Therefore, this study refines Lindmark's interpretation regarding the absence of a conflict between these models. Both structures had their respective function in explaining the social order and in discouraging listeners from any kind of social unrest.

However, the circumstances of local communities led to differences in the presentation of the social order. As earlier studies have pointed out, formulations and concepts were used in a conventional manner when describing society.[72] Still, the varying local contexts frequently impart different implications to seemingly standard expressions. There are evident variations in the topics of discourse. In the socio-economically homogeneous agrarian parishes, the differences in wealth or household relations were often more important issues than the social hierarchy. In fact, the nuances in respect of social diversities or different occupations even paled, as we can see especially in the case of agrarian Suonenjoki, or were expressed as an abstract theme, as in the case of the poorhouse of Gothenburg. Even the sources of livelihood in different kinds of local communities affected teaching about society in different ways, as can be seen, for example, in Offerdal and maritime towns. But in the sermons of every clergyman the common good was a goal for instruction about the social order, irrespective of local applications. Even in the towns of Jakobstad and – especially – Malmö, where social diversity and differences with regard to members and orders of society were especially evident, the idea of a societal system was solidly based on harmonious, unbroken and God-given vocations, or callings.

Major political, social and intellectual shifts during the Age of Revolution brought wide-ranging changes to the respective context and external circumstances of sermons, but the changes in the overall discourses of local clergymen were actually relatively modest.

---

72 On the weight of conventions in Norwegian eighteenth-century sermons, see Viken, *Frygte Gud og ære Kongen*, pp. 428–30, 442–6; Slettebø, *In Memory of Divine Providence*, pp. 476–7, 486–7. See also Ihalainen, *Protestant*, pp. 70–1.

In Swedish and Finnish sermons during the Age of Revolution, the teaching of Lutheran societal doctrines was firmly based on the idea of stability and on the fixed duties of different orders of society. Clergymen liked to follow the inherited, conventional discursive patterns. But as we see in the example of Widberg, reconsiderations of the political role of the individual did take place in 1810s Sweden. The function of the political Estates was not questioned; indeed, it was emphasized in that the political activity of a subject inside their respective Estate was brought up in sermons. Notably, ideas about popular sovereignty found their way into local sermons in the 1810s. This underscores the dynamism inherent in Nordic sermons with respect to adherence to trends in contemporary political language, as well as to intellectual changes, as earlier studies have suggested.

The present chapter has shown that the ideas contained within the three-estate doctrine were applied locally, and that the various modes of application display both similarities and divergences. Even though the basic idea of the corporate society might have been much the same for different members of the clergy, and we can detect a wide range of conventions in their discourse, there were a number of ways in which that basic idea could be expressed before listeners. The local clergymen thus adapted the Lutheran doctrine according to local, social and temporal circumstances. Consequently, even the teaching of the core doctrines of Lutheranism was not beyond the impact of circumstances in different parishes and local communities. The local adaptations in the teaching of social relations reflect that local sermons were a vivid and active arena of political culture during the Age of Revolution. This realization engenders a significant perspective on the nature of relations between Lutheranism and the state, a perspective which incorporates local reactions to the currents of the Age of Revolution in the Nordic countries.

Bibliography

Archival sources

Gothenburg

Riksarkivet, Gothenburg (RG)
  Göteborgs Stifts arkiv – predikosamlingar mm (GSA): Predikningar, föredrag m fl handlingar (AI: v. 49–55)

Helsinki

Kansallisarkisto, Helsinki (KH)
Kaarle Fr. Berghin arkisto (KFBA): Saarnat (v. 1–2, 5)
Suomen kirkkohistoriallisen seuran arkisto (SKHS): Saarnat ja puheet (C: v. 86, 95b, 96, 96a)

Malmö, Sweden

Malmö stadsarkiv (MSA)
Nils Quiding Jönssons predikosamling (NQJP): v. 1799–1816

Östersund, Sweden

Riksarkivet, Östersund (RÖ)
Olof Nordenströms samling (ONS): Predikningar (v. 1–7)

Printed sources and literature

Andersson, Bertil, *Göteborgs historia*, II: *Näringsliv och samhällsutveckling: Från fästningsstad till handelsstad 1619–1820* (Stockholm: Nerenius & Santérus, 1996).
Antonsson, Niklas and Joonas Tammela, 'Postillor och predikanten: en undersökning av Erik Levans (1746–1837) användning av predikolitteratur', *Historisk Tidskrift för Finland*, 106:2 (2021), 215–48.
Aronsson, Peter, *Bönder gör politik: Det lokala självstyret som social arena i tre smålandssocknar, 1680–1850* (Lund: Lund University Press, 1992).
——, 'Hustavlans värld: folklig mentalitet eller överhetens utopi?', in Christer Ahlberger and Göran Malmstedt (eds), *Västsvensk fromhet* (Gothenburg: University of Gothenburg, 1993), pp. 11–42.
Bregnsbo, Michael, *Samfundsorden og statsmagt set fra prædikestolen: danske præsters deltagelse i den offentlige opinionsdannelse vedrørende samfundsordenen og statsmagten 1750–1848, belyst ved trykte prædikener: en politisk-idéhistorisk undersøgelse* (Copenhagen: Museum Tusculanum, 1997).
Bregnsbo, Michael and Pasi Ihalainen, 'Gradual reconsiderations of Lutheran conceptions of politics', in Pasi Ihalainen and others (eds), *Scandinavia in the Age of Revolution: Nordic Political Cultures, 1740–1820* (Farnham: Ashgate, 2011), pp. 107–19.
Carlsson, Sten, *Ståndssamhälle och ståndspersoner 1700–1865: Studier rörande det svenska ståndssamhällets upplösning* (Lund: Gleerup, 1949).
Christensson, Jakob, *Lyckoriket: Studier i svensk upplysning* (Stockholm: Atlantis, 1996).

Edgren, Henrik, *Publicitet för medborgsmannavett: Det nationellt svenska i Stockholmstidningar 1810–1831* (Uppsala: Uppsala University, 2005).
Edgren, Lars, *Stadens sociala ordning: Stånd och klass i Malmö under sjuttonhundratalet* (Lund: Lund University, 2021).
Francis, Keith A. and William Gibson (eds), *The Oxford Handbook of the British Sermon* (Oxford: Oxford University Press, 2012).
Helander, Olle, 'Stadens historia 1719–1820', in Oscar Bjurling (ed.), *Malmö stads historia*, II (Malmö: Malmö stad, 1977), pp. 351–537.
Ihalainen, Pasi, *Protestant Nations Redefined: Changing Perceptions of National Identity in the Rhetoric of the English, Dutch and Swedish Public Churches, 1685–1772* (Leiden: Brill, 2005).
——, 'The Enlightenment sermon: towards practical religion and a sacred national community', in Joris van Eijnatten (ed.), *Preaching, Sermon and Cultural Change in the Long Eighteenth Century* (Leiden: Brill, 2009), pp. 219–60.
Ihalainen, Pasi and Karin Sennefelt, 'General introduction', in Pasi Ihalainen and others (eds), *Scandinavia in the Age of Revolution: Nordic Political Cultures, 1740–1820* (Farnham: Ashgate, 2011), pp. 1–13.
Ihalainen, Pasi and Anders Sundin, 'Continuity and change in the language of politics at the Swedish Diet, 1769–1810', in Pasi Ihalainen and others (eds), *Scandinavia in the Age of Revolution: Nordic Political Cultures, 1740–1820* (Farnham: Ashgate, 2011), pp. 169–92.
Johansson, Egil, 'Den kyrkliga lästraditionen i Sverige – en konturteckning', in Mauno Jokipii and Ilkka Nummela (eds), *Läskunnighet och folkbildning före folkskoleväsendet*, XVIII: *Nordiska historikermötet i Jyväskylä 1981. Mötesrapport* (Jyväskylä: University of Jyväskylä, 1981), pp. 169–92.
Koskinen, Ulla and others (eds), *Uudistuva maakunta: Satakunnan historia*, VI: *1750–1869* (Pori: Satakunnan museo, 2014).
Laine, Esko M. and Tuija Laine, 'Kirkollinen kansanopetus', in Jussi Hanska and Kirsi Vainio-Korhonen (eds), *Huoneentaulun maailma: Kasvatus ja koulutus Suomessa keskiajalta 1860-luvulle* (Helsinki: Suomalaisen Kirjallisuuden Seura, 2010), pp. 258–306.
Laine, Tuija, *Aapisen ja katekismuksen tavaamisesta itsenäiseen lukemiseen: Rahvaan lukukulttuurin kehitys varhaismodernina aikana* (Helsinki: Suomalaisen Kirjallisuuden Seura, 2017).
Leufvén, Edvard, *Upplysningstidens predikan*, I: *Frihetstiden* (Stockholm: Svenska kyrkans diakonistyrelse, 1926).
Linde, Martin, *I fädrens spår? Bönder och överhet i Dalarna under 1700-talet* (Hedemora: Gidlund, 2009).
Lindmark, Daniel, *Uppfostran, undervisning, upplysning: Linjer i svensk folkundervisning före folkskolan* (Umeå: Umeå University, 1995).
Malmström, Carl, 'Landskapsbildens förändringar i Halland under de senaste 300 åren', in Jerker Rosén and others (eds), *Hallands historia*, II: *Från freden i Brömsebro till våra dagar* (Halmstad: Hallands läns landsting, 1959), pp. 589–616.

McCullough, Peter and others (eds), *The Oxford Handbook of the Early Modern Sermon* (Oxford: Oxford University Press, 2011).
Melkersson, Martin, *Staten, ordningen och friheten: En studie av den styrande elitens syn på statens roll mellan stormaktstiden och 1800-talet* (Uppsala: Uppsala University, 1997).
Nordbäck, Carola, *Lycksalighetens källa: Kontextuella närläsningar av Anders Chydenius budordspredikningar 1781–82* (Turku: Åbo Akademi, 2009).
Normann, Carl-E. (ed.), *Cleri comitialis cirkulär 1723–1772* (Stockholm: Svenska kyrkans diakonistyrelse, 1952).
Olofsson, Sven, *Till ömsesidig nytta: Entreprenörer, framgång och sociala relationer i centrala Jämtland ca 1810–1850* (Uppsala: Uppsala University, 2011).
Östlund, Joachim, *Lyckolandet: Maktens legitimering i officiell retorik från stormaktstid till demokratins genombrott* (Lund: Sekel, 2007).
Pleijel, Hilding, *Hustavlans värld: Kyrkligt folkliv i äldre tiders Sverige* (Stockholm: Verbum, 1970).
Ropponen, Jari, *Suonenjoen historia: Pitäjien takamaasta mansikkakaupungiksi* (Suonenjoki: Suonenjoen kaupunki, 1993).
Skinner, Quentin, *Visions of Politics*, I: *Regarding Method* (Cambridge: Cambridge University Press, 2002).
Slettebø, Thomas Ewen Daltveit, *In Memory of Divine Providence: A Study of Centennial Commemoration in Eighteenth-Century Denmark–Norway (1717–1760)* (Bergen: University of Bergen, 2016).
Söderhjelm, Alma, *Jakobstads historia*, II: *Andra perioden – daningens tid 1721–1808* (Helsinki: Akademiska Bokhandeln, 1909).
Tammela, Joonas, 'Yhteiskunnan rakentuminen ruotsalaisen ja suomalaisen paikallispapiston saarnoissa noin 1790–1820' (thesis, forthcoming in 2023).
Tunefalk, Martin, *Äreminnen: Personmedaljer och social status i Sverige cirka 1650–1900* (Lund: Nordic Academic Press, 2015).
Viitaniemi, Ella, *Yksimielisyydestä yhteiseen sopimiseen: Paikallisyhteisön poliittinen kulttuuri ja Kokemäen kivikirkon rakennusprosessi 1730–1786* (Tampere: University of Tampere, 2016).
Viken, Øystein Lydik Idsø, *Frygte Gud og ære Kongen: Preikestolen som politisk instrument i Noreg 1720–1814* (Oslo: University of Oslo, 2014).
Virrankoski, Pentti, *Pohjanlahden ja Suomenselän kansaa: Kahdeksan vuosisataa Keski-Pohjanmaan historiaa* (Kokkola: Keski-Pohjanmaa-säätiö, 1997).
Wichman, Holger, 'Befolkning och bebyggelse', in Holger Wichman (ed.), *Jämtlands och Härjedalens historia*, IV: *1720–1880* (Stockholm: P. A. Norstedt & Söner, 1962), pp. 63–99.
―――, 'Handeln', in Holger Wichman (ed.), *Jämtlands och Härjedalens historia*, IV: *1720–1880* (Stockholm: P. A. Norstedt & Söner, 1962), pp. 197–237.

Wiking-Faria, Pablo, *Freden, friköpen och järnplogarna: Drivkrafter och förändringsprocesser under den agrara revolutionen i Halland 1700–1900* (Gothenburg: University of Gothenburg, 2009).

Wirilander, Kaarlo, *Herrskapsfolk: Ståndspersoner i Finland 1721–1870*, trans. Eva Stenius (Stockholm: Nordiska museet, 1982, first edition 1974).

——, *Savon historia*, III: *Savo kaskisavujen kautena. 1721–1870* (Kuopio: Savon säätiö, 1960).

Part II

Dealing with the Catholic past (and present)

5
In the midst of thick and wretched darkness: enlightened orthodoxy and the heritage of the medieval Church

Terese Zachrisson

> Our honourable theologians have most happily averted the invocation of the saints, and to that end they have had their images removed, so that the ignorant need not be reminded of an old and harmful delusion; but the poor, that in these parts are somewhat more *in obscuro* and further removed from *medicis*, have persisted longer in their superstition and claimed, as of the Catholic fables, to have been helped in their needs and illnesses by St Olaf.[1]

The words above were penned by the most prominent representative of the Swedish Enlightenment, Carl Linnaeus, after he had visited the church of St Olaf in Scania in 1749. Linnaeus was far from alone in making distinct connections between the concept of Roman Catholicism and ignorance and superstition, as well as between the concept of Lutheranism and reason and clarity. While the Enlightenment movement in France in the circles of the *philosophes* often denounced the teachings of institutionalized religion, Swedish Enlightenment ideas were often firmly embedded in the theology of the national Lutheran Church. As opposed to Linnaeus, who was never ordained into the priesthood, many scholars of the eighteenth century were both scientists and scholars while also being men of the cloth. This combination frequently produced a

---

1 'Efter Catholiska tiden hafwa wåra hederwärda Theologi lyckeligen afbögt Helgonens åkallande, och til den ändan afskaffat deras bilder, at de enfaldige ej af dem måtte påminnas om en gammal och skadelig inbillning; men det fattiga folket, som här ligger, liksom något mer in obscuro, och längre skildt ifrån Medicis, har trägnare hållit uti med sin widskeppelse, och förment sig, efter Catholiske dikterne, af St. Olof kunna få någon hjelp i sin nöd och sjukdom'; Carl Linnaeus, *Carl Linnæi Skånska resa, på höga öfwerhetens befallning förrättad år 1749: Med rön och anmärkningar uti oeconomien, naturalier, antiquiteter, seder, lefnadssätt. Med tilhörige figurer. Med kongl. Maj:ts allernådigste privilegio* (Stockholm: Lars Salvius, 1751), p. 155. All translations mine.

Figure 5.1 Sketch of a sculpture of St Olaf, from Carl Linnaeus' *Skånska resa*, 1751. Photo: The National Library of Sweden.

fierce rejection of Roman Catholicism in general, and of the medieval Church in particular.[2]

The present chapter discusses how central themes of Enlightenment thought shaped the learned view of medieval Christianity in eighteenth-century Sweden, mainly in relation to its surviving physical traces. Two main types of sources will be used to this end: antiquarian, historical and topographical publications on the one hand and visitation records on the other. While the first category will provide insights into general modes of thought, the visitation records will show how the learned priesthood argued and acted in practice when confronted with the medieval heritage in the line of their day-to-day work. The authors behind the sources used in this essay were either academics or ecclesiastics, but in practice a majority combined these two fields of activity. Andreas Rhyzelius (1677–1761), for instance, whose works will feature in the following, published several extensive historical works while Bishop of Linköping. Rooted in Lutheran orthodoxy, he was critical of the more radical ideas of the Enlightenment; but he incorporated several of the ideals commonly associated with the movement in his rhetoric regarding knowledge and rationality.[3] Some of the individuals whose texts will be featured were members of the local clergy who acted as informants for collectors such as Samuel Rogberg (1698–1760) and Sven Wilskman. In these cases, it is difficult to assess the extent to which the texts were edited and rephrased by the collectors themselves. In this particular context, however, this aspect is not of fundamental importance, since the wording is of interest regardless of whether they were penned word-by-word by a member of the lower clergy or summarized by collectors.

The light of the Reformation

> Now, it was like a new world; darkness gave way and Evangelical light took its place. Human reason started to gaze upwards, once it had been freed from the shackles of superstition.[4]

---

2 Henrik Ågren, *Erik den helige – landsfader eller beläte? En rikspatrons öden i svensk historieskrivning från reformationen till och med upplysningen* (Lund: Sekel, 2012), pp. 447–9.

3 Oxell, 'Andreas O. Rhyzelius', in *Svenskt biografiskt lexikon*, https://sok.riksarkivet.se/sbl/artikel/6655 [accessed 30 September 2020].

4 'Här blef nu lika som en ny wärld; mörkret måste wika och det ewangeliska ljuset intog des ställe. Det menniskliga förnuftet började se up, sedan det blifwit löst från widskepelsens bojor, under hwilka det hade legat fängsladt';

In the topographical, antiquarian and historical works of the era, pre-Reformation religious life was depicted in gloomy colours and functioned as a stark contrast to the light and freedom of the Lutheran Church, as depicted in the passage quoted above, written in 1765 by economist Emanuel Ekman (1737–1801) in a description of the Province of Värmland. Likewise, in another topographical piece on the same province, Pastor Erik Fernow (1735–1791), writing in the 1770s, summarized 'what thick and wretched darkness our ancestors have dwelled in.'[5] A dichotomy of light and darkness was frequently used when the Lutheran Reformation was debated. In embracing key concepts of the Enlightenment vocabulary – reason, clarity, freedom and intellectual understanding – learned members of the Swedish priesthood assumed a distinctly anti-Catholic stance. Olof Broman (1676–1750), pastor, schoolmaster and author of *Glysisvallur* – an ethnographic, historical and topographical account of the Province of Hälsingland – depicted the Reformation in the following terms:

> When this all-too-thick darkness [heathendom] with much effort came to be repelled from the sky of the Church, and small glimmers of light were lit by the brightness of Truth, it did not take long before the harmful fog and poisonous haze rose from the wide and deep Popish swamp and mire, that confused both brain and vision; so that the people here fared no better, nay worse, [than before], as was also the case elsewhere in Europe; until God in his great mercy awoke King Gustaf Eriksson I to – like Emperor Constantine – liberate and defend the congregation from devilish human beings and human-like devils.[6]

Emanuel S. Ekman, *Wärmeland i Sitt Ämne Och i Sin Upodling, Första Delen Beskrifwit Af Emanuel S. Ekman* (Uppsala: Kongl. Acad. Tryckeriet, 1765), p. 192.

5 Erik Fernow, *Beskrifning öfver Värmland afdelad i sex tidehvarf: tvänne under hedendomen och lika många under påfvedömet och lutherska tiden: jemte en kort inledning om landets läge, namn, vattendrag, bergsträckningar, skogar m.m. utgifven af Erik Fernow* (Karlstad: H. O. Norstedt, 1898), p. 258.

6 'När tå thetta alt för tiocka mörkret med mycken mödo kom at fördrifwas på kyrkohimelen, och små liusa strimor uplysa af Saningens lius, warade intet länge för än then skadeliga töcknen och förgiftiga dimban upsteg utur wida och diupa Påfwiska träsket och myran, som förwillade både hiärnan och synen; så at folket här intet bätre, utan snarare wärre råkade ut, såsom på andra orter i Europa; til thes Gud af sin stora barmhärtighet upwäckte Konung Gudstaf Eriksson I:ste, at lika som Keyser Constantinus Magnus, frja och förswara Församlingen ifrån diefwulska Meniskor och menskliga diäflar'; Olof Johansson Broman, *Glysisvallur: och övriga skrifter rörande Helsingland D. 2* (Uppsala: Gestrike-Helsinge nation, 1912–1953), p. 50.

Roman Catholicism was associated with darkness, bondage, superstition and deceit. The general populace of pre-Reformation times was represented as naive, gullible and taken advantage of by scheming monks driven by greed and hunger for power.[7] These attitudes were projected onto objects surviving from this era which were regarded as physical testimony to the corruptness of medieval Christendom. During the eighteenth century, a large part of the still-surviving medieval mural paintings disappeared when churches were rebuilt and whitewashed, and countless medieval sculptures and altarpieces were destroyed.

From *res indifferentes* to danger

The depiction of the medieval past as a world of darkness partly originated in the Reformation era, where an insistence on understanding and knowledge in opposition to incomprehension was a key feature of the reformers' didactic discourse.[8] The trope of cunning monks and priests deliberately misleading the common folk featured heavily in Reformation-era polemics on the British Isles, as did a general disdain for material expressions of faith and the cult of the saints.[9] Though it did occur to some degree, this kind of language was less pronounced during the Swedish Reformation. In the Church Ordinance of 1571, Roman Catholic practices were renounced. But the ordinance also positioned itself against the Reformed churches, and in particular against the iconoclastic practices associated with them. Images, altars, vestments and liturgical vessels were all stated to be *res indifferentes* – objects that in themselves were neither harmful nor beneficial to religious practice.[10] The emphasis on material objects as *res indifferentes* was more pronounced during the earlier years of the Reformation than later; but

---

7 Marie Lennersand and Linda Oja, 'Responses to witchcraft in late seventeenth- and eighteenth-century Sweden', in Willem de Blécourt and Owen Davies (eds), *Beyond the Witch Trials: Witchcraft and Magic in Enlightenment Europe* (Manchester: Manchester University Press, 2004), pp. 61–80 (p. 69).
8 Kajsa Brilkman [Weber], *Undersåten som förstod: Den svenska reformatoriska samtalsordningen och den tidigmoderna integrationsprocessen* (Skellefteå: Artos, 2013), pp. 222–24.
9 Helen L. Parish, *Monks, Miracles and Magic: Reformation Representations of the Medieval Church* (London: Routledge, 2005), pp. 52–60, 74–82.
10 Laurentius Petri, 'Then swenska kyrkeordningen: Lärer all ting ährligha och skickeliga tilgå', in *Kyrko-ordningar och förslag dertill före 1686: Första Afdelningen* (Stockholm: P. A. Norstedt, 1872), pp. 3–180 (pp. 3–19, 98–104).

during the late sixteenth century, these aspects became more controversial owing to the re-Catholizing efforts of King John (Johan) III (r. 1569–1592).[11]

Seventeenth-century scholars and learned members of the clergy sometimes had a hesitant relationship with the material objects of the pre-Reformation church. This is well illustrated in the highly influential *Ethica Christianæ*, published between 1617 and 1621 by future archbishop Laurentius Paulinus Gothus (1565–1646). In this work, in a manner similar to that of the ordinance of 1571, Lutheran orthodoxy positioned itself not only against Roman Catholicism, but also against Calvinism and the Reformed churches. With regard to images, Gothus rhetorically asked what to make of images 'that by the Papists are held in great veneration, but by the Calvinists are wholly rejected', answering that, 'Both parties are in error, the Papists in that they go too far in these matters and abuse images for worship, the Calvinists in that they denounce the matter too much and banish images from all of their churches'.[12]

From a European perspective, early modern Sweden had an unusually strict legislation regarding religious freedom, or rather the lack of it. Roman Catholicism had been outlawed as early as 1617, and Reformed Protestants only had a limited right to practise their religion. Even Pietism, a movement within Lutheranism itself, was repressed.[13] The struggle to create an essentially mono-confessional cultural environment in all likelihood had an impact on Enlightenment-era clergy and scholars. The first part of the eighteenth century saw hardened attitudes towards all non-orthodox religious beliefs. The 1726 Conventicle Act made all religious gatherings beyond the framework provided by the national religion illegal, and the 1735

---

11 Martin Berntson, *Kättarland: En bok om reformationen i Sverige* (Skellefteå: Artos, 2017), pp. 209–11.
12 'Hwad skal Man halla vtaff Beleten, huilka hos Papisterna ära i stor Wyrdning, Men aff the Calwinister warda aldeles förkastade? Begge Parterna fara wille: Papisterna i thet the Klijffua här medh alt för högt, och missbruka beleten til Gudstienst. Calvinisterna i så motto, at the saken mycket förringa och Beleten vthaff alla theras Kyrkior vthmönstra och förkasta'; Laurentius Paulinus Gothus, *Ethica Christianæ pars prima, de ratione bene vivendi. Thet är: Catechismj förste deel, om Gudz lagh* (Stockholm: Christoffer Reusner, 1617), pp. 72–3.
13 Johannes Ljungberg, *Toleransens gränser: Religionspolitiska dilemman i det tidiga 1700-talets Sverige och Europa* (Lund: Lund University, 2017), pp. 7–8.

Act on Religion enabled pastors to actively seek out and report anyone harbouring irregular religious views.[14] These edicts, and the inquests leading up to them, were primarily aimed at rooting out Pietism; but they illustrate an increasing concern with Lutheran orthodoxy and religious unity that seems to have had an impact on clerical views on all heterodox thoughts and actions.

Attitudes to the medieval heritage

The clergy of this era usually employed a distancing idiom when discussing medieval material culture, especially images of the saints; but the modes of marking this distance took several forms. First, objects could be criticized in a historical light, in which the author in question lamented the sorry state of medieval Christendom, often with more than a hint of sarcasm and ridicule. Secondly, they could also be rejected with an eye towards the future – in these cases, altars, shrines and images were regarded as the weights that kept the population down, preventing them from embracing rationality, freedom and a true relationship with God. A third mode of marking one's distaste for these objects was that of silence and oblivion, in which the authors marked the total irrelevance of the objects by means of a – genuine or feigned – lack of understanding of them. These three approaches will be discussed in greater detail in the following section.[15]

---

14 'Kongl. Maj:tz förnyade Placat och Förbud, angående the oloflige Sammankomster, hwilka vti enskylte Hus til en särskild och enkannerlig Gudstienst förrättande anställas; Samt theras straff, som ther med beträdas. Stockholm i Råd-Cammaren then 12 Januarii Åhr 1726', in Anders Anton von Stiernman (ed.), *Samling Vtaf åtskillga, tid efter annan, vtkomna Kongliga Stadgar, Bref och Förårdningar Angående Religion Giord vppå Hans Kongl. Maj:ts Nådigaste Befallning* (Stockholm: Kongl. Tryckeriet, 1744), pp. 200–7; 'Kongl. Maj:ts Rådige Stadga och Påbud, til Hämmande af hwarjehanda willfarelser, och theras vtspridande, emot then rena Evangeliska Läran. Gifwit Stockholm i Råd-Cammaren then 20. Martii 1735', in Anders Anton von Stiernman (ed.), *Samling Vtaf åtskillga, tid efter annan, vtkomna Kongliga Stadgar, Bref och Förårdningar Angående Religion Giord vppå Hans Kongl. Maj:ts Nådigaste Befallning* (Stockholm: Kongl. Tryckeriet, 1744), pp. 225–37.

15 These three modes of distancing discourse invite comparison with the four strategies for taming the medieval heritage in Denmark as identified by Wangsgaard Jürgensen in this volume.

Crafty monks and bloodied knees

In all discussions of the faults of the medieval Church, no group seem to have been more to blame than monks and friars. In his *Glysisvallur*, composed around 1720, Olof Broman (1676–1750) writes that during the early days of Christendom, the greed and craftiness of monks soon became so great that eventually the Benedictines became known as the 'Benefictines', whereas the Dominicans were called 'Dæmonicans', the Franciscans 'Fraudciscans' and the Carmelites 'Carnalites'.[16] This kind of abuse was repeated by Bishop Andreas Rhyzelius, also a historian, in his *Monasteriologia Sviogothica* from 1740.[17]

Though it sometimes occurred, it was much rarer for the secular clergy of the pre-Reformation era to be attacked in the same manner. One reason for this discrepancy might have been that the parish system was in many respects only slightly altered by the Reformation, and criticism levelled at the parish priests of the fourteenth century could spill over on to their eighteenth-century successors. As noted by Henrik Ågren, a denunciation of the priesthood of the Middle Ages could also function as a masked critique of the contemporary Lutheran Church.[18] Criticizing monks will have been a much safer proceeding than directing open criticism at contemporary clergy, and monasticism provided Enlightenment-era scholars with an ideal outlet for any possible traces of the anti-clericalism that was so characteristic of the French Enlightenment. In eighteenth-century Britain, the term 'priestcraft' was often used in the same pejorative

---

16 'Munkarne hafwa warit kiäcke TaskSpelare och öfwat sitt hocus pochus; alt på förtjänst och at richta pungen; ju längre ju mera, så att theßa Munkar af S. Bengts Orden, eller Benedictiner, blefwo nämde Benefictiner; lika som the Dominicaner, Dæmonicaner; Carmeliter, Carnaliter; Franciscaner, Fraudiscaner; o. s. w. Thet af Krönikorna allom kunigt är; hwilket war mächta stort hinder til rena läran och Christendomen'; Broman, *Glysisvallur*, p. 86.
17 Andreas Olavi Rhyzelius, *Monasteriologia Sviogothica, eller Klosterbeskrifning, vti hwilken vpräknas, med berettelse om hwad om them kunnat igenfinnas och vpspanas, alla the kloster och helg-andshus, som, vnder påfwedömet, vti Swea- och Götharike, såsom begripande the otta gambla sticht: Vpsala, Linköping, Skara, Strengnäs, Wästerås, Wägsiö, Åbo och Lund, blefwit byggde och vnderhållne, samt om the munke-order, som i Swerige haft kloster; bestående af tio böker, och en tilleggning om jesuit-orden* (Linköping: Petter Pelican, 1740), p. 17.
18 See Ågren, *Erik den helige*, p. 264.

ways as 'witchcraft', and it could be applied not only to Catholic priests but to Protestant clergy as well.[19] This rhetoric was mainly applied in a political context, and it would not have been relevant to works of the kind investigated in the present chapter.

According to Broman, cunning missionaries first made use of the pagans' habit of worshipping wooden idols and converted them by introducing images that were made to 'weep, speak and perform miracles'.[20] The trope of the crafty monk using mechanics to fool the populace into believing a sculpture was miraculous appears frequently in other Enlightenment-era writings as well. Several sculptures in the church of Luleå in the northernmost part of the country were claimed by topographer Abraham Hülphers (1734–1798) to be such devices. An image of the Virgin had little cavities 'between the eyes and the skull', allowing the monks to bring about tears with the use of a damp sponge, while other sculptures had string devices enabling movement and alleged miracles.[21] In a 1740s description of Tolånga parish church in Scania, its pastor claimed that a statue of the Virgin had been made to appear to weep. The head of the sculpture was hollow, and when water was poured into it, it would slowly drip from the eyes and down the cheeks of the statue.[22] Historian and topographer Carl Fredric Broocman (1709–1761) published a topographical description of the Province of Östergötland in 1760, and when discussing the old Bridgettine abbey in Vadstena, he especially commented on the collection of surviving medieval sculptures, stating that

> [a]mong these [sculptures] there is an image of St Bridget, remarkable in that through this image, which is so large and hollow that a human being may fit within it, the monks have often spoken to the congregation, in order to blind and deceive the simple crowds.[23]

---

19 James A. T. Lancaster and Andrew McKenzie-McHarg, 'Priestcraft: anatomizing the anti-clericalism of early modern Europe', *Intellectual History Review*, 28:1 (2018), 7–22 (10).
20 Broman, *Glysisvallur*, p. 27.
21 Abraham Abrahamsson Hülphers, *Samlingar til en beskrifning öfwer Norrland: Femte samlingen om Westerbotten* (Västerås: Joh. L. Horrn, 1789).
22 Mattias Karlsson (ed.), *Sockenbeskrivningar från Färs härad 1746–1747, utgivna med inledning och kommentarer av Mattias Karlsson* (Lund: Kungl. humanistiska vetenskapssamfundet i Lund, 2009), p. 38.
23 'ibland hwilka är S:t Britas Bild, theraf märkwerdig, at Munkarna genom thetta belätet, som är stort och utholkadt, at en menniskia kan rymas theruti, ofta talat til menigheten, at thermed förblinda och bedraga then enfaldiga

When mentioning objects that were perceived to have been used in connection with punishment, authors often included detailed descriptions of the bodily torments that the medieval Church was imagined to have inflicted upon its members. This is evident as early as the beginning of the eighteenth century, when church historian Petter Dijkman (1647–1717) described various humiliating punishments for sinners, such as being forced to beat oneself with rods and scourges and to eat among dogs and cats, as well as being shackled and even walled up alive.[24] In his description of the Province of Dalarna, Abraham Hülphers discussed a former chapel in Grangärde parish which, in his view, resembled a diabolical maze. According to this description, several buildings had been erected on top of one another with narrow passages between them where sinners had been made to crawl, tormenting and forcing their bodies 'all in accordance with the gravity of their sin'.[25] A similar arrangement was claimed to have been in place underneath the church of Stora Tuna (near Borlänge in the Province of Dalecarlia/Dalarna), according to Dean Magnus Sahlstedt (1686–1752) in a topographical description published in 1743. Sinners had to crawl through a narrow passage that had been dug out beneath the altar, to their great 'harm and shame'.[26] At a place called 'Taveltäkten' in the parish of Tuna in the Province of Hälsingland, Olof Broman mentioned in his *Glysisvallur* a wayside cross. The cross had sharp rocks at its base, where

---

hopen'; Carl Fredric Broocman, *Beskrifning öfwer the i Öster-Götland befintelige städer, slott, sokne-kyrkor, soknar, säterier, öfwer-officers-boställen, jernbruk och prestegårdar, med mera* (Norrköping: Johan Edman, 1760), p. 170.

24 Petter Dijkman, *Antiquitates ecclesiasticæ, Eller gamle Swenske Kyrkie-Handlingar Angående wåra förfäders Christeliga Troos och Kyrckio-Ceremoniers beskaffenheter några hundrade åhr tilbakas; sammanplåckade vthur gamla stycker, som runstenar, kyrckior, rijmstafwar, bref, griftestenar, pergament, recesser, afhandlingar, beläten, åthskillige Swea provinciers lag- och agende-böcker, och vnder wisza flåckar förde af Petter Dijkman* (Stockholm: Michaele Laurelio, 1703), p. 340.

25 Abraham Abrahamsson Hülphers, *Dagbok Öfwer en resa igenom de under Stora Kopparbergs Höftingedöme lydande Lähn och Dalarne år 1757* (Västerås: Joh. Laur. Horrn, 1762), p. 618.

26 Magnus Sahlstedt, *Stora Tuna i Dahlom och Bergom minnes-döme: Thet är: vtförlig beskrifning och vnderrettelse om then ort och christeliga församling, som har namn af Stora Tuna, och är belägen i Öster-Dahls bergslagen* (Falun: Falu nya boktryckeri, 1955), pp. 369–70.

those who had merited punishment, or who wished to show their remorse, had to crawl around the cross on their bare knees across these sharp stones, until their skin was shed and the blood was flowing. This is the origin of the popular phrase ... 'go to Tuna and learn your manners!'[27]

Pre-Reformation objects as harmful influences

The small stave church of Skaga was a well-known votive church in the Province of Västergötland, and it was a continuous source of trouble for the diocesan chapter.[28] According to the collections of cathedral dean and historian Sven Wilskman, all the 'superstition' and misconduct taking place there originally stemmed from a sculpture of the head of St John the Baptist, 'planted there during the Popish darkness', which the people had been tricked into believing was miraculous.[29] Images of the saints often seem to have been viewed as potential instigators for superstition among the uneducated.

Linguistic scholar and bishop Daniel Juslenius (1676–1752) can be seen to have embodied the heightened hostility of his time against the medieval heritage of the Church. As Bishop of Skara, a position he held from 1746 up to his death in 1752, he continuously battled

---

27 'De som woro skyllige til något straff, eller skulle wisa boot och bättring, måste på bar knäen, krypa så länge kring korset, öfwer theßa hwaßa klappur-stenar, at huden afnöttes och blodet utran; hwar utaf thet ordspråket är kommit: Gack til Tuna, kryp til kry, och Lär weta huut; eller som thet nu kortare säjes: Gå til Tuna, och Lära weta huut': Broman, *Glysisvallur*, p. 243.

28 A votive church (*Offerkyrka* in Swedish, *Lovekirke* in Norwegian) was a church building that was considered especially holy, to which those in hope of healing and other divine interventions travelled or sent offerings. This tradition is well attested throughout the early modern era in Scandinavia. See Monica Weikert, *I sjukdom och nöd: Offerkyrkoseden i Sverige från 1600-tal till 1800-tal* (Gothenburg: University of Gothenburg, 2004), pp. 4–8; Henning Laugerud, *Reformasjon uten folk: Det katolske Norge i før- og etterreformatorisk tid* (Oslo: St Olavs, 2018), pp. 268–83. For two Danish examples of this phenomenon, see Wangsgaard Jürgensen's section on the Krogstrup and Stora Heddinge parish churches in this volume.

29 'Har af urminnes tider warit ett offer Capell, hwilken widskepelse, som ei ännu kunnat utrotas, är ifrån det Påfwiska mörkret ditplantad, då itt hufwud af träd, bildat efter S. Johanni Baptistas hufwud, är ditsatt, och folket inbillat att det skulle hafwa en miraculös werkan til mongas hiälp'; Skara, Skara stifts- och landsbibliotek, Sven Wilskmans samling [collection], De Singulis in Diocesi Scarensi Parochiis I: 613.

both popular 'superstition' and Pietism. The visitation acts from his episcopate reveal an aversion towards pre-Reformation artworks that bordered on the iconoclastic. At one point, during a visitation in Norra Ving in 1746, he ordered images of the Virgin Mary and some other saints to be smashed up before being buried in a deep pit because the images were being 'misused for all manner of superstitions'.[30] Ever-present in his criticism was the fear that these objects may mislead parishioners towards superstitious thoughts and actions. An artistic representation that he seems to have considered especially harmful was that of Mary as Queen of Heaven. In Norra Fågelås parish church, the bishop ordered the removal of two images of the crowned Virgin during the visitation of 1748. One of them stood on the main altarpiece; the other is likely to have been a depiction belonging to the still-preserved early fifteenth-century Marian shrine that is today housed at the Swedish Historical Museum, a shrine from which a sculpture of a standing Madonna has been removed.[31] In Häggum parish church, the entire altarpiece was removed during a visitation in 1749, because of 'the crown on Mary's image on the altarpiece, which could have caused many opportunities for harm'.[32] In the church of Gudhem, parishioners were apparently allowed to keep their image of the Virgin on condition that her crown and the words *ora pro nobis* were removed.[33] The image of Mary was also to be removed in the parish church of Skölvene, as it displayed a 'Popish delusion' – a phrasing that reaffirms the alleged connection between Roman Catholicism and a lack of reason that was discussed above.[34]

An instance that is representative of the changed attitudes towards medieval images is the visitation record from Husaby parish church in 1747. On this occasion, the pastor of the parish was ordered by Bishop Juslenius to make sure that an image of Mary, which was placed on the northern wall, was removed in order to prevent superstition.[35] In all likelihood, this command referred to the

---

30 Riksarkivet, Gothenburg (RG), Norra Vings kyrkoarkiv [parish archive], KI:1, visitation record of 1746.
31 RG, Norra Fågelås kyrkoarkiv, N:1, visitation record of 1748.
32 RG, Häggums kyrkoarkiv, C:1, visitation record of 1749.
33 RG, Gudhems kyrkoarkiv, C:1, visitation record of 1749.
34 'J. Mariae bild på Altaretaflan skal med första borttagas, aldenstund den samma utwisar den Påfwiske wilfarelsen, och kan altså mycken förargelse förorsaka'; RG, Skölvene kyrkoarkiv, C:1, visitation record of 1748.
35 RG, Husaby kyrkoarkiv, N:2, visitation record of 1747.

In the midst of thick and wretched darkness 141

Figure 5.2 Remnants of a Marian tabernacle shrine from Norra Fågelås parish church, early fifteenth century. Photo: Lennart Karlsson, Swedish Historical Museum.

still-preserved standing Madonna originating from a late fourteenth-century altarpiece. The sculpture had, together with the images of a holy bishop and an apostle, been rearranged into a secondary altarpiece in 1671.[36] By the mid-eighteenth century, objects that had been deemed worthy of renovation less than a century before were hence viewed as vessels of superstition.

Bishop Juslenius was also critical of depictions of the saints in two-dimensional form. In the parish of Jung, one of the chalices was engraved with the name of Mary. During his visitation in 1746, the bishop demanded that the letters be erased. Likewise, when visiting Sunnersberg the year before, he had decided that an embroidered text on a chasuble saying *O Beate Paule, Ora Pro Nobis* was to be removed.[37]

It is well known that the majority of medieval mural paintings in Swedish churches were whitewashed in the eighteenth century, rather than in the Reformation era. There were several motivational forces behind this destruction. The murals were at odds with the neo-classical aesthetics that came to dominate a large part of the eighteenth century. Even the post-Reformation wall-paintings in the wooden church of Stenberga, removed in 1778, were described as 'old and useless' in the collections of Samuel Rogberg, the judgement being uttered by the local pastor.[38] An ambition to literally enlighten church space through enlarged windows often meant demolishing part of the walls, and in connection with such renovations it was not uncommon for the remaining walls to be whitewashed. But apart from being the objects of purely aesthetics-induced disdain, these murals were also perceived to be harmful because of their theological content. When visiting the church of Börstig in 1746, Juslenius took the opportunity to condemn both the church's altarpiece and its murals:

> His Eminence the Doctor and Bishop observed that the middle part of the sculpture work on the altarpiece in Börstig church should be

---

36 *Medeltidens bildvärld*: 92051952.
37 RG, Jungs kyrkoarkiv, LI:1, visitation record of 1746; RG, Sunnersberg KI:1, visitation record of 1745.
38 'sirad med gammal och usel målning'; Samuel Rogberg, *Historisk beskrifning om Småland i gemen, i synnerhet Kronobergs och Jönköpings lähner, ifrån äldsta, til närwarande tid, om thesz politie, natural-historia, bergwärk, kyrko-stat, folkmängd, hushållning, kyrkor, slott och herregårdar, med mera mines wärdt* (Karlskrona: Kongl. Amiralitets boktryckeriet, 1770), p. 719. *Bebyggelseregistret*: Vetlanda Stenberga Stom 1:4.

removed as being idolatrous and popish, and that a crucifix or some other decoration should be put there instead. Also, the chancel roof should be lime-washed, in order to obliterate the saints of the Papists that are painted there and may be expected to cause vexation among some persons at some time.[39]

The particular language used in this case – that the saints are to be 'obliterated' (*utplånade* in Swedish) – highlights the same intense aversion that featured in the visitation record from Norra Ving, mentioned earlier in this section, where images were to be 'smashed' (*sönderslås*) and 'buried' (*nedgrävas*).

Feigned ignorance

On some occasions, eighteenth-century clergy distanced themselves from pre-Reformation objects with an air of feigned ignorance. In the famous church of Husaby between Lakes Vänern and Vättern in Sweden, a sculpture of St Elmo was mentioned in a dismissive tone by Rector Jonas Marchander as a 'wooden image, with something like a papal cap on its head, standing with its feet in a cauldron, which is supposedly meant to be a depiction of some martyr'.[40] Though it is certainly possible that Marchander could not identify St Elmo on the basis of the iconography of the image, this way of denying knowledge of the saints was also applied to depictions where the identity of the figure in question should have been apparent to the viewer. In Samuel Rogberg's description of the churches of the Province of Småland, published in 1770 and based on reports from local clergy, an image of St Olaf in Dädesjö parish church was described as 'an image of a man, which seems to show the likeness of a king with sceptre and apple in his hand, trampling a man lying underneath'.[41] During the

---

39 'Påminte H. Herr Doctorn och Biskopen, at det medlerste Bildthuggare wärket på AltarTaflan i Börstigs kyrka bör borttagas såsom afgudiskt och påfwiskt, och ett Crucifix eller någon annan Zirat sättias i stellet. Äfwen bör Taket fram i Choret öfwerstrykas med lim, at utplåna de Påfwiskas helgon, som der stå målade och torde wid tilfälle lända någon til förargelse'; RG, Börstigs kyrkoarkiv, N:1, visitation record of 1746.
40 'Neder i Kyrkan synes ock en hvit Bild af Trä med likasom en Påfvemösa på hufvudet, stående med föttren i en gryta, som förmenas vara en afbild af någon Martyr'; Skara, Skara stifts- och landsbibliotek, Olof Sundholms samling, 75 Husaby.
41 'Likaledes finnes en mans-bild, som tyckes föreställa en Konung med spira och äple i handen, trampande på en underliggande man'; Rogberg, *Historisk beskrifning om Småland i gemen*, p. 284.

Middle Ages, St Olaf was immensely popular in Scandinavia, perhaps only rivalled by the Virgin Mary. He continued to be a figure of great importance in historical narratives as well as in folklore and popular piety throughout the early modern era, which makes it unlikely that the rector of Dädesjö would have been unable to recognize the motif. In 1749 the diocesan chapter of Åbo/Turku issued a call for the pastors of the diocese to report what historical monuments were to be found in their churches; in a response from the parish of Huittinen, the pastor stated that the church possessed 'an image of a woman, with a child sitting on her knee', stowed away in a tool-shed.[42] That the pastor should have been unable to identify the image of the Virgin seems absurd. In denying the precise identity of an object, it was effectively disarmed of all its dangerous potential as a vestige of 'popery'. Also, in the descriptions of these objects, the persons depicted were only referred to as a 'man' and a 'woman'. Not only were the exact identities of these saints obscured, but so was their very status as saints.

An even more radical way of marking the lack of importance of these objects was by entirely omitting to mention them. The questionnaires that were sent out by topographers and antiquarians to the clergy of various dioceses usually included variants of the question of what 'monuments' were preserved in their churches. The questionnaire issued by Count Fredrik Adolf Ulric Cronstedt (1744–1829), Provincial Governor of Gävleborg, in 1790 included at least two opportunities for respondents to describe medieval ecclesiastical objects: 'The church's paintings, images, pulpit, altarpiece, organ, etc. – what are they like?' and 'What old monuments are there, such as copes, thuribles, etc.?'[43] Despite these direct questions, Rector Johan Sjöström of Segersta parish failed to mention a fourteenth-century crucifix as well as a gilded fifteenth-century altarpiece depicting the Virgin, St Barbara and St Catherine, among others.[44] In the report from Norrala parish in the Province of Hälsingland,

---

42 Anders Anton von Stiernman, *Presterskapets redogörelser om forntida minnesmärken i Finlands kyrkor* (Helsinki: Reinold Hausen, 1882), p. 200.
43 'Kyrkans målningar, bilder, Prädikstol, Alltartafla, Orgvärk, m. m. hurudana? Hvilka ållderdoms lemningar, såsom Chor-Kåpor, rökelse-kar, m. m. Där förvaras?'; Nils-Arvid Bringéus (ed.), *Sockenbeskrivningar från Hälsingland 1790–1791, tillkomna på anmodan av landshövdingen F. A. U. Cronstedt, med efterskrift och register utgivna av Nils-Arvid Bringéus* (Uppsala: A.-B. Lundequistska bokhandeln, 1961), p. 7.
44 Bringéus, *Sockenbeskrivningar från Hälsingland*, p. 44.

the still-preserved sculptures of the Virgin and St Anne were not mentioned, and neither were the three crucifixes, the image of St Olaf or the early sixteenth-century altarpiece from Ilsbo.[45] This failure to mention medieval artefacts was by no means unique to the Cronstedt questionnaire; it may be observed in the responses to several other such surveys, too, such as the questionnaire issued by Olof Sundholm (1752–1819) in the Diocese of Skara in the 1780s.

Side altars, reliquaries, thuribles and other objects

Most of the examples in the sections above have dealt with sculptures, and these were probably the most common and eye-catching manifestations of the medieval past in early modern church space. But eighteenth-century writers also occasionally discussed other kinds of objects.

Multiple altars in churches had been banned as early as 1562, with the exception of cathedrals and large town churches; but in practice, side altars remained in many churches throughout the seventeenth century and to some extent into the eighteenth.[46] When discussing side altars in a historical context, Bishop Rhyzelius of Linköping (1677–1761) often lingered on their multitude and overabundance. Another matter that was frequently criticized was the stipends attached to the altars, by which a superfluity of idle ecclesiastics would enrich themselves. During a visitation in the parish of Vist in 1750, Rhyzelius made a historical note in the parish register: 'The church was at that time enlarged, only for this reason, that there would be made room for more altars and images of the saints, to the greater seduction of the people.'[47] In his 1753

---

45 Bringéus, *Sockenbeskrivningar från Hälsingland*, pp. 44, 155–6, 226. *Medeltidens bildvärld*: 900901S3, 900901S2, 900901S1, 900901A2, 900901A1, 900924S8, 900925S10, 900927S4 and 930812A1.

46 *Svenska riksdagsakter jämte andra handlingar som höra till statsförfattningens historia under tidehvarfvet 1521–1718, Andra delen, 1, 1561–1592* (Stockholm: Riksarkivet, 1899), pp. 6–7, 61. See also Terese Zachrisson, *Mellan fromhet och vidskepelse: Materialitet och religiositet i det efterreformatoriska Sverige* (Gothenburg: University of Gothenburg, Department of Historical Studies, 2017), pp. 57–82.

47 'Kyrkian är then tiden vtbyggd på längden endast til then ändan, at thervti skulle blifwa rum för flere altare och helgona-beläten, til menighetens större förförelse'; Riksarkivet, Vadstena, Vists kyrkoarkiv, C:3, church description from 1750.

work on the history of the Swedish dioceses, *Episcoposcopiæ Sviogothicæ*, he noted that the cathedral of Strängnäs had, before the Reformation, been 'on almost every side piled up with altars, where countless requiems were held, bought with wills, testaments, gifts and donations, from which not only deans and canons, but a vast huddle of prebendaries, rectors, altar priests and others had their bountiful upkeep'.[48] In a more practical setting, other problems with side altars were addressed when bishops and deans encountered them *in situ* in parish churches throughout the country. In his home parish of Od in Västergötland, Bishop Rhyzelius in 1754 described the removal of Our Lady's altar in 1711 by stating that the altar had been 'unnecessary, and serving superstition and harm'.[49] Similarly, a women's altar was to be torn down in Hov, also in Västergötland, in 1764, since it took up much-needed space, but also because it was 'an old remnant of the Papacy, and as such all-together unnecessary'.[50]

If Bishop Rhyzelius had a clear opinion as to the side altars, his view on reliquaries seems to have been marked by some insecurity. This is evident from his notes on the Eriksberg reliquary, which is now kept in the Swedish Historical Museum. On the one hand, he could not deny the sheer beauty and artistic qualities of the shrine, stating that 'its likeness could scarcely be found in the entire country'.[51] On the other hand, however, he emphasized that

---

48 'Hon war ock nästan å alla sidor vpfyld med altare, therwid oräkneliga Siälameßor blefwo hållna, som warit köpte med testamenten, gåfwor och Siälagifter, af whilka, vtom Domherrerna och Kanikerna, en weldig hop Præbendater, Vicarier, Altaristæ och andre slike hade sin rikeliga nödtorft'; Andreas Olavi Rhyzelius, *Episcoposcopiæ Sviogothicæ, Eller En SweaGöthisk Sticht- och Biskops-Chrönika, Om alla Swea- och GöthaRikets Sticht och Biskopar, ifrå början, in til närwarande tid; Bestående af twå Delar. Med några anmerkningar Och fullkomligt Register* (Linköping: Gabriel Biörckegren, 1752), p. 205.
49 RG, Ods kyrkoarkiv, C:1, church description from 1754.
50 'som tyckes wara en gammal öfwerlefwa af Påfwedömet, och således aldeles onödig'; Carl-Martin Bergstrand, *Kulturbilder från 1700-talets Västergötland, andra delen* (Gothenburg: N. J. Gumperts bokhandel, 1934), p. 179. Many medieval altars of Our Lady were retained in post-Reformation churches under the names of 'women's altars', 'churching altars' or 'cake altars', and used in churching rituals during the seventeenth century; see Zachrisson, *Mellan fromhet och vidskepelse*, pp. 154–5.
51 'På thet wälvtzirade och med vtarbetad mässing öfwertäckta helgedoma-kar, som ännu finnes wti Eriksbergs Kyrkio, och ellierst näpeligen hafwer sin lika i hela landet'; RG, Eriksbergs kyrkoarkiv, C:1, church description from 1720.

the reliquary had been used for 'unscrupulous fraud' by the monks, and concluded his description with a prayer:

> Eternal thanks be to God, who has delivered us from such deceivers, and brought us to the clear Evangelical light! May the same God keep us and our descendants therein until the end of time, for the sake of our Lord, Jesus Christ. Amen!![52]

Medieval thuribles, altar bells and other metal objects were often preserved in eighteenth-century churches, usually tucked away in the sacristy as unused artefacts. While frequently mentioned in church descriptions of the era, they usually seem to have been regarded as purely historical objects; as such, there seems to have been little need to criticize them – though one of the rectors in the collections of Olof Sundholm stated that the church of Kölaby had a small thurible made of metal, which was 'preserving the memory of the Catholic buffoonery'.[53] Unlike images in painted or sculptured form, these do not seem to have presented a possible threat to orthodoxy and were therefore usually not described in the same hostile manner by topographers, collectors and clergy.

Enlightenment and the 'end of superstition'?

Several authors drew clear parallels between the forces of Enlightenment and progress and the decline in 'superstitious' traditions among the peasantry. In the 1750s, in his description of the Province of Blekinge, schoolmaster and rector Christopher Cronholm (1711–1789) attributed the decline in visits to holy wells to the establishment of 'proper' mineral spas.[54] Several of the pastors who contributed to the parish descriptions of Olof Sundholm from the 1780s onwards proudly declared that their parishioners had mostly abandoned their old, superstitious ways in favour of

---

52 'Gudi ware ewig tack, som oss ifrå sådana bedragare förlossat och fördt oss til thet klara Ewangeliska liuset! Samma nådige Gud bibehålle oss och wåra efterkommande ther wid in til wår och werldens ända, för wår Herras Jesu Christi skul. Amen!!'; RG, Eriksbergs kyrkoarkiv, C:1, church description from 1720.
53 'Intet märkvärdigt finnes der, utom et litet Rökelse Kar af malm, som förvarar minnet af Catholska Gykleriet'; Skara stifts- och landsbibliotek, Olof Sundholms samling: 132 Åsarp.
54 Christopher Cronholm, *Blekings beskrivning författad av Christopher Cronholm år c:a 1750–1757* (Malmö: Blekingia, 1976), pp. 90–1.

more enlightened modes of thought.[55] This triumphant view is also apparent in the visitation records of the latter half of the century. In 1776, visiting the parish of Vilske-Kleva, Bishop Forssenius of Skara (1708–1788) – who had composed a thesis on St Helen of Skövde as early as 1734, in which he criticized the then-practised veneration of her holy well – stated that 'the superstitions of former times ... are altogether abandoned in this parish'.[56]

The language used by Enlightenment-era scholars and clerics in depicting the pre-Reformation church had its origins in Reformation-era polemics.[57] That being the case, similar statements may be found in the works of the two great Swedish reformers, brothers Olaus (1493–1552) and Laurentius Petri (1499–1573). But the polemics of the reformers was considerably milder than that of their contemporaries in other parts of Europe, as well as that of their domestic Enlightenment-era successors. Anti-Catholicism alone cannot account for these sentiments; similar themes can be found in enlightened Catholicism as well. During this era, Catholic clergy too displayed an increased concern with 'superstition' and articulated scepticism towards 'material' aspects of faith, such as miraculous images, the veneration of relics and even the saying of the rosary. Just like their Protestant counterparts, they rooted their arguments in terms of both 'rationality' and morality.[58]

In comparison to the situation in most other parts of Protestant Europe, pre-Reformation ecclesiastical objects were preserved to an unprecedented degree in Scandinavia. When English ambassador Bulstrode Whitelocke (1605–1675) visited Uppsala Cathedral in 1654, he found it so full of images and crucifixes that the church was 'little different therein from the Popish churches'.[59]

---

55 Skara stifts- och landsbibliotek, Olof Sundholms samling: 85 Larv; 81 Källby; 83 Kinne-Kleva.
56 'Förra tiders widskeppelser, samt andra mißbruk och oseder, såsom skjutande om Påskafton och wid Bröllop m. m. äro här i församlingen aldeles aflagde'; RG, Vilske-Kleva kyrkoarkiv, KI:3, visitation record of 1776. Anders Forssenius, *Specimen historicum de Schedvia Westergothiæ urbe, antiqua S. Helenæ sede* (Uppsala: Uppsala University, 1734), pp. 30–1.
57 S. J. Barnett, *Idol Temples and Crafty Priests: The Origins of Enlightenment Anticlericalism* (New York: Palgrave Macmillan, 1999), pp. 123–4.
58 Ulrich L. Lehner, *The Catholic Enlightenment: The Forgotten History of a Global Movement* (New York: Oxford University Press, 2016), pp. 125–6, 156–58.
59 Bulstrode Whitelocke, *Journal of the Swedish Embassy in the Years 1653 and 1654*, ed. C. Morton, 2 vols (London: Longman, 1855), II, p. 232.

Although hostility towards religious images and other pre-Reformation church furnishings could be found among individual seventeenth-century clergymen, there seems to have been a general level of acceptance – and even embracing of – the medieval heritage.[60] This situation changed during the eighteenth century. The latter half of that century saw the beginning of the process during which countless medieval churches were demolished in order to make way for the white neo-classical buildings that may still be seen scattered across the Swedish countryside. The reasons behind this development were partly practical; the Romanesque churches were becoming too small for a growing population, and side altars, rood-screens and sculptures took up space that could be put to better uses. But the ideological engine behind this development was that of enlightened orthodoxy. At a first glance, religious orthodoxy and Enlightenment ideals may seem a most peculiar pairing; but the two combined created a milieu that was to change the structure of the physical religious landscape for a long time to come.

In the response to Count Cronstedt's questionnaire from the parish of Gnarp, its rector supplied a detailed description of the completion of the new church building in 1785, on top of the foundations of the 'narrow and defective' thirteenth-century church. The account of the neo-classical whitewashed building oozes with pride. The church was 'one of the finest in the entire country', and when light from two of the ten new large windows hit the altarpiece – consisting of a bare shrouded cross with an allegorical figure – it was a truly beautiful sight.[61]

Bibliography

Archival sources

Gothenburg

Riksarkivet, Gothenburg (RG)
  Börstigs kyrkoarkiv [parish archive], N:1

---

60 Inga Lena Ångström, 'Avdammad madonna åter på tronen – Maria i 1600-talets kyrkorum', in Sven-Erik Brodd and Alf Härdelin (eds), *Maria i Sverige under tusen år: Föredrag vid symposiet i Vadstena 6–10 oktober 1994, Bok 2: Marias tillbakaträngade* (Skellefteå: Artos, 1996), pp. 647–76 (pp. 647, 653).

61 Bringéus, *Sockenbeskrivningar från Hälsingland 1790–1791*, pp. 248–50.

Eriksbergs kyrkoarkiv, C:1
Husaby kyrkoarkiv, N:2
Häggums kyrkoarkiv, C:1
Gudhems kyrkoarkiv, C:1
Jungs kyrkoarkiv, LI:1
Norra Fågelås, N:1
Norra Vings kyrkoarkiv, KI:1
Ods kyrkoarkiv, C:1
Skölvene kyrkoarkiv, C:1
Sunnersbergs kyrkoarkiv, KI:1
Vilske-Kleva kyrkoarkiv, KI:3

Skara, Sweden

Skara stifts- och landsbibliotek
  Olof Sundholms samling [collection], 75 Husaby
  Olof Sundholms samling, 81 Källby
  Olof Sundholms samling, 83 Kinne-Kleva
  Olof Sundholms samling, 85 Larv
  Olof Sundholms samling, 132 Åsarp
  Sven Wilskmans samling, De Singulis in Diocesi Scarensi Parochiis 1

Vadstena, Sweden

Riksarkivet, Vadstena
  Vists kyrkoarkiv, C:1

Digital sources

Bexell, Oloph, 'Andreas O. Rhyzelius', in *Svenskt biografiskt lexikon*, https://sok.riksarkivet.se/sbl/artikel/6655 [accessed 30 September 2020].

Riksantikvarieämbetet, 'Vetlanda Stenberga stom 1:4', in *Bebyggelseregistret*, www.bebyggelseregistret.raa.se/bbr2/sok/searchResult.raa?ts=1676360115823 [accessed 12 February 2021].

Statens historiska muséer, '900901S3' [Crucifix from Ilsbo], in *Medeltidens bildvärld*, http://medeltidbild.historiska.se/medeltidbild/visa/foremal.asp?objektid=900901S3 [accessed 12 February 2021].

Statens historiska muséer, '900901S2' [Crucifix from Ilsbo], in *Medeltidens bildvärld*, http://medeltidbild.historiska.se/medeltidbild/visa/foremal.asp?objektid=900901S2 [accessed 12 February 2021].

Statens historiska muséer, '900901S1' [Crucifix from Ilsbo], in *Medeltidens bildvärld*, http://medeltidbild.historiska.se/medeltidbild/visa/foremal.asp?objektid=900901S1 [accessed 12 February 2021].

Statens historiska muséer, '900901A2' [St Olaf from Ilsbo], in *Medeltidens bildvärld*, http://medeltidbild.historiska.se/medeltidbild/visa/foremal. asp?objektid=900901A2 [accessed 12 February 2021].
Statens historiska muséer, '900901A1' [Altarpiece from Ilsbo], in *Medeltidens bildvärld*, http://medeltidbild.historiska.se/medeltidbild/visa/foremal. asp?objektid=900901A1 [accessed 12 February 2021].
Statens historiska muséer, '900924S8' [St Anne with Virgin and Child from Norrala], in *Medeltidens bildvärld*, http://medeltidbild.historiska.se/medeltidbild/visa/foremal.asp?objektid=900924S8 [accessed 12 February 2021].
Statens historiska muséer, '900925S10' [Madonna from Norrala], in *Medeltidens bildvärld*, http://medeltidbild.historiska.se/medeltidbild/visa/foremal.asp?objektid=900925S10 [accessed 12 February 2021].
Statens historiska muséer, '900927S4' [Crucifix from Segersta], in *Medeltidens bildvärld*, http://medeltidbild.historiska.se/medeltidbild/visa/foremal. asp?objektid=900927S4 [accessed 12 February 2021].
Statens historiska muséer, '920519S2' [Wooden sculpture from Husaby], in Medeltidens bildvärld http://medeltidbild.historiska.se/medeltidbild/visa/foremal.asp?objektid=920519S2 [accessed 13 February 2023].
Statens historiska muséer, '930812A1' [Altarpiece from Segersta], in *Medeltidens bildvärld*, http://medeltidbild.historiska.se/medeltidbild/visa/foremal.asp?objektid=930812A1 [accessed 12 February 2021].

Printed sources and literature

Ågren, Henrik, *Erik den helige – landsfader eller beläte? En rikspatrons öden i svensk historieskrivning från reformationen till och med upplysningen* (Lund: Sekel, 2012).
Ångström, Inga Lena, 'Avdammad madonna åter på tronen – Maria i 1600-talets kyrkorum', in Sven-Erik Brodd and Alf Härdelin (eds), *Maria i Sverige under tusen år: Föredrag vid symposiet i Vadstena 6–10 oktober 1994, Bok 2: Marias tillbakaträngade* (Skellefteå: Artos, 1996), pp. 647–76.
Barnett, S. J., *Idol Temples and Crafty Priests: The Origins of Enlightenment Anticlericalism* (New York: Macmillan, 1999).
Bergstrand, Carl-Martin, *Kulturbilder från 1700-talets Västergötland, andra delen* (Gothenburg: N. J. Gumperts bokhandel, 1934).
Berntson, Martin, *Kättarland: En bok om reformationen i Sverige* (Skellefteå: Artos, 2017).
Brilkman, Kajsa, *Undersåten som förstod: Den svenska reformatoriska samtalsordningen och den tidigmoderna integrationsprocessen* (Skellefteå: Artos, 2013).
Bringéus, Nils-Arvid (ed.), *Sockenbeskrivningar från Hälsingland 1790–1791, tillkomna på anmodan av landshövdingen F. A. U. Cronstedt, med efterskrift och register utgivna av Nils-Arvid Bringéus* (Uppsala: A.-B. Lundequistska bokhandeln, 1961).

Broman, Olof Johansson, *Glysisvallur: och övriga skrifter rörande Helsingland D. 2* (Uppsala: Gestrike-Helsinge nation, 1912–1953).
Broocman, Carl Fredric, *Beskrifning öfwer the i Öster-Götland befintelige städer, slott, sokne-kyrkor, soknar, säterier, öfwer-officers-boställen, jernbruk och prestegårdar, med mera* (Norrköping: Johan Edman, 1760).
Cronholm, Christopher, *Blekings beskrivning författad av Christopher Cronholm år c:a 1750–1757* (Malmö: Blekingia, 1976).
Dijkman, Petter, *Antiquitates ecclesiasticæ, Eller gamle Swenske Kyrkie-Handlingar Angående wåra förfäders Christeliga Troos och Kyrckio-Ceremoniers beskaffenheter några hundrade åhr tilbakas; sammanplåckade vthur gamla stycker, som runstenar, kyrckior, rijmstafwar, bref, griftestenar, pergament, recesser, afhandlingar, beläten, åthskillige Swea provinciers lag- och agende-böcker, och vnder wisza flåckar förde af Petter Dijkman* (Stockholm: Michaele Laurelio, 1703).
Ekman, Emanuel S., *Wärmeland i Sitt Ämne Och i Sin Upodling, Första Delen Beskrifwit Af Emanuel S. Ekman* (Uppsala: Kongl. Acad. Tryckeriet, 1765).
Fernow, Erik, *Beskrifning öfver Värmland afdelad i sex tidehvarf: tvänne under hedendomen och lika många under påfvedömet och lutherska tiden: jemte en kort inledning om landets läge, namn, vattendrag, bergsträckningar, skogar m.m. utgifven af Erik Fernow* (Karlstad: H. O. Norstedt, 1898).
Forssenius, Anders, *Specimen historicum de Schedvia Westergothiæ urbe, antiqua S. Helenæ sede* (Uppsala: Uppsala University, 1734).
Gothus, Laurentius Paulinus, *Ethica Christianæ pars prima, de ratione bene vivendi. Thet är: Catechismj förste deel, om Gudz lagh* (Stockholm: Christoffer Reusner, 1617).
Hülphers, Abraham Abrahamsson, *Dagbok Öfwer en resa igenom de under Stora Kopparbergs Höftingedöme lydande Lähn och Dalarne år 1757* (Västerås: Joh. Laur. Horrn, 1762).
———, *Samlingar til en beskrifning öfwer Norrland. Femte samlingen om Westerbotten* (Västerås: Joh. L. Horrn, 1789).
Karlsson, Mattias (ed.), *Sockenbeskrivningar från Färs härad 1746–1747, utgivna med inledning och kommentarer av Mattias Karlsson* (Lund: Kungl. Humanistiska vetenskapssamfundet i Lund, 2009).
'Kongl. Maj:tz förnyade Placat och Förbud, angånde the oloflige Sammankomster, hwilka vti enskylte Hus til en särskild och enkannerlig Gudstienst förrättande anställas; Samt theras straff, som ther med beträdas. Stockholm i Råd-Cammaren then 12 Januarii Åhr 1726', in Anders Anton von Stiernman (ed.), *Samling Vtaf åtskillga, tid efter annan, vtkomna Kongliga Stadgar, Bref och Förårdningar Angående Religion Giord vppå Hans Kongl. Maj:ts Nådigaste Befallning* (Stockholm: Kongl. Tryckeriet, 1744), pp. 200–7.
'Kongl. Maj:ts Nådige Stadga och Påbud, til Hämmande af hwarjehanda willfarelser, och theras vtspridande, emot then rena Evangeliska Läran.

Gifwit Stockholm i Råd-Cammaren then 20. Martii 1735', in Anders Anton von Stiernman (ed.), *Samling Vtaf åtskillga, tid efter annan, vtkomna Kongliga Stadgar, Bref och Förårdningar Angående Religion Giord vppå Hans Kongl. Maj:ts Nådigaste Befallning* (Stockholm: Kongl. Tryckeriet, 1744), pp. 225–37.

Lancaster, James A. T. and Andrew McKenzie-McHarg, 'Priestcraft: anatomizing the anti-clericalism of early modern Europe', *Intellectual History Review*, 28:1 (2018), 7–22.

Laugerud, Henning, *Reformasjon uten folk: Det katolske Norge i før- og etterreformatorisk tid* (Oslo: St Olavs, 2018).

Lehner, Ulrich L., *The Catholic Enlightenment: The Forgotten History of a Global Movement* (New York: Oxford University Press, 2016).

Lennersand, Marie and Linda Oja, 'Responses to witchcraft in late seventeenth- and eighteenth-century Sweden', in Willem de Blécourt and Owen Davies (eds), *Beyond the Witch Trials: Witchcraft and Magic in Enlightenment Europe* (Manchester: Manchester University Press, 2004), pp. 61–80.

Linnaeus, Carl, *Carl Linnæi Skånska resa, på höga öfwerhetens befallning förrättad år 1749: Med rön och anmärkningar uti oeconomien, naturalier, antiquiteter, seder, lefnadssätt. Med tilhörige figurer. Med kongl. Maj:ts allernådigste privilegio* (Stockholm: Lars Salvius, 1751).

Ljungberg, Johannes, *Toleransens gränser: Religionspolitiska dilemman i det tidiga 1700-talets Sverige och Europa* (Lund: Lund University, 2017).

Parish, Helen L., *Monks, Miracles and Magic: Reformation Representations of the Medieval Church* (London: Routledge, 2005).

Petri, Laurentius, 'Then swenska kyrkeordningen: Lärer all ting ährligha och skickeliga tilgå', in *Kyrko-ordningar och förslag dertill före 1686. Första Afdelningen* (Stockholm: P. A. Norstedt, 1872), pp. 3–180.

Rhyzelius, Andreas Olavi, *Monasteriologia Sviogothica, eller Klosterbeskrifning, vti hwilken vpräknas, med berettelse om hwad om them kunnat igenfinnas och vspspanas, alla the kloster och helg-andshus, som, vnder påfwedömet, vti Swea- och Götharike, såsom begripande the otta gambla sticht: Vpsala, Linköping, Skara, Strengnäs, Wästerås, Wägsiö, Åbo och Lund, blefwit byggde och vnderhållne, samt om the munke-order, som i Swerige haft kloster; bestående af tio böker, och en tilleggning om jesuit-orden* (Linköping: Petter Pelican, 1740).

——, *Episcoposcopiæ Sviogothicæ, Eller En SweaGöthisk Sticht- och Biskops-Chrönika, Om alla Swea- och GöthaRikets Sticht och Biskopar, ifrå början, in til närwarande tid; Bestående af twå Delar. Med några anmerkningar Och fullkomligt Register* (Linköping: Gabriel Biörckegren, 1752).

Rogberg, Samuel, *Historisk beskrifning om Småland i gemen, i synnerhet Kronobergs och Jönköpings lähner, ifrån äldsta, til närwarande tid, om thesz politie, natural-historia, bergwärk, kyrko-stat, folkmängd, hushållning, kyrkor, slott och herregårdar, med mera mines wärdt* (Karlskrona: Kongl. Amiralitets boktryckeriet, 1770).

Sahlstedt, Magnus, *Stora Tuna i Dahlom och Bergom minnes-döme. Thet är: vtförlig beskrifning och vnderrettelse om then ort och christeliga församling, som har namn af Stora Tuna, och är belägen i Öster-Dahls bergslagen* (Falun: Falu nya boktryckeri, 1955).

Stiernman, Anders Anton von, *Presterskapets redogörelser om forntida minnesmärken i Finlands kyrkor* (Helsinki: Reinold Hausen, 1882).

Svenska riksdagsakter jämte andra handlingar som höra till statsförfattningens historia under tidehvarfvet 1521–1718, Andra delen, 1, 1561–1592 (Stockholm: Riksarkivet, 1899).

Weikert, Monica, *I sjukdom och nöd: Offerkyrkoseden i Sverige från 1600-tal till 1800-tal* (Gothenburg: University of Gothenburg, 2004).

Whitelocke, Bulstrode, *Journal of the Swedish Embassy in the Years 1653 and 1654*, ed. C. Morton, 2 vols (London: Longman, 1855), II.

Zachrisson, Terese, *Mellan fromhet och vidskepelse: Materialitet och religiositet i det efterreformatoriska Sverige* (Gothenburg: University of Gothenburg, Department of Historical Studies, 2017).

6
A problematic legacy: negotiating the medieval past in Danish eighteenth-century church interiors

Martin Wangsgaard Jürgensen

In the eighteenth-century Danish Church, the past gradually began to pose a problem, at least to some church authorities, church owners and congregations at large. Whereas the Danish Lutheran Reformation of 1536 naturally resulted in changes inside churches, these modifications were far from thorough and far-reaching. As can be gleaned from much older research on the topic, medieval furnishings and decorations kept a strong presence within Danish churches – as they still do today, one might add. A German study edited by Johann Michael Fritz in 1997 carries the apt title *Die bewahrende Kraft des Luthertums* (The preserving power of Lutheranism), and in his introduction Fritz correctly points to the large amount of medieval church furniture preserved in Lutheran churches compared to the churches of other confessions.[1] Indeed, many have endeavoured to explain this fact from different angles since the appearance of *Die bewahrende Kraft*.[2] However, these

---

I am grateful for the advice and suggestions of my colleague Birgitte Bøggild Johannsen, who has made her as-yet-unpublished material available to me. Her publication on the subject at hand is eagerly anticipated.

1 Johann Michael Fritz (ed.), *Die bewahrende Kraft des Luthertums: Mittelalterliche Kunstwerke in evangelischen Kirchen* (Munich: Schnell & Steiner, 1997).

2 See such works as Sergiusz Michalski, *The Reformation and the Visual Arts: The Protestant Image Question in Western and Eastern Europe* (London and New York: Routledge, 1993); Peter Poscharsky, *Die Bilder in den lutherischen Kirchen: Ikonographische Studien* (Munich: Scaneg, 1998); Bridget Heal, '"Better Papist than Calvinist": art and identity in later Lutheran Germany', *German History*, 29 (2011), 584–609; Martin Wangsgaard Jürgensen, *Ritual and Art across the Danish Reformation: Changing Interiors of Village Churches, 1450–1600* (Turnhout: Brepols, 2018); Justin Kroesen, 'The survival of medieval furnishings in Lutheran churches: notes towards a comparison between Germany and Scandinavia', *ICO: Iconographisk Post*, 3–4 (2018), 4–39.

pre-Reformation survivals became troublesome in the eighteenth century, as the ideals of rationalism or Enlightenment began to spread throughout the Danish realm.

This chapter delves into Danish church interiors of the eighteenth century and explores how they interacted with their heritage from the Middle Ages. Late medieval churches were diversely furnished, filled with numerous different objects more or less related to liturgy and private devotion. Many of these were uncontroversial in the eyes of the reformers and were hence left out of Reformation debates in the sixteenth century. The truly problematic items which sparked heated discussion were ultimately altars, altar furnishings and devotional art at large – particularly images on altars and images connected with specific acts of veneration.

A resurgent disapproval of the vestiges of Catholicism can in other words be discerned among the authorities of the eighteenth century, who wanted to combat what they perceived as old superstition and the relics of 'popery', which threatened to contaminate weak minds and pollute the evangelical message. By way of tracts and actual refurnishing of parish churches, several campaigns led by theologians and church owners were set in motion with a view to adapting the church building as well as its rituals to prevailing ideas of rational thinking.

It should be stated from the outset that this eagerness for reform was by no means a universally accepted attitude or interest. Rather, the preoccupation with the purging of the churches was carried through by zealous individuals or clusters of communities spread all over the country. Furthermore, economic and regional factors influenced this otherwise strictly theological issue, as the most widespread renovation and refurnishing work implemented during the eighteenth century often took place in such prosperous parts of the country as eastern Jutland and the islands of Funen and Zealand. Theology was certainly a prominent motivational force for the renewal of church interiors; but a better-performing economy also enabled church owners to follow the artistic fashions of the period much more closely than in other parts of the country, where fists were necessarily tighter. There were undoubtedly ideals behind most renewals; but as we shall see, we also find voices explicitly proclaiming their ideology in areas where otherwise little change was set in motion in churches because of a lack of funds.

Present-day scholarship has access to records of many eighteenth-century reactions to the medieval heritage, and a number of different strategies for dealing with the past can be discerned among them.

In the following, I shall try to demonstrate some of these strategies through a number of small case studies where their implications will be pointed out and discussed. The case studies should be compared with the strikingly similar findings of Terese Zachrisson in her chapter in this volume on religious material culture in Sweden. However, before I embark on the case studies, a few general words need to be said about Danish churches in the first centuries after the evangelical Reformation of 1536.

Some notes on the Reformation of Danish churches

While the Lutheran reformers of the sixteenth century specifically changed the status of the religious image, they also changed the perception of church furnishings and devotional objects, such as three-dimensional sculptures that had been in place prior to the Reformation. Some were removed from altars and preserved as so-called *Gedenkbilder*; some were destroyed, altered or adjusted; others were left in place; and some came to be integrated into new ritual and devotional contexts.[3] In his handbook from the middle of the sixteenth century concerning the visitation of churches, the Danish superintendent Peter Palladius (1503–1560) could suggest:

> That is why churchwardens can dismantle these [side altars] ... The retables and images can be put up on the wall [elsewhere in the church]. When people know whom they depict, they may use them as mirrors [i.e. examples of pious living].[4]

The immediate need was to stop the previous devotional and liturgical activities practised in churches, and one of the ways of doing so was to remove or reposition the objects which had traditionally been used in worship, thereby disrupting the association between object and ritual. Altarpieces displaying saints as the primary motif were often removed from altars and the altars themselves broken up and taken away or repurposed, while other liturgical equipment, such as censers, were put to different uses. In this context, it is important to note that most of these changes applied to side

---

3 Caroline Bynum, 'Are things "indifferent"? How objects change our understanding of religious history', *German History*, 34:1 (2016), 88–112; Jürgensen, *Ritual*.
4 Lis Jacobsen (ed.), *Peder Palladius' Danske Skrifter*, 5 vols (Copenhagen: Thiele, 1911–1926), V (1925–1926), p. 36. Translations throughout the chapter are mine.

altars found in the nave and chapels attached to the churches; the decoration on the high altar in the chancel would mostly be left untouched because the altarpiece here usually had the crucifixion or the Passion story as the central theme, and this was, according to Luther and most of his followers, unproblematic. Nevertheless, not all altarpieces portraying the Passion embodied a solely Christological iconography: Mariological as well as hagiographical themes could be intertwined in the composition of a retable, the consequence being, in principle, that unwanted content was at times left on the altar as vestiges of outmoded beliefs. To this we may add the wall-paintings and stained-glass windows which all carried pre-Reformation imagery but were rarely the objects of direct veneration and accordingly mostly left untouched and unmentioned by reformers. The superintendent Jacob Madsen (1538–1606), visiting the churches on the island of Funen during the last decade of the sixteenth century, almost exclusively mentions altar decorations in his visitation reports; Madsen is more or less silent about all the other paraphernalia and imagery in the churches he visited, because he simply found them of little consequence.[5]

What we are to take from all this is that a substantial number of medieval church furnishings and decorations were left inside churches following the Reformation – not always in their originally designated places, but still visible and, at times, also still in use. While the alteration of altar decorations and liturgical equipment was certainly an expression of an iconoclastic approach to the Reformation of the church space, it was a very moderate one, as a substantial amount of pre-Reformation devotional art was left visible.[6] All of this led to an intricate and highly variable pattern of attitudes within the Lutheran sphere, a pattern which not only changed from one church region to another but also from church to church in neighbouring parishes. Time and time again, it sparked renewed discussion of the harmful nature of pre-Reformation or Catholic

---

5 A. R. Idum (ed.), *Den fyenske Biskop Mester Jacob Madsens Visitatsbog* (Odense: Historisk Samfund for Odense og Assens Amter, 1929).

6 Fritz, *Die bewahrende*; Jürgensen, *Ritual*. See, furthermore, Anita Hansen and Birgitte Bøggild Johannsen, 'Imo licet: Omkring Niels Hemmingsens billedsyn', in Peter Sjömar and others (eds), *Kirkearkeologi og kirkekunst: Studier tilegnet Sigrid og Håkon Christie* (Øvre Ervik: Akademisk förlag, 1993), pp. 181–98; and Sven Rune Havsteen, 'Lutheran theology and artistic media: responses to the theological discourse on the visual arts', in Andrew Spicer (ed.), *Lutheran Churches in Early Modern Europe* (Farnham: Ashgate, 2012), pp. 221–40.

images and the status of church furnishings in general. Not until the Evangelical-Lutheran Church was able to settle on the concept of *adiaphora* after the discussions in the Colloquy of Montbéliard (1586) did the debate more or less end, and it was now – within certain boundaries – left to individual interpretation to choose which images and types of objects were proper to have and not to have.[7] We can also see the discussion about *adiaphora* in the Lutheran community as a way of coming to terms with aspects of the pre-Reformation past. During the latter part of the sixteenth century and particularly in the seventeenth century, in what is often named the period of Lutheran orthodoxy, new furnishings came into Danish churches – particularly new altarpieces and pulpits, but also wall-paintings and numerous other types of objects. While this probably led to the complete removal of medieval objects in many places, these new installations often seem simply to have been added on, like the rings of a tree, another chronological period joining the steadily growing number of images and objects inside the churches.

This brings us to the situation which church owners and authorities faced in the eighteenth century, when the revolutionary ideals of Enlightenment and rationalism sparked an urge to clear the house of God and unsentimentally recreate it without what was felt to be the superstition and unenlightened clutter of past centuries. As we shall see, the ultimate aim was to reinstate conditions like those in the early Church of late Antiquity; but this dream rarely came to fruition, and where it succeeded the changes were almost always rolled back during the nineteenth century, when the aesthetic ideals of the Enlightenment reformers had more or less lost their appeal.

For many hectic decades following the Reformation, the Danish Crown sold or gave the rights and control over most parish churches to the nobility, who regarded the churches – or rather the tithes – as a steady source of income. In principle, church owners could do what they wanted with their churches as long as the buildings were kept in good repair and the necessary services were provided to the community. This could at times give rise to conflict when too little care was shown in the maintenance of the buildings.

---

7 Concerning *adiaphora* and images, see Jill Raitt, *The Colloquy of Montbéliard: Religion and Politics in the Sixteenth Century* (Oxford: Oxford University Press, 1993); R. B. Sdzuj, *Adiaphora und Kunst: Studien zur Genealogie ästhetischen Denkens* (Tübingen: Max Niemeyer, 2005); Andrew Spicer, 'Adiaphora, Luther and the material culture of worship', *Studies in Church History*, 56 (2020), 246–72.

Figure 6.1 Interior of the church of Bellinge on the island of Funen. Medieval and post-medieval furnishings and decorations side by side. Photo: Arnold Mikkelsen.

Danish eighteenth-century church interiors

Financial, nostalgic and devotional interests were all blended with the use and perception of the church, and it was by no means always easy simply to purge it of all previous furnishings and install new ones in tune with new ideals, if the owner wished to do so.[8] I will therefore turn to a number of case studies showing how this problem of the presence of the medieval past was handled within some rural parishes.

The first case: criticizing superstitious practices

The first case takes us to Krogstrup on the island of Zealand. In the rural parish church there, a shrine was in all likelihood established at some point during the late Middle Ages in honour of St Denis or Dionysius of Paris.[9] We have no medieval sources confirming the existence of the cult; but as we shall see, the afterlife of this veneration makes it likely that the shrine became a popular pilgrimage site in the region around the early sixteenth century, and a centre to which rural people from nearby villages would travel in order to find cures for their ailments. We know little about this cult of St Dionysius except that the depiction of the saint was probably on display in a chapel added to the church around 1500 and specifically designated for this purpose. Many such shrines dotted the sacred topography of late medieval Denmark, but what is particularly interesting in the present context is the post-Reformation survival of devotion to the saint.[10] After the Reformation, we hear of this cult in 1606 when King Christian IV ordered the chapel to be cleared and the image of St Dionysius taken down and removed owing to the blasphemous adoration of this effigy.[11]

---

8 A vivid impression of the negotiations and conflicts between Church, pastor and church owner can be gained from Charlotte Appel and Morten Fink-Jensen, *Når det regner på præsten: En kulturhistorie om sognepæster og sognefolk 1550–1750* (Gjern: Hovedland, 2009).
9 *Danmarks Kirker: Frederiksborg Amt*, pp. 2725–53, http://danmarkskirker. natmus.dk/uploads/tx_tcchurchsearch/Frederiksborg_2725-2753.pdf [accessed 23 February 2023]. See also Chr. Axel Jensen, 'Katolsk kirkeinventars skæbne efter Reformationen: Studier og exempler', in *Aarbøger for Nordisk Oldkyndighed og Historie* (1921), pp. 167–204.
10 An overview of a substantial number of Danish shrines is presented in Christoph Daxelmüller and Marie-Louise Thomsen, 'Mittelalterliches Wallfahrtswesen in Dänemark: Mit einem Kultstätten-Katalog', *Jahrbuch für Volkskunde* 1 (1978), 155–204.
11 *Danske Magazin*, 1 (Copenhagen, 1745–1752), p. 96.

Figure 6.2 Krogstrup Church on Zealand with the sacristy and chapel attached to the chancel. Photo: National Museum of Denmark.

As far as we know, the chapel was duly cleared in accordance with the King's command. Only the royal decree has been preserved, and no response that might have confirmed the intervention which the local authorities were to perform in the church. It seems fair to assume that the orders were indeed carried out, and one would think that the veneration displayed at Krogstrup was eradicated as a result. However, this was not the case. In 1764 Bishop Erik Pontoppidan, whom we shall meet again shortly, could report that owing to old superstitious practices, peasants from the region around Krogstrup were travelling to the church or sending couriers with money for the alms box, when their children had fallen seriously ill or women experienced trouble during pregnancy.[12] The church of Krogstrup was hence still a place to which one could turn in order to seek cures and succour more than two hundred years after the Reformation. St Dionysius himself in all likelihood disappeared in 1606, but the place retained his healing functions. Rather than donating alms specifically to the saint, as would have been done in the late Middle Ages, the focus was shifted to the church building

---

12 Erik Pontoppidan (ed.), *Den Danske Atlas eller Konge-Riget Dannemark*, 7 vols (Copenhagen, 1763–1781), II, p. 95.

as a space which was believed to possess special, blessed powers. King Christian's order to remove the saint was successful insofar as it rendered the cult surrounding the church of Krogstrup faceless – it was no longer to a specific entity that the peasants travelled – but the cult itself remained active and transformed itself according to post-Reformation conditions.

In Store Heddinge Church, also on Zealand, the pastor complained that parishioners sought the help of a figure of the Virgin Mary with her child kept in the church, as well as of a crucifix hanging by the entrance, which the peasants sought out to counter toothaches and difficulties during pregnancy. On 6 January 1787 he was given permission by Bishop Nicolai Edinger Balle (1744–1816), of whom more below, to take down the medieval sculptures and burn them, with the addendum that a matching amount of firewood should be given to the needy in the parish.[13] We have many such instances recorded from the eighteenth century, testifying to the fact that communities retained certain practical attitudes to the past as a means of finding help which was otherwise not to be had in their community, and in a sense they thereby kept some ownership of their past and religion. Yet this was clearly unwanted from the outset of the Reformation, and downright embarrassing to many authorities in the eighteenth century who felt as alienated from the practices of rural communities as they probably did from the urban and intellectual spheres that promoted the new ideals of the time.

There is a ritual aspect to such ceremonial destruction of the past, an aspect to which I shall return in the next case. However, what we should note here is the attempt to establish order or to better the community through acts of simple destruction. Such attitudes bring out the charged nature of these acts of *damnatio memoriae* and the forces that the agents of Enlightenment confronted in their zeal.[14] The result, as the case of Krogstrup demonstrates, was far from always successful, as it was simply the exterior or surface of the practice that was eliminated, not the need that fuelled the undesirable devotions in the church. While we should perhaps be wary of reading the cult at Krogstrup as a direct continuation of late medieval practice, we may see it as an expression of a

---

13 *Danmarks Kirker: Præstø Amt*, pp. 65–6, http://danmarkskirker.natmus.dk/uploads/tx_tcchurchsearch/Praestoe_0053-0071.pdf [accessed 23 February 2023].

14 Concerning iconoclasm, see Lee Palmer Wandel, *Voracious Idols and Violent Hands* (Cambridge: Cambridge University Press, 1999).

traditional religion which again and again clashed with the expectations of church authorities, first with Lutheran orthodoxy and then again with the idealism of Enlightenment. As a coping strategy, the destruction of the deprecated objects should furthermore be considered the first and oldest of the strategies presented here and an expedient reaching back to the Reformation debates of the sixteenth century.

The second case: exposing superstition

The second case also involves a cult of St Dionysius. This time we have moved to a rural parish church in western Jutland, a rather poor region in medieval and early modern Denmark with limited farming possibilities. Yet here we find the rural church of Ejsing, which was much enlarged during the late Middle Ages.[15] The church thereby became a substantial regional landmark by rural standards and especially so for a church in western Jutland. Among the additions to the fabric was a chapel which was in all likelihood dedicated to the cult of St Dionysius, and we should undoubtedly envision activities taking place here that were very similar to those presented in connection with the church of Krogstrup. However, one big difference sets Krogstrup and Ejsing apart. Instead of being eradicated, the saints' cult at Ejsing was 'exposed as superstition'. The figure of St Dionysius was not removed, but retained on display in the church. The effigy was moved from the dismantled altar and placed in front of its former chapel, positioned for all to see, with the following text (rhymed in the original Danish) written above it:

> This chapel, one here sees, in the days of the Pope was where Dionysius and others were the teachers. From him [St Dionysius] it has its name from ancient times. Now it [the chapel] has found better use and he is here no more located. As a mark of worship a little altar of stone was once erected here. On this lurked without flesh and bones this wooden monk [the effigy of St Dionysius] who has [now] been removed.[16]

---

15 *Danmarks Kirker: Ringkøbing Amt*, pp. 2941–79, 3010, 3068, http://danmarkskirker.natmus.dk/uploads/tx_tcchurchsearch/Ringkobing_2941-3104.pdf [accessed 23 February 2023].

16 'Dette capel som mand heer seer: I pavedom har været: Hvor Dionysius med fleer: Paa sin maneer har læret. Af hannem hæfver det sit nafn, Til en ældgammel minde. Nu brugis det til bedre gafn sligt er ei meer at finde. Til kiende tegn var her af steen et lidet altar muret. Der stod foruden kjød oc been: Den munch af træ oc luret. Mand tog det bort.'

Danish eighteenth-century church interiors

Figure 6.3 St Dionysius from Ejsing Church in western Jutland, *c.* 1500.
Photo: Arnold Mikkelsen.

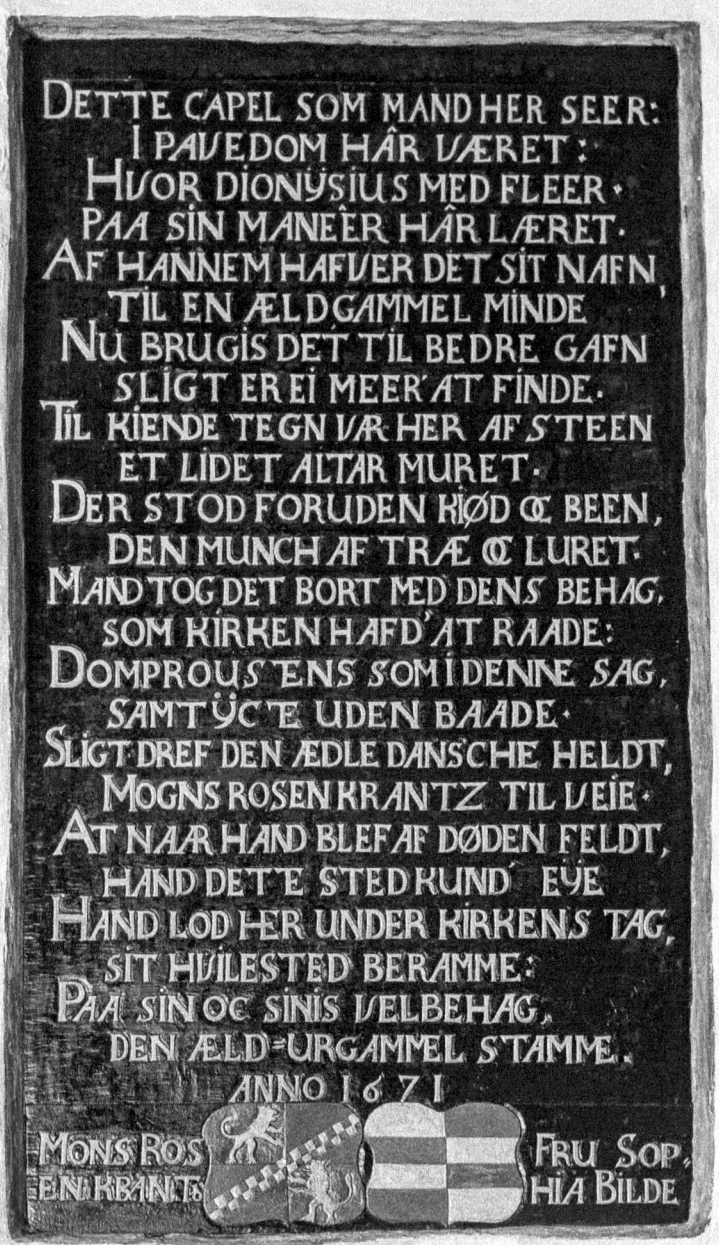

Figure 6.4 Plaque from 1671 above the figure of St Dionysius in Ejsing Church, western Jutland. Photo: Arnold Mikkelsen.

According to the inscription, which was made in 1671, the reason for the removal of the altar was that the chapel was to be cleared and used for burials. The proceedings were, of course, very early in the light of the chronological scope of this chapter; but they are relevant because this is one of the first salient examples of dealing with the medieval past in such a manner. The interesting thing in this connection is the strange paradox of the commemoration itself. The statue of St Dionysius was placed on the wall along with the text, which exposes and disempowers the saint while demonstrating his redundancy to the community. First of all, this is a clear break with the ideas of both Luther and Superintendent Peder Palladius (1503–1560), who regarded the potential of these depictions of saints as favourable influences on the congregation. Here the reverse is the case, and we are told that the saint belongs to the unenlightened past. But to my mind a curious or ambivalent quality creeps into the process as well: by putting the saint on display in the church in such a prominent way, the exact opposite is also happening. The saint's power seems reconfirmed and his place in the community is upheld, despite now being almost put in the pillory within the church, which again points to the extremely charged nature of these interactions with the past. We have no records of the cult of St Dionysius at Ejsing, neither in the Middle Ages nor after the Reformation, but the memory of his cult was nevertheless secured through the attempts made by the churchwardens to expose it.

A less striking but parallel example concerns the church of Vindinge on the island of Funen, where we find an interesting note in the topographical survey *Den Danske Atlas* (The Danish Atlas), published between 1763 and 1781. In the description of the church, we read that the altarpiece was at some point replaced or perhaps merely altered, but on the retable present in the middle of the eighteenth century a text was written, stating that '[h]ere was St Matthew shown on the altar'.[17] Again, we encounter the curious dual movement of simultaneously commemorating the presence and the abolition of the saint. This phenomenon certainly smacks of an elitist approach to the betterment of the congregation, who could hardly be expected to follow the rhetorical strategy in play here. As I shall show below, the strategy of ridicule also posed the danger of further alienating the rural faithful, who would not necessarily be party to it. The rhetoric could be counterproductive to the message.

---

17 'Hir vard St. Mathæus vor dem Altar dot *gestocken*'. Pontoppidan, *Den Danske Atlas*, III:4, p. 693.

The third case: explaining superstition

In 1765, Ditlev Mortensen Kirketerp (1734–1792) bought an obsolete altarpiece, produced c. 1500, from the large late medieval church of St Morten in the town of Randers in eastern Jutland.[18] On the retable we see the Mercy Seat depicted in the middle, flanked by the Virgin with child and St Martin of Tours, while saints are portrayed on the wings of the piece. Kirketerp had the retable installed on the altar of the rural parish church of Hald, also in eastern Jutland, which he owned. However, before he had the piece placed on the altar, he equipped it with new rhymed inscriptions in Danish underneath the central images – images which can only be seen as traditional late medieval motifs, and which would have had unquestionable Catholic connotations in 1765. Beneath the Virgin, the new text reads: 'Mary does not hear our prayer / we only adore her Son',[19] and under the Mercy Seat we read: 'We honour the invisible God / images we can do without'[20], while the text beneath St Martin reads: 'St Martin's image may stand here / [but] we build on the words of the apostles'.[21]

Two things are striking in this context. First and foremost, it is remarkable that the church owner, Kirketerp, bought and installed the altarpiece in his church only to have the very images he was putting on display countered through the added inscriptions. It should be stressed that the retable is a very fine piece and certainly a valuable object from the final decades prior to the Reformation, but it very obviously belongs to a wholly different religious sphere. We thus get a sense of the church owner negotiating with himself. On the one hand, he must have been taken with the sheer quality of the work and therefore found it fitting for his parish church; on the other, it clearly was a disturbing piece which had to be disarmed somehow. As we have seen, Luther was of the opinion that a church might harbour images if such were needed, but preferably there should not be any. Kirketerp was clearly of a different opinion,

---

18 See Hans Jørgen Frederiksen, 'Da Maria fik skæg', *ICO: Iconographisk Post*, 2 (1983), 17–29; Hans Jørgen Frederiksen, in Ole Høiris and Thomas Ledet (eds), 'Kristendom, oplysning og billedpolemik', *Oplysningens Verden: Idé, historie, videnskab og kunst* (Aarhus: Aarhus Universitetsforlag, 2007), pp. 383–92.
19 'Maria hører ey vor Bøn / vi kun tilbede hendes Søn'.
20 'Den usynlige Gud vi ære / Billeder vi kan undvære'.
21 'St: Mortens billed her maa staae / Apostlers Ord vi bygge paa'.

Figure 6.5 The retable from *c.* 1500 in Hald Church in eastern Jutland. Photo: National Museum of Denmark.

finding it better to have the old medieval retable on show rather than displaying something else or nothing at all. In other words, he preferred a spectacular medieval altarpiece to anything new that had been created specifically for the building. We do not know what he paid for the retable; it might have been cheap, but the purchase still points to the growing veneration of old precious objects from the pre-Reformation period which became increasingly evident during the latter half of the eighteenth century. One may, for instance, note a similar regard for the rich alabaster retables from the early fifteenth century found in the churches of Borbjerg and Vejrum in western Jutland, as well as numerous other similar cases which show how the sheer age of the objects began to modify their essence from highly charged Catholic instruments into historical relics.[22] Consequently, we observe how Enlightenment ideals fostered the budding antiquarianism which allowed for a preoccupation with the medieval past in a secularized manner, the objects being transformed from charged and religiously dangerous idols into

---

22 *Danmarks Kirker: Ringkøbing Amt*, pp. 1872–87; 2203–22, http://danmarkskirker.natmus.dk/uploads/tx_tcchurchsearch/Ringkobing_1839-1922.pdf [accessed 23 February 2023].

Figure 6.6 The altarpiece in Borbjerg Church, western Jutland.
Photo: Kristian Hude (1908).

historical curiosities.[23] This is clearly the case with the two above-mentioned alabaster pieces; but in Hald, there is still a sense of danger attached to the retable. It retained some of its power, a power which needed to be curbed lest the parishioners should be misled by the beauty and material wealth of the piece – its aesthetic

---

23 Concerning the general trend of antiquarianism, see Rosemary Sweet, 'Antiquaries and antiquities in eighteenth-century England', *Eighteenth-Century Studies*, 34:2 (2001), 181–206; Bernd Roling (ed.), *Boreas Rising: Antiquarianism and National Narratives in 17th- and 18th-Century Scandinavia* (Berlin: De Gruyter, 2019).

qualities clearly being the reason why Kirketerp put it in his church in the first place.

This brings me to my second point. The added inscriptions, unlike the inscription at Ejsing, do not mock the images but rather take a different approach. They teach the reader how to understand them, so that the altarpiece in a contradictory way makes itself obsolete by stating that the congregation should have no use for it. Still, it is here and it is put in the role of the teacher, instructing the beholder what to think of itself as an image in the church by pointing to its nature as a mere depiction and nothing divine. Placing didactic inscriptions on objects in order to explain their proper use or meaning was a strategy which quickly spread during the decades following the Reformation.[24] One might think of the altar in Svindinge Church, dating from 1578, on the island of Funen, which explains what the altar is not but completely fails to explain what it is and why it is there.[25] On one side of the altar, for instance, we read: 'I desire loving-kindness and not sacrifice, [as well as] knowledge of God and not burnt offerings';[26] but if the altar is not for sacrifice, what is it for? On this question the inscriptions are silent. We could similarly turn to a small group of chalices, also found on Funen, where we find the following inscription: 'I am to be used in the manner of Christ, and not according to the Pope's erroneous teaching'.[27] These words are inscribed on a chalice from 1634 in the small rural church of Bjerreby.

Such convoluted rhetorical manoeuvring was clearly a part of what has been called the process of confessionalization after the reformations, yet this didactic approach became ever more common during the eighteenth century in the slipstream generated by the spread of Enlightenment ideals. It was a tool employed by the authorities to reduce and reshape what were perceived as lax attitudes among the primarily rural congregations. While the pastor could explain the content and nature of the church through his sermons

---

24 Ragne Bugge, 'Effigiem Christi, qui transis, semper honora: verses condemning the cult of the sacred images in art and literature', *Acta ad archaeologiam et atrium historiam pertinentia*, 6 (1975), 127–39.
25 Jürgensen, *Ritual*, pp. 103–5.
26 'Jeg haffver lyst til miskundhed oc icke til offer oc til at kiene gud oc icke til brendoffer'.
27 'Jeg skal bruges efter Christi skik, och ey efter Pavfens vrange dict 1634'; Finn Grandt-Nielsen, *Fynsk Kirkesølv. Fynske Studier XII* (Odense: Odense Bys Museer, 1983), p. 75.

and theological writings, the very objects within the church buildings could also be given a voice and in a sense speak directly to both their user and an audience, as when, in 1736, the new pulpit in the town church of Elsinore on Zealand was inscribed, on the steps leading up to the podium (again, the original is in rhyme): 'Two hundred years in time / it is now in Denmark, since / we escaped from monkish ways / and found the true faith'.[28] The inscription, of course, first and foremost commemorates the bicentennial of the Danish Reformation; but it also feeds into the idea of the objects in the church as having a voice of their own, addressing their pre-Reformation counterparts and explaining that they are better and different, just as the pulpit here clearly states that something new is now preached in this church. Like the attempt to remove specific, troublesome objects (as in the first case), this way of giving a voice to the church interior was among the oldest strategies for handling the past, and it is noteworthy that the Enlightenment attempts at explaining what was the proper use of, say, a chalice – attempts intended to discredit old beliefs and so-called superstitions – in many cases produced a different effect, leading to the preservation of troublesome objects which might otherwise have been peremptorily discarded because of their medieval origins.

The fourth case: narrowing the focus

In this last case, I want to point out a specific tendency in eighteenth-century church decoration rather than discussing a particular church. If we take a step back and look at developments in church decoration from the seventeenth century and into the late eighteenth century, a shift becomes clear. At the beginning of this period, the amount and fullness, or elaboration, of church furnishings was increasing, church spaces being filled with compact expressions of Baroque material splendour. Materiality came to be the crucial element when giving expression to notions of sanctity, sacred presence or transcendence.[29] During the seventeenth century,

---

28 'Tvende hundred Aar i Tiiden / Er det nu i Danmark, Siden / Wi slap ud af Munke-Skik / Og den Sande Lære fik'; *Danmarks Kirker: Frederiksborg Amt*, pp. 170–6, http://danmarkskirker.natmus.dk/uploads/tx_tcchurchsearch/Frederiksborg_0039-0289.pdf [accessed 23 February 2023].
29 Martin Wangsgaard Jürgensen, 'The rhetoric of splendour: matter and the invisible in seventeenth-century church art', *Transfiguration: Journal of Religion and the Arts* (2013/14), 163–87.

Danish eighteenth-century church interiors

in other words, the size, volume or sheer material presence in churches became a way, through a form of non-iconography, to express what the late medieval period prior to the reformations of the sixteenth century could show through, for instance, specific depictions of the sacred. The sacred was now to be an abstract presence, felt through the very abundance of matter in the churches – richly carved retables, extremely ornate pulpits and huge sepulchral tablets, to name but the most obvious elements. While this idea remained strong up until the late seventeenth century, it changed during the 1700s in the course of what might be called a narrowing of focus. Rather than artistic emphasis on the whole of the church, the focus came to rest on the key places or spaces within the church – the baptismal font, altar and pulpit – whereas a gradual abandonment of the decoration of the church interior in general became apparent. That is not to say that a growing carelessness was setting in, but rather that attention was concentrated on the places in the church which held the greater theological importance. It might be said that by not demonstrating the same degree of care and splendour, the places which did receive attention would then stand out more clearly to the beholder.

An example of this development is the fragmented mural decoration in the parish church of Greve on Zealand, dating from around 1700.[30] Here the walls and vaults were whitewashed and then painted with angels blowing horns and carrying palm leaves. The painting was executed in grisaille and was remarkably simple, considering the dense colours usually employed up until this point. Compared to previous modes of wall-painting, a certain sense of the understated could be detected at Greve, which then again would enable the gilded pulpit of 1617 and the now lost altarpiece of 1619 to stand out in the interior.[31] To take a better preserved but somewhat less striking example, one could look at the large painted drapery surrounding the altar and altarpiece in Magleby Church, also on Zealand, painted *c.* 1750–1775.[32]

---

30 Mette Kristine Jensen, 'Pæn og hvid', in Eva Louise Lillie (ed.), *Danske Kalkmalerier: 1536–1700* (Copenhagen: Nationalmuseet, 1992), pp. 172–3.
31 *Danmarks Kirker: Københavns Amt*, pp. 967–72, http://danmarkskirker.natmus.dk/uploads/tx_tcchurchsearch/kob_amt_958-976.pdf [accessed 23 February 2023].
32 *Danmarks Kirker: Præstø Amt*, pp. 999–1007, http://danmarkskirker.natmus.dk/uploads/tx_tcchurchsearch/Praestoe_0999-1007.pdf [accessed 23 February 2023].

174 Dealing with the Catholic past (and present)

Figure 6.7 One of the painted angels from around 1750–1775 in Greve Church. Photo: National Museum of Denmark.

The delicacy which these artistic representations express, compared to the same type of art from the middle of the previous century, can be illustrated by the church of Mary Magdalene in eastern Jutland. Here the church received a remarkable altarpiece in 1757, commemorating the church owner Jørgen Fogh Wilster (1714–1756) and donated by his widow Anne Margrethe Galten (1730–1797).[33] The splendid retable is a Rococo-style altarpiece with a highly stylish frame incorporating typical period ornament, framing a Last Supper scene. On the flanks of the retable Christ and Moses are carved as three-dimensional sculptures, while the top-piece is crowned by a putto sitting above the Jahve name

---

33 See the description of the church in J. P. Trap, *Danmark*, 5th edn, 15 vols (Copenhagen: Gads, 1953–1972), VII (1963), pp. 876–8.

Figure 6.8 Altar decoration in Magleby Church on Zealand, painted
c. 1750–1775. Photo: author's own.

written in Hebrew. The retable is a lush vista of gold and rich sculptural carving, with an expressive use of forms that seem to bulge out into the space of the chancel, yet retaining a sense of a slim and upward-pointing whole. The effect is a strong focal point in the church, comprised of elements from different periods and without any sense of strict unity. Nonetheless, in the chancel the

Figure 6.9 The retable from 1756 in Maria Magdalene church in Eastern Jutland. Photo: Kristian Hude (1908).

altarpiece outshines the other elements and becomes the central and most splendid part of the church.

In light of the theme under consideration, these changes serve to demonstrate the ways in which the authorities tried to refocus the church interior and cleanse it of the most troubling elements

Danish eighteenth-century church interiors

from the past. They form a gradual movement; its thinking is very much rooted in the recurrence of pleasure in materiality and splendour that arose during the seventeenth century.

The past as a problem

The powerful polemical denunciations of the cult of saints and everything 'popish' that characterized the sixteenth century still lingered as relevant objections in the Lutheran community in the eighteenth. They were gradually reactivated as arguments for a reform of the Church, not solely to remove it from previous superstition but also to wrest it free of the most cumbersome elements of the Lutheran past and attune the church building and its rituals to the present. With renewed force, the Middle Ages came to be a symbol of all that should be left behind; and to many leading intellectual figures of the time, the ghost of the pre-Reformation age – or what became the Catholic past – always loomed as a threat to the religious hegemony of the realm. Over time, a change is nevertheless apparent in the way the medieval heritage was addressed. Whereas the rhetoric of the 1500s and 1600s directly influenced the Reformation and the ensuing consolidation of a confessional identity in the Lutheran sphere, we find a somewhat different line of thought in the 1700s.[34] Here the medieval Church and all its ritual trappings were clearly becoming a thing of the past, with only vestiges left, as can be seen from the case studies above. These vestiges, however, were still regarded as troublesome symbols by pastors and learned scholars writing about the great superstition which, they felt, still beset the 'simple people', especially in the countryside.[35] As pastor Frederik Christian Hjort (1760–1820) notes in his fascinating treatise on religion among the peasantry:

> I venture to say that the true religion of the heart is all too rare among the peasantry; the outwardly apparently good deeds found among them are more often fruits of a hope for favours in return than a truthful and living acknowledgement of obligations, which should always, after all, be the force impelling the true Christian to practise [Christian] virtues.[36]

---

34 Thomas Kaufmann, *Konfession und Kultur: Lutherischer Protestantismus in der zweiten Hälfte des Reformationsjahrhundert* (Tübingen: Mohr, 2006).
35 See for instance Frederiksen, 'Da Maria', 17–29.
36 'Jeg tør påstå, at den sande og hjertets religion er alt for sjælden blandt landalmuen; at de så udvortes skingode gerninger, som findes blandt mængden,

The dichotomy between learned and urban culture on the one hand and the rural communities on the other was felt, by some at least, to be a wide and unacceptable gap which could only be bridged through the stern enlightenment of the unlearned.[37] A prime example of this, writing on the very cusp of the rationalistic Enlightenment movement in Denmark, would be the already-mentioned Erik Pontoppidan, bishop of the Diocese of Bergen in Norway, who published a small treatise against superstition in Latin entitled *Everriculum fermenti veteris* in 1736.[38] The title of the work, in translation, means 'Broom to remove the old sourdough', and the metaphor signifies that all ancient superstition should be swept out of the Church. In his work, Pontoppidan states:

> I am somewhat in doubt if I, in this age of superstition, should be surprised by the practical character of the vices or their great age. We are positioned as the complete heirs of the Papists and the Papists of the Pharisees, because one should not believe that this has come into being yesterday or the day before.[39]

What Pontoppidan does here is to trace a lineage of superstition running from his day through the Middle Ages and back to biblical times, whereupon he blames the Jews for being at the root of much of it.[40] In addition, he defines everything between the Bible and Luther as a dark age of misguided effort and pure invention,

---

oftere er frugter af håb om gentjenester, end af den sande og levende pligternes erkendelse, som dog burde være driveren for den sande kristne til dydernes udøvelse'; F. Chr. Hjorth, *Tanker til Eftertanke om Religion og Sæderne blandt den danske Landalmue* (Copenhagen, 1784), p. 20.

37 See this discussed in Palle O. Christensen, *A Manorial World: Lord, peasants and cultural distinctions on a Danish estate 1750–1980* (Copenhagen: Scandinavian University Press, 1996); Peter Henningsen, 'Det antropologiske bondebegreb', *Fortid og Nutid*, 1 (2000), 29–58, and the same author's 'Den rationelle bonde: en historisk-antropologisk analyse af traditionalismen i dansk bondekultur', *Historisk Tidsskrift*, 100 (2000), 329–81.

38 The volume was translated and republished as Erik Pontoppidan, *Fejekost, til at udfeje den gamle surdejg eller de i de danske lande tiloversblevne og her for dagen bragte levninger af saavel hedenskab som papisme*, 1736, trans. Jørgen Olrik (Copenhagen: Schønbergske, 1923).

39 'Om jeg ved dette en overtroisk Tidsalders practiske Kætteri mest skal forundre mig over dets lastværdige Art eller ærværdige Alder, er jeg noget i Tvivl om. Vi ere indsatte til dets Universal-Arvinger af Papisterne, og Papisterne atter efter Pharisæerne, for at man ikke skal tro det opkommet igaar eller iforgaars'; Pontoppidan, *Fejekost*, p. 34.

40 Pontoppidan, *Fejekost*, pp. 34–5.

thereby attempting to remove any quality of 'true religion' from both Catholicism and Judaism. A similar rhetoric is found among many of the Lutheran theologians who wrote during the following decades as Enlightenment ideas were spreading, primarily from Copenhagen, to pastors and manor houses throughout the country. And as we have seen, one of the agendas clearly was to emasculate the authority of the past by moving the conversation from religion and into the realm of folk magic and superstition.[41]

What further complicates the matter is that the strict opposition between learned elite and unlearned rustics was to a certain degree an old trope in theological thinking, and it was by no means only made popular again by the reformers of the eighteenth century. To supply just two examples countering the idea of a vast, utterly unlearned rural population in need of enlightenment, we can first note how the rural parish church of Snesere on Zealand received a new altarpiece in 1728 as a replacement for a medieval retable. The reason for this exchange is said to be that the altarpiece was 'replaced not only owing to [its] fragility, but also because of the many images standing upon it to the indignation of the congregation'.[42] Here we get a sense that the process of renovation within the church, and the discarding of the medieval altarpiece, was not just a top-down process but one supported by at least a number of parishioners. Resistance to, as well as support of, change and Enlightenment could, in other words, be found on all levels in some communities. A second example, again from Zealand, illustrates the same thing. Here, Bishop Nicolai Edinger Balle makes an interesting comment in the records of his 1786 visitation of the rural parish of Spjellerup, where he was to examine the congregation in matters of faith. An added interest was that Henrik Paulin Sandal (1751–1833) was present during the visitation. Sandal was the author of at least two books critical of the lack of learning among the peasantry, and in particular he wrote a small book questioning whether Luther's *Small Catechism* was a useful tool in the education of the young.[43] Much to

---

41 This topic is explored in a wider context in the classic study of Keith Thomas, *Religion and the Decline of Magic: Studies in Popular Beliefs in Sixteenth and Seventeenth-Century England* (London: Penguin, 2003; first published in 1971).
42 'ikke alene formedelst skrøbelighed, men også for de mange til menighedens förargelse derpå stående billeder'; *Danmarks Kirker: Præstø Amt*, p. 856, http://danmarkskirker.natmus.dk/uploads/tx_tcchurchsearch/Praestoe_0852-0860_01.pdf [accessed 23 February 2023].
43 See H. P. Sandal, *En Skolelærers Undersøgelse hvor vidt Luthers Katekismus er skikket til at være Lærebog for Ungdommen* (Copenhagen, 1786).

Bishop Balle's delight, Sandal afterwards congratulated him and told him that he had certainly managed to educate his parishioners into more than 'babble-machines' (*Plapper-Maskiner*). While grateful, the bishop rather wryly closes his comment on the episode by stating:

> when the mighty Enlighteners themselves would come out and take in the so-called Egyptian Darkness, which they find themselves obligated to banish through illumination, even by the use of thunder and lightning, the tune might get another sound, or they might perhaps be silent, which perhaps would be for the better.[44]

It is to be noted that Bishop Balle acknowledged the timeliness of reforms within the Church, but he was by no means a radical, and he felt the need to stay in touch with traditions within the Lutheran Church.[45] His flippant remark about Sandal is no surprise, but what is noteworthy in the present context is the fact that the farmers at Spjellerup were given good marks by both the bishop and the reformer. All was not 'Egyptian Darkness', and to a certain extent the learned theologians thundering from Copenhagen about the beliefs of the rural population were pushing at an open door. We should consequently be careful about following the seminal conclusions by Robert W. Scribner too closely; Scribner saw the eighteenth century as exactly the type of religious battleground that the reformers of the period envisioned themselves as entrenched in.[46] Things were much more muddled than Scribner made them seem. Not only had changes spurred by agents of the Enlightenment gained supporters in the countryside, too; all the arguments and strategies had, as we have seen in the case studies, roots going back to the Reformation in the sixteenth century.

While the sharp pens of pastors and scholars poked fun at Catholic religion and peasant beliefs, the effect of their joint efforts was

---

44 'naar vore mægtige Opklarere vilde selv komme ud og beskue det saakaldte Ægyptiske Mørke, for hvilket at bortdrive de holde sig forpligtede til at skaffe Lysning, om det end skal være ved Torden og Lynild; Saa fik vel Tonen en anden Lyd, eller man tav i det mindste stille, som maaske kunde være det tieneligste'; Christian Larsen (ed.), *Biskop Balles Visitationsindberetninger 1783–1793* (Copenhagen: Selskabet for Udgivelse af Kilder til Danmarks Historie, 2002), pp. 55–6.
45 Concerning the work and theological attitude of Bishop Balle, see the introduction to Larsen, *Biskop Balles* and the engaging L. Koch, *Biskop Nicolai Edinger Balle* (Copenhagen: Gad, 1876).
46 Robert W. Scribner, 'The Reformation, popular magic, and the "disenchantment of the world"', *Journal of Interdisciplinary History*, 23 (1993), 475–94.

probably limited. Indeed, if we look at the arguments formulated by the second half of the nineteenth century, hands-on devotion or liturgical veneration of, for instance, saints was out of the question; but the saints as exemplary individuals were still understood as an expression of the profound piety of the Middle Ages, and in particular the piety of the laity, not the clergy. What the theologians of the later decades of the 1700s mockingly defined as peasant superstition could thus in the early nineteenth century be interpreted by such extremely influential theologians as N. F. S. Grundtvig (1783–1872) as an expression of the pure, honest faith of ordinary parishioners, who were far removed from the intellectual, theological movers and shakers who came and went over time.[47] In other words, the medieval past seemingly went on offering something to the community, or filled a devotional void in the congregation, during both the eighteenth and the nineteenth centuries; some would argue that it still does.[48]

As was stated at the beginning of this chapter, the changes set in motion through the ideas and agents of the Enlightenment were regionally scattered and often driven by individuals or small groups. While my case studies have primarily dealt with the reaction against these new ideals, it should not be forgotten that in many places changes were accepted, and at times accepted eagerly. Reactions to the Enlightenment ideals were by no means uniform, which is probably why much was accepted but still more was quickly rejected. At least, the most radical ideas of change regarding the furnishing of churches and the liturgy were rapidly abandoned.[49] Today, it may be difficult to fully appreciate what the reformers of the eighteenth century saw as the perfect or model church, because most of the changes that came about during their century disappeared

---

47 Jens Rasmussen, *Vækkelser i dansk luthersk fælleskultur: Andagtsbøger og lægmandsforsamlinger (1800–1840)* (Odense: University of Southern Denmark, 2016). On Grundtvig, see Anders Holm, *Grundtvig: En introduktion* (Copenhagen: Filo, 2018), and the same author's *To Samtidige: En historisk-systematisk undersøgelse af Kierkegaards og Grundtvigs kritik af hinanden* (Århus: Aarhus University, 2007).
48 Martin Wangsgaard Jürgensen, 'Protestants and the uncomfortable sainthood', in Ivert Angel, Hallgeir Elstad and Eivor Andersen Oftestad (eds), *Were we ever Protestants? Essays in Honor of Tarald Rasmussen* (Berlin: De Gruyter, 2019), pp. 37–72.
49 For a close presentation of the primary sources, see L. Koch, *Oplysningstiden i den danske Kirke 1770–1800* (Copenhagen: Selskabet for Danmarks Kirkehistorie, 1914).

again in the 1800s. Nevertheless, it is worthwhile mentioning some of the most striking features in these reforms, as they show how different an Enlightenment vision of a church interior was from the traditional parish church with its assemblage of medieval and early modern furnishings and decorations.

How, then, did the reformers envisage their new churches without the fetters of the medieval past? As discussed in the fourth case above, there was an ambition to clear the church in order to make space for the primary functions of the Eucharist, the sermon and baptism. These changes were all quickened by a wish for liturgical reform. Not all the changes happening within the churches were directly related to the new liturgical developments, but where these ideas were implemented, changes to the layout of the building became necessary. Of the changes in the liturgy, the most important for the church interior as a whole was the wish that the pastor should conduct the service facing the congregation. Most medieval high altars had been moved up against the east wall of the chancel at some point prior to the Reformation, making it impossible for anyone to stand behind the altar and face the congregation.[50] Furthermore, altarpieces would make such a position on the part of the priest or pastor impossible in almost all churches. One of the strong reformatory voices, Peter Christian Steenvinkel (1742–1799), in his brief pamphlet *Forslag og Ønsker om en Forbedring i det udvortes af Gudstjenesten* ('Suggestions and wishes for the improvement of the outer aspects of the service') of 1785, thus argued for free-standing altars or even mobile altar tables like those found in the Calvinist tradition. This necessitated drastic changes in the furnishings of the chancel.[51] The medieval altar had to be removed along with its altar decorations and everything else blocking the line of sight, or making it difficult for the congregation to gather for the Eucharist during the service. This change was without a doubt the most important of Steenvinkel's recommendations, but other changes followed this rethinking of the chancel. He of course urged that all obsolete objects without any function should be removed from the building. The clear target was first and foremost medieval furnishings, which had no place in a modern house of worship; but he was equally critical of confessionals and memorial

---

50 Jürgensen, *Ritual*, pp. 82–90.
51 Peter Christian Steenvinkel, *Forslag og Ønsker om en Forbedring i det udvortes af Gudstjenesten* (Odense, 1785).

Figure 6.10 The cleansed, white interior of Melby Church with the pulpit from *c.* 1820, altarpiece from 1916 and pews from 1927. Photo: Arnold Mikkelsen.

tablets from the seventeenth century, along with chancel screens and other trappings belonging to prior centuries. Just as in Sweden, the ideal was a whitewashed, well-lit interior with only one interesting attempt at a sense of staging. Steenvinkel suggested that it should be possible to dim the lighting through drapes during the Eucharist in order to create a 'pious atmosphere' parallel to what he believed prevailed in the early Church. The idea that dimming the light would bring the church interior into touch with the first Christian communities is of course in highly questionable in a factual sense, but it is noteworthy that he felt the need to have something which could appeal to the senses on a mystical level, which was otherwise exactly what the reformers of the century were opposing. It is also noteworthy that Steenvinkel thereby makes the same rhetorical stride as Pontoppidan does in his *Everriculum fermenti veteris* by bridging the medieval period and attuning the contemporary Church with late Antiquity, thus suppressing everything in between.

Such reforming ideals were followed throughout the country; yet, as we have seen, in many places the changes were quickly erased during the second half of the nineteenth century.[52]

---

[52] Concerning the interplay between church owner and the Reformation of parish churches during the eighteenth century, see Ebbe Nyborg and Birgitte

On Funen, for instance, Baroness Constance Frederikke Henriette of Gyldensteen (1772–1827) had the churches in her possession altered according to some of these ideals during the first decade of the 1800s. This meant a whitening of the walls, new altarpieces (the altars in these cases not being moved) and the insertion of new, large windows along with a re-colouring of the interior in lighter shades. Once renovated, her churches must have looked strikingly different from what they presented before the changes were set in motion.[53]

An example of how this trend developed even further was the manner in which the temple architecture of Classicism filtered into the new churches during the late eighteenth century.[54] Here the idea of narrowing the focus to the few specific points in the church that were of particular importance becomes even more evident and indeed striking. At that stage, the trends discussed here had perhaps also reached a point where the effect began to alienate rather than captivate the viewer or congregation. At least, the strict ideals of Classicism never gained a proper foothold in the Danish Church, and by the middle of the nineteenth century the style was heavily censured. Christian Molbech (1783–1857), an esteemed antiquarian and scholar of the period, famously wrote in a commentary on contemporary church architecture in 1855: 'One cannot in this day and age, neither in the North nor in the South, worship God in Greek temples or live in Pompeian houses'.[55] To Molbech, the idea of a Christian service in a building shaped like the pagan temples of Antiquity was an absurdity, especially in the north. To him and many others at this time, the aesthetic ideals of Enlightenment had failed completely in the matter of church furnishing and ecclesiastical architecture, resulting in a distancing from the qualities which nurtured the piety and devotion of the congregation.

Bøggild Johannsen, 'Herregård og kirke', in John Erichsen and Mikkel Vengeborg (eds), *Herregården: Menneske, samfund, landskab, bygninger* (Copenhagen: National Museum of Denmark, 2005), pp. 241–90.

53 An example of a church with preserved furnishings inserted by Baroness Gyldensteen is Guldbjerg Church; see *Danmarks Kirker: Odense Amt*, pp. 5750–65, http://danmarkskirker.natmus.dk/uploads/tx_tcchurchsearch/Odense_5739-5772.pdf [accessed 23 February 2023].

54 Claus M. Smidt, 'Folkekirkens tid', in Hugo Johannsen and Claus M. Smidt (eds), *Danmarks Arkitektur: Kirkens huse* (Copenhagen: Gyldendal, 1981), pp. 163–97.

55 'Man vil og kan i vore Dage, hverken i Nord eller Syd, dyrke Gud i græske templer, eller boe i pompeiiske Huse'; Christian Molbech, *Anmærkninger*

Figure 6.11 The interior of Vonsild Church in Jutland. Photo: National Museum of Denmark.

The development of the Protestant confessions and the dismissal of medieval religion have often been interpreted as paving the way for the secularization of Western culture in general.[56] While this may or may not have been the case, it is worth noting how, for instance, the renewed harsh stance towards the cultic practices of the past during the eighteenth century softened in the 1800s. To the Lutherans of the late nineteenth century, romantic notions about the medieval past enabled them to be in touch with a spirituality that extended the range of devotional culture, and they facilitated the potential for the experience of an almost mystical bond across time within the community. As has been pointed out, the theologians of the Enlightenment reacted strongly against such ideas; but even in the midst of what can only be described as a clear-cut rationalistic Protestant or Lutheran dismissal of everything that was not tied to what Berndt Hamm would call the normative centre of faith,

---

over nyere Tiders Architectur særdeles i Danmark og i Kiøbenhavn, med nogle Ord om Fornyelsen af gammel Bygningsstil i Sverige (Copenhagen: Bianco Lunos Bogtrykkeri, 1855), p. 40.

56 See, for instance, Brad S. Gregory, *The Unintended Reformation: How a Religious Revolution Secularized Society* (Cambridge, MA: Harvard University Press, 2012).

Bishop Pontoppidan nonetheless states in his introduction to the *Everriculum*:

> But guard yourself from believing that we here intend to bring to light and expose to laughter all of those things, each and every one, which smack of the sourdough of either heathendom or Papism, and which would stir nausea and soon give rise to worry in every just judge of evangelical purity. There are things which a not unreasonable piety of today would argue are better covered by the cloak of love and kindness than exposed and shattered.[57]

While the presence of the medieval past within the eighteenth-century context can help us understand the degree of fluidity in religious identities beneath the surface of seemingly firmly set beliefs, we must also be aware of the process of translation that made the past available to a Lutheran present. As was noted in the case studies, authorities were keen to dismiss any 'popery' while still accepting the medieval past into their churches, often in the guise of figures of saints. What they in effect did was to 'evangelize' the past, often encapsulated in the figured saint. They discarded all previous ideas of liturgical veneration and, most importantly, cut all ties between these relics from the past and any notion of what was deemed serious religion. And because the past was retained, it kept a voice and a poetic and very 'irrational' presence which the Enlightenment, however strongly it tried, could not replace.

Conclusion

Most of the strategies for coping with the medieval past presented here testify to the fact that it could be ridiculed and devalued, but still kept its presence and seemed to offer something to the community. While the agents of Enlightenment could record with horror the religious misdemeanours of the rural population, their attempts to change the setting for religion were, in the end, unsuccessful. They could change rituals and wordings, but the actual church building in a sense resisted change. The reasons for this are manifold; but

---

[57] 'Men vogt dig for at tro, at vi have i Sinde paa dette Sted at bringe for Lyset og udsætte for Latteren alle de Ting, hver og én, som smage enten af Hedenskabts eller af Papismens Surdejg, og som hos retsindige Dommere om evangelisk Renhed snart opvække Væmmelse, snart fremkalde Bekymring. Der gives Ting, som en ikke ubesindig Fromhed for Tiden snarere mener at burde dække med Kærlighedens og Godhedens Kaabe end at burde afsløre og gennemhegle'; Pontoppidan, *Fejekost*, p. 3.

one of the most important is without a doubt what Bishop Erik Pontoppidan observed, namely that religion always borders on the irrational and mystical, no matter what words are employed to explain it. Max Weber famously wrote about the disenchantment of the world and the resilient poetic formulae employed to explain what is difficult to express.[58] In that sense one could argue that the eighteenth century began to reformulate the medieval past into a poetic symbol which came to represent ideals of devout piety and truthful, inner spirituality. This, at least, was the dialectic response to the enlightened attempts at purifying both the church buildings and religion as such during the late eighteenth century.

The Romantic movement, so closely connected to concepts of rationalism, seized upon this poetic potential in the past and emphasized it, yet never or at least only very rarely turned to actual medieval or Catholic practices within the Church. The Middle Ages were kept as a symbol, becoming a guiding light in attempts to counter the changes set in motion by the reformers of the eighteenth century. Thus, many of the church renovations executed during the late 1700s and the early 1800s lost their appeal with noteworthy speed and came to be replaced with church furnishings, colours and materials much more closely aligned with romantic notions of the past. When looking at Danish churches today, we may note that the reformers of the eighteenth century won victories and accomplished some of their aims, but in the end their project failed because ultimately the past could not be rationalized or replaced. The Middle Ages kept returning, perhaps not in exactly the same guise, but they remained a presence and are still felt when we enter most rural parish churches today.

Bibliography

Appel, Charlotte and Morten Fink-Jensen, *Når det regner på præsten: En kulturhistorie om sognepræster og sognefolk 1550–1750* (Gjern: Hovedland, 2009).

Bugge, Ragne, 'Effigiem Christi, qui transis, semper honora: verses condemning the cult of the sacred images in art and literature', *Acta ad archaeologiam et atrium historiam pertinentia*, 6 (1975), 127–39.

---

58 As Weber for instance argues in his famous lecture of 1917. Reprinted in Max Weber, *Wissenschaft als Beruf* (Berlin: Reclam, 1995; first published in 1919).

Bynum, Caroline, 'Are things "indifferent"? How objects change our understanding of religious history', *German History*, 34:1 (2016), 88–112.
Christensen, Palle O., *A Manorial World: Lord, peasants and cultural distinctions on a Danish estate 1750–1980* (Copenhagen: Scandinavian University Press, 1996).
Danmarks Kirker (Copenhagen: National Museum of Denmark, 1933–).
Danske Magazin, 1 (Copenhagen, 1745–1752).
Daxelmüller, Christoph and Marie-Louise Thomsen, 'Mittelalterliches Wallfahrtswesen in Dänemark: Mit einem Kultstätten-Katalog', *Jahrbuch für Volkskunde*, 1 (1978), 155–204.
Frederiksen, Hans Jørgen, 'Kristendom, oplysning og billedpolemik', in Ole Høiris and Thomas Ledet (eds), *Oplysningens Verden: Idé, historie, videnskab og kunst* (Aarhus: Aarhus Universitetsforlag, 2007), pp. 383–92.
——, 'Da Maria fik skæg', *ICO: Iconographisk Post*, 2 (1983), 17–29.
Fritz, Johan Michael (ed.), *Die bewahrende Kraft des Luthertums: Mittelalterliche Kunstwerke in evangelischen Kirchen* (Munich: Schnell & Steiner, 1997).
Grandt-Nielsen, Finn, *Fynsk Kirkesølv: Fynske Studier XII* (Odense: Odense Bys Museer, 1983).
Gregory, Brad S., *The Unintended Reformation: How a Religious Revolution Secularized Society* (Cambridge, MA: Harvard University Press, 2012).
Hansen, Anita, and Birgitte Bøggild Johannsen, 'Imo licet: Omkring Niels Hemmingsens billedsyn', in Peter Sjömar and others (eds), *Kirkearkeologi og kirkekunst: Studier tilegnet Sigrid og Håkon Christie* (Øvre Ervik: Akademisk förlag, 1993), pp. 181–98.
Havsteen, Sven Rune, 'Lutheran theology and artistic media: responses to the theological discourse on the visual arts', in Andrew Spicer (ed.), *Lutheran Churches in Early Modern Europe* (Farnham: Ashgate, 2012), pp. 221–40.
Heal, Bridget, '"Better Papist than Calvinist": art and identity in later Lutheran Germany', *German History*, 29 (2011), 584–609.
Henningsen, Peter, 'Det antropologiske bondebegreb', *Fortid og Nutid*, 1 (2000), 29–58.
——, 'Den rationelle bonde: en historisk-antropologisk analyse af traditionalismen i dansk bondekultur', *Historisk Tidsskrift*, 100 (2000), 329–81.
Hjorth, F. Chr., *Tanker til Eftertanke om Religion og Sæderne blandt den danske Landalmue* (Copenhagen, 1784).
Holm, Anders, *Grundtvig: En introduktion* (Copenhagen: Filo, 2018).
——, *To Samtidige: En historisk-systematisk undersøgelse af Kierkegaards og Grundtvigs kritik af hinanden* (Århus: Aarhus University, 2007).
Idum, A. R. (ed.), *Den fyenske Biskop Mester Jacob Madsens Visitatsbog* (Odense: Historisk Samfund for Odense og Assens Amter, 1929).
Jacobsen, Lis (ed.), *Peder Palladius' Danske Skrifter*, 5 vols (Copenhagen: Thiele, 1911–1926), V (1925–1926).

Jensen, Chr. Axel, 'Katolsk kirkeinventars skæbne efter Reformationen: Studier og exempler', in *Aarbøger for Nordisk Oldkyndighed og Historie* (1921), pp. 167–204.
Jensen, Mette Kristine, 'Pæn og hvid', in Eva Louise Lillie (ed.), *Danske Kalkmalerier: 1536–1700* (Copenhagen: Nationalmuseet, 1992), pp. 172–3.
Jürgensen, Martin Wangsgaard, 'Protestants and the uncomfortable sainthood', in Ivert Angel, Hallgeir Elstad and Eivor Andersen Oftestad (eds), *Were We Ever Protestants? Essays in Honor of Tarald Rasmussen* (Berlin: De Gruyter, 2019), pp. 37–72.
———, 'The rhetoric of splendour: matter and the invisible in seventeenth-century church art', *Transfiguration: Journal of Religion and the Arts* (2013/14), 163–87.
———, *Ritual and Art across the Danish Reformation: Changing Interiors of Village Churches, 1450–1600* (Turnhout: Brepols, 2018).
Kaufmann, Thomas, *Konfession und Kultur: Lutherischer Protestantismus in der zweiten Hälfte des Reformationsjahrhundert* (Tübingen: Mohr, 2006).
Koch, L., *Biskop Nicolai Edinger Balle* (Copenhagen: Gad, 1876).
———, *Oplysningstiden i den danske Kirke 1770–1800* (Copenhagen: Selskabet for Danmarks Kirkehistorie, 1914).
Kroesen, Justin, 'The survival of medieval furnishings in Lutheran churches: notes towards a comparison between Germany and Scandinavia', *ICO: Iconographisk Post*, 3–4 (2018), 4–39.
Larsen, Christian (ed.), *Biskop Balles Visitationsindberetninger 1783–1793* (Copenhagen: Selskabet for Udgivelse af Kilder til Danmarks Historie, 2002).
Michalski, Sergiusz, *The Reformation and the Visual Arts: The Protestant Image Question in Western and Eastern Europe* (London and New York: Routledge, 1993).
Molbech, Christian, *Anmærkninger over nyere Tiders Architectur særdeles i Danmark og i Kiøbenhavn, med nogle Ord om Fornyelsen af gammel Bygningsstil i Sverige* (Copenhagen: Bianco Lunos Bogtrykkeri, 1855).
Nyborg, Ebbe, and Birgitte Bøggild Johannsen, 'Herregård og kirke', in John Erichsen and Mikkel Vengeborg (eds), *Herregården: Menneske, samfund, landskab, bygninger* (Copenhagen: National Museum of Denmark, 2005), pp. 241–90.
Pontoppidan, Erik (ed.), *Den Danske Atlas eller Konge-Riget Dannemark*, 7 vols (Copenhagen, 1763–1781).
———, *Fejekost, til at udfeje den gamle surdejg eller de i de danske lande tiloversblevne og her for dagen bragte levninger af saavel hedenskab som papisme, 1736*, trans. Jørgen Olrik (Copenhagen: Schønbergske, 1923).
Poscharsky, Peter, *Die Bilder in den lutherischen Kirchen: Ikonographische Studien* (Munich: Scaneg, 1998).

Raitt, Jill, *The Colloquy of Montbéliard: Religion and Politics in the Sixteenth Century* (Oxford: Oxford University Press, 1993).
Rasmussen, Jens, *Vækkelser i dansk luthersk fælleskultur: Andagtsbøger og lægmandsforsamlinger (1800–1840)* (Odense: University of Southern Denmark, 2016).
Roling, Bernd (ed.), *Boreas Rising: Antiquarianism and National Narratives in 17th- and 18th-Century Scandinavia* (Berlin: De Gruyter, 2019).
Sandal, H. P., *En Skolelærers Undersøgelse hvor vidt Luthers Katekismus er skikket til at være Lærebog for Ungdommen* (Copenhagen, 1786).
Scribner, Robert W., 'The Reformation, popular magic, and the "disenchantment of the world"', *Journal of Interdisciplinary History*, 23 (1993), 475–94.
Sdzuj, R. B., *Adiaphora und Kunst: Studien zur Genealogie ästhetischen Denkens* (Tübingen: Max Niemeyer, 2005).
Smidt, Claus M., 'Folkekirkens tid', in Hugo Johannsen and Claus M. Smidt (eds), *Danmarks Arkitektur: Kirkens huse* (Copenhagen: Gyldendal, 1981), pp. 163–97.
Spicer, Andrew, 'Adiaphora, Luther and the material culture of worship', *Studies in Church History*, 56 (2020), 246–72.
Steenvinkel, Peter Christian, *Forslag og Ønsker om en Forbedring i det udvortes af Gudstjenesten* (Odense, 1785).
Sweet, Rosemary, 'Antiquaries and antiquities in eighteenth-century England', *Eighteenth-Century Studies*, 34:2 (2001), 181–206.
Thomas, Keith, *Religion and the Decline of Magic: Studies in Popular Beliefs in Sixteenth and Seventeenth-Century England* (London: Penguin, 2003; first published in 1971).
Trap, J. P., *Danmark*, 5th edn, 15 vols (Copenhagen: Gads, 1953–1972), VII (1963).
Wandel, Lee Palmer, *Voracious Idols and Violent Hands* (Cambridge: Cambridge University Press, 1999).
Weber, Max, *Wissenschaft als Beruf* (Berlin: Reclam, 1995; first published in 1919).

7
Saints and Enlightenment: St Erik of Sweden in eighteenth-century Swedish history-writing

Henrik Ågren

In the early modern period, the intellectual milieu of Western Europe, including Sweden, experienced two major challenges: the Reformation and the Enlightenment. Which of these made the greatest difference may be debated. Traditional views on the Enlightenment have been challenged by revisionist historians. For example, the idea that Europe experienced one uniform revolutionary turn of the intellectual climate in the eighteenth century is now disputed.[1] Especially from a Swedish perspective, it would be difficult to argue that the impact of the Enlightenment is comparable to that of the Reformation, even when it comes to intellectual history. While the Swedish Reformation brought new theological doctrines, new religious practices and a new educational and cultural landscape (the isolation from Roman Catholic universities, for example), the Enlightenment was much less dramatic.[2] The Swedish Enlightenment scholars were mostly sincere Lutherans, loyal to

---

1 Roy Porter, *Enlightenment: Britain and the Creation of the Modern World* (London: Allen Lane, 2000), p. xviii; J. G. A. Pocock, 'Historiography and enlightenment: a view of their history', *Modern Intellectual History*, 5:1 (2008), 83–96; Erik Sidenvall, 'Förnuftets och teologins kritik: ett bidrag till förståelsen av frihetstidens historieskrivning', *Historisk tidskrift*, 139:2 (2019), 223–50 (229).
2 For recent overviews of the effects of the Reformation in Sweden, see Jakob Evertsson, 'Den långsamma reformationen i Sverige: fyra exempel från Uppsala ärkestift', *Uppsala Stiftshistoriska Sällskap: Årsskrift*, 2 (2019), 5–18; Kajsa Brilkman, Morten Fink-Jensen and Hanne Sanders (eds), *Reformation i två riken: Reformationens historia och historiografi i Sverige och Danmark* (Gothenburg: Makadam, 2019). A shorter overview in English can be found in Ole Peter Grell, 'Intellectual currents', in E. I. Kouri and Jens E. Olesen (eds), *The Cambridge History of Scandinavia*, II: *1520–1870* (Cambridge: Cambridge University Press, 2016), pp. 89–100.

the Swedish government.³ Their main concern was to promote economic and moral utility, not to rebel against the authorities.⁴ It has even been suggested that Sweden never truly experienced an Enlightenment. According to this standpoint, there were definitely ideas that were similar to, and probably inspired by, those of continental and British Enlightenment scholars; but these were never particularly influential.⁵ Even if that claim may be somewhat presumptuous, it is hard to deny that the Swedish Enlightenment differed from Enlightenment in other countries. For example, an effective and rationally managed society was more important than freedom of thought, even though ideas about freedom of religion started to become more common.⁶

This chapter does not aim to argue for or against the idea of a weak Swedish Enlightenment. It does, however, claim that with regard to the attitude towards the past – more precisely, Sweden's medieval pre-Reformation era – and the domestic saints who had been venerated role models during that time, the Enlightenment did have a bigger impact on intellectual life in Sweden than the Reformation. The present chapter shows that while change in the depiction of these characters had been mild in the sixteenth and seventeenth centuries, it was much more dramatic in the eighteenth. The focus here is on King St Erik (d. 1160), who held a special position among Swedish saints. By virtue of being the sole Swedish

---

3 Nils Eriksson, *Dalin, Botin, Lagerbring: Historieforskning och historieskrivning i Sverige 1747–1787* (Gothenburg: University of Gothenburg, 1973), pp. 18–50; Sten Lindroth, *Svensk lärdomshistoria*, III: *Frihetstiden* (Stockholm: Norstedts, 1978), pp. 615–16; Jouko Nurmiainen, 'Past, present and future in eighteenth-century Swedish history writing', in Petri Karonen (ed.), *Hopes and Fears for the Future in Early Modern Sweden, 1500–1800* (Helsinki: Finnish Literature Society, 2009), pp. 291–314 (p. 294).
4 Jakob Christensson, *Lyckoriket: Studier i svensk upplysning* (Stockholm: Atlantis, 1996), pp. 48–9; Peter Hallberg, 'History and ethics in prerevolutionary Sweden', in Jóhann Páll Árnason and Björn Wittrock (eds), *Nordic Paths to Modernity* (New York: Berghahn Books, 2012), pp. 111–42 (p. 121).
5 Tore Frängsmyr, *Sökandet efter upplysningen: En essä om 1700-talets svenska kulturdebatt* (Höganäs: Wiken, 1993), pp. 183–4.
6 Lindroth, *Svensk lärdomshistoria*, p. 613; Gunnar Granberg, *Gustav III: en upplysningskonungs tro och kyrkosyn* (Uppsala: Acta Universitatis Upsaliensis, 1998), pp. 66–9; Carola Nordbäck, *Lycksalighetens källa: Kontextuella närläsningar av Anders Chydenius budordspredikningar 1781–82* (Turku: Åbo Akademis Förlag, 2009), pp. 380–4.

royal saint, he symbolized not only Christianity and the Church but also the state and the Swedish nation.

The state of history-writing in eighteenth-century Europe and Sweden

A comparison between Enlightenment-era Swedish history-writing and that of other countries reveals both significant similarities and distinguishing differences. Historical writing in Western Europe experienced considerable development throughout the entire early modern era.[7] It is, however, fair to claim that the eighteenth century brought extraordinary changes in this regard. On the basis of the scientific revolution of the seventeenth century, a new epistemological perspective affected several academic disciplines. For historical writing specifically, it meant that natural factors, rather than divine intervention, were emphasized as causes of various occurrences and changes. Growing empiricism also inspired a more critical attitude towards given facts, especially if these facts came from old or obscure sources. These new attitudes meant, among other things, that scepticism towards miracles grew as early as the end of the seventeenth century.[8] A feature that is less obviously connected to the scientific revolution, but still forms a distinctive trait in Enlightenment history-writing, has to do with the idea of a glorious past: nostalgic backward looks towards a lost golden age were replaced by developmental optimism and contempt for past eras if their values differed from those of the present. The last fact, combined with a general mistrust of ecclesiastical authorities, meant that historians in general held the Middle Ages in low esteem.[9]

There were differences between countries as well as between individuals, however. Several of the more prominent Enlightenment figures, both from Roman Catholic and from Protestant countries, held an unfavourable view of the medieval Church. Famous names in this context are Voltaire and David Hume (1711–1776), although in their cases it was not a matter of displaying specific animosity towards either Roman Catholicism or the Middle Ages; both were

---

7 Harry Elmer Barnes, *A History of Historical Writing* (Norman, OK: University of Oklahoma Press, 1938), pp. 136–7.
8 James Westfall Thompson, *A History of Historical Writing*, II: *The Eighteenth and Nineteenth Centuries* (New York: Macmillan, 1942), p. 28.
9 Barnes, *A History of Historical Writing*, p. 152.

critical of the Reformation, too.[10] Among people known primarily as historians, the picture differs somewhat. Edward Gibbon (1737–1794), who may arguably be called the main representative of eighteenth-century history-writing, entertained some understanding of, but mostly aversion against, Christianity in general and the medieval Church in particular. Among other things, he blamed Christianity for the fall of the Roman Empire.[11] William Robertson (1721–1793), Scottish Historiographer Royal, was more specific and a more loyal Protestant. He disapproved of medieval Catholicism, but viewed the Reformation as a turning point for the better in European history.[12]

This attitude was also prevalent among German history-writers, especially Lutherans, who were generally more traditional and less oppositional towards both Church and state than their French or British counterparts. They shared the contempt for the Middle Ages, but took a more favourable view of the past in general. In their opinion, history-writing did not only serve as a search for *exempla* in the past but also as a pursuit geared towards emphasizing continuity.[13] Differences between schools and individuals were present among the Germans as well. Johann Lorenz von Mosheim (1693–1755), active during the first half of the century, was in many ways a traditionalist; and although he was cautious towards sources and did not approve of early Christianity, he was not fully sceptical in his view on miracles. On the other hand, Ludwig Spittler (1752–1810), who was active during the second half of the century, was secular and had liberal sympathies, but Spittler too held the Middle Ages in low esteem.[14] The starting points of these scholars were hence different, but the outcome was the same.

The last comment may also be applied to Swedish historians during the same time. Like other Swedish Enlightenment thinkers and writers, historians were not particularly hostile towards the contemporary authorities. On the other hand, their dislike of

---

10 Barnes, *A History of Historical Writing*, pp. 154–6.
11 Barnes, *A History of Historical Writing*, pp. 159–61; Donald R. Kelley, *Faces of History: Historical Inquiry from Herodotus to Herder* (New Haven, CT: Yale University Press, 1998), p. 231.
12 Barnes, *A History of Historical Writing*, pp. 156–7.
13 Thompson, *A History of Historical Writing*, pp. 103, 126; Kelley, *Faces of History*, p. 244.
14 Thompson, *A History of Historical Writing*, pp. 120–4.

Saints and Enlightenment: St Erik of Sweden 195

Roman Catholicism and the Middle Ages is well known, and it was embraced by both orthodox traditionalists and more profiled Enlightenment thinkers.[15]

The best-known representatives of these views were all active during the middle and/or second half of the century: professional historians like Professor Sven Lagerbring (1707–1787) or royal historiographers Olof von Dalin and Anders Schönberg the younger (1737–1811); publishers like Carl Christopher Gjörwell (1731–1811) or top civil servants like Anders af Botin (1724–1790). Most of these people combined a critical method with suspiciousness of or disdain for older times, especially the Middle Ages. Even so, they were also generally loyal to the leaders and values of the society they lived in.[16] Another important trait found in this time's history-writing was that its intended audience became broader: history books were not only written for other scholars or for men of the state, but also for people in general. Among other things, that wider audience meant that more books, and books by less well-known authors, were published.[17]

The earliest decades of the eighteenth century have attracted less attention from modern historians than those of its second half. That does not, however, mean that no important works on history were published during this period, or that it did not bring certain changes. Both international and domestic factors affected history-writing at that time. The sceptical attitude towards the notion of divine intervention in history that is seen internationally at the end of the seventeenth century may be observed in Sweden as well at approximately the same time.[18] Domestically, Sweden's loss of its position as the great power of Northern Europe in the 1710s also meant that a new and more modest attitude came to characterize history-writing. Representatives of this school include the Swedish archbishop Erik Benzelius the younger (1675–1743) and the history

---

15 Tore Frängsmyr, *Svensk idéhistoria: Bildning och vetenskap under tusen år*, I: *1000–1809* (Stockholm: Natur och kultur, 2004), pp. 327–9. See also Eriksson, *Dalin, Botin, Lagerbring*, pp. 22–44.
16 See Eriksson, *Dalin, Botin, Lagerbring* for a good overview.
17 Carl Arvid Hessler, '"Aristokratfördömandet": En riktning i svensk historieskrivning', *Scandia*, 15 (1943), 209–66 (212); Hallberg, 'History and ethics', p. 134.
18 Henrik Ågren, *Erik den helige – landsfader eller beläte? En rikspatrons öde i svensk historieskrivning från reformationen till och med upplysningen* (Lund: Sekel, 2012), p. 269.

professor Jacob Wilde (1679–1755).[19] Other prominent historians from this era were, among others, the antiquarian Johan Peringskiöld (1654–1720) and the church historian Claudius Örnhjelm (1627–1695). Even though they did not embrace the new view of history to any remarkable degree, it can still be traced in their works.[20] What that meant for the presentation of Sweden's medieval royal saint will be shown after something has been said about the saint himself.

Historical background

St Erik's regency is mainly known through his legend, which may have been written as late as a century after his death. It is therefore of questionable source value for information about Erik's own life.[21] That problem is not of any great concern for this study, though. What is important is that in early modern Sweden the legend was believed to be reasonably accurate, and that it served as a base for all history-writing about St Erik. On the basis of that source, Erik was a pious, just and good king, who promoted both the Church and the realm and took good care of his people. Among his most prominent deeds was a crusade to Finland, where he christened the Finns and brought their lands under the Swedish Crown. His personal life was distinguished by his good character, manifested in fasting and sexual abstinence, generosity with alms and moderation with taxes, and the like. King Erik's death was the tragic result of an attack by his rival for the throne Magnus Henriksen when he was celebrating mass in Uppsala; after he was killed, miracles occurred at that site.[22]

St Erik's cult was never extensive, and it is possible that he was more important as a political symbol for the Swedish government than as a symbol for the Church, even before the Reformation.[23]

---

19 Urpilainen, Erkki, 'Algot Scarin och historievetenskapen i början av 1700-talet', *Historisk tidskrift för Finland*, 76 (1991), 347–57 (347).
20 Ågren, *Erik den helige*, pp. 272–73.
21 Ågren, *Erik den helige*, p. 69.
22 Bengt Thordeman (ed.), 'Erik den heliges legend på latin, fornsvenska och modern svenska' (written c. 1270), in *Erik den helige: Historia. Kult. Reliker* (Stockholm: Nordisk rotogravyr, 1954), pp. xviii–xx.
23 Biörn Tjällén, *Church and Nation: The Discourse on Authority in Ericus Olai's Regni Gothorum (c. 1471)* (Stockholm: Stockholm University, 2007), p. 81; Sara Ellis Nilsson, *Creating Holy People and Places on the Periphery: A Study of the Emergence of Cults of Native Saints in the Ecclesiastical*

Nevertheless, as a saint, his name and person were connected to Catholic Christianity. It is therefore reasonable to presume that Protestant historians would have presented an unfavourable picture of Erik, or at least marked some distance from him. He could, in theory, have been used as an example of the evils inherent in the old system.

Anyone looking for such judgements in Reformation-era Swedish history-writing will be disappointed, though. Throughout the sixteenth century, and most of the seventeenth, St Erik was still described as a role model for both kings and Christians in general. His rule and general characteristics were as praiseworthy as his piety.[24] The only major difference compared to Roman Catholic Swedish history-writing was that the more obvious medieval Catholic traits of his faith were consistently omitted or markedly toned down. Giving alms was described as a sign of good character, mortification or fasting were viewed as signs of an ascetic temperament, and so on.[25] This indicates that the early Protestant historians were not unaware of the problems associated with Erik, on the contrary. The fact that they passed by these qualities in presentations that were otherwise both detailed and true to earlier history-writing shows not only that medieval Catholic customs were thought to be embarrassing, but also that Erik still possessed a function as a role model whose memory needed to be protected. Harmony between past and present was the main concern in this history-writing, not conflict between what was considered to be right or wrong.

Changes during the Enlightenment era

All this began to change rather suddenly at a specific point in time, namely 1689. The year before, Samuel Pufendorf (1632–1694) had published his *Inledning till svenska historien* ('Introduction to Swedish history') in which the traditional picture of Erik was provided: completely laudatory, and faithful to earlier sources.[26] Now, however, in Claudius Örnhjelm's *Historia Sveonum Gothorumque*

Provinces of Lund and Uppsala from the Eleventh to the Thirteenth Centuries (Gothenburg: University of Gothenburg, 2015); Christian Oertel, *The Cult of St Erik in Medieval Sweden: Veneration of a Christian Saint, Twelfth–Sixteenth centuries* (Turnhout: Brepols, 2016), p. 7.

24 Ågren, *Erik den helige*, p. 5.
25 Ågren, *Erik den helige*, pp. 152, 158.
26 Samuel von Pufendorf, *Inledning till svenska historien* (Stockholm: Johann Eberdt, 1688), pp. 75–7.

Ecclesiastica ... ('Swedish church history'), hints of criticism were starting to permeate the narrative. For example, Örnhjelm states that Erik was not a better king than most of his contemporaries.[27] This is of course not criticism in and of itself, and it was hardly voiced as such either. However, the statement is noteworthy for two reasons. One is that Erik was no longer necessarily seen as a particularly glorious regent, rather one among many. A more nuanced characterization than previous accounts had provided was presented. The other is that Örnhjelm was also questioning the known facts about Erik. With a few exceptions, particularly during the middle of the Reformation era, previous history-writing had mostly been reproducing a one-sided, glorifying picture.[28]

From this modest beginning, a drastic change in the descriptions of St Erik took place over the course of the eighteenth century. Even though a mainly favourable picture survived the entire period, a detached attitude, a degree of scepticism and even criticism became more common and more explicit, too. Before the different aspects of this change are presented, a brief overview of the development is in order.

Looking at history-writing several decades into the eighteenth century, any critique of Erik was still rare. When it did occur, it was never aimed at his general character, which was still praised. Instead, only particular traits or deeds were questioned, often in an almost sympathetic way. Some authors, for example, argued that Erik should have been more cautious when he received news that Magnus Henriksen's superior army was approaching.[29] Others presented the opinion that while the crusade against the Finns was justified, maybe it should have been less violent.[30] To the extent that open criticism was voiced, it was aimed at the miracles and the cult connected to the dead saint, not at the living king. Especially, the people who had believed in and spread these stories – in other words, priests and monks of the medieval Church – were ridiculed.[31]

---

27 Claudius Örnhjelm, *Historia Sveonum Gothorumque Ecclesiastica ...* (Stockholm: Nicolaus Wankivius, 1689), p. 480.
28 For one of the exceptions, see Laurentius Petri, 'Svenska Chrönika', in Eric Michael Fant, Erik Gustaf Geijer and Johan Henrik Schröder (eds), *Scriptores rerum Svecicarum Medii Aevi*, 3 vols (Uppsala: Palmblad et soc., 1818–1876), (written *c.* 1560), II:b (1828), pp. 1–160 (p. 64).
29 Örnhjelm, *Historia Sveonum*, p. 474; Haquin Spegel, *Then svenska kyrkiohistorian*, 2 vols (Linköping: Kempe, 1707–8), II (1708), p. 15.
30 Stockholm, Kungliga biblioteket (KB), D-collection 385, p. 27.
31 Uppsala universitetsbibliotek (UUB), Nordin collection 766, p. 41; KB, Engeström collection B.III.1.39, pp. 39, 92, 202.

Saints and Enlightenment: St Erik of Sweden 199

Three observations may be made on the basis of these facts. One is that such criticism against Erik as was expressed was either mild and nuanced or indirect. Another is that the criticism was mainly aimed at aspects of Erik that can be labelled religious or even Roman Catholic: crusades, choosing mass over defence, miracles, as well as the cult that emerged after his death.[32] Erik's general traits and his worldly deeds were still praised. Finally, the circumstances recapitulated in the preceding paragraph show that scepticism towards the credibility of earlier traditions and history-writing was an alternative to hostility or ridicule. That attitude may stem from a change in epistemological values rather than in theological ones, but the effect was the same. Scepticism of this kind is a significant component in Enlightenment mentality, but in this case it encompasses an evident anti-Catholic or anti-medieval angle.

In the second half of the eighteenth century, attitudes towards St Erik continued to deteriorate. In more ways than one, the criticism became less restrained and limited. The dominating sentiment was still one of approval, but an increasing number of scholars interpreted a larger part of Erik's story in a negative way, and they were more explicit in their judgements. The main difference was that Erik was now (occasionally) criticized for his general persona and not only for traits or deeds with particularly Roman Catholic connotations. For example, the Finnish expedition was now not only criticized on the grounds that it was wrong to spread Christianity through war, but also that the accepted reason behind the attack on Finland – Finnish piracy against Swedish coasts – did not excuse the brutality committed by Erik's forces.[33] In other cases, Erik was described as a well-meaning and good-natured person, but also as weak and perhaps not too bright.[34] Even though such statements were rare, they do show that opinions were changing. What these changes consisted of in detail, and how they can be interpreted, will be examined below.

---

32 Protestants did not deny the possibility of miracles; but they were generally suspicious of non-biblical ones, especially if they were of medieval origin. See Ralph Del Colle, 'Miracles in Christianity', in Graham H. Twelftree (ed.), *The Cambridge Companion to Miracles* (Cambridge: Cambridge University Press, 2011), pp. 235–53 (p. 241); Sidenvall, 'Förnuftets och teologins kritik', 245.

33 [Fredrik Conrad Broman], *Anteckningar uti svenska kyrkohistorien* (Stockholm: A. J. Nordström, 1782), p. 54.

34 Anders af Botin, *Utkast till svenska folkets historia*, 4 vols (Stockholm: Lars Salvius, 1757–1764), IV (1764), p. 162.

Categories of criticism

Criticism against Erik may be roughly categorized into three – not mutually exclusive – categories. The first has already been touched upon and is probably the most obvious: Protestant criticism. It was also the most common type, especially during the first half of the eighteenth century. This kind of criticism manifested itself in condemnation of, or sometimes a sense of distance or scepticism towards, details which Swedish scholars of the time perceived as particularly Roman Catholic. Among these were miracles and the Erik cult, as mentioned above, but there were other aspects as well. To begin with, Erik's personal life included practices that were unseemly from a Protestant point of view. For example, Claudius Örnhjelm and Sven Lagerbring were of the opinion that wearing a horsehair shirt was a vain attempt to appear pious.[35] Anders af Botin was even more hostile. He referred to mortification as the 'at these times often practised external sermon' and went on to condemn other types of religious practices of a physical nature: extensive prayers, waking, fasting, cold baths and sexual abstinence, the last being in conflict with 'the voice of nature', 'marital duty' and 'legitimate needs'.[36] As we can see, af Botin thought Erik's religious practices perverted. He did not explicitly mention medieval Catholic faith; but the fact that he placed the practices in the past ('at these times') is a clear hint that this is what he had in mind. So is the fact that one important component of Protestant criticism against Roman Catholicism was that it was too fixated on ceremonies, practices and material aspects of faith, and less so on spiritual (or internal, to paraphrase af Botin) aspects.

While we may not agree with af Botin's and other Swedish eighteenth-century historians' harsh comments, or even accept that fasting and so on are defining aspects of Roman Catholic faith, it is easy to recognize their criticism as a typical Protestant attack on medieval Catholicism, in the same manner as antipathy against the Erik cult or the scepticism towards miracles mentioned above. There are, however, certain other aspects of Erik's life which are not as obviously Catholic in character but were still viewed as such among

---

35 Örnhjelm, *Historia Sveonum*, p. 465; KB, D-collection 385, pp. 275–76.
36 Anders af Botin, *Svenska folkets historia*, 2 vols (Stockholm: Johan A. Carlbohm, 1789– 1792), II (1792), p. 58.

Saints and Enlightenment: St Erik of Sweden 201

eighteenth-century historians. One is the crusade against Finland. Early modern Protestants were not against religious war or defending the faith by violence as such. The Thirty Years' War is one of many examples of that. This may also be one reason why seventeenth-century historians had been so favourably disposed towards Erik's Finnish campaign. During the eighteenth century, however, there were many examples of historians who disapproved of the crusade, which they thought excessive and morally questionable. Their opinion was often expressed as attacks on the Pope and his priests, who were said to have instigated the attack on the Finns.[37]

Other examples of the changing attitude towards St Erik are found in passages dealing with his concern for the state of Christianity in his realm. Two efforts of his were, and had always been, emphasized: one was Erik's commission of ecclesiastical buildings and the other his support for priests. Both might seem praiseworthy even from a Protestant point of view. However, they also contained aspects that were problematic. Erecting or maintaining churches was not, and had never been, frowned upon by Protestants. Stories about how Erik founded monasteries raised another question, though. That pursuit clearly belonged within the field of Catholic Christianity. Therefore, it is a little surprising to notice that even though no one commended Erik for such actions, criticism of or distancing from them was restrained during the entire eighteenth century. Some scholars doubted that Erik had actually been involved in setting up monasteries at all.[38] Others argued that the idea behind monasteries was good – they were meant to be institutions for education – and that founders could not be held accountable if a monastery was used to 'support and feed a crowd of useless and pernicious people'.[39] From this perspective, Erik was protected even by eighteenth-century scholars. However, the fact that they admitted that some details in the stories about him were problematic was a novelty. Seventeenth-century Protestant historians had passed over these details in silence.[40]

---

37 Olof von Dalin, *Svea rikes historia ifrån dess begynnelse till våra tider*, 4 vols (Stockholm: Lars Salvius, 1747–1761), II (1750), p. 106; Sven Lagerbring, *Svea rikes historia ifrån de äldsta tider till de närvarande*, 5 vols (Stockholm: Carl Stolpe, 1769–1987), II (1773), p. 155; Botin, *Svenska folkets historia*, p. 54.
38 Lagerbring, *Svea rikes historia*, p. 160.
39 [Nils Erik Lundström], *Kärnan av Svea rikes historia*, 2 vols (Stockholm: Peter Hesselberg, 1760), II (1760), p. 388.
40 Ågren, *Erik den helige*, p. 137.

The attitude towards Erik's relation to the clergy was similar. The claim that he had taken specific care of priests and monks and given them particular privileges had not normally been mentioned in seventeenth-century works.[41] In the eighteenth century, though, that claim began to appear. Often it was simply mentioned without comment, especially in the early decades.[42] Sometimes, however, an author clearly stated that the King's benevolence towards men of the cloth affected Sweden in a bad way. Some of these authors mainly put the blame on the clergy's schemes to trick Erik, and other early medieval Swedish kings, into giving them more power.[43] Other writers were more frank and claimed that Erik deliberately gave the clergy too much influence, as a consequence of his misguided views on piety and Christian values. Common points in this criticism are that the inheritance laws became too Church-friendly, and that Rome and the Pope were given too much influence over Sweden.[44] In other words, the criticism clearly had Protestant features, in these cases also with a hint of nationalism.[45]

Protestant dogma was obviously an important part of the negative sentiments towards St Erik. However, it was not the only or even primary reason why he was being re-evaluated. If that had been the case, the change would have occurred sooner, during the Reformation. Furthermore, in many of the examples mentioned above, viewpoints other than Protestant ones are discernible.

One such viewpoint may be called rational. What is and what is not rational is, of course, debatable. In the present case, the term

---

41 Ågren, *Erik den helige*, p. 141.
42 Johan Peringskiöld, *Monumenta Ullerakerensia cum Upsala Nova Illustrata eller Ulleråkers härads minningsmärken med nya Uppsala* (Stockholm: Horn, 1719), p. 48; Jacob Wilde, *Sueciae Historia Pragmatica* (Stockholm: Gercken, 1731), p. 341; KB, D-collection 356:1, p. 96.
43 Dalin, *Svea rikes historia*, p. 109; [Lundström], *Kärnan av Svea rikes historia*, pp. 400–1; Anders Schönberg, *Anders Schönbergs historiska brev om det svenska regeringssättet i äldre och nyare tider*, I (Stockholm: P. A. Norstedt, 1849 [1778]), pp. 37, 140.
44 Botin, *Utkast till svenska folkets historia*, p. 163; [Samuel Loenbom], *Kort inledning till svenska historien och statskunskapen* (Stockholm: Kungl. tryckeriet, 1768), p. 24; Christian Wåhlin, *Fäderneslandets historia för begynnare* (Lund: Johan Lundblad, 1791), p. 33.
45 Several early modern Protestant countries used anti-Catholicism to build national identity; see Pasi Ihalainen, *Protestant Nations Redefined: Changing Perceptions of National Identity in the Rhetoric of the English, Dutch and Swedish Public Churches, 1685–1772* (Leiden: Brill, 2005), p. 5.

is used to describe how eighteenth-century historians viewed themselves. These historians sometimes based their criticism of Erik and his time on the assumption that he and the Middle Ages were inherently irrational, whereas they themselves and the eighteenth century were rational. More precisely, this means that these men presented a picture in which people in the Middle Ages were prone to believe in preposterous stories about extraordinary occurrences, whereas they themselves had a more sceptical and down-to-earth mindset.

The most common example of the rational attitude on the part of eighteenth-century historians is the dismissal of medieval miracles as manifestations of misconceptions that modern people were too enlightened to believe in, at least in Sweden. An early representative of that view, Örnhjelm claimed that these miracles were fabricated, and he emphasized that belief in them belonged to times past.[46] Similar opinions were expressed throughout the century. The Erik miracles were called 'unsavoury and made up',[47] 'only trumped up by monks to fool common people into parting with their money',[48] or 'so great, so many and so childish that they lacked nothing except maybe truth and decency'.[49] The canonization was 'a foolish arrangement',[50] typical of 'that superstitious era'.[51] It is obvious that while earlier Protestant historians had tried to play down the differences between the present and the past, these differences were now put forward and used to emphasize the distinction between an older, superstitious era and the sound – or enlightened – eighteenth century.

This censorious attitude was expressed during the entire time period. The quotations above were not aimed at Erik as a person, though they do point in the same direction as the overt judgements of him in the second half of the century. One of the kinder judgements was that Erik's faith seems to have been honest 'although mixed with false belief'.[52] Other historians were less understanding. Anders af Botin, in his criticism of Erik's sexual abstinence, claimed that

---

46 Örnhjelm, *Historia Sveonum*, p. 480.
47 KB, Engeström collection B.III.1.39, p. 92.
48 KB, F-collection m16:1, c. 5.
49 Botin, *Utkast till svenska folkets historia*, p. 165.
50 Lagerbring, *Svea rikes historia*, p. 163.
51 [Loenbom], *Kort inledning*, p. 24.
52 Jöran Jakob Thomæus, *Sveriges historia uti kort sammandrag för den spädare ungdomen* (Kristianstad: F.F. Cedergréen, 1812), p. 15.

it was 'false belief and superstition'[53] that made him go against his conjugal duty and the voice of nature. Obviously, af Botin was of the opinion that he himself and people of his time had a better understanding of twelfth-century people's real needs than a saintly king from their own era.

This brings us to the last aspect of the Enlightenment alienation from St Erik and the Middle Ages. One way of interpreting the quotation from af Botin is that he was of the opinion that the biological urges of human beings were more important than spirituality. Of course, it could just be a manifestation of the common opinion that it was medieval piousness in particular that was flawed. However, other statements make it clear that secularism was another aspect of the increasingly unfavourable sentiments towards Erik and the Middle Ages. This dimension comes out in different contexts. One is the story about Erik's last stand. Several historians stated that he should have thought more about survival than about the spiritual values he honoured by staying in the church before facing his opponents. Among these historians, the most interesting example is Carl Christopher Gjörwell, who calls Erik's action an expression of 'excessive godliness, which we now call superstition'.[54] For Gjörwell, not only the nature of Erik's faith but also its intensity qualified as superstition. In the previously mentioned examples, both the criticism as such and the word 'superstition' alluded to a certain kind of belief, a belief that is Roman Catholic and medieval in character. In this case, no such specification is made. The problem was simply that Erik cared too much for religion. It seems that in Enlightenment-era Sweden, it was possible to be *too* Christian. Such comments might be expected from modern authors; but in still officially Christian eighteenth-century Sweden, they are somewhat surprising. From a Christian perspective, whether Catholic or Protestant, it could actually be argued that it was more rational to prepare your soul just before a battle than to prepare your forces.

Such secular sentiments can also be found in comments on other parts of St Erik's life. Sometimes they are specifically aimed at Roman Catholicism, as when the schoolbook author Christian Wåhlin (1761–1829) stated that Erik 'resembled or rather surpassed

---

53 Botin, *Svenska folkets historia*, p. 58.
54 Carl Christopher Gjörwell, *Caracteren av Sveriges regenter alltifrån överdrotten Oden till Konung Gustaf III* (Stockholm: Johan A. Carlbohm, 1793), p. 210. See also Lagerbring, *Svea rikes historia*, p. 161 and note 29 above.

the monks in religious fervour'.[55] More often the criticism was less specific and focused more on worldly than celestial ideals, without explicit digs at Roman Catholic faith. One example which is probably anti-Catholic, but definitely secular, concerns the established fact that Erik cared much about his subjects' material well-being. To begin with, he was said to be generous with alms to the poor. Furthermore, he also refused to accept revenues from his subjects. Some versions of this story concern taxes; others involve fines and still others are concerned with voluntary gifts. In any case, Erik's refusal was almost always presented as an example of his good character as a king. Quite often it was omitted or toned down by Protestant historians. This can be explained by the fact that a king who refused taxes was a sensitive subject in almost any feudal society, especially one as dependent on domestic incomes as Sweden in the early modern era.[56] Even so, there are a few cases where authors took up another standpoint. Two of them come from Anders af Botin, who opined that refusal to accept fines encouraged criminals and that generosity with alms filled the country with idlers.[57] Another comes from a handwritten chronicle by an essentially unknown author named Johan Hermansson. He comments that refusal of taxes accustomed people to not paying.[58] To be sure, these examples are few; but if compared to some of the more approving comments on the same stories, they paradoxically display the same values. Several historians interpreted Erik's reluctance to accept taxes as a sign that he knew how to manage his resources well. They also commented that a prosperous population was the base for a thriving country.[59] Even though these comments represent more or less the opposite viewpoint from that of Hermansson and af Botin, they were born from the same value system. In these situations, St Erik's deeds are judged on the basis of the general consequences for society, more specifically its economic gains. Consequently, they show not only a secular but even a mercantilist attitude. Concern about the wealth of the nation was typical of the Swedish Enlightenment, a feature which manifested itself in different ways.

---

55 Wåhlin, *Fäderneslandets historia*, p. 21.
56 Ågren, *Erik den helige*, p. 131.
57 Botin, *Utkast till svenska folkets historia*, pp. 163–4.
58 UUB, Nordin collection 775, p. 34.
59 KB, F-collection, e13A [1.], no page; Lagerbring, *Svea rikes historia*, p. 154; Gjörwell, *Caracteren av Sveriges*, p. 210.

If concern for Sweden's economic prosperity sometimes resulted in eighteenth-century historians being less concerned about the well-being of their compatriots than their predecessors, there is one instance where they acted in a more soft-hearted manner. As mentioned above, there was growing criticism of Erik's actions in Finland. To some extent that criticism was based on a Protestant world view, as stated above, but also on a more secular one. Fighting against heathens was no longer an excuse for the use of excessive violence; that practice was said to belong to a cruel and uncivilized past.[60] Still, it is worth noticing that Protestant historians from earlier centuries did not object to Erik's violent methods against the Finns. There are also comments from the eighteenth century that make it clear that conversion by force was generally condemned. A greater concern for people's lives than for their souls was becoming apparent, and starting wars on religious grounds was now regarded as, generally speaking, reprehensible.[61] The most remarkable expression of this sentiment was once again made by Anders af Botin. According to the older historiography, Erik had displayed the goodness of his heart by crying over the dead Finns whose souls, he believed, were now in hell, when they could have been blessed if they had willingly accepted the Christian faith. Instead, af Botin made this reflection: 'Surely, Erik expressed regret at the condemnation of so many souls, but absolutely no concern over the loss of so many innocent lives.'[62] In this quotation, secularism approaches atheism. Of course, the statement in itself is not a denial of the existence of a deity. However, the consequence of investing as much concern in earthly life as in eternal fate does come close to such a position, and af Botin's well-known criticism of medieval Christianity has a general reputation of being more than just Protestant.[63] Even if the author himself would not have agreed with that interpretation, it is at least clear that negative feelings towards St Erik and his piety were more than merely an expression of Lutheran anti-Catholicism.

---

60 KB, D-collection 356:1, pp. 95–6; [Broman], *Anteckningar uti svenska*, p. 54 and the following notes.
61 UUB, E-collection 61, no page; KB, D-collection 385, p. 272; Lagerbring, *Svea rikes historia*, p. 155.
62 Botin, *Svenska folkets historia*, p. 55.
63 B—lk, 'Recension', *Skandia: Tidskrift för vetenskap och konst*, 4 (1834), 313–451 (321) and repeated among others by Eriksson, *Dalin, Botin, Lagerbring*, p. 31.

On the other hand, such anti-Catholicism was indeed present in most of the criticism levelled at Erik. Deeds and traits that were, in one way or another, associated with medieval Catholic Christianity inspired most of the disapproving comments: miracles, the cult of a saint, crusades, monasteries and their inhabitants, independent priests, or fasting, self-mortification and alms. By clearly stating that these phenomena were typical of a past, superstitious and less-developed period, Enlightenment-era historians managed to simultaneously criticize a competing faith system and mark their own time as civilized and rational.[64] Taken altogether, whether the arguments were Protestant, rational, secular or a mixture of all these, they all expressed Enlightenment attitudes. The entire century was characterized by an idea of development, where – unlike in the sixteenth and seventeenth centuries – differences from earlier epochs were emphasized, not similarities. Previous research has observed a profound optimism with regard to development among some of the more influential Swedish eighteenth-century historians, something that fits well with this conclusion.[65] The eighteenth century differs more from the sixteenth and seventeenth centuries in respect of attitudes towards the Middle Ages than those centuries do from the view that the Middle Ages had of their own era. In other words: the Enlightenment had a bigger impact than the Reformation with regard to the re-evaluation of Sweden's Catholic past.

Bibliography

Archival sources

Stockholm

Kungliga biblioteket (KB)
  D-collection, 356:1, 'Wallwiks anmärkningar ur svenska historien' [1769]
  ———, 385, Sven Bring (Lagerbring): 'Föreläsningar över Doct Erich Benzelii collegium i svenska historien …' 1749
  Engeström collection, B.III.1.39, Gustaf Benzelstierna: 'Historisk avhandling om konung Erik den helige' s. a.
  F-collection, e13A [1.], Niklas Keder: 'Imagines Regum Priscorum Suecia ex Antiquis …' s. a.

---

64 This has also been noted by Sidenvall.
65 Barnes, *A History of Historical Writing*, p. 148; Eriksson, *Dalin, Botin, Lagerbring*, p. 208.

———, m16:1, Fabian Törner: 'Collegium de Antiqvitatibus Sveogothias ...'
s. a.

Uppsala, Sweden

Uppsala universitetsbibliotek (UUB)
E-collection, 61, 'Prof. Fabiani Törners observationes in historiam' [1710]
Nordin collection, 766, Fabian Törner: 'Historia regum regni Sueciae in Collegio private ...' 1700
———, 775, Johan Hermansson: 'Collegium i svensk historia' s. a.

Printed sources and literature

Ågren, Henrik, *Erik den helige – landsfader eller beläte? En rikspatrons öde i svensk historieskrivning från reformationen till och med upplysningen* (Lund: Sekel, 2012).
B—lk, 'Recension', *Skandia: Tidskrift för vetenskap och konst*, 4 (1834), 313–451.
Barnes, Harry Elmer, *A History of Historical Writing* (Norman, OK: University of Oklahoma Press, 1938).
Botin, Anders af, *Utkast till svenska folkets historia*, 4 vols (Stockholm: Lars Salvius, 1757–1764), IV (1764).
———, *Svenska folkets historia*, 2 vols (Stockholm: Johan A. Carlbohm, 1789– 1792), II (1792).
Brilkman, Kajsa, Morten Fink-Jensen and Hanne Sanders (eds), *Reformation i två riken: Reformationens historia och historiografi i Sverige och Danmark* (Gothenburg: Makadam, 2019).
[Broman, Fredrik Conrad], *Anteckningar uti svenska kyrkohistorien* (Stockholm: A. J. Nordström, 1782).
Christensson, Jakob, *Lyckoriket: Studier i svensk upplysning* (Stockholm: Atlantis, 1996).
Dalin, Olof von, *Svea rikes historia ifrån dess begynnelse till våra tider*, 4 vols (Stockholm: Lars Salvius, 1747–1761), II (1750).
Del Colle, Ralph, 'Miracles in Christianity', in Graham H. Twelftree (ed.), *The Cambridge Companion to Miracles* (Cambridge: Cambridge University Press, 2011), pp. 235–53.
Ellis Nilsson, Sara, *Creating Holy People and Places on the Periphery: A Study of the Emergence of Cults of Native Saints in the Ecclesiastical Provinces of Lund and Uppsala from the Eleventh to the Thirteenth Centuries* (Gothenburg: University of Gothenburg, 2015).
Eriksson, Nils, *Dalin, Botin, Lagerbring: Historieforskning och historieskrivning i Sverige 1747–1787* (Gothenburg: University of Gothenburg, 1973).
Evertsson, Jakob, 'Den långsamma reformationen i Sverige: fyra exempel från Uppsala ärkestift', *Uppsala Stiftshistoriska Sällskap: Årsskrift*, 2 (2019), 5–18.

Saints and Enlightenment: St Erik of Sweden 209

Frängsmyr, Tore, *Svensk idéhistoria: Bildning och vetenskap under tusen år*, I: *1000–1809* (Stockholm: Natur och kultur, 2004).
——, *Sökandet efter upplysningen: En essä om 1700-talets svenska kulturdebatt* (Höganäs: Wiken, 1993).
Gjörwell, Carl Christopher, *Caracteren av Sveriges regenter alltifrån överdrotten Oden till Konung Gustaf III* (Stockholm: Johan A. Carlbohm, 1793).
Granberg, Gunnar, *Gustav III: en upplysningskonungs tro och kyrkosyn* (Uppsala: Acta Universitatis Upsaliensis, 1998).
Grell, Ole Peter, 'Intellectual currents', in E. I. Kouri and Jens E. Olesen (eds), *The Cambridge History of Scandinavia*, II: *1520–1870* (Cambridge: Cambridge University Press, 2016), pp. 89–100.
Hallberg, Peter, 'History and ethics in pre-revolutionary Sweden', in Jóhann Páll Árnason and Björn Wittrock (eds), *Nordic Paths to Modernity* (New York: Berghahn Books, 2012), pp. 111–42.
Hessler, Carl Arvid, '"Aristokratfördömandet": En riktning i svensk historieskrivning', *Scandia*, 15 (1943), 209–66.
Ihalainen, Pasi, *Protestant Nations Redefined: Changing Perceptions of National Identity in the Rhetoric of the English, Dutch and Swedish Public Churches, 1685–1772* (Leiden: Brill, 2005).
Kelley, Donald R., *Faces of History: Historical Inquiry from Herodotus to Herder* (New Haven, CT: Yale University Press, 1998).
Lagerbring, Sven, *Svea rikes historia ifrån de äldsta tider till de närvarande*, 5 vols (Stockholm: Carl Stolpe, 1769–1787), II (1773).
Lindroth, Sten, *Svensk lärdomshistoria*, III: *Frihetstiden* (Stockholm: Norstedts, 1978).
[Loenbom, Samuel], *Kort inledning till svenska historien och statskunskapen* (Stockholm: Kungl. tryckeriet, 1768).
[Lundström, Nils Erik], *Kärnan av Svea rikes historia*, 2 vols (Stockholm: Peter Hesselberg, 1760), II (1760).
Nordbäck, Carola, *Lycksalighetens källa: Kontextuella närläsningar av Anders Chydenius budordspredikningar 1781–82* (Turku: Åbo Akademis Förlag, 2009).
Nurmiainen, Jouko, 'Past, present and future in eighteenth-century Swedish history writing', in Petri Karonen (ed.), *Hopes and Fears for the Future in Early Modern Sweden, 1500–1800* (Helsinki: Finnish Literature Society, 2009), pp. 291–314.
Oertel, Christian, *The Cult of St Erik in Medieval Sweden: Veneration of a Christian Saint, Twelfth–Sixteenth centuries* (Turnhout: Brepols, 2016).
Örnhjelm, Claudius, *Historia Sveonum Gothorumque Ecclesiastica ...* (Stockholm: Nicolaus Wankivius, 1689).
Peringskiöld, Johan, *Monumenta Ullerakerensia cum Upsala Nova Illustrata eller Ulleråkers härads minningsmärken med nya Uppsala* (Stockholm: Horn, 1719).
Petri, Laurentius, 'Svenska Chrönika', in Eric Michael Fant, Erik Gustaf Geijer and Johan Henrik Schröder (eds), *Scriptores rerum Svecicarum*

Medii Aevi, 3 vols (Uppsala: Palmblad et soc., 1818–1876), (written *c.* 1560), II:b (1828), pp. 1–160.

Pocock, J. G. A., 'Historiography and enlightenment: a view of their history', *Modern Intellectual History*, 5:1 (2008), 83–96.

Porter, Roy, *Enlightenment: Britain and the Creation of the Modern World* (London: Allen Lane, 2000).

Pufendorf, Samuel von, *Inledning till svenska historien* (Stockholm: Johann Eberdt, 1688).

Schönberg, Anders, *Anders Schönbergs historiska brev om det svenska regeringssättet i äldre och nyare tider*, I (Stockholm: P. A. Norstedt, 1849 [1778]).

Sidenvall, Erik, 'Förnuftets och teologins kritik: ett bidrag till förståelsen av frihetstidens historieskrivning', *Historisk tidskrift*, 139:2 (2019), 223–50.

Spegel, Haquin, *Then svenska kyrkiohistorian*, 2 vols (Linköping: Kempe, 1707–8), II (1708).

Thomæus, Jöran Jakob, *Sveriges historia uti kort sammandrag för den spädare ungdomen* (Kristianstad: F. F. Cedergréen, 1812).

Thompson, James Westfall, *A History of Historical Writing*, II: *The Eighteenth and Nineteenth Centuries* (New York: Macmillan, 1942).

Thordeman, Bengt (ed.), 'Erik den heliges legend på latin, fornsvenska och modern svenska' (written *c.* 1270), in *Erik den helige: Historia. Kult. Reliker* (Stockholm: Nordisk rotogravyr, 1954), pp. xviii–xx.

Tjällén, Biörn, *Church and Nation: The Discourse on Authority in Ericus Olai's Regni Gothorum (c. 1471)* (Stockholm: Stockholm University, 2007).

Urpilainen, Erkki, 'Algot Scarin och historievetenskapen i början av 1700-talet', *Historisk tidskrift för Finland*, 76 (1991), 347–57.

Wåhlin, Christian, *Fäderneslandets historia för begynnare* (Lund: Johan Lundblad, 1791).

Wilde, Jacob, *Sueciae Historia Pragmatica* (Stockholm: Gercken, 1731).

8
A history of its own? The Catholic era as presented in Norwegian history-writing during the eighteenth century

Rolv Nøtvik Jakobsen

In 1814, after more than four hundred years of union with Denmark, Norway was suddenly declared an independent kingdom. This put an end to a complicated relationship. Since 1660, Norway and Denmark had been kingdoms with an equal status under the same king, and Norway was no longer regarded as a vassal state but rather as part of 'the twin monarchies' of Denmark–Norway. The political influence of the nobility had been dramatically reduced in 1660, as the Assembly of the Estates of the Realm in Copenhagen decided to give the king absolute power and even make the throne hereditary. The Norwegian Council of the Realm, which had been led by the Catholic archbishop in Norway up until the Reformation, had not been in operation since 1537. Ludvig Holberg saw a turning point in Norwegian history in the events of 1660: from now on, Norway was no longer regarded as a 'province', but rather as a kingdom of its own right under the absolute king.[1]

The new political situation after 1660 paved the way for written presentations of Norway and its history, much in the same way as already published books on Danish history.[2] One favoured way of creating such presentations was by making use of the older texts which were rediscovered and translated in the latter half of the seventeenth century, such as the numerous Icelandic sagas, many

---

1 Ståle Dyrvik, *Truede tvillingriker: 1648–1720. Danmark-Norge 1380–1814*, III (Oslo: Universitetsforlaget, 1998), pp. 19–32. For Holberg's argument, see Ludvig Holberg, *Dannemarks Riges Historie: Tomus 3* (Copenhagen, 1735), p. 15. It is of course not coincidental that Holberg, who had referred to Hobbes' argumentation for political absolutism in his own introduction to natural law from 1716, made use of the Hobbesian terms 'sovereign' and 'sovereignty' in his history of Denmark.
2 See Karen Skovgaard-Petersen, '"Nutildags er vores forhold til Norge venligt": om Norges plads i 1600-tallets officielle historieskrivning', *Teologisk Tidsskrift*, 7 (2018), 188–97 (196–7).

of which dealt with Norwegian history. Snorri's sagas of the Norwegian kings were especially suitable for the purpose. According to Snorri, the Norwegian kingdom was hereditary from the beginning and the king portrayed as an absolute ruler. Later historians took a cue from Snorri. The political order of Medieval Norway could in fact be invoked in order to impart a sense of historical legitimacy to the absolutism that was introduced in Denmark in the latter half of the seventeenth century.

The writing of such histories called for careful handling, however. Until the union with Denmark in 1387, Norway had been an independent, and Catholic, kingdom. Moreover, Catholic ecclesiastics had played a crucial role in the Norwegian resistance to the Lutheran Reformation instigated by the Danish king. In comparison to Denmark and Sweden, very few, if any, citizens in the Norwegian part of the kingdom were Lutherans or Protestants in the 1530s. The opposition to the King's Reformation was led by the Norwegian Assembly of Estates, with the last Catholic archbishop, the Norwegian-born Olaf Engelbrektsson (c. 1480–1538), as its leader. The Archbishop resided in Trondheim, at the shrine of the 'eternal king of Norway', St Olaf. Engelbrektsson had to flee the country in 1537. In order to erase the memory and the cult of the so-called eternal king of Norway, Danish officials buried the body of St Olaf in an unknown grave some years after the Reformation (a course of events markedly different to the treatment of St Erik in Sweden following the Reformation; see Chapter 7). As the Danish king had all of a sudden declared the Norwegians to be Lutherans, the memory of St Olaf and the Norwegian Catholic past could potentially threaten the union of Norway and Denmark under one Danish and Lutheran king.

Consequently, authors of historical chronicles had to somehow portray the history of Norway in a way that legitimated the ideology of the twin monarchy of Denmark–Norway, without making its Catholic past a burden. Starting with Tormod Torfæus' (1636–1719) magnum opus *Historia Rerum Norvegicarum* from 1711, this chapter will investigate the ways in which the ambiguity of the histories of the twin kingdoms came to be displayed in the Norwegian and Danish historiography of the eighteenth century. In a given political situation, such stories of an independent Norwegian kingdom could trigger ideas of political independence from Denmark, because it could be argued that a once-independent kingdom might benefit from regaining its independence. This was clearly the interpretation of Norwegian historians of the late nineteenth century, writing in the aftermath of Norwegian independence from Denmark in 1814.

The main part of the present chapter deals with the works of the historians Ludvig Holberg, Gerard Schøning (1722–1780) and Peter Suhm (1728–1798), and it ends with a reading of some literary works by the poet and playwright Johan Nordahl Brun (1745–1816). The authors discussed here have four qualities in common: they were all loyal servants of the Danish king; they had close connections to Norway; they were Lutherans; and finally, as a consequence of this last point, they shared an anti-Catholic attitude. With the exception of the Icelander Torfæus and the Danish Suhm, who both lived in Norway for some time, they were all born in Norway. I have argued elsewhere that Holberg was a loyal servant to the Danish Crown all his life.[3] This goes for Holberg's followers as well, for Bishop Johan Ernst Gunnerus (1718–1773) and for Professor Schøning, who was appointed to a position as the Royal *Geheimearchivar* in 1775. Brun, who was appointed Bishop of Bergen by the King in 1804, in all likelihood shared Holberg's and his two mentors' position regarding the King and the union between Denmark and Norway.

Tormod Torfæus' *Historia Rerum Norvegicarum*

Torfæus was born on Iceland and was thus able to read the sagas and other manuscripts from the Icelandic Middle Ages, part of which he had himself discovered and brought to Denmark. In the following years, Torfæus moved to Norway as a royal official, bringing some of the valuable manuscripts with him. The writing of the history of the Norwegian past was delayed by a variety of official tasks after he was appointed as a royal historiographer in 1684. The project, a history of all the kings of Norway from the beginnings until the union with Denmark, including a concise geographical description of the country, was a vast one. Torfæus took more than thirty years

---

3 For example in Rolv Nøtvik Jakobsen, 'General church history', in Knud Haakonssen and Sebastian Olden-Jørgensen (eds), *Ludvig Holberg (1684–1754): Learning and Literature in the Early Nordic Enlightenment* (London and New York: Routledge, 2017), pp. 182–95, and the same author's 'Politikkmakeren: Dannelsen av det profesjonelle byråkrati og Holbergs Den Politiske Kandestøber', in Knut Ove Eliassen, Helge Jordheim and Tue Andersen Nexø (eds), *Staten: Fra utopi til bureaukrati, Europæisk litteratur 1500–1800*, II (Aarhus: Aarhus Universitetsforlag, 2015), pp. 157–78.

to complete the huge historical work. His main historical opus, written in Latin, was finally published in 1711 in four luxurious and expensive volumes counting 3,500 pages. In his foreword, Torfæus dedicates the work to the present king, Frederik IV (r. 1699–1730), also thanking both the previous regents, Frederik III (r. 1648–1670) and Christian V (r. 1670–1699), and his editor Christian Reitzer for their interest and generous financial support.

Part of the explanation for the sheer voluminousness of the work was, according to Torfæus, that he wanted to present the Icelandic manuscripts which formed his unique sources. It was not at all his intention to select from among different versions of the historical events in order to present a coherent version of the history, readable for the common public. Instead, Torfæus took great care to present the documents he relied on. This makes Torfæus' work invaluable as a historical source and presentation of the Icelandic sagas dealing with Norwegian history. On the other hand, the writer's refusal to make selections, and to assume a critical attitude to the information given in the older text, is apt to try a latter-day reader's patience. Torfæus' choice of writing in Latin rather than the Danish language was due to the fact that his intended readers were primarily the King and his officials, as well as the learned European audience.[4] His choice of language, however, meant that this important work was inaccessible to the general reading public. The first translation of the Latin text into Norwegian did not in fact appear in print until 2008 to 2014.[5]

The lengthy title of the work clearly states Torfæus' project. He promises to supply a description of Norway, especially dealing with the heroes and kings before and after the foundation of the institution of kingdom (*tam ante quam post Monarchiam institutam*). For Torfæus, Håkon Hårfagre was the first Norwegian king. The Norwegian kingdom was meant to be absolute and hereditary from the start, just as the Danish-Norwegian kingdom of 1660 was. Following Torfæus' preface, a salient feature in the initial parts of

---

4 Some of the Latin terms Torfæus made use of in order to make the context understandable were in themselves confusing. The best example is his translations of 'Vikings' as *pirata*. As this was written during a period later named 'the Golden Age of Piracy' and especially after the so-called Turkish pirate raid on Iceland in 1627, the concept of 'pirates' had more ambiguous connotations than 'Vikings'. For Torfæus, the term 'giants' (*gigantes*) covered both what the sagas named *troll*, *tusser* and *jotner*.

5 Tormod Torfæus, *Norges historie*, ed. Torgrim Titlestad, 5 vols (Bergen: Eide förlag, 2008–2011), I (2008).

A history of its own? 215

this work are the harsh conflicts – some of them instigated by disputes between Christians and non-Christians, others by 'false' kings who claimed their right to inherit the throne – that haunted the young Norwegian domain. The last part of the story, from King Sverre who, Torfæus believed, was 'by blood' a true heir to the kingdom, represented for him the best part of the history. The history ended as happily as possible, with the Danish queen Margrete (r. 1387–1412) as the new monarch in Norway.[6] In this way, Torfæus depicted a historical continuity, based on the institution of a Norwegian hereditary monarchy. The Danish Oldenburgian family, to which the royal dedicatees of Torfæus' work all belonged, could then clearly be described as legitimate heirs to the Norwegian throne. The voluminous work was thus able to serve as a historical legitimation of the Danish institution of absolute monarchy from 1660.[7]

This historical reconstruction encountered some problems of its own. The fundamental challenge was of course that a depiction of Norway as an independent kingdom could serve as a reminder of the possibility that it might once more be a kingdom in its own right. By showing that a Danish queen was a legitimate heiress ('by blood') to the Norwegian throne, and that this union was meant to last 'forever', Torfæus emphasized that the possibility of a future independent Norwegian kingdom was clearly a misreading of history. Another dilemma, on a different scale, was how to deal with the harsh words that some of the Norwegian kings reportedly used against their Danish opponents. Torfæus was clearly intrigued by this dilemma, as is documented in his letters. For instance, was it justified to put the words of King Olaf Trygvason, in a battle against a Danish fleet, on record? On this occasion, Olaf allegedly remarked: 'I do not fear those cowards; they are no braver than deer. Never have Danes defeated Norwegians, nor will they do it today'.[8] Following his instincts as a historiographer, Torfæus not

---

6 Torfæus, *Norges historie*, p. 73.
7 See Karen Skovgaard-Petersen, 'The first post-medieval history of Norway in Latin: the *Historia Rerum Norvegicarum* (Copenhagen 1711) by Tormod Torfæus', in E. Kessler and H. C. Kuhn (eds), *Germania latina – Latinitas teutonica: Politik, Wissenschaft, humanistische Kultur vom späten Mittelalter bis in unsere Zeit*, II, 1st edn (Paderborn: Fink, 2008), pp. 707–20 for convincing arguments for the official use of Torfæus' work.
8 'Non timeo timidos illos; neque enim ii damis animosiores sunt: nunquam Dani Norvegos vicerunt, neque hodie vincent'; Skovgaard-Petersen, 'The first', pp. 715, n. 16, referring to Tormod Torfæus, *Historia Rerum Norvegicarum*, 4 vols (Copenhagen, 1711), II, p. 445.

only chose to include such potentially harmful statements in the printed version of his book; he also recounted some even more undiplomatic variants of what was said from other manuscripts. Torfæus justified this choice to his friends by making it clear that the King uttered these words on a specific historic occasion. The reproduced words were hence not at all to be understood as meaningful outside that context.[9]

The first part of Torfæus' work describes the history of Norway from pre-historic times up to the founding of the institutionalized kingdom in great detail. His account of Norwegian history before the foundation of its kingdom, in the modern Norwegian translation comprising nearly seven hundred pages, makes use of ancient texts from the Bible and from Classical Greek literature. The biblical stories of the Great Deluge and of the building of the Tower of Babel, as well as the Classical Greek myths and histories, could, in Torfæus' view, demonstrate the ancient lineage of the Norwegians. For the modern reader, most of his reading and use of ancient literature appears dubious to say the least. The reason why Torfæus chose to include these curious readings in a work dedicated to the Danish-Norwegian king in 1711 was probably, as Karen Skovgaard-Petersen points out, that it was 'first and foremost a message about Norway being part of the civilized world'.[10] Especially, of course, the portrayals of the Classical ancestry of the Norwegians are to be read in the context of the various contemporaneous Swedish attempts to prove the historical uniqueness of the Swedes, such as by Olof Rudbeck the elder (1630–1702), on the basis of biblical and Classical texts.[11]

Torfæus' account of the ancient Norwegian 'giants' is a telling example of the way in which he utilized these ancient texts. On the basis of the biblical stories of giant 'Sons of God' in Genesis 6, Torfæus tried to show how the early Norwegian landscape came to be populated with the offspring of these biblical giants. In this way, the giants were portrayed as closely related to Noah's son Ham. Torfæus questions the biblical version in which the ancient giants were exterminated and argues for the historical possibility

---

9 Skovgaard-Petersen, 'The first', pp. 715, n. 17.
10 Skovgaard-Petersen, 'The first', p. 712.
11 Carl S. Petersen writes about Danish jealousy (*Misundelse*) and desire for resources against the weak arguments of Swedish ancient history ('som Kampmidler mod Sveriges kun svagt underbyggede Oldhistorie') in his *Illustreret dansk litteraturhistorie*, I (Copenhagen, 1929), p. 800.

that the giants immigrated via Germany and Sweden.[12] The vivid account of the lives of these early Norwegians, based on very weak historical foundations, covers three chapters (2–4) in the third part of the first volume.[13] According to Torfæus, the giants were in themselves strong and independent persons living in the mountainous area of Jotunheimen and Dovre. By using classical and European literature in order to document the existence of these early Norwegians, Torfæus demonstrates that Norwegian history is closely related to both sacred and global history from the very outset.

Ludvig Holberg as a historical writer

The Norwegian-born historian and author Ludvig Holberg made his literary debut in 1711, the same year as Torfæus published his main historical work. In comparison to Torfæus' four volumes, Holberg's book was a minor work presenting an introduction to the most important European states (*Introduction Til de fornemste Europæiske Rigers Historier*). Just like Torfæus, Holberg ends his introduction to Norwegian history with the union with Denmark in 1387. He concludes by stating that Norway and Denmark have formed a union ever since, and that 'the kings have always had their residence in Denmark'.[14] Holberg refers readers who wish to learn more about Norwegian history after 1387 to his chapter on Denmark.[15] The information about Norway provided in that chapter is quite scanty, though.

Holberg was a staunch adherent to the views regarding absolutism professed by Thomas Hobbes (1588–1679) and the Swedish-German scholar Samuel Pufendorf. Holberg used parts of his *Almindelig Kirke-Historie* ('General church history') from 1738 to argue against the legitimacy of the political powers of the Catholic Church.[16] Referring to natural law, he maintained that the secular sovereign, and not the Church, should have the last word within all sectors

---

12 Torfæus, *Norges historie*, p. 250.
13 Torfæus, *Norges historie*, pp. 244–55.
14 'Siden den Tid haver Dannemarck og Norge væred foreenede, og Kongerne stedse resideret udi Dannemarck'; Ludvig Holberg, *Introduction Til de fornemste Europæiske Rigers Historier* (Copenhagen, 1711), p. 36.
15 'Om dem tales kortelig udi den Danske Historie, hvorhen jeg vil den gunstige Læser henviise'; Holberg, *Introduction Til de fornemste Europæiske Rigers Historier*.
16 Jakobsen, 'General church history', pp. 182–95.

of society. Holberg was a consistent exponent of Erastianism, according to which the state or sovereign was to rule the Church. He concluded his *Almindelig Kirke-Historie* with an account of the Reformation. According to Holberg, the Reformation resulted in the formation of national churches which formed integral parts of society at large, governed by the regent. For Holberg, this was a beneficial solution, ending the harmful power struggles between Church and state. Consequently, when Holberg wrote about the Norwegian archbishop's struggle against the King's Reformation in 1537, he showed no signs of sympathy either for the archbishop or for the Norwegian case.[17]

The most important difference between these two historians was their choice of language. As an exponent of early Enlightenment ideals about the usefulness of knowledge, Holberg, albeit well versed in Latin, decided to publish most of his works in Danish. In ensuing works, Holberg argues vehemently against the use of Latin and German in texts meant to be read by Danish subjects. In the dedication to the King in his *Introduction Til Naturens- Og Folke-Rettens Kundskab* ('Introduction to natural and public law', 1716), Holberg states that the work, like all his other writings, is written in Danish, in order for it to be useful to all people who did not understand Latin or other foreign languages.[18] For Holberg the German language, which had a prominent place in the Danish administration and was also the language of the court up to the 1770s, was clearly one of these 'foreign' languages. Holberg's literary programme was to present the Danish public with readable, entertaining and instructive books in different academic disciplines as well as in a variety of genres of fiction, including his popular comedies. He stuck to this programme for most of his life, producing a vast historical and literary output.[19]

---

17 'Udi Norge derimod blev Reformationens Fremgang noget hindret af Erke-Bisp Oluf Lunge, som var Hovet for de Norske, og havde stiftet stort Oprør udi samme Rige, som tilforn er omtalt'; Ludvig Holberg, *Dannemarks Riges Historie. Tomus 2* (Copenhagen, 1733), pp. 349–59.
18 'saa vel som mine andre Skrifter, jeg har skrevet paa Dansk, at alle, besynderlig de, som ikke forstaa Latin, eller andre fremmede Sprog, kunne have nytte deraf'; Ludvig Holberg, *Introduction Til Naturens- Og Folke-Rettens Kundskab* (Copenhagen, 1716), Dedication, A3.
19 Updated introductions to Holberg's vast literary output are given in the anthology edited by Haakonssen and Olden-Jørgensen, *Ludvig Holberg (1684–1754)*. For Holberg's historical works, see also the Norwegian anthology by Jørgen Magnus Sejersted and Sebastian Olden-Jørgensen (eds), *Historikeren Ludvig Holberg* (Oslo: Scandinavian Academic Press, 2014).

A history of its own? 219

On several occasions, Holberg did compliment Torfæus on his outstanding work, as 'one of the most impressive and wonderful histories ever to have seen the light of day'.[20] Even if he seldom made such explicit references to Torfæus, Holberg obviously made use of Torfæus' works in his own historical publications. Holberg supported Torfæus in his critical stance towards Saxo's twelfth-century account of the early and even pre-historic Danish kings (found in *Gesta Danorum*). However, Holberg was clearly not convinced or even amused by Torfæus' inventive reconstructions of the early pre-history of the Norwegian tribes, for instance the stories of the biblical giants in the mountains. As historians, Torfæus and Holberg embodied two different historical ideals: while Torfæus was first and foremost a collector, Holberg (just like Olof von Dahlin in Chapter 7) wanted to be a popular author, writing exciting 'histories' of different subjects that could be instructive as well as a good read. It goes without saying that neither one of them was a critical historian in the modern sense.

The scientific and critical pioneers in Danish-Norwegian historiography were all closely connected to Holberg, and most of them shared his positive attitude to the Danish language. Holberg's friend and contemporary Hans Gram (1685–1748) was in many ways the first critical historian in Denmark. His work was continued by his pupil Jakob Langebek (1710–1775), who was also the founder in 1745 of the first Danish society for history and language, *Det danske Selskab for Fædrelandets Historie og Sprog*. Some years later, in 1751, two of Gram's pupils – both friends of Langebek – left Copenhagen in order to move permanently to Trondheim in Norway. In time, both Gerhard Schøning and Peter Suhm were to establish themselves as historiographers in their own right.[21]

Schøning, Suhm and the Royal Norwegian Society for science and arts

Schøning had already published a geographical treatise of the Nordic countries, especially Norway, in 1751. Together with Suhm,

---

20 Ludvig Holberg, *Epistler 2*, ed. Laurids Kristian Fahl and Peter Zeeberg (Copenhagen, DSL/Aarhus universitetsforlag, 2017), p. 294. Holberg describes the work as 'en af de anseligste og prægtigste historier som nogen tid er kommet for lyset, og at det med al rette fortjener at hedde et 30 års værk'.
21 For a detailed introduction to different forms of historical writings in Norway from this period, see Anne Eriksen, *Livets læremester: Historiske kunnskapstradisjoner i Norge 1650–1840* (Oslo: Pax, 2020).

who after his marriage to Karen Angell (1732–1788) in Trondheim was one of the wealthiest men in the country, Schøning started a small study group. Among other subjects, the members of the group taught themselves Icelandic and Old Norse in order to read historical documents. Their joint labour resulted in the publication in 1756 of a historical treatise of Danish and Norwegian kings, *Forsøg til Forbedringer i den gamle Danske og Norske Historie* ('An attempt at improvements in the Old Danish and Norwegian historical accounts'). In the preface, Suhm explains that the five historical portraits of Danish and Norwegians kings supplied in the book were also meant to be read as exemplary stories, describing different types of kings: the first king is seen as 'great', the next is described as 'good', while the third is 'depraved'. The fourth of the kings, the Norwegian Harald Hardråde, is said to be 'a wise and combative king'.[22] By adopting this outline, Suhm points out that the historical work could be read as 'a mirror-for-princes', a *Speculum regale* in the tradition of the well-known thirteenth-century Norwegian instruction book for princes.[23] In his detailed portrait of Harald Hardråde, Schøning presents a nuanced description of the conflict between the King and the local leader Einer Tambeskielver, based on both Snorri and Torfæus.[24] Schøning introduced his exemplary biography by describing King Harald as no less than a king 'who without doubt has been one of the bravest, wisest, most experienced and tried, as well as most firm kings in our Northern realms, if not the greatest of them all'.[25]

In 1758 the Norwegian-born scholar Johan Ernst Gunnerus was appointed Bishop of Trondheim. Gunnerus had studied and taught theology and natural law at the universities in Halle, Jena and finally in Copenhagen, where he had chosen Holberg to be his tutor. Gunnerus met Schøning and Suhm in Trondheim and soon began

---

22 Peter Suhm and Gerhard Schøning, *Forsøg til Forbedringer i den gamle Danske og Norske Historie* (Copenhagen, 1756), p. 157.
23 Rolv Nøtvik Jakobsen, 'The Trondheim connection: Johan Nordahl Bruns to skodespel frå 1772 og den kulturelle utvekslinga mellom den trønderske stiftsstaden og Kongens by i det lange 1700-talet', in Anne Fastrup, Gunnar Foss and Rolv Nøtvik Jakobsen (eds), *Opplysninger: Festskrift til Knut Ove Eliassen på 60-årsdagen 26. oktober 2019* (Oslo: Novus, 2019), pp. 131–44.
24 Suhm and Schøning, *Forsøg til Forbedringer*, pp. 243–409.
25 'uden al Tvil har været en af de tapperste, klogeste, mest bereiste og forsøgte, samt myndigste Konger i vor Norden, om ei heri den ypperste blant dem'; Suhm and Schøning, *Forsøg til Forbedringer*, pp. 244–5.

A history of its own? 221

to draft the organization of a scientific society. The society, which was given the name *Det Kongelige Norske Videnskabers Selskab* (Royal Society of Science and Letters) some years later, was organized in 1760, modelled on the various scientific societies Gunnerus had known from his years in Germany.[26] Gunnerus also became the editor of the journal of the society, *Skrifter* ('Writings'), now the oldest Norwegian scientific journal in existence. At its inception, *Skrifter* was published in Danish. Although the journal was also translated into German in its early years, Gunnerus made it clear from the beginning that the working language of the society was to be Danish. By doing this – and thereby excluding the alternatives (Latin and German) – the society as a whole adhered to Holberg's political line regarding the choice of language.

In 1765, after years of intensive cooperation in the study of Nordic history, Suhm and Schøning both returned to Denmark. Schøning went to the Royal Academy in Sorø as a professor of history and rhetoric, whereas Suhm continued his life as an independent intellectual and author in his huge library, firmly placed in his palace Pustervig in Copenhagen. Both of them continued to publish historical works about their respective home countries. Suhm managed to write a comprehensive history of Denmark, *Historie af Danmark*, in fourteen large volumes, some of them published posthumously. The Norwegian-born Schøning, for his part, published *Norges Riiges Historie* ('History of the Norwegian realm') in three volumes from 1771 to 1781. In the first volume, which leads up to the first king, Harald Hårfagre, Schøning writes about the pre-history of Norway, making connections with biblical and ancient history in a vein similar to Torfæus. Schøning tried to convince his readers from the start that the biblical Japheth, son of Noah, was the ancestor of the first Norwegians.[27] The mountains of Armenia, where the ark of Noah settled, bore close similarities to the Norwegian mountains. As a patriotic Norwegian, Schøning suggests that this is probably the reason why some of the descendants of Japheth found their home in Norway. Schøning finds it probable that some of these first Norwegians were giants (*Kiemper*) living in this beautiful and

---

26 See Rolv Nøtvik Jakobsen, *Gunnerus og nordisk vitskapshistorie* (Oslo: Scandinavian Academic Press, 2015), pp. 244–5.
27 Gerhard Schøning, *Norges Riiges Historie, Første Deel, indeholdende Riigets ældste Historie fra dets Begyndelse til Harald Haarfagers Tiide* (Sorø, 1771), pp. 3–11; compare Anne Eriksen, *Topografenes verden* (Oslo: Pax, 2007), pp. 34–40.

healthy climate.²⁸ Referring explicitly to Torfæus, he also argues for the existence of 'trolls' and *tusser*.²⁹ Several of the arguments of Torfæus, both regarding the biblical ancestry and the existence of Norwegian giants, had been under discussion for several years when Schøning published his historical works. In this respect Schøning differs from Holberg, who barely mentions the suggested biblical pre-history and the giants in his works.

The learned theologian Erik Pontoppidan mentions Torfæus' theory of the giants in the second part of his *Norges Naturlige Historie* ('Natural history of Norway'), published in 1753 while Pontoppidan was still Bishop of Bergen. Pontoppidan takes great care to underline that his readers have to decide for themselves whether this theory of what he, in Danish, characterizes as *Kiæmpe-Art* is at all trustworthy. He goes on to describe some findings of bone material in Norway that could suggest that there really were giants in pre-historic times. He does, however, also leave this to his readers to decide.³⁰ During his travels in Norway in the 1770s, Schøning took great care to document every archaeological finding of bones that might imply the existence of such giants or *Kiemper*.

Censorship and political ambiguity: Johann Nordahl Brun's literary output

After the death of his father in 1766, Christian VII became the new absolute king of the twin kingdoms Denmark and Norway. Officially, he reigned until his death in 1808. Owing to his mental illness, however, Christian VII was in reality unable to serve as king for most of this time. From the beginning of 1770 until the coup on 14 January 1772, the King's German-speaking personal physician, Johann Friedrich Struensee, was de facto ruler of the kingdoms.

In 1770 Struensee ordered Gunnerus, then still Bishop of Trondheim, to come to Copenhagen in order to assist with a plan for reforming the university.³¹ From his contacts in Copenhagen, Gunnerus knew that in the unstable political situation, the task

---

28 Schøning, *Norges Riiges Historie*, pp. 23–5.
29 Schøning, *Norges Riiges Historie*, p. 102.
30 Erich Pontoppidan, *Norges Naturlige Historie, Anden Deel* (Copenhagen, 1753), pp. 386–8.
31 See John Peter Collett, 'Johan Ernst Gunnerus as a university reformer of the Enlightenment', in *Det Kongelige Norske Videnskabers Selskabs Skrifter* (2011), pp. 23–62.

could easily turn out to be dangerous for those involved. Gunnerus decided to ask the young secretary of the society, the Norwegian-born theologian Johan Nordahl Brun, to accompany him to Copenhagen as his secretary. Brun, however, was not fluent in German, the administrative language of the kingdoms, and he was therefore deemed not suitable for the position. Brun thus ended up in Copenhagen with no occupation. Following a challenge from the (likewise Norwegian-born) director of the Royal Theatre to write a tragedy in Danish, in a few months Brun wrote a play based on a classical subject. The result of this work, Zarine, in fact won the prize for the first tragedy originally written in Danish, and it was successfully performed at the Royal Theatre. The premiere was on 14 February 1772, exactly one month after the coup against Struensee. Today, Brun's first tragedy is mostly known through a friendly parody called Kierlighed uden Strømper ('Love without stockings') written by Brun's friend, the Norwegian-born Johan Herman Wessel (1742–1785).

Following his success as a dramatist, Brun was approached by the court. Persons close to the King, he later told his biographer, congratulated him and challenged him to write a new tragedy, this time with a subject chosen from the history of the nation (fra Fædrenelandets Historie).[32] Brun did as he was told, or as he believed he was told. He began writing a new tragedy to follow up the success of the first. The subject he chose was the conflict between the Norwegian king Harald Hardråde and his influential warlord Einer Tambeskielver. Brun probably used the above-mentioned treatise by his teacher from Trondheim, Gerhard Schøning, as a basis for writing the play. The issue that started the conflict between the two main characters is no less than a dispute about whether Norway should go to war with Denmark. The King, according to Schøning one of the best, strongly desires a new war with Denmark. His more experienced warlord, on the other hand, argues vehemently against such a venture. Einer, who at one point mistakenly believes that the King has killed his son, rushes against Harald in order to kill him. He is thus close to committing the most heinous crime in an absolute monarchy, the crime of regicide. After he discovers his mistake, Einer is a mere shadow of his former self for the remainder

---

32 Jens Zetlitz, 'Johan Nordahl Brun, Biskop over Bergens Stift', in G. L. Lahde (ed.), Portrætter med Biographier af Danske, Norske og Holsteenere, Tredje Hefte (Copenhagen, 1805), p. 21.

of the drama, begging the King to punish him for this grave offence against the throne.

The tragedy *Einer Tambeskielver* was printed in 1772. The play was, however, heavily attacked by the press; and most importantly, it was not performed at the Royal Theatre. Instead, the authorities made Brun a chaplain in the area of his birth, Byneset in Norway. Back in his home country, Brun wondered what he had done wrong in following the call to write a play based on the history of 'our nation'. He concluded that he still did not know whether the expression 'our nation', as employed by those who encouraged him, referred to Denmark or Norway. Anyway, the result was the same: the play was not performed.[33]

The political situation in Denmark after the coup against Struensee was complicated and tense. Immediately after the fall of the King's German minister, Suhm published an open letter addressed to Christian VII, pleading that the Danish king should speak and write in Danish, as well as make this language of his home country, and not German, the common language of the administration of the kingdoms, as well as the military. Suhm's letter in fact marked the final success of Holberg's programme for language reform in Denmark. At the same time, the Danish authorities were informed that the Swedish king was considering invading Norwegian territory again (Gustav III of Sweden had successfully carried out his own coup in August 1772). In such a tense situation, it is understandable that the authorities would not have been keen to allow a tragedy where one of the heroic Norwegian kings argues for a war with Denmark.

Most of the Norwegian historians who have written about this incident tend to agree with Brun. In a tense political situation, the authorities deemed that the play might be interpreted as an argument for a more independent Norwegian state. On the other hand, it is possible that it was the theatre itself which decided against performing the play. While *Einer Tambeskielver* was slightly better than *Zarine*, it was still not a strikingly good text that would have been suitable for theatrical performance on its own.

Be that as it may, Brun, safely back in his homeland, wrote a strongly polemical article directed against the commentators who had criticized his second tragedy. For him, as well as for all his fellow Norwegians, there was no conflict, as the critics had implied,

---

33 Zetlitz, 'Johan Nordahl Brun', p. 20.

between Norwegian patriotism on the one hand and fidelity to the Danish king on the other. On the contrary, for Brun it was obvious that Norwegians could simultaneously love their own country and be faithful subjects of the Danish king.[34]

Some years later, in 1786, Brun made a strange comment in his preface to a collection of his own hymns: 'I have never written a song to be sung in company [*Selskabs Sang*] that was meant for publication by the press.'[35] The song that Brun obviously wrote with no intention of having it printed, if we are to believe him, was nevertheless published in the posthumous collection of Brun's *Mindre Digte* ('Minor poems') from 1818, edited by his son Christian. The song is called 'Norges Skaal' ('A toast to Norway'), and at the time of publication it was – and still is – a popular song at Norwegian parties and celebrations. The Danish authorities in Brun's time, however, suspected that the song was a patriotic Norwegian hymn making unsound arguments for Norwegian independence from Denmark. Performing it was, therefore, forbidden.

Brun's text was clearly inspired by Schøning's description, following Torfæus, of the ancient Norwegian giants and their idyllic environment in the Norwegian mountains. The opening line proposed a toast to Norway, birthplace of giants ('For Norge, Kjæmpers Fødeland'). The song continues by stating that the singers will 'sweetly dream of freedom'. Brun then claims on behalf of all Norwegians that 'we will wake someday, and break chains, bonds and coercion'. Given the tense political situation of the time, it is not difficult to understand why Danish authorities wanted to ban this song as rebellious. Whether the author Brun was actually arguing for Norwegian independence from Denmark in the song is still under discussion. What remains clear is that the text was interpreted in such a way, especially after Norway was declared an independent nation in 1814 in the aftermath of the Napoleonic wars. Brun's son Christian, who published the text of the song in 1818, took care to inform readers in a note that it was written well before the

---

34 The polemical text was aptly named 'Til Nordmænd om Troeskab mod Kongen og Kierlighed til Fædrelandet i Anledning af Einer Tambeskielver' ('To Norwegians about Fidelity to the King and Love for one's Native Land in Connection with Einer Tambeskielver', 1773). See Rolv Nøtvik Jakobsen, 'Johan Nordahl Bruns polemikk', in Trond Berg Eriksen and Egil Børre Johnsen (eds), *Norsk litteraturhistorie: Sakprosa fra 1750 til 1995*, I: *1750–1920* (Oslo: Universitetsforlaget, 1998), pp. 69–71.
35 Johan Nordahl Brun, *Evangeliske Sange* (Bergen, 1786), 'Forerindring' ('Preface').

French Revolution. This remark was, however, made in a collection of poems which Christian dedicated to the Swedish king Karl XIV Johan (1763–1844), who become the new king of Norway in 1818. In the dedication, Christian points out that his father had loved and been faithful both to his country and the King.

There are good reasons for believing the Bruns, father and son, when they claimed that the elder Brun had been loyal to the Danish king for most of his life – that is, up to 1814. Once back in Norway, Brun even wrote a sort of follow-up to the tragedy of Einar in 1790. This light 'Singspiel', *Endres og Signes Brøllup*, ended in a spectacular celebration of the union between Norway and Denmark.

Conclusion

The different accounts of Norwegian history published in the eighteenth century were all composed and written by authors who claimed to be, and who actually were, loyal servants of the Danish king. In fact, it could be argued that the historical works of both Torfæus and Holberg had a clear tendency: to legitimate and support the historical rights of the Danish king as an absolute and hereditary ruler, by birth a true heir to the throne of Norway. Holberg even supported these royal claims by arguments drawn from contemporary natural law. Paradoxically, the sheer richness of the material, made accessible to common readers by Holberg's and Schøning's historical publications in Danish, made these historical treatises into archives filled with stories and information about a once-upon-a-time independent kingdom with a glorious past and even an ancient pre-history.

None of Torfæus, Holberg or Schøning regarded the Roman Church in Norway as an integral part of the heroic and independent past of the nation. In fact, they do not seem to have been particularly interested in the pre-Reformation part of Norwegian history. Torfæus and Schøning did not even cover the Reformation in their respective histories of Norway. For them, the pre-Christian history of the early Vikings was important and a less problematic aspect of Norwegian history than the strong influence of the Church under Christian kings. They therefore downplayed the political role of the Church in their histories. In times of political conflict between the Church and the monarchy, for example between King Sverre and Pope Innocent III in the twelfth century, the historians sided with the regent. For Torfæus, the rule of King Sverre marked the beginning of the best part of Norwegian royal history. Holberg once more resorted to natural law to support the King against the political claims of the Church.

Johan Nordahl Brun, who used some of the historical material from Torfæus and Schøning as inspiration when writing a tragedy based on Norwegian history as well as a popular nationalist ode, composed for celebrations with fellow Norwegians, was as loyal to the Danish king as Holberg and Schøning. Even though it was not by any means Brun's intention, both the play and the song were clearly interpreted as a call for Norwegian independence both by Danish authorities and by the Norwegian public. Interestingly enough, in a historical situation in which the King was weak and the relationship with other countries – especially the rival kingdom of Sweden – was tense, some of the historic depictions of the early Norwegian kings and of Norway's pre-history began to appear ambivalent. Suddenly the curious stories of Torfæus and Schøning regarding the Norwegian giants, linking the Norwegians to biblical and Classical forebears, could sound like a call for national independence. Likewise, the narrative of a Norwegian king and hero who wanted to go to war with Denmark started to sound suspicious to the authorities.

A reason why these old narratives suddenly began to take on new meanings is found in their genre and the language in which they were published. Torfæus' massive tomes were written in Latin, as already mentioned, inaccessible to most people in Denmark–Norway. Holberg's and Schøning's versions of the early history were much more accessible to the general reading public that now emerged. However, when Brun made use of Schøning's description of the life of the Norwegian king Harald Hardråde in a tragedy which was going to be performed in public, something new happened. There is a vast difference between reading a historical narrative on one's own and witnessing a theatre performance in which actors speak about a possible war between Norway and Denmark. The same could be said about the difference between the private reading of a poem and collective, and celebratory, singing. When Norwegians started to sing, not only read, about Norwegian giants and yearning for freedom, the words became more emotional and more persuasive. And, of course, the sound of a collective of Norwegians singing together appeared much more menacing to the Danish authorities.

Later Norwegian historians were to dwell on the role played by the Catholic Church in the struggle against the Reformation of the Danish king; as we have seen, this was not a topic that appealed either to the eighteenth-century historians mentioned in this chapter or to the writer Brun. One of the consequences of the Norwegian Reformation, imposed from above and from abroad, was the end of the Norwegian Assembly of Estates. Holberg's own staunch anti-Catholicism, as well as the anti-Catholic attitude of his pietistic contemporary Erik Pontoppidan, probably made it impossible to describe the cult of the eternal king of Norway, St Olaf – as well as the Norwegian archbishop's struggle against the Danish Lutheran Reformation – in a favourable light that might be utilized in support of Norwegian independence. This state of things was going to change significantly in the latter half of the nineteenth century, in the years after the Norwegian independence from Denmark. That, however, is another story.

Bibliography

Brun, Johan Nordahl, *Evangeliske Sange* (Bergen, 1786).
Collett, John Peter, 'Johan Ernst Gunnerus as a university reformer of the Enlightenment', in *Det Kongelige Norske Videnskabers Selskabs Skrifter* (2011), pp. 23–62.
Dyrvik, Ståle, *Truede tvillingriker: 1648–1720. Danmark-Norge 1380–1814*, III (Oslo: Universitetsforlaget, 1998).
Eriksen, Anne, *Livets læremester: Historiske kunnskapstradisjoner i Norge 1650–1840* (Oslo: Pax, 2020).
———, *Topografenes verden* (Oslo: Pax, 2007).
Holberg, Ludvig, *Dannemarks Riges Historie. Tomus 2* (Copenhagen, 1733).
———, *Dannemarks Riges Historie. Tomus 3* (Copenhagen, 1735).
———, *Epistler 2*, ed. Laurids Kristian Fahl and Peter Zeeberg (Copenhagen: DSL/Aarhus universitetsforlag, 2017).
———, *Introduction Til de fornemste Europæiske Rigers Historier* (Copenhagen, 1711).
———, *Introduction Til Naturens- Og Folke-Rettens Kundskab* (Copenhagen, 1716).
Jakobsen, Rolv Nøtvik, 'General church history', in Knud Haakonssen and Sebastian Olden-Jørgensen (eds), *Ludvig Holberg (1684–1754): Learning and Literature in the Early Nordic Enlightenment* (London and New York: Routledge, 2017), pp. 182–95.
———, *Gunnerus og nordisk vitskapshistorie* (Oslo: Scandinavian Academic Press, 2015).
———, 'Johan Nordahl Bruns polemikk', in Trond Berg Eriksen and Egil Børre Johnsen (eds), *Norsk litteraturhistorie: Sakprosa fra 1750 til 1995*, I: *1750–1920* (Oslo: Universitetsforlaget, 1998), pp. 69–71.
———, 'Politikkmakeren: Dannelsen av det profesjonelle byråkrati og Holbergs Den Politiske Kandestøber', in Knut Ove Eliassen, Helge Jordheim and Tue Andersen Nexø (eds), *Staten: Fra utopi til bureaukrati, Europæisk*

litteratur 1500–1800, II (Aarhus: Aarhus Universitetsforlag, 2015), pp. 157–78.

———, 'The Trondheim connection: Johan Nordahl Bruns to skodespel frå 1772 og den kulturelle utvekslinga mellom den trønderske stiftsstaden og Kongens by i det lange 1700-talet', in Anne Fastrup, Gunnar Foss and Rolv Nøtvik Jakobsen (eds), *Opplysninger: Festskrift til Knut Ove Eliassen på 60-årsdagen 26. oktober 2019* (Oslo: Novus, 2019), pp. 131–44.

Petersen, Carl S., *Illustreret dansk litteraturhistorie*, I (Copenhagen, 1929).

Pontoppidan, Erich [Erik], *Norges Naturlige Historie, anden Deel* (Copenhagen, 1753).

Schøning, Gerhard, *Norges Riiges Historie, Første Deel, indeholdende Riigets ældste Historie fra dets Begyndelse til Harald Haarfagers Tiide* (Sorø, 1771).

Sejersted, Jørgen Magnus and Sebastian Olden-Jørgensen (eds), *Historikeren Ludvig Holberg* (Oslo: Scandinavian Academic Press, 2014).

Skovgaard-Petersen, Karen, 'The first post-medieval history of Norway in Latin: the *Historia Rerum Norvegicarum* (Copenhagen 1711) by Tormod Torfæus', in E. Kessler and H. C. Kuhn (eds), *Germania latina – Latinitas teutonica: Politik, Wissenschaft, humanistische Kultur vom späten Mittelalter bis in unsere Zeit*, II, 1st edn (Paderborn: Fink, 2008), pp. 707–20.

———, '"Nutildags er vores forhold til Norge venligt": om Norges plads i 1600-tallets officielle historieskrivning', *Teologisk Tidsskrift*, 7 (2018), 188–97.

Suhm, Peter and Gerhard Schøning, *Forsøg til Forbedringer i den gamle Danske og Norske Historie* (Copenhagen, 1756).

Torfæus, Tormod, *Historia Rerum Norvegicarum*, 4 vols (Copenhagen, 1711).

———, *Norges historie*, ed. Torgrim Titlestad, 5 vols (Bergen: Eide förlag, 2008–2011), I (2008).

Zetlitz, Jens, 'Johan Nordahl Brun, Biskop over Bergens Stift', in G. L. Lahde (ed.), *Portrætter med Biographier af Danske, Norske og Holsteenere, Tredje Hefte* (Copenhagen, 1805).

9
Gustav III, Enlightenment and religion: ecumenical visions and Catholicizing strategies

Yvonne Maria Werner

Gustav III, who ascended the Swedish throne in 1771 and whose reign tragically ended with his assassination in 1792, is generally portrayed as a typical representative of the Enlightenment. Described as an 'enlightened' monarch, he introduced several reforms, for example a liberalization of criminal justice and religious legislation, liberal economic reforms and measures geared to strengthening the position of the lower Estates; and he was one of the first heads of state to establish relations with the United States of America. In his younger years he corresponded with leading *philosophes* such as Voltaire, and he promoted art and culture, among other things by founding the Swedish Academy and the Royal Dramatic Theatre. Through a *coup d'état* in 1772, he established a new constitution, increasing the Crown's power at the expense of the Swedish parliament, the *Riksdag*. This development towards royal autocracy was completed with the Union and Security Act of 1789, which at the same time reduced the privileges of the nobility and opened new career paths for bourgeois commoners in the state bureaucracy.[1]

Sweden was a Protestant country, based on the Lutheran Augsburg confession, with a previously severe religious legislation. As part of the 'enlightened' reform activity, Gustav III issued an Edict of Tolerance for 'foreign believers' on 24 January 1781. This law allowed Catholic immigrants to practise their religion publicly. The members of the Reformed communities had already been granted the same rights, and in 1782 Jewish immigration was permitted,

---

1 Gunnar von Proschwitz, 'Gustaf III – En upplyst kosmopolit', in Hans Medelius (ed.), *Himla många kungar: Historier kring Den Svenska Historien* (Enskede: Fataburen, 1993), pp. 231–49; Harry Lenhammar, *Sveriges kyrkohistoria*, V: *Individualismens och upplysningens tid* (Stockholm: Verbum, 2000), pp. 124–70; Erik Lönnroth, *Den stora rollen: kung Gustaf III spelad av honom själv* (Stockholm: Norstedt, 2008).

although residence was restricted to certain towns. Previous research has argued that these laws were issued primarily for economic reasons, with the purpose of making it easier for wealthy non-Lutheran foreigners to establish themselves in the country.[2] This was undoubtedly a decisive reason in respect of Jews and Reformed communities. With regard to Catholics, however, I will argue that another reason came into play, namely the King's fascination with Catholic liturgy and church life.

The present chapter proposes and discusses this hypothesis, showing how the King's Catholic sympathies came to shape his ecclesiastical policies in a direction that ran counter to the ideals of the Enlightenment. In line with this, I will also question the tendency prevalent in previous research to contrast the 'enlightened' Gustav III with backward-looking Lutheran clergy. Yet, the question is whether the leading churchmen appeared to be more marked by Enlightenment ideals than the King in respect of important matters. They represented what may be labelled 'enlightened orthodoxy'.

Gustav III and the Catholic mission

In the early modern period Rome, capital of the Papal States in central Italy, had developed into a cosmopolitan city, attracting not only Catholic pilgrims but also an ever-growing number of non-Catholic travellers, including many Scandinavians. Gustav III was one of them. The city was an obvious destination for young noblemen's educational journeys, the so-called 'grand tour'; but it also attracted scholars, artists, craftsmen, merchants and religious seekers. It was during this time that it became fashionable among the cultural elite to visit Rome and admire its art treasures, both secular and religious.[3] The Catholic ecclesiastical authorities kept an eye

---

2 Arne Palmqvist, *Die Römisch-katholische Kirche in Schweden nach 1781: Das Apostolische Vikariat 1783–1820* (Uppsala: Almqvist & Wiksell, 1954), pp. 76–87; Gunnar Granberg, *Gustav III: en upplysningskonungs tro och kyrkosyn* (Uppsala: Acta Universitatis Upsaliensis, 1998), pp. 78–88. See also Magnus Nyman, *Press mot friheten: opinionsbildning i de svenska tidningarna och åsiktsbrytningar om minoriteter 1772–1786* (Uppsala: Almqvist & Wiksell, 1988).
3 Peter A. Mazur, *Conversion to Catholicism in Early Modern Italy* (New York and London: Routledge, 2016); Ola Winberg, *Den statskloka resan: Adelns peregrinationer 1610–1680* (Uppsala: Uppsala University, 2018), pp. 278–309; Hanns Gross, *Rome in the Age of Enlightenment: The Post-Tridentine Syndrome and the Ancien Régime* (Cambridge: Cambridge University Press, 2004).

on these Protestant visitors, as they wanted to prevent them from spreading Protestant teachings but also because they hoped to win them for the Catholic faith. For this purpose, religious guest houses for foreigners, so-called *Casa dei catecumeni*, were set up, where Jews, Muslims and Protestants were offered free food and lodging and were taught the Catholic faith. Converts included many Scandinavians.[4]

One of these Nordic converts was Lorenz Birger Thjulén (1746–1833) from Gothenburg, who encountered the Catholic faith when living in Southern Europe in his youth. After being taught by Jesuits in Ferrara in northern Italy, he was received into the Catholic Church in January 1769. Two years later, he was accepted as a novice at the Jesuit college in Bologna, which belonged to the Papal States. The papal decree on the dissolution of the Jesuit order in August 1773 forced him to leave the college and complete his priestly formation at the diocesan seminary. After his ordination the following year, he served as a military chaplain, teacher and writer in Bologna. Thjulén wrote articles against the revolutionary movements of the time but also about Gustav III, and he defended the Swedish position in connection with the Russian war of 1788–1790. If Gustav III had not been murdered, Thjulén would have returned to Sweden in 1792 and served as a Catholic priest in Stockholm. On 5 March that year, Gustav III had signed a resolution giving him the right to return to his homeland with the right to practise his Catholic faith. However, the King's death three weeks later meant that Thjulén did not dare to trust that he would be able to return to Sweden without suffering reprisals.[5]

At this time there were about two thousand Catholics in Sweden, most of them in Stockholm. Gustav III himself had several Catholics in his service. The legations of the Catholic powers in Stockholm had long been allowed to have a priest, but only for the pastoral care of their own employees. The above-mentioned Edict of Toleration confirmed this practice, developed in the early eighteenth century; but it also provided an opportunity to build churches and establish Catholic parishes. A similar edict was issued in 1781 by Emperor

---

4 Ricarda Matheus, *Konversionen in Rom in der Frühen Neuzeit: Das Ospizio dei Convertendi 1673–1750* (Berlin and Boston: De Gruyter, 2012); Anu Raunio, *Conversioni al cattolicesimo a Roma tra Sei e Settecento: La presenza degli scandinavi nell'Ospizio dei Convertendi* (Turku: University of Turku, 2009).

5 Palmqvist, *Die Römisch-katholische Kirche*, pp. 243–58.

Joseph II (r. 1765–1790) for the Protestants in the Habsburg hereditary lands, an edict which was supplemented in the following year to include Jews as well.[6]

Even so, these liberties only applied to the religious dissenter groups in question, and changes of religious affiliation were not allowed. This meant that it was a criminal offence to apostatize from the Lutheran faith, and for a Swedish subject who converted to the Catholic Church, emigration was hence the sole option.[7] To provide for the Catholic immigrants, Gustav III initiated negotiations with the Holy See; these negotiations resulted in the establishment of an Apostolic Vicariate in 1783, directly subordinate to the Roman congregation of mission, the Propaganda Fide. Pope Pius VI (r. 1775–1799) appointed the French priest Nicolaus Oster apostolic vicar. A Catholic parish was created in Stockholm, and soon more priests were sent to Sweden, among them the Italian Paulo Moretti (1759–1804). The latter came from Bologna, and it was on his initiative that Thjulén came into consideration as a missionary priest and future apostolic vicar in Sweden.[8]

The visit to Italy and papal Rome

Gustav III's journey to Rome and Italy in 1783–1784 was to be of great importance in this context. The travelling party included Baron Gustaf Mauritz Armfelt (1757–1814), the governor of Stockholm Baron Carl Sparre (1723–1791), Count Axel von Fersen (1755–1810), son of the influential former parliamentary leader with the same name, the national antiquarian Gudmund Jöran Adlerbeth (1751–1818) and the sculptor Johan Tobias Sergel (1740–1814). During the trip, the President of the Chancellery, Count Gustaf Philip Creutz (1731–1785), handled government affairs in Stockholm; and in letters to him, the King communicated his impressions of the trip.[9] To avoid official representation, the King travelled incognito as the Count of Haga. This strategy was

---

6 Harm Klueting, 'Catholic Enlightenment in Austria or the Habsburg Lands', in Ulrich Lehner and Michael Printy (eds), *A Companion to the Catholic Enlightenment in Europe* (Leiden: Brill, 2010), pp. 127–64.
7 Lenhammar, *Individualismens*, p. 124.
8 Palmqvist, *Die Römisch-katholische Kirche*, pp. 96–150.
9 Correspondence in Uppsala universitetsbibliotek (UUB), Gustavianska samlingen, F479. See Henning Stålhane, *Gustaf III:s resa till Italien och Frankrike* (Stockholm: Nordisk Rotogravyr, 1953), pp. 90–160.

common among European royals at the time. At the same time as the King, Emperor Joseph II made such an incognito journey, as usual under the name Count von Falkenstein.[10] The two monarchs met on several occasions. Gustav III's trip was formally motivated by his need to cure an arm injury by visiting the bathing establishments 'in Pisa and elsewhere', as it was formulated in his doctor's assessment. The real reason, however, was his wish to complete the trip abroad that he made as Crown Prince, a trip which had been interrupted by his father's death in 1771.[11]

This time, the destination was Italy, and the high point of the trip was Rome. Here the King was received by Pope Pius VI, who personally showed him around in the Vatican's art collections. Gustav III showed great interest in the Catholic liturgy and visited a great number of churches. He participated in the papal mass in St Peter's Basilica on Christmas Day and in the Sistine Chapel on New Year's Day, as well as in the masses celebrated by the Pope during Holy Week and Easter. He also visited the House of Saint Bridget at Piazza Farnese where the saint had spent the last twenty years of her life, a house which had long served as a centre for Swedish Catholic converts. He strolled in the park at Corsino Palace, where Sweden's Queen Christina (1626–1689) had resided a hundred years before. The King showed great interest in this predecessor of his, who renounced the Swedish throne in order to become a Catholic. He was anxious to see objects and items that had belonged to her.[12]

It was customary for Catholic princes to be received in audience by the Pope when they visited Rome. For a ruling Protestant prince to do so was unusual to say the least. The Danish king Frederik IV had visited Rome as Crown Prince in 1692 in connection with his grand tour, and his brother Prince Charles did the same six years later. Both attended Catholic services and experienced Pope Innocent XII (1615–1700) in various liturgical functions, and they were cared for by papal dignitaries. But they did not make any personal visits to the Pope, and their attendance at papal liturgical

---

10 Gustav III met the Emperor first in Florence and then in Rome, which was reported in Swedish newspapers. See Granberg, *Gustav III*, pp. 110–12.
11 Stålhane, *Gustaf III*, pp. 9–28 (quotation on p. 16).
12 Gudmund Jöran Adlerbeth, *Gustaf III:s resa i Italien: Anteckningar utgifna af Henrik Schück* (Stockholm: Bonnier, 1902), pp. 64–105, 152–96; Stålhane, *Gustaf III*, pp. 85–107, 126–45.

ceremonies rather had the character of participatory observation.[13]

This was not the case with Gustav III, who according to contemporary testimonies participated in Catholic liturgical services. He had several personal meetings with Pius VI, and members of his entourage attended papal audiences. The King's younger brother, Duke Frederik Adolf (1750–1803), had been received by the Pope during a visit to Rome in 1776. It was in connection with this visit that the contacts between Gustav III and the Roman Curia began. The French ambassador to Rome, Cardinal François-Joachim de Pierre de Bernis (1715–1794), acted as a mediator, and it was he who arranged an audience with Pius VI for the Duke.[14] During Gustav III's stay in the Eternal City, the Cardinal served as his cicerone and organized tours focusing on the religious cultural heritage. Cardinal de Bernis, who served as a 'cultural diplomat' in the broadest sense, also took care of other Protestant royal personages and arranged meetings with the Pope; however, they were not regents at the time.[15] Gustav III was the only ruling Protestant monarch thitherto received in the Vatican in this manner. The German historian Ludwig von Pastor, who provides a detailed account of the King's activities in Rome in his history of the popes, sees this event as the beginning of a new era.[16]

The importance Gustav III attached to his experiences in the Vatican is illustrated by the two paintings that were made to immortalize these occasions. He commissioned the French artist Bénigne Gagneraux (1756–1795) to paint his visit to the Vatican art collections together with Pius VI, and his presence at the papal Christmas mass in St Peter's Basilica is documented in a painting by Louis Jean Desprez (1743–1804), a French artist whom the King

---

13 Louise Bobé, 'Danske Fyrstebesøg i Rom: Kronprins Frederik 1692, Prins Carl 1698', in Louise Bobé (ed.), *Rom og Danmark gennem Tiderne*, 2 vols (Copenhagen: Levin & Munksgaard, 1935–1937), I (1935), pp. 91–7.
14 Granberg, *Gustav III*, pp. 112–17.
15 Adlerbeth, *Gustaf III*, pp. 67–85. Regarding Cardinal de Bernis as a cultural diplomat, see Virginie Larre, 'Le Cardinal de Bernis à Rome, une figure emblématique de la diplomatie et des arts (1769–1791)', in Marc Favreau and others (eds), *De l'usage de l'art en politiques* (Clermont-Ferrand: Presses Universitaire Blaise-Pascal, 2009), pp. 24–36. See also Gilles Montègre, *Le Cardinal de Bernis: le pouvoir de l'amitié* (Paris: Tallandier, 2019).
16 Ludwig Freiherr von Pastor, *Geschichte der Päpste seit dem Ausgang des Mittelalters*, XVI:3, *Pius VI, 1775–1799* (Freiburg/Br.: Herder, 1933), pp. 71–81.

also engaged for a number of other assignments.[17] Gustav III made several visits to the Propaganda Fide, where he was honoured with a tribute poem, recited in forty-six languages. He also witnessed how five priests celebrated mass simultaneously, each at his own altar and according to a different rite: a manifestation of the worldwide character of the Catholic Church. The fact that one of the priests was Black aroused some astonishment among the Swedish visitors. In connection with these visits, the King was in talks with the prefect, Cardinal Leonardo Antonelli (1730–1811), regarding the position of Catholics in Sweden.[18]

With papal permission, Gustav III organized the celebration of a Lutheran service in Rome on Easter Sunday, 11 April 1784; at the same time, the apostolic vicar Oster celebrated the first public Catholic Easter mass in Stockholm since the sixteenth century. The Protestant service in Rome was held in Palazzo Torlonia near St Peter's Basilica, which Gustav III used as a residence during his second stay in Rome. The Catholic Easter mass in Stockholm was celebrated in the southern City Hall in the presence of State Secretary Elis Schröderheim (1747–1795) and Duke Charles (1748–1818), the later Charles XIII (r. 1809–1818).[19] Schröderheim, who helped Oster obtain permission to print Catholic devotional literature, reported in a letter to Gustav III in Rome about the Catholic mass and the favourable impression it had made.[20] The two religious services may be regarded as a manifestation of religious tolerance in an enlightened spirit, and so they were described in the influential newspaper *Stockholms Posten*.[21] There is much to suggest that the King also wished them to be seen as expressions of mutual ecclesiastical recognition. The Catholic hierarchy did not accept this kind of reciprocity, however. Whereas government representatives attended the Catholic Easter mass in Stockholm, there were no papal dignitaries present at the Protestant Easter service in Rome.

From a Catholic point of view, the Protestant countries were, as before, regarded as mission areas which should be brought back to

---

17 Granberg, *Gustav III*, pp. 114–15.
18 Adlerbeth, *Gustaf III*, pp. 90–1; Palmqvist, *Die Römisch-katholische Kirche*, pp. 185–90.
19 Adlerbeth, *Gustaf III*, p. 182; Granberg, *Gustav III*, pp. 119–26.
20 Schröderheim to Gustav III, 13 April 1784, in Elof Tegnér (ed.), *Från tredje Gustafs dagar: Anteckningar och minnen af E. Schröderheim, G.G. Adlerbeth och G.M. Armfelt* (Stockholm: Beijer, 1892–1894), pp. 221–3; Granberg, *Gustav III*, pp. 120–2.
21 *Stockholms Posten*, 17 July 1784. See Nyman, *Press mot friheten*, pp. 27–9.

Figure 9.1 King Gustav III guided by Pope Pius VI in the Vatican sculpture gallery, painted by Bénigne Gagneraux. Photo: National Museum of Sweden.

Figure 9.2 King Gustav III attending Christmas mass in St Peter's Cathedral, painted by Louis Jean Desprez. Photo: National Museum of Sweden.

the community of the Catholic Church in the long run. A first goal was to establish parish structures, and Oster planned the construction of a large Catholic church in the capital and the establishment of a Catholic school for boys. As far as the church was concerned, he could count on royal support. In his reports to Rome, Oster relates a conversation with the court chaplain and *pastor primarius* in Stockholm, Baron Carl Edvard Taube (1746–1785), and others about a re-Catholization of Sweden and the Swedish Church's reunification with Rome. However, his eagerness to spread the Catholic faith led to conflict with the Stockholm City Consistory, where Taube was chairman. In this capacity, Taube could not show the same benevolence towards the apostolic vicar as he did on other occasions, and Oster was forced to promise not to receive Lutherans into the Catholic Church.[22]

However, these events reinforced anti-Catholic sentiments among the Swedish clergy and led to dissatisfaction with the policy of religious tolerance. Moreover, rumours circulated that the King was about to become a Catholic, rumours fuelled by reports in the media from his visit to Rome.[23] When reading the correspondence and reports concerning Gustav III's stay in Rome, there is much that reminds us of a Protestant convert's journey to the Catholic faith. The King visited churches and attended religious services; and at the Christmas mass in St Peter's, he participated in the service in the same manner as the Catholics, being seen kneeling beside Emperor Joseph II. He mentions this in a letter to Schröderheim, where he states that he considers himself as Catholic as the Emperor and more apostolic, since he, unlike the Emperor, held on to the faith of his nation, in his case the creed of the Synod of Uppsala.[24]

Here it is worth noting that the King chose to put forward the Synod of Uppsala as an example when highlighting his Catholicity. This synod, held in 1593, admittedly confirmed the three classic Christian creeds but also rejected the 'Papist' Church and its traditions, not least the Catholic mass. Yet this seemed to be no problem for Gustav III, who apparently constructed his own interpretation concerning the character of the doctrinal foundation of Swedish society and the national Church. According to Schröderheim, the King had even intended to issue the 1785 Intercession Day placard, a kind of annual government declaration read out in Swedish

---

22 Palmqvist, *Die Römisch-katholische Kirche*, pp. 181–84, 191–97.
23 Granberg, *Gustav III*, pp. 126–29.
24 Gustav III to Schröderheim, 28 January 1784, in Tegnér, *Från tredje*, p. 210.

churches, in Rome. He was dissuaded by his advisers, however, and the placard was signed at the Castle of Gripsholm instead.[25]

Gustav III's attraction to Catholicism

Previous research has described Gustav III's interest in Catholic liturgical life as an expression of his aesthetic interests. In the two biographies written by historian Erik Lönnroth and the literary scholar Leif Landen, the interest the King took in Catholic worship during his visit to Rome is thus explained by his aesthetic disposition.[26] Church historian Bertil Rehnberg, in his book on the religious debate in Sweden during the Gustavian era, emphasizes Gustav III's interest in pomp and ceremonies. He further asserts that the King had an attraction to 'the occult and superstitious', and that he, according to testimonies by contemporary church officials, would have been alien to the Christian faith. In her biography of the King, historian Beth Hennings states that, although he occasionally showed interest in Christian mysticism, he did not absorb any lasting impressions of the Christian faith. According to her, he used religion mainly to emphasize his serene royal position.[27]

Historian Claes Theodor Odhner presents a different picture in his 1896 study of the reign of Gustav III. He gives examples of the King seeking consolation in the Christian faith in connection with conflicts and devoting himself to Bible reading and religious meditations. According to Odhner, the transcendent dimensions of Christianity were what interested the King.[28] This is in line with the impressions Cardinal de Bernis conveys in a report from July 1784 to the French foreign minister, Count Charles Gravier de Vergennes (1717–1787), in which he emphasizes the King's great interest in liturgy but also that he seemed 'attaché' to his religion.[29]

---

25 Granberg, *Gustav III*, pp. 130–1.
26 Leif Landen, *Gustaf III: En biografi* (Stockholm, Wahlström & Widstrand, 2004), pp. 244–50; Lönnroth, *Den stora rollen*, pp. 97–103.
27 Bertil Rehnberg, *Prästeståndet och religionsdebatten 1786–1800* (Uppsala: Almqvist & Wiksell, 1966), pp. 94–6; Beth Hennings, *Gustav III: En biografi* (Stockholm: Norstedt, 1957), pp. 172–7.
28 Theodor Odhner, *Sveriges politiska historia under konung Gustaf III:s regering*, 3 vols (Stockholm: Norstedt, 1885–1905), II (1896), pp. 187–9.
29 Bernis to Vergennes, 14 July 1784, in Anatole de Montaiglon and Jules Guiffrey (eds), *Correspondance des directeurs de l'Académie de France à Rome avec les surintendants des bâtiments, 1780–1784*, 18 vols (Paris: Charavay, 1895), XIV (1895), p. 430.

Church historian Gunnar Granberg, who examines Gustav III's church policy in his 1998 dissertation, argues that the King's view of the Church was characterized both by Lutheran ideals of unity and by a quest for renewal in the spirit of Enlightenment. Like previously mentioned scholars, Granberg highlights the King's aesthetic interest as a source of motivation in the context of ecclesiastical reform policy, asserting that Gustav III found inspiration not only in the Catholic Church but also in the Anglican tradition. He does not, however, manage to support this claim other than by pointing at some Swedish priests who had good relations with representatives of the Anglican Church.[30] A somewhat different picture of Gustav III's ceremonial and aesthetic manifestations is supplied by the historians Mikael Alm and Henrika Tandefelt, who both claim that this was an expression of his technique as a ruler. But the significance of religion and religious symbolism in this context is hardly mentioned. Moreover, Tandefelt seems to lack knowledge of the confessional systems of the time and the conflicts between denominations. She states, for example, that Gustav III organized a Protestant service at St Peter's during his visit to Rome – an impossibility then as now.[31]

Enlightenment and ecclesiastical reform policy

Recent research has fundamentally altered the previously common view that 'enlightened' rulers took an unfavourable view of religion. Several researchers have shown how religious policy was an integral part of reform projects of various kinds. The overall goal was to make the practice of religion more rational and to eradicate everything that could be associated with superstition.[32] One example is the liturgical reforms introduced in Denmark under the influence of the theologian and court preacher Christian Bastholm,

---

30 Granberg, *Gustav III*, pp. 184–6, 262–4.
31 Mikael Alm, *Kungsord i elfte timmen: Språk och självbild i det gustavianska enväldets legitimitetskamp 1772–1809* (Stockholm: Atlantis, 2002); Henrika Tandefelt, *Konsten att härska: Gustaf III inför sina undersåtar* (Helsinki: Svenska litteratursällskapet i Finland, 2007), p. 97.
32 See, for example, William J. Bulman and Robert G. Ingram (eds), *God in the Enlightenment* (Oxford: Oxford University Press, 2016); David Sorkin, *The Religious Enlightenment: Protestants, Jews, and Catholics from London to Vienna* (Princeton, NJ: Princeton University Press, 2008); Pasi Ihalainen, *Protestant Nations Redefined: Changing Perceptions of National Identity in the Rhetoric of the English, Dutch and Swedish Public Churches, 1685–1772*

whose writings served as inspiration for Swedish churchmen as well. His target was simple worship free of ceremonies and Christian preaching with a focus on ethics and edification. This ideal of worship was also cherished by the Pietists, who – although the movement was subject to certain restrictions – exercised a strong influence in Scandinavia, especially in Denmark.[33]

In Catholic countries, reform policies in the spirit of the Enlightenment mainly took the form of restrictions on processions, devotions, pilgrimages and other popular religious practices. The most radical reforms were carried out in the Habsburg hereditary lands as part of Joseph II's centralization efforts, aimed at strengthening state control over the Church. By a decree of 1782, contemplative monasteries were abolished and their property confiscated to be used for pastoral and charitable purposes, and several apostles' feasts were abolished. Another distinguishing feature was the effort to tone down the ceremonial character of worship in favour of the educational and ethical dimensions of the Christian faith.[34] This kind of liturgical reform activity played a central role in the popular education projects of the Enlightenment era.

Admittedly, Gustav III too had carried out a reduction of the number of holy days at the beginning of his reign,[35] and he seems to have shown no interest in preserving the medieval heritage of the country. Even during his reign, several medieval churches were, as is shown in Zachrisson's contribution to this volume, demolished to be replaced by neo-classical buildings. Yet when it came to liturgy and worship, the King's ideas and visions went contrary to the ideals of the Enlightenment. He opposed the efforts to simplify religious services and committed himself to a richer and more ceremonial liturgy. This inclination was expressed already in connection with his coronation in May 1772, whose rituals he himself designed in minuscule detail. At the coronation, depicted afterwards on a painting by Carl Gustav Pilo (1711–1793), Archbishop Magnus

---

(Leiden: Brill, 2005); Jürgen Overhoff and Andreas Oberdorf (eds), *Katholische Aufklärung in Europa und Nordamerika* (Göttingen: Wallstein, 2019); Ulrich L. Lehner, *Die katholische Aufklärung: Weltgeschichte einer Reformbewegung* (Paderborn: Schöningh, 2017).

33 Martin Schwarz Lausten, *A Church History of Denmark* (Burlington, VT: Ashgate, 2002), pp. 173–6, 189–94.

34 Klueting, 'Catholic Enlightenment in Austria', pp. 139–56.

35 Göran Malmstedt, *Helgdagsreduktionen: övergången från ett medeltida till ett modernt år i Sverige 1500–1800* (Gothenburg: Department of History, 1994).

Gustav III, Enlightenment and religion 243

Beronius (1692–1775) wore a mitre in accordance with the King's wish. This item of Catholic liturgical insignia was abolished during the Reformation era, reintroduced by the Catholic-orientated King John III's *Nova ordinantia* (1575) and then banned by the aforementioned Synod of Uppsala in 1593.[36]

As part of his liturgical reform project, Gustav III reintroduced both the mitre and the crosier as episcopal insignia. He also planned to introduce the pectoral cross in connection with the upcoming celebration of the bicentennial of the Synod of Uppsala by personally handing over such a cross to all the bishops. But his death prevented the implementation of this project. In addition to this, the King had plans to adopt the use of incense at services, but was persuaded not to present such a proposal.[37]

Several scholars have understood Gustav III's liturgical visions and his passion for the mystical dimensions of Christian faith in connection with his interest in Freemasonry. The Masonic Order was founded in England in the early eighteenth century and introduced in Sweden in 1752, when the first lodge was established in Stockholm. In his younger years, Gustav III, like his brothers, was actively engaged in the Masonic Order. What interested him was the chivalric mysticism that appeared in the northern European branch of the order and the religious symbolism that characterized its rites, which were partly taken from Catholic liturgy. While southern European Freemasonry was strongly influenced by rationalist ideals and had (and has) an anti-clerical orientation, the Swedish branch had an esoteric character with ten degrees, in which members were gradually inaugurated and admitted through solemn ceremonies. Swedish Freemasonry drew inspiration from the so-called strict observance, a system which developed in Germany in the 1750s and gave Freemasonry an even more mysterious and ceremonial character.[38]

Gustav III's interest in Freemasonry waned considerably after his Italian journey. He left the Masonic activities to his brother Duke

---

36 Granberg, *Gustav III*, pp. 193–5, 232–6. The printed ritual comprises 54 pages, divided into 259 paragraphs.
37 Rehnberg, *Prästeståndet och religionsdebatten*, p. 106; Granberg, *Gustav III*, pp. 146–7, 193–7.
38 Lenhammar, *Individualismens*, pp. 153–57; Göran Anderberg, *Frimuraren Gustaf III – Bakgrund, visioner, konspirationer, traditioner* (Partille: Warne, 2009), pp. 30–73. Regarding Freemasonry, see Mark Stavish, *Freemasonry: Rituals, Symbols and History of the Secret Society* (Woodbury, MN: Llewellyn, 2007); Helmuth Reinalter, *Die Freimaurer* (Munich: C. H. Beck, 2010).

Charles, who had been head of the Swedish lodges since 1774. The King's visit to the then supreme leader or Grand Master of the order, the Catholic pretender to the English throne, Prince Charles Edward Stuart (1720–1788), in Florence, was disappointing. The prince had no secrets to convey, and moreover, the Catholic liturgy probably completely overshadowed the Masonic rituals. Gustav III, however, promised to pay a pension to Stuart in exchange for taking over the title of Grand Master at his death.[39] It should be added that the Catholic Church condemned Freemasonry as incompatible with the Catholic faith, which made it problematic for Stuart to be engaged as its leader.[40]

Instead of Freemasonry, Gustav III focused on the royal orders, instituted by King Frederik I (r. 1720–1751) in 1748, namely the Order of the Seraphim, the Order of the Sword and the Order of the Pole Star. He also founded a new order, the Vasa Order, with three degrees, and he planned a special order for clerics, called the Jehovah Order. But he had to drop that project due to opposition from the clergy.[41] However, Gustav III's liturgical visions were neither historically orientated nor motivated by any a desire to revitalize Swedish medieval heritage. The historical epochs in Swedish history that were his main sources of inspiration were the reign of Gustav Vasa (1523–1560) and the Great Power era (the sixteenth and seventeenth centuries). The national costume he introduced was designed with elements from the latter period.[42] For him, liturgy was about the present and about giving eternal religious principles a symbolic shape, not about reviving a historical heritage. The negative image of the religious heritage of the Middle Ages, examined in a previous chapter, had no relevance in this context.[43]

---

39 Gustaf Mauritz Armfelt, *Resan till Italien, Gustaf Mauritz Armfelts resedagbok 1783–1784* (Stockholm: Atlantis, 1997), p. 60; Anderberg, *Frimuraren Gustaf III*, pp. 74–80; Leif Landen, *Gudmund Jöran Adlerbeth om Gustaf III:s italienska resa 1783–84* (Vejbystrand: Litteraturtjänst, 1998), pp. 89–92.
40 Richard Mathieu, *Freimaurerei und katholische Kirche: Geschichte und kirchenrechtliche Einordnung eines 300-jährigen Streits* (Leipzig: Salier, 2015).
41 Granberg, *Gustav III*, pp. 223–7.
42 Landen, *Gustaf III*, pp. 52–3.
43 Erik Sidenvall, 'Förnuftets och teologins kritik: ett bidrag till förståelsen av frihetstidens historieskrivning', *Historisk tidskrift*, 139:2 (2019), 223–50.

Liturgy and hierarchy – Catholicizing tendencies

The restorative alignment of Gustav III's ecclesiastical reform policy was clearly expressed in connection with episcopal installations carried out during his reign. He started with abolishing remaining offices of diocesan superintendents in 1772; henceforth, all heads of dioceses were to be named bishops. At the same time, he decreed that a bishop should have the exclusive right to ordain clergymen. Until then, this principle had been considered a Catholic practice. As a result, ordinary clergymen performed ordinations as well, and the ordination of bishops had long been regarded as a confirmation of the appointment, not as an act of consecration. Gustav III ensured that the sacred character of the bishop's installation was restored, and it was clearly marked when new bishops were enthroned.[44]

This ritual was first used at the ordination of the Bishop of Gothenburg, Johan Wingård (1738–1818), in the Royal Chapel in Stockholm in June 1780, where thirty-three clergymen in chasubles participated and the court orchestra was responsible for the music. The ordination was performed by Archbishop Carl Fredrik Mennander (1712–1786), who wore a cope and a mitre and carried a crosier. A particularly solemn episcopal ordination was that of Jacob Lindblom, former professor of eloquence and poetics at Uppsala University, in the cathedral of Linköping in March 1787. Two hundred clerics participated in the solemn consecration, which was performed by Archbishop Uno von Troil (1746–1803). Of great importance in this context was the consecration of the above-mentioned court chaplain Baron Taube in Uppsala Cathedral in November 1783. Taube was ordained bishop in his capacity as holder of a newly established bishopric attached to the Order of the Seraphim. Gustav III decided that the bishop of the order should have the same dignity as a diocesan bishop. His jurisdiction was, however, limited to the royal court.[45]

The King liked to see noblemen included in his clerical entourage, and it was because of the King's encouragement that Taube, who originally served as a military officer, embarked upon a clerical career. The fact that the episcopate was thus made into a career path for nobles gave rise to dissatisfaction within the Clerical Estate.

---

44 Sven Kjöllerström, *Sätt till att ordinera en vald biskop, 1561–1942* (Lund: Gleerup, 1974), pp. 134–6; Granberg, *Gustav III*, pp. 161–3, 187–92.
45 Granberg, *Gustav III*, pp. 170–1, 174–6.

Here, too, we can see an inspiration from the Catholic Church, where a large part of the ecclesiastical dignitaries belonged to the nobility.[46] It should be added, however, that a majority of the just over fifty court chaplains who served during the reign of Gustav III were commoners, and that several came from a comparatively modest background. Taube shared the King's liturgical preferences, and as president of the Stockholm City Consistory he was committed to countering the prevailing tendency to simplify the liturgy.[47]

In the spring of 1784 Taube was summoned to Rome to officiate at the Lutheran services which were celebrated with papal permission in a provisional chapel in the Palazzo Torlonia on Easter Day and Easter Monday that year. He was assisted by the court chaplain Anders Norberg (1745–1840), who was also ordered to come to Rome solely for this purpose. The Protestant services in Rome were celebrated according to the order of worship for the palace chapels, designed by the King himself and established in the court regulations of 1778. It stipulated that the service was to be celebrated by two clergymen in chasubles when the King was present, that parts of it should be sung, and that the blessing should be given from the altar, not from the pulpit. Particularly magnificent were the services celebrated within the framework of the royal orders, but they were open only to members and specially invited guests.[48]

For the Easter mass, the first public Protestant service to be celebrated in Rome, many people had gathered, both Romans and northerners staying in the city. The King and some of the Protestants went to communion. Two clergymen were wearing red chasubles procured in Rome, and Taube wore a mitre and a magnificent cope. According to Norberg, the service made a deep impression on those present, and he noted with surprise the respectful treatment he and Taube received at the papal court.[49] As was pointed out above, the King did not content himself with these Protestant services.

---

46 See Erwin Gatz and Clemens Brodkorb (eds), *Die Bischöfe des Heiligen Römischen Reiches, 1448 bis 1648: ein biographisches Lexikon* (Berlin: De Gruyter, 1996).
47 Granberg, *Gustav III*, pp. 144, 172–3, 201–3, 208–18, 223–5.
48 Granberg, *Gustav III*, pp. 119–24.
49 UUB, Strödda handlingar 1019, Anders Norberg, 'Berättelse om Kon. Gustaf III:s Nattvardsgång i Rom'. See Stålhane, *Gustaf III*, pp. 153–4. Gustav III gives a short account in a letter to Creuz, of 14 April 1784, where he mentions the friendly reception the two Swedish prelates received from the Pope; see UUB, Gustavianska samlingen, F479.

His entourage included his close friend Armfelt, who documented the stay and supplied accounts of the King's cultural and religious activities in Rome. For example, Armfelt notes that the King fasted on Good Friday and that he participated in the Good Friday service with Tenebrae litanies and veneration of the cross in the Sistine Chapel.[50]

A more extensive description of the King's countless visits to churches, excursions and social gatherings is given by Adlerbeth, who served as the King's secretary during the journey.[51] Adlerbeth supplies a detailed account of the religious services of different kinds in which Gustav III participated. An interesting detail that he mentions is that the King attended the consecration of a nun in a Clarist convent, where he as an anointed and crowned monarch was let into the enclosure and could watch the ceremonies up close. According to Catholic teaching, a crowned king is included in the clergy, a rule which Gustav III could invoke despite not being a Catholic.[52] Gustav III's notion of kingship was marked, as clearly manifested at his coronation, by a theocratic conception of the king as God's chosen and anointed servant. He drew parallels between the coronation and the ordination of priests and bishops. At the reception of a deputation from the clergy in 1789, he thus emphasized, according to one of those present, that clergymen were the only officials in the kingdom who were consecrated into their office in the same way as he himself.[53] This is in line with the Catholic concept but does not fit in with a more rational view of the monarchy and the clergy.

With regard to the importance of apostolic succession, Gustav III's view is also consistent with that of the Catholic Church. He considered the Church of Sweden to have preserved the apostolic succession during the Reformation era, a circumstance which he emphasized in his relations with the Holy See. This was the case, for example, in connection with a meeting with the papal nuncio in Cologne, Carlo Bellisomi (1736–1808), at the health resort Spa in Germany in the summer of 1780. In letters to the Propaganda Fide, Bellisomi reported that the King had told him that the Church in Sweden had not changed

---

50 Armfelt, *Resan till Italien*, pp. 83–106, 137–54.
51 Adlerbeth, *Gustaf III*, pp. 79–83, 173–83, 192–6. See also Landen, *Gudmund Jöran Adlerbeth*.
52 Adlerbeth, *Gustaf III*, pp. 79–83, 173–83, 192–6; Pastor, *Geschichte der Päpste*, p. 79.
53 Granberg, *Gustav III*, pp. 231–40.

to any great degree at the Reformation. He also noted the King's discussions of the issue of what separated and united Lutherans and Catholics, respectively, thereby proving, according to the nuncio, how well informed the King was in religious matters.[54]

During his stay in Rome, Gustav III had similar conversations with Cardinal de Bernis (1715–1794), who provided a series of dinners and parties for the King and his entourage. De Bernis' reports to Vergennes reveal that the King showed great interest in liturgical matters and studied the ceremonies and practices of the Catholic Church with great zeal, and that he expressed a Catholic view regarding the edifying character of religious ceremonies. The Cardinal further noted that the King attended Catholic services during Holy Week with greater reverence than most Catholics, and that he was deeply touched by the papal blessing on St Peter's Square.[55] Gustav III developed a real friendship with the Cardinal, as evidenced by the correspondence between the two. It is mainly about political matters, but more personal issues are discussed as well, including some of a religious nature. The King uses the address 'mon cher Cardinal', and in a letter from August 1786 he refers to himself as the Cardinal's 'pénitent du Nord'. Bernis, for his part, describes himself as the King's 'confesseur extraordinaire' and conveys greetings to the Pope in this capacity.[56] Interestingly, the King received a copy of this letter and personally noted the sender.[57]

It may be assumed that Gustav III also discussed religious and liturgical issues with Pius VI, with whom he had several meetings, the last of them just before the King's departure from Rome on 19 April 1784. By all accounts, the Pope appreciated the King, who from a Catholic point of view admittedly represented a heretical Church but who also showed great interest in Catholic worship and had legalized Catholic religious practice in Sweden through his tolerant reforms. The prefect of the Propaganda Fide, Cardinal Leonardo Antonelli (1730–1811), emphasized in a letter to the

---

54 Palmquist, *Die Römisch-katholische Kirche*, pp. 87–92.
55 Bernis to Vergennes, 28 December 1783; 16 March; 6, 14 April and 14 July 1784, in de Montaiglon and Guiffrey, *Correspondance*, pp. 396–8, 419–20, 425, 428–33.
56 Gustav III to Bernis, 24 August 1784, 8 March 1788; Bernis to Gustav III, 6 December 1788, 23 March 1787, undated 1789, 10 March 1792, published in Carlos Sommervogel, 'Gustave III et le Cardinal de Bernis', *Etudes religieuses, historiques et littéraires*, 16 (1869), 185–208.
57 Stockholm, Kungliga biblioteket (KB), Gustav III:s historia, D 1019.

apostolic vicar in Stockholm that the King had shown great respect and benevolence towards the Pope and the Holy See, which he hoped would benefit the Catholic cause in Sweden.[58] On his last night in Rome, Gustav III was honoured with a magnificent firework display. In a letter to Creutz in Stockholm, the King writes that Rome was the only place, since he left Sweden, that caused him to feel 'a real loss' (*en verklig saknad*). He also notes that Taube was well received by the Pope, which he interpreted as implying that Taube was recognized as a proper bishop.[59]

Anti-Catholic reactions

Gustav III's stay in Rome gave echo in the press. The official newspaper in Rome, *Diario ordinario*, reported on the King's various programmes and excursions. Much of this was translated and published in the Swedish newspaper *Stockholms Post-Tidningar*. For example, there were reports about the King's visit to Rome's main churches and about how he participated in Catholic religious services and inspected famous relics. *Diario ordinario* also reported on the King's interest in Queen Christina and his repeated visits to the Propaganda Fide.[60]

This led, as mentioned, to rumours that the King was about to become a Catholic, and that this was the reason for his benevolent treatment of Catholics in Sweden. The King's many encounters with the Pope only served to fuel these rumours. Count Axel von Fersen, who had been at the forefront of opposition to the King since the *coup d'état* in 1772, did his part in spreading them.[61] Taube too was suspected of having converted to the Catholic faith, and Schröderheim reported that there were rumours to the effect that he was about to introduce a Catholic-inspired liturgy. In his reply, the King tried to downplay these fears by stressing that the papacy was approaching its doom after the Emperor had given it its

---

58 Palmqvist, *Die Römisch-katholische Kirche*, pp. 186–90.
59 Gustav III to Creutz, 17 April 1794, in UUB, Gustavianska samlingen, F479.
60 *Stockholms Post-Tidningar*, nos. 25, 33 and 36–8, 1784.
61 Axel von Fersen, *Riksrådet och fältmarskalken m.m. grefve Fredrik Axel von Fersens historiska skrifter*, ed. R. M. Klinckowström, 8 vols (Stockholm: Norstedts, 1867–1872), V (1870), pp. 190–3, 199–200, 209–10. He was kept informed of events in Rome by his son of the same name, who was in the King's entourage.

'extreme unction', referring to Joseph II's church policy.[62] In a letter to Cardinal de Bernis, the King, speaking of these rumours, ironically emphasized that he was no more Catholic than the Emperor, an ambiguous statement to say the least.[63]

These rumours contributed to increasing the deep-rooted anti-Catholic sentiments in Sweden. Several of the King's closest associates shared this critical attitude towards the Catholic Church. Adlerbeth described its teachings as an expression of 'human blindness', and he criticized the allegedly unedifying character of ceremonial Latin worship. Others, von Fersen among them, expressed themselves even more critically; the Count characterized Catholicism as a religion embossed by clericalism and an 'exaggerated pride and splendour'.[64] Such anti-Catholic criticism forced Gustav III to be more restrained in voicing sympathies for the Catholic Church. He stuck to his plans to build a Catholic church in the capital, however, and commissioned Desprez to draw up a proposal.[65] He also continued his efforts to reform and ritualize the worship of the Church of Sweden in a Catholic spirit.

Not unexpectedly, the strongest opposition to the King's ecclesiastical reform policy came from the clergy. In previous research, this disagreement has often been described as a conflict between the King's enlightened ideas and the Lutheran orthodoxy of the clergy.[66] As far as the tolerance laws are concerned, the matter can to some extent be understood in this way. Several representatives of the Clerical Estate opposed the liberalization of religious legislation, and here concerns about Catholic proselytizing activities played an important role. But there were also clergymen in the *Riksdag* who advocated increased religious tolerance, and the initiative in this matter was actually taken in the Clerical Estate. The Finnish clergyman Anders Chydenius, supported by like-minded

---

62 Schröderheim to Gustav III, 30 November 1783; Gustav III to Schröderheim, 28 January 1784, in Tegnér, *Från tredje*, pp. 207, 209–10. The Swedish envoys in Hamburg, Dresden and Regensburg were commissioned to deny rumours that the King should have secretly become a Catholic. Palmqvist, *Die Römisch-katholische Kirche*, pp. 187–90.
63 Gustav III to Bernis, undated 1786, in Sommervogel, 'Gustave III et le Cardinal de Bernis', 193–4.
64 Adlerbeth, *Gustaf III*, pp. 184–6; Fersen, *Riksrådet och fältmarskalken*, p. 72.
65 Granberg, *Gustav III*, pp. 131–4.
66 Lenhammar, *Individualismens*, pp. 140–52; Rehnberg, *Prästeståndet och religionsdebatten*, pp. 73–9, 486–9.

clerics such as Bishop Wingård and Archbishop-to-be von Troil, presented a memorial to the *Riksdag* of 1778 which included a proposal of religious freedom for foreign believers. Some scholars suggest that the King was behind the proposal, but there is no clear evidence to support that claim. The King gave his support to the memorial, which after being accepted by the other three Estates was finally voted through in the Clerical Estate in January 1779. That the Edict of Toleration was issued on Gustav III's birthday on 24 January 1781 illustrates the importance that the King attached to this reform for the benefit of Catholics in the kingdom.[67]

Anti-Catholic tendencies were clearly expressed in connection with the celebration of the bicentennial of the Synod of Uppsala in March 1793. Several speakers pointed out how Christian doctrine, through the Reformation, had been freed from 'papist' delusions and cleansed from abuse, superstition and unnecessary ceremonies. Here, the propagandistic rhetoric of the Reformation about the purchase of remission of sins and the worship of saints was repeated. The Catholic religious heritage was thus, in the same way as illustrated in other chapters of this volume, connected with abuse and decay. This unfavourable picture contrasted with religious Enlightenment, the progress of science and the development of a more rational interpretation of the Bible. In addition, and alluding to the ongoing French Revolution, 'pure evangelical doctrine' was praised as a safeguard against revolutionary fanaticism.[68]

Gustav III and the clergy

Gustav III advocated a greater measure of freedom of conscience within the Swedish Church. The Moravians were allowed to erect chapels in Stockholm and Gothenburg, and the King intervened in some cases in favour of people who had been subjected to repressive measures for activities that were in conflict with the religious legislation at the time. This was the case, for example, with the pietist preacher Anders Collin (1754–1830), who was taken into custody but released upon the King's command.[69]

---

67 Granberg, *Gustav III*, pp. 78–100.
68 *Handlingar rörande jubel-festen uti Upsala 1793* (Uppsala: J. Edmans enka, 1793), pp. 135–45, 151–7. See also Harry Lenhammar, 'Jubelfesterna 1693, 1793 och 1893', *Kyrkohistorisk årsskrift*, 93 (1993), 29–32.
69 Granberg, *Gustav III*, pp. 88–9.

Yet the Conventicle Act of 1726, which forbade unlicensed religious gatherings, remained in force, and there is no indication that the King intended to remove this restriction on religious freedom of conscience. Ecclesiastical censorship continued, and the King sanctioned measures against pietist and other nonconformist literature.[70] Gustav III thus had no intention of breaking up the Swedish ecclesiastical system founded on the basis of Lutheran doctrine. At the end of his reign, it was still forbidden for Swedish subjects to leave the established Lutheran Church and join another Christian denomination. The King advocated freedom of conscience within the framework of the existing ecclesiastical system along with the right to practise one's ancestral religion, not religious freedom in the sense we attribute to the concept today.

The clergy supported the policy of religious tolerance, despite some criticism. However, the King's liturgical renewal policy met with compact opposition, and the proposals presented in the Clerical Estate went in the opposite direction. This was clearly expressed at the *Riksdag* of 1786 and 1789, where several members advocated a more Enlightenment-orientated liturgy with a focus on ethics and morality. An example is the Turku theologian Jacob Tengström (1755–1832), later Finland's first archbishop, who in 1786 presented a proposal to simplify the liturgy and to play down the supernatural elements of worship. Other members of the Clerical Estate criticized the Enlightenment ideas, however, highlighting their unfavourable impact on church life; that theatres were allowed to be open on Sundays was regarded as part of this problem.[71]

The opposition to the King's liturgical reform policy was accentuated at the *Riksdag* of 1789. The *Riksdag* was summoned as a result of the war against Russia and the rebellious officers' confederation at Anjala in Finland, formed the previous autumn as a protest against a renewed war effort. With support from the three lower Estates, the King enforced a constitutional amendment, the Union and Security Act, which strengthened his position of power and weakened the influence of the nobility.[72] The fact that the King, in a situation where he was under considerable pressure, addressed a special letter to the Clerical Estate in February 1789 containing proposals for liturgical reforms shows the importance he attached

---

70 Rehnberg, *Prästeståndet och religionsdebatten*, pp. 30–2, 81–4; Granberg, *Gustav III*, pp. 140–1.
71 Rehnberg, *Prästeståndet och religionsdebatten*, pp. 43–50, 57–61, 69–71.
72 Lönnroth, *Den stora rollen*, p. 201.

to this matter. The royal letter, which was geared towards the impending jubilee celebration of the bicentennial of the Synod of Uppsala in 1793, also raised the question of the planned revision of the Service Book and the Hymnal. Diocesan chapters were invited to submit proposals for this purpose.[73]

The King's proposal provoked a lively debate in the Clerical Estate, and several members expressed requests for a simplified liturgy. The court chaplain Joel Jacob Petrejus (1732–1804) stood out in particular. In a memorial he argued for a removal of baptismal exorcism, the sign of the cross and other, in his view, un-biblical elements in the service. At the same time, he warned – with a clear hint against the King's liturgical ideas – that the introduction of new ceremonies would turn public worship into a theatre. These positions were in line both with the pietist conception of worship and with the liturgical views held by the proponents of Enlightenment ideas. However, the Bishop of Växjö, Olof Wallquist, whose activities are examined by Sidenvall in this volume, intervened and ensured that the issue was postponed and that Petrejus withdrew his memorial. Without his intervention, the Clerical Estate would probably have voted in favour of a simplification of the liturgy, contrary to the King's wishes.[74] The new Service Book, adopted at the *Riksdag* of 1811, went in this direction. A number of 'classic' liturgical practices and prayers, including the Nicene Creed, were abandoned or simplified.[75]

In his memorial, Petrejus held up the liturgical reform work in Denmark and Germany as a model. Like many others, among them Archbishop von Troil, he was inspired by the Danish theologian and court chaplain Christian Bastholm, who was one of the main representatives of rationalist Enlightenment theology and who advocated a church reform in this spirit. Bastholm's ideas had a considerable impact on Danish church life and led to the removal of a number of older practices which were regarded as superstitious and useless. Gustav III, not unexpectedly, was strongly opposed to this kind of reform, which, as he noted in a conversation with

---

73 Rehnberg, *Prästeståndet och religionsdebatten*, pp. 90–7.
74 Rehnberg, *Prästeståndet och religionsdebatten*, pp. 98–111; Granberg, *Gustav III*, pp. 150–4.
75 A detailed account is supplied in Dick Helander, *Den liturgiska utvecklingen i Sverige*, I: *Tillkomsten av 1811 års kyrkohandbok* (Lund: Svenska Kyrkans Diakonistyrelses bokförlag, 1934). See also Rehnberg, *Prästeståndet och religionsdebatten*, pp. 131–4, 159–75.

the clergyman and historian (later bishop) Carl Gustaf Nordin (1749–1812), had given the Danish religious services a poor and 'simple' character.[76]

This is just another example of how badly Gustav III's ideals of Christian worship fitted in with the liturgical reform ideas in the spirit of the Enlightenment. While the representatives of Enlightenment advocated a simplified liturgy, the King committed himself to a richer and more solemn religious service. He saw the liturgy as a tool to convey devotion and communion with God, not as an instrument of moral education. Gustav III was anxious to emphasize the apostolic succession of the Church of Sweden and the sacred character of its clergy. In this respect, his ideals were more in line with incipient Romanticism than with the Enlightenment.[77]

Conclusion

In several ways, Gustav III represented the ideals of the Enlightenment. This orientation was manifested in his political reforms, not least within the religious field. However, his ecclesiastical reform policy went contrary to these ideals. The King did not have any time for the Enlightenment's visions of a rational worship service, nor for a Christian faith where ethics instead of the Christian mystery was foregrounded. Despite his legislation of religious tolerance, he showed no intention of abandoning the system of ecclesiastical unity. Nor was there ever any question of repealing the ban on private religious gatherings or of allowing Swedish subjects to convert to another Christian denomination. At this point, Gustav III's policy of religion was completely in line with the confessional principles of the pre-modern system, where restricted tolerance, not individual religious freedom, was the norm.

The King's idea of kingship was firmly rooted in a pre-modern world view. He was keen to emphasize the divine character of kingship, and he stressed the connection between the royal and the clerical office. This is in line with what was then Catholic doctrine, but it runs counter to rationalist views of society. Gustav III drew

---

76 Carl Gustaf Nordin, *Historiska handlingar*, VI: *Dagboksanteckningar för åren 1786–1792 af Carl Gustaf Nordin* (Stockholm: Haeggströms, 1868), p. 6. Granberg, *Gustav III*, pp. 141–3.
77 See Jonathan B. Fine, 'The birth of aestheticized religion out of the counter-enlightenment attraction to Catholicism', *European Romantic Review*, 26:1 (2017), 17–57.

his inspiration partly from older Swedish liturgical traditions, but above all from the Catholic Church. Here the impressions from his visit to Rome in 1783–1784 played an important role. According to several testimonies, he participated diligently in Catholic services and events, and Pope Pius VI received him almost as if he had been a Catholic monarch.

The Catholic influence was evident in Gustav III's ecclesiastical reform policy. He reformed the Swedish episcopal college in a Catholic spirit by reviving the bishop's installation as a liturgical act of consecration and reintroducing episcopal insignia. He also committed himself to a richer and more ceremonial mode of worship. Here the liturgy used in the court chapels, which the King had designed himself, served as a model. The two Protestant services that the King, with papal permission, organized in Rome at Easter 1784 were conducted according to this order. At the Catholic Easter mass celebrated at the same time in Stockholm, high state dignitaries were present, and Gustav III's religious tolerance policy especially benefited the Catholics.

There is, however, no evidence that the King would have embraced the teachings of the Catholic Church apart from the liturgy and the hierarchical order. Yet, he showed great interest in theological matters and in the question of what separated and united Lutherans and Catholics. In conversations with the papal nuncio in Cologne, he argued that the Swedish Church had not changed to any great extent at the Reformation. He was thus anxious to convince his Catholic interlocutor that the Lutheran Swedish Church was a Catholic Church with roots in the apostolic age. To strengthen, consolidate and manifest this status was the overall aim of his ecclesiastical reform policy.

In this respect, Gustav III's ecclesiastical visions thus remind us of the present-day Swedish High Church movement, and perhaps even more of Archbishop Nathan Söderblom's (1866–1931) idea of ecumenism and 'evangelical catholicity'.[78] Yet, in the same way as these twentieth-century Swedish churchmen, Gustav III had to realize that the Catholic hierarchy did not regard the Swedish Church as a legitimate local Catholic Church. An expression of this stance on the part of the Catholic leaders was that neither representatives of the papal court nor Catholic clerics were present at the celebration

---

78 See Klas Hansson, 'Nathan Söderblom's ecumenical cope: a visualization of a theological and ecumenical concept', *Studia Theologia: Nordic Journal of Theology*, 66:1 (2012), 62–79.

of the Protestant services that the King caused to be arranged in Rome. From a Catholic point of view, the Protestant countries were seen as mission fields which had to be brought back to the Catholic fold in the long run.

The King's church reforms provoked opposition from the Lutheran clergy, not least his Catholicizing liturgical endeavours. Contrary to the King's intentions, this opposition contributed to the revival and reinforcement of anti-Catholic sentiment. As for the perception of worship, many of the leading representatives of the clergy were influenced by the purist ideals of the Enlightenment, which to them appeared more in conformity with the Lutheran tradition than the ceremonial Catholic liturgy. Gustav III used the ideas of the Enlightenment to adapt the breakup of the system of confessional uniformity and bring the Lutheran state-Church system more up to date. At the same time, he questioned parts of the Enlightenment project and instead tied in with the ideals of the upcoming Romanticism with its appreciation of religious mysticism and Catholic liturgical aesthetics.

Bibliography

Archival sources

Stockholm

Kungliga biblioteket (KB)
  Strödda handlingar till Gustav III:s historia, D 1019

Uppsala, Sweden

Uppsala Universitetsbibliotek (UUB)
  Gustavianska samlingen, F479
  Strödda handlingar, 1019

Printed sources and literature

Adlerbeth, Gudmund Jöran, *Gustaf III:s resa i Italien: Anteckningar utgifna af Henrik Schück* (Stockholm: Bonnier, 1902).

Alm, Mikael, *Kungsord i elfte timmen: Språk och självbild i det Gustavianska enväldets legitimitetskamp 1772–1809* (Stockholm: Atlantis, 2002).

Anderberg, Göran, *Frimuraren Gustaf III: Bakgrund, visioner, konspirationer, traditioner* (Partille: Warne, 2009).

Armfelt, Gustaf Mauritz, *Resan till Italien: Gustaf Mauritz Armfelts resedagbok 1783–1784* (Stockholm: Atlantis, 1997).
Bobé, Louise, 'Danske Fyrstebesøg i Rom: Kronprins Frederik 1692, Prins Carl 1698', in Louise Bobé (ed.), *Rom og Danmark gennem Tiderne*, 2 vols (Copenhagen: Levin & Munksgaard, 1935–1937), I (1935), pp. 91–7.
Bulman, William J. and Robert G. Ingram (eds), *God in the Enlightenment* (Oxford: Oxford University Press, 2016).
Fersen, Axel von, *Riksrådet och fältmarskalken m.m. grefve Fredrik Axel von Fersens historiska skrifter*, ed. R. M. Klinckowström, 8 vols (Stockholm: Norstedts, 1867–1872), V (1870).
Fine, Jonathan B., 'The birth of aestheticized religion out of the counter-enlightenment attraction to Catholicism', *European Romantic Review*, 26:1 (2017), 17–57.
Gatz, Erwin and Clemens Brodkorb (eds), *Die Bischöfe des Heiligen Römischen Reiches, 1448 bis 1648: ein biographisches Lexikon* (Berlin: De Gruyter, 1996).
Granberg, Gunnar, *Gustav III: en upplysningskonungs tro och kyrkosyn* (Uppsala: Acta Universitatis Upsaliensis, 1998).
Gross, Hanns, *Rome in the Age of Enlightenment: The Post-Tridentine Syndrome and the Ancien Régime* (Cambridge: Cambridge University Press, 2004).
Handlingar rörande jubel-festen uti Upsala 1793 (Uppsala: J. Edmans enka, 1793).
Hansson, Klas, 'Nathan Söderblom's ecumenical cope: a visualization of a theological and ecumenical concept', *Studia Theologia: Nordic Journal of Theology*, 66:1 (2012), 62–79.
Helander, Dick, *Den liturgiska utvecklingen i Sverige*, I: *Tillkomsten av 1811 års kyrkohandbok* (Lund: Svenska Kyrkans Diakonistyrelses bokförlag, 1934).
Hennings, Beth, *Gustav III. En biografi* (Stockholm: Norstedt, 1957).
Ihalainen, Pasi, *Protestant Nations Redefined: Changing Perceptions of National Identity in the Rhetoric of the English, Dutch and Swedish Public Churches, 1685–1772* (Leiden: Brill, 2005).
Kjöllerström, Sven, *Sätt till att ordinera en vald biskop, 1561–1942* (Lund: Gleerup, 1974).
Klueting, Harm, 'Catholic Enlightenment in Austria or the Habsburg Lands', in Ulrich Lehner and Michael Printy (eds), *A Companion to the Catholic Enlightenment in Europe* (Leiden: Brill, 2010), pp. 127–64.
Landen, Leif, *Gudmund Jöran Adlerbeth om Gustaf III:s italienska resa 1783–84* (Vejbystrand: Litteraturtjänst, 1998).
———, *Gustaf III: En biografi* (Stockholm, Wahlström & Widstrand, 2004).
Larre, Virginie, 'Le Cardinal de Bernis à Rome, une figure emblématique de la diplomatie et des arts (1769–1791)', in Marc Favreau and others (eds), *De l'usage de l'art en politiques* (Clermont-Ferrand: Presses Universitaire Blaise-Pascal, 2009), pp. 24–36.

Lehner, Ulrich L., *Die Katholische Aufklärung: Weltgeschichte einer Reformbewegung* (Paderborn: Schöningh, 2017).
Lenhammar, Harry, *Sveriges kyrkohistoria, V: Individualismens och upplysningens tid* (Stockholm: Verbum, 2000).
——, 'Jubelfesterna 1693, 1793 och 1893', *Kyrkohistorisk årsskrift*, 93 (1993), 29–32.
Lönnroth, Erik, *Den stora rollen: kung Gustaf III spelad av honom själv* (Stockholm: Norstedt, 2008).
Malmstedt, Göran, *Helgdagsreduktionen: övergången från ett medeltida till ett modernt år i Sverige 1500–1800* (Gothenburg: Department of History, 1994).
Matheus, Ricarda, *Konversionen in Rom in der Frühen Neuzeit: Das Ospizio dei Convertendi 1673–1750* (Berlin and Boston: De Gruyter, 2012).
Mathieu, Richard, *Freimaurerei und katholische Kirche: Geschichte und kirchenrechtliche Einordnung eines 300-jährigen Streits* (Leipzig: Salier, 2015).
Mazur, Peter A., *Conversion to Catholicism in Early Modern Italy* (New York and London: Routledge, 2016).
Montaiglon, Anatole de and Jules Guiffrey (eds), *Correspondance des directeurs de l'Académie de France à Rome avec les surintendants des bâtiments, 1780–1784*, 18 vols (Paris: Charavay, 1895), XIV (1895).
Montègre, Gilles, *Le Cardinal de Bernis: le pouvoir de l'amitié* (Paris: Tallandier, 2019).
Nordin, Carl Gustaf, *Historiska handlingar*, VI: *Dagboksanteckningar för åren 1786–1792 af Carl Gustaf Nordin* (Stockholm: Haeggströms, 1868).
Nyman, Magnus, *Press mot friheten: opinionsbildning i de svenska tidningarna och åsiktsbrytningar om minoriteter 1772–1786* (Uppsala: Almqvist & Wiksell, 1988).
Odhner, Theodor, *Sveriges politiska historia under konung Gustaf III:s regering*, 3 vols (Stockholm: Norstedt, 1885–1905), II (1896).
Overhoff, Jürgen and Andreas Oberdorf (eds), *Katholische Aufklärung in Europa und Nordamerika* (Göttingen: Wallstein, 2019).
Palmqvist, Arne, *Die Römisch-katholische Kirche in Schweden nach 1781: Das Apostolische Vikariat 1783–1820* (Uppsala: Almqvist & Wiksell, 1954).
Pastor, Ludwig Freiherr von, *Geschichte der Päpste seit dem Ausgang des Mittelalters*, XVI:3, Pius VI, 1775–1799 (Freiburg/Br.: Herder, 1933).
Proschwitz, Gunnar von, 'Gustaf III – En upplyst kosmopolit', in Hans Medelius (ed.), *Himla många kungar: Historier kring Den Svenska Historien* (Enskede: Fataburen, 1993), pp. 231–49.
Raunio, Anu, *Conversioni al cattolicesimo a Roma tra Sei e Settecento: La presenza degli scandinavi nell'Ospizio dei Convertendi* (Turku: University of Turku, 2009).
Rehnberg, Bertil, *Prästeståndet och religionsdebatten 1786–1800* (Uppsala: Almqvist & Wiksell, 1966).

Reinalter, Helmuth, *Die Freimaurer* (Munich: C. H. Beck, 2010).
Schwarz Lausten, Martin, *A Church History of Denmark* (Burlington, VT: Ashgate, 2002).
Sidenvall, Erik, 'Förnuftets och teologins kritik: ett bidrag till förståelsen av frihetstidens historieskrivning', *Historisk tidskrift*, 139:2 (2019), 223–50.
Sommervogel, Carlos, 'Gustave III et le Cardinal de Bernis', *Etudes religieuses, historiques et littéraires*, 16 (1869), 185–208.
Sorkin, David, *The Religious Enlightenment: Protestants, Jews, and Catholics from London to Vienna* (Princeton, NJ: Princeton University Press, 2008).
Stålhane, Henning, *Gustaf III:s resa till Italien och Frankrike* (Stockholm: Nordisk Rotogravyr, 1953).
Stavish, Mark, *Freemasonry: Rituals, Symbols and History of the Secret Society* (Woodbury, MN: Llewellyn, 2007).
Stockholms Posten.
Stockholms Post-Tidningar.
Tandefelt, Henrika, *Konsten att härska: Gustaf III inför sina undersåtar* (Helsinki: Svenska litteratursällskapet i Finland, 2007).
Tegnér, Elof (ed.), *Från tredje Gustafs dagar: Anteckningar och minnen af E. Schröderheim, G.G. Adlerbeth och G.M. Armfelt* (Stockholm: Beijer, 1892–1894).
Winberg, Ola, *Den statskloka resan: Adelns peregrinationer 1610–1680* (Uppsala: Uppsala University, 2018).

Part III
Milestones of Enlightenment challenged

10
Melancholy diagnostics: on pietist introspection and forensic psychiatry *in statu nascendi*

Tine Reeh and Ralf Hemmingsen

Did the pietist preoccupation with the 'inner person' influence the general awareness and perception of mental health among the population at large? Can we trace the impact of pietist anthropology and interest on the individual subject beyond the religious praxis, and did this pietist 'gaze' influence societal developments in Denmark–Norway during the century of the Enlightenment?

The present chapter examines these questions, using a source material which focuses on the perception of impaired mental states within the legal system, specifically on the assessment of melancholy. After a brief introduction to the ambivalence surrounding the concept in the eighteenth century, we consider the era's legal framework regarding 'insanity defence'. We then turn to examples of pietist literature on introspection and diagnosis of the inner person before finally exploring three illustrative court cases of so-called melancholic murder. This leads to a presentation of a subsequent formal change in legal practice and changes in institutional response. These changes promoted new statutory rights on the part of the individual, but they were not driven by enlightened or humanitarian ideas. By way of conclusion, we return to the dynamics between pietist anthropology and pre-medicalized forensic psychiatry.

Melancholia on trial

Before the eighteenth century, criteria for insanity defence mirrored the definitions of severe mental illness, hence focusing on outward symptoms limited to aggressive, disorganized or antisocial behaviour.[1] Thus, *melancholia* and introversion were not generally considered impaired mental states comparable to insanity.

---

1 Mary Lindemann, 'Murder, melancholy and the insanity defence in eighteenth-century Hamburg', in Roberta Bivins and John V. Pickstone (eds), *Medicine,*

The idea that an individual could or perhaps should under certain circumstances be granted diminished responsibility for their actions can be traced to Classical Antiquity. However, while the Greeks and Romans recognized mental disorders, they did not as a rule exempt the sufferer from penal consequences.[2] In general, insanity and impaired mental health were considered as punishment inflicted by the gods but not as acquittal from human justice. In *The Laws*, Plato recommended that if a person was insane, his kinsfolk should watch over him as best they could under a penalty or fine.[3] This viewpoint was retrieved in Roman law, where a madman is considered to be punished by his madness itself, and the family is regarded as being responsible for the care and custody of the sufferer. The various classical descriptions of the troubled individual were used in courts in the eighteenth century as well, namely *furiosus, mente captus, non compos mentis* and *insanus*.[4] According to the Romans, these states of mind on the one hand required that the family assume responsibility for the sufferer, and on the other rendered the individual unaccountable for his or her actions to some degree. At the same time, we encounter an awareness that such a condition may not be permanent, and that a sufferer may have periods of sanity or bright moments, described as *lucida intervalla* or *intervalla sensu saniore*.[5]

The Roman line of thought was to some degree transmitted within canon law. In *Decretum Gratiani*, we also find scattered developments of the principle of guilt. Not only should a deed be offensive by nature and perpetrated by the accused, it should also be considered something that the accused could have avoided doing under the circumstances. Factors such as age and accountability,

---

Madness and Social History: Essays in Honour of Roy Porter (Basingstoke: Palgrave Macmillan, 2007), pp. 161–72; German E. Berrios, *The History of Mental Symptoms* (Cambridge: Cambridge University Press, 1996); Ralf Hemmingsen, 'Sindssygdomsbegrebet i det 18. århundrede', in Mads Julis Elf and Lasse Horne Kjældgaard (eds), *Mere Lys! Indblik i oplysningstiden i dansk litteratur og kultur* (Hellerup: Forlaget Spring, 2002), pp. 231–9; Catherine Beck, 'Patronage and insanity: tolerance, reputation and mental disorder in the British navy, 1740–1820', *Historical Research*, 94 (2021), 73–95 (73–9).

2 Nigel Walker, 'The insanity defense before 1800', *Annals of the American Academy of Political and Social Science*, 477:1 (1985), 25–30 (26).
3 Walker, 'The insanity defense before 1800', 26.
4 Knud Waaben, *Retspsykiatri og Strafferet i Historiens Lys* (Copenhagen: Janssen-Cilag, 1997), p. 14.
5 Waaben, *Retspsykiatri og Strafferet*, p. 14.

as well as negligence and intent or *mens rea*, became matters of consideration.[6] This connects to the role of the wrongdoer's will, and in the case of insanity the absence of will or the loss of control over such will as was deemed to be present. Canon law had a strong influence on Danish provincial codes (e.g. *Jyske Lov*) regarding civil and criminal law;[7] concepts and considerations regarding guilt as well as will are part of this legacy.

The Danish Code of 1683 continued many of these policies. Two of its sections concern insanity and insanity defence. The first, §1-19-7, states that if a person is furious (*rasende*) or insane (*galind*), anyone who wishes to do so can bind the person and take him before the governing assembly – the *Thing*. Here, in parallel with Classical Antiquity, the person is to be offered to his or her family, who are obliged to confine the person if they have the resources to do so. If not, the authorities should take the sufferer into custody. The second, §6-6-17, states that if a homicide is committed in delirium (*Vildelse*) or fury (*Raseri*), the killer should not be punished with the death penalty, but should instead pay blood money to the heirs of the deceased. This comes as an exception to the general rule found in §6-6-1, according to which a person who kills another person should lose their own life according to the biblical principle of *jus talionis*, referring to Exodus 21:23–5. The paragraph on murder is the only mention of an insanity defence in the Danish Code; and even though it was formally limited to homicide, it was interpreted throughout the eighteenth century as a general rule on the criteria for exemption from punishment. In other words, delirium and fury de facto defined the legal concept of insanity, and §1-19-17 served as a legal consequence or sanction in criminal cases where insanity was ascertained.[8]

There were no rules regarding the assessment of the suspect's mental condition. However, in addition to the delinquent's own behaviour and testimonials, statements by witnesses as well as by local clergy – and in critical cases the assessments of medical doctors

---

6 Waaben, *Retspsykiatri og Strafferet*, p. 12.
7 Jørgen Stenbæk, 'En kirkeretslig vurdering af Danske Lovs 6. bog – strafferetten', in *Kirkehistoriske Samlinger* (1972), pp. 58–90; Waaben, *Retspsykiatri og Strafferet*, p. 17.
8 Tage Holmboe, 'Højesteret og strafferetten', in Povl Bagge and others (eds), *Højesteret 1661–1961*, 2 vols (Copenhagen: Gads Förlag, 1961), II, p. 174; Troels G. Jørgensen, *Højesteret fra 1790 til Grundloven* (Copenhagen: Frost-Hansens Förlag, 1950), p. 137.

and the Copenhagen Faculty of Theology – were taken into consideration. The form of legal procedure in the Danish Code of 1683 was predominantly the accusatorial, with the prosecutor investigating and presenting the crime at a public trial where the verdict would be passed by an impartial judge or jury, most often lay assessors or judges with little in the way of legal training.[9] During the eighteenth century, however, the inquisitorial form of legal procedure was adopted, a development supported by, among other things, the introduction of a degree in law at the University of Copenhagen in 1736.[10] The inquisitorial principle, deriving from canonical law, allowed and stimulated judges to play a more active role in the investigation of crimes, as well as to question the accused. Its adoption led to an altogether more thorough, uniform and professional practice.[11]

However, preliminary studies from Denmark–Norway have also indicated that beginning at the height of Pietism in the region, the courts showed an increased interest not only in facts, intention and premeditation, but also in the subjective outlook or mental state of the criminal.[12] Studies have shown that the courts began to discuss a de facto extension of the narrow insanity-defence criteria in a number of cases from the 1740s – long before the official legal change.[13]

---

9 P. U. Knudsen, *Lovkyndighed og vederhæftighed: Sjællandske byfogeder 1682–1801* (Copenhagen: Jurist- og Økonomforbundet, 2001); Ditlev Tamm and E. Slottved (eds), *Københavns Universitet 1479–1979: Det Rets- og Statsvidenskabelige Fakultet* (Copenhagen: Københavns Universitet, 2005).
10 The first formal change in procedure was decreed on 21 May 1751, and was regulated by an additional decree on 3 June 1796. The stated grounds for the 1751 change in principle were that cases were not handled with due diligence and gravity everywhere, and were quite often treated more roughly.
11 Ditlev Tamm and Jens Ulf Jørgensen, *Dansk retshistorie i hovedpunkter: Fra landskabslovene til Ørsted*, 2 vols (Copenhagen: Gad, 1973–1978; repr. Akademisk förlag, 1987).
12 Tyge Krogh, *Oplysningstiden og det magiske: Henrettelser og korporlige straffe i 1700-tallets første halvdel* (Copenhagen: Samleren, 2000); Riikka Miettinen, *Suicide, Law, and Community in Early Modern Sweden* (Cham: Palgrave Macmillan, 2019); Ralf Hemmingsen and Tine Reeh, 'Mentale tilstande hos kvindelige barnemordere i det 18. århundrede', *Bibliotek for Læger – tidsskrift for medicinens historie, kultur, filosofi og metode* (2019), 100–33.
13 Krogh, *Oplysningstiden*, Appendix C; Tine Reeh, 'Cross trade and innovations: judicial consequences of German historical exegesis and pietistic individualism in Denmark', in Stefanie Stockhorst and Søren Peter Hansen (eds), *Deutsch-dänische Kulturbeziehungen* (Trykkeby: Vandenhoeck & Ruprecht, 2018), pp. 41–53.

This could indicate a dynamic of developments alternative to the top-down narrative of absolutism, as well as to the pattern of explanations usually presented in subsequent legal and intellectual history. Instead, the pressure for developments in legal practice could be seen to emerge, at least partly, from opinions or pressure from below. The court records and other documents relate to the actual processing of citizens' individual cases, and from these it becomes apparent that those on trial almost exclusively represented society's lowest social classes. Furthermore, assessors and judges in the lower courts at this time were mainly practical people of the merchant and bourgeois class; the sources hence lend expression not only to the experiences of sufferers but also to lay assessments and general views.[14]

Consequently, the experiences and perspectives of those attending trials in cases where elements of melancholy were present may not only provide fresh insight into but also supplement the understandings of the contemporary professional and academic elites, thereby challenging certain mainstream narratives of the past. In the following, using a rarely tapped source, we thus explore what could be termed knowledge of 'lay' perception and experience, with regard to both theology and medicine.

Concepts of melancholy and pietist introspection

While melancholy is a central concept in pietist literature on introspection, its character is ambiguous.[15] On the one hand, melancholy could signify a state on the way to conversion or rebirth, thus embodying a constructive potential. On the other, remaining or dwelling in a melancholic state could be considered a sign of destructive self-absorption or lack of faith, which made it not only sinful but extremely dangerous – even deadly. In addition, the Pietists' preoccupation with the (constructive) use of melancholy elicited criticism from proponents of the Enlightenment, and

---

14 Knudsen, *Lovkyndighed og vederhæftighed*; Tamm and Jørgensen, *Dansk retshistorie i hovedpunkter*.
15 Markus Mattias, 'Bekehrung und Wiedergeburt', in Ulrich Gäbler and others (eds), *Geschichte des Pietismus*, 6 vols (Göttingen: Vandenhoeck & Ruprecht, 1993–2004), IV: *Glaubenswelt und Lebenswelten*, ed. Hartmut Lehmann (2004), pp. 49–79; Jonathan Strom, *German Pietism and the Problem of Conversion* (University Park, PA: Penn State University Press, 2018). See also Jonathan Strom, 'Bekehrung', in W. Breul (ed.), *Pietismus Handbuch* (Tübingen: Mohr Siebeck, 2021), pp. 368–78.

previous research points to a connection between the diagnosis of melancholia and the criticism of religion in the second half of the eighteenth century.[16]

At the same time, melancholy is a key concept in the development of the discipline of psychiatry. Its polysemantic connotations in the seventeenth and eighteenth centuries are illustrated in Burton's seminal *Anatomy of Melancholy* (1621), which mixes religious and medical approaches. A century later, the article *Mélancholie* in the *Encyclopédie*, attributed to Diderot, combines sections on ancient medicine with expositions of *Mélancholie religieuse*. Among the phenomena ascribed to melancholy in the article are delirium combined with sadness; a dark mood; sad, pensive misanthropy; megalomaniac ideation; lycanthropy; demonic possession; nihilistic bodily experiences; grief; anxiety; despair; revenge; homesickness; and transformations into animals.[17] The article also encompasses a large number of hypotheses about pathological bodily correlates to melancholy.

Consequently, the eighteenth-century conception of melancholy cannot be reduced to the modern term 'depression'. Rather, it should be regarded as a broader category of sufferings, incorporating key elements from pietistic theology as well as from psychiatric phenomenology *in statu nascendi*.

The ambiguous perception of melancholy combined with an increasing interest in the phenomenon is also reflected in eighteenth-century Pietism's preoccupation with the religious status of the individual, or the 'inner man'. Palpable examples may be seen in pamphlets and prints distributed in the first half of the eighteenth century.[18] Introspection, or self-examination, soon became a significant element in Hallensian Pietism and spread in the kingdom of Denmark–Norway in the first half of

---

16 Hans-Jürgen Schings, *Melancholie und Aufklärung: Melancholiker und ihre Kritiker in Erfahrungskunde und Literatur des 18. Jahrhunderts* (Stuttgart: J. B. Metzler, 1977).
17 Denis Diderot and Jean Le Rond d'Alembert (eds), *Encyclopédie: Ou dictionnaire raisonné des sciences, des arts et des métiers*, 28 vols (Paris: Briasson, 1751–1772), X (1761), pp. 307–11.
18 I owe thanks and credit to Sigrid Nielsby Christensen, who drew my attention to the collection of these materials in Det Kongelige Bibliotek (Royal Library): Thottske Samlinger 1591, 4°. See also Sigrid Nielsby Christensen, 'Enevold Ewalds selvprøvelsesprogram', in *Kirkehistoriske Samlinger* (2020), pp. 7–30.

the eighteenth century.[19] The claim was that introspection was helpful, or even necessary, for the regeneration of the pious individual and the way to salvation. Here, we find melancholy described in terms of being troubled, heavy-hearted and depressed, as well as experiencing self-hatred, pessimism, animosity towards the world and hostility towards one's own life.

An example of the many self-help publications and relatively detailed promotions of introspection current at the time is the pamphlet *Et Aandeligt Speyl* ('A spiritual mirror').[20] The eight-page publication describes three overall conditions of the human being, namely whether he or she is living outside divine law, within divine law or in a state of grace. After a general introduction and definition of the three categories of human life, the pamphlet is divided into three columns, each with ten numbered characteristics of the 'condition of a human being' living in each of the three categories. The following pages continue with this structure of three columns corresponding to the overriding three human conditions, each with sixty clauses or items to identify the 'condition' of a human being within that particular stage. The items include both external symptoms, such as 'to desire food and drink in abundance',[21] and internal symptoms of a more subjective nature, such as feeling alienated from the world or focused on its deceitfulness and

---

19 In turn, early German Pietism was inspired by Puritan devotional literature and spiritual guides on self-observation or introspection. See Markus Mattias, 'Pietism and Protestant orthodoxy', in Markus Mattias and Douglas H. Shantz (eds), *A Companion to German Pietism 1660–1800* (Leiden: Brill, 2015), pp. 17–49 (pp. 21–2). See also Udo Sträter, *Sonthom, Bayly, Dyke und Hall: Studien zur Rezeption der englischen Erbauungsliteratur in Deutschland im 17. Jahrhundert* (Tübingen: Mohr, 1987). On the situation in Denmark, see Knud Heiberg, 'Fra den religiøse brydningstid i Aarene o. 1725–59', in *Kirkehistoriske Samlinger* (1905–1907), pp. 435–67 and 694–702; Holger Frederik Rørdam, 'Kirkelige brydninger i aaret 1733', in *Kirkehistoriske Samlinger* (1909–1911), pp. 657–770; Thomas Bredsdorff, *Den brogede oplysning: Om følelsernes fornuft og fornuftens følelse i 1700-tallets nordiske litteratur* (Copenhagen: Gyldendal, 2003).
20 Anon., 'Et Aandeligt Speyl, hvorved man kand kiende og prøve sig selv og andre, efter Menniskernes tredobbelte Tilstand, udi det Aandelige', Copenhagen, Det Kongelige Bibliotek, Thottske Samlinger 1591, IV. For a more detailed description, see Sigrid Nielsen Christensen, 'Skriftemål og Selvprøvelse' (unpublished master's thesis, University of Copenhagen, 2018).
21 'De som beherskes af Vellyst, ere letsindige, begierærlige efter Overdådighed i Mad og Drikke, og tilbøyelige til Ødselhed'; in 'Et Aandeligt Speyl' (see note 20), 4, column 1 no. 15.

illusions.[22] In the present context, the forty-first clause is of potential interest as it focuses on the person's religious state, signified by his or her perception of death. It states that persons in the stage of the first column – that is, a human life outside or in absence of the law – 'do not wish to die' as long as life is treating them well, but that they are 'often very afraid of death'.[23] The corresponding forty-first clause in the second column, regarding those in the state of living within the law, suggests that they still wish to live for a while in order to experience a rebirth.[24] The third column's forty-first clause identifies those who live a life in a state of grace as being characterized by a 'wish to depart from this world and be with Christ'.[25]

In total, the pamphlet supplies 210 symptoms or signifiers by which to diagnose the situation of the inner person. This particular publication, however, proved too radical for the authorities and was therefore banned and confiscated. Nevertheless, attention to different states and constitutions on the part of the individual or subject spread in numerous other publications, simultaneously increasing within theological and pietistic milieus. In addition, we would argue that this growth in attention had an impact outside the narrow applications within theology and religion, namely its influence on what went on in contemporary court rooms.

Three cases of melancholy

On the night between 18 and 19 May 1733, Anna Marie Truelsdatter cut the throat of her infant girl, Anne Kirstine.[26] Truelsdatter was examined in the City Court in Copenhagen on 1 July, where she gave an elaborate statement, telling how two weeks before, around

---

22 'Et Aandeligt Speyl' (see note 20), 4, column 2 no. 12.
23 'De vil ikke gierne døe, saa længe de i deres Lyster have god Fremgang; og ere ofte meget bange for Døden'; in 'Et Aandeligt Speyl' (see note 20), 6, column 1 no. 41.
24 'De ønske, at de maatte endnu leve noget, paa det de kunde ret af gandske hierte blive omvendte'; in 'Et Aandeligt Speyl' (see note 20), 6, column 2 no. 41.
25 'De have Lyst til, at fare herfra, og være med Christo'; in 'Et Aandeligt Speyl' (see note 20), 6, column 3 no. 41.
26 The handwritten archival files and sources on this case are found in Copenhagen, Statens Arkiver (SAr), Københavns Bytingsprotokol 1733 fol. 299b–301a, fol. 314b–15a; SAr, Reviderede Regnskaber, Københavnske Regnskaber, Byfogedregnskaber, 1733 no. 186–8, 222–5; SAr, Københavns Universitet, Det teologiske fakultet, Kopibog 1733, pp. 70–3.

10 a.m., she had given birth alone in the kitchen, gripping a barrel. Her husband, Thomas Jensen, a dismissed sailor and now a skilled rope-maker, had left for work early in the morning. After she had delivered the baby, one of her elder children, seven-year-old Hans Christiansen, entered the kitchen. Truelsdatter told him to go fetch a German soldier's wife, who then came and left right away to bring the midwife, Kirstine Sørensdatter. The latter had assisted Truelsdatter with earlier deliveries and knew that she had suffered from a 'troubled mind' ('uroelig i Hovedet') in connection with previous childbirths. When the midwife arrived, she separated the child from Truelsdatter, who had continued to stand paralysed by the barrel. Gently taking the child, the midwife wrapped it and led Truelsdatter to bed, where she stayed until the fatal night, one week later, when her mind was disturbed ('hun faldt i griller') and she lay pondering her own destitution. She felt that she was despised, as no one would come to see her. With her husband asleep, and after nursing her infant, she took a knife with a black handle which was lying on the table, and stood at length in two minds, beset by evil thoughts ('i beraad med onde tancker'). Overcome by one such evil thought, she cut the throat of the child so swiftly that the baby did not even make a noise but died instantly. She then woke her husband and told him to look at what she had done. He sent for the security guard from the nearby gate, Nørre Port, and he stayed with her until the night watchman arrived to escort her to the city jail. Now, one week after the incident, she expressed to the court that she was deeply repentant of her folly. She regretted having felt a wish to leave this world owing to her poverty and the feeling of being looked down on, as well as to her desperate plight with four surviving young children. Truelsdatter had given birth nine times, and her eldest was nine years old. She had married her first husband thirteen years previously, but he had died, and she had subsequently lost everything she owned in the great Copenhagen Fire of 1728. Three years before the incident, she had remarried.

After an interrogation of her husband, Thomas Jensen, who confirmed his wife's detailed testimony, the court adjourned to summon further witnesses. They resumed two weeks later, on 15 June 1733. At this point, the midwife, Kirstine Sørensdatter, testified to having assisted Truelsdatter during three previous births. This time she had not noticed her having a disturbed mind ('Uroelighed i Sindet'); but she had noticed that Truelsdatter lay in bed, silent and still, neither speaking nor responding when asked a question. When the midwife tried to give her beer, she took it with apathy and somewhat enigmatically said she did not want any more. Two more witnesses testified that they had visited Truelsdatter, who had replied to their questions with sensible answers; these witnesses thus did not consider her to be suffering from insanity. During these testimonials, it became evident that Truelsdatter had had to borrow swaddling bands as well as nappies, caps and clothes, as she did not own any nor had the means to buy the baby clothes she needed. In other words, she appeared to be desperately poor. Finally, the husband of Truelsdatter's sister testified that he had visited her six births ago, recalling that after giving birth she had experienced fainting fits and delirium ('Besvimelser og nogen phantasie'), but he could not confirm an impaired mind. During the court's investigations, a post-mortem was performed by the surgeon Hendrichson and his assistant Vederkampt, and they confirmed Truelsdatter's explanation. Finally, the defence argued that the Danish Code §6-6-17 applied, since Truelsdatter had committed the murder with a troubled mind – delirium along with delusions due to her extreme poverty.

The court, however, did not go along with the arguments of the defence. On 13 July 1733, Truelsdatter was sentenced to death by the city recorder (*byfoged*) and eight lay assessors – in accordance with §6-6-1. She appealed to the magistrate's court, which confirmed the verdict on 29 July, and a new appeal was sent to the Supreme Court.

On 31 October, before the final verdict of the Supreme Court, the King sent a request to the Faculty of Theology at the University of Copenhagen. They were to help in bringing out the truth of the matter, in view of Truelsdatter's claims to have suffered from melancholy and fury. In their response to the hearing request, the faculty underlined that Truelsdatter voluntarily confessed to the murder, as well as to a temporary wish to die owing to her desperate poverty and to her feeling that she was the object of contempt. They found that the exculpation of §6-6-17 could not apply, as neither Truelsdatter's husband nor the midwife assessed her to be insensible, attesting that she had lain silent and still in bed. Thus, though she may very well have suffered from strong melancholy, she could not have suffered from fury, the formal criterion of exculpatory insanity.

In the *vota* and statements of the Supreme Court, we find an emphasis on the fact that even though Truelsdatter may have suffered from 'a troubled mind and melancholic whims' ('Sindets U Roelighed [*sic*] og Melancholiske Griller') – possibly exacerbated by her poverty and desperate situation – there is no positive evidence that she was 'delirious or deprived of her senses' ('har Phantaseret, eller saa aldeles berøvet hendes forstand') to such a degree that she did not know what she was doing. Consequently, she could not be excused for her actions and was required to pay for a life with her life. The Supreme Court confirmed the previous verdicts on 21 November 1733.

On the very same day, Anna Marie Truelsdatter wrote a petition to the Queen, probably assisted by her counsel and pastor. While largely resembling her initial testimony in the City Court, the retelling of her story uses the legal terms 'fury' (*Vildelse*), 'melancholic' (*Melancholisk*) and 'confused' (*forvildet*) to describe her state of mind at the moment of committing the crime. On this basis, she begged for her life. On 24 November, Truelsdatter added a petition to the King, merely pleading to be buried at the cemetery for the poor at Trinity Church. In this, there is no mention of any religious consideration or preoccupation with the destiny of her soul; rather, it appears to have been a matter of saving her surviving husband and children from the shame that would accompany the dishonourable treatment of her body. There is also a mention of the possibility for alms for her husband, who suffered from consumption (*Svindsot*) and was now to become the household's sole breadwinner. In addition, she asked if her eldest – who would be orphaned by her own demise – might be admitted to the newly established orphanage, Vajsenhuset.[27] Finally, she pleaded that her husband and children might be able to obtain the bed linen that she had used during her stay in the city jail after her execution, so that they would not freeze to death in the approaching cold of winter. Truelsdatter's petition was supported by a brief enclosed statement by her pastor, C. Holst, bearing witness to her penitent and faithful character. Subsequently, on 4 December, the King assented to Truelsdatter's pleas regarding her burial and support for her husband and children, and she was executed on 10 December 1733.

In this case, it appears obvious and agreed among those concerned – the accused, the witnesses and those handling her court case – that Truelsdatter had been suffering from some sort of impaired mental state, one they tended to connect to the birth of her child and her state of desperate poverty. There is evidently a lack of

---

27 Københavns Vajsenhus was established after a Hallensian model in the autumn of 1727; see Christian Ottesen, *Det Kgl. Vajsenhus gennem to hundrede aar* (Copenhagen: Det Kgl. Vajsenhus, 1927).

psychiatric nomenclature; her comprehensive and detailed description of events and her experience thereof only mentions a troubled and disturbed mind as well as evil thoughts. One could also note that there were various assessments as to the pathological nature of this suffering. Despite the attempts made by the defence to push the interpretation of Truelsdatter's plight in the direction of exemption on the grounds of insanity, her obvious apathy and lack of outward reactions prevented the application of this section of the law, as she was clearly neither furious nor delirious. Also, the royal inquiry at the Faculty of Theology indicates that the new king, Christian VI (r. 1730–1746), was uncomfortable with the sentence and the assessment made by the court system. While the formal framework clearly still prevailed, a degree of uneasiness over the old principles would appear to emerge at this time.

To illustrate these developments, we shall move to a case from the 1760s. Anna Lisbeth Greisdatter, widow of the sailor Jacob Jacobsen, killed her own child, a seven-year-old boy who bore his father's name, Jacob Jacobsen.[28] The murder took place on 30 August 1763. When Greisdatter's son returned from school around 11 a.m., she sent her daughter, Anna Maria, to run an errand. As soon as the daughter left home, the mother grabbed the boy by the head, threw him flat on his face and cut his throat with a bread knife. She then went out into the street in search of someone to denounce her to the authorities; right outside the door she encountered her daughter, whom she told of her deed. The daughter helped her inside again and went to her mother's chamber, where she found her brother lying on the floor, gushing blood. Greisdatter then told her landlord, Morten Nielsen, that she had cut her son's throat, requesting arrest. Nielsen immediately summoned the guard, who brought her to the city jail. A post-mortem performed by the surgeon Hintze established three cuts that would have caused immediate death.

On the basis of the *corpus delicti* and the confession of Greisdatter herself, the Admiralty's Combined Court consequently found the sailor's widow guilty of murder on 30 August 1762, and the verdict was confirmed by a royal resolution of 24 February 1763. She was sentenced to death according to an extended death penalty prescribed

---

28 The handwritten archival files on this case are found in SAr, Generalauditøren (Søetaten) Betænkninger (til kongen) 23 February 1763; SAr, Kombinerede ret, Domssager, 23 February 1763.

by the decree from 7 February 1749. This meant that she was first to be pinched with red-hot tongs outside the place of the murder, then three times in the square and finally again at the site of execution, where her right hand was to be cut off prior to decapitation by axe and the subsequent display of the dismembered body on wheels and a stake.

In connection to this case, we find an interesting enclosure from Peder Kofod Ancher (1710–1788), a Danish theologian and jurist.[29] Kofod Ancher became Professor of Law at the University of Copenhagen in 1748; but because of his fragile health, he was relieved of teaching duties. In 1753 he was appointed Judge Advocate General (*Generalauditør*) of the Navy, judge of the Supreme Admiralty's Court and Supreme Court judge. His renowned works include his preparations for the case against Johann Friedrich Struensee in 1772. Owing to Kofod Ancher's capacity as Naval Judge Advocate General, the sailor's widow Anna Lisbeth Greisdatter came within his jurisdiction, and this occasioned Kofod Ancher to send a comprehensive statement to the King on 23 February 1763.

Kofod Ancher states that the post-mortem and the confession of the accused herself prove that Greisdatter committed the murder. Furthermore, there is no doubt that she committed the murder with intent, in a calculated manner and *mens rea* ('frie Forsæt og beraad Hue'). In addition, there is reason to conclude that the motive was to end her own life, or *taedium vitae*. This is indicated by her immediate wish to turn herself in, as well as her own testimony in which she stated that she committed the act while brooding on her wretched condition and despair regarding the sustenance of both herself and her child. To Kofod Ancher, this proved that her desperate concern over the necessities of life led her to wish to end her misery by bringing an end to the child's life as well as her own. Her premeditation and intent further demonstrate that her melancholy did not rob her of reason ('Fornuftens Brug').

This led Kofod Ancher to pose what might appear to be a rhetorical question: would His Majesty, out of royal clemency, be able

---

29 Ditlev Tamm, 'Peder Kofod Ancher', Dansk Biografisk Leksikon, https://biografiskleksikon.lex.dk/Peder_Kofod_Ancher [accessed 30 March 2021]. Peder Kofod Ancher received his degree in theology in 1730 from the University of Copenhagen, graduated in law in 1738 and was created doctor by the Faculty of Law in 1742 (also in Copenhagen); among his many distinctions, he is considered to be the founder of the study of Danish legal history.

to mitigate a sentence of this type without weakening the general safety of society and the purpose of punishment? Kofod Ancher acknowledges that in cases where a homicide is committed out of the murderer's own wish to die, it is problematic to define the right and adequate punishment with a view to ensuring that the chosen punishment will frighten other people and thereby deter them from committing similar crimes. To achieve this preventive purpose of punishment, Kofod Ancher finds two options. One is not to punish the murderer with death but rather by imposing an agonizing life on him or her. The other is to augment the simple death penalty by means of measures geared to making death painful. As the first option is the lightest or most lenient, it is to be recommended as the safest and most righteous *in dubio*. In this way, the perpetrator will not achieve his or her objective, but will rather be placed in a state that they themselves – and like-minded persons after their way of thinking ('efter deres egen Tænkemåde') – consider horrible.

However, in the case of murder – a deed as gross and unnatural as that committed by Anna Lisbeth Greisdatter – Kofod Ancher does not dare to recommend suspending the death penalty. This would weaken the sense of justice among the general public, who often fail to realize why a murder has been committed and are not cognizant of the relevant causal factors. He therefore recommends the use of the extended death sentence in the decree from 1749, especially as this type of 'desperate' murder, as he describes it, continues to occur on a regular basis. That the latter circumstance could be seen as an argument in favour of a life sentence does not seem to bother Kofod Ancher. He moves on to an explanation of how the uneducated public may interpret an execution as a so-called good death,[30] adding that such ignorance can lead to

---

30 Hans Christian Erik Midelfort, 'Selbstmord im Urteil von Reformation und Gegenreformation', in Wolfgang Reinhard and Heinz Schilling (eds), *Die Katholische Konfessionalisierung* (Münster: Aschendorff, 1995), pp. 296–310; Volker Leppin, 'Preparing for death', in Tarald Rasmussen and Jon Øygarden Flæten (eds), *Preparing for Death, Remembering the Dead* (Göttingen: Vandenhoeck & Ruprecht, 2015), pp. 9–23; Lindemann, 'Murder, melancholy and the insanity defence'; Tyge Krogh, *A Lutheran Plague: Murdering to Die in the Eighteenth Century* (Leiden: Brill, 2012); Riikka Miettinen, '"Lord, have mercy on me": spiritual preparations for suicide in early modern Sweden', in Anu Lahtinen and Mia Korpiola (eds), *Dying Prepared in Medieval and Early Modern Northern Europe* (Leiden: Brill, 2017), pp. 160–86.

an abuse of the penal system.[31] This only proves, Kofod Ancher concludes, that for those in a 'desperate' state, capital punishment is dysfunctional unless it is increased by way of a painful and disgraceful death.

The last case is Marie Jensdatter, who killed her two-year-old daughter with a knife on 28 April 1766.[32] In the City Court, Jensdatter confessed the crime but also explained that she did so owing to a troubled mind ('uroelige Tanker'), stating that she had previously been out of her mind ('fra Forstanden') as she suffered from melancholy ('Tungsindighed') and mental illness ('Sygdom i Forstanden'), and was in a state of delirium at the moment of the crime. It is indicated and presumed that her husband had triggered her to lose her mind ('gaa fra Forstanden'). This had caused her to be tormented in her heart ('Hjerteklemmelse'), and her husband had previously put her under surveillance. An earlier and possibly ongoing impaired mental state is thus more than indicated in this case. Pastoral certificates with evaluations of her condition had already been obtained from the lower court, declaring that Jensdatter was afflicted with heavy melancholy ('beladt med Tungsindighed'). In the very first sentence, the verdict states that it is well-evidenced and proven ('vel oplyst og beviist') that before the crime was committed, she had occasionally suffered from depression and melancholy. This is further established by the pastoral assessments, certifying that she was suffering from melancholy both shortly before and after the time of the crime. However, before the murder her melancholy had been caused by miserable conditions that had made her weary of life, whereas after the murder she was extremely anxious to preserve her life ('hendes Livs Conservation'). It is also established that she had had *intervalla* in which she was able to use her intellect, and she must therefore be deemed to possess an inconstant mental constitution.

---

31 This is also the perception of the contemporary theologian Peder Hersleb (1689–1757), and it accounts for his suggestion to moderate pastoral participation as well as his ideas concerning the Church's elaborate ceremonial connection to executions; see Poul Georg Lindhardt (ed.), *Kirke-Ritualet og Pietismen: Biskop Peder Herslebs betænkning over Danmarks og Norgis Kirke-Ritual af 1685* (Copenhagen: Akademisk Förlag, 1986). See also Pieter Spierenburg, *The Spectacle of Suffering: Executions and the Evolution of Repression: From a Preindustrial Metropolis to the European Experience* (Cambridge: Cambridge University Press, 1984).
32 The handwritten archival sources on this case are found in SAr, Højesterets voteringsprotokol 11 October 1766; SAr, Reviderede Regnskaber, 1766, no. 117–19, no. 161–2.

The vocabulary used in this connection parallels the terminology used in the literature on religious introspection, including its focus on changes or developments within the individual. In addition, there was a debate in court regarding the origins of such an impaired state – bad blood, hard circumstances, bad marriage or guilty conscience – but no conclusion is reached on the matter. In the end, the main issue in terms of the court's decision appears to be the danger that such a person constitutes to public safety, as reflected in the law. On 30 June 1766 the city recorder and eight lay assessors consequently sentenced Marie Jensdatter to death. A parallel evaluation, expressed with regret, was the result of the second ruling, announced by the magistrates' court on 28 July 1766. This second court verdict also recognizes and stresses the proven melancholy; but at the same time, it establishes that such suffering cannot exempt the accused from the punishment laid down by law, thus confirming the previous sentence.

Jensdatter then submitted an appeal to the Supreme Court. The ensuing debate among the Supreme Court judges displays an important transformation that took place during these years. The assessor, Koren, opens his statement with the fact that Jensdatter had previously been so tormented by pressures on her heart that her husband had arranged for her to be placed under surveillance, and that there were numerous signs of disturbance and an impaired mind ('Uroelighed og Sinds Forvirrelse').

Immediately, the first Supreme Court judge replied that melancholy did not qualify as an insanity defence according to §6-6-17 of the Danish Code ('Melancholie er ej af den slags udi 6-6-17 fastsettes'). However, five of the judges agreed with Koren and voted in favour of confinement for life. Still, seven held on to the extended death penalty of 1749. The Supreme Court thus confirmed the death sentence by seven votes to five on 11 October 1766. In his subsequent consideration of the case and of the Supreme Court's verdict, the King emphasized the pastoral assessments and witness statements on the perpetrator's melancholy, stressing that this suffering appears proven beyond doubt; but he did not suspend the punishment for murder according to the law. However, on 7 November 1766 the King commuted Jensdatter's sentence to life at a correctional institution, Børnehuset, on the basis of the fact that she had previously been troubled, melancholic, out of her mind and placed under surveillance. It is noted on this occasion that she 'owned nothing' except the clothes she wore, and she was registered as entering the institution on 11 November 1766.

Melancholy diagnostics

The case of Marie Jensdatter is characterized by a much more elaborate nomenclature than the ones antedating the general advance of Pietism from the mid-1730s onwards. The proliferation of vocabulary used not only by professionals but also by Jensdatter herself is germane to the descriptions of the inner person found in pietist literature: for example, 'tormented in her heart', 'subjected to pressures on the heart', 'depressed' and 'melancholic'. There is also a clear development in the interpretation of melancholy as a notable pathological quality, in that it is described as an illness of the mind or an impairment in a way corresponding to delirium. Also, the proceedings from the first trial onwards display an extensive interest in the subjective experience and state of the accused, exemplified in the questions put to her as well as in a wish for a more accurate diagnosis and assessment of her mental state – not her morality or Christian conduct – from her pastors. Melancholy obviously acquires a different and greater weight when the scale of the impaired state and the disturbance of the will – and thus the degree of responsibility – is considered. Even so, an element of ambivalence is still present in the discussion of the causal factors, while the criteria pertaining to insanity defence in the law remain unchanged.

A formal change in the legal practice was on the way, though. It came in 1767 with the so-called decree on melancholic murders, which abolished the death penalty for suicidal murderers. This change was, however, not driven by medical nor enlightened or humanitarian influences.[33] Rather, it must be considered as justified on moral or utilitarian grounds. The first official proposal regarding this law came in 1757 from Henrik Stampe (1713–1789), the chief legal adviser to the Danish king. Thus, Peder Kofod Ancher's ample exposition to the King is not only a matter of rhetoric but very much a contribution to what must be considered an ongoing debate at the time.

In Henrik Stampe's arguments for a fundamental legal change, he states that there are two ways for authorities to provide safety and peace for citizens. One is to improve the guilty criminal, *poenae emendatrices*. These punishments are indeed valuable but,

---

33 See, for instance, Jørgensen, *Højesteret fra 1790 til Grundloven*, p. 44. In his two-volume dissertation and standard work on historical studies of forensic psychiatry, Hans Adserballe calls the decree 'gruesome' and adds that it illustrates that there was still a long way to go before even slightly humane measures were introduced for all types of mental illness; see Hans Adserballe, *Frihedsberøvelse og tvang i psykiatrien*, 2 vols (Copenhagen: FADL, 1977), I, p. 84.

unfortunately, they are often not enough. Therefore, there is a need for the second type, exemplary punishments of certain criminals, in order to discourage or prevent others from committing the same crime; these are the so-called *poenae exemplares*. When determining this punishment, one should take into account that a penalty does not always make the same impression on different persons. When fixing exemplary penalties or punishments, one must therefore consider the different types of personalities or diverse subjectivities, their different reactions and, in particular, which types are most likely to commit the crime in question. One should consider 'what could tempt them the most' and what creates feelings of 'fright, horror and disgust' at their particular stage. Here, one could draw a clear parallel to pietistic considerations regarding the inner person and the religious subject.

This insight is important, Stampe claims, when it comes to a crime such as a murder committed by a melancholiac. To sentence this type of murderer to death is actually to be considered as granting them their wish, or rewarding their misdeed.[34] When a depressed or melancholic person is then publicly executed, says Stampe, it does not have the intended preventive or exemplary effect on other potential melancholic murderers – quite the contrary. Instead, the right punishment should take into account the criminal subject's state or type – melancholy or *taedium vitae* – and accordingly make life even more terrible and painful for the perpetrator than it had been before the crime. Their lives should be made so horrible that ordinary people of a more common constitution could not possibly view the new punishment as a pardon.[35]

The debate on Stampe's proposal was heated and extensive. The proposal did not pass the first time. But ten years later, in 1767, it passed almost verbatim and without debate.

Conclusion: the birth of a pietist clinic?

The so-called melancholic murders form one of the obvious sites to investigate when looking for evidence regarding the dynamics

---

34 Ditlev Tamm and Morten Kjær (eds), *Henrik Stampe – enevældens menneskelige ansigt* (Copenhagen: Jurist- og økonomforbundet, 2013), p. 32.

35 Instead of losing their lives, these criminals should be confined to hard labour and branded and whipped every year on the day of the crime, and, when death finally catches up with them, their bodies should suffer the humiliating display of a murderer; Tamm and Kjær, *Henrik Stampe*, pp. 35–6.

between pietist diagnostics of the inner person and pre-medical forensic psychiatry. The frequency of this type of murder in the eighteenth century is not debated in this chapter, and nor is the contested role of Lutheran religion as a causative factor.[36] Rather, we wish to draw attention to this material as a basis for investigating assessments of mental issues and developments within legal practice. Our thorough investigation of forty-eight female and sixteen male child murderers in Copenhagen from 1697 to 1779 demonstrates a substantial element of mental suffering in many cases, as displayed in the examples above.[37] Owing to the contemporary legal criteria in the Danish Code of 1683, insanity needed to be explicit, aggressive or extrovert to be diagnosed; consequently, even evident suffering

---

36 Hellmuth von Weber, German professor of law, first claimed that erroneous orthodox Lutheran ideas played a key role in a type of murder that he termed indirect suicide; see Hellmuth von Weber, 'Selbstmord als Mordmotiv', *Monatsschrift für Kriminalbiologie und Strafrechtsreform*, 28 (1937), 161–81. Tyge Krogh developed Weber's viewpoint, identifying Lutheran Pietism as a causal explanation; see Krogh, *A Lutheran Plague*. However, other studies have opposed confession as a determining factor and have found numerous cases in Catholic and Reformed areas; see Jeffrey R. Watt, *Choosing Death: Suicide and Calvinism in Early Modern Geneva* (Kirksville, MI: Truman State University Press, 2001); Kathy Stuart, 'Suicide by proxy: the unintended consequences of public executions in eighteenth-century Germany', *Central European History*, 41:3 (2008), 413–45; Kathy Stuart, 'Melancholy murderers: suicide by proxy and the insanity defence', in Marjorie E. Plummer (ed.), *Ideas and Cultural Margins in Early Modern Germany: Essays in Honor of H. C. Erik Midelfort* (London: Routledge, 2009), pp. 63–77. Lately, Miettinen and others have accounted for the religious ideas in connection to suicide as predominantly a matter of popular belief, referable to overwintering Catholic or folklore perceptions of, for example, sleepless souls; see Miettinen, *Suicide, Law, and Community*. Krogh himself also ends his book by pointing to the phenomenon of 'suicide by cop' in a contemporary American (that is, a secular or, if Christian, predominantly Calvinist) context; Krogh, *A Lutheran Plague*, p. 170.

37 A pilot study was published in Tine Reeh and Ralf Hemmingsen, 'Common sense, no magic: a case of female child murderers in the eighteenth century', *Sjuttonhundratal*, 15 (2018), 110–34. Further cases were examined in Hemmingsen and Reeh, 'Mentale tilstande'. A complete work on the females is forthcoming in Tine Reeh and Ralf Hemmingsen. '"...the greater fault is in their reason": religious and mental components in cases of suicide murder in 18th century Copenhagen' (forthcoming). The male murderers are examined in Tine Reeh and Ralf Hemmingsen, 'Mentale tilstande hos mandlige barnemordere i 1700-tallet. En case-baseret undersøgelse af mentale begreber og deres anvendelse i retssager', *Bibliotek for Læger – tidsskrift for medicinens historie, kultur, filosofi og metode*, 211 (2022), 126–53.

with a recognizable subjective mental condition – of the kind that characterizes such states as severe depression and psychosis – was difficult for the legal and penal system to acknowledge. Hence, the murders officially had to be labelled as 'groundless', that is to say unwarranted or without obvious motive.

The legal change brought about by the decree in 1767 constituted a break with previous legislation, and the debate on the abolition of the death penalty for such crimes took place remarkably early; the archives reveal that the Danish debate even predated the seminal work of Cesare Beccaria, *On Crimes and Punishments*,[38] as well as Voltaire's famous commentary on this argument for reform. Also, it was clearly not driven by humanist, Enlightenment thinking but rather by utilitarian and moral arguments. There are no signs of any critique of the death penalty as cruel or inhumane. Rather, the motivation and precondition for change appear to be an awareness of differing mental states and individual subjective perceptions, including the subjective position of the perpetrator, the options open to him or her and the perspectives on punishment that might be applied in the individual case.

In conclusion, one might ask whether the Pietists' passionate interest in the inner person objectified the mental state of the individual subject, and if this contributed to a development towards modernity in the Nordic countries. While in Pietism the object of the inner person was identified with the person per se, criminal court cases indicate that the intense focus on the subject stimulated a fresh awareness of mental health, as demonstrated in the questions, vocabulary, 'nomenclature' and perceptions of impaired or pathological mental states. In the wake of the Pietists' focus on the inner person, we begin to detect a more detailed examination of the individual's subjective experience. Moreover, the inner person or mental constitution is no longer the quality that defines the criminal on trial. In other words, the perpetrator's mental state is objectified as something separate from the person affected by it. In their focus

---

38 Cesare Beccaria, *On Crimes and Punishments and Other Writings* (Cambridge: Cambridge University Press, 1995; first published as *Dei delitti e delle pene* in 1764). See also Reeh, 'Cross trade'; Tine Reeh, 'Pietistic subjectivity as an agent of legal change? On theologians' arguments regarding punishment for murder in 18th century Denmark–Norway', *Pietismus und Neuzeit*, 45 (Göttingen: Vandenhoeck & Ruprecht, 2021), 69–83. For an analysis of developments in this area in Sweden, see Erik Anners, *Humanitet och rationalism: Studier i upplysningstidens strafflagsreformer – särskilt med hänsyn till Gustav III:s reformlagstiftning* (Stockholm: Nordiska Bokhandeln, 1965).

on mitigating circumstances in criminal offences, mental assessments in court cases hence constitute a valuable framework for investigating developments in pietist perceptions and practices, as well as their possible influences on the general – and modern – awareness of mental health.

Bibliography

Archival sources

Copenhagen

Det Kongelige Bibliotek (The Royal Library)
　Thottske Samlinger 1591, 4° and IV
Statens Arkiver (SAr)
　Generalauditøren (Søetaten) Betænkninger (til kongen) 23 February 1763
　Højesterets voteringsprotokol, 11 October 1766
　Københavns Bytingsprotokol 1733 fol. 299b–301a, fol. 314b–315a
　Københavns Universitet, Det teologiske fakultet, Kopibog 1733, pp. 70–3
　Kombinerede ret, Domssager, 23 February 1763
　Reviderede Regnskaber, Københavnske Regnskaber, Byfogedregnskaber, 1733 no. 186–8, 222–5; 1766, no. 117–19, no. 161–2

Digital sources

Tamm, Ditlev, 'Peder Kofod Ancher', *Dansk Biografisk Leksikon*, https://biografiskleksikon.lex.dk/Peder_Kofod_Ancher [accessed 30 March 2021].

Printed sources and literature

Adserballe, Hans, *Frihedsberøvelse og tvang i psykiatrien*, 2 vols (Copenhagen: FADL, 1977), I.
Anners, Erik, *Humanitet och rationalism: Studier i upplysningstidens strafflagsreformer – särskilt med hänsyn till Gustav III:s reformlagstiftning* (Stockholm: Nordiska Bokhandeln, 1965).
Beccaria, Cesare, *On Crimes and Punishments and Other Writings* (Cambridge: Cambridge University Press, 1995).
Beck, Catherine, 'Patronage and insanity: tolerance, reputation and mental disorder in the British navy, 1740–1820', *Historical Research*, 94 (2021), 73–95.
Berrios, German E., *The History of Mental Symptoms* (Cambridge: Cambridge University Press, 1996).
Bredsdorff, Thomas, *Den brogede oplysning: Om følelsernes fornuft og fornuftens følelse i 1700-tallets nordiske litteratur* (Copenhagen: Gyldendal, 2003).

Christensen, Sigrid Nielsby, 'Enevold Ewalds selvprøvelsesprogram', in *Kirkehistoriske Samlinger* (2020), pp. 7–30.

——, 'Skriftemål og Selvprøvelse' (unpublished master's thesis, University of Copenhagen, 2018).

Diderot, Denis and Jean Le Rond d'Alembert (eds), *Encyclopédie: Ou dictionnaire raisonné des sciences, des arts et des métiers*, 28 vols (Paris: Briasson, 1751–1772), X (1761).

Heiberg, Knud, 'Fra den religiøse brydningstid i Aarene o. 1725–59', in *Kirkehistoriske Samlinger* (1905–1907), 435–67 and 694–702.

Hemmingsen, Ralf, 'Sindssygdomsbegrebet i det 18. århundrede', in Mads Julis Elf and Lasse Horne Kjældgaard (eds), *Mere Lys! Indblik i oplysningstiden i dansk litteratur og kultur* (Hellerup: Forlaget Spring, 2002), pp. 231–9.

Hemmingsen, Ralf and Tine Reeh, 'Mentale tilstande hos kvindelige barnemordere i det 18. århundrede', in *Bibliotek for Læger – tidsskrift for medicinens historie, kultur, filosofi og metode*, 211 (2019), 100–33.

Holmboe, Tage, 'Højesteret og strafferetten', in Povl Bagge and others (eds), *Højesteret 1661–1961*, 2 vols (Copenhagen: Gads Förlag, 1961), II.

Jørgensen, Troels G., *Højesteret fra 1790 til Grundloven* (Copenhagen: Frost-Hansens Förlag, 1950).

Knudsen, P. U., *Lovkyndighed og vederhæftighed: Sjællandske byfogeder 1682–1801* (Copenhagen: Jurist- og Økonomforbundet, 2001).

Krogh, Tyge, *A Lutheran Plague: Murdering to Die in the Eighteenth Century* (Leiden: Brill, 2012).

——, *Oplysningstiden og det magiske: Henrettelser og korporlige straffe i 1700-tallets første halvdel* (Copenhagen: Samleren, 2000).

Leppin, Volker, 'Preparing for death', in Tarald Rasmussen and Jon Øygarden Flæten (eds), *Preparing for Death, Remembering the Dead* (Göttingen: Vandenhoeck & Ruprecht, 2015), pp. 9–23.

Lindemann, Mary, 'Murder, melancholy and the insanity defence in eighteenth-century Hamburg', in Roberta Bivins and John V. Pickstone (eds), *Medicine, Madness and Social History: Essays in Honour of Roy Porter* (Basingstoke: Palgrave Macmillan, 2007).

Lindhardt, Poul Georg (ed.), *Kirke-Ritualet og Pietismen: Biskop Peder Herslebs betænkning over Danmarks og Norgis Kirke-Ritual af 1685* (Copenhagen: Akademisk Förlag, 1986).

Mattias, Markus, 'Bekehrung und Wiedergeburt', in Ulrich Gäbler and others (eds), *Geschichte des Pietismus*, 6 vols (Göttingen: Vandenhoeck & Ruprecht, 1993–2004), IV: *Glaubenswelt und Lebenswelten*, ed. Hartmut Lehmann (2004), pp. 49–79.

——, 'Pietism and Protestant orthodoxy', in Markus Mattias and Douglas H. Shantz (eds), *A Companion to German Pietism 1660–1800* (Leiden: Brill, 2015), pp. 17–49.

Midelfort, Hans Christian Erik, 'Selbstmord im Urteil von Reformation und Gegenreformation', in Wolfgang Reinhard and Heinz Schilling (eds),

Die Katholische Konfessionalisierung (Münster: Aschendorff, 1995), pp. 296–310.
Miettinen, Riikka, '"Lord, have mercy on me": spiritual preparations for suicide in early modern Sweden', in Anu Lahtinen and Mia Korpiola (eds), *Dying Prepared in Medieval and Early Modern Northern Europe* (Leiden: Brill, 2017), pp. 160–86.
———, *Suicide, Law, and Community in Early Modern Sweden* (Cham: Palgrave Macmillan, 2019).
Ottesen, Christian, *Det Kgl. Vajsenhus gennem to hundrede aar* (Copenhagen: Det Kgl. Vajsenhus, 1927).
Reeh, Tine, 'Cross trade and innovations: judicial consequences of German historical exegesis and pietistic individualism in Denmark', in Stefanie Stockhorst and Søren Peter Hansen (eds), *Deutsch-dänische Kulturbeziehungen* (Trykkeby: Vandenhoeck & Ruprecht, 2018), pp. 41–53.
———, 'Pietistic subjectivity as an agent of legal change? On theologians' arguments regarding punishment for murder in 18th century Denmark–Norway', *Pietismus und Neuzeit*, 45 (Göttingen: Vandenhoeck & Ruprecht, 2021), 69–83.
Reeh, Tine and Ralf Hemmingsen, 'Common sense, no magic: a case of female child murderers in the eighteenth century', *Sjuttonhundratal*, 15 (2018), 110–34.
———, '"… the greater fault is in their reason": religious and mental components in cases of suicide murder in 18th century Copenhagen' (forthcoming).
———, 'Mentale tilstande hos mandlige barnemordere i 1700-tallet. En case-baseret undersøgelse af mentale begreber og deres anvendelse i retssager', *Bibliotek for Læger – tidsskrift for medicinens historie, kultur, filosofi og metode* (2022), 126–53.
Rørdam, Holger Frederik, 'Kirkelige brydninger i aaret 1733', in *Kirkehistoriske Samlinger* (1909–1911), pp. 657–770.
Schings, Hans-Jürgen, *Melancholie und Aufklärung: Melancholiker und ihre Kritiker in Erfahrungskunde und Literatur des 18. Jahrhunderts* (Stuttgart: J. B. Metzler, 1977).
Spierenburg, Pieter, *The Spectacle of Suffering: Executions and the Evolution of Repression: From a Preindustrial Metropolis to the European Experience* (Cambridge: Cambridge University Press, 1984).
Stenbæk, Jørgen, 'En kirkeretslig vurdering af Danske Lovs 6. bog – strafferetten', in *Kirkehistoriske Samlinger* (1972), pp. 58–90.
Sträter, Udo, *Sonthom, Bayly, Dyke und Hall: Studien zur Rezeption der englischen Erbauungsliteratur in Deutschland im 17. Jahrhundert* (Tübingen: Mohr, 1987).
Strom, Jonathan, 'Bekehrung', in W. Breul (ed.), *Pietismus Handbuch* (Tübingen: Mohr Siebeck, 2021), pp. 368–78.
———, *German Pietism and the Problem of Conversion* (University Park, PA: Penn State University Press, 2018).

Stuart, Kathy, 'Melancholy murderers: suicide by proxy and the insanity defence', in Marjorie E. Plummer (ed.), *Ideas and Cultural Margins in Early Modern Germany: Essays in Honor of H. C. Erik Midelfort* (London: Routledge, 2009), pp. 63–77.

———, 'Suicide by proxy: the unintended consequences of public executions in eighteenth-century Germany', *Central European History*, 41:3 (2008), 413–45.

Tamm, Ditlev and Jens Ulf Jørgensen, *Dansk retshistorie i hovedpunkter: Fra landskabslovene til Ørsted*, 2 vols (Copenhagen: Gad, 1973–1978; repr. Akademisk förlag, 1987).

Tamm, Ditlev and Morten Kjær (eds), *Henrik Stampe – enevældens menneskelige ansigt* (Copenhagen: Jurist- og økonomforbundet, 2013).

Tamm, Ditlev and E. Slottved (eds), *Københavns Universitet 1479–1979: Det Rets- og Statsvidenskabelige Fakultet* (Copenhagen: Københavns Universitet, 2005).

Waaben, Knud, *Retspsykiatri og Strafferet i Historiens Lys* (Copenhagen: Janssen-Cilag, 1997).

Walker, Nigel, 'The insanity defense before 1800', *Annals of the American Academy of Political and Social Science*, 477:1 (1985), 25–30.

Watt, Jeffrey R., *Choosing Death: Suicide and Calvinism in Early Modern Geneva* (Kirksville, MI: Truman State University Press, 2001).

Weber, Hellmuth von, 'Selbstmord als Mordmotiv', *Monatsschrift für Kriminalbiologie und Strafrechtsreform*, 28 (1937), 161–81.

11
Changing practices of censorship: the Faculty of Theology at the University of Copenhagen, 1738–1770

Jesper Jakobsen and Lars Cyril Nørgaard

As a socially embedded practice, early modern censorship aimed to preserve public order. Accordingly, negotiations between censors, authors and printers reflect changing ideas about the public. This chapter examines different rationalities of censorship in eighteenth-century Denmark, focusing on the Faculty of Theology at the University of Copenhagen.[1] It might have been expected that, for instance, religious books were evaluated according to monolithic standards of Lutheran orthodoxy, and indeed theological conflicts are seen to have affected practices of censorship; but these practices cannot easily be reduced to a simple framework. Instead, we argue that the relationship between theological censorship and Enlightenment ideals is complex and somewhat misunderstood in overarching narratives of secularization, which often point to the Struensee regime (1770–1772) as a watershed between robust censorship and freedom of print.

In the Danish monarchy, institutionalized forms of censorship regulation were introduced in the sixteenth century, following the spread of print culture. The Church Ordinance of 1537/1539 stated that nothing could be printed without the approval of the university and the clergy.[2] The twenty-first chapter of the second book of the

---

1 This chapter builds on results from Jesper Jakobsen's unpublished doctoral thesis about censorship practices in eighteenth-century Denmark – Jesper Jakobsen, 'Uanstændige, utilladelige og unyttige skrifter: en undersøgelse af censuren i praksis 1746–1773' (unpublished doctoral thesis, University of Copenhagen, 2017) – which has been further developed within the research programme of the Danish National Research Foundation Centre for Privacy Studies (DNRF 138).
2 Martin Schwarz Lausten, *Kirkeordinansen 1537/39* (Copenhagen: Akademisk Förlag, 1989), p. 232. On censorship in Denmark–Norway between the Reformation and 1770, see Henning Matzen, *Kjøbenhavns Universitets Retshistorie 1479–1879* (Copenhagen: J. H. Schultz, 1879); Ludvig Koch,

Danske Lov ('Danish Code', 1683) confirmed such pre-publication censorship, which remained the legal foundation of later practices.[3] By contrast, unrestricted freedom of print was introduced in 1770 under the regime of Johann Friedrich Struensee. On 14 September 1770, King Christian VII signed off on this unprecedented freedom.[4] Unbridled debates immediately ensued; and as early as October 1771, the authorities proclaimed that defamation in print was still considered a crime. An Act of October 1773 further prescribed the imposition of severe fines to combat defamatory speech. In 1799 pre-publication censorship was partly reintroduced, as such a procedure became required of authors who had previously been punished for 'abusing' the freedom of print. Despite the short-lived period of the unrestricted freedom of print, the 1770 decree remains a milestone of the Enlightenment and an important step towards the abolition of religiously motivated censorship.[5] Struensee's decree

---

'Bidrag til Censurens Historie under Fredrik V', *Historisk Tidsskrift*, 2 (1889), 67–94; Charlotte Appel, *Læsning og bogmarked i 1600-tallets Danmark*, 2 vols (Copenhagen: Museum Tusculanum, 2001), I, pp. 367–454; Øystein Rian, *Sensuren i Danmark-Norge: Vilkårene for offentlige ytringer 1536–1814* (Oslo: Universitetsforlaget, 2014), pp. 144–93.

3 Vilhelm Adolf Secher (ed.), *Kong Christian den femtis Danske Lov* (Copenhagen: Gads, 1929), p. 204. The censorship laws in the *Danske Lov* of 1683 were a codification of older laws, of which the most important was the *Censurforordning* of 6 May 1667. For a discussion on the connections between the Law of 1667 and the *Danske Lov*, see Appel, *Læsning og bogmarked*, pp. 367–454. This document, however, did not apply in the provinces of Schleswig and Holstein: this exemption also applied to the town of Altona with its thriving print business, which constituted a nodal point in the network of distribution; see Dagmar Cochanski, *Präsidial- und Oberpräsidialverfassung in Altona 1664–1746* (Hamburg: Selbstverlag Verein für Hamburgische Geschichte, 1984), pp. 30–2; Holger Bönig, *Welteroberung durch ein neues Publikum: die deutsche Presse und der Weg zur Aufklärung: Hamburg und Altona als Beispiel* (Bremen: Edition Lumière, 2002).

4 In 1766 Sweden had issued legally guaranteed freedom-of-print regulations. However, they involved several exemptions relating to religious and political literature; see Jonathan Israel, 'Northern varieties: contrasting the Dano-Norwegian and the Swedish-Finnish Enlightenments', in Ellen Krefting, Aina Nøding and Mona Ringvej (eds), *Eighteenth-Century Periodicals as Agents of Change* (Leiden: Brill, 2012), pp. 17–45; Jonas Nordin and John Christian Laursen, 'Northern declarations of freedom of the press: the relative importance of philosophical ideas and of local politics', *Journal of the History of Ideas*, 81:2 (2020), 217–37.

5 Harald Jørgensen, *Trykkefrihedsspørgsmaalet i Danmark 1799–1848* (Copenhagen: Munksgaard, 1944), pp. 15–47; John Christian Laursen,

did not come as a bolt from the blue, though. Before pre-publication censorship was removed, social changes had taken place – changes which, albeit incrementally, paved the way for what was to come.[6]

Throughout the eighteenth century, the robust requirements of censorship had increasingly become an obstacle to the expanding print culture and the successful business of print houses. This was especially true of print shops located outside the capital. Slowly but steadily, the official system had to adapt to a growing commercial market which developed outside Copenhagen's city walls. Initially, this adaptation was able to base itself on existing practices because local authorities had long taken an active part in the process of censoring religious manuscripts. Printers outside of Copenhagen were thus accustomed to interacting with bishops and, through these interactions, to securing a written assessment which allowed them to submit manuscripts to the Faculty of Theology. Indeed, bishops would increasingly be entrusted with the evaluation of minor works dealing with religion, while works containing more substantial argumentation still had to be shipped off to Copenhagen. During the 1730s and 1740s, printers in Viborg, Trondheim and Aalborg

---

'Spinoza in Denmark and the fall of Struensee, 1770–1772', *Journal of the History of Ideas*, 61:2 (2020), 189–202; Israel, 'Northern varieties'. For an in-depth discussion of the short period of unrestricted freedom of print and the rise of a new public order, see Henrik Horstbøll, Ulrik Langen and Frederik Stjernfelt, *Grov Konfekt: Tre vilde år med trykkefrihed, 1770–73*, 2 vols (Copenhagen: Gyldendal, 2020). For discussions on the restrictions in 1771 and 1773, see Horstbøll and others, *Grov Konfekt*, II, pp. 131–57, 399–410.

6 Since the 2010s, historians have unveiled how an increasing focus on commerce and economic theory became a vector for book circulation; the rise of a new culture of public debate in the eighteenth century was closely tied to this circulation. The Norwegian historian Jakob Maliks has demonstrated that the Danish-Norwegian government increasingly prioritized issues of commerce, thereby transforming the public sphere into a sphere of critical discussion and foreshadowing the abolishment of pre-publication censorship during the Struensee years. Maliks' doctoral thesis from 2011 sadly remains unpublished, but some key results are presented in Jakob Maliks, 'Imprimatur i provinsen – Sensuren av det trykte ord utenfor København 1737–1770', in Eivind Tjønneland (ed.), *Kritikk før 1814* (Oslo: Dreyer, 2014), pp. 78–102, and the same author's 'To rule is to communicate: the absolutist system of political communication in Denmark–Norway 1660–1750', in Ellen Krefting, Aina Nøding and Mona Ringvej (eds), *Eighteenth-Century Periodicals as Agents of Change* (Leiden: Brill, 2015), pp. 134–52. Importantly, these insightful studies do not focus on the actual practices of censorship and their logic, which form the focal point of the present chapter.

were also allowed to exercise local censorship; and following the expansion of the book market around the mid-eighteenth century, similar permissions were granted to printers in other provincial towns.[7] Centralized censorship seems to have adapted to general developments in society and thereby lost, or at least loosened, its iron grip on the public sphere.[8]

The present chapter focuses on such small-scale changes in censorship. These changes not only emerged among local authorities but also in the censorship undertaken at the Faculty of Theology. This development is documented in a surviving protocol that details the censoring of minor works during the period from 1738 until 1770.[9] The following discussion concentrates on this protocol and the historical period after 1737, when two institutional bodies in the Danish capital became charged with censoring religious writings. This situation was brought about by changes within the religious system itself: these changes deeply affected censorship, moving its exercise from a 'traditional' type of authority to the anonymous realm of institutional authority. We present the actual censorship as it is recorded in the protocol: this source reveals how a variety of concerns informed censorship, ranging from theological, stylistic

---

7 For an overview and discussion of provincial censorship in Denmark and Norway, see Maliks, 'Imprimatur'. As argued in Jesper Jakobsen, 'Der Klagen über das verdorbene Christenthum: om interessekonflikter og censurprocedure vedrørende oversættelsen af et teologisk skrift i 1739', *Fund og Forskning*, 50 (2011), 259–78, these local practices were influenced by and, to some extent, mirrored the agenda of the censorship authorities based in Copenhagen.

8 The expanding book market was of course a general European trend that Rolf Engelsing correctly labelled as a 'Leserevolution'; see Rolf Engelsing, *Der Bürger als Leser: Lesergeschichte in Deutschland, 1500–1800* (Stuttgart: Metzler, 1974). On this topic, see also James Van Horn Melton, *The Rise of the Public in Enlightenment Europe* (Cambridge: Cambridge University Press, 2001), and Henrik Horstbøll, *Menigmands medie: Det folkelige bogtryk i Danmark 1500–1840* (Copenhagen: Museum Tusculanum, 1999).

9 This key source of eighteenth-century Danish censorship practices has attracted relatively little attention in historical studies. It was first studied in an article by the theologian Ludvig Koch (1837–1917), which focuses on the reign of King Frederik V; see Koch, 'Bidrag til Censurens Historie'. An overview of relevant manuscripts dating from 1738 to 1746 can be found in Jesper Jakobsen, 'Omorganiseringen af den teologiske censur', *Historisk Tidsskrift*, 111:1 (2011), 1–36, which focuses on the censorship practices of the *Generalkirke-inspektionskollegiet* (Collegium for the general inspection of the Church, hereafter 'the Collegium'). An analysis and discussion of the whole protocol is found in Jakobsen, 'Uanstændige', pp. 75–92.

and grammatical to juridical and economic concerns. The latter aspect is discussed with respect to the importation of books, as this activity was perceived in terms of economic theory and in the words of the university professors.

Institutional anonymity

The censorship procedures that were codified in the *Danske Lov* of 1683 stated that censors were personally responsible for their assessments of manuscripts, and thus the individual censor's professional evaluation of a manuscript was easily associated with his private conscience. However, with the introduction of the censorship protocols in 1738 the traditional printed personal assessment was replaced by an anonymized protocol, which effectively separated the censor's official/public duties from his private beliefs and consciousness.

King Christian VI's reign, lasting from 1730 until 1746, has often been associated with his pious beliefs and ambition to reorganize the Church. Christian and his advisers also implemented financial policies that facilitated what would later be known as 'den florissante periode' – that is, the flourishing period (1778–1807).[10] Often overlooked, royal piety also affected the structures of censorship. Strongly inspired by the Hallesian brand of Pietism that had been initiated by August Hermann Francke (1663–1727), the King, among other initiatives, established the Collegium on 1 October 1737. This institutional body was given the task of administering clerical and theological matters pertaining to the Church itself, but also to schools and to the University of Copenhagen. Its duties included the supervision of censorship of theological and religious writings. The emergence of this institution has attracted interest from historians; but little attention has been paid to the actual, and sometimes creative, practices of censorship. Consequently, our focus is on these practices as they unfolded at the Faculty of Theology after the foundation of the Collegium.[11]

---

10 Olaf Olsen (ed.), *Gyldendal og Politikens Danmarkshistorie*, 16 vols (Copenhagen: Gyldendal, 1988-1991), IX: *Ole Feldbæk, Den lange fred: 1700-1800* (1990), pp. 296-307.

11 For an overview of the relevant scholarship and of the censorship carried out by this institutional body, see Jakobsen, 'Omorganiseringen'; Jakob Maliks, 'Vilkår for offentlighet: sensur, økonomi og transformasjonen af det offentlige rom i Danmark-Norge 1730–1770' (unpublished doctoral

For a long period, during the first decades of the eighteenth century, Christen Worm (1672–1737) had served as Dean of the Faculty of Theology and as Bishop of Zealand. In an unprecedented move, Worm's successor, Peder Hersleb (1689–1757), declined to head the theological professors. Instead, Hersleb was awarded a prominent position within the Collegium, leaving the Faculty of Theology without a dean. On 24 September 1738, therefore, the professors petitioned King Christian VI that this prominent position should be made a temporary one: each professor should hold office as dean for either six or twelve months. The professors suggested that, alternatively, their most senior member be elected: this would have left Hans Steenbuch (1664–1740) in charge, but owing to old age and failing health Steenbuch had already requested not to be taken into consideration. In further support of making the dean's position temporary, the professors added that this would help ease the burden of censoring all theological works, which, as 'the heaviest workload ... surpasses the powers of one man'.[12] In the vacuum of 1737, brought about by religious conflicts, the professors were suggesting a rationalization of their organization.

The Crown consulted the Collegium before answering the faculty's petition. Its members approved the request on condition that an additional change be introduced, a change directly related to the practice of censorship: the name of the professor who acted as censor was no longer to appear on the printed page, where it had featured beneath the imprimatur up to that point. This might seem like a trivial detail, but it was not. The removal of the institutional sign and the censor's name is accounted for by reference to 'the reputation of a righteous theologian'. More specifically, the public might infer 'that a censor is of the same opinion as the book that he has approved'.[13] We must conclude that the proposed disassociation of the censor's name from the right to print was intended to facilitate the dissemination of religious literature – that is, pietistic literature – which professors at the Faculty of Theology found questionable.

---

thesis, Norges teknisk-naturvitenskapelige universitet, 2011), pp. 92–5; Rian, *Sensuren i Danmark-Norge*, pp. 398–410.

12 'det tungeste arbeide ...overgaaer een Mands Kræfter'; Copenhagen, Statens arkiver (SAr), Koncepter og indlæg til ST 1738 (D21-79), Nr. 578; compare Jakobsen, 'Uanstændige', p. 76.

13 'en retskaffen Theologi Reputation'; 'at en Censor er af lige Meening med den af ham approberede bog'; SAr, Koncepter og indlæg til ST 1738 (D21-79), Nr. 578; compare Jakobsen, 'Uanstændige', p. 76.

This was undoubtedly an important motive for the faculty's petition. However, the deletion of the censor's name, identifying a professional evaluation with a private individual, also has more profound, societal consequences.[14] The Collegium's suggestion purposefully uprooted any monolithic framework for censorship. It indirectly implied the emergence of a public order wherein theological semantics was gradually losing its relevance while social subsystems and their semantics exercised an increasing influence. This differentiation, and the increase in societal complexity that followed from it, was rooted in the religious system itself. It was not external forces but rather internal conflicts that brought about this professionalization of censorship. This initiative was primarily a means to a theological end: members of the Faculty of Theology could now approve books of a pietistic flavour, although they would not want to be publicly associated with this stance. The anonymity afforded by the protocols has been recognized by other scholars, but the underlying reasons have been interpreted in different ways. For instance, Jakob Maliks has argued that the protocols were introduced as an attempt to conceal the academic discord at the faculty from the public eye.

The Crown implemented what the Collegium suggested, and on 17 October 1738, the Faculty of Theology therefore began keeping two record books or protocols. One protocol, dedicated to 'major works', is presumably lost, while a second protocol on 'minor works' survives.[15] These protocols constitute a system of support that had not been required before the advent of the Collegium, when the faculty's dean had overseen all matters of censorship.

In order to document its institutional decision-making processes, the Faculty of Theology kept a special record. At a time when the censor's name was kept away from the public, the protocols disclose who had carried out individual acts of censorship. In public, readers faced the anonymous 'Imprimatur In Fidem Protocolli Facultatis'

---

14 On the reorganization of censorship during the reign of Christian VI, and on motives for introducing the protocols, see Jørgen Lundbye, *Kirkekampen i Danmark 1730–1746* (Copenhagen: Schønbergske, 1947); Erik Reitzel-Nielsen, 'Censuren af Pontoppidans katekismus', *Kirkehistoriske Samlinger*, 7:4 (1960–1962), 12–48; Jakobsen, 'Omorganiseringen'; Maliks, 'Vilkår'; Jakobsen, 'Uanstændige', pp. 75–7. In 1765, after the Collegium had lost influence, the name of the censor was reintroduced on the printed page. This return to a more personalized type of authority was a desperate attempt from a failing system to reassert itself.

15 'større skrifter'; 'smaae skrifter'; SAr, Københavns Universitet, Sager vedrørende censur af teologiske skrifter (3106-01).

('printed in accordance with the protocols of the Faculty'), while the protocols identify the professors behind the institution's faceless mask.

Censors in action

The protocol on minor works holds information about more than seven hundred manuscripts.[16] Close to 80 per cent of the submitted manuscripts were approved for printing, whereas 7 per cent were accepted on condition that they undergo some revision. Only 5 per cent could not be printed. A small number of manuscripts were labelled as being outside the faculty's expertise, while other manuscripts were transferred to the lost protocol on major works. We only find a small number of Latin works, which probably implies that the censored manuscripts targeted a relatively broad readership. Small formats in the vernacular were a popular commodity. Manuscripts in German appear regularly, which is unsurprising since this language was widely spoken and written within the kingdom. We find no manuscripts in French, the preferred language of European courts.

Between 1738 and 1770, ten professors censored minor works submitted to the faculty: Søren Bloch (1696–1753), Erik Pontoppidan the younger, Marcus Wøldike (1699–1750), Jeremias Friedrich Reuss (1700–1777), Christian Langemach Leth (1701–1764), Johann August Seidlitz (1704–1751), Peder Rosenstand-Goiske (1704–1769), Peder Jakobsen Holm (1706–1777), Hans Otto Bang (1712–1764) and Johan Andreas Cramer (1723–1788). These men either held a chair at or were otherwise associated with the Faculty of Theology. In the hands of these professors, state-sponsored Lutheranism served as the standards of censorship. Authors were readily rejected when they did not abide by such standards.[17] In 1750, Seidlitz censored a translation that he could not allow to be printed:

---

16 This section is based on and develops insights from the unpublished thesis by Jakobsen, 'Uanstændige', pp. 75–92. For a detailed overview of the annual distribution of the manuscripts in the protocol on minor works, see Jakobsen, 'Uanstændige', p. 256.
17 In his pioneering study of eighteenth-century Danish censorship, Ludvig Koch characterized the main task of the faculty's censorship as preventing the dissemination of Moravian texts. This was indeed one aim of censorship in eighteenth-century Denmark–Norway, but certainly not the sole objective of this societal practice.

These canticles that, for the most part, have been translated into Danish from the German by the Moravian Brethren cannot be approved, since they are blemished throughout by ridiculous, mistaken formulations and Zinzendorf's senseless tautologies.[18]

This entry is telling because of the theological tone of the record-keeping, but the professors' censorship also reveals concerns that lie beyond theology proper. Clearly, standards were not simply a matter of theological orthodoxy; commercial questions and the expectations of buyers come into view as well. Those who exercised censorship seem to have been aware of an expanding market for printed texts, a market where stylistic correctness and aesthetic quality mattered. This aspect comes to the fore in Peder Holm's assessments.[19] Holm was born in what is now Norway. His theological stance remains unstudied, but he seems to have been critical of the Pietists. A professor from 1738, he was not awarded a chair at the faculty until 1746. The protocol has him active from 1739 until 1769, and he was by far the most productive of all censors. Holm assessed more than 160 manuscripts, of which he only rejected 11. Concerning a manuscript of 1749, Holm concluded that it was fit for printing, 'but the style and spelling, which are everywhere filled with mistakes, should first be corrected by someone who knows how to write correctly'.[20] Two years later, he again approved a manuscript on the condition of certain improvements:

> With adequate carefulness, these pious reflections have been either dictated or written by the author, this is evident, but they are badly transcribed by a most inexperienced man, and this to such an extent that it is beyond all measure. Repeatedly, so many mistakes distort

---

18 'Cantilenas hasce maximam partem ex germanicis Herrnhuthanis in linguam Danicam conuersas approbare non possum; quia erronibus phrasibus ludicris, et ineptis Tautologiis Zinzendorffianis passim sunt commaculatae'; SAr, Københavns Universitet, Sager vedrørende censur af teologiske skrifter (3106-01), 9 January 1750.

19 For information on Holm, see Albert Thorvald Jantzen, 'Peder Holm', in Carl Frederik Bricka (ed.), *Dansk biografisk Lexikon, tillige omfattende Norge for tidsrummet 1537–1814*, 19 vols (Copenhagen: Gyldendal, 1887–1905), VII (1893), pp. 584–6; Knud Banning, 'Det teologiske Fakultet 1732–1830', in Svend Ellehøj (ed.), *Københavns Universitet 1479–1979*, 14 vols (Copenhagen: Gad, 1979–2005), IV: *Det teologiske fakultet*, ed. Leif Grane (1980), pp. 213–82 (pp. 259–60).

20 'Men Stiilen og Bogstavringen der over alt er saa meget urigtig, burde dog først rettes af én, som forstaaer at skrive ret'; SAr, Københavns Universitet, Sager vedrørende censur af teologiske skrifter (3106-01), 10 June 1749.

the very meaning itself. This distorted copy should not have been
handed in for theological censorship. When the most honoured author
has truly corrected everything that originates from the transcriber's
ignorance and negligence, he will recognize and better attend to just
how easily a mistake is made: he will then be permitted to add the
censor's rubric, also on the first page: Imprimatur.[21]

On other occasions, Holm would praise the authors and their manuscripts. In 1760 he assessed a manuscript version of a song that had allegedly been composed by Svendina Finger, the ten-year-old daughter of a vicar from a town near Flensburg. In the protocol, Holm notes that he had actually met the girl and made enquiries about the song before arriving at the conclusion that the young girl had written it: 'To the many objections, the little maiden answered with such conviction and surprise that I found myself confounded by it and took it not to be beyond belief that she could have authored the song'.[22] Holm was clearly impressed by the girl and passed her manuscript for publication, merely adding that the minor errors 'must be regarded as permissible at her age'.[23] Concerning a Danish translation of *A Sure Guide to Hell*, Holm strikes a more uncompromising note:

---

21 'Piæ hæ meditationes ab Auctore quidem accurate satis sive dictatæ sive scriptæ fuerunt, quod satis apparet, at ab imperitissimo homine vitiose adeo supra omnem modum descriptæ sunt, ut tot mendis, ipsum sæpe sensum depravantibus, foedatum exemplar censuræ Theologiæ tradi haud debuisset. Quando vero emendari auctor plur(imum) reu(erendus) quicquid descriptoris inscitiâ atque neglegentiâ peccatum esse facile observabit, curaverit, licebit censuræ loco titulo et folio primo inscribere: Imprimatur'; SAr, Københavns Universitet, Sager vedrørende censur af teologiske skrifter (3106-01), between 6 and 17 May 1751. The censored work was authored by Hans Mossin (1716–1794) and later published in Bergen. Mossin was influenced by Pietism and tried, on several occasions, to earn a chair at the Faculty of Theology; see Daniel Smith Tharp, 'Hans Mossin', in Carl Frederik Bricka (ed.), *Dansk biografisk Lexikon, tillige omfattende Norge for tidsrummet 1537–1814*, 19 vols (Copenhagen: Gyldendal, 1887–1905), XI (1897), pp. 481–3. In 1751 Erik Pontoppidan secured him a position as chaplain at Nykirken in Bergen. Here, Mossin obtained royal privilege to run his own printing press. Without the manuscript that Mossin handed in, it is impossible to verify whether the author followed Holm's advice.
22 'Den lille Jomfrue svarede med saadan fermetet og overraskelse paa adskillige Indvendinger, at jeg forundret mig derover, og holder det ej utroeligt, at hun kand have forfattet Sangen'; SAr, Københavns Universitet, Sager vedrørende censur af teologiske skrifter (3106-01), 31 July 1760.
23 'maa holdes hende til gode i den alder'; SAr, Københavns Universitet, Sager vedrørende censur af teologiske skrifter (3106-01), 31 July 1760.

Although the work's intention seems to be good, this way of writing seems not to be such that it would be fitting for it to be approved for publication by a theological censor, because it is also to be expected that many could learn and perceive much that is evil from this work, which they would not otherwise have thought of themselves.[24]

Similar concerns were voiced in relation to a catechism entitled *Fattig mands tanker til Gudelige Hiemsbrug, som Bønder og Børn, Der har liten tiid, og mindre nemme, at Føre til videre* ('A poor man's thoughts: for the godly use in the home by people who, like peasants and children, have little time and ability to educate').[25] The catechism was dated 18 November 1745 in the protocol, and Marcus Wøldike was charged with the task of censoring its seventy-eight pages.[26] After studying in Wittenberg and Jena, Wøldike had returned to Copenhagen, where he found employment at the Royal Library. In 1732 he became a professor at the Faculty of Theology, where he remained until his death in 1750. Wøldike was the first professor to lecture on church history, and his *Positiones fidei christianæ* (1740) was highly influential. The protocol documents Wøldike's activities as a censor from 1738 until 1750; in 1748 he approved *Fattig mands tanker*, adding interlinear corrections in the manuscript. In accordance with procedures, the manuscript with the signed 'Imprimatur in fidem Protocolli Facult[atis] Theolog[i]' was passed on to the Collegium, which, in this instance, decided against Wøldike and announced

---

24 'Skiønt hensigten af Skriftet synes at være god, saa synes dog den Skrivemaade ikke at være saadan, at det kand skikke sig ret vel at approbere samme ved en Theologisk Censur til Trykken, som det og ej er uventeligt, at mange deraf kunde lære og see meget ont, som de ikke ellers selv vare falden paa'; SAr, Københavns Universitet, Sager vedrørende censur af teologiske skrifter (3106-01), 9 February 1757. First published in 1750 or 1751 and purportedly written by Beelzebub, *A Sure Guide to Hell* is a playful response to the nonconformist pastor Joseph Alleine (1634–1668) and his *A Sure Guide to Heaven* (1671). The latter offers advice to parents, to youth, to those whose minds are possessed, to a good king, to the first minister of state, to the clergy and to young women.
25 The original manuscript is preserved in the archives of the Collegium: SAr, Kirkekollegiet (F4.18.3).
26 For information on Wøldike, see Albert Thorvald Jantzen, 'Marcus Wöldike', in Carl Frederik Bricka (ed.), *Dansk biografisk Lexikon, tillige omfattende Norge for tidsrummet 1537–1814*, 19 vols (Copenhagen: Gyldendal, 1887–1905), XIX (1905), pp. 257–8; Banning, 'Det teologiske Fakultet', pp. 220–2.

its disapproval of the manuscript.[27] Members of this body argued that similar books of higher quality were already available. One member remarked: 'I am of the opinion that we should prevent not only hateful books but also useless books, since the buyer is deceived by the latter, and this [deception] causes disgust among our countrymen'.[28] Evidently, censors of religious literature cared not only about orthodoxy but also about quality and supply on the book market.

Pragmatic orthodoxy

No references to atheistic writings are found in the preserved protocol, and explicit criticism of the monarch, the Church or the government is equally absent. However, this does not mean that such writings were not in circulation within the realm of the Danish king. They certainly were; but for obvious reasons, their authors and printers had no reason to hand them in for official approval – such writings travelled through unofficial networks.[29] Even so, the censors sometimes saw manuscripts they thought would be inappropriate to print; but even when confronted by texts which originated outside the Lutheran cultural sphere, they occasionally exercised a remarkable pragmatism.

---

27 It was not the first time that *Generalkirkeinspektionskollegiet* overruled his assessments. In 1737, before the emergence of the Collegium, Wøldike had approved a Danish translation of Julius Bernhard von Rohr's *Einleitung zu der Klugheit zu Leben, oder, Anweisung: wie ein Mensch zu Beförderung seiner zeitlichen Glückseeligkeit seine Actiones vernünfftig anstellen soll* (1730). Given the book's content, its censorship assessment was carried out by the Faculty of Philosophy; but two chapters dealt with theological matters, and therefore Wøldike became involved. However, the newly established Collegium decided to overrule the theology professor. In 1738, members of the Collegium found Rohr's two theological chapters in opposition to Hallensian teachings, and Wøldike's approval had to be withdrawn. On this conflict in censorship, see Jakobsen, 'Omorganiseringen', 20–2.

28 'Jeg er af de tanker at mand burde hindre ej alene Hadlige, men unyttige bøger, thi ved de sidste bedragis kiøberen og det foraarsager vore landsmænd væmmelse'; SAr, Kirkekollegiet (Generalkirkeinspektionskollegiet), Diverse Sager (F4.18.3).

29 Gina Dahl's research on private collections in eighteenth-century Norway shows that controversial texts in foreign languages made their way to the north; see Gina Dahl, *Books in Early Modern Norway* (Leiden: Brill, 2011), and the same author's *Libraries and Enlightenment: Eighteenth-Century Norway and the Outer World* (Aarhus: Aarhus University Press, 2014).

In December 1739 Holm censored a manuscript entitled *Eenfoldigt Bibellys, sat imod det exegetiske Mørk*. Its author, Hans Tulle (1711–1743), was renowned for his mastery of Hebrew, and in 1736 he had handed in a disputation on how to translate the Bible. His *Bibellys* actually identifies several mistakes in the Danish translation of 1739. Despite the young man's obvious talents, his methods did not go down well with the faculty.[30] Furthermore, Holm remarks about the manuscript version of the *Bibellys* that a specific section should include a prohibition in order for the work to be in accordance with the *Danske Lov*.[31] The section in Tulle's work that Holm refers to is entitled 'on the marriage of stepchildren', and the censor thus evokes a larger, theological issue.[32] At the University of Copenhagen, the first professor of natural law, Andreas Højer (1690–1739), had caused heated debate with his *De nuptiis propinquorum jure divino non prohibitis* ('On marriages between closely related persons which are not prohibited according to divine law'). This brief treatise was not just an intellectual challenge; as the main administrative body of the university, the Consistory possessed the *tamperret* – that is, the authority to decide in such matters – and its members frequently had to consider petitions from Zealanders who wished to marry a not very distant relative. Now, Højer claimed that incest was not a crime because it violated a divine order of things; rather, incest was a punishable offence because it violated a rational ordering of the social world.[33]

---

30 Tulle's preface outlines his scientific approach to Scripture, which is rather idiosyncratic and cannot easily be identified as, for example, pietistic; see H. L. Tulle, 'Fortale', in *Bibellys, sat imod det exegetiske Mørk* (Copenhagen: Andreas Hartvig Godiche, 1740). To our knowledge, no study of Tulle and his work exists.

31 See SAr, Københavns Universitet, Sager vedrørende censur af teologiske skrifter (3106-01), 10 December 1739.

32 'om sammenbragte Børns Ægteskab'. On the early elaboration of this question in the seventeenth century, see Benjamin T. G. Mayes, *Counsel and Conscience: Lutheran Casuistry and Moral Reasoning after the Reformation* (Göttingen: Vandenhoeck & Ruprecht, 2011), pp. 137–42. On this issue and its relation to the new and social model of marriage which followed in the wake of the Lutheran upheaval, see also John Witte, Jr, *From Sacrament to Contract: Marriage, Religion, and Law in the Western Tradition* (Louisville, KY: Westminster John Knox, 2011), pp. 119–36.

33 Besides being a professor of law at the University, Andreas Højer was also the driving force behind the creation of *Generalkirkeinspektionskollegiet*. For discussions of Højer, see Holger Rørdam, *Historiske Samlinger og Studier vedrørende danske Forhold og Studier især i det 17 århundrede* (Copenhagen:

In Holm's censoring of Tulle, ideas like those of Højer loom large. The emerging scientific field of biblical exegesis, spearheaded by the Pietists, was raising issues of debate, and Holm's assessment chimes well with the overall renewal of Old Testament exegesis that made it increasingly problematic to lift juridical precepts from the biblical texts.[34]

While Holm's engagement with Tulle is in accordance with an emerging critical rationality within theology, his censorship also involves elements that are more surprising. Since 1729, a popular devotional work had circulated which carried the Danish title *Armelle Nicolas gemeenlig kaldet den gode Armelle hendes daglige Omgang med Gud* ('Armelle Nicolas, commonly called the good Armelle, her everyday relations with God'). Originally written in French and published in 1676, the work was ascribed to Jeanne de la Nativité (1731–1798), an Ursuline nun and the superior of a convent in Vannes.[35] This text celebrates the mystical experiences of Armelle Nicolas (1606–1671), who was never canonized by Rome but played an important role in French religious worship. Including testimonies by the Jesuits, who had directed the conscience of 'la bonne Armelle', the French text was republished several times. In 1704 Pierre Poiret (1646–1719) reedited Armelle's *vita*,[36] and shortly thereafter, in

---

Gads, 1891–1902); Johannes Pedersen, *Fra Brydningen mellem Orthodoksi og Pietisme, 1704–1712*, 2 vols (Copenhagen: Gads, 1945–1948), II: *Mellem theologer 1712–1730* (1948), pp. 65–80; Tyge Krogh, *Oplysningstiden og det magiske: Henrettelser og korporlige straffe i 1700-tallets første halvdel* (Copenhagen: Samleren, 2000), pp. 158–90; M. Langballe Jensen, 'Libertas philosophandi and natural law in early eighteenth-century Denmark–Norway', *Intellectual History Review* 30:2 (2021), 209–31. On his connection to Pietism, see Kristian Mejrup, 'Andreas Hojer (1690–1739) – the standard-bearer of Danish-Norwegian Pietism', in Kjell Å. Modéer and Helle Vogt (eds), *Law and the Christian Tradition in Scandinavia: The Writings of Great Nordic Jurists* (London: Routledge, 2021), pp. 180–95.

34 On this issue, see Tine Reeh and Ralf Hemmingsen's contribution to this volume.
35 Jeanne de la Nativité, *Le triomphe de l'amour divin dans la vie d'une grande servante de Dieu, nommée Armelle Nicolas décédée l'an de Notre-Seigneur 1671*, 2 vols (Vannes: Jean Galles, 1676).
36 Olivier Échallard [and Jeanne de la Nativité], *L'Ecole du pur Amour de Dieu, ouverte aux savants et aux ignorans, dans la vie merveilleuse d'une pauvre fille idiote, païsanne de naissance, et servante de condition, Armelle Nicolas, vulgairement dite la bonne Armelle, décédée depuis peu en Bretagne: Par une Fille Religieuse de sa connaissance* (Cologne: Jean de la Pierre, 1704).

1708, Poiret's edition was translated into German.[37] The first Danish edition of 1729 is based on this German version.[38] Ten years later, in November 1739, the Faculty of Theology received an official request for publishing the book. This request was filed on behalf of the Danish-German printer Ernst Heinrich Berling (1708–1750); we might infer that Berling recognized that this book was in demand, but before publishing an official edition he had to secure an approval. The initial translation might actually have circulated among clandestine Catholics living in Copenhagen,[39] but Berling's request implies that a broader readership existed for this kind of literature. On 10 November 1739 Holm formulated the following concise censure: 'I find that this short story of the life and sayings of Armelle should by no means be printed. Laws forbid that it is published together with Pirckheimer's small book'.[40] What are we to make of this suggestion? The professor opposes any straightforward publication of this devotional text, but he also rejects Berling's attempt to publish the popular Catholic text together with a text from a certain Pirckheimer. Now, it is not entirely clear which specific text Holm is referring to. It might be the *Denkwürdigkeiten* by Caritas Pirckheimer (1467–1563), who was the abbess of a convent of Poor Clares in Nuremberg. This journal describes the period from 1524 until 1528, and the abbess documents how her community struggled as Lutheranism was introduced in the city.[41] We have

---

37 *Die Schule der reinen Liebe Gottes Eröffnet den Gelehrten und Ungelehrten in dem Wunder Leben Einer armen unwissenden Weibs-Person / die von Geburt eine Bäurin / und dem Stande nach eine Dienst-Magd gewesen, Armelle Nikolas. Sonsten die gute Armelle genannt, welche vor weniger Zeit in Klein-Britannien gestorben. Durch eine ihr bekandte Kloster-Jungfrau / anjetzo aus dem Frantzösischen getreulich ins Teutsche übersetzt* (Regensburg: Johann Martin Hagen, 1708).

38 *Den fromme Tieneste Pige Armelle Nicolas i aldmindelighed kaldet den gode Armelle, hendes daglig omgiengelse med Gud uddragen af hendes under-levnets andendeel, som Anno 1708 er oversat i det Tüdske og nu i det danske Tungemaal dennem som elsker et helligt Levnet til en opmuntring* (n.p., 1729).

39 Urban Schrøder, 'Den gode Armelle', *Catholica*, 13:4 (1956), 155–62 (158).

40 'Narratiunculam hanc de Armellæ vita et dictis imprimi haud debere censeo. Additus vero Pirkheimeri libellus quin edatur leges haud prohibent'; SAr, Københavns Universitet, Sager vedrørende censur af teologiske skrifter (3106-01), 10 November 1739.

41 For modern editions, see Josef Pfanner (ed.), *Die 'Denkwürdigkeiten' der Caritas Pirckheimer* (Landshut: Caritas Pirckheimer Forschung, 1962);

not found a translation of this work, and it seems a rather strange fit, since Pirckheimer never submitted to the Lutheran authorities.[42] Another and more likely fit is a booklet that Caritas' younger brother, the humanist Willibald Pirckheimer (1470–1530), published in 1524 and entitled *Wie alle Closter vnd sonderlich Junckfrawen Clöster in ein Christlichs wesen möchten durch gottes gnaden gebracht werden* ('How all religious houses, especially convents housing women who are not nuns, may be brought to a Christian character by the grace of God'). This work was published pseudonymously.[43] Willibald offers several suggestions for reform, including that all convents should acquire as many books as possible by Luther, Melanchthon and Bugenhagen.[44] Furthermore, the author maintains that convents need not be abolished if they work for the common good of society and offer poor relief.[45] This booklet seems a more likely complement to the book on Armelle: Berling's suggestion for an intertext reveals an expectation to be able to revise the Catholic work and the intentions of its cloistered author.[46]

Economic reasoning

Since the 1980s, scholars of pre-revolutionary France have pointed to the fact that French censors often prioritized financial concerns

---

Caritas Pirckheimer, *Caritas Pirckheimer: A Journal of the Reformation Years, 1524–1528*, trans. Paul A. MacKenzie (Cambridge: D. S. Brewer, 2006).

42 In face-to-face meetings with Philipp Melanchthon (1497–1560), Caritas remained true to her beliefs, and her account offers a rather harsh depiction of, for instance, how nuns were forced to listen to the new doctrine of the Lutherans for hours on end; see Kenneth G. Appold, 'Taking a stand for Reformation: Martin Luther and Caritas Pirckheimer', *Lutheran Quarterly*, 32:1 (2018), 40–59.

43 Noricus Philadelphus [Willibald Pirckheimer], *Wie alle Closter vnd sonderlich Junckfrawen Clöster in ein Christlichs wesen möchten durch gottes gnaden gebracht werden* (Augsburg: Philipp Ulhart, 1524).

44 Philadelphus, *Wie alle Closter*, unpag. [pp. 5–6].

45 Philadelphus, *Wie alle Closter*, unpag. [pp. 14–15].

46 Whatever its precise nature, Holm's suggestion was not followed, as Berling never published an edition of 'the good Armelle'. A small portion of the work, just forty-eight small pages, was later published: *Dend fromme Tieneste Pige Armelle Nicolas i aldmindelighed kaldet dend gode Armelle, hendes daglig omgiengelse med Gud uddragen af hendes under-levnets andendeel, som Anno 1708 er oversat i det Tüdske og nu i det danske Tungemaal dennem som elsker et helligt Levnet til en opmuntring* (Copenhagen: Stein, 1764). This translation carries no imprimatur.

over religious orthodoxy; this was true of censorship in eighteenth-century Denmark as well, both in terms of censorship practice and on a legislative level.[47] During the 1740s, the censors of songs and ballads would sometimes issue tacit printing permissions but specifically asked not to have their names on the printed texts.[48] They hereby avoided having their private names associated with popular cheap prints, while not hindering printers from producing what was a lucrative commodity.[49] Consequently, the popularity of prints – that is, their value in the market place – was able to circumvent rigid control of their content: the societal ideals of censorship remained intact, but economic concerns seem increasingly to encroach upon this practice. In general, these concerns chimed with mercantilist principles and, most prominently, with the idea that accumulation of wealth in the national treasuries was a key to prosperity. Indeed, many European governments implemented customs schemes, restrictions on imports and other instruments of protectionism: money flowing outside of a given territory was perceived as detrimental to state finances. In 1759 Erik Pontoppidan expressed similar thoughts in his work *Oeconomiske Balance eller uforgribelige Overslag paa Dannemarks naturlige og borgerlige Formule til at giøre sine Indbyggere lyksalige, saavidt som de selv*

---

47 As argued by Robert Darnton in his studies of royal censorship in eighteenth-century France, censorship is embedded in the societies where it unfolds, and consequently it follows different societal norms; see Robert Darnton, *The Forbidden Best-Sellers of Pre-Revolutionary France* (New York: Norton, 1996). Raymond Birn documents how the censors' assessments were affected by their academic taste, which paved the way for fluctuating rationalities and practices within the institution; see Raymond Birn, *Royal Censorship of Books in Eighteenth-Century France* (Stanford, CA: Stanford University Press, 2012).

48 Popular songs were censored by the Faculty of Philosophy, and this faculty did not use an anonymizing protocol like that of the Faculty of Theology. Instead, the professor's name and permission were required to be printed on the front page.

49 See Harald Ilsøe, 'Censur og approbation: lidt om bogcensurens administration i 16–1700-tallet', in John T. Lauridsen and Olaf Olsen (eds), *Umisteligt* (Copenhagen: Museum Tusculanum, 2007), pp. 119–35. On the legal proceedings concerning the cases from the 1740s, see Jesper Jakobsen, '"...At I for saadant Eders u-tilladelige forhold skal vorde anseet og straffet...": Bogtrykkeren Johan Jørgen Høpfner mellem politimyndighed og akademisk censur i 1740'ernes København', in Sofie Lene Bak and others (eds), *'Kildekunst' Historiske og kulturhistoriske studier: Festskrift til John T. Lauridsen* (Copenhagen: Museum Tusculanum, 2016), pp. 165–83.

ville skiønne derpaa og benytte sig deraf. After completing his studies in 1718, Pontoppidan had travelled in England and Holland, where he was influenced by, among others, Friedrich Adolph Lampe (1683–1729), who was attempting to translate pietistic trends into a Calvinistic framework. Upon his return to Denmark, Pontoppidan became vicar on the island of Als in the Baltic Sea, and his pietistic leanings soon earned him both enemies and supporters. In 1734 he was awarded a position affiliated to the parish of Hillerød and, more specifically, to the Castle of Frederiksborg. Pontoppidan became professor extraordinarius in 1738, and he maintained this position even after 1748, when he became Bishop of Bergen. He returned to Copenhagen in 1754 and later became pro-chancellor of the university. The protocol on censorship of minor works informs us that between 1738 and 1764, Pontoppidan censored seventy-seven manuscripts. In some instances, he employs a rather uncompromising tone: he rejects one manuscript by abruptly stating that 'this foolish accumulation of words must be suppressed'.[50] Despite such harsh rejections, Pontoppidan also argued for a more lenient regulation of the book market, and this standpoint was clearly motivated by contemporary economic theories. Indeed, Pontoppidan relied heavily upon trends in European mercantilism and, more specifically, German cameralism.[51] Thus, a substantial part of Pontoppidan's *Oeconomisk Balance* is dedicated to the negative effects of imports, which the author describes

---

50 'supprimatur inepta verborum congeries'; SAr, Københavns Universitet, Sager vedrørende censur af teologiske skrifter (3106-01), 30 September 1740. The title of the censored manuscript is: *En omhygelig Huusfaders gudelige Omhue for sin af Gud betroede Familie og Huuhstyrende, med Morgen- Middags og Aften Andagter, som af hellige tyske Evangeliske Mænds Skrifter er uddraget* ('An attentive house-father's pious care for his God-given family and household, including morning, noon, and evening prayers, which have been selected from the writings of holy German evangelical authors').

51 The immense influence of German cameralism on mid-eighteenth-century economical thought is also stressed in Maliks, 'To rule is to communicate', p. 144. For a brief introduction to the spread of mercantilist and cameralist ideas in eighteenth-century Denmark, see Erik Oxenbøll, *Dansk økonomisk tænkning 1700–1770* (Copenhagen: Akademis Förlag, 1977). On the discussion of luxury goods during the period, see Mikkel Venborg Pedersen, *Luksus: forbrug og kolonier i Danmark i det 18. Århundrede* (Copenhagen: Museum Tusculanum, 2013). See also Petterson's contribution to this volume.

as draining the gutters of the treasury.⁵² Even so, the professor of theology remarked how the import of books from Germany, France and the Netherlands was inevitable.⁵³ Until domestic book production met the standards of foreign printers, this influx would be impossible to avoid; the failure of Danish printers to match international production standards posed a financial problem, and also raised the danger that controversial literature would steadily flow into the kingdom.⁵⁴ Accordingly, Pontoppidan suggested that the best way to control the importation of books was to ease restrictions on domestic printers and publishers.⁵⁵

Did such opinions influence the practice of censorship? The protocol on minor works does not provide us with sufficient information to answer to this question. However, a series of legal memoranda corroborate that the faculty was attempting to strike a difficult balance between religious orthodoxy on the one hand and the market conditions of printers situated outside Copenhagen on the other. These memoranda were drafted in response to the petitions of printers who applied for special rights or complete exemption from censorship. In 1757 the Jewish printer Coppel Samson Bloch (d. 1772) and his brother applied for permission to establish a Jewish print shop in Copenhagen. The Faculty of Theology was asked for a response; while not enthusiastic about the endeavour, the professors' memorandum includes an important financial consideration: the print shop could potentially be a source of income, and the brothers could thereby be able to 'make a living, and conserve some money in the nation, as well as attract money from elsewhere'.⁵⁶ In their

---

52 Erik Pontoppidan, *Oeconomiske Balance eller Uforgribelige Oberslag paa Dannemarks Naturlige og Borgerlige Formue Til at giøre sine Indbyggere lyksalige, saavidt som de selv ville skiønne derpaa og benytte sig deraf* (Copenhagen: Godiche, 1759), p. 229.
53 For a more detailed discussion on the importation of books, see Jakobsen, 'Uanstændige', pp. 65–9.
54 In early modern Europe, texts prohibited in one country were often printed in another country from where they could then be imported; see Darnton, *The Forbidden*. In Copenhagen, the French-speaking Swiss printer Claude Philibert (1709–1784) printed controversial French literature and distributed it to France; compare Henrik Horstbøll, 'En bogtrykker og boghandler i København: Claude Philiberts forbindelse med Societé typographique de Neuchatel 1771–1783', *Fund og Forskning*, 44 (2012), 311–35.
55 Pontoppidan, *Oeconomiske Balance*, p. 228.
56 'fortienne Deres Brød, samt at menagere nogle Penge i Landet, sa vel og at trekke Penge anden Steds fra herind'; SAr, Københavns Universitet,

response, the theologians seem sensitive to a mercantilist and cameralist line of reasoning. They take state finances into consideration, and despite theologically motivated suspicions against Jews, the professors allow for the establishment of the print shop. As part of the increasing rationalization of society, economics – in theory and practice – influenced the practice of censorship. Indeed, Pontoppidan was both a censor and an active proponent of such theories and practices.[57]

In the first half of the eighteenth century, local censorship administration was introduced for provincial printing houses in both Denmark and Norway. Jakob Maliks has argued that the de-monopolization of the university's censorship administration was an attempt by the Royal Chancellery in Copenhagen to reclaim control of all material that left the printing presses within the kingdom, as 'the provincial printers seem to have managed to avoid sending non-controversial print material to the capital for censoring'.[58] We will argue that the practice of establishing local censorship administration was, on the contrary, perceived by the university as a weakening of control over printed materials. However, during the 1760s the university still approved the further establishing of local censorship administration; in this process, the university clearly prioritized business conditions for the provincial printing houses over the maintenance of religious orthodoxy. In 1765 the aforementioned Hans Mossin argued that his print shop, situated in Bergen, was suffering from unnecessary expenditure because manuscripts had to be forwarded to the Faculty of Theology in Copenhagen. He asked permission for the local bishop, Frederik Arentz (1699–1779), to assess and approve manuscripts prior to printing. The Faculty of Theology was asked to formulate an official response to Mossin's request, and this memorandum recognizes the validity of his complaint; the professors even welcome the

---

Konsistoriums kopibog (1213-11), 399. On this and the ensuing memoranda, see Jakobsen, 'Uanstændige', pp. 148–64.

57 Between 1757 and 1764 Pontoppidan was also the editor of the periodical *Danmarks og Norges Økonomiske Magazin*. This financial periodical was the first of its kind in eighteenth-century Denmark, and it invited 'patriots' to publish their suggestions as to how state finances might be improved. Thus, and as argued by Maliks, the introduction of this state-sponsored journal facilitated a space for critical discourse, although this space was closely monitored and regulated; Maliks, 'To rule is to communicate', pp. 144–5.

58 Maliks, 'To rule is to communicate', p. 140.

prospect of having less work on their plates. However, they also maintain that a less centralized system of censorship would allow texts to be published which should have been suppressed. Furthermore, the professors remark:

> Today, caution is much more required than two hundred years ago, as a portion of the worst writings, classifiable as of the crudest kind, which are being imported from Germany and other countries, are now being published with the greatest audacity and in several languages.[59]

Finally, in 1767 the printer Emanuel Balling (1733–1795), who had established his shop in the town of Elsinore, handed in a request like Mossin's. Located fifty kilometres north of Copenhagen, his shop was just four kilometres from the Swedish coast. Balling therefore argued that he hoped to attract customers from across the Øresund, but this venture 'would vanish completely' if Swedish authors were to be committed to letting themselves be censored in Copenhagen, and could not be censored in the same location where the printing was done.[60] In their response, the professors again recognize the need to ease restrictions and rationalize conditions, but they also reiterate the potential risk of 'private concern or private affiliation between censor and author'.[61] This challenge is specific to the relatively small social milieu of a provincial town like Elsinore. It was unclear to the professors at the university how impartiality could be secured outside of the capital.

Conclusion

Before freedom of print was introduced in Denmark on 14 September 1770, an increase in societal complexity caused debates and conflicts. We might perceive such debates and conflicts

---

59 'i disse tider behøves forsigtighed langt meere end i nestforige 200de Aar, da henhører end og af det Allergroveste Slags nu med største dristighed i adskillige Sprog udgive i trycken én Mængde af de værste Skrifter som fra Tydskland og andre Lande her indføres'; SAr, Københavns Universitet, Konsistoriums kopibog (1213-12), 684.
60 'vilde ganske forsveinde, dersom Svendske forfattere skulle være forbunden til at lade sig Censurere i København og ikke kunde have Censuren paa samme Stæd, hvor Trykningen skeede'; SAr, Københavns Universitet, Konsistoriums kopibog (1213-13), 17.
61 'privat interesse eller privat Conexion imellem Censores og forfatteren'; SAr, Københavns Universitet, Konsistoriums kopibog (1213-13), 18.

as precursors of the historical moment when Enlightenment became not the answer to a question, but rather the question that societies had (and still have) to pose to themselves. Since the 2010s, scholars of the eighteenth century have nuanced our understanding of these emerging spaces of public debate. During this century, the Danish monarchy underwent a reorganization that opened its public sphere to an unprecedented level of debate about, for example, economics. Furthermore, pre-publication censorship had slowly but surely been undermined. Struensee's introduction of an unrestricted freedom of print was the crest of wave that had long been rising. The professors of theology took an active part in this process as well. The introduction of competing frameworks for religious authority became an important factor driving societal changes that would later be recognized as secular. Less rigid practices of censorship constitute one example of changes that were not imposed upon the religious system but rather developed inside it.

Bibliography

Archival sources

Copenhagen

Rigsarkivet (SAr)
    Danske Kancelli Koncepter og indlæg til Sjællandske Tegnelser (D21)
    Københavns Universitet, Konsistoriums kopibog (1213)
    Københavns Universitet, Sager vedrørende censur af teologiske skrifter (3106-01)
    Kirkekollegiet (Generalkirkeinspektionskollegiet), Diverse Sager (F4.18.3)

Printed sources and literature

Appel, Charlotte, *Læsning og bogmarked i 1600-tallets Danmark*, 2 vols (Copenhagen: Museum Tusculanum, 2001).

Appold, Kenneth G., 'Taking a stand for Reformation: Martin Luther and Caritas Pirckheimer', *Lutheran Quarterly*, 32:1 (2018), 40–59.

Banning, Knud, 'Det teologiske Fakultet 1732–1830', in Svend Ellehøj (ed.), *Københavns Universitet 1479–1979*, 14 vols (Copenhagen: Gad, 1979–2005), IV: *Det teologiske fakultet*, ed. Leif Grane (1980), pp. 13–82.

Birn, Raymond, *Royal Censorship of Books in Eighteenth-Century France* (Stanford, CA: Stanford University Press, 2012).

Bönig, Holger, *Welteroberung durch ein neues Publikum: die deutsche Presse und der Weg zur Aufklärung: Hamburg und Altona als Beispiel* (Bremen: Edition Lumière, 2002).
Cochanski, Dagmar, *Präsidial- und Oberpräsidialverfassung in Altona 1664–1746* (Hamburg: Selbstverlag Verein für Hamburgische Geschichte, 1984).
Dahl, Gina, *Books in Early Modern Norway* (Leiden: Brill, 2011).
———, *Libraries and Enlightenment: Eighteenth-Century Norway and the Outer World* (Aarhus: Aarhus University Press, 2014).
Darnton, Robert, *The Forbidden Best-Sellers of Pre-Revolutionary France* (New York: Norton, 1996).
Échallard, Olivier [and Jeanne de la Nativité], *L'Ecole du pur Amour de Dieu, ouverte aux savants et aux ignorants, dans la vie merveilleuse d'une pauvre fille idiote, païsanne de naissance, et servante de condition, Armelle Nicolas, vulgairement dite la bonne Armelle, décédée depuis peu en Bretagne. Par une Fille Religieuse de sa connaissance* (Cologne: Jean de la Pierre, 1704).
Engelsing, Rolf, *Der Bürger als Leser: Lesergeschichte in Deutschland, 1500–1800* (Stuttgart: Metzler, 1974).
Horstbøll, Henrik, 'En bogtrykker og boghandler i København: Claude Philiberts forbindelse med Societé typographique de Neuchatel 1771–1783', *Fund og Forskning*, 44 (2012), 311–35.
———, *Menigmands medie: Det folkelige bogtryk i Danmark 1500–1840* (Copenhagen: Museum Tusculanum, 1999).
Horstbøll, Henrik, Ulrik Langen and Frederik Stjernfelt, *Grov Konfekt: Tre vilde år med trykkefrihed, 1770–73*, 2 vols (Copenhagen: Gyldendal, 2020).
Ilsøe, Harald, 'Censur og approbation: lidt om bogcensurens administration i 16–1700-tallet', in John T. Lauridsen and Olaf Olsen (eds), *Umisteligt* (Copenhagen: Museum Tusculanum, 2007), pp. 19–35.
Israel, Jonathan, 'Northern varieties: contrasting the Dano-Norwegian and the Swedish-Finnish Enlightenments', in Ellen Krefting, Aina Nøding and Mona Ringvej (eds), *Eighteenth-Century Periodicals as Agents of Change* (Leiden: Brill, 2012), pp. 17–45.
Jakobsen, Jesper, '"… At I for saadant Eders u-tilladelige forhold skal vorde anseet og straffet …": Bogtrykkeren Johan Jørgen Høpfner mellem politimyndighed og akademisk censur i 1740'ernes København', in Sofie Lene Bak and others (eds), *'Kildekunst' Historiske og kulturhistoriske studier: Festskrift til John T. Lauridsen* (Copenhagen: Museum Tusculanum, 2016), pp. 165–83.
———, 'Der Klagen über das verdorbene Christenthum: om interessekonflikter og censurprocedure vedrørende oversættelsen af et teologisk skrift i 1739', *Fund og Forskning* 50 (2011), 259–78.
———, 'Omorganiseringen af den teologiske censur', *Historisk Tidsskrift*, 111:1 (2011), 1–36.

———, 'Uanstændige, utilladelige og unyttige skrifter: en undersøgelse af censuren i praksis 1746–1773' (unpublished doctoral thesis, University of Copenhagen, 2017).
Jantzen, Albert Thorvald, 'Marcus Wöldike', in Carl Frederik Bricka (ed.), *Dansk biografisk Lexikon, tillige omfattende Norge for tidsrummet 1537–1814*, 19 vols (Copenhagen: Gyldendal, 1887–1905), XIX (1905), pp. 257–8.
———, 'Peder Holm', in Carl Frederik Bricka (ed.), *Dansk biografisk Lexikon, tillige omfattende Norge for tidsrummet 1537–1814*, 19 vols (Copenhagen: Gyldendal, 1887–1905), VII (1893), pp. 584–6.
Jensen, M. Langballe, 'Libertas philosophandi and natural law in early eighteenth-century Denmark–Norway', *Intellectual History Review*, 30:2 (2020), 209–31.
Jørgensen, Harald, *Trykkefrihedsspørgsmaalet i Danmark 1799–1848* (Copenhagen: Munksgaard, 1944).
Koch, Ludvig, 'Bidrag til Censurens Historie under Fredrik V', *Historisk Tidsskrift*, 2 (1889), 67–94.
Krogh, Tyge, *Oplysningstiden og det magiske: Henrettelser og korporlige straffe i 1700-tallets første halvdel* (Copenhagen: Samleren, 2000).
Laursen, John Christian, 'Spinoza in Denmark and the fall of Struensee, 1770–1772', *Journal of the History of Ideas*, 61:2 (2020), 189–202.
Lausten, Martin Schwarz, *Kirkeordinansen 1537/39* (Copenhagen: Akademisk Förlag, 1989).
Lundbye, Jørgen, *Kirkekampen i Danmark 1730–1746* (Copenhagen: Schønbergske, 1947).
Maliks, Jakob, 'Imprimatur i provinsen – Sensuren av det trykte ord utenfor København 1737–1770', in Eivind Tjønneland (ed.), *Kritikk før 1814* (Oslo: Dreyer, 2014), pp. 78–102.
———, 'To rule is to communicate: the absolutist system of political communication in Denmark–Norway 1660–1750', in Ellen Krefting, Aina Nøding and Mona Ringvej (eds), *Eighteenth-Century Periodicals as Agents of Change* (Leiden: Brill, 2015), pp. 134–52.
———, 'Vilkår for offentlighet: sensur, økonomi og transformasjonen af det offentlige rom i Danmark-Norge 1730–1770' (unpublished doctoral thesis, Norges teknisk-naturvitenskapelige universitet, 2011).
Matzen, Henning, *Kjøbenhavns Universitets Retshistorie 1479–1879* (Copenhagen: J. H. Schultz, 1879).
Mayes, Benjamin T. G., *Counsel and Conscience: Lutheran Casuistry and Moral Reasoning after the Reformation* (Göttingen: Vandenhoeck & Ruprecht, 2011).
Mejrup, Kristian, 'Andreas Hojer (1690–1739) – the standard-bearer of Danish-Norwegian Pietism', in Kjell Å. Modéer and Helle Vogt (eds), *Law and the Christian Tradition in Scandinavia: The Writings of Great Nordic Jurists* (London: Routledge, 2021), pp. 180–95.
Melton, James Van Horn, *The Rise of the Public in Enlightenment Europe* (Cambridge: Cambridge University Press, 2001).

Nativité, Jeanne de la, *Le Triomphe de l'amour divin dans la vie d'une grande servante de Dieu, nommée Armelle Nicolas décédée l'an de Notre-Seigneur 1671* (Vannes: Jean Galles, 1676).

Nordin, Jonas and John Christian Laursen, 'Northern declarations of freedom of the press: the relative importance of philosophical ideas and of local politics', *Journal of the History of Ideas*, 81:2 (2020), 217–37.

Olsen, Olaf (ed.), *Gyldendal og Politikens Danmarkshistorie*, 16 vols (Copenhagen: Gyldendal, 1988–1991), IX: *Ole Feldbæk, Den lange fred: 1700–1800* (1990).

Oxenbøll, Erik, *Dansk økonomisk tænkning 1700–1770* (Copenhagen: Akademis Förlag, 1977).

Pedersen, Johannes, *Fra Brydningen mellem Orthodoksi og Pietisme, 1704–1712*, 2 vols (Copenhagen: Gads, 1945–1948), II: *Mellem theologer 1712–1730* (1948).

Pedersen, Mikkel Venborg, *Luksus: forbrug og kolonier i Danmark i det 18. Århundrede* (Copenhagen: Museum Tusculanum, 2013).

Pfanner, Josef (ed.), *Die 'Denkwürdigkeiten' der Caritas Pirckheimer* (Landshut: Caritas Pirckheimer Forschung, 1962).

Pirckheimer, Caritas, *Caritas Pirckheimer: A Journal of the Reformation Years, 1524–1528*, trans. Paul A. MacKenzie (Cambridge: D. S. Brewer, 2006).

Philadelphus, Noricus [Willibald Pirckheimer], *Wie alle Closter vnd sonderlich Junckfrawen Clöster in ein Christlichs wesen möchten durch gottes gnaden gebracht werden* (Augsburg: Philipp Ulhart, 1524).

Pontoppidan, Erik, *Oeconomiske Balance eller Uforgribelige Oberslag paa Dannemarks Naturlige og Borgerlige Formue Til at giøre sine Indbyggere lyksalige, saavidt som de selv ville skiønne derpaa og benytte sig deraf* (Copenhagen: Godiche, 1759).

Reitzel-Nielsen, Erik, 'Censuren af Pontoppidans katekismus', *Kirkehistoriske Samlinger*, 7:4 (1960–1962), 12–48.

Rian, Øystein, *Sensuren i Danmark-Norge: Vilkårene for offentlige ytringer 1536–1814* (Oslo: Universitetsforlaget, 2014).

Rørdam, Holger, *Historiske Samlinger og Studier vedrørende danske Forhold og Studier især i det 17 århundrede* (Copenhagen: Gads, 1891–1902).

Schrøder, Urban, 'Den gode Armelle', *Catholica*, 13:4 (1956), 155–62.

Secher, Vilhelm Adolf (ed.), *Kong Christian den femtis Danske Lov* (Copenhagen: Gads, 1929).

Tharp, Daniel Smith, 'Hans Mossin', in Carl Frederik Bricka (ed.), *Dansk biografisk Lexikon, tillige omfattende Norge for tidsrummet 1537–1814*, 19 vols (Copenhagen: Gyldendal, 1887–1905), XI (1897), pp. 481–3.

Tulle, H. L., 'Fortale', in *Bibellys, sat imod det exegetiske Mørk* (Copenhagen: Andreas Hartvig Godiche, 1740).

Witte, John, Jr, *From Sacrament to Contract: Marriage, Religion, and Law in the Western Tradition* (Louisville, KY: Westminster John Knox, 2011).

12
Sabbath crimes in a city of Enlightenment: religious and commercial (dis)order in eighteenth-century Altona

Johannes Ljungberg

What do Sabbath crimes have to do with the Enlightenment? Civil legislation to keep Sunday holy was issued in several Protestant states in the course of the seventeenth century, by way of implementing the Third Commandment of the Decalogue.[1] In the Danish monarchy, an extensive ordinance regarding church discipline, published in 1629, declared that failure to attend the Sunday sermon was a crime, to be punished by the local clergyman. The ordinance was motivated by the need to practise collective repentance as a united community faithful to God. Consequently, fighting Sabbath crimes became an integrated part of the reforms linked to Lutheran confessionalization.[2] About one century later, in 1735, an updated version of the ordinance

---

This research has been funded by the Danish National Research Foundation Centre for Privacy Studies (DNRF 138).

1 Jonathan Willis, *The Reformation of the Decalogue: Religious identity and the Ten Commandments in England, c. 1485–1625* (Cambridge: Cambridge University Press, 2017); John Witte, Jr, *Law and Protestantism: The Legal Teachings of the Lutheran Reformation* (Cambridge: Cambridge University Press, 2002), pp. 134–5; Kyle J. Dieleman, *The Battle for the Sabbath in the Dutch Reformation: Devotion or Desecration?* (Göttingen: Vandenhoeck & Ruprecht, 2019); Kyle J. Dieleman, 'Conceiving of the Sabbath in 17th-century Kampen: "disorderly", "public" and "scandalous" desecration', *Dutch Crossing*, 42:1 (2018), 28–36; Kenneth L. Parker, *The English Sabbath: A Study of Doctrine and Discipline from the Reformation to the Civil War* (Cambridge: Cambridge University Press, 1988), pp. 217–19; Jürgen Kaiser, *Ruhe der Seele und Siegel der Hoffnung: Die Deutungen des Sabbats in der Reformation* (Göttingen: Vandenhoeck & Ruprecht, 1996); Markus M. Totzeck, *Die politischen Gesetze des Mose als Vorbild: Entstehung und Einflüsse der politia-judaica-Literatur in der Frühen Neuzeit* (Göttingen: Vandenhoeck & Ruprecht, 2019).

2 Ditlev Tamm, 'Danmark/Dänemark', in Ditlev Tamm (ed.), *Repertorium der Policeyordnungen der Frühen Neuzeit*, 9.1: *Danmark og Slesvig-Holstein/ Dänemark und Schleswig-Holstein* (Frankfurt am Main: Klostermann, 2008),

introduced a number of exceptions to the general obligation to rest from activities, especially for selected commercial business pursuits. Such mitigations of confessional legislation might typically be ascribed to the arrival of the Age of Enlightenment, with reference to the gradual separation of religion from law.[3] However, while such a characterization captures a significant conceptual shift in the foundations of law-making, it does not tell us how the still-existing confessional legislation functioned in the everyday world of local officials, as well as of inhabitants of the realm.

The Danish Sabbath ordinance remained an active element in legislation until as late as 1845. Focusing on the eighteenth century, one could not very well argue that the issue of whether this law should remain in force was simply a matter of a conflict between remaining orthodoxy and emerging Enlightenment. The Sabbath ordinance could be used, neglected and opposed for a variety of purposes.

First, Sabbath regulation served as an instrument for those who wished to keep on reforming habits in accordance with the Third Commandment, such as the highly influential Lutheran Pietists.[4] The revised ordinance of 1735 was itself formulated in harmony with the pietist ethos of King Christian VI, highlighting the importance of letting oneself be edified by the word of God instead of wasting time on 'unnecessary occupations' such as worldly enjoyment or pure vice.[5] As a direct application of that view, the eighth paragraph

---

pp. 1–5; Jürgen Mührmann-Lund, *Borgerligt regemente: Politiforvaltningen i købstæderne og på landet under den danske envelde* (Copenhagen: Museum Tusculanum, 2019), pp. 99–101.

3 Sören Koch and Kristian Mejrup, 'Introduction: the Enlightenment', in Kjell Å Modéer and Helle Vogt (eds), *Law and the Christian Tradition in Scandinavia: The Writings of Great Nordic Jurists* (London: Routledge, 2021), pp. 153–61.

4 Juliane Engelhardt, 'Performing faith and structuring habitus: sociological perspectives on the propagation of Pietism in Denmark–Norway in the first half of the eighteenth century', *Pietismus und Neuzeit*, 45 (2021), 48–68 (50–2); Johannes Ljungberg, *Toleransens gränser: Religionspolitiska dilemman i det tidiga 1700-talets Sverige och Europa* (Lund: Lund University, 2017), pp. 89–93; Urban Claesson, *Kris och kristnande: Olof Ekmans kamp för kristendomens återupprättande vid Stora Kopparberget 1689–1713: pietism, program och praktik* (Gothenburg: Makadam, 2015), p. 132.

5 'unnöthigen Verrichtungen'; Copenhagen, Statens arkiver (SAr), Tyske Kancelii, Trykte kgl. Forordninger (1567–1770), p. 112. The quotation was taken from the official German translation of the Sabbath ordinance, which was distributed by the German Chancellery in Copenhagen on 16 April 1736. All translations mine.

of the ordinance instructed local clergy to teach the parish youth for thirty minutes after the end of the sermon on Sunday mornings.[6] This focus was emphasized by the introduction in the same year of mandatory confirmation.[7] But the renewed Sabbath regulation contained more than these pious concerns.

Second, the 1735 ordinance was also presented as a remedy against so-called tumult in the streets. The responsibility for pursuing this task was transferred from the clergy to the existing civil authorities in the form of the local bailiff or, in cities where public professionalized offices were increasing in number, the police master.[8] In this way, the issue of Sabbath crimes was intertwined with safeguarding, or protesting against, ideals pertaining to 'good polic[ing]' (*god politi*). As far back as the early seventeenth century, confessional legislation in both Nordic realms had been partly motivated by the desire to maintain such ideals.[9] But in the early eighteenth century, police regulation also developed as a scientific novelty. Professors of cameral science were installed in various parts of the Lutheran world – in Halle (1727), Frankfurt (Oder) (1727), Rinteln (1730) and Uppsala (1741) – and growing literature on 'good police' triggered institutional reforms.[10] In theological terms, police regulation earned recognition from Christian Wolff, who connected its focus on order and security to ideals regarding welfare and societal perfection.[11]

---

6 SAr, Tyske Kancelii, Trykte kgl. Forordninger (1567–1770), p. 119.
7 Ingrid Markussen, *Til Skaberens Ære, Statens Tjeneste og Vor Egen Nytte: Pietistiske og kameralistiske idéer bag framvæksten af en offentlig skole i landdistrikterne i 1700-tallet* (Odense: Odense Universitetsforlag, 1995), pp. 18–53.
8 However, the local clergy were still encouraged to report violations against Sabbath regulation, and they were promised a reward in the form of a third of the payable fine; SAr, Tyske Kancelii, Trykte kgl. Forordninger (1567–1770), p. 113.
9 For the Danish realm, see Tamm, 'Danmark/Dänemark'. For the Swedish realm, see Pär Frohnert, 'Sverige', in Karl Härter and others (eds), *Repertorium der Policeyordnungen der Frühen Neuzeit*, 12.1: *Kungariket Sverige och hertigdömerna Pommern och Mecklenburg* (Frankfurt am Main: Klostermann, 2017), pp. 21–4.
10 Lars Magnusson, 'On happiness: welfare in cameralist discourse in the seventeenth and eighteenth centuries', in Ere Nokkala and Nicholas B. Miller (eds), *Cameralism and the Enlightenment: Happiness, Governance and Reform in Transnational Perspective* (New York: Routledge, 2019), pp. 23–46 (pp. 26–30).
11 Hans-Martin Bachmann, *Die naturrechtliche Staatslehre Christian Wolffs* (Berlin: Duncker & Humblot, 1977).

Besides such visionary ideals, research on police regulation has detected rather more practical ambitions arising from a wish to prevent conflicts between townsmen, and to balance ordinances against local circumstances.[12]

Third, the Sabbath ordinance was also perceived as securing a weekly rhythm of work and rest. The existing scholarship on the regulation of time in the eighteenth century has demonstrated how the prescribed Sunday rest was largely confirmed, and even invigorated, in the paradigmatic calendar reforms of the mid- and late eighteenth century. These reforms specifically targeted the holy days inherited from the medieval Church. Consequently, they supported a regular weekly rhythm which included both more days of work and a routinized Sunday rest.[13] Research on religiously moderate voices that experienced these shifting tendencies in the Protestant world has pointed to a persistent ideal of keeping Sunday holy; but that ideal coexisted with increasing flexibility in respect of reinterpreting the function of the Sunday as a day of rest. While Protestant reformers of the seventeenth century considered complete rest pure idleness, mid-eighteenth-century thinkers praised the lack of activities on the resting day as corresponding to ideals of simplicity.[14]

Initiating a discussion on Sabbath crimes thus amounted to opening a multifunctional toolbox. Despite these multiple views and functions of Sabbath regulation in the eighteenth century, research on its practical implementation in this period has been scant. As Kyle Dieleman has rightly remarked regarding the early modern Netherlands, there is especially a lack of studies on 'how the Sabbath was policed and practiced'.[15]

---

12 André Holenstein, 'Die Umstände der Normen – die Normen der Umstände: Policeyordnungen im kommunikativen Handeln von Verwaltung und lokaler Gesellschaft im Ancien Régime', in Karl Härter (ed.), *Policey und frühneuzeitliche Gesellschaft* (Frankfurt am Main: Klostermann, 2000), pp. 1–46.

13 Jens Toftgaard Jensen, 'Sekularisering af tiden? Den danske helligdagsreduktion 1770', *Den Jyske Historiker*, 105 (2004), 73–93; Göran Malmstedt, *Helgdagsreduktionen: övergången från ett medeltida till ett modernt år i Sverige 1500–1900* (Gothenburg: Department of History, 1995); Christopher Hill, *Society and Puritanism in Pre-Revolution England* (London: Secker & Warburg, 1964), pp. 141–211.

14 For examples of moderate voices, see Stephen Miller, *The Peculiar Life of Sundays* (Cambridge, MA: Harvard University Press, 2008), pp. 100–1. Concerning the view of Protestant reformers, see Dieleman, *The Battle*, pp. 194–5; Parker, *The English Sabbath*, pp. 24–7.

15 Dieleman, *The Battle*, p. 232.

The present chapter investigates how Sabbath legislation was discussed and implemented in the case of Altona.[16] This was the first commercial free town of the Danish monarchy, and its inhabitants enjoyed freedom of trade, tolls and religion. Obviously, a legislation aiming to honour religious practice by sacrificing working hours did not go well with the concept of a free town. Nevertheless, the Danish Lutheran ordinance against Sabbath-breaking was severely implemented here in 1754, during the very heyday of Enlightenment ideas. As we will see, the reason for this unexpected timing was the introduction of a professional police regulation for the city. In accordance with Danish standards, the very first part of the new police instruction for Altona, issued in 1754, announced strict measures against breaches of the Sabbath. It was not there only for formal reasons. Intriguingly, Altona's second police director, Johann Peter Willebrand (who served in that capacity from 1759 to 1766), defended Sabbath regulation in the very name of the Enlightenment. In his most prominent book concerning 'good police' in towns and cities, Willebrand concisely stated that 'enlightened' governments should take care that Sunday was kept sacred in order to maintain a functioning religious pluralism. This apparent paradox, as well as other entanglements between Enlightenment ideas and confessional legislation in mid-eighteenth-century Altona, is in the focus of this chapter. The present study hence contributes to the recent scholarship on early modern Denmark, which has characterized the eighteenth century as a period when ambitions to foster good Christians and good citizens were intertwined in various ways.[17]

This chapter analyses the process of implementing Sabbath legislation in Altona, starting with the discussions that followed upon the request from the townsmen. These discussions involved the city council, the Supreme President and the German Chancellery

---

16 On implementation, see Achim Landwehr, *Policey im Alltag: Die Implementation frühneuzeitlicher Policeyordnungen in Leonberg* (Frankfurt am Main: Klostermann, 2000); Mührmann-Lund, *Borgerligt regemente*, pp. 39–45.

17 Nina Javette Koefoed, 'Den gode kristne og den gode borger', in Nina Javette Koefoed and others (eds), *Religion som forklaring? Kirke og religion i stat og samfund* (Aarhus: Aarhus Universitetsforlag, 2018), pp. 213–29, Per Ingesman, 'Reformation and confessionalisation in early modern Denmark', in Lars Ivar Hansen and others (eds), *The Protracted Reformation in Northern Norway: Introductory Studies* (Stamsund: Orkana Akademisk, 2014), pp. 29–48; Tine Reeh (ed.), *Religiøs oplysning: studier over kirke og kristendom i 1700-tallets Danmark-Norge* (Copenhagen: Kirkehistoriske Samlinger, 2018).

in Copenhagen. Their correspondence reveals both practical problems with Sabbath-breaking and suggestions on how these might be resolved. The analysis then returns to police director Willebrand's statement on the reasons why enlightened governments should care about Sabbath legislation, looking at how these ideals were reflected in his practical service as police director. What makes Willebrand especially interesting is that he constitutes an intriguing combination of a theorist and a practitioner. His books set forth his ideas about the purposes of Sabbath legislation; and his practical work as the police director of Altona gives us an idea of his struggles to implement the royal police instruction to the best of his ability. First, however, something needs to be said about the particular case of Altona as well as about the emergence and development of Sabbath ordinances as a legislative tool.

Altona: the Enlightenment city

Eighteenth-century Altona, which was the third largest city of the Danish monarchy after Copenhagen and Bergen, is far from being representative of Nordic cities at the time in question. Still, it offers the most striking opportunity for a case study examining how mono-Lutheran legislation was applied when directly confronted with distinct markers of Enlightenment.

Like other free towns of the Holy Roman Empire and the United Provinces, Altona developed its Enlightenment features in an urban setting based on a combination of commercial interest and religious pluralism.[18] At its foundation in 1601, the Holstein-Pinneberg Duke Ernst von Schaumburg (1569–1622) invited persecuted religious minorities to settle freely in the city without paying any taxes. The purpose was to benefit from North Sea trade, particularly from business connected to Hamburg, the trade hub of the region, which was situated a mere three kilometres from the north-eastern Altonian city gate. This policy attracted numerous Mennonites and French Huguenots, who were granted permission to erect their own church buildings in Altona – churches which subsequently attracted members of those communities who lived in Hamburg but went to Altona

---

18 This was by no means a unique initiative in the Holy Roman Empire, to which Altona belonged. A similar strategy was adopted in around forty so-called refugee-cities; see Benjamin J. Kaplan, 'The legal rights of religious refugees in the "refugee-cities" of early modern Germany', *Journal of Refugee Studies*, 32:1 (2018), 86–105 (89).

on Sundays for worship. Reformed Germans also established both their business and their site of worship in the city, as did the Catholic minority and German as well as Portuguese Jews.

After becoming part of the Danish realm, Altona was made its first free town (although Catholics had to wait twenty years extra for official recognition). It was soon followed by Fredericia on eastern Jutland (1682) as well as by Fredrikstad (1682) and Kristiansand (1686) in southern Norway.[19] Following a major fire in 1713 which destroyed as much as two-thirds of its buildings, King Frederik IV issued another royal letter in French, German and Dutch, inviting people to settle in Altona without paying taxes, regardless of confession.[20] Eighteenth-century Altona hence functioned as an intellectual cradle for numerous key agents of the Enlightenment. It was here that the radical royal counsellor Johann Friedrich Struensee started his career by teaching at the city's school of midwifery in the 1760s. In the same decade, the prominent moral philosopher Johann Bernhard Basedow was transferred from the Sorø Academy to a school in Altona after having been accused of heterodoxy. And before that, Altona had attracted several iconic free-thinkers in religious matters, such as Jean de Labadie (1610–1674) and Johann Conrad Dippel (1673–1734).[21]

---

19 Franklin Kopitzsch, *Grundzüge einer Sozialgeschichte der Aufklärung in Hamburg und Altona* (Hamburg: Hans Christian, 1982), pp. 217–19; Jens Glebe-Møller, 'Kommerz versus Theologie im dänischen Gesamtstaat', in Sascha Salatowsky and Winfried Schröder (eds), *Duldung religiöser Vielfalt – Sorge um die wahre Religion: Toleranzdebatten in der Frühen Neuzeit* (Stuttgart: Franz Steiner, 2016), pp. 183–94; Michel Driedger, *Obedient Heretics: Mennonite Identities in Lutheran Hamburg and Altona during the Confessional Age* (Burlington, VT: Ashgate, 2002); Erwin Freytag, 'Nichtlutherische Religionsgemeinschaften unter dem landesherrlichen Kirchenregiment', in *Schleswig-Holsteinische Kirchengeschichte*, IV: *Orthodoxie und Pietismus*, Schriften des Vereins für Schleswig-Holsteinische Kirchengeschichte, 29 (Neumünster: Karl Wachholtz, 1984), pp. 233–64; Gerhard Specht, 'Der Streit zwischen Dänemark und Hamburg aus Anlass der Erhebung Altonas zur Stadt', in Martin Ewald (ed.), *300 Jahre Altona: Beiträge zu seiner Geschichte* (Hamburg: Hans Christian, 1964), pp. 19–28.
20 Agathe Wucher, 'Die gewerbliche Entwicklung der Stadt Altona im Zeitalter des Merkantilismus 1664–1803', in Ewald, *300 Jahre Altona*, pp. 49–102 (p. 55).
21 Lorenz Hein, 'Außenseiter der Kirche', in *Schleswig-Holsteinische Kirchengeschichte*, IV: *Orthodoxie und Pietismus*, pp. 173–214. On the context of Struensee and Basedow, see the introduction to this volume.

The religious minorities of Altona each possessed one site of worship that was announced as a public building on official maps (Figs 12.1 and 12.2). The façades of these churches and synagogues clearly announced the type of building. At first glance, the public status of the buildings may come across as an unusual sign of official recognition. In most early modern cities where religious minorities found a safe haven, including the Dutch cities that were famous for practising religious toleration, minority groups were only allowed to gather for worship inside private houses which were demonstratively hidden from the street and did not signal the type of building with any outside decoration or marker. Despite this lack of visibility, such private arrangements were somewhat public secrets. The sites were neither clandestine nor illicit, and information about their location was widely accessible in popular guidebooks.[22] Both research on police regulation and research on religious minorities have pointed to this kind of private arrangement as particularly successful examples of furtive practices that went beyond the increasing control of public authorities in the early modern period.[23] This implies, somewhat paradoxically, that the public status of the Altonian minority churches made them a more direct target for public surveillance once police regulation was implemented. The lists of 'public spaces' that would be patrolled regularly according to the instructions for the police director, as well as according to the instruction for the street bailiff, mentioned the churches and churchyards.[24] This means that the implementation

---

22 Steven Mullaney, Angela Vanhaelen and Joseph Ward, 'Religion inside out: Dutch house churches and the making of publics in the Dutch Republic', in Bronwen Wilson and Paul Yachnin (eds), *Making Publics in Early Modern Europe* (Abingdon: Routledge, 2009), pp. 25–36 (p. 26); Benjamin J. Kaplan, 'Fictions of privacy: house chapels and the spatial accommodation of religious dissent in early modern Europe', *American Historical Review*, 107:4 (2002), 1031–64; Benjamin J. Kaplan, *Divided by Faith: Religious Conflict and the Practice of Toleration in Early Modern Europe* (Cambridge, MA: Belknap, 2007), pp. 174–7.
23 Willem Frijhoff, 'How to approach privacy without private sources? Insights from the Franco-Dutch network of the Eelkens family around 1600', in Michaël Green, Lars Cyril Nørgaard and Mette Birkedal Bruun (eds), *Early Modern Privacy: Sources and Approaches* (Leiden: Brill, 2021), pp. 105–34 (pp. 107, 121–4).
24 SAr, Tyske Kancelli, Slesvig-holsteinsk-lauenburgske Kancelli, Patenten (1670–1770), B5:1754, p. 375; Landesarchiv Schleswig-Holstein (LSH), Abt 65.2, Nr. 3886, Reglement für die Gaßen-voigte in Altona.

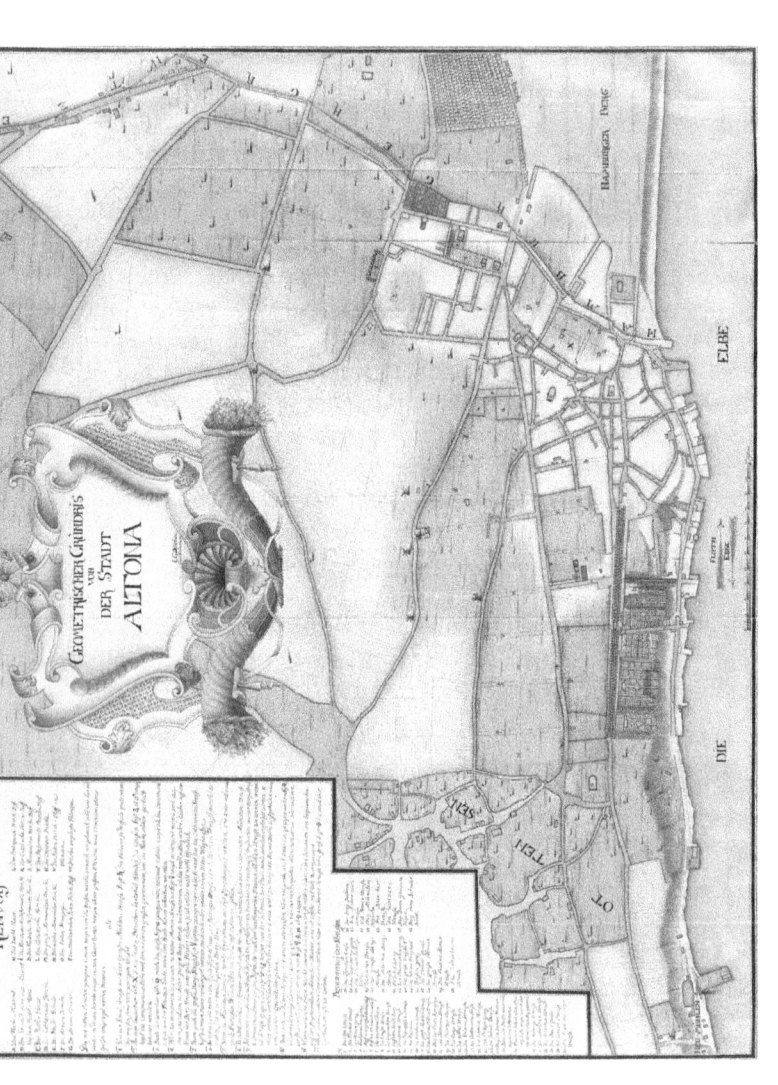

Figure 12.1 Sketch of Altona listing the minority churches among the noteworthy buildings of the town. Note the dense area of minority churches in the north-eastern corner of the city, called 'The Freedom', 'Die Freiheit' in German. Photo: The Royal Library in Copenhagen.

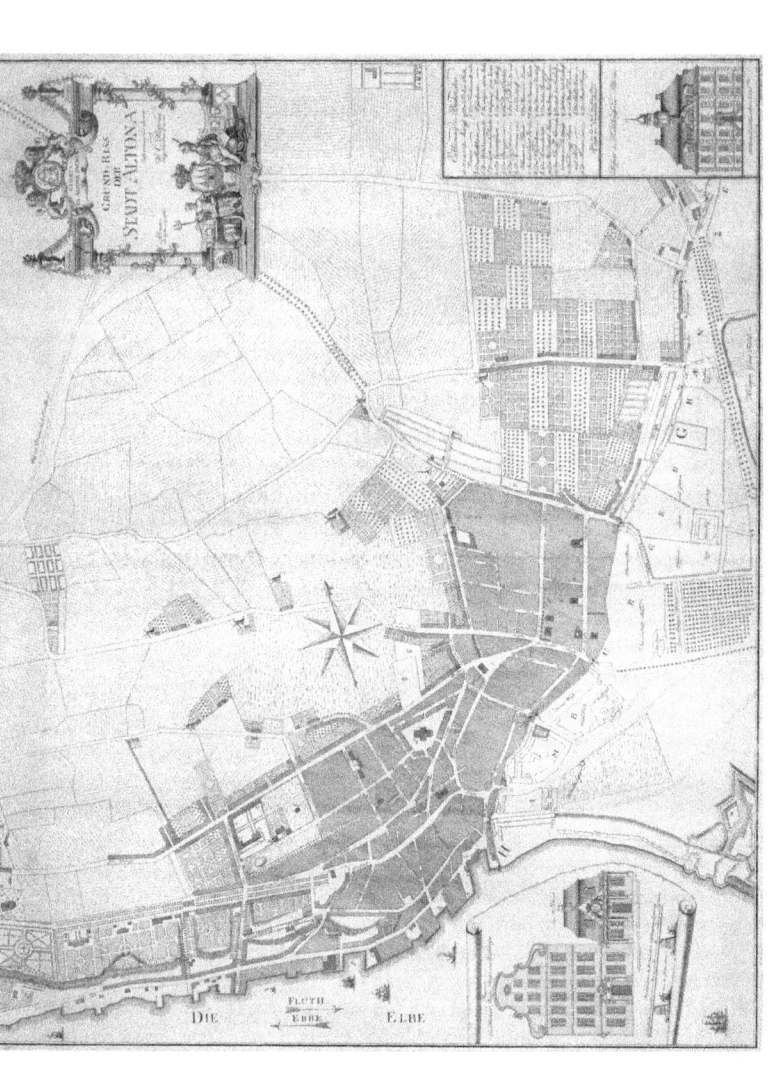

Figure 12.2 Copper engraving of Altona listing the minority churches among the noteworthy buildings of the town, from C. Praetorius, *Grund-Riss der Stadt Altona*, 1780. Photo: The Royal Library in Copenhagen.

of Sabbath legislation jeopardized not only the freedom of commerce but also the mosaic of religious pluralism in the free town.

Sabbath legislation between confessional culture and public order

Prior to the Reformation era, the Third Commandment was generally interpreted in symbolical terms as a call for spiritual rest.[25] Certainly, disturbing the peace on Sundays and holy days was categorized as a violation that encompassed a dimension of sacrilege.[26] But there was no demand for a complete cessation of activities until the late sixteenth century, when Puritan movements in England and rigid branches of the Dutch Reformed tradition introduced literal interpretations of the Third Commandment. In these groups, issues regarding Sunday profanation were closely linked with attempts to form a unique confessional identity as a contrast to Roman Catholics and less pious Protestants.[27] In the Swedish realm, the Clerical Estate raised the question of introducing Sabbath legislation at the *Riksdag* in 1617, but without managing to persuade the other three Estates of its necessity. When the question had been raised repeatedly for almost half a century, an ordinance against

---

25 R. J. Bauckham, 'Sabbath and Sunday in the medieval Church in the West', in D. A. Carson (ed.), *From Sabbath to Lord's Day: A biblical, historical and theological investigation* (Grand Rapids, MI: Zondervan, 1982), pp. 299–309; Tiziana Faitini, 'Shaping the profession: some thoughts on office, duty, and the moral problematisation of professional activities in the Counter-Reformation', *Journal of Early Modern Christianity*, 7:1 (2020), 177–200 (185–7).
26 See Göran Inger, 'Sacrilegium', in Johannes Brønsted and others (eds), *Kulturhistorisk leksikon for nordisk middelalder fra vikingatid til reformationstid*, 22 vols (Copenhagen: Rosenkilde & Bagger, 1956–1978), XIV: *Regnebræt–samgäld*, ed. John Danstrup (1969), pp. 639–46.
27 Anselm Schubert, 'Einleitung', in Anselm Schubert (ed.), *Sabbat und Sabbatobservanz in der Frühen Neuzeit* (Göttingen: Güterloher Verlagshaus, 2016), pp. 11–18; Susan Juster, 'Heretics, blasphemers, and Sabbath breakers', in Chris Beneke and Christopher S. Grenda (eds), *The First Prejudice: Religious Tolerance and Intolerance in Early America* (Philadelphia, PA: University of Pennsylvania Press, 2011), pp. 123–42; Dieleman, *The Battle*, pp. 111–30; Parker, *The English Sabbath*, p. 70. The Moravians also stressed the importance of the Sabbath, and they included both Saturday and Sunday in their eclectic version; see Johannes Hartlapp, 'Zinzendorf und der Sabbat', in Anselm Schubert (ed.), *Sabbat und Sabbatobservanz in der Frühen Neuzeit*, pp. 225–64.

Sabbath-breaking was finally established in 1665. It focused on combating various activities, such as gluttony, drinking and dancing, on Sundays and holy days.[28] The Swedish church historian Hilding Pleijel has characterized the Sabbath ordinance of the realm as a general tool for keeping order during Sweden's thirty-eight years of absolute rule (1680–1718).[29]

The introduction of Sabbath legislation in the Danish realm was quicker. In accordance with the 1629 ordinance, the local clergy were instructed to record cases of drinking, gambling and guild celebrations which, in practice, replaced Sunday service and led to 'neglect of the sermon and abuse of the Holy Day'.[30] A fixed fine of 1 rigsdaler was set for the crime. This fine was to be paid unless the sinner repented after having experienced a 'secret, Christian, meek, brotherly admonition'.[31] The Sabbath regulations were further specified in the Penal Law of the Danish Code issued in 1683, of which the first ten sections consisted of legal prescriptions issuing from each of the Ten Commandments. The Code declared each paterfamilias responsible for not letting his children play outside the church, or fail to participate in catechism class after the service. The law text also introduced some exceptions. For example, it stated that city gates must be opened for clergymen on duty and animals in need of pastures.[32]

The revised ordinance of 1735 briefly repeated the risk of provoking God's wrath by dishonouring the Sabbath. However, it devoted more space to expanding the list of exceptions. Now taverns were allowed to serve drinks after 5 p.m., if handled with moderation, and they were also allowed to serve travellers and sick people before that hour. Bakers were permitted to conduct their business

---

28 Göran Malmstedt, 'In defence of holy days: the peasantry's opposition to the reduction of holy days in Sweden', *Cultural History*, 3:2 (2014), 103–25; Malmstedt, *Helgdagsreduktionen*, pp. 35, 106–14.
29 Hilding Pleijel, *Svenska kyrkans historia*, V: *Karolinsk kyrkofromhet, pietism och herrnhutism, 1680–1772* (Stockholm: Svenska kyrkans diakonistyrelse, 1935), p. 96.
30 Vilhelm Adolf Secher (ed.), *Corpus constitutionum Daniæ: Forordninger, Recesser og andre kongelige Breve, Danmarks Lovgivning vedkommende 1558–1660*, 6 vols (Copenhagen: Klein, 1887–1918), IV (1897), pp. 453–5.
31 'hemmeligt, christelig, sactmodig, broderlig advarsel'; Secher, *Corpus constitutionum Daniæ*, p. 454.
32 *The Danish Laws, or, The Code of Christian the Fifth: faithfully translated For the Use of the English Inhabitants of the Danish Settlements in America* (London: N. Gibson, 1756), pp. 385–9.

on Sundays, except during the sermons in the morning and in the afternoon. People were allowed to work in the fields even on the Sabbath during harvest seasons, and when the weather offered beneficial circumstances. Pharmacies were permitted to stay open day and night, including Sundays. The only type of business that was explicitly identified as having no excuse for not stopping their work completely was retail.[33] Now we will look at what happened when this legislation was applied in the free town of Altona.

Discussing Sabbath crimes in Altona, 1752–1754

It all started with a petition. In March 1752, a group of townsmen wrote to the Danish king asking for a police master. They also attached an outline for a set of instructions for the police (hereafter 'police instruction').[34] The request from the citizens emphasized that the police master should be educated in law, especially in 'the ordinances and city constitutions regarding police regulation', a reference to cameralist sciences.[35] Since these tasks were being carried out at the time by the local bailiff, the townsmen's request was fundamentally a call for professionalization.[36] 'Spiritual matters' was the headline of the first section of the draft. In several respects, the townsmen requested stricter application of the Sabbath ordinance, whereas the local authorities expressed their unwillingness to accept most of the suggested changes. The specification of the original request, as well as the responses to it, reveal the various dimensions at play when discussing Sabbath crimes in an eighteenth-century free town.

First, exceptions were discussed from the perspective of commercial concerns. Here, the petitioners suggested a delimitation of the restrictions for producers of liquor (*Brandtwein Brenner*) to comprise Sundays only, not other holy days. Otherwise, they simply maintained that the Sabbath ordinance should be applied.[37] Supreme President Henning von Qualen (1703–1785) argued against this, declaring that Altona could not be treated in the same way as other cities of the realm. He suggested that taverns should count as a general

---

33 SAr, Tyske Kancelii, Trykte kgl. Forordninger (1567–1770), pp. 114–15.
34 LSH, Abt 65.2, Nr. 3749, Stadt Altona: Magistrat 1732–1846, 27 May 1752, pp. 1–23.
35 LSH, Abt 65.2, Nr. 3749, 27 May 1752, p. 4.
36 LSH, Abt 65.2, Nr. 3749, 21 August 1753, p. 23.
37 LSH, Abt 65.2, Nr. 3749, 27 May 1752, p. 13.

exception for travellers – as stipulated in the Danish Sabbath ordinance – but also for the regular guests from Hamburg who paid a visit to Altona over the day, which resulted in considerable business.[38] His predecessor, Bernhard Leopold Volkmar von Schomburg (1705–1771), supported this argument in a letter sent to the German Chancellery in Copenhagen, in which he pointed out that Altona had derived huge benefits from Sunday business ever since Hamburg introduced a Sabbath ordinance in 1741, during his presidency. Schomburg stressed that Altona's sole source of prosperity was what he referred to as 'conversation, trade and flux', thereby interestingly highlighting the informal conversations that would typically take place at taverns as something that the city could not afford to lose for economic reasons. Consequently, keeping the city open on Sundays offered a valuable opportunity to benefit economically from more social interaction, and this was business that Altona could ill afford to lose.[39] The city council argued that taverns could be kept open on Sundays, as long as guests avoided 'music, noisy games and fights' during the time when sermons were delivered in the morning and in the afternoon.[40] The limited time-span of the two sermons coincided with the mitigated Sabbath ordinance of 1735; but the suggestion to keep all taverns open, and merely reduce the level of sound from them, amounted to a further scaling-down of the restrictions. Moreover, the townsmen's request to introduce these additional exceptions was a flagrant violation of the Sabbath ordinance, which condemned excursions that omitted a Sunday service.[41]

Second, the petitioners expressed their wishes to prevent 'sectarians' and 'forbidden conventicles' from gathering in the city.[42] This request was turned down as well and even deemed illegitimate by the local authorities. Both the city council and the Supreme President declared that the city privileges of 1664 guaranteed all religious minorities (except the Socinians!) the right to practise their religion freely, and they added that any complaints about the character of religious activities should be directed to church

---

38 LSH, Abt 65.2, Nr. 3749, 21 August 1753, pp. 42–3.
39 'Conversation, Handel und Wandel'; LSH, Abt 65.2, Nr. 3740, 'Gedanken über die Stadt Altona in Absicht derselben Lage', p. 60.
40 '*Music*, lärmende Spiele und Schlägereyen'; LSH, Abt 65.2, Nr. 3749, 21 April 1753, p. 22.
41 SAr, Tyske Kancelii, Trykte kgl. Forordninger (1567–1770), p. 117.
42 LSH, Abt 65.2, Nr. 3749, 27 May 1752, pp. 11–12.

authorities instead.[43] Nevertheless, the occurrence of this request once more demonstrates how townsmen expressed confession-related wishes when the implications of Sabbath regulations were at play. Their wishes were heard. The city's first police instruction of 1754 confirmed the formulations used by the townsmen, stipulating that the police master should protect the city from any 'public outbreaks carried out by mockers of religion'.[44] The instruction also made clear that it was the clergy's responsibility to 'maintain the purity of religion', thereby confirming that that purity was still a legitimate concern.[45] The discussion around this question reveals loopholes for religious dissenters; but it also confirms the persistent legitimacy of church authorities against those whose reduced engagement was viewed as directed against the official Church. This focus on targeting the public character of activities – often designated as scandals – while sparing those that were concealed corresponded well to the tendency of the time when it came to dealing with religious dissenters.[46]

Third, the petitioners listed churches and churchyards among their preferred sites of surveillance (besides streets and public houses). In doing so, they involved the spaces of the religious minorities. They specified their wish that the police master should make sure he punished those who actively acted in a provoking or disturbing way during divine service. They also expressed a specific demand that the city's Jewish butchers keep their commerce closed on Sundays and holy days.[47] While local authorities defended taverns that were

---

43 LSH, Abt 65.2, Nr. 3749, 21 April 1753, pp. 19–20; 21 August 1753, p. 43. Despite the religious pluralism of the city, people could not expect to make up their own beliefs in any way they liked. For example, one person who denied infant baptism without being a part of the Mennonite community was punished by the Lutheran consistory; LSH, Abt 65.2, Nr. 3799, Separatisten in Altona.
44 'öffentliche Ausbrüche der Religions-Spötter'; SAr, Tyske Kancelli, Slesvig-holstein-lauenburgske Kancelli, Patenten (1670–1770), B5:1754, pp. 374–5.
45 'die Sorge für die Erhaltung der Reinigkeit derselben [die Religion]'; SAr, Tyske Kancelli, Slesvig-holstein-lauenburgske Kancelli, Patenten (1670–1770), B5:1754, pp. 374.
46 Kaplan, 'Fictions of privacy'; Mullaney and others, 'Religion inside out'; Johannes Ljungberg, 'Threatening piety: perceptions and interpretations of pietist activities during the early phase of Sweden's Age of Liberty', *Pietismus und Neuzeit*, 45 (2021), 27–47.
47 LSH, Abt 65.2, Nr. 3749, 27 May 1752, p. 12. The words used here are 'einiger Muthwillen oder ander Aergerniß wärenden Gottes Dienstes, verübt und begangen werden'.

staying open on Sundays, they did not argue along the same lines regarding shops, presumably as shops did not serve the same purpose as taverns when it came to supporting publicly profitable interaction with people visiting from Hamburg. In any case, the discussions between responsible authorities in Altona reveal that there was also another concern at play in relation to people from Hamburg. In a letter sent to the German Chancellery in Copenhagen, Supreme President von Qualen passed on complaints from the French Reformed community about particular shopkeepers in the city:

> A major scandal is caused by Jewish butchers, who not only hang out meat publicly during Sundays and Feast days, also during the sermon; they also behave badly in general. Lately, close to the Reformed Churches, even during the ongoing service, they were doing business, offering their products to people coming out of the church, and thereby causing anger and a bad impression of the police in Altona, especially among the French Reformed people from Hamburg.[48]

The geography of the recounted conflict is revealing. The French Reformed church was situated in the north-eastern quarter of the city called 'the Freedom' ('die Freiheit' in German), on the road connecting Altona with Hamburg. Ideally, this was the area of the city that was to fulfil the dual promises of freedom of religion and trade, as well as expanding contacts with the powerful neighbouring city. Most sites of worship were situated here, but so were numerous shops and taverns. As a result, while some people took to 'the Freedom' to eat and drink, thereby violating the Sabbath, others came with the contrary intent to honour the Sabbath by partaking in the religious services on offer. This was obviously not appreciated by the Reformed community, which was known for harbouring the strictest Sabbatarians, a view of them that formed part of the Reformed confessional identity in pluralist environments.[49] Irritation over Jewish business activities in proximity to the church

---

48 'Ein hauptsächliches *Scandalum* wird von den jüdischen Schlachtern dadurch gegeben, daß erstere an den Sonn- und Festtagen auch unter den Predigten, nicht allein das Fleich öffentlich aushängen, sondern auch gemeiniglich an diesen Tagen einzuschlechte pflegen; letztere aber bey denen reformirten Kirchen, sogar bey noch währende Gottes Dienst, gleichsam eine Börse halten, sich denen aus der Kirche kommende Leute mit ihren Waaren aufbringen, und dadurch, besonders denen französisch Reformirten aus Hamburg ein grosses Aargerniss und eine sehr schlechte idee von der Altonaischen Policey erwecken'; LSH, Abt 65.2, Nr. 3749, 21 August 1753, p. 44.
49 Dieleman, *The Battle*, pp. 24–25, 232.

during the time of worship was channelled through the discussion on how to apply the existing Sabbath regulation. In this regard, the public status of the minority church actually served to promote the wish to establish surveillance around it. Ironically, this complaint about Sabbath-breaking was directed against members of a Jewish community for following the original concept of keeping the Sabbath on Saturdays holy instead of that on Sundays.

Johann Peter Willebrand: an agent of Enlightenment

There is good reason to speak about Altona's second police director, Johann Peter Willebrand, as an agent of Enlightenment. With a background as a Doctor of Law, educated in Halle – the first university to introduce a chair in cameral sciences – he was appointed police director of Altona in 1759.[50] The introductory paragraph of his book on police regulation, published in French during the final year of his service under the title *Abrégé de la Police* (1765), echoes the Wolffian theology that was topical for Lutheran Enlightenment. Here, the fundament of police regulation is defined as '[t]he fear of God, founded in the knowledge of the natural and revealed light, and opposed to superstition and atheism'.[51] Furthermore, God's invisible arm is depicted as the supporting element of the police director's vocation.[52] It follows that the above-mentioned statement according to which rules against the profanation of the Sunday must be kept emanates from this point of departure; it does not constitute a remnant from the past but outlines a highly desirable active intervention which could be expected from 'enlightened governments':

> Enlightened governments have issued wise ordinances in order to celebrate Sundays and feast days with highest dignity [Fr. *Décence*], so that those who participate in public services in churches, or private devotions in their homes [Fr. *dévotions particuliéres chez eux*], would not be troubled in any way. Therefore, it is the task of the police to keep a watchful eye on the implementation of these salutary ordinances.[53]

---

50 Magnusson, 'On happiness', p. 30.
51 'La crainte de Dieu, fondée sur la connoissance de la lumière naturelle & révélée, en tant qu'opposée à la superstition & à l'Athéisme'; Johann Peter Willebrand, *Abrégé de la Police, accompagné de réflexions sur l'accroissement des villes* (Hamburg: Chez l'Estienne et fils, 1765), pp. 34–5.
52 Willebrand, *Abrégé de la Police*, p. 35.
53 'Des Gouvernements éclairés ont rendu de sages Ordonnances, pour faire célébrer les Dimanches & jours de Fêtes avec toute la Décence imaginable, afin

According to Willebrand, then, the overarching reason behind the implementation of Sabbath regulation was a desire to support dignity. There is no direct mention of collective duties within a religious community, which were what originally motivated the introduction of Sabbath laws. Instead, the principle presented to the reader was one of non-interference: the value of not disturbing those who performed religious practices, no matter whether they took place in private homes or in public churches. This reasoning is imbued with ideals of tolerance, and it is noteworthy that it was written in French only three years after Voltaire published his famous treaty on the subject.[54]

If the quotation above supported religious practices carried out in private, another passage in Willebrand's book idealized functioning religious pluralism by taking the example of the tolerant environment in Altona, highlighting amiable everyday relations among Christians and Jews:

> It is generally known that a great number of sects are tolerated in Altona, a large city without walls, fortress or stronghold, and it is not rare to see a Jew and a Christian live as closest neighbours, and a Roman Catholic, a Protestant, a Mennonite, and a Lutheran under the same roof. I add that during my six years as police director, I cannot remember a single incident of turbulence among the sectarian strangers.[55]

Before ascribing the tone in this passage exclusively to the French Enlightenment, we should take the fifth paragraph of the Danish Sabbath legislation into account. Willebrand was entirely committed to abiding by the regulating documents for his service as police director. Here, all inhabitants were exhorted to 'show all Christian

---

que ceux, qui assistent au Culte public dans les Eglises, ou ceux qui vaquent à des dévotions particuliéres chez eux, ne soient troublés en aucune manière. Il est donc du devoir de la Police de veiller attentivement, à l'exécution de ces Ordonnances salutaires'; Willebrand, *Abrégé de la Police*, p. 54.

54 Voltaire, *Traité sur la tolérance* (Paris: Gallimard folio, 2016 [1763]).
55 'Il est généralement connu, qu'un grand nombre de Sectes est toléré à Altona, Ville fort spacieuse, sans murs, sans Remparts & sans Garnison; & l'on n'y voit pas peu souvent dans le même Etage un Juif & un Chrétien être les plus proches Voisins, & dans une même Maison un Catholique Romain, un Protestant, un Mennonite & un Luthérien habiter sous le même toit. J'ajoute que dans l'espace des six années que la Direction de la Police m'a été confiée, je ne me rappelle aucun événement qui ait donné lieu à des émeutes entre les Etrangers sectaires'; Willebrand, *Abrégé de la Police*, p. 58.

and appropriate veneration' when taking part in the Sunday service. According to Willebrand, such veneration was extended to all devotional activities in the city.[56] The coincidence regarding the formulation of the Sabbath regulation thus indicates that Willebrand's terminology was not only embedded in the symbolic world of the Enlightenment, seemingly paraphrasing Voltaire; at the same time, it corresponded to the Danish Sabbath legislation. Consequently, the Sabbath ordinance of 1735 could – perhaps unexpectedly – be taken to support peaceful religious pluralism in a free town where such a condition was, by way of exception, allowed and regulated. The outcome was a more generally motivated obligation to show veneration towards practices of devotion conducted on Sundays.

As a man who emphasized the value of education, Willebrand particularly valued Sundays as the day when young people received public teaching in catechism classes. This attachment was the reason behind his best-documented conflict with a group of Jews in the city. In correspondence with his superiors in Copenhagen, Willebrand recounted that some Jewish men in Altona let children work on Sundays, with the devastating consequence that they were deprived of 'the first fundament of their religion'.[57] He stressed that this was not only an offence against the Sabbath ordinance, which instructed parents to let their children receive one hour of catechism teaching on Sundays, but also in a wider sense an attack on the value of education. In his theoretical work, Willebrand argued that education prepares the young generation for becoming citizens, and that all education that is based on love for God moulds them so that they become 'virtuous and reasonable'.[58] Indeed, when catechism teaching was made compulsory in the eighteenth century, this was often the context in which children learnt to read, write and recite. The example shows that Willebrand's preference for catechism education once more targeted the Jewish minority specifically. In the conflict about children working on Sundays, he bluntly stated that the Jewish community belonged to the 'tolerated religions', which had to adapt to 'the dominant religion' of the country determined by the government.[59] This was Lutheran Christendom, which both in

---

56 'alle Christliche und geziemende *Veneration* bezeigen'; SAr, Tyske Kancelii, Trykte kgl. Forordninger (1567–1770), p. 118. The Danish original reads: 'opføre sig med al christelig og sømmelig Veneration'.
57 'ersten Grundlage ihrer Religion'; LSH, Abt 65.2, Nr. 3886, p. 50.
58 'vertueux & raisonnable'; Willebrand, *Abrégé de la Police*, p. 98.
59 LSH, Abt 65.2, Nr. 3886, p. 50; Willebrand *Abrégé de la Police*, p. 57.

the matter of education and the matter of Sunday rest shared views with the Christian minorities of the city, for example the French Huguenots who complained about business activities on Sundays conducted by Jewish shopkeepers.

Willebrand's handwritten log containing more than 700 fines imposed between 1759 and 1764, preserved at Landesarchiv Schleswig-Holstein, confirms that the Jewish minority was particularly targeted when fighting Sabbath crimes, at least in the beginning. When the category 'profanation of the Sunday' first occurs in the log, 6 and 10 January 1760, for instance, six Jews were fined for profaning the Sunday; and for the rest of the year, all fines posted in the register under this category concerned Jews.[60] Interestingly, these notifications also include a case concerning a Jewish man who had allegedly disturbed Jewish worship by bad manners and commercial activities ('liederliche Conduite und Zählerei') on a Friday evening. The offender was reported by another Jewish man, and he was sentenced to two days in prison on bread and water.[61]

After 1760, however, only a small number of Sabbath-violation cases involved the Jewish population.[62] Instead, the logged police interventions mainly targeted public houses (inns and taverns) that exceeded the permitted opening hours in the evenings and on Sundays and holy days, and addressed the issue of games taking place.[63] In addition, the police director worked proactively by warning a shopkeeper close to the Reformed church that if he were to offer products for sale on another Sunday morning, he would have to pay a substantial fine. Willebrand is likely to have been impelled by a wish to prevent any further conflict with Sabbatarian-minded Reformed Christians from Hamburg, who frequented the church.[64]

On New Year's Day 1762 Willebrand initiated a third type of campaign against Sabbath offenders, as he penned a rather extensive

---

60 LSH, Abt 65.2, Nr. 3888, Polizeiregistraturen und Manuskripte des Polizeidirektors Willebrandt 1759–1766, 6 January 1760, 10 January 1760, 8 June 1760, 10 June 1760, 13 June 1760, 8 January 1761.
61 'Stöhrung des Jüdischen Gottesdienstes'; LSH, Abt 65.2, Nr. 3888, p. 144.
62 The only cases concerning Jews that were noted in the register of fines hereafter concerned butchers hanging out their meat on Sundays; see LSH, Abt 65.2, Nr. 3888, e.g. 10 June 1761; 8 January, 15 January, 27 January, 21 June 1762; 23 February, 12 May 1763; 26 April 1764.
63 LSH, Abt 65.2, Nr. 3888, 16 April, 4 June, 8 July, 4 September 1761.
64 LSH, Abt 65.2, Nr. 3888, 22 July 1761.

account to his superiors in Copenhagen complaining that local farmers were profaning the Sabbath by trailing their milk carts into the city on Sunday mornings. Three days later, a handful of farmers were charged for the crime, and the same procedure followed on two other Sundays that winter.[65]

These temporary and variegated campaigns against, in chronological order, the Jewish population, public houses and local farmers bear witness to a selective and impromptu implementation of Sabbath regulations. In all these matters, the police director gave up his ambitions after a limited period of intensified efforts. This was certainly not because he was reluctant to apply the legislation. No less than 9.4 per cent (63 out of 679) of the entries in his fines log concerned profanation of the Sunday.[66] The instruction to the police assistants in 1766, which was launched as an effort to improve the efficiency of the police, exhorted these servants of the law to keep a vigilant eye on Jewish shopkeepers on Sundays, as well as on public houses. With regard to the latter, he instructed his assistants not to allow sitting guests at the time when sermons were being preached in churches (9–11 a.m. and 2–3 p.m.), which means that he preferred the stricter policy stated in the Sabbath ordinance to the exemption suggested by local authorities.[67] Similarly, the sale of milk on Sundays – which Willebrand counteracted by punishing the farmers who came with their carts on Sunday mornings – appears in the scholarly literature as a recurring example of commercially motivated exceptions to Sabbath regulation.[68] His efforts met with varying degrees of success. On 14 March 1762 Willebrand noted that he had fined a shoemaker for commissioning his journeyman to repair his own shoes on a Sunday, while on 8 May 1763 he noted that he had failed to forbid people to go to work in one of the city's major factories on Sunday mornings.[69] On Christmas Day 1761 the police director successfully closed down the city's confectioner's sale of Christmas pastry – even though bakers were listed among the exceptions in the 1735 ordinance.[70]

---

65 LSH, Abt 65.2, Nr. 3888, 4 January, 25 January, 6 February 1762.
66 LSH, Abt. 65.2, Nr. 3888.
67 LSH, Abt 65.2, Nr. 3887, Stadt Altona: Polizeikommissar, Polizeiassistent, Polizeidiener sowie Gassen- und Armenvogt 1736–1844, Anweisung was nach der Königl. Instruction des Herrn Policey Directoris, auch sonst nach dem befinden deßelben, § 13.
68 Miller, *The Peculiar Life of Sundays*, p. 86
69 LSH, Abt 65.2, Nr. 3888, 14 March 1762, 8 May 1763.
70 LSH, Abt 65.2, Nr. 3888, 25 December 1761.

The correspondence between Willebrand and his superiors in Copenhagen offers revealing annotations about the agony behind these twists and turns. Under the resigned headline 'Lack of police in Altona', the police director blamed the failures of his various efforts on the fact that Altona was situated on the outskirts of Hamburg, where hardly any rules applied at all.[71] Moreover, he stressed that the tradition of the free town was strong, which meant that 'there is no reason to fear that the Sunday ordinance will be applied to the letter beyond what circumstances allow'.[72] Here, Willebrand might have put too much blame on Altona's status as a free town. According to Jørgen Mührmann-Lund's thorough study of police regulation during the eighteenth century in Aalborg, Sabbath crimes were only punished in transient campaigns in the northern Danish city as well.[73] Nevertheless, and importantly for this book, Willebrand's note reveals an ambition to increase control over Sabbath-breaking more than proved possible, partly for reasons attached to Enlightenment ideas, partly with reference to the sovereignty of what he referred to as the dominant religion.

Three passages in Willebrand's book on ideal police regulation in cities comment on precisely the imperfection of regulations in practice. In a section regarding the matter of imposing fines on citizens, he declared that 'if [ordinances] are moderate, they are lasting; if they are rigorous, they cease of their own accord', adding that it was not possible to apply them to cases that occur every day.[74] In another passage, he declared that rigorous measures 'hold back strangers instead of accelerating expansion and tranquillity'.[75] And when commenting on the profanation of Sunday during the weekends of the relocating seasons around Ascension Day in May and Saint Martin's Day in November, when large numbers of people were permitted to use the time for moving in and out of households, the police director travestied a certain

---

71 LSH, Abt 65.2, Nr. 3888, p. 112.
72 'So ist dahero nicht zu befurchten, daß der Buchstab der Sonntags-Verordnung in Altona genauer beobachtet werden, als die Umstände erhieschen'; LSH, Abt 65.2, Nr. 3886, pp. 48–119.
73 Mührmann-Lund, *Borgerligt regemente*, p. 130. The findings in Dieleman's study on Sabbath regulation in the United Provinces during the seventeenth century point in the same direction; see Dieleman, *The Battle*, pp. 29–30.
74 'Si elles sont modérées, elles sont durables; sont elles rigoureuses, elles cessent d'elles mêmes'; Willebrand, *Abrégé de la Police*, pp. 25–6.
75 Willebrand, *Abrégé de la Police*, p. 119.

biblical idiom about flexibility, stating that 'unfortunately, there are sometimes circumstances when one must remind oneself that the Sabbath was made for human beings, and not human beings for the Sabbath'.[76]

Conclusion

So, what did Sabbath crimes have to do with the Enlightenment? This chapter has demonstrated that legislation against Sabbath crimes modelled in the mono-Lutheran North had its place even in a city much marked by the Enlightenment, such as Altona. The Sabbath ordinance was not handled as an obsolete remnant from the past. On the contrary, it functioned as a productive element of available legislation as the city was reformed by the introduction of topical police regulation. The discussion between townsmen and various authorities concerning stricter implementation of Sabbath regulation included confessional standpoints, pragmatic exceptions and mediating solutions to conflicting ideals of routinized Sunday practices.

Sabbath legislation in eighteenth-century Altona was multifunctional. It supported collective pauses in the rhythm of urban public life during Sunday sermons, public education for children in the form of catechism classes and respect for the traditions of Christian minorities. Conversely, the Jewish minority was obliged to adapt to the Christian concept of the Sabbath, which demonstrates how Sabbath legislation still carried an element of confessional strife. Each of these key elements of eighteenth-century Sundays deserves more thorough study from the perspective of what changes, adaptations and continuations the Age of Enlightenment entailed in actual practice: rest, churchgoing, catechism teaching, public order and potentially the day for the articulation of sovereignty over the Jewish population (real or imagined).

Three markers of the Enlightenment formed the special dynamics inherent in the implementation of the ordinance in Altona: commercial concerns, religious pluralism and Enlightenment-driven reforms, which included Sabbath regulation. All these markers were particularly strong in Altona; but as the century wore on,

---

76 'Malheureusement il y a des circonstances, où il faut se dire quelquefois, que le Sabbat est fait pour les hommes, & non les hommes pour le Sabbat'; Willebrand, *Abrégé de la Police*, p. 55 (quoting Mark 2:27).

they became increasingly tangible for the Nordic countries at large. The legal intervention sparked a typical tension between religion and commerce, or between God and Mammon, to use a biblical idiom. Interestingly, the religious concerns included complaints expressed by members of one of the city's religious minorities, the French Huguenots, against members of another, Jewish businessmen. For an in-depth understanding of such conflicts, confessional culture and Enlightenment need to be understood as coexisting and intertwined phenomena in the eighteenth century.

In conclusion, the case of Altona provides an example of what a focus on practices and institutions as sites of interaction can tell us about the relationship between confessional legislation and ideas of the Enlightenment in the Nordic countries. The implementation of Danish Sabbath legislation was carried out with numerous exceptions and mitigations, but the result was nevertheless increased control over Sunday practices. The bureaucracy that was set up to achieve the ideals posed by regulation was equipped with contradicting instructions: both for making exceptions and for boosting public surveillance. This raises questions concerning contentions between the furtive religious practices established as a response to confessional antagonism and the increasing public control over religious minorities which came with the official recognition: did religious minorities benefit from public recognition, or did such recognition in fact create fresh problems related to the minority status? And did the extensive lists of exceptions increase not only permission for but also rejection of what was not included among the exceptions? One thing is clear: while public control may have increased, so did flexibility in the application of Sabbath regulation, at least from the perspective of local officeholders. And such a flexibility was not only linked to the decline of orthodoxy. Police director Johann Peter Willebrand's book on ideals of regulation is instructive in that it shows how local authorities could find legitimacy in biblical references for choosing moderation over strictness. Ultimately, the coexistence of divergent standpoints in the form of the duty to keep Sunday holy, the detailed discussions about exceptions to the rule to rest from activities and, finally, the legitimacy of a moderate approach to Sabbath regulation all show that Sabbath crimes remained a relevant concern in the Enlightenment city as elsewhere.

Bibliography

Archival sources

Schleswig, Germany

Landesarchiv Schleswig-Holstein (LSH)
  Abt. 65.2, Deutsche Kanzlei zu Kopenhagen ab 1730
  ———, Nr. 143, Berichte zu Grenzbesichtigungen
  ———, Nr. 3740, Stadt Altona: Ausbau der abgebrannten Stadt und Vorschläge zu ihrer Wiederaufhelfung 1737–1769
  ———, Nr. 3749, Stadt Altona: Magistrat 1732–1846
  ———, Nr. 3799, Separatisten in Altona 1747–1767
  ———, Nr. 3886, Stadt Altona: Polizeimeister und Polizeydirektor 1736–1846
  ———, Nr. 3887, Stadt Altona: Polizeikommissar, Polizeiassistent, Polizeidiener sowie Gassen- und Armenvogt 1736–1844
  ———, Nr. 3888, Stadt Altona: Polizeiregistraturen und Manuskripte des Polizeidirektors Willebrandt 1759–1766

Copenhagen

Statens arkiver (SAr)
  Tyske Kancelii, Trykte kgl. Forordninger (1567–1770)
  Slesvig-holstein-lauenburgske Kancelli, Patenten (1670–1770)
  Det Kongelige Bibliotek, Frederik den Femtes Atlas, Bd. 29, Tvl. 76, C. G. Dilleben, *Geometrischer Grundris von der Stadt Altona* (1745)
  ———, Altona-0-1780/1, W. C. Praetorius, *Grund-Riss der Stadt Altona* (Hamburg 1780)

Printed sources and literature

Bachmann, Hans-Martin, *Die naturrechtliche Staatslehre Christian Wolffs* (Berlin: Duncker & Humblot, 1977).

Bauckham, R. J., 'Sabbath and Sunday in the medieval Church in the West', in D. A. Carson (ed.), *From Sabbath to Lord's Day: A biblical, historical and theological investigation* (Grand Rapids, MI: Zondervan, 1982), pp. 299–309.

Claesson, Urban, *Kris och kristnande: Olof Ekmans kamp för kristendomens återupprättande vid Stora Kopparberget 1689–1713: pietism, program och praktik* (Gothenburg: Makadam, 2015).

The Danish Laws, or, The Code of Christian the Fifth: faithfully translated for the Use of the English Inhabitants of the Danish Settlements in America (London: N. Gibson, 1756).

Inger, Göran, 'Sacrilegium', in Johannes Brønsted and others (eds), *Kulturhistorisk leksikon for nordisk middelalder fra vikingatid til reformationstid* (Copenhagen: Rosenkilde & Bagger, 1956–1978), XIV: *Regnebræt–samgäld*, ed. John Danstrup (1969), pp. 639–46.

Dieleman, Kyle J., *The Battle for the Sabbath in the Dutch Reformation: Devotion or Desecration?* (Göttingen: Vandenhoeck & Ruprecht, 2019).

———, 'Conceiving of the Sabbath in 17th-century Kampen: "disorderly", "public" and "scandalous" desecration', *Dutch Crossing*, 42:1 (2018), 28–36.

Driedger, Michael D., *Obedient Heretics: Mennonite Identities in Lutheran Hamburg and Altona during the Confessional Age* (Burlington, VT: Ashgate, 2002).

Engelhardt, Juliane, 'Performing faith and structuring habitus: sociological perspectives on the propagation of Pietism in Denmark–Norway in the first half of the eighteenth century', *Pietismus und Neuzeit*, 45 (2021), 48–68.

Faitini, Tiziana, 'Shaping the profession: some thoughts on office, duty, and the moral problematisation of professional activities in the Counter-Reformation', *Journal of Early Modern Christianity*, 7:1 (2020), 177–200.

Freytag, Erwin, 'Nichtlutherische Religionsgemeinschaften unter dem landesherrlichen Kirchenregiment', in *Schleswig-Holsteinische Kirchengeschichte*, IV: *Orthodoxie und Pietismus*, Schriften des Vereins für Schleswig-Holsteinische Kirchengeschichte, 29 (Neumünster: Karl Wachholtz, 1984), pp. 233–64.

Frijhoff, Willem, 'How to approach privacy without private sources? Insights from the Franco-Dutch network of the Eelkens family around 1600', in Michaël Green, Lars Cyril Nørgaard and Mette Birkedal Bruun (eds), *Early Modern Privacy: Sources and Approaches* (Leiden: Brill, 2021), pp. 105–34.

Frohnert, Pär, 'Sverige', in Karl Härter and others (eds), *Repertorium der Policeyordnungen der Frühen Neuzeit*, 12.1: *Kungariket Sverige och hertigdömerna Pommern och Mecklenburg* (Frankfurt am Main: Klostermann, 2017), pp. 21–4.

Glebe-Møller, Jens, 'Kommerz versus Theologie im dänischen Gesamtstaat', in Sascha Salatowsky and Winfried Schröder (eds), *Duldung religiöser Vielfalt – Sorge um die wahre Religion: Toleranzdebatten in der Frühen Neuzeit* (Stuttgart: Franz Steiner, 2016), pp. 183–94.

Hartlapp, Johannes, 'Zinzendorf und der Sabbat', in Anselm Schubert (ed.), *Sabbat und Sabbatobservanz in der Frühen Neuzeit* (Göttingen: Gütersloher Verlagshaus, 2016), pp. 225–64.

Hein, Lorenz, 'Außenseiter der Kirche', in *Schleswig-Holsteinische Kirchengeschichte*, IV: *Orthodoxie und Pietismus*, Schriften des Vereins für Schleswig-Holsteinische Kirchengeschichte, 29 (Neumünster: Karl Wachholtz, 1984), pp. 173–214.

Hill, Christopher, *Society and Puritanism in Pre-Revolution England* (London: Secker & Warburg, 1964).

Holenstein, André, 'Die Umstände der Normen – die Normen der Umstände: Policeyordnungen im kommunikativen Handeln von Verwaltung und lokaler Gesellschaft im Ancien Régime', in Karl Härter (ed.), *Policey und frühneuzeitliche Gesellschaft* (Frankfurt am Main: Klostermann, 2000), pp. 1–46.

Ingesman, Per, 'Reformation and confessionalisation in Early Modern Denmark', in Lars Ivar Hansen and others (eds), *The Protracted Reformation in Northern Norway: Introductory Studies* (Stamsund: Orkana Akademisk, 2014), pp. 29–48.

Jensen, Jens Toftgaard, 'Sekularisering af tiden? Den danske helligdagsreduktion 1770', *Den Jyske Historiker*, 105 (2004), 73–93.

Juster, Susan, 'Heretics, blasphemers, and Sabbath breakers', in Chris Beneke and Christopher S. Grenda (eds), *The First Prejudice: Religious Tolerance and Intolerance in Early America* (Philadelphia, PA: University of Pennsylvania Press, 2011), pp. 123–42.

Kaiser, Jürgen, *Ruhe der Seele und Siegel der Hoffnung: Die Deutungen des Sabbats in der Reformation* (Göttingen: Vandenhoeck & Ruprecht, 1996).

Kaplan, Benjamin J., *Divided by Faith: Religious Conflict and the Practice of Toleration in Early Modern Europe* (Cambridge, MA: Belknap, 2007).

———, 'Fictions of privacy: house chapels and the spatial accommodation of religious dissent in early modern Europe', *American Historical Review*, 107:4 (2002), 1031–64.

———, 'The legal rights of religious refugees in the "refugee-cities" of early modern Germany', *Journal of Refugee Studies*, 32:1 (2018), 86–105.

Koch, Sören, and Kristian Mejrup, 'Introduction: the Enlightenment', in Kjell Å Modéer and Helle Vogt (eds), *Law and the Christian Tradition in Scandinavia: The Writings of Great Nordic Jurists* (London: Routledge, 2021), pp. 153–61.

Koefoed, Nina Javette, 'Den gode kristne og den gode borger', in Nina Javette Koefoed and others (eds), *Religion som forklaring? Kirke og religion i stat og samfund* (Aarhus: Aarhus Universitetsforlag, 2018), pp. 213–29.

Kopitzsch, Franklin, *Grundzüge einer Sozialgeschichte der Aufklärung in Hamburg und Altona* (Hamburg: Hans Christian, 1982).

Landwehr, Achim, *Policey im Alltag: Die Implementation frühneuzeitlicher Policeyordnungen in Leonberg* (Frankfurt am Main: Klostermann, 2000).

Ljungberg, Johannes, 'Threatening piety: perceptions and interpretations of pietist activities during the early phase of Sweden's Age of Liberty', *Pietismus und Neuzeit*, 45 (2021), 27–47.

———, *Toleransens gränser: Religionspolitiska dilemman i det tidiga 1700-talets Sverige och Europa* (Lund: Lund University, 2017).

Magnusson, Lars, 'On happiness: welfare in cameralist discourse in the seventeenth and eighteenth centuries', in Ere Nokkala and Nicholas B. Miller (eds), *Cameralism and the Enlightenment: Happiness, Governance and Reform in Transnational Perspective* (New York: Routledge, 2019), pp. 23–46.

Malmstedt, Göran, *Helgdagsreduktionen: övergången från ett medeltida till ett modernt år i Sverige 1500–1900* (Gothenburg: Department of History, 1994).

——, 'In defence of holy days: the peasantry's opposition to the reduction of holy days in Sweden', *Cultural History*, 3:2 (2014), 103–25.

Markussen, Ingrid, *Til Skaberens Ære, Statens Tjeneste og Vor Egen Nytte: Pietistiske og kameralistiske idéer bag framvæksten af en offentlig skole i landdistrikterne i 1700-tallet* (Odense: Odense Universitetsforlag, 1995).

Miller, Stephen, *The Peculiar Life of Sundays* (Cambridge, MA: Harvard University Press, 2008).

Mührmann-Lund, Jørgen, *Borgerligt regemente: Politiforvaltningen i købstæderne og på landet under den danske enevælde* (Copenhagen: Museum Tusculanum, 2019).

Mullaney, Steven, Angela Vanhaelen and Joseph Ward, 'Religion inside out: Dutch house churches and the making of publics in the Dutch Republic', in Bronwen Wilson and Paul Yachnin (eds), *Making Publics in Early Modern Europe* (Abingdon: Routledge, 2009), pp. 25–36.

Parker, Kenneth L., *The English Sabbath: A Study of Doctrine and Discipline from the Reformation to the Civil War* (Cambridge: Cambridge University Press, 1988).

Pleijel, Hilding, *Svenska kyrkans historia*, V: *Karolinsk kyrkofromhet, pietism och herrnhutism, 1680–1772* (Stockholm: Svenska kyrkans diakonistyrelse, 1935).

Reeh, Tine (ed.), *Religiøs oplysning: Studier over kirke og kristendom i 1700-tallets Danmark-Norge* (Odense: Syddansk Universitetsforlag, 2018).

Schubert, Anselm, 'Einleitung', in Anselm Schubert (ed.), *Sabbat und Sabbatobservanz in der Frühen Neuzeit* (Göttingen: Güterloher Verlagshaus, 2016), pp. 11–18.

Secher, Vilhelm Adolf (ed.), *Corpus constitutionum Daniæ: Forordninger, Recesser og andre kongelige Breve, Danmarks Lovgivning vedkommende 1558–1660*, 6 vols (Copenhagen: Klein, 1887–1918), IV (1897).

Specht, Gerhard, 'Der Streit zwischen Dänemark und Hamburg aus Anlass der Erhebung Altonas zur Stadt', in Martin Ewald (ed.), *300 Jahre Altona: Beiträge zu seiner Geschichte* (Hamburg: Hans Christian, 1964), pp. 19–28.

Tamm, Ditlev, 'Danmark/Dänemark', in Ditlev Tamm (ed.), *Repertorium der Policeyordnungen der Frühen Neuzeit*, 9.1: *Danmark og Slesvig-Holstein/Dänemark und Schleswig-Holstein* (Frankfurt am Main: Klostermann, 2008), pp. 1–5.

Totzeck, Markus M., *Die politischen Gesetze des Mose als Vorbild: Entstehung und Einflüsse der politia-judaica-Literatur in der Frühen Neuzeit* (Göttingen: Vandenhoeck & Ruprecht, 2019).

Voltaire, *Traité sur la tolérance* (Paris: Gallimard folio, 2016 [1763]).

Willebrand, Johann Peter, *Abrégé de la Police, accompagné de réflexions sur l'accroissement des villes* (Hamburg: Chez l'Estienne et fils, 1765).

Willis, Jonathan, *The Reformation of the Decalogue: Religious identity and the Ten Commandments in England, c. 1485–1625* (Cambridge: Cambridge University Press, 2017).

Witte, John, Jr, *Law and Protestantism: The Legal Teachings of the Lutheran Reformation* (Cambridge: Cambridge University Press, 2002).

Wucher, Agathe, 'Die gewerbliche Entwicklung der Stadt Altona im Zeitalter des Merkantilismus 1664–1803', in Martin Ewald (ed.), *300 Jahre Altona: Beiträge zu seiner Geschichte* (Hamburg: Hans Christian, 1964), pp. 49–102.

13
A commercial alliance between agents of Enlightenment: Struensee's statecraft and the Moravian Brethren

Christina Petterson

In 1771 the Minister of Finance of Denmark–Norway, Carl August Struensee (1735–1804) – brother to the then de facto regent of the kingdom, Johann Friedrich Struensee – extended an invitation to the Moravian leadership in Herrnhut to settle in the Duchy of Schleswig. Thanks to successful negotiations, and by extending a wide range of economic privileges to the community, he became one of the few government officials who were able to entice the much-courted Moravian leadership to establish a settlement in Schleswig at a time when other governments of Europe (Sweden, Bohemia, Austria, Poland, Russia, Georgia and many German principalities) failed.[1] The concession for Christiansfeld, as the town was eventually named, was signed in 1772, and building commenced the following year. This marked the end of almost five decades of government indecision towards the Moravian Brethren in the Danish regions. It also represented the beginning of a time in Denmark–Norway when religious reasons were not the primary factor in dealings with the Moravians. Previously, the attitude towards Moravians had been characterized by either support for or dismissal of their teaching and spiritual practices.

The new approach towards Moravians comes through very clearly in the text under examination in the present chapter, namely the document written by Carl August Struensee at his trial in 1772, where he explains his actions as Minister of Finance.[2] This document

---

1 See, for example, Joanna Kodzik, 'Vom Glauben zum Nutzen: Bestrebungen des polnischen Adels zur Ansiedlung der Herrnhuter in Polen-Litauen im 18. Jahrhundert', in Claudia Mai, Rüdiger Kröger and Dietrich Meyer (eds), *250 Jahre Unitätsarchiv: Beiträge der Jubiläumstagung vom 28. bis 29. Juni 2014* (Herrnhut: Herrnhuter Verlag, 2017), pp. 73–99.
2 Carl August Struensee, 'Justitsraad Carl August Struensees Forsvarsskrift', in Holger Hansen (ed.), *Inkvisitionskommissionen af 20. Januar 1772:*

has not been analysed in depth before, but it offers us important insights into the impetus for founding the Moravian settlement and the economic reasoning behind it.[3] We turn to this text after a short background sketch of the Moravian Brethren.

Government and Moravians

The Pietist reform movement that began in the second half of the seventeenth century across German principalities had several branches and offshoots, one of which was the controversial community in Herrnhut (founded in 1722), known as the Moravian Brethren and also known as the (Herrnhuter) Brüdergemeinde, or Unitas Fratrum. The leader, Count Zinzendorf (1700–1760), had attended August Hermann Francke's school for aristocratic boys in Halle, because his grandmother Henrietta von Gersdorff (1648–1726) was a fervent Pietist and a great admirer of Philipp Jakob Spener (1635–1705) and August Hermann Francke. Zinzendorf, an imperial count of Austrian heritage, bought an estate in Berthelsdorf not far from his grandmother's estate in Grosshennersdorf, and gave permission to a group of German-speaking Moravian refugees to settle and set up a religious community. Herrnhut, as the settlement was called, was initially inspired by Halle; but after Francke's death, the already-strained relations between Halle and Herrnhut deteriorated and broke down completely in the late 1730s.[4] From then on, Herrnhut took its own very distinct path. On the surface a matter of religious taste as well as personal animosity, the schism had deep roots and created significant fault-lines within the Danish and German ruling class.[5]

Udvalg af dens papirer og brevsamlinger til oplysning om Struensee og hans medarbejdere (Copenhagen: Gad, 1927), pp. 38–104. The document is published in full in the first volume of Holger Hansen's five-volume collection (1927–1941) of documents from the trial of the Struensee government in 1772. All translations from this document are mine.

3 Holger Hansen has written an extensive and thorough article on the founding of Christiansfeld, where he uses this document as well as correspondence also found in the case files. He does not, however, elaborate on the economic politics involved, but connects the settlement with a new tolerance; Holger Hansen, 'Christiansfelds Anlæggelse', *Jyske Samlinger*, 4:4 (1924), 1–26.

4 Hans Schneider, 'Die "Zürnenden Mutterkinder": Der Konflikt zwischen Halle und Herrnhut', *Pietismus und Neuzeit*, 29 (2004), 37–66.

5 Thomas Grunewald, *Politik für das Reich Gottes? Der Reichsgraf Christian Ernst zu Stolberg-Wernigerode zwischen Pietismus, adligem Selbstverständnis und europäischer Politik* (Halle: Verlag der Franckeschen Stiftungen, 2020).

Hallensian Pietism was a comparatively institutionally palatable form of Christianity, whereas the Moravian version was more excessive in all kinds of ways. Hallensian Pietism had a wide range of patrons from the aristocracy, while the Moravians – operating with a different organizational structure – had many *members* from the German aristocracy, as well as sympathizers at the Danish court. These are all circumstances which influenced the Moravian presence in Denmark.

When Christian VI became king in 1730, he found himself thrown into a power struggle between Zinzendorf and Count Ernst von Stolberg-Wernigerode (1691–1771), a staunch Hallensian. While Stolberg managed to gain influence over the King, Zinzendorf had a number of high-ranking allies; however, they fell away in the years 1733–1735, as the various branches of Pietism, radical and Hallensian, resulted in substantial civil unrest in Denmark.[6] From the orthodox point of view, as Juliane Engelhardt points out, the difference between Hallensians and Moravians was one of degree rather than of kind. And for the Hallensians, as Jørgen Lundbye and also Knud Heiberg observe, it was imperative to distinguish themselves from the Moravians. The most convenient way of doing so consisted in aligning Zinzendorf with the radical Pietist and separatist Johann Conrad Dippel, whose followers had caused considerable upheaval in Sweden and in Denmark.[7] Indeed, Zinzendorf's refusal to distance himself from Dippel meant that many of his aristocratic sympathizers shifted their allegiance to the Hallensian branch of Pietism,[8] and that Zinzendorf was blamed for the unrest.[9]

---

6 Juliane Engelhardt, 'Pietismus und Krise: Der Hallesche und der Radikale Pietismus im Dänischen Gesamtstaat', *Historische Zeitschrift*, 307:2 (2018), 341–69; Jørgen Lundbye, *Herrnhutismen i Danmark: Det attende hundredaars indre mission* (Copenhagen: Karl Schønberg, 1903).
7 Lundbye, *Herrnhutismen i Danmark*, pp. 60–6; Knud Heiberg, 'Kirkelige Brydninger i Aaret 1733', *Kirkehistoriske Samlinger*, 5:1 (1909), 509–45.
8 Lundbye, *Herrnhutismen i Danmark*, pp. 54–5.
9 In a letter dated 1 February 1735, from the Lord Chamberlain Carl Adolph von Plessen (1678–1758) to Zinzendorf. The letter concerned a group of Moravian members who were to travel to St Croix to work as overseers on Plessen's plantations. Plessen had chartered a ship to sail to St Croix and was anxious as to whether the Moravians would be there in time to board, because if they missed the ship they would *not* be permitted to stay in Copenhagen 'because of the thousands of extravagant acts that visionary prophets have initiated here, and which people associate with the Moravian Brethren' ('à cause de mille Extravagances, que des Visionaries se sont mis en tête icy, et que le Public met sur le compte des Frerès de Moravie

In a letter dated 22 July 1733, Stolberg lists Zinzendorf's alleged theological and social aberrations in nine points: the first six are theological (justification, sacraments, original sin and public confession of sins, emphasis on the writings of the Moravian Brethren at the expense of the Bible and indifference with regard to religion), whereas the last three concern the institutions of the Moravians and their disregard for rank, the alienation of believers from their rightful teachers and, finally, the issue of Zinzendorf's truthfulness, which Stolberg describes as fluid and ad hoc.[10] Stolberg is trying to paint Zinzendorf as a separatist while positioning himself as being in line with the Augsburg confession, which underpinned the absolute monarchy in Denmark in that one of the central elements in both the Danish Code (*Danske Lov*) and the King's Code (*Kongeloven*) was that the king was (and is) bound to the Augsburg confession.[11] While Stolberg succeeded in his machinations over against the King and court, there were large groups within the population which were not favourably attuned to the individualist impetus of Pietism.[12] Nevertheless, what is of interest here is that these objections are mainly theological, albeit with serious political and constitutional implications. Besides, we may well ask what changed between 1733–1735 and 1772. One thing that is easy to demonstrate is the change in the Moravian Brethren. After Zinzendorf's death in 1760, Moravian theology was shorn of its more radical elements, such as female leadership as well as controversial theological elements and sexuality; instead we find a new leadership structure implemented, and a concerted PR campaign conducted through centrally approved publications.[13] As we shall see in the following, however, religious reasons were not the primary factor in dealings with the Moravians in 1772. Whether this was due to a diminished role for religion and its relegation to the status of a mere supporting act, rather than constituting a primary purpose, is a major question which cannot be examined within the confines of a single chapter; but it makes a brief reappearance in the

---

[i.e. Zinzendorf]'); Plessen to Zinzendorf, 1 February 1735, Herrnhut, Unity Archives, R.20.C.3.d, letter 136.
10 Listed in Heiberg, 'Kirkelige Brydninger', 520–2.
11 Engelhardt, 'Pietismus', 344.
12 The main point in Engelhardt, 'Pietismus'.
13 Paul Peucker, *A Time of Sifting: Mystical Marriage and the Crisis of Moravian Piety in the Eighteenth Century* (University Park, PA: Penn State University Press, 2015), pp. 147–64.

final section. Now it is time to look at Struensee's explanation of the permission granted to the Moravian Brethren.

Struensee's projects

The key moment in the shift to a primary concern with economic matters in Denmark–Norway came with the Struensee government's economic reforms, which is why we need to look at Carl August Struensee's specific contribution. While economic thinking as a distinct theoretical exercise began to emerge during the eighteenth century,[14] innovative economic practice had been under way since the Renaissance, most memorably embodied in the Contrôleur général des finances to King Louis XIV, Jean-Baptiste Colbert (1619–1683), in the seventeenth century.[15] Studies on how or whether economic theory translated into practice and vice versa are only just beginning to appear,[16] mainly because there has been a reluctance in historiography to address this relationship between

---

14 Early examples in the German principalities include C. H. Amthor's *Project der Oeconomie in Form einer Wissenschaft* (1716), J. B. von Rohr's *Einleitung zu der allgemeinen Land- und Feld-Wirthschafts-Kunst derer Teutschen* (1720) and J. H. G. von Justi's two works, *Staatswirtschaft oder systematische Abhandlung aller ökonomischen und Cameralwissenschaft* (1755; 2nd edn, 1758) and *Vollständige Abhandlung von denen Manufakturen und Fabriken*, 2 vols (1758–1761). Later examples outside Germany include François Quesnay's *Tableau Économique* (1759), Anne Robert Jacques Turgot's *Reflections on the Formation and Distribution of Wealth* (1766) and Adam Smith's magnum opus *Inquiry into the Nature and Causes of the Wealth of Nations* (1776). For discussions on early economics in German-speaking areas, see Keith Tribe, *Governing Economy: The Reformation of German Economic Discourse 1750–1840* (Cambridge: Cambridge University Press, 1988) and the same author's *Strategies of Economic Order: German Economic Discourse, 1750–1950* (Cambridge: Cambridge University Press, 1995). On the latter works, see the chapter on economics in Jonathan I. Israel, *The Enlightenment that Failed: Ideas, Revolution, and Democratic Defeat, 1748–1830* (Oxford: Oxford University Press, 2019).
15 Charles Woolsey Cole, *Colbert and a Century of French Mercantilism*, 2 vols (New York: Columbia University Press, 1939).
16 Simon Adler, *Political Economy in the Habsburg Monarchy 1750–1774: The Contribution of Ludwig Zinzendorf* (London: Palgrave Macmillan, 2020); Rolf Straubel, *Adlige und bürgerliche Beamte in der Friderizianischen Justiz- und Finanzverwaltung: Ausgewählte Aspekte eines sozialen Umschichtungsprozesses und seiner Hintergründe (1740–1806)* (Berlin: Berliner Wissenschafts-Verlag, 2010).

theory and practice.[17] Another, and more practical, reason is that the instrumentalization of new economic principles at government level are rarely laid out in clear detail but must be ferreted out from enormous amounts of archival material, from council meetings and the activities of other administrative bodies.[18]

In the case of Denmark–Norway, the figure of Privy Councillor of Economy and Enterprise to the Prussian Court Carl August Struensee should be of particular interest. As mentioned at the start of this chapter, Struensee was, for a brief period in the year 1771, the Minister of Finance in Denmark, a period during which he experimented with liberalized economic practices.[19] While there are surprisingly few studies that look at his career and achievements in Prussia, there is even less interest in his activities in Denmark.[20] This could be due both to the brevity of his service and to his being somewhat overshadowed by the more dramatic career and spectacular end of his brother.[21] Carl August Struensee escaped his brother's fate of decapitation and dismemberment, but he was

---

17 As admirably mapped out and dissected in Andre Wakefield, *The Disordered Police State: German Cameralism as Science and Practice* (Chicago, IL: University of Chicago Press, 2009).

18 See, for example, Paul Beckus, *Hof und Verwaltung des Fürsten Franz von Anhalt-Dessau (1758–1817): Struktur, Personal, Funktionalität* (Halle (Saale): Mitteldeutscher Verlag, 2016); Marten Seppel and Keith Tribe (eds), *Cameralism in Practice: State Administration and Economy in Early Modern Europe* (Woodbridge: Boydell & Brewer, 2017).

19 Hans Christian Johansen, 'Carl August Struensee: reformer or traditionalist?', *Scandinavian Economic History Review*, 17:2 (1969), 179–98; Peter Krause and Horst Mühleisen, 'Carl August von Struensee (1735–1804)', *Aufklärung*, 6:2 (1992), 97–9.

20 This is certainly the case in Rolf Straubel, *Carl August von Struensee: Preußische Wirtschafts- und Finanzpolitik im ministeriellen Kräftespiel (1786–1804/06)* (Potsdam: Verlag für Berlin-Brandenburg, 1999).

21 Thus, Kersten Krüger's article on reforms during the Struensee period does not mention Carl August Struensee at all, despite his central position; see Kersten Krüger, 'Möglichkeiten, Grenzen und Instrumente von Reformen im Aufgeklärten Absolutismus: Johann Friedrich Struensee und Andreas Peter Bernstorff', in Klaus Bohnen and Sven-Aage Jørgensen (eds), *Der Dänische Gesamtstaat: Kopenhagen · Kiel · Altona* (Tübingen: Max Niemeyer, 1992), pp. 23–47. Jonathan Israel also fails to mention Carl August Struensee in his assessment of the Enlightenment and the Struensee years in Denmark–Norway; see Israel, *The Enlightenment that Failed*, Chapter 8. For a survey of the scholarship on Johann Friedrich Struensee, see Ulrik Langen, *Struensee* (Aarhus: Aarhus Universitetsforlag, 2018).

nevertheless imprisoned and put on trial, and his documents and papers were seized and examined. For his trial, Carl August Struensee produced a defence writ in which he defends himself against a number of charges and accusations, one being the permission for a Moravian settlement. An especially interesting feature of this document is that here Struensee speaks from the point of view of 'political economy' and describes the measures he took to transform the financial management of the country, as well as his council, for further development. Not only does this give us interesting insights into 'an economic practitioner' and the implementation of cameralism; we will also see how the Moravian issue was an economic decision and, as such, a concrete outcome of political-economic considerations. The following presents a close reading of sections of the document that relate both to his position as Minister of Finance and to the Moravian settlement.

Reorganization of financial management

Carl August Struensee arrived in Copenhagen in late December 1770/early January 1771. After an interview with the Danish king, Christian VII, he sought his departure from the service of the Prussian king, Friedrich II (r. 1740–1786). Johann Friedrich Struensee told his brother that Christian VII's intentions amounted to, first, a desire to set the nation's finances on a firm footing and, second, imposing a better shape on the 'chamber'. In preparation for the first task, Carl August was informed of the Danish finances by his brother; and in the second task he was instructed by the first Deputy of Finances, Jørgen Erik Scheel (1737–1795), as to how matters were decided in the treasury, *Rentekammeret*. Struensee subsequently requested 'all papers which related to chamber matters'; but instead, he received an objection from the treasury and Privy Councillor Caspar Herman von Storm (1718–1777).[22] The latter concerned the establishment of three chambers in Copenhagen,

---

22 One of Storm's claims to fame is his enormous collection of books, mathematical instruments, natural history specimens and shells, which were sold at an auction in 1772. See Gina Dahl, *Books in Early Modern Norway* (Leiden: Brill, 2011), pp. 176–7. Through an analysis of the categorization of the historical works in Storm's possession, Dahl further demonstrates that Storm was also interested in the development of the category of history and its distinct nature from that of the fable.

Christiania (Oslo) and Rendsburg.[23] He was also sent an essay by Finance Councillor Georg Christian von Oeder (1728–1791) on establishing a Finance College (*Finanz Collegium*).[24] The essay by Oeder indicates that some activity geared towards reforming the 'chamber' was already in motion.

Struensee notes that a cameralist understanding of 'chamber' is not simply an auditing agency focused on the correctness of the accounts regarding the income and expenditure of the state (as in earlier understandings), but a collegium which, 'besides calculation, is supposed to deal with everything that concerns agriculture, the population, industry, commerce and other related matters in the state'.[25] In Denmark, Struensee remarks, these things were taken

---

23 In a footnote, Hansen points out that the order to assess the establishment of the three chambers is extant, but that the objections raised are not; see Struensee, 'Forsvarsskrift', p. 41, n. 2.

24 Oeder was a trained physician and botanist and is perhaps most famous for his initiative to map the flora of Denmark–Norway, Schleswig and Holstein and the North Atlantic colonies, also known as *Flora Danica*, of which he was editor-in-chief between 1753 and 1771. See Henning Knudsen, *The Story Behind Flora Danica* (København: Lindhardt og Ringhof, 2016). However, he also published a number of essays and studies on socio-economic issues, such as a pamphlet on the liberation of and granting property rights to peasants; see Georg Christian Oeder, *Bedenken über die Frage wie dem Bauernstande Freyheit und Eigenthum in den Ländern, wo ihm beydes Fehlet, Verschaffet werden könne?* (Frankfurt and Leipzig, 1769), which came out in a Danish translation in 1769, and an edition with added considerations in 1771. This contains, according to Hans Friedl, the kernel of his early liberal ideas in relation to the reforms of state and society; see Hans Friedl, 'Oeder, Christian von', in *Neue Deutsche Biographie* (1953–) XVIIII (1998), pp. 425–6. To this we might add that these early liberal ideas are also evident in Oeder's opposition to Linnaeus' classification system, a structure which he felt violated the individuality of the animal and plant kingdoms. See Ib Friis, 'G.C. Oeder's conflict with Linnaeus and the implementation of taxonomic and nomenclatural ideas in the monumental Flora Danica project (1761–1883)', *Gardens' Bulletin Singapore*, 71:2 (2019), 53–85. On Linnaeus' system as an expression of the Classical episteme, see Michel Foucault, *Les Mots et les choses: Une archéologie des sciences humaines* (Paris: Éditions Gallimard, 1966); trans. Alan Sheridan as *The Order of Things: An Archaeology of the Human Sciences* (New York: Vintage Books, 1994), Chapter 5.

25 Struensee, 'Forsvarsskrift', p. 42. In his article on cameralism and the sciences of the state, Keith Tribe notes this difference between earlier domanial management and the later understanding of cameralism as economic administration in his discussion of Wilhelm von Schröder's *Fürstliche Schatz- und*

care of by different collegia: The Exchequer (*Rentekammeret*), the *Oeconomie und Commerz Collegium*, the Department of Taxation and the Privy Council. He then continues:

> These circumstances raised two questions for me. 1. Whether it would be a good thing that these matters, which directly concern the welfare of the state and of all individual inhabitants, should be taken care of by such different colleges? 2. If it were proved that it would be advantageous to treat them in one place on the same principle, which college could deal with it most easily, surely, and in the most useful manner? There were few difficulties in answering the first question. Everyone who knows how necessary it is that these important matters are treated according to a principle, according to a general plan extending to the whole, can see for himself that these matters are more suitably taken care of by one rather than by several colleges. And the many collisions that arise when several departments, which do not work according to one plan, deal with the state economy have shown clearly enough the necessity of the unity of this college. This gave me the idea of advising the King to set up a college which would have general oversight over the state economy and which would, above all, develop the principles and plan according to which this economy was to be conducted. This college might be called the Finance College.[26]

The matters which this one college should address were agriculture and the population, industry, commerce (internal as well as external), including money and coinage, credit, bank loans and public debts, and finally taxes and the spending of royal funds. This college, however, was not to deal with the details of the relevant issues; rather, participants would liberate their minds and become adequately acquainted 'with the great and the sublime of the state economy' ('mit dem Grossen und dem Sublimen der Staatswirtschaft'). To manage the lower level of detail, three subordinated colleges were established according to the provinces within the kingdom, namely the chambers for Denmark, Norway and the German duchies.

Struensee notes that because the previous organization was preoccupied at the level of local detail and mountains of accounting, it

---

Rent-Kammer (1686); see Keith Tribe, 'Cameralism and the sciences of the state', in Mark Goldie and Robert Wokler (eds), *The Cambridge History of Eighteenth-Century Political Thought* (Cambridge: Cambridge University Press, 2006), pp. 525–49 (p. 529).
26 Struensee, 'Forsvarsskrift', pp. 42–3.

could never arise to the level of principle which is necessary for good governance. What we see here, in this dialectical move, is the early formation of the liberal state. Struensee sets the existing structure on its feet and places the primary focus at the level of the state economy, from which various levels of detail and subordinated categories and departments can be generated. He was well ahead of his time. The subsequent execution of his brother and his own dismissal in 1772 suspended this process, but the seeds had been sown and would germinate in due course.[27]

The development of the Danish economy

Given its geographical situation and its diverse regions, it was a wonder that Denmark was not flourishing economically, and Struensee set out to find the reasons by examining various sources of information. A significant reason was, according to Struensee, that 'no plan was made for the Danish state economy' (*dänische Staatswirthschaft*). Struensee had planned to draw one up; but at the time in question, in 1772, it consisted of 'immature thoughts' which needed to be thoroughly honed.[28] Nevertheless, his reorganization of the chambers seems to have been part of such a plan, as were his recommendations to make the most of Denmark's resources and the path he indicated for future development. He recommended that Denmark itself should be based primarily on agriculture and animal husbandry; in Norway, he suggested mining, forestry and fishing, and in the duchies, a push for all kinds of manufacture (*Fabriquen*). 'In Denmark', he states, 'it is not yet the time for manufactories'.[29] Rather, he notes, it was more pressing first to 'cultivate the undeveloped moors, dry up the marshes, improve the mechanics of farming, and when people then multiply because of the increased amount of food, then think of the finer industry'. Here again, we note another cameralist motif, namely the emphasis on population management and increase

---

27 He acknowledges that the process is yet imperfect; Struensee, 'Forsvarsskrift', p. 46. Ingrid Markussen sees the age of reform setting in in the 1780s and 1790s; see Ingrid Markussen, 'Johan Ludvig Reventlow's master plan at the Brahetrolleborg Estate: cameralism in Denmark in the 1780s and 1790s', in Seppel and Tribe, *Cameralism in Practice*, pp. 203–20.
28 Struensee, 'Forsvarsskrift', p. 49.
29 Struensee, 'Forsvarsskrift', p. 48.

as a basis for wealth.[30] Struensee is not advocating the abolishment of already existing manufactories; rather, he says, they should not be made the primary industry of Denmark at the present time. And if one nevertheless were to establish manufactories, it should be linen, wool and cotton, leaving finer luxuries out of production. Even at this early point in time, it is evident that settling the Moravians in the Duchy of Schleswig aligns with these recommendations. He then goes on to note that the geographical layout of Denmark makes it the most fortunate place in Europe for trade, owing to the entrance from the Baltic Sea and the outflow of the Elbe and Weser. He also touches upon a planned free-port project along the lines of Livorno and Marseille, which would require storage facilities. Permission to construct these facilities was, according to Hansen, given in March 1771; but construction was to be at the merchants' own expense, rather than as a state project, and so was not carried out.[31] This was in line with one of Struensee's main tasks, namely that of restraining the King's expenditure and increasing his income. As will be seen below, that was also an incentive behind the Moravian settlement – Moravians being willing to carry the financial burden.

The Moravian settlement

In turning to the settlement of the Moravians in the Duchy of Schleswig, the immediate context of the relevant section in the document is interesting. It should be borne in mind that this is a document of defence in a trial, and Struensee is responding to a list of accusations against his person and his actions. Consequently, the

---

30 Marten Seppel, 'Cameralist population policy and the problem of serfdom, 1680–1720', in Seppel and Tribe, *Cameralism in Practice*, pp. 91–110 (p. 92). Thomas Dorfner rightly sees the desire for the kings and princes of Europe to attract Moravians as a concrete *Peuplierungspolitik*; see Thomas Dorfner, 'Von "Bösen Sektierern" zu "Fleißigen Fabrikanten": Zum Wahrnehmungswandel der Herrnhuter Brüdergemeinde im Kontext kameralistischer Peuplierungspolitik (Ca. 1750–1800)', *Zeitschrift für historische Forschung*, 45:2 (2018), 283–313 (287–8, 297).
31 Struensee, 'Forsvarsskrift', p. 49, n. 1. The freeport of Copenhagen was not established until 1891. For the port of Copenhagen in the eighteenth century, see Per Boye, *Vejen til velstand – marked, stat og utopi: Om dansk kapitalismes mange former gennem 300 år. Tiden 1730–1850* (Odense: Syddansk Universitetsforlag, 2014), pp. 80–1.

order and context of the accusations against Struensee and the Moravians are of great interest, as the following list of items shows. After a number of accusations pertaining to embezzlement,[32] the subsequent points are raised:

9. Whether I [Struensee] wanted to obtain advantages in this country for the king of Prussia, and whether this does not follow from the King of Prussia's judgement of me as written above?
10. Concerning my talks with von Arnim [Joachim Erdmann von Arnim, the Prussian emissary in Copenhagen].
11. Concerning the establishment of the Moravians on the Tyrstrup estate.
12. Whether I wanted to attract foreigners to the country, to obtain commissions for them.
13. Whether I have corresponded with foreigners concerning the local finances.[33]

The accusations then return to questions of embezzlement and to the accused's relationship with his brother, Johann Friedrich Struensee. What the above points indicate, however, is that the founding of the Moravian settlement is embedded within a series of accusations pertaining to what we today would call espionage, nationalism and preferential treatment.[34] The invitation to the Moravians thus belongs within the context of concerns over the maintenance of the sovereignty of the kingdom, and the anxiety which foreigners generated.[35] Perhaps this was intended to support an accusation of

---

32 As Wakefield points out, this was a typical accusation levelled against 'bad Cameralists' in the seventeenth century, namely that they did everything for their own good and financial benefit, rather than for the good of the state. See Wakefield, *The Disordered Police State*, pp. 6–13. Though Struensee lived in an age where 'good Cameralists' were recognized and appreciated, the accusations against him smack of seventeenth-century sentiment, which – given the reactionary nature of his accusers – should perhaps not be surprising.
33 Hansen, 'Christiansfelds Anlæggelse', 13–14. The Tyrstrup estate, Tyrstrupgård, had become Crown land during the reign of Christian IV and was sold off by Christian VII because of the state of the royal finances.
34 Ole Feldbæk, 'Dänisch und Deutsch im dänischen Gesamtstaat im Zeitalter der Aufklärung', in Klaus Bohnen and Sven-Aage Jørgensen (eds), *Der Dänische Gesamtstaat: Kopenhagen · Kiel · Altona* (Tübingen: Max Niemeyer, 1992), pp. 7–22 (pp. 17–18).
35 In the early days, the Moravians did have a reputation for being socially disruptive. The orthodox Lutheran minister Johann Gottlob Seidel in Rennersdorf, near Herrnhut, called them 'a plague of state and church'

treason against the Crown, which was then coupled with a charge of atheism. At any level, it is a significant leap from the situation in Copenhagen in the 1730s, where most of the objections were theological in nature, recalling Count Stolberg's letter to Zinzendorf.[36]

The defence of the settlement is presented as a discussion between Struensee and the King, where Struensee distinguishes between the viewpoint of a financier and that of a theologian, and spends some lines dismissing theological objections. It might seem odd that Struensee's defence of the invitation focuses on theological elements; but, as we will see, financial considerations were the real reason for the establishment, and this required overturning former decisions in the realm of theology and church politics. Struensee writes:

> When I first visited His Majesty the King as Deputy of Finance, I mentioned factories, whereby His Majesty came to think of his journey and told me that in Holland he had seen one of the colonies of the Moravian Brethren, which had pleased him greatly. I told him that I had seen such institutions in Saxony and Silesia, and that I had enjoyed their modes of organization and their factories immensely. Then His Majesty said that he might wish to have such establishments in his lands. I replied that this depended only on His Majesty's will, but that it was known to me that in former times it was forbidden to admit Moravians here.[37]

Here Struensee refers to the Danish authorities' intervention against the Moravians as expressed in two anti-Moravian decrees from 1744 and 1745.[38] He then goes on to say that were he to give his

---

and accused them of being a state within the state; see Christina Petterson, '"A plague of the State and the Church": a local response to the Moravian enterprise', *Journal of Moravian History*, 16:1 (2016), 45–60.

36 Even the questions raised during the trial itself, of which four concern the Moravians, are more concerned with Struensee's flagrant disregard for the laws of the land against the Moravians, and with advice from his parents concerning the devious, greedy nature of the Moravians. On the basis of this knowledge, it was asked, how could he defend himself against letting them into the country, given that they were of no use to the state and a danger to the 'pure religion'? See Hansen, 'Christiansfelds Anlæggelse', 17.

37 Struensee, 'Forsvarsskrift', p. 75.

38 The decree of 20 November 1744 forbade certain unruly elements to visit Herrnhut in Saxony and Marienborn in the Wetterau, two central Moravian settlements in the German states. It was also forbidden to send one's children there for schooling, and nobody who had been educated there could hold a clerical position in Denmark. The decree from 29 January 1745 stated that anyone leaving Denmark and Norway to settle in Moravian

opinion as a financier, it would be a statement to the effect that the Moravians would be of use in the country: experience had shown that money from the royal purse spent on factories in the Danish realm had been wasted, and Struensee was morally convinced that the Moravians would streak ahead of any competitor with factories within a year, without being a burden on the treasury.

In relation to the religious objections, Struensee presented four arguments. First, the Moravians claimed to be true (*ächte*) Lutherans. The Lutheran nature of the Moravian Brethren had been a contentious topic in the history of Moravians in Denmark; as was pointed out above, they were regarded as separatists and sectarian, and as such they were deemed to be dangerous to both state and Church. While the Moravians themselves had always claimed to conform to the articles of faith in the Lutheran *Confessio Augustana*, some of their early practices had been seen as calling this into question.[39] The emphasis now placed on their true Lutheran nature is thus more a question of guaranteeing their conformity with Danish-Norwegian state ideology. Indeed, as Ole Fischer points out, the Moravians were not only granted the right to build a church 'for private and public services' but also released from the control of the Lutheran church in Tyrstrup.[40] Struensee's second point is that, judging from experience, the establishing of a Moravian settlement might have a favourable impact on the faith of the 'common mob' in the area, in that they would become acquainted with practical knowledge, as well as with a deeper sense of God, virtue and honesty. The Moravian settlers would thus serve as good role models for their neighbours. Third, the Moravians' way of life was so distinctive that there was no need to fear that they would attract the masses. So while their presence would be regarded as having a good effect on the spiritual life of the surroundings, their idiosyncratic practices would ensure that large numbers of people would not be drawn to the settlement. There should have been no fear, then, that the entire region would become Moravian – as was the fear of the clergy in

---

  communities would forfeit their property and their inheritance rights. The decrees are reprinted in Hansen, 'Christiansfelds Anlæggelse', 2–4.
39 For an example of the Lutheran response in Germany, see Petterson, 'A plague of the State and the Church'.
40 Ole Fischer, 'Wirtschaftliche Prosperität und religiöse Erweckung: Das Handwerk in der Herrnhutersiedlung Christiansfeld', in Detlev Kraack and Martin Rheinheimer (eds), *Aus der Mitte des Landes: Klaus-Joachim Lorenzen-Schmidt zum 65. Geburtstag* (Neumünster and Hamburg: Wachholtz Verlag, 2013), pp. 175–94 (p. 177).

the 1730s and 1740s – but rather that the region would, generally speaking, be spiritually improved. Finally, given that the Moravians had been allowed to operate in Tranquebar, in Greenland, in Guinea and in the Danish West Indies, why should they not be permitted to settle in this country?[41] By way of advice, Struensee proposed that the colony should be set up in the German provinces, where the towns of Altona and Friedrichstadt already tolerated many different religious groups.[42]

The King asked how this could be brought about, and Struensee contacted Lorenz Praetorius (1708–1781), legal counsel appointed to the German chamber. Praetorius was also a member of the Moravian community and founder of the society in Copenhagen. Once contact was established, negotiations commenced, and the whole matter was examined in the German chamber and presented to the King. According to Struensee's knowledge, the report of the Finance College and the Chancellery had been used as a basis for the agreement and privilege granted. Struensee adds, 'if the Moravians come here, the success [of the settlement] will show whether my conclusions and guesses were correct'.[43]

He then notes that his father, Adam Struensee (1708–1791), Superintendent General in Rensborg, was displeased with the move towards a Moravian settlement in the realm. Struensee points out that this aversion was due to the Moravians' behaviour during Zinzendorf's time, especially in Herrnhaag and in connection with several acrimonious encounters with Zinzendorf and Moravians. Now, however, if they were to achieve the same success in Denmark as in Herrnhut, Barby, Gnadenfrey, Gnadenberg, Neusalz and so

---

41 As mentioned earlier, the Moravians were very active missionaries in the Danish colonies. The two most extensive missions in the Danish-Norwegian realm were the missions to Greenland and the West Indies. At this time in Greenland, the Moravians had two large settlements, one called Neuherrnhut (1733), next to the Danish-Norwegian settlement of Godthaab (present-day Nuuk), and the other, Lichtenfels (1758), to the south, near the Danish settlement of Fiskenæsset (present-day Qeqertarsuatsiaat). In the Danish West Indies, mission stations were in place on all three islands, St Thomas, St Croix and St John. Interestingly enough, the freedom granted to the Moravians in Denmark also meant that they acquired freedom from the state-sponsored mission in Greenland, to whose control they had been subjected before. See Finn Gad, *Grönlands Historie*, II (Copenhagen: Nyt Nordisk Förlag Arnold Busck, 1969), p. 465.
42 Struensee, 'Forsvarsskrift', pp. 75–6.
43 Struensee, 'Forsvarsskrift', p. 77.

on, and if they were to behave in the same manner as in those places, then not even Struensee senior could have anything against such an establishment. 'At this point I do not want to add anything more than that a government can be very tolerant of various religious groups without being indifferent to religion itself'.[44] While other religions had been accepted in free towns such as Altona, Friedrichstadt and Fredericia, religious tolerance was not quite as prevalent in the rest of the kingdom, despite Ludvig Holberg's agitations.[45] Not until later would it become more widespread.[46] Both Struensee brothers had to defend themselves against charges of atheism.[47] However, advocating economic priority before religion would be, and is, regarded as atheism. The palace coup in January 1772, which removed the Struensee brothers from power, nevertheless ratified the agreement with the leadership in Herrnhut and permitted the settlement to proceed; and the royal concession was signed on 13 August 1772.

State and settlement

In an article comparing the economic histories of Halle and Herrnhut, Guntram Phillip states that the Moravians as a rule had to fight hard for their fundamental freedoms, such as church independence, freedom of settlement, self-management and freedom from guild participation as well as from military service, and that these freedoms were obtained through loans to territorial lords. He reluctantly acknowledges a role for the state in the founding of two Moravian settlements, namely Christiansfeld and Sarepta on Volga (1765), as corresponding to 'the mercantilist ideas of the enlightened European princes and cameralists',[48] but otherwise Phillip

---

44 Struensee, 'Forsvarsskrift', p. 77.
45 Thomas Bredsdorff, *Den brogede oplysning: Om følelsernes fornuft og fornuftens følelse i 1700- tallets nordiske litteratur* (Copenhagen: Gyldendal, 2003).
46 Martin Schwarz Lausten, 'Tolerance and Enlightenment in Denmark: the theologian Christian Bastholm (1740–1819) and his attitude toward Judaism', *Nordisk Judaistik: Scandinavian Jewish Studies*, 19/1–2 (1998), 123–39; see also Bredsdorff, *Den brogede oplysning*.
47 Jens Glebe-Møller, *Struensees vej til skafottet: Fornuft og åbenbaring i oplysningstiden* (Copenhagen: Museum Tusculanum, 2007), pp. 35–46. See also John Christian Laursen, 'Spinoza in Denmark and the fall of Struensee, 1770–1772', *Journal of the History of Ideas*, 61:2 (2000), 189–202 (202).
48 Guntram Philipp, 'Halle und Herrnhut: Ein wirtschaftsgeschichtlicher Vergleich', in Christian Soboth and Thomas Müller-Bahlke (eds), *Reformation*

regards the relationship between the states and the Moravians as fundamentally antagonistic. Such a view does not take the changing relation of the state to religious minorities such as the Moravians into account, but stays with the early views of the European states towards religious subgroups.

As we have seen, however, the Danish state's religious concerns – originally paramount – had shifted and become less significant at this point, and economic issues were now central to the policies of the state. As Thomas Dorfner has argued, the Moravians received settlement offers from more than fifty noble estates with substantial concessions and privileges between 1758 and 1804.[49] Indeed, of the sixteen settlements on mainland Europe, only five were settled after 1758, making Christiansfeld one of the few invitations that were accepted by the Unity Board.[50] In this respect, Sarepta and Christiansfeld were indeed exceptions; but they stood out as such at a time when the Moravians had become desirable settlers, and hence in a position to negotiate their terms. Dorfner also connects this state of things with the specific population strategy of cameralism, and thus with an overall change in economic policy. That is also the line followed here. So, rather than viewing the founding of Christiansfeld as one of two 'exceptional cases' in Moravian history, I regard it as implying a change in state policy.

The founding of Christiansfeld should be set within a wider context of social change in the Danish realm, which manifested itself through the significant political, economic and cultural transformations that took place from the early 1770s up to the ratifications of the 'November constitution' (*Novemberforfatningen*) in 1863 and the implementation of liberal democracy in Denmark and Schleswig. The state Church

---

und Generalreformation: Luther und der Pietismus (Halle: Verlag der Franckesche Stiftungen, 2012), pp. 125–205 (p. 135).
49 Dorfner, 'Von "Bösen Sektierern"'.
50 The sixteen settlements were: Heerendijk, Ijsselstein (1736); Pilgerruh, Holstein (1737); Herrnhaag, Isenburg-Büdingen (1738); Niesky, Oberlausitz (1742); Gnadenfrei, Prussia (1743); Neusalz, Prussia (1743); Gnadenberg, Prussia (1745); Zeist (1746), Ebersdorf, Duchy of Reuss-Ebersdorf (1746); Neuwied, Wied (1750); Neudietendorf, Duchy of Sachsen-Gotha-Altenburg (1753); Sarepta, Russian Empire (1765); Gnadau, Saxony (1767); Christiansfeld, Duchy of Schleswig (1773); Gnadenfeld, Prussia (1780); Königsfeld, Württemberg (1807).

was losing its dominance,[51] which increased influences in law and sexual relations of both secular and pietist provenances;[52] patriotism was rising, providing a new way of thinking about 'belonging';[53] tolerance was becoming central;[54] censorship was relinquished;[55] human rights were preached from the pulpits;[56] a public sphere was emerging;[57] and agricultural reforms were implemented.[58] While the settlement of Christiansfeld does not necessarily relate to all of these changes, the presence of the Moravian Brethren touches upon issues beyond mere religion. The Moravians' individualism and egalitarianism were attractive to those seeking tolerance, human rights and new ideas of belonging which differed from former notions of estate and

---

51 Per Ingesman, 'Kirke, stat og samfund i historisk perspektiv', in Tim Knudsen (ed.), *Den Nordiske Protestantisme og velfærdsstaten* (Århus: Aarhus Universitetsforlag, 2000), pp. 65–86.

52 Nina Javette Kofoed, *Besovede kvindfolk og ukærlige barnefædre: Køn, ret og sædelighed i 1700-tallets Danmark* (Copenhagen: Museum Tusculanum, 2008); Tine Reeh, 'Gud ud af retssalen: Fromme ønsker om sekularisering af dansk retspraksis i 1700-tallet', in Thomas Bredsdorff and Søren Peter Hansen (eds), *Det Lange Lys: 2000-Tals Spørgsmål, 1700-Tals Svar* (Copenhagen: U Press, 2017), pp. 107–31.

53 Juliane Engelhardt, 'Patriotism, nationalism and modernity: the patriotic societies in the Danish conglomerate state, 1769–1814', *Nations and Nationalism*, 13:2 (2007), 205–24; Tine Damsholt, 'The fatherland, the nations and the good citizens: rituals and symbols in Danish 18th-century patriotic culture', in Ton Dekker, John Helsloot and Carla Wijers (eds), *Roots and Rituals: The Construction of Ethnic Identities* (Amsterdam: Het Spinhuis, 2000), pp. 229–38.

54 Bredsdorff, *Den brogede oplysning*.

55 Charlotte Appel, *Læsning og bogmarked i 1600-tallets Danmark*, 2 vols (Copenhagen: Museum Tusculanum, 2001).

56 Michael Bregnsbo, *Samfundsorden og statsmagt set fra prædikestolen: danske præsters deltagelse i den offentlige opinionsdannelse vedrørende samfundsordenen og statsmagten 1750–1848, belyst ved trykte prædikener: en politisk-idéhistorisk undersøgelse* (Copenhagen: Museum Tusculanum, 1997).

57 Ulrik Langen, 'Defending citizenship, defining citizenship: rumours, pamphleteering and the general public in late eighteenth century Copenhagen', in *Gender in Urban Europe: Sites of Political Activity and Citizenship, 1750–1900*, in Krista Cowan, Nina Javette Kofoed and Åsa Karlsson Sjögren (eds), *Gender in Urban Europe: Sites of Political Activity and Citizenship, 1750–1900* (London: Routledge, 2014), pp. 42–57.

58 Birgit Løgstrup, *Bondens frisættelse: De danske landboreformer 1750–1810* (Copenhagen: Gad, 2015).

social stratification.[59] In other words, the future welcomed the Moravians with open arms. So, while Struensee's reasons for inviting them were economic, the presence of the Moravians as such would certainly be in line with the comparatively liberal ideals of the brothers Struensee. That the opposition to the settlement would come from the orthodox clergy is perhaps indicated in Struensee's arguments, although these could, as surmised above, be connected to the issue of supporting the state. If that was indeed the case, this connection would indicate a subordination of Church matters to those of the state, as well as a definite weakening of the influence of Christianity as state ideology. Even though they were depicted as true Lutherans, the settlement of the Moravians in Denmark helped pave the way for the liberal civil society and the concomitant weakening of religion in the public sphere.

Bibliography

Archival sources

Herrnhut, Germany

Unity Archives, R.20.C.3.d, 136.

Printed sources and literature

Adler, Simon, *Political Economy in the Habsburg Monarchy 1750–1774: The Contribution of Ludwig Zinzendorf* (London: Palgrave Macmillan, 2020).

Appel, Charlotte, *Læsning og bogmarked i 1600-tallets Danmark*, 2 vols (Copenhagen: Museum Tusculanum, 2001).

Beckus, Paul, *Hof und Verwaltung des Fürsten Franz von Anhalt-Dessau (1758–1817): Struktur, Personal, Funktionalität* (Halle (Saale): Mitteldeutscher Verlag, 2016).

Boye, Per, *Vejen til velstand – marked, stat og utopi: Om dansk kapitalismes mange former gennem 300 år. Tiden 1730–1850* (Odense: Syddansk Universitetsforlag, 2014).

---

[59] I touch upon matters of individual/community and egalitarianism in Christina Petterson, *The Moravian Brethren in a Time of Transition: A Socio-Economic Analysis of a Religious Community in Eighteenth-Century Saxony*, Historical Materialism Book Series, 231 (Leiden: Brill, 2021).

Bredsdorff, Thomas, *Den brogede oplysning: Om følelsernes fornuft og fornuftens følelse i 1700-tallets nordiske litteratur* (Copenhagen: Gyldendal, 2003).
Bregnsbo, Michael, *Samfundsorden og statsmagt set fra prædikestolen: danske præsters deltagelse i den offentlige opinionsdannelse vedrørende samfundsordenen og statsmagten 1750–1848, belyst ved trykte prædikener: en politisk-idéhistorisk undersøgelse* (Copenhagen: Museum Tusculanum, 1997).
Cole, Charles Woolsey, *Colbert and a Century of French Mercantilism*, 2 vols (New York: Columbia University Press, 1939).
Dahl, Gina, *Books in Early Modern Norway* (Leiden: Brill, 2011).
Damsholt, Tine, 'The fatherland, the nations and the good citizens: rituals and symbols in Danish 18th century patriotic culture', in Ton Dekker, John Helsloot and Carla Wijers (eds), *Roots and Rituals: The Construction of Ethnic Identities* (Amsterdam: Het Spinhuis, 2000), pp. 229–38.
Dorfner, Thomas, 'Von "Bösen Sektierern" zu "Fleißigen Fabrikanten": Zum Wahrnehmungswandel der Herrnhuter Brüdergemeinde im Kontext kameralistischer Peuplierungspolitik (Ca. 1750–1800)', *Zeitschrift für historische Forschung*, 45:2 (2018), 283–313.
Engelhardt, Juliane, 'Patriotism, nationalism and modernity: the patriotic societies in the Danish conglomerate state, 1769–1814', *Nations and Nationalism*, 13:2 (2007), 205–24.
———, 'Pietismus und Krise: Der Hallesche und der Radikale Pietismus im Dänischen Gesamtstaat', *Historische Zeitschrift*, 307:2 (2018), 341–69.
Feldbæk, Ole, 'Dänisch und Deutsch im dänischen Gesamtstaat im Zeitalter der Aufklärung', in Klaus Bohnen and Sven-Aage Jørgensen (eds), *Der Dänische Gesamtstaat: Kopenhagen · Kiel · Altona* (Tübingen: Max Niemeyer, 1992), pp. 7–22.
Fischer, Ole, 'Wirtschaftliche Prosperität und religiöse Erweckung: Das Handwerk in der Herrnhutersiedlung Christiansfeld', in Detlev Kraack and Martin Rheinheimer (eds), *Aus der Mitte des Landes: Klaus-Joachim Lorenzen-Schmidt zum 65. Geburtstag* (Neumünster and Hamburg: Wachholtz Verlag, 2013), pp. 175–94.
Foucault, Michel, *Les Mots et les choses: Une archéologie des sciences humaines* (Paris: Éditions Gallimard, 1966); trans. Alan Sheridan as *The Order of Things: An Archaeology of the Human Sciences* (New York: Vintage Books, 1994).
Friedl, Hans, 'Oeder, Christian von', in *Neue Deutsche Biographie* (1953–), XVIII (1998), pp. 425–6.
Friis, Ib, 'G.C. Oeder's conflict with Linnaeus and the implementation of taxonomic and nomenclatural ideas in the monumental Flora Danica project (1761–1883)', *Gardens' Bulletin Singapore*, 71:2 (2019), 53–85.
Gad, Finn, *Grönlands Historie*, II (Copenhagen: Nyt Nordisk Förlag Arnold Busck, 1969).

Glebe-Møller, Jens, *Struensees vej til skafottet: Fornuft og åbenbaring i oplysningstiden* (Copenhagen: Museum Tusculanum, 2007).
Grunewald, Thomas, *Politik für das Reich Gottes? Der Reichsgraf Christian Ernst zu Stolberg-Wernigerode zwischen Pietismus, adligem Selbstverständnis und europäischer Politik* (Halle: Verlag der Franckeschen Stiftungen, 2020).
Hansen, Holger, 'Christiansfelds Anlæggelse', *Jyske Samlinger*, 4:4 (1924), 1–26.
Heiberg, Knud, 'Kirkelige Brydninger i Aaret 1733', *Kirkehistoriske Samlinger*, 5:1 (1909), 509–45.
Ingesman, Per, 'Kirke, stat og samfund i historisk perspektiv', in Tim Knudsen (ed.), *Den Nordiske Protestantisme og velfærdsstaten* (Århus: Aarhus Universitetsforlag, 2000), pp. 65–86.
Israel, Jonathan I., *The Enlightenment that Failed: Ideas, Revolution, and Democratic Defeat, 1748–1830* (Oxford: Oxford University Press, 2019).
Johansen, Hans Christian, 'Carl August Struensee: reformer or traditionalist?', *Scandinavian Economic History Review*, 17:2 (1969), 179–98.
Knudsen, Henning, *The Story Behind Flora Danica* (Copenhagen: Lindhardt og Ringhof, 2016).
Kodzik, Joanna, 'Vom Glauben zum Nutzen: Bestrebungen des Polnischen Adels zur Ansiedlung der Herrnhuter in Polen-Litauen im 18. Jahrhundert', in Claudia Mai, Rüdiger Kröger and Dietrich Meyer (eds), *250 Jahre Unitätsarchiv: Beiträge der Jubiläumstagung vom 28. bis 29. Juni 2014* (Herrnhut: Herrnhuter Verlag, 2017), pp. 73–99.
Kofoed, Nina Javette, *Besovede kvindfolk og ukærlige barnefædre: Køn, ret og sædelighed i 1700-tallets Danmark* (Copenhagen: Museum Tusculanum, 2008).
Krause, Peter and Horst Mühleisen, 'Carl August von Struensee (1735–1804)', *Aufklärung*, 6:2 (1992), 97–9.
Krüger, Kersten, 'Möglichkeiten, Grenzen und Instrumente von Reformen im Aufgeklärten Absolutismus: Johann Friedrich Struensee und Andreas Peter Bernstorff', in Klaus Bohnen and Sven-Aage Jørgensen (eds), *Der Dänische Gesamtstaat: Kopenhagen · Kiel · Altona* (Tübingen: Max Niemeyer, 1992), pp. 23–47.
Langen, Ulrik, 'Defending citizenship, defining citizenship: rumours, pamphleteering and the general public in late eighteenth century Copenhagen', in Krista Cowan, Nina Javette Kofoed and Åsa Karlsson Sjögren (eds), *Gender in Urban Europe: Sites of Political Activity and Citizenship, 1750–1900* (London: Routledge, 2014) pp. 42–57.
———, *Struensee* (Aarhus: Aarhus Universitetsforlag, 2018).
Laursen, John Christian, 'Spinoza in Denmark and the fall of Struensee, 1770–1772', *Journal of the History of Ideas*, 61:2 (2000), 189–202.
Lausten, Martin Schwarz, 'Tolerance and Enlightenment in Denmark: the theologian Christian Bastholm (1740–1819) and his attitude toward Judaism', *Nordisk Judaistik: Scandinavian Jewish Studies*, 19/1–2 (1998), 123–39.

Løgstrup, Birgit, *Bondens frisættelse: De danske landboreformer 1750–1810* (Copenhagen: Gad, 2015).
Lundbye, Jørgen, *Herrnhutismen i Danmark: Det attende hundredaars indre mission* (Copenhagen: Karl Schønberg, 1903).
Markussen, Ingrid, 'Johan Ludvig Reventlow's master plan at the Brahetrolleborg Estate: cameralism in Denmark in the 1780s and 1790s', in Marten Seppel and Keith Tribe (eds), *Cameralism in Practice: State Administration and Economy in Early Modern Europe* (Woodbridge: Boydell & Brewer, 2017), pp. 203–20.
Oeder, Georg Christian, *Bedenken über die Frage wie dem Bauernstande Freyheit und Eigenthum in den Ländern, wo ihm beydes Fehlet, Verschaffet werden könne?* (Frankfurt and Leipzig, 1769).
Petterson, Christina, *The Moravian Brethren in a Time of Transition: A Socio-Economic Analysis of a Religious Community in Eighteenth-Century Saxony*, Historical Materialism Book Series, 231 (Leiden: Brill, 2021).
——, '"A plague of the State and the Church": a local response to the Moravian enterprise', *Journal of Moravian History*, 16:1 (2016), 45–60.
Peucker, Paul, *A Time of Sifting: Mystical Marriage and the Crisis of Moravian Piety in the Eighteenth Century* (University Park, PA: Penn State University Press, 2015).
Philipp, Guntram, 'Halle und Herrnhut: Ein wirtschaftsgeschichtlicher Vergleich', in Christian Soboth and Thomas Müller-Bahlke (eds), *Reformation und Generalreformation: Luther und der Pietismus* (Halle: Verlag der Franckesche Stiftungen, 2012), pp. 125–205.
Reeh, Tine, 'Gud ud af retssalen: Fromme ønsker om sekularisering af dansk retspraksis i 1700-tallet', in Thomas Bredsdorff and Søren Peter Hansen (eds), *Det Lange Lys: 2000-Tals Spørgsmål, 1700-Tals Svar* (Copenhagen: U Press, 2017), pp. 107–31.
Schneider, Hans, 'Die "Zürnenden Mutterkinder": Der Konflikt zwischen Halle und Herrnhut', *Pietismus und Neuzeit*, 29 (2004), 37–66.
Seppel, Marten, 'Cameralist population policy and the problem of serfdom, 1680–1720', in Marten Seppel and Keith Tribe (eds), *Cameralism in Practice: State Administration and Economy in Early Modern Europe* (Woodbridge: Boydell & Brewer, 2017), pp. 91–110.
Seppel, Marten and Keith Tribe (eds), *Cameralism in Practice: State Administration and Economy in Early Modern Europe* (Woodbridge: Boydell & Brewer, 2017).
Straubel, Rolf, *Adlige und bürgerliche Beamte in der Friderizianischen Justiz- und Finanzverwaltung: Ausgewählte Aspekte eines sozialen Umschichtungsprozesses und seiner Hintergründe (1740–1806)* (Berlin: Berliner Wissenschafts-Verlag, 2010).
——, *Carl August von Struensee: Preußische Wirtschafts- und Finanzpolitik im ministeriellen Kräftespiel (1786–1804/06)* (Potsdam: Verlag für Berlin-Brandenburg, 1999).

Struensee, Carl August, 'Justitsraad Carl August Struensees Forsvarsskrift', in Holger Hansen (ed.), *Inkvisitionskommissionen af 20. Januar 1772: Udvalg af dens papirer og brevsamlinger til oplysning om Struensee og hans medarbejdere* (Copenhagen: Gad, 1927), pp. 38–104.

Tribe, Keith, 'Cameralism and the sciences of the state', in Mark Goldie and Robert Wokler (eds), *The Cambridge History of Eighteenth-Century Political Thought* (Cambridge: Cambridge University Press, 2006), pp. 525–46.

——, *Governing Economy: The Reformation of German Economic Discourse 1750–1840* (Cambridge: Cambridge University Press, 1988).

——, *Strategies of Economic Order: German Economic Discourse, 1750–1950* (Cambridge: Cambridge University Press, 1995).

Wakefield, Andre, *The Disordered Police State: German Cameralism as Science and Practice* (Chicago, IL: University of Chicago Press, 2009).

14
New medical knowledge in the parish: mass vaccinations in rural Finland, 1802–1825

Esko M. Laine

A smallpox epidemic raged throughout Finland in the late eighteenth and early nineteenth centuries.[1] Most of the available statistical information about it is based on annual reports (*tabeller*) from the parishes, written by the local clergy. From 1749 onwards, rectors in every parish were obliged to record annually, as exactly as possible on a printed form, the number of infants born and deceased persons in each parish, categorized according to age, gender and social status. As such, the documentation requested and administered by the Swedish Table Office (*Tabellverket*) is considered to be among the world's oldest demographic statistics.[2] The clergy were responsible for reporting demographic data from their parishes to the Commission of Statistics (*Tabellkommissionen*), which operated under the Royal Chancery (*Kanslikollegium*). Besides the number of persons deceased, clergymen were supposed to record the causes of death, the ages of women who gave birth and the character of recent accidents. Pastors were also expected to make notes on weather conditions, the quality of crops and the circumstances of farming in general.

---

1 Markus Brummer-Korvenkontio, *Virusten ja prionien luonnonhistoriaa: Myyräkuumeesta SARS: iin, Ebolasta AIDS:iin ja arboviruksesta lintuinfluenssaan*. (Helsinki: Helsinki University Press, 2007), pp. 45, 61–2; Susanne Hakkarainen and Henna Sinisalo, *Tappava tauti, pelätty pelastaja – isorokon ja rokotuksen historiaa* (Helsinki: Suomen lääketieteen historian seura, 2012), pp. 140–1; Johanna Viitaharju, 'Rippikoulun käynyt ja rokotettu', http://kulperi.blogspot.com/2020/11/rippikoulun-kaynyt-ja-rokotettu.html [accessed 1 November 2021]. In 1980 the World Health Organization declared smallpox to be the first epidemic whose natural strain has been totally defeated.
2 Peter Sköld, 'The birth of population statistics in Sweden', *The History of the Family*, 9:1 (2004), 5–21.

The idea of annual reports from parishes originated in the lively discussion about national resources that took place in mid-eighteenth-century Sweden. There was not only anxiety about the decline in population after the great famine from 1696 to 1698 and the plague epidemics that lasted until the 1710s; the debate also reflected the new European interest – which grew steadily throughout the eighteenth century – in taxonomy as a new form of information. Statistics helped not only to classify detailed information but also to handle large amounts of it, enabling conclusions and demographic comparisons between different areas. Beyond its practical use, all this information in itself was considered valuable. In collecting and utilizing this data, the Table Office had something in common with the extensive encyclopaedias of the *philosophes*.[3]

The annual reports submitted by pastors prove that smallpox varied significantly from year to year and from one parish to another. In 1799 the total population of Finland was about 830,000. That year almost 6,000 individuals died of smallpox in Finland out of a total number of deceased persons of around 22,600. In many parishes, such as Lappeenranta, Janakkala and Lapua, smallpox was the most frequent cause of death in 1799.[4] Occasionally, the annual toll was less than 1,000 individuals, but in 1803 nearly 7,200 persons died of the disease. A good thirty years later, in the late 1830s, the number of victims was nearly the same, 7,000. The disease was endemic and highly contagious. Most of the victims were infants, small children or young people, which accentuated the significance of inoculation of babies and young children.[5]

---

3 Thomas Ihre, *Abraham Bäck: Mannen som reformerade den svenska sjukvården* (Stockholm: Atlantis, 2012), p. 65; Elina Maaniitty, 'Befolknings- och folkhälsofrågornas framväxt i Sverige på 1700-talet', *Historisk tidskrift för Finland*, 105:4 (2020), 441–69 (445–9).
4 Mikkeli, Kansallisarkisto Mikkeli (KM), Lappeenranta seurakunna arkisto ('parish archive', SeA), Kuolleet 1786–1801, I C:3, p. 174; Hämeenlinna, Kansallisarkisto Hämeenlinna (KHä), Janakkala SeA, Väkilukutaulukot 1749–1844; Vaasa, Kansallisarkisto Vaasa (KV), Lapua SeA, Väkilukutaulukot 1774–1877, II Df:4.
5 Stockholm, Riksarkivet, Collegium Medicum, E 3 Årsberättelser från provinsialläkare, IV (1801–1807); Bertel Bonsdorff, *The History of Medicine in Finland 1828–1918* (Helsinki: Societas scientarum fennica, 1975), p. 91; Seppo Koskinen and others, *Suomen väestö* (Gaudeamus: Helsinki, 2007), p. 61; Frank M. Snowden, *Epidemics and Society: From the Black Death to the Present* (New Haven, CT: Yale University Press, 2019), pp. 89–90.

From 1804 onwards, local clergymen started to make preliminary notes in the margins of the annual reports concerning vaccinated individuals in their parishes.[6] In 1807, in order to help the clergy identify a proper practicable vaccine, the chapter of Porvoo diocese sent illustrations of 'genuine' and 'not-genuine' vaccines to the parishes.[7] From the outset, the vaccination project was a typical phenomenon of the Enlightenment in that it was based on new, experimental knowledge. In 1796 a British country physician, Edward Jenner (1749–1823), invented a new method of vaccination based on his observations on a self-limiting disease, cowpox, which was caused by another orthopox virus closely related to smallpox. Jenner was the first physician to use this virus type as a prophylaxis against smallpox. Thanks to Jenner's observations, patients no longer needed to contract smallpox itself, either naturally or via inoculation, in order to achieve immunity.[8] The first person in Finland to perform a vaccination with cowpox vaccine instead of variolation was Anders Boxström (1766–1849), who served as acting district physician in Turku in 1802. Vaccine taken from cowpox was called 'not-genuine'.

---

6 Gösta Lext, *Studier i svensk kyrkobokföring 1600–1946* (Gothenburg: Göteborgs universitet, 1984), pp. 92, 135–6, 177, 212, 322–3.

7 Turku, Kansallisarkisto Turku (KT), Huittinen SeA, II Df: 3.Väkilukutaulut 1805–1850; Joensuu, Kansallisarkisto Joensuu (KJ), Kuopio SeA, II Bk: 3. Aidolla rokotteella rokotettujen luettelo 1848; KM, Käkisalmi SeA, Rokotusluettelo 1845; Porvoon tuomiokapitulin kiertokirje joulukuussa 1807, as reprinted in A. J. Hornborg, *Sammandrag af Domkapitlets i Borgå härförinnan otryckta Cirkulärbref (1725–1829) i alfabetisk och kronologisk följd utarbetadt* (Borgå, 1872), p. 263; Heikki S. Vuorinen, *Tautinen Suomi 1851–1865* (Vaajakoski: Tampere University Press, 2006), p. 162. In Swedish, the variolation method was called *ympning med skyddskoppor* ('grafting the protective poxes'), Jenner's method of vaccination. In Vanaja the pastor recorded in 1804 that eight children were inoculated (*ympade*). The next year, 1805, he used the word 'vaccination'. Whether or not this indicates a change from variolation to Jenner's method is impossible to know, however; KHä, Vanaja SeA, Väkilukutaulukot 1749–1805.

8 Elizabeth A. Fenn, *Pox Americana: The great smallpox epidemic of 1775–82* (New York: Hill and Wang, 2001), p. 33. 'Inoculation' is the accurate term for variolation and vaccination by Jenner's method. Inoculation in the sense of implanting the germs of a disease to produce immunity is first recorded in English in 1722, vaccination as the practice of vaccinating in 1800; see Robert K. Barnhart, *Dictionary of Etymology* (Edinburgh and New York: Chambers, 2006), p. 1191. In Finnish and Swedish, the corresponding words are *rokonistutus/ympning* (inoculation) and *rokotus/vaccinering* (vaccination); Hakkarainen and Sinisalo, *Tappava tauti*, p. 139.

In the course of time, however, the meaning of that concept varied; factitious vaccines of different kinds could be called by that name.[9] Because of its utility and undeniable benefits for public health, vaccination became an essential part of a patriotic endeavour pursued by learned societies supported by the (Swedish) Crown.

The aim of this chapter is twofold: to map how vaccination of the masses was carried out in rural Finnish parishes between 1802 and 1825, and to explore in what ways the reactions of the common people reveal something about their general attitudes towards the new practice that came with the Enlightenment. The study is based on an extensive investigation of Finnish parish archives. There are two kinds of source material for a study of vaccination practices in the early nineteenth-century Finnish Church: the annual reports of pastors and vaccination records, including diaries, usually recorded by sextons.[10] The latter provide a great deal of useful information about vaccination practices and the vaccinators themselves. Vaccination records containing names, ages and the social status of vaccinated individuals before the year 1825 are preserved from twelve Finnish parishes (Iitti, Ilmajoki, Kisko, Liljendal, Liperi, Loppi, Mouhijärvi, Puumala, Sahalahti, Rautalammi, Somero and Vihti). Apart from Liperi, Puumala and Rautalammi, all were located in the southern or western parts of country. Altogether, there are twenty-seven vaccination records in digitized form from Finland from 1805 to 1927. The oldest preserved vaccination record from the year 1805 (Ilmajoki) contains, besides thirty-seven names, additional information on the age and social status of the vaccinated individuals.

Vaccination carried out in practice

In most cases, sextons vaccinated children and young people in the villages. In some parishes, low-ranking clergy participated in this

---

9 In some parishes the vaccinators tried to compensate for a shortage of vaccine by using vaccine taken from already vaccinated children who had developed immunity; Hakkarainen and Sinisalo, *Tappava tauti*, p. 149, and Snowden, *Epidemics and Society*, p. 87.
10 There is no equivalent term in English for the Finnish word *lukkari* (Swedish *klockare*), which has been translated as 'precentor and organist' or 'sexton'. Besides singing and assisting the pastor, other duties of the *lukkari* included teaching small children and various other services. In this chapter, the term 'sexton' best reflects the role of the *lukkari* as performing various ecclesiastical assignments and as vaccinator.

work as well. In Kannus (Mid-Ostrobothnia), for example, the sexton Jacob Nikander and the chaplain Johan Gabriel Borg together vaccinated 264 children in one summer. In Vihti (Uusimaa), the chaplain Adolph Bäckvall was in charge of vaccination. In 1807 the chapter in Porvoo advised parishes to delegate vaccination to the clergy if the sexton in a parish was unable to manage it alone. The condition for transferring this responsibility was that it could be done without hampering the spiritual duties of the clergy. In Mouhijärvi (Satakunta) the rector's wife, Catharina Polviander, got down to business by vaccinating sixty-six children in 1814 alone. According to the annual report from Suodenniemi in 1807, Madame Polviander had also vaccinated a young girl there seven years earlier.[11] In Liljendahl (Uusimaa), the parish would have preferred a midwife as vaccinator but could not afford to hire one. Therefore, the local clergy had to take care of that task themselves until 1908, when the first midwife in the area began her work.[12] In Suonenjoki (Savo), in addition to the sexton, the assistant vicar Karl Fredrik Bergh, assisted by two students, also implemented the vaccination programme in 1822 after a long wait for the vaccine.[13]

Before the vaccination, the preacher called on parishioners to enrol their children for the programme at Sunday service. His duty was limited to informing parish members about vaccination; if necessary, he encouraged, exhorted or enlightened them about its benefits. In 1803 the chapter reminded the clergy of their duties in this regard for the first time. However, it did not supply any detailed instructions as to how the clergy were supposed to carry out this task. The clergy are likely to have employed tactics similar to those of the Swedish kings in persuading the peasantry to participate in castle-building in Ostrobothnia: pointing to benefit and protection for themselves. In 1815 the Economic Society noted the difficulties the clergy were facing in advocating vaccination. It suggested that every parish should establish a committee under the pastor, which

---

11 KT, Mouhijärvi SeA, Rokotusluettelot 1814–1843; KV, Kannus SeA, Väkilukutaulut 1805–1877; Porvoon tuomiokapitulin kiertokirje, 23 February 1807, reprinted in Hornborg, *Sammandrag af Domkapitlets*, p. 263; Seppo Myllyniemi, *Vihdin historia 1800–1918: Vihti Venäjän vallan aikana* (Jyväskylä: Vihdin kunta, 1990), p. 243. Suodenniemi is a neighbouring parish of Mouhijärvi.
12 Anders Allardt, *Liljendals sockens historia* (Lovisa: Östra Nylands förlag, 1980), p. 370.
13 KJ, Suonenjoki SeA, Piisp. tark. pk. 4–5 August 1822, § 16.

would share the clergy's burden by dispelling the fears common people had about vaccination. If resistance against it was zealous, governors ordered civil servants to calm tempers at the parish assemblies.[14]

Before 1827, clergy could not compel parents to permit the vaccination of their children. Their authority was based solely on the ability to convince and persuade the suspicious parents by advising them. This perfectly reflects the true Lutheran belief in the spoken word as a powerful tool. In the autumn of 1802 Professor Josef Pipping, a passionate advocate of vaccination, appealed to the 'enlightened clergy' in the newspaper *Åbo Tidning*, urging them to do everything in their power to stop the spread of false rumours concerning the dangers of vaccination. He did not specify what kind of rumours he had heard, though.[15]

The sextons and the lower clergy vaccinated children either separately or, in rare cases, together. The vaccinator advised the parents to return in a week for inspection. Some parents refused to do so, however, because they feared that the vaccinator would take vaccine from the immune child in order to use it for somebody else. They believed that the use of factitious vaccine produced by vaccinated individuals would diminish the immunity in the body of the first-vaccinated child.[16]

In the event of failure, the parents were advised to return after a while. In Liljendal, for example, a one-year-old infant, Carolina Gustava, daughter of a maid, had to be vaccinated twice in 1805 because the first attempt failed. In the case of an eight-year-old boy, Isaac Andersson, the procedure had to be repeated twice after two earlier failures.[17] In some parishes, such as Sahalahti (Häme), the

---

14 Porvoon tuomiokapitulin kiertokirje, 8 October 1803, reprinted in Hornborg, *Sammandrag af Domkapitlets*, p. 262; Myllyniemi, *Vihdin historia*, p. 243. On persuasion techniques in early modern Finland, see Maria Julku, '"For your own benefit and defence:" persuading peasants to participate in castle building in early modern Ostrobothnia', in Kari Alenius, Maija Kallinen and Maria Julku (eds), *Tieto vai mielikuvat? Kohtaamiset, representaatiot ja yhteisöt muuttuvassa maailmassa* (Rovaniemi: Societas Historica Finlandiae Septentrionalis, 1986), pp. 115–30.
15 *Åbo Tidning*, 4 September 1802; Gunnar Soininen, 'Suomalaisen almanakan lääketieteellisistä kirjoituksista', in Kustaa Vilkuna (ed.), *Suomen almanakan juhlakirja* (Helsinki: Helsingin yliopisto, 1957), pp. 97–106.
16 Porvoon tuomiokapitulin kiertokirje, 8 October 1803, reprinted in Hornborg, *Sammandrag af Domkapitlets*, p. 262; Myllyniemi, *Vihdin historia*, p. 243.
17 KHä, Liljendahl SeA, Rokotusluettelot 1805–1822.

sexton commented on the efficiency of the vaccine in the margin of the vaccination diary. In 1816 the vaccine had not met expectations in ten cases out of forty-six.[18] It is possible that failures of these kinds diminished the peasants' confidence in the vaccination. The youngest known vaccinated child in Finland was only six months, the oldest in her teens.[19] The vaccination of infants and young children was based on an idea that was typical of the medicine of that period: being infected under the age of four was considered a bad sign for the prognosis.[20] Most vaccinations took place in villages. In this way, vaccination made the Enlightenment tangible in the midst of everyday life for the peasantry. A sexton started in one village and later moved on to the next. The vaccination season normally began by July at the latest (but in Kisko as early as April) and continued until November, to take advantage of the best travelling conditions.[21] After finishing their work, vaccinators handed over the records to pastors who read them aloud at the parish council in the presence of adult parishioners, recording the number of vaccinated people in the annual report. The parish council confirmed that the records were correctly compiled. From 1803 to 1825, a total 37.8 per cent of children and young people in Finland were vaccinated.[22] After the first quarter of the nineteenth century, the numbers of those who had been exposed to smallpox or had been infected decreased significantly. Minor new epidemics nevertheless occurred after 1825,

---

18 KHä, Sahalahti SeA, Rokotusluettelot 1816–1878, 2.
19 KV, Ilmajoki SeA, Rokotusluettelo 1805–1863, 2; KM, Iitti SeA, I He: 1 Rokotettujen lasten luettelo 1811–1857. In Iitti (south-east Häme) in 1811, the youngest vaccinated child was likewise six months, the oldest four years old.
20 Rosén von Rosenstein, quoted in Martin Jägervall, *Nils Rosén von Rosenstein och hans lärobok i pediatrik* (Lund: Studentlitteratur, 1990), p. 84.
21 KM, Puumala SeA, I He: 1. Rokotusluettelot 1814–1888; KHä, Sahalahti SeA, Rokotusluettelot 1816–1878; KT, Kisko SeA, I He: 1. Rokotettujen lasten luettelo 1814–1871; KJ, Liperi SeA, I He: 1. Rokotuspäiväkirjat- ja luettelot 1815–1899.
22 Kaarlo Jalkanen, *Lukkarin- ja urkurinvirka Suomessa 1809–1870* (Helsinki: Suomen kirkkohistoriallinen seura, 1976), pp. 164–5. Besides sextons and district physicians, midwives and lower clergy also practised vaccination; Oiva Turpeinen, 'Lastensuojelu ja väestökehitys: Lastensuojelun lääkinnällinen ja sosiaalinen kehitys Suomessa', in Panu Pulma and Oiva Turpeinen (eds), *Suomen lastensuojelun historia* (Helsinki: Lastensuojelun Keskusliitto, 1986), pp. 269–470 (pp. 334–5).

New medical knowledge in the parish 371

but the vaccination of children between 1803 and 1825 had a crucial impact on the development of smallpox in Finland.[23]

Before turning to the implementation of the vaccination policy in rural Finnish parishes, the medical debate with a focus on variolation in eighteenth-century Finland and Sweden should be considered.

Variolation as an instrument against smallpox

Inoculation had been utilized for hundreds of years in Asia and Africa, but the method was almost unknown among Europeans until the early seventeenth century. The procedure consisted of deliberately implanting the live *Variola* virus in an incision on the patient's hand or arm. The inoculator sucked up vaccine from a pustule on a person who was infected but still in relatively good condition. Then, with the parents' permission in the case of children, he applied the vaccine evenly to the skin. English physicians reportedly used the variolation method by the 1720s. In Finland, Herman Dietrich Spöring (1701–1747), who had been appointed professor of medicine at the Academy of Turku in 1728, mentioned this treatment for the first time as early as 1737.[24]

The first variolation experiment in Scandinavia was performed by Professor Johan Haartman. He used this technique to protect young Maria, daughter of his predecessor in the office, Johan Leche (1704–1764), on 19 November 1754. Leche's three other children, who were not inoculated, later died of smallpox. In Turku, Haartman experimentally inoculated eighty-two individuals, both gentry and common people, using variolation. At that point it became generally accepted in Finland, and from 1757 also in mainland Sweden.[25]

---

23 Koskinen and others, *Suomen väestö*, p. 61.
24 Fenn, *Pox Americana*, p. 32; Arno Forsius, 'Spöring, Herman Diedrich (1701–1747)', in *Biografiskt lexikon för Finland*, 4 vols (Helsinki: Svenska litteratursällskapet i Finland, 2008–2011), I (2008), pp. 628–30; 'Ylioppilasmatrikkeli 1640–1852', https://ylioppilasmatrikkeli.helsinki.fi/henkilo.php?id=U653 [accessed 1 November 2021]; *Almanacka eli ajan-tieto meidän Wapahtajam Christuxen syndymän jälkeen wuonna* (Turku, 1805), p. B 2ʳ; Iréne Sjögren, *Mannen som förlängde människolivet: En trilogi* (Stockholm: Carlssons, 2006), p. 26; Hakkarainen and Sinisalo, *Tappava tauti*, p. 143.
25 Sjögren, *Mannen som förlängde*, pp. 32–3. The Danish anatomist Thomas Bartholin (1616–1680) displayed the variolation method in 1666 in Europe, but it did not arouse much interest in learned circles at the time.

It is recorded that the variolation method was in use during the eighteenth century, at least in Ostrobothnia, where district physicians showed a genuine enthusiasm for it. The district physician Barthold Hast (1724–1784), for example, asserted that he had vaccinated as many as sixteen thousand children there between 1768 and 1784. This personal claim, however, is unconfirmed and probably heavily exaggerated. In addition, the rector of Karleby, Anders Chydenius, was well known for his predilection for travelling around his parish vaccinating people.[26] According to the annual reports of district physicians to the *Collegium Medicum*, medical professionals in mainland Sweden in the eighteenth century were often too busy with the increasing numbers of people with venereal diseases to be able to vaccinate as much as their Finnish colleagues did, particularly in Ostrobothnia.[27]

Haartman's role model at this time was the distinguished Swedish *archiater* Nils Rosén von Rosenstein (1706–1773). In his home Dr Haartman advocated Rosenstein's cures and highly valued his views on smallpox. Rosenstein, especially in his almanacs, spoke strongly in favour of vaccination. He believed firmly that mass inoculation, combined with burying the clothes of children killed by smallpox, would enable humankind to get rid of smallpox permanently.[28]

Besides Haartman in the Academy of Turku, Pehr Gadd (1727–1797), professor of chemistry, also spoke up for inoculation. In the thesis *Om förmon af kopp-ympningens widtagande i Finland*

---

26 Turpeinen, 'Lastensuojelu ja väestökehitys', p. 331; Peter Sköld, *The Two Faces of Smallpox: A Disease and its Prevention in Eighteenth- and Nineteenth-Century Sweden* (Umeå: Umeå University, 1996), p. 270; Forsius, 'Haartman, Johan (1725–1787)', in *Suomen Kansallisbiografia*, 10 vols (Helsinki: Suomalaisen Kirjallisuuden Seura, 2003–2007), IV (2004), pp. 425–7; Mattia Haltia and Antti Vaheri, 'Johan Haartman – Suomen lääketieteen isä', *Duodecim*, 122:23 (2006), 2919–28.

27 For example, in Bergslagen County in Sweden, the district physician Carl Blom only vaccinated fifty people in 1771. The number of vaccinated people did not increase between 1769 and 1771; see Stockholm, Riksarkivet, Collegium Medicum, E 3 Årsberättelser från provinsialläkare, I: Årsberättelser från provinsialläkare (1769–1779).

28 Joh[an] Joh[ans]son Haartman, *Tydelig underrättelse, om de mäst gångbara sjukdomars kännande och motande genom lätta och enfalliga hus-medel, samt et litet res- och hus-apothek* (Åbo, 1765), p. 228; Turpeinen, 'Lastensuojelu ja väestökehitys', pp. 330–1; Jägervall, *Nils Rosén von Rosenstein*, pp. 78–9; Sjögren, *Mannen som förlängde*, pp. 27–33. According to Brummer-Korvenkontio, *Virusten ja prionien luonnonhistoriaa*, pp. 47–9, the variolation method was an invention by Indo-Iranian physicians.

(1763), Gadd eloquently described the intrusion of smallpox into the remotest parts of Finland. Like Haartman and Rosenstein, he considered smallpox the most damaging of all the infectious 'foreign epidemics'. He also shared their opinion that inoculation was the safest available method for relieving the symptoms of the infected and obstructing the transmission of smallpox in the population. On the basis of the learned literature of his time, he was convinced that inoculation would work for everyone equally, regardless of age, body weight or gender.[29]

Nevertheless, a comparison of the death rates of infants and children before (1751–1775) and after (1776–1800) inoculation by the variolation method in Finland shows that the differences in favour of inoculation are surprisingly small. The factual basis in which the learned scientists had believed so firmly turned out to be a disappointment.[30]

Sextons become vaccinators

Vaccination was promoted early by the Finnish Economic Society (*Finska hushållningssällskapet*).[31] Shortly after its establishment in 1797, it approached the governors asking for advice on how it could best promote vaccination efforts in the country. However, it had no staff at its command to implement the decisions made by the board. District physicians were obviously involved in the vaccination programmes from the very beginning, but in the early nineteenth century there were only twenty of them in the entire country.[32]

Besides the Economic Society, the *Collegium Medicum*, the highest authority on medical matters in Sweden, grappled with the same problem. In 1794 Swedish physicians had been discussing the idea of using parish sextons for some minor medical jobs, but

---

29 Pehr Gadd and Otto Bökman, *Politico-oeconomisk afhandling, om förmon af kopp-ympningens widtagande i Finland* (Åbo, 1763), pp. 5–8; Haartman, *Tydelig underrättelse*, p. 228.
30 Turpeinen, 'Lastensuojelu ja väestökehitys', p. 332.
31 Jani Marjanen, *Den ekonomiska patriotismens uppgång och fall: Finska hushållningssällskapet i europeisk, svensk och finsk context 1720–1840* (University of Helsinki: Helsinki, 2013), pp. 8–10, 14–16, 19.
32 Bonsdorff, *The History of Medicine in Finland*, pp. 22–3; Mervi Naakka-Korhonen, 'Kuu ja terveys', in Eija Starck and Laura Starck (eds), *Kansanomainen ajattelu* (Helsinki: Suomalaisen Kirjallisuuden Seura, 2007), pp. 79–96 (p. 79).

at that time it had led nowhere. Subsequently, Professor Josef Pipping (1760–1815) advocated providing that kind of employment for sextons. Unlike the majority of common people, sextons could usually read and write fluently. In addition, their duties had already been expanded from purely ecclesiastical functions towards medical tasks, as the royal edict of 1755 had required them to practise medicine as phlebotomists.[33] The governor of Savo-Karelia Province, A. H. Ramsay, agreed with the proposal. The chapter in Porvoo, however, opposed it, fearing that new obligations would disturb the sextons' 'actual duties' as teachers of children in elementary instruction and as church musicians. The chapter in Turku contented itself with merely recording the proposal without any comment. The Economic Society accepted the idea and proposed it to the King in Council. In March 1803 King Gustav IV Adolf (r. 1792–1809) confirmed the charter for sextons as vaccinators. He repeated this assent in April 1804, simultaneously with the authorization of the Economic Society as the official actor and supervisor of vaccination activities in the country.[34] In 1803 the Economic Society founded a vaccination committee, which would be in charge of vaccination efforts on its behalf. It tried to promote vaccination by rewarding sextons and clergy for every successful vaccination with a premium of 12 shillings. Each district physician was responsible for vaccination in his area. In parishes all over the country, the responsibility, in practice, was in the hands of the clergy.[35] In his study on the role of sextons in Finland between 1809 and 1870, Kaarlo Jalkanen concludes that approximately half of all vaccinators were sextons.[36] They practised vaccination in parishes for years, gradually gaining experience and polishing their often rather modest medical skills.

---

33 Kaarlo Jalkanen, *Lukkarin- ja urkurinvirka Suomessa 1721–1809* (Helsinki: Suomen kirkkohistoriallinen seura, 1986), p. 72.
34 Bonsdorff, *The History of Medicine in Finland*, p. 22; Jalkanen, *Lukkarin- ja urkurinvirka Suomessa 1809–1870*, pp. 161–2; Arno Forsius, *Sosiaali- ja terveydenhuollon kehitys Hollolassa ja Lahdessa vuoteen 1865* (Hämeenlinna: Lahden kaupunki, 1982), pp. 97–8; Vuorinen, *Tautinen Suomi*, p. 162.
35 KT, Turun tuomiokapitulin arkisto, A I: 29, 430. Turun tklin pk. 9 October 1799; Jalkanen, *Lukkarin- ja urkurinvirka Suomessa 1809–1870*, p. 162.
36 Jalkanen, *Lukkarin- ja urkurinvirka Suomessa 1809–1870*, p. 362.

The first parishes to implement vaccinations (1803–1804)

Vaccination by Jenner's method began earlier in some Finnish parishes than in other parts of the Swedish realm.[37] First in line was the tiny Nauvo, located about fifty-five kilometres from Turku by road and thus close to the city from which the policy was dictated. As early as 1803, a total of 308 children were vaccinated there 'without fatalities', as the pastor pointed out in his annual report. In the next year, 1804, the vaccination project got off to a good start, not only in the city of Turku but also in Pöytyä, Sauvo, Vampula, Halikko and Rymättylä (Varsinais-Suomi), Eurajoki, Suodenniemi and Vesilahti (Satakunta), Närpiö, Korsnäs and Pörtom (Ostrobothnia), Porvoo, Sipoo and Siuntio (Uusimaa), Akaa, Sääksmäki, Vanaja (Häme) and Tohmajärvi (Karelia). Apart from Tohmajärvi, all these parishes were located in western Finland. The parishes that started vaccination in 1805 included further parishes in southern Finland around Helsinki, as well as along the west coast – Pertteli, Raisio (Varsinais-Suomi), Perho, Siipyy, Veteli, Ylihärmä (Ostrobothnia), Pohja, Tenhola, Vihti, Espoo, Helsinki (Uusimaa), Hattula and Renko (Häme). These observations show that the vaccination project was surprisingly successful in the in the west and south; but the further north or east it proceeded, the more problems and obvious yet passive resistance it encountered.

A typical congregation among those parishes where vaccination began early was Pöytyä. It was small but located twenty-four kilometres from Turku. According to the annual report, the pastor recorded the vaccination of fourteen children as early as 1804. From 1806 onwards, however, vaccination seems to have ceased totally, until 1811. The explanation for this sudden break was probably the progression of the disease: in that particular year, no one died of it in Pöytyä.[38]

In the nineteenth century, the post of sexton was life-long. Nevertheless, the old sexton of Pöytyä, Matti Matinpoika Tenlund, gradually lost his ability to work. In 1779 he asked the parish to hire his son Mikko to assist him. The parish council declined this request for two reasons. The young Tenlund, unlike his father, was

---

37 Anto Leikola, 'Eurooppalainen luonnontiede', in Matti Klinge (ed.), *Kuninkaallinen Turun Akatemia 1640–1808: Helsingin yliopisto 1640–1990* (Helsinki: Otava, 1987), pp. 679–703 (p. 703).
38 KT, Pöytyä SeA, Väkilukutaulukot 1804–1811.

in their opinion a maverick who did not show due respect to his elders, including his own father. Moreover, his ability to read music was not satisfactory. In short, he was immature in many respects. Young Tenlund was, however, talented at bloodletting. He knew the most frequent internal diseases, and he could vaccinate. He had even extracted teeth. In addition, the younger Tenlund was known to be a good teacher. In this situation, the members of the parish council had to deliberate as to whether they should attach greater value to the skills of the old school or prefer the new. Their choice, to elect young Tenlund, reflected their preparedness for the new era and its challenges. This decision made Pöytyä one of the first parishes in the entire country when it came to vaccination.[39]

In the Province of Häme, developments were similar in outline. In Renko and Vanaja, for example, one sexton, alongside his other duties, vaccinated seventy people in the spring of 1805, and an additional seventy-three children later in the same year. During the following years the urgent need for vaccination seemed not to have been fulfilled until 1814, when the sexton again vaccinated seventy-six children in Renko in one year.[40] In Siuntio, too, in the western part of the Province of Uusimaa, the same pattern was repeated.

Parishes like Pöytyä are especially interesting in the context of the Enlightenment, because they illustrate how quickly innovations could spread in the Finnish countryside in the late eighteenth century if the circumstances were favourable. They also show how the reception of innovations was dependent on the needs of the peasantry on the one hand – that is, the practical usefulness of the new knowledge – and on the degree of activity on the part of the clergy or sextons when it came to implementing vaccination on the other.

In most cases, it is difficult to tell who was the *primus motor* behind local vaccination. Sometimes enlightened clergy encouraged sextons on their own initiative, but there were also examples of the opposite. In Oulunsalo in northern Ostrobothnia, the rector

---

39 Aulikki Ylönen, *Pöytyän, Yläneen ja Oripään historia vuoteen 1865* (Helsinki: Pöytyän, 1969), pp. 850–2. In Munsala in 1797, the parish granted a 'pension' to the decrepit sexton Mats Svedjelin in order to get rid of him, even though the entire concept was unknown in Church Law; see Bertel Nyholm, *Kyrkan i Munsala: en historisk översikt med anledning av Munsala kyrkas 200 års jubileum 1992* (Munsala: Munsala evang. luth. församling, 1992), p. 279.
40 KHä, Renko SeA; KHä, Vanaja SeA, Väkilukutaulukot 1804–1813; KHä, Siuntio SeA, Väkilukutaulukot 1804–1816.

recorded in the annual report that he did not know how many persons were vaccinated in the parish in 1813, because he had not received the list of vaccinated persons from the sexton.[41] Similarly unaware of vaccination efforts in their own parishes were the rectors in Elimäki in 1807, Käkisalmi in 1812, and Rautu and Hämeenkyrö in 1814.[42] In Pernaja the initiative lay entirely in the hands of the chaplain Samuel Ceder, who besides his ordinary pastoral duties at an iron mill vaccinated children in area of Pernaja and Strömfors. Instead of the rector, it was he who kept a record of vaccinated children as well. In these cases, the duties of rectors seem to have been limited to the passive recording of children vaccinated by others.[43]

What the clergy actually knew about vaccination can scarcely be studied in detail. However, it is possible to make some observations by analysing their book collections. According to Tuija Laine, the most important source of information for clergy on medical issues was a 'house-doctor' manual called *Tydelig underrättelse om de mäst gångbara sjukdomars kännande och motande* ('Clear information about the identification and prevention of the most frequent diseases'), which was written by Johan Haartman (1725–1789) in 1763. It was often found in parish book collections because the author, in 1774, voluntarily donated 1,200 copies to clergy in the dioceses in Sweden and Finland 'for the good of the common people'.[44] In this book, Haartman described the nature and progression of smallpox in four stages, conveying useful knowledge about how infected patients should be treated and medicated. Intended for those who did not have access to a physician, Haartman's book concentrated on practical advice.

Besides academic publications, the early Finnish- or Swedish-speaking press distributed information on smallpox and its treatment by means of almanacs and articles intended for the common people, simultaneously advocating vaccination as a means of

---

41 Oulu, Kansallisarkisto Oulu (KO), Oulunsalo SeA, II Df:1 Väkilukutaulukot 1810–1814.
42 KM, Käkisalmi SeA, Rokotusluettelot 1842–1847; KM, Rautu SeA, II Df: 2 Väkilukutaulukot 1812–1814; KHä, Hämeenkyrö SeA, Väkiluku- ja kuolleisuustaulukot 1812–1814; KM, Elimäki SeA, II Dg:2 Kuolleisuustaulukot (Väkilukutaulut) 1811–1877.
43 KHä, Pernaja SeA, Väkilukutaulukot 1807–1813.
44 Tuija Laine, 'Katederilta kansan pariin: Suomalainen lääketieteellinen kirjallisuus 1600- ja 1700-luvuilla', in Raimo Jussila and others (eds), *Tieto ja kirja* (Helsinki: Suomen tietokirjailijat ry, 2001), pp. 190–210 (pp. 197–8).

preventing smallpox.[45] The first article concerning smallpox, 'Cuinga yhteisen kansan pitä heidän Lapsians Wartoman, jotca tulewat rupuljin' ('How common people should take care of children who are infected with smallpox'), was published in the Finnish almanac of 1764. In the previous year, 1763, roughly 23 per cent of the population had died of smallpox. In that article, the writer, presumably Professor Johan Leche, advised various treatments for infected children, ranging from healthy nutrition to vinegar-water and buttermilk, and with pleas to protect children from draughts, cold and damp. Inoculation, however, was not a part of his toolbox.[46]

Parishes with delayed implementation (1814–1817)

Other parishes started later but nevertheless implemented vaccination relatively soon. One example is Rantsila (northern Ostrobothnia). Judging from the annual report from 1814, there is no evidence of any vaccination in the parish before that year. After the first twenty-three vaccinated children, the sexton continued his efforts the next year, 1815, by vaccinating sixty-two children. In 1816 the rate was slightly lower; but in 1817, again, a further twenty-six children were vaccinated.[47] Almost the same can be noticed in Lapinjärvi (eastern Uusimaa). Vaccination efforts there too began rather late, in 1812. In the next year vaccination hit record heights, with 308 vaccinated children. In 1814 this rate fell sharply to 179, and in 1815 to 36. Vaccinations began late in both cases; but by avoiding interruptions, both parishes managed to keep smallpox under control despite the late start.[48]

---

45 'Lyhyt Historia Rokosta eli Rupulista', *Turun Wiikko-Sanomat*, 3 February 1821. In 1805 the Economic Society assumed responsibility for the content of the Finnish almanacs; see Aulis J. Alanen, 'Almanakka talouden ja sivistyksen opastajana', in *Suomen almanakan juhlakirja* (Helsinki: Helsingin yliopisto & Weilin & Göös, 1957), pp. 117–18.
46 Soininen, 'Suomalaisen almanakan lääketieteellisistä kirjoituksista', pp. 97–8.
47 KO, Rantsila SeA, II Df:1 Väkilukutaulut 1814–1817.
48 KHä, Lapinjärvi SeA, Väkilukutaulukot 1812–1815. Other examples are Hauho (Häme), Haukivuori (southern Savo), Valkeala (eastern Häme), Tyrnävä (southern Ostrobothnia) and Ilomantsi (northern Karelia). In Hauho, only 2 children were vaccinated in 1812. The next year the number rocketed to 115. Corresponding rates in Haukivuori were 5 and 80, and in Valkeala 0 and 115, respectively. In Tyrnävä (Southern Ostrobothnia), the number of vaccinated persons rose in one year from 10 to 134.

In the parish of Huittinen (Satakunta), vaccination began relatively late, in 1810. The subject had, however, been discussed during the dean's inspection in 1804. The dean expressed his gratitude to the sexton, Johan Savonius, for his good work as a phlebotomist and a teacher. He accepted the excuse for the delay in vaccination, which was allegedly due to the ongoing training of Savonius in the relevant skill. In Huittinen Savonius was known not only for his proficiency but also for his sobriety, a characteristic which in many parishes could not be taken for granted.

In Kisko, vaccination only began in 1816, and partly for the same reason. The old sexton, Jonas Lydman, had served the parish honourably for twenty-six years. In his last years, however, he was unfit for work without assistance. Finally, in 1815, the parish council elected a new sexton, Emmanuel Lindroth, who started vaccination immediately. For his devoted labours in respect of medical care, the *Collegium Medicum* granted Lindroth a silver goblet as a reward.[49] In 1813 the Economic Society similarly awarded a young sexton, Mikko Kääriä in Joutseno (Karelia), a medal for his 'industrious and successful use of instruments in vaccination'. Kääriä had started vaccination in Joutseno in 1807. In 1813 the parish expressed satisfaction with his work by raising his salary for the same reason. This gesture was remarkable because some years before, parishioners had adopted quite a different attitude to vaccination and to the young sexton.[50] The coming of the new generation of sextons substantially speeded up vaccination efforts in many parishes. They managed to win parishioners' trust and convince them of the utility of the new knowledge. From this point of view, the young sextons can be considered the true torchbearers of the Enlightenment, one of the many neglected categories of Enlightenment agents in the European North.

Implemented vaccination as an obligation (1812)

In 1812 the civil authorities added a spot in the template for the annual report where the local pastor was expected to fill in the

---

49 KT, Huittinen SeA, II Cd: 1, 131. Rov.tark.pk. 3 July 1804 § 43; Seija Väärä, 'Kiskon ja Suomusjärven historia historiallisen ajan alusta kunnallishallinnon uudistamiseen 1347–1865', in Anja Sarvas and Seija Väärä (eds), *Kiskon ja Suomusjärven historia*, I (Jyväskylä: Kiskon ja Suomusjärven kuntien ja seurakuntien historiatoimikunta, 1998), pp. 105–629 (pp. 440–1).

50 Jari Ropponen, *Joutsenon historia* (Jyväskylä: Joutsenon kunta ja seurakunta, 1997), pp. 216–17.

number of vaccinated children in his parish. This revision implied that a pastor could not just ignore this issue without running the risk of being held responsible for misconduct in office. The sources indicate that this reform led to a significantly increasing number of vaccinated children in Finnish parishes all over the country, including Koski, Isokyrö, Jokioinen, Karjalohja, Karttula, Kauhajoki, Laukaa, Sotkamo and Tampere.[51]

In Askola (Uusimaa) the rector spoke openly in favour of vaccination, but his words went unheard. In order to exculpate himself with regard to the lack of recorded vaccinations, he copied his words to the parish assembly in his annual report for 1811, stating that 'vaccination should not be neglected'. In 1812, however, he was reluctantly compelled to record 'none' in answer to the question about the number of vaccinated persons. Finally, in 1813, he had his way when the parents of fourteen children allowed them to be vaccinated. Later in the same year, twenty-nine other children were vaccinated.[52]

Not only the parish clergy but also bishops reminded parents and clergy of the importance of vaccination during episcopal inspections. In Juva (Savo), for example, in the spring of 1816 the local clergy gave an account of vaccination efforts in the parish to the bishop in the presence of the congregation. The bishop urged mothers to ensure that their children were vaccinated in due time, using the 'genuine vaccine' for the purpose. To the clergy, he pointed out that the supervision of vaccination was one of their duties.[53]

Among the Finnish clergy, there were nevertheless some individuals who got away with hardly doing anything to promote vaccination for a surprisingly long time, despite increased pressure from above. In Hankasalmi and Eräjärvi (northern Häme), for example, no

---

51 KT, Koski SeA, Väkilukutaulukot 1813–1815; KV, Isonkyrö SeA, II Df:3, 31. Väkilukutaulukko 1812; KHä, Jokioinen SeA, Väkilukutaulukot 1812–1814; KHä, Karjalohja SeA, Väkilukutaulukot II Df:3 1802–1811 ja II Df:4, 1812–1813; KJ, Karttula SeA, II Df:1, 82. Väkilukutaulukot 1775–1877; Jyväskylä, Kansallisarkisto Jyväskylä (KJy), Laukaa SeA, Väkilukutaulukot 1812–1815; KO, Sotkamo SeA, II Df:1, 197–209. Tilastot ja väkilukutaulukot 1812–1815; KHä, Tampere SeA, Väkilukutaulukot 1812–1822.

52 KHä, Askola SeA, Väkilukutaulukot 1811–1812. In Nummi (Uusimaa), the pastor recorded in his report 'Vaccinering försummat' ('vaccination neglected'); KHä, Nummi SeA, Väkilukutaulukko 1811.

53 KM, Juva SeA, Piisp. tark. pk. 9 March 1816.

children were vaccinated before 1821.[54] In Loppi (southern Häme), vaccination began in 1817; in Viljakkala (northwest Häme), it only started in 1825. In Karvia (Satakunta), the first eight children were vaccinated in 1813. After a break of four years, vaccination was resumed, with sixty-five vaccinated individuals in 1817.[55]

In some parishes, such as Eräjärvi, the delay was caused by two factors. The old sexton was famously capable in his duties as precentor and phlebotomist, but such duties as teaching, not to mention vaccination, were beyond his ability. At the same time, the parishioners complained during an inspection by the dean in 1812 that the chaplain who was in charge of the dependent parish was seldom present. The absence of a pastor and the limited ability of the sexton in combination led to a failure to start vaccination until 1821.[56]

The Vaccination Act of 1804 did not explicitly require sextons to undertake vaccination. In the absence of proper sanctions, sextons who neglected their duties as vaccinators could easily get away with it unpunished. This was considered fair if the sexton was practically unfit for work because of old age but had diligently served the parish for decades.[57] In Viljakkala, for example, the unimpressive performance of a sexton in the teaching of children, for which the dean rebuked him at an inspection in 1825, probably implied poor skills in the other duties of a sexton as well.[58] In Kankaanpää the sexton Matti Tesolin was by all appearances an honourable person and a skilled professional; but his frequent long absences from his post, for unknown reasons, significantly exacerbated the problems in respect of vaccination during the years 1810–1836.[59]

Parishes with poor implementation of the vaccination policy

Some parishes, mostly located in northern and eastern Finland and far away from the major coastal cities in the south, were prevented

---

54 KJy, Hankasalmi SeA, Väkilukutaulut 1812–1821; KHä, Eräjärvi SeA, Väkilukutaulu 1821.
55 KHä, Loppi SeA, Väkilukutaulukko 1816; KHä, Loppi SeA, Rokotusluettelot; KHä, Viljakkala SeA, Väkilukutaulut 1806–1826; KT, Karvia SeA, II Df:1,19, Väkilukutaulukot 1805–1840.
56 KHä, Eräjärvi SeA, Rov.tark.pk. 7 July 1812, 4, 10.
57 Jalkanen, *Lukkarin- ja urkurinvirka Suomessa 1809–1870*, p. 166.
58 KHä, Viljakkala SeA, Rov. tark. pk. 25 March 1825, § 42.
59 KT, Kankaanpää SeA, II Df:1. Väkilukutaulukot 1805–1850; Martta Sevio, *Kankaanpään seurakunnan vaiheita vuoteen 1970* (Rauma: Kankaanpään seurakunta, 1970), pp. 52–3.

from implementing vaccination due to various problems. The worst of those is likely to have been the poor availability of vaccine. Although it was not a very complicated chemical product in the early nineteenth century compared to modern vaccines, neither clergy nor sextons were usually able to produce it themselves. In order to be able to vaccinate locally they needed the vaccine, which was kept in the central stores of the Economic Society in Turku.[60]

In Suonenjoki (northern Savo), Karl Fredrik Bergh complained about the lack of vaccine in his annual report for 1810: no child could be vaccinated under these conditions. Shortage of vaccine had forced the parish to live in distress and anxiety for years because the Economic Society had not delivered the orders from Turku. The first remarks on vaccination found in annual reports from Suonenjoki are from 1804. The attempts made by the local clergy to solve the supply problem were a bitter failure.[61] The same pattern was repeated in Haapajärvi (mid-Ostrobothnia) in 1813. When new consignments of vaccine arrived the next year, it was possible to vaccinate 196 children and young people. In Artjärvi (Uusimaa), the rector tried to explain that no one had been vaccinated in 1815 by claiming that there was no vaccine there. In the context of relatively unimpressive numbers before and after, however, it is possible that lack of vaccine was an excuse for some other problem.[62]

In Maaninka (northern Savo), vaccination was significantly delayed because of the lack of a suitable vaccinator. In 1812 the rector was convinced that there was nobody in the surrounding area who could run the vaccination efforts. In the years that followed, he repeatedly had to face the same problem, until the parish finally managed in 1816 to find an energetic vaccinator who vaccinated 231 children in the course of one year.[63]

Most sextons only practised as vaccinators within the limits of their own parishes, but there were exceptions. For example, the sextons in Hirvensalmi and Masku, Eric Relander and Henric Lundelin, travelled around the provinces of Savo and Viborg

---

60 Jalkanen, *Lukkarin- ja urkurinvirka Suomessa 1809–1870*, p. 162.
61 KO, Reisjärvi SeA, II Df:1,13,18. Väkilukutaulukot 1806–1814; KJ, Suonenjoki SeA, Väkilukutaulut 1804–1810.
62 KO, Alavieska SeA, II Df:2, 25–31. Väkilukutaulukot 1811–1814; KO, Haapajärvi SeA, Väkilukutaulukot 1813–1814; KHä, Artjärvi SeA, Väkilukutaulukot 1814–1816.
63 KJ, Maaninka SeA, Väkilukutaulukot 1812–1819.

New medical knowledge in the parish 383

as vaccinators. On these visits, Eric Relander vaccinated eight hundred children, simultaneously training followers to continue his job as vaccinator in the most remote villages. P. W. Sumelius, the sexton of Kangasala (Häme), vaccinated almost one thousand children in his own parish and in addition a large number of others in the surrounding area.[64] In the old mother parishes, as in Kokkola (Mid-Ostrobothnia), each dependent parish (Veteli, Ala-Veteli, Perho, Kaustinen) had a sexton of its own. This permitted a division of duties. According to an agreement, the sexton of Ala-Veteli, Mats Kaitfors, dedicated himself to medical matters including vaccination. Because of this arrangement, vaccinating could be started in the area in the spring of 1804. Up until 1869, good results in respect of vaccination based on a sexton's medical skills created opportunities for skilful and experienced sextons to seek better-paid posts in the wealthier parishes. The new Ecclesiastical Act (1869), however, no longer included any requirements pertaining to medical readiness or skills.[65]

In most parishes where there was overt resistance to vaccination, it was passive by nature. In Säkylä (Satakunta) in 1806, the pastor lamented the unwillingness of parents to have their children vaccinated. Despite encouraging words and educational leaflets, nobody had taken up the opportunity. The vaccination of the first children in Säkylä was delayed until 1814. Both there and in Viljakkala, resistance to vaccination reflected old-fashioned thinking. Perhaps simple indolence also played a part in the neglect of vaccination.[66] In Säkylä, the number of deaths from smallpox was relatively small in comparison to other causes of death in the 1790s. In Viljakkala, though, smallpox killed several farmers up until 1808, when the epidemic suddenly eased off for a while.[67] It is possible that this

---

64 Jalkanen, *Lukkarin- ja urkurinvirka Suomessa 1809–1870*, p. 165.
65 KV, Veteli SeA, Piisp.tark.pk. 23 February 1804, § 5; Reija Satokangas, 'Isostavihasta seurakuntahallinnon uudistukseen (1722–1864)', in Kyösti Elo, Reija Satokangas and Jouko Vahtola (eds), *Iin seurakunnan historia* (Jyväskylä: Iin seurakunta, 1998), pp. 97–176 (pp. 137–8); Reija Satokangas, 'Seurakunta muuttuvassa maailmassa (1865–1980)', in *Iin seurakunnan historia*, pp. 177–331 (pp. 231–2).
66 KT, Säkylä SeA, Väkilukutaulut 1806–1819; Raili Nurminen, *Säkylän historia*, I (Jyväskylä: Säkylän Kunta ja Seurakunta, 1970), pp. 381–3; Hakkarainen and Sinisalo, *Tappava tauti*, pp. 150–1.
67 KHä, Viljakkala SeA, Väkilukutaulut 1806–1860, 1, 13, 19, 43 and 47; KT, Säkylä SeA, Väkilukutaulut 1805–1810, 6, 8, 16 and 18; KT, Säkylä SeA, Väkilukutaulut 1815–1875, 7 and 24.

change lulled the peasants into a false sense of security. In Juva (Savo) in 1812, only one family showed up for vaccination. In the next year, 1813, the pastor lamented that all his efforts to promote vaccinations had come to a dead end. The number of people who died of smallpox in Juva fell rapidly from twenty in 1812 to only two in 1813; but in 1814 it once again rose alarmingly, to fifty-seven. In 1815 the parents of fifty children were willing to permit vaccination.[68]

Social differences played a part as well. In the annual report submitted by rectors, there were separate columns for vaccinated individuals among the gentry and among the common people. In most parishes, differences between the social groups as regards vaccination were not significant. In Luhanka (northern Häme), however, that was not the case. According to the records, no vaccination occurred there before 1815. In that year, finally, three children with a social background in the gentry were vaccinated. Until 1818, when the first child with a peasant background was vaccinated in Luhanka, vaccination was a concern for people of rank alone. Kontturi's study of Ostrobothnia district physicians' reports to the *Collegium Medicum* in the eighteenth century indicates that, at least initially, the main reason for avoiding vaccination among the common people was fear. The peasantry refused to have their children inoculated even though both the procedure and the vaccine itself were free of charge for everybody. A significant share of all the inoculated children in eighteenth-century Finland was thus made up of children whose families belonged to the gentry.[69]

Concluding discussion

This chapter has demonstrated the key role played by parishes, and particularly sextons, in implementing vaccination policies in rural Finland at the end of the long eighteenth century. A variety of starting points for the implementation has emerged in the course

---

68 KM, Juva SeA, II Df: 1. Väkilukutaulut 1812–1841.
69 Saara-Maija Kontturi, *Suomen varhaisen piirilääkärilaitoksen tavoitteet ja niiden toteutuminen* (Helsinki: Suomen lääketieteen historian seura, 2015), p. 101. According to the report of the district physician from the Province of Turku and Pori to the *Collegium Medicum* in 1800, most of the inoculated people belonged to gentry families; see Stockholm, Riksarkivet, Collegium Medicum, E3, Berättelse om gångbara sjukdomar i Björneborgs län 1800.

of the analysis. The poor implementation in areas far from major cities is striking and calls for further exploration. The available sources offer little explanation as to why such a large proportion of the common people in these parishes was not vaccinated. What this study has demonstrated is that they did in fact have ample opportunities to receive the new health-promoting measure. However, previous research on the culture and beliefs of the common folk in rural Finland may offer some hypotheses. Besides fear and prejudice, folk medicine – which still flourished in the early nineteenth century, especially in eastern Finland – is likely to have affected the willingness of parents to allow their children to be vaccinated. Remedies which were believed to be as effective as the vaccine were sauna, tar, salt and liquor. Different kinds of mixtures made of tar, honey, beer, camphor or vinegar were in common use as medication. Among the uneducated peasantry until the mid-nineteenth century, there was a strong faith in the healing power of fresh air or objects such as the teeth of a bear, rags from the clothes of deceased people and snake grease. Resorting to spells or magic was not excluded either.[70]

Although folk medicine and vaccination were based on different concepts of medical knowledge, there were nevertheless some similarities in their practices. Old folk ways of curing smallpox consisted of spreading a compound made of burbot's liver on the patient's skin. Unlike the vaccinator, the natural healer did not nick the skin of the patient. For many people in eastern and northern Finland in the early nineteenth century, the issue at stake was the difference between old and new, and between popular and academic knowledge. The vaccination efforts on the part of the Church and the Crown only made such differences visible in the everyday life of the common people in remote localities. Acceptance of the new knowledge encapsulated in vaccination took longer in rural areas far from the major cities.

Gary B. Ferngren has drawn attention to the rapid naturalization of medical theory in the eighteenth century as the specific causes of many diseases were discovered within a matter of a few decades.

---

70 U. K. Teittinen, 'Uudenkaupungin rauhasta kunnallishallinnon perustamiseen', in Martti Ruuth (ed.), *Juvan historia* (Pieksämäki: Juvan seurakunta ja kunta, 1957), pp. 173–455 (pp. 318–23); Naakka-Korhonen, 'Kuu ja terveys', pp. 80, 83–92; Mikko Europaeus, 'Kansankulttuuri', in *Pitäjä ison kiven takana: Lemin historia* (Jyväskylä: Lemin kotiseutuyhdistys & Lemin kunta, 2009), pp. 198–203.

According to him, belief in God's direct and immediate involvement in human sickness had begun to diminish long before this in the central areas of Europe and in the United States – even in the minds of the devout – with the rise of rational-speculative medical theories.[71]

Vilkuna has scrutinized the consequences of these events in detail. According to him, the sacred authority based on the law and divine order crumbled during the long years of Russian occupation.[72] Both Juva and Vilkuna point to the diminished confidence of the Finnish common people in direct divine intervention in crises as an outgrowth of the perceived absence of protective divine power during the atrocities of the Russian occupation. These interpretations may explain the rapid naturalization of medical attitudes as well. In areas where losses in both material and mental/psychological terms were comparatively serious, the common people were more willing to accept vaccination. In the rural parishes of northern and eastern Finland, by contrast, simple faith in Providence linked to folk medicine may have survived to a greater extent because of fewer bitter experiences of divine abandonment during crises.

In his circular letter of 1799, the Bishop of Turku, Jacob Tengström, harshly criticized the stubbornness of the common people in their attitudes to medicine, encouraging the clergy to enlighten the peasantry in favour of the new treatments. According to him, these 'wrong and harmful concepts' (beliefs to the effect that smallpox was a scourge sent from God) threatened to obstruct the work of vaccinators seeking to save the lives of innocent children. As a true patriot and supporter of the Enlightenment, he strongly emphasized the significance of reason as a gift from God for the benefit of the fatherland and humankind. Tengström firmly rejected the idea of immediate divine interference as heresy.[73] His letter brought the juxtaposition of old and new knowledge to the centre of the vaccination debate.

Judging by the absence of peasants from vaccination records in certain parishes, the idea of passive resistance might – as Tengström wrote – have included a perception of God's will. If infection by a horrible illness was God's will, then recovery would likewise lie

---

71 Gary B. Ferngren, *Medicine and Religion: A Historical Introduction* (Baltimore, MD: Johns Hopkins University Press, 2014), p. 172.
72 Kustaa H. J. Vilkuna, *Paholaisen sota* (Helsinki: Teos, 2006), pp. 580–1, 584–5.
73 KT, Turun tuomiokapitulin kirjekirja (missive) B I: 66, 342–9. Tklin kiertokirje, 27 November 1799.

solely in his hands. From that point of view, vaccination appeared to be unnecessary.[74] The scepticism of the Finnish peasants in northern and eastern Finland towards the new science is probably best understood from this perspective.[75] Apparently, two concepts of medical knowledge, the old and the new, coexisted among the Finnish peasantry. In most parishes located close to major cities, an early breakthrough for the new knowledge of 'Enlightenment', in the shape of vaccination, was a fact. At the same time, however, suspicions still prevailed for many reasons, at least in the remote countryside.

Bibliography

Archival sources

Hämeenlinna, Finland

Kansallisarkisto Hämeenlinna (KHä)
  Artjärven seurakunnan arkisto (Artjärvi SeA), Väkilukutaulukot 1815–1845
  Askolan seurakunnan arkisto (Askola SeA), Väkilukutaulukot 1802–1840
  Eräjärven seurakunnan arkisto (Eräjärvi SeA), Väkilukutaulukot 1774–1879
  ——, Rovastintarkastus pöytäkirjat 1812–1880
  Hämeenkyrön seurakunnan arkisto (Hämeenkyrö SeA), Kuolleisuustaulukot 1811–1877, II Dg:2
  Janakkalan seurakunnan arkisto (Janakkala SeA), Väkilukutaulukot 1749–1844, I S:1
  Jokioisten seurakunnan arkisto (Jokioinen SeA), Väkilukutaulukot 1748–1833
  Karjalohjan seurakunnan arkisto (Karjalohja SeA), Väkilukutaulukot 1802–1811, 1812–1824, II Df:3, II Df:4
  Lapinjärven seurakunnan arkisto (Lapinjärvi SeA), Väkilukutaulukot 1749–1877
  Liljendalin seurakunnan arkisto (Liljendal SeA), Rokotusluettelot 1805–1822

---

74 Turpeinen refers to 'religious prejudice' against variolation in the late eighteenth century; but in the documents composed by the clergy in the time of mass vaccination, these kinds of protests are conspicuous by their absence; see Turpeinen, 'Lastensuojelu ja väestökehitys', p. 311.
75 Ferngren, *Medicine and Religion*, p. 172.

Lopen seurakunnan arkisto (Loppi SeA), Väkilukutaulukot 1749–1875
———, Rokotusluettelot 1817–1927
Nummen seurakunnan arkisto (Nummi SeA), Väkilukutaulukot 1749–1877
Pernajan seurakunnan arkisto (Pernaja SeA), Väkilukutaulukot 1749–1824
Rengon seurakunnan arkisto (Renko SeA), Väkilukutaulukot 1811–1877
Sahalahden seurakunnan arkisto (Sahalahti SeA), Rokotusluettelot 1816–1878
Siuntion seurakunnan arkisto (Siuntio SeA), Väkilukutaulukot 1749–1900
Tampereen tuomiokirkkoseurakunnan arkisto (Tampere SeA), Väkilukutaulukot 1802–1860
Vanajan seurakunnan arkisto (Vanaja SeA), Väkilukutaulukot 1749–1805
Viljakkalan seurakunnan arkisto (Viljakkala SeA), Rovastintarkastusten pöytäkirjat 1825–1857
———, Väkilukutaulut 1806–1860

Joensuu, Finland

Kansallisarkisto Joensuu (KJ)
Karttulan seurakunnan arkisto (Karttula SeA), Väkilukutaulukot 1775–1877, II Df:1
Kuopion maa- ja kaupunkiseurakunnan arkisto (Kuopio SeA), Kyytivuoroluettelo 1831–1881, Sarjaan sisältyvät rokotusluettelot vuosilta 1848–1851, II Bk:3
Liperin seurakunnan arkisto (Liperi SeA), Rokotuspäiväkirjat ja -luettelot 1815–1889, I He:1
Maaningan seurakunnan arkisto (Maaninka SeA), Väkilukutaulukot 1802–1877
Suonenjoen seurakunnan arkisto (Suonenjoki SeA), Piispantarkastusten pöytäkirjat 1794–1857, Väkilukutaulukot 1802–1811 and 1812–1821

Jyväskylä, Finland

Kansallisarkisto Jyväskylä (KJy)
Hankasalmen seurakunnan arkisto (Hankasalmi SeA), Väkilukutaulut 1803–1869
Laukaan seurakunnan arkisto (Laukaa SeA), Väkilukutaulukot 1749–1875

Mikkeli, Finland

Kansallisarkisto Mikkeli (KM)
Elimäen seurakunnan arkisto (Elimäki SeA), Kuolleisuustaulukot 1749–1810, II Dg:1
Iitin seurakunnan arkisto (Iitti SeA), Rokotettujen lasten luettelo 1811–1857, I He:1
Juvan seurakunnan arkisto (Juva SeA), Piispantarkastusten pöytäkirjat 1790–1848

———, Väkilukutaulut 1812–1841, II Df:1
Käkisalmen seurakunnan arkisto (Käkisalmi SeA), Rokotusluettelot 1842–1847
Lappeen seurakunnan arkisto (Lappeenranta SeA), Kuolleet 1786–180, I C: 3; Väkilukutaulukot 1812–1877
Puumalan seurakunnan arkisto (Puumala SeA), Rokotusluettelot 1814–1888, I He:1
———, Rovastintarkastusten pöytäkirjat 1825–1846, II Cg:1
Raudun seurakunnan arkisto (Rautu SeA), Väkilukutaulukot 1812–1877, II Df:2

Oulu, Finland

Kansallisarkisto Oulu (KO)
Alavieskan seurakunnan arkisto (Alavieska SeA), Väkilukutaulukot 1778–1850, II Df:2
Haapajärven seurakunnan arkisto (Haapajärvi SeA), Väkilukutaulukot 1749–1849
Oulunsalon seurakunnan arkisto (Oulunsalo SeA), Väkilukutaulukot 1805–1840, II Df:1
Rantsilan seurakunnan arkisto (Rantsila SeA), Taulukot väkiluvuista 1775–1877, II Df:1
Reisjärven seurakunnan arkisto (Reisjärvi SeA), Väkilukutaulukot 1806–1835, II Df:1
Sotkamon seurakunnan arkisto (Sotkamo SeA), Tilastot ja väkilukutaulukot 1749–1854, II Df:1

Stockholm

Riksarkivet, Stockholm
Collegium Medicum, Årsberättelser från provinsialläkare, E 3/4, 1769–1779, 1801–1807

Turku, Finland

Kansallisarkisto Turku (KT)
Huittisten seurakunnan arkisto (Huittinen SeA), Piispantarkastusten pöytäkirjat 1651–1928, II
———, Cd:1; Väkilukutaulut 1805–1850, II Df:3
Kankaanpään seurakunnan arkisto (Kankaanpää SeA), Väkilukutaulukot 1805–1850, II Df:1
Karvian seurakunnan arkisto (Karvia SeA), Väkilukutaulukot 1805–1840, II Df:1
Kiskon seurakunnan arkisto (Kisko SeA), Rokotettujen lasten luettelo 1814–1871, I He:1

Kosken (Hämeenkoski) seurakunnan arkisto (Koski SeA), Väkilukutaulukot 1813–1855
Mouhijärven seurakunnan arkisto (Mouhijärvi SeA), Rokotusluettelot 1814–1843
Pöytyän seurakunnan arkisto (Pöytyä SeA), Väkilukutaulukot 1749–1811
Säkylän seurakunnan arkisto (Säkylä SeA), Väkilukutaulut 1805–1810, 1815–1875
Turun tuomiokapitulin arkisto, Pöytäkirjojen pääsarja 1799, A I: 29

Vaasa, Finland

Kansallisarkisto Vaasa (KV)
Ilmajoen seurakunnan arkisto (Ilmajoki SeA), Rokotusluettelo 1805–1863
Isonkyrön seurakunnan arkisto (Isonkyrö SeA), Väkilukutaulukoita 1802–1850, II Df:3
Kannuksen seurakunnan arkisto (Kannus SeA), Väkilukutaulut 1805–1877
Lapuan seurakunnan arkisto (Lapua SeA), Väkilukutaulukot 1774–1877, II Df:4
Vetelin seurakunnan arkisto (Veteli SeA), Piispantarkastusten pöytäkirjat 1732–1825

Digital sources

Viitaharju, Johanna, 'Rippikoulun käynyt ja rokotettu', https://kulperi.blogspot.com/2020/11/rippikoulun-kaynyt-ja-rokotettu.html [accessed 1 November 2021].
'Ylioppilasmatrikkeli 1640–1852', https://ylioppilasmatrikkeli.helsinki.fi [accessed 1 November 2021].

Printed sources and literature

Åbo Tidning
Alanen, Aulis J., 'Almanakka talouden ja sivistyksen opastajana', in *Suomen almanakan juhlakirja* (Helsinki: Helsingin yliopisto & Weilin & Göös, 1957).
Allardt, Anders, *Liljendals sockens historia* (Lovisa: Östra Nylands förlag, 1980).
Almanacka eli ajan-tieto meidän Wapahtajam Christuxen syndymän jälkeen wuonna (Turku, 1805).
Barnhart, Robert K., *Dictionary of Etymology* (Edinburgh and New York: Chambers, 2006).
Bonsdorff, Bertel, *The History of Medicine in Finland 1828–1918* (Helsinki: Societas scientarum fennica, 1975).
Brummer-Korvenkontio, Markus, *Virusten ja prionien luonnonhistoriaa: Myyräkuumeesta SARS: iin, Ebolasta AIDS:iin ja arboviruksesta lintuinfluenssaan* (Helsinki: Helsinki University Press, 2007).

New medical knowledge in the parish 391

Europaeus, Mikko, 'Kansankulttuuri', in *Pitäjä ison kiven takana: Lemin historia* (Jyväskylä: Lemin kotiseutuyhdistys & Lemin kunta, 2009).
Fenn, Elizabeth A., *Pox Americana: The Great Smallpox Epidemic of 1775–82* (New York: Hill and Wang, 2001).
Ferngren, Gary B., *Medicine and Religion: A Historical Introduction* (Baltimore, MD: Johns Hopkins University Press, 2014).
Forsius, Arno, *Sosiaali- ja terveydenhuollon kehitys Hollolassa ja Lahdessa vuoteen 1865* (Hämeenlinna: Lahden kaupunki, 1982).
——, 'Haartman, Johan (1725–1787)', in *Suomen Kansallisbiografia*, 10 vols (Helsinki: Suomalaisen Kirjallisuuden Seura, 2003–2007), IV (2004), pp. 425–7.
——, 'Spöring, Herman Diedrich (1701–1747)', in *Biografiskt lexikon för Finland*, 4 vols (Helsinki: Svenska litteratursällskapet i Finland, 2008–2011), I (2008).
Gadd, Pehr and Otto Bökman, *Politico-oeconomisk afhandling, om förmon af kopp-ympningens widtagande i Finland* (Åbo, 1763).
Haartman, Joh[an] Joh[ans]son, *Tydelig underrättelse, om de mäst gångbara sjukdomars kännande och motande genom lätta och enfalliga hus-medel, samt et litet res- och hus-apothek* (Åbo, 1765).
Hakkarainen, Susanna and Henna Sinisalo, *Tappava tauti, pelätty pelastaja – isorokon ja rokotuksen historiaa* (Helsinki: Suomen lääketieteen historian seura, 2012).
Haltia, Matti and Antti Vaheri, 'Johan Haartman – Suomen lääketieteen isä', *Duodecim*, 122:23 (2006), 2919–28.
Hornborg, A. J., *Sammandrag af Domkapitlets i Borgå härförinnan otryckta Cirkulärbref (1725–1829) i alfabetisk och kronologisk följd utarbetadt* (Borgå, 1872).
Ihre, Thomas, *Abraham Bäck: Mannen som reformerade den svenska sjukvården* (Stockholm: Atlantis, 2012).
Jägervall, Martin, *Nils Rosén von Rosenstein och hans lärobok i pediatrik* (Lund: Studentlitteratur, 1990).
Jalkanen, Kaarlo, *Lukkarin- ja urkurinvirka Suomessa 1809–1870* (Helsinki: Suomen kirkkohistoriallinen seura, 1976).
Julku, Maria, '"For your own benefit and defence." Persuading peasants to participate in castle building in early modern Ostrobothnia', in Kari Alenius, Maija Kallinen and Maria Julku (eds), *Tieto vai mielikuvat? Kohtaamiset, representaatiot ja yhteisöt muuttuvassa maailmassa* (Rovaniemi: Societas Historica Finlandiae Septentrionalis, 1986), pp. 115–30.
Kontturi, Saara-Maija, *Suomen varhaisen piirilääkärilaitoksen tavoitteet ja niiden toteutuminen* (Helsinki: Suomen lääketieteen historian seura, 2015).
Koskinen, Seppo and others, *Suomen väestö* (Gaudeamus: Helsinki, 2007).
Laine, Tuija, 'Katederilta kansan pariin: Suomalainen lääketieteellinen kirjallisuus 1600- ja 1700-luvuilla', in Raimo Jussila and others

(eds), *Tieto ja kirja* (Helsinki: Suomen tietokirjailijat ry, 2001), pp. 190–210.

Leikola, Anto, 'Eurooppalainen luonnontiede', in Matti Klinge (ed.), *Kuninkaallinen Turun Akatemia 1640–1808: Helsingin yliopisto 1640–1990* (Helsinki: Otava, 1987), pp. 679–703.

Lext, Gösta, *Studier i svensk kyrkobokföring 1600–1946* (Gothenburg: Göteborgs universitet, 1984).

Maaniitty, Elina, 'Befolknings- och folkhälsofrågornas framväxt i Sverige på 1700-talet', *Historisk tidsskrift för Finland*, 105:4 (2020), 441–69.

Marjanen, Jani, *Den ekonomiska patriotismens uppgång och fall: Finska hushållningssällskapet i europeisk, svensk och finsk context 1720–1840* (University of Helsinki: Helsinki, 2013).

Myllyniemi, Seppo, *Vihdin historia 1800–1918: Vihti Venäjän vallan aikana* (Jyväskylä: Vihdin kunta, 1990).

Naakka-Korhonen, Mervi, 'Kuu ja terveys', in Eija Starck and Laura Starck (ed.), *Kansanomainen ajattelu* (Helsinki: Suomalaisen Kirjallisuuden Seura, 2007), pp. 79–96.

Nurminen, Raili, *Säkylän historia*, I (Jyväskylä: Säkylän Kunta ja Seurakunta, 1970).

Nyholm, Bertel, *Kyrkan i Munsala: en historisk översikt med anledning av Munsala kyrkas 200 års jubileum 1992* (Munsala: Munsala evang. luth. församling, 1992).

Ropponen, Jari, *Joutsenon historia* (Jyväskylä: Joutsenon kunta ja seurakunta, 1997).

Satokangas, Reija, 'Isostavihasta seurakuntahallinnon uudistukseen (1722–1864)', in Kyösti Elo, Reija Satokangas and Jouko Vahtola (eds), *Iin seurakunnan historia* (Jyväskylä: Iin seurakunta, 1998), pp. 97–176.

——, 'Seurakunta muuttuvassa maailmassa (1865–1980)', in Kyösti Elo, Reija Satokangas and Jouko Vahtola (eds), *Iin seurakunnan historia* (Jyväskylä: Iin seurakunta, 1998), pp. 177–331.

Sevio, Martta, *Kankaanpään seurakunnan vaiheita vuoteen 1970* (Rauma: Kankaanpään seurakunta, 1970).

Sjögren, Iréne, *Mannen som förlängde människolivet: En trilogi* (Stockholm: Carlssons, 2006).

Sköld, Peter, 'The birth of population statistics in Sweden', *The History of the Family*, 9:1 (2004), 5–21.

——, *The Two Faces of Smallpox: A Disease and its Prevention in Eighteenth- and Nineteenth-Century Sweden* (Umeå: Umeå University, 1996).

Snowden, Frank M., *Epidemics and Society: From the Black Death to the Present* (New Haven, CT: Yale University Press, 2019).

Soininen, Gunnar, 'Suomalaisen almanakan lääketieteellisistä kirjoituksista', in Kustaa Vilkuna (ed.), *Suomen almanakan juhlakirja* (Helsinki: Helsingin yliopisto, 1957), pp. 97–106.

Teittinen, U. K., 'Uudenkaupungin rauhasta kunnallishallinnon perustamiseen', in Martti Ruuth (ed.), *Juvan historia* (Pieksämäki: Juvan seurakunta ja kunta, 1957), pp. 173–455.

Turpeinen, Oiva, 'Lastensuojelu ja väestökehitys: Lastensuojelun lääkinnällinen ja sosiaalinen kehitys Suomessa', in Panu Pulma and Oiva Turpeinen (eds), *Suomen lastensuojelun historia* (Helsinki: Lastensuojelun Keskusliitto, 1986), pp. 269–470.

Turun Wiikko-Sanomat.

Väärä, Seija, 'Kiskon ja Suomusjärven historia historiallisen ajan alusta kunnallishallinnon uudistamiseen 1347–1865', in Anja Sarvas and Seija Väärä (eds), *Kiskon ja Suomusjärven historia*, I (Jyväskylä: Kiskon ja Suomusjärven kuntien ja seurakuntien historiatoimikunta, 1998), pp. 105–629.

Vilkuna, Kustaa H. J., *Paholaisen sota* (Helsinki: Teos, 2006).

Vuorinen, Heikki S., *Tautinen Suomi 1851–1865* (Vaajakoski: Tampere University Press, 2006).

Ylönen, Aulikki, *Pöytyän, Yläneen ja Oripään historia vuoteen 1865* (Helsinki: Pöytyän, 1969).

Epilogue: the piety of Enlightenment – much more than rationalism

Anders Jarlert

A change of emphasis

Music is a different space of experience which reveals new horizons of expectation to the attentive listener. The oratorio *The Creation* by Josef Haydn (1732–1809), composed 1797–1798 with texts from the Bible and Milton's *Paradise Lost*, may serve as an example. Here, what I have described as 'the Now in Church History' in another context is concentrated in one single point. In Haydn's depiction of the creation, the horizon of expectation is being rolled up for new worlds. It is no longer the Creator or his Word of creation that is placed in the centre, but the effect of the Word, that is the Light. This shows how Enlightenment was by no means atheistic or even merely deistic; instead, it shifted the emphasis from revelation and eternity into creation and its mysteries. God's creative Word is being whispered by the choir, while the created Light is presented almost as a horizon of expectation for the not yet launched 'Big Bang'. My example is from immediately after the introduction's depiction of chaos:

> No. 2 Recitative and Chorus
> RAPHAEL. In the beginning God created the heaven and the earth.
>   And the earth was without form, and void; and darkness was upon
>   the face of the deep.
> CHORUS. And the Spirit of God moved
>   upon the face of the waters.
>   And God said, Let there be light:
>   and there was light.
> URIEL. And God saw the light, that it was good: and God divided
>   the light from the darkness.

Epilogue: the piety of Enlightenment

The British historian Mark Berry describes this as 'Haydn's greatest coup de théâtre'.[1] It is clear that God is still the Creator of the world, who creates by his Word only, and separates the light from the darkness; but the emphasis, and thus the interest of this Christian oratorio and its audiences, has moved from God to the created light.

A long-term influence exercised by a kind of pious Enlightenment practice was the strange Swedish custom of a Good Friday performance of Haydn's *Creation* in some churches. This custom persisted for most of the nineteenth century until finally the Baroque Renaissance of late Romanticism in the 1890s paved the way for the passion music of Heinrich Schütz (1585–1672) and Johann Sebastian Bach (1685–1750), which thus entailed a return to a religious context that emphasized and entered into the liturgical and homiletical context of the day, instead of trying to escape from it.

Enlightenment changed the emphasis from revelation to creation and its mysteries. This should not be taken to mean that early modern or Lutheran orthodox theology had not included creation and nature. On the contrary, early modern theology spoke of the two books, the Book of Nature and the Book of Grace. This concept was further developed by enlightened scientists like Linnaeus and others in the physico-theological tradition. Nature was studied as a book, written by God. This Book of Nature could be read just like the Bible.[2] Thus, Linnaeus interpreted creation by modern means within the old framework. However, an emphasis could change without destroying the system; but even a small change of emphasis could change the world view, though without excluding God or traditional orthodoxy.

The vital importance of empiricism

In his most influential thesis on the Enlightenment, *Försök til en afhandling om uplysningen* (1793), the Swedish philosopher and

---

1 Mark Berry, 'Haydn's *Creation* and Enlightenment Theology', *Austrian History Yearbook*, 39 (2008), 25–44 (34). This paragraph is derived from Anders Jarlert, 'Kyrkohistoriens nu', *Svensk Teologisk Kvartalskrift*, 95:4 (2019), 237–53 (243–44).
2 For more information on Linnaeus' thoughts on the books, see Uppsala University's Linné online website – http://www2.linnaeus.uu.se/online/ide/natursyn.html.

highly engaged official Nils von Rosenstein stressed the importance of empiricism. In his definition of Enlightenment, he took his starting point in material experience, including its hidden properties.[3] Enlightenment is further defined as true, sufficient and applicable knowledge.[4] Rosenstein declares that mathematical methods cannot be used in philosophy, but also that human passions may lead the scientist astray. He especially mentions curiosity, pride, fear, impatience, feebleness and delusion.[5] Furthermore, Rosenstein distinguishes between knowledge, learning and Enlightenment – as well as between the characteristics knowledgeable, learned and enlightened.[6] His entire thesis is supported by the empiricism of John Locke (1632–1704) as well as by the state doctrine of Montesquieu, in service of the social bliss of mankind.[7] Rosenstein's thesis was published only a few years after Immanuel Kant's essay pondering the question 'What is Enlightenment?', where Kant tried to synthesize early modern rationalism and empiricism.[8]

Some Enlightenment ideas were also of great importance to Christian revival movements. For example, Count Zinzendorf and the Moravians emphasized the value of philosophy, religious liberty, the importance of the human side of the Bible and its optimistic views on human bliss.[9] In Pietism, spiritual experience became a main interest. Emphasis shifted from theory to empiricism, the Bible being understood as a book of spiritual experience rather than as a book of doctrinal teaching and proof.

---

3 Nils von Rosenstein, *Försök til en afhandling om uplysningen, til dess beskaffenhet, nytta och nödvändighet för samhället, understäldt kongl. vetenskaps-academien vid præsidii nedläggande den 26 augusti 1789 ...* (Stockholm: Johan A. Carlbom, 1793), pp. 5–6.
4 Rosenstein, *Försök til en afhandling om uplysningen*, p. 24.
5 Rosenstein, *Försök til en afhandling om uplysningen*, pp. 16–17.
6 Rosenstein, *Försök til en afhandling om uplysningen*, p. 33.
7 Torkel Stålmarck, 'Nils von Rosenstein', in *Svenskt Biografiskt Lexikon* (Stockholm: Norstedts, 1918–), XXX (1998–2000), p. 439; Sten Lindroth, *Svensk lärdomshistoria*, II: *Stormaktstiden* (Stockholm: Norstedts, 1975), p. 192.
8 Michael Rohlf, 'Immanuel Kant', in Edward N. Zalta (ed.), *The Stanford Encyclopedia of Philosophy* (Stanford, CA: Stanford University, Metaphysics Research Lab, 2020), https://plato.stanford.edu/entries/kant/ [accessed 1 November 2021].
9 Emanuel Linderholm, *Sven Rosén och hans insats i frihetstidens radikala pietism* (Uppsala: Almqvist & Wiksell, 1911), p. 47.

Separation as a key concept of Enlightenment

As early as 1689, King Charles XI of Sweden had allowed philosophical freedom at Swedish universities, though it was not to interfere with Christian faith or doctrine, or with the contents of the Bible. The King tried to strike a compromise leading to a separation between the philosophical and theological areas, each with its own particular responsibilities.[10] During the eighteenth century, 'the separation of religion from law gradually increased'.[11] Philosophy was separated from theology, and reason from experience. This observation is also applicable in many other areas, including religious ones.

Johan Peter Boström (1764–1814) of Berghem in western Sweden, an ordinary country rector, had defended a thesis in Greifswald in 1788 in which he energetically rejected a poetic reading of the book of Joshua, asserting that the sun and moon actually stood still in the sky. Whether he was in fact the author of the thesis is of no importance here. But when, in 1805, he left his post as a teacher in Uddevalla on the west coast of Sweden, this town was described as a place 'where people have never forgotten his dignified and moving presentation of the sacred truths of Religion',[12] a mode of expression highly germane to enlightened ways of speaking about the Christian faith. An orthodox position could hence be defended in an uncompromising way at the same time as this position no longer seemed to have any function for the practical description of religion. This example reveals that a separation could sometimes be made between the formal demands of orthodoxy and practical needs involved in describing the religious map, even when experienced by the very same theologian.

Enlightenment as language

During the 'enlightened' era, the language and style of the Enlightenment were also employed by persons who would not and

---

10 Gunnar Eriksson (ed.), *Svensk lärdomshistoria*, IV: *Gustavianska tiden* (Stockholm: Norstedts, 1981), pp. 464–5.
11 Sören Koch and Kristian Mejrup, 'Introduction: the Enlightenment', in Kjell Å. Modéer and Helle Vogt (eds), *Law and the Christian Tradition in Scandinavia: The Writings of Great Nordic Jurists* (London: Routledge, 2021), pp. 153–61 (p. 153).
12 'där man sedan aldrig glömt hans värdiga och rörande framställningssätt av Religionens heliga sanningar'; Elias Trägård and Johannes Boström resp., *Dissertatio academica de quiete solis ac lunæ, Jos. Cap. X. 12–14* (Greifswald, 1788), p. 11, § 5.

cannot be labelled 'enlightened', or at least not exclusively described as such. A couple of examples illustrate this.

In Sven Johansson Hjerton's (1741–1809) sermon when the local clergy swore allegiance to new Swedish king Gustaf IV Adolf in 1792, fervid sentiments coexisted with a serious wonder at the passivity of Providence at the murder of King Gustav III. References to 'our mildest king' and similar expressions are mixed with an orthodox, biblical rhetoric of mourning, including a traditional reference to Lamentations 5:16 ('The crown is fallen from our head; woe unto us, that we have sinned!'). This verse had, for example, been quoted in the funeral sermons for Queen Dowager Hedvig Eleonora (1717) and King Charles XII (1719), but it still occurred in the Jewish lamentation for all synagogues on the lamentation day after the death of Gustav III (1792).[13]

A perhaps even better example is to be found in a funeral sermon of 1747 by Petrus Eneroth (d. 1761) on the rather enlightened theme 'About the Highest Wisdom: 1. The teachers of the Highest Wisdom, 2. The doctrine of the Highest Wisdom'. However, the exposition could by no means be described as 'enlightened' in any significant sense: it is a Christocentric sermon with a strong flavour of Moravianism.[14] One may wonder if this phenomenon is merely a 'neutral' matter of terminology, or if it might have something to do with theological censorship. An 'enlightened' addition in a Moravian sermon would of course more easily slip through the hands of the censor than a sermon that favoured Moravianism in an obvious manner.

---

13 Mattias Steuchius, 'I dag Konung, i morgon död': Matthias Steuchius likpredikan över Riksänkedrottningen Hedvig Eleonora och Änkehertiginnan Hedvig Sofia. Utg. med inledning och kommentar av Anders Jarlert, Meddelanden från Kyrkohistoriska arkivet i Lund, 11 (Lund: Lunds universitets kyrkohistoriska arkiv, 2015), p. 69; Hugo Valentin, Urkunder till judarnas historia i Sverige (Stockholm: Bonniers, 1924), p. 94.

14 'Om den högsta Visheten: 1. Den högsta vishetenes Lärare, 2. Den högsta vishetenes Lära'; Petrus Eneroth, Siälenes hwila och sötaste ro, Med tilflycht i sann och lefwande tro til Frälsaren, fins i thess namn, blod och år, Then äger högst wisshet som nåden åtrår. Förestäldt i Enfaldig Lik-Predikan, Tå fordom Probsten för Kinds Härad, Samt Kyrckoherden för Giellstads Församlingar, Then Högähreuwyrdige och Höglärde Herren, Nu Salig hos Gud, Herr Daniel Ödman, Efter långsam och med beständigt tolamod öfwerwunnen siukdom, i Guds Sons tro den 4 Aug. Saligen afled... den 15 Sept. Åhr 1747 (Gothenburg: Joh. Georg Lange junior, 1747).

Epilogue: the piety of Enlightenment 399

A third example is a sermon by Clas Henrik Cramer (1762–1835), preached in Gothenburg Cathedral in 1797. Here the language is of a mixed character. The theme is 'Some advantages, which a man who has become spiritually wise, gains through his good company in meekness and wisdom'. Among expressions such as 'the Eternal Wisdom' and 'blissful' are some fierce attacks on 'the false light which, in our so-called enlightened time, is so fiercely and eagerly scattered', and the total impression is Christocentric with an emphasis on Christ both as redeemer and as a model. Whether the target of this sermon was radical philosophy or the rational mysticism of Emanuel Swedenborg (1688–1772) is hard to tell, but it emphasizes the dual face of the Enlightenment. Cramer also has direct references to conservative Pietism and most notably to Stockholm minister Anders Nohrborg's (1725–1767) much-used collection of sermons.[15]

A rational mysticism

The new emphasis on the Light also paved the way for a rational mysticism. As Linnaeus' systematization of nature had by no means diminished his astonishment before the Creator and the creation, the technicalities of the eighteenth century were quite compatible with sometimes rather strange mysteries in both thought and cult. Swedenborg, the Swedish mystic and Christian anti-Trinitarian, was also a scientist and inventor who was a member of several scientific academies, national and foreign. His transition from science to mysticism has fascinated his biographers, who have not always understood that this combination, rather than being incomprehensible, is actually quite significant for his time, and still more for the following decades. Swedenborg regarded his dreams as empirical material, and he labelled himself a *mystikos* – that is, an initiated person.[16] To be initiated is to be enlightened in a special way.

---

15 'Några fördelar, hwilka en människa, som blifwit andeligen wis, winner genom sin goda umgängelse i sagtmodighet och wisdom'; 'Här finns visserligen tidstypiska uttryck som "lycksalig" och "den Eviga Wisheten", men C angriper "det falska sken, som uti wår så kallade uplysta tid, så häftigt och ifrigt kringsprides"'; quoted in Anders Jarlert, *Göteborgs stifts herdaminne 1620–1999*, III: *Fässbergs, Älvsyssels södra och norra kontrakt* (Gothenburg: Tre Böcker, 2016), p. 589.
16 Lars Bergquist, *Swedenborgs hemlighet: Om Ordets betydelse, änglarnas liv och tjänst hos Gud: En biografi* (Stockholm: Natur och Kultur, 1999), p. 451, based on Swedenborg's *Arcana Caelestia* § 4099.

Rational mysticism became highly modern towards the end of the century, especially in the rituals and ceremonies of the Masonic and other orders. Spreading Enlightenment through initiation and secret wisdom, these orders were in their turn caricatured by poets such as Johan Henric Kellgren (1751–1795) and Carl Michael Bellman (1740–1795). Simultaneously, the esoterism of Swedenborg was attacked by both the Lutheran orthodox and the Moravians, who defended the Christian teaching on the Holy Trinity and redemption against all attempts to supplement or 'correct' the biblical word with subjective revelations.

Several enlightenments

The picture of the Enlightenment era as spiritually arid, with an exclusive cult of reason and a prudent proclamation of utility, became commonly accepted, even though this identification ultimately stems from its contemporary counter-currents.[17]

From the sixteenth century onwards, 'enlightened' had primarily been applied in connection with the enlightenment of the Holy Spirit, as Martin Luther describes it in his explanation of the third article of the Creed. The Enlightenment, however, entailed an emphasis on rationality, whereas the esoteric movements of the late eighteenth century used 'enlightened' with reference to the special knowledge transmitted by secret rituals.[18] It is important to observe that these different meanings of 'enlightenment' did not succeed one another in time or space, but coexisted. Historians must note that 'enlightenment' in its old theological sense was actual and relevant long after 1775, and may thus have coloured the ideological understanding of this term as well.[19] The three meanings of the term 'enlightenment' described above would then coexist side by side, though not without contact or conflict. The situation is made complex by the combination of theological and profane dimensions when speaking of 'the enlightenment of the understanding'.[20]

---

17 Inge Jonsson, 'Förord', in Martin Lamm, *Upplysningstidens romantik: Den mystiskt sentimentala strömningen i svensk litteratur*, 2 vols (Enskede: Hammarström & Åberg, 1981), I, pp. v–ix (p. vii).
18 See also Daniel Lindmark, *Uppfostran, undervisning, upplysning: Linjer i svensk folkundervisning före folkskolan* (Umeå: Umeå University, 1995).
19 Lindmark, *Uppfostran, undervisning, upplysning*, p. 85.
20 'förståndets upplysning/upplyst förstånd'; Lindmark, *Uppfostran, undervisning, upplysning*, p. 88.

Epilogue: the piety of Enlightenment

The great Swedish poet Bishop Esaias Tegnér (1782–1846) used his light metaphors without any clear distinction between Christian enlightenment in the old, Lutheran sense and the later, philosophical use of the term. His understanding of 'enlightenment' was not secularized but spiritualized in a manner that surprised both contemporary readers of the catechism and the philosophers. In this, emphasis shifted from the Holy Spirit to a somewhat indeterminate, dual spiritual enlightenment. But the most self-evident understanding of 'enlightened' in a liturgical context was still the blessing: 'The LORD make his face shine upon thee', as it was read in the old Swedish translation: 'Herren upplyse sitt ansigte öfver eder' – that is, 'The LORD enlighten his face upon you'. Consequently, enlightenment is not limited to the enlightenment in the human being, from God or from man, but includes in ritual repetition what we may call the self-enlightenment of God: God reveals himself and lets his face be enlightened and known to humanity.[21]

Bible criticism and Romanticism could be combined in one person, such as the lector and pastor Johan Gothenius (1721–1809), who was the first in Sweden to apply the methods of comparative exegesis. Simultaneously, Gothenius was the first person in Swedish literary history who noticed and was captivated by the Poems of Ossian.[22]

Moderate Enlightenment ideas influenced representatives of Romanticism such as the bishop and hymn writer Frans Michael Franzén (1772–1847). The natural religion of the Enlightenment went willingly hand in hand with revealed religion, and its optimistic world view saw in each natural phenomenon and in every event a sign of the goodness of God and the expediency of creation.[23]

'Enlightened' reforms

From 1993 onwards, Swedish historian of ideas Tore Frängsmyr declared that Sweden had no Enlightenment worth

---

21 Anders Jarlert, 'Hördes ljuset? Den kyrkliga receptionen av Esaias Tegnér', in Jerker Blomqvist (ed.), *Esaias Tegnér, Texter och läsningar* (Lund: Tegnérsamfundet, 2011), pp. 69–83 (pp. 81–2).
22 Gösta Lundström, 'Johan Gothenius', in *Svenskt Biografiskt Lexikon* (Stockholm: Norstedts, 1918–), XVII (1967–1968), pp. 185–6.
23 Martin Lamm, *Upplysningstidens romantik: Den mystiskt sentimentala strömningen i svensk litteratur*, 2 vols (Stockholm: Geber, 1918–1920; repr. Enskede: Hammarström & Åberg, 1981), I, p. 220.

mentioning.[24] However, like other expressions describing patterns and flows of thought and ideas, 'Enlightenment' has sometimes been shortened and simplified in such a way that the important differences between the radical French Enlightenment and the more moderate German one have been equalized. Emphasis has often been put on philosophical and political Enlightenment more than on the ecclesiastical or pious variants of it. A reason for this obvious fact, as Tine van Osselaer has stated, is that Christian Enlightenment was expressed in new practices rather than in theoretical reflections, and that this activism resulted in numerous reforms in various countries. The Belgian example saw pious Enlightenment confronting French rationalist Enlightenment, the latter having influenced the irreligion and moral decay of a whole region since the French Revolution.[25] Thus, 'enlightened' influences laid the foundations of modern alterations in piety; but these changes worked in very different directions. As I have shown in my introduction to the volume *Piety and Modernity*, 'enlightened' reforms might concern Bible translation, devotion, education, or pastoral and social care. An extreme example of an 'enlightened' Bible translation project is the 'long' Bible committee in Sweden at work from 1773 until the final royal confirmation of the new translation in 1917.

The general sensitivity of rationalism has often been neglected. Rationalism was not only about draining swamps or growing potatoes. Paradoxically, it was not only based on reason, but open towards knowledge beyond representations produced by our senses – even though, like Christian orthodoxy, rationalism would not and could not rely on emotions as its foundation.

The success of enlightened reforms in devotion, public and private, was dependent on different historical and political circumstances in different countries. It is hence not surprising that the distinction between Pietism and pious Enlightenment could sometimes be subtle, since many aspects of education and pastoral care were common to the Pietists and the 'enlightened'. In a country like Sweden, Pietism almost always found itself confronting state regulations of religion,

---

24 Tore Frängsmyr, *Sökandet efter upplysningen: En essä om 1700-talets svenska kulturdebatt* (Höganäs: Wiken, 1993).
25 Tine van Osselaer, 'Reform of piety in the southern Netherlands/Belgium', in Anders Jarlert (ed.), *Piety and Modernity*, The Dynamics of Religious Reform in Northern Europe 1780–1920, 3 (Leuven: Leuven University Press, 2012), pp. 101–24 (p. 102).

ecclesiastical authorities and local opinion; but pietistic and enlightened churchmen nevertheless shared an individualist approach, as has long been observed in ecclesiastical historical research.[26]

Around 1810–1815 some of the reformers, influenced by Romanticism, embarked on a new course, satisfying some of the orthodox demands (a new emphasis on the incarnation, atonement and resurrection of Christ, as well as on eternity and eternal salvation), though still maintaining the enlightened accent on education and the individual. Compared to Catholic Enlightenment, the differences are undeniable; but a common striving for purity in devotional life is obvious. The historical dimension inherent in Romanticism encouraged emphases on other ideals: religious originality, pious heroism and a new mysticism. Romanticism often tried to cast a shadow across pious Enlightenment as being a faith apprehended by the mind but not by the heart.[27] However, this should not overshadow their similarities.

The dual face of the Enlightenment may be observed in Voltaire and Christian von Wolff, or in Sweden in Queen Lovisa Ulrika (1720–1782) and also in the influential parish theologian Henric Schartau (1757–1825), in whom orthodoxy, Pietism and rationalism came together.[28] The understanding of the pious Enlightenment as a faith apprehended by the mind but not by the heart obscures the fact that Romanticism actually draws on pious Enlightenment. This was, of course, rooted in philosophical Wolffianism and its logical rationalism, rather than in Voltairianism.

Communication and dialogue as a personal complement

Written communication and printed media were used in new ways, and the emphasis on preaching and catechetical instruction was extended to conversation or dialogue. Literary historian

---

26 See, for example, Wolfgang Schmidt, *Lars Lefrén – en herrnhutisk upplysningsteolog vid Åbo Akademi* (Åbo: Åbo Akademi, 1940), in which Moravianism is combined with Enlightenment in the very same theologian, or, more recently, Kelly Joan Whitmer, *The Halle Orphanage as Scientific Community: Observation, Eclecticism, and Pietism in the Early Enlightenment* (Chicago, IL: University of Chicago Press, 2005), where science and Pietism are seen to be combined in the Halle Orphanage.
27 Anders Jarlert, 'Introduction', in Jarlert, *Piety and Modernity*, pp. 7–24 (pp. 13–14).
28 Tore Hulthén, *Jesu regering: En studie i Henric Schartaus teologiska åskådning i jämförelse med ortodox, pietistisk och wolffiansk lärouppfattning* (Lund: Gleerup, 1969).

Ann Öhrberg has shown that the 'new' rhetoric of Moravianism is not a great innovation, but a creative reusage and refunctionalization of established rhetorical techniques. Sensibility and authenticity became central values, and the texts' means of collective identification.

Towards the end of the century, classical rhetoric was dethroned. In eighteenth-century Sweden, classical rhetoric can be seen as 'directly connected with the creation of formal power, the contemporary political system and the production of gender'. A characteristic feature is the promotion of equality (social and gender-orientated): 'the ideal communication should be shaped as a dialogue between equals'.[29]

The conversation was instrumentalized by pietist movements, such as Moravianism and Württemberg Pietism. The dialogue books by Magnus Friedrich Roos (1727–1803), translated from German, were accepted in the conservative movement that originated with Schartau, and they were used as a complement and alternative to traditional methods of instruction. To their readers, the dialogue books could also serve as a substitute for novels and worldly travel stories. They contain dialogues for certain professional groups, such as soldiers, seamen or rural people; dialogues pertaining to a certain stage of life, such as old age; but also dialogues on a biblical book such as the Revelation of St John. The Roos books combine traditional Lutheran teaching on the three estates and their responsibilities with an emphasis on the new life of the faithful according to pietistic principles.[30]

Eschatology and the Theodicy problem

During the eighteenth century, the previously strong consciousness of the impending end of the world was transformed into a more personal interest in eschatological matters. In the revival movements, the question was more a matter of personal motivation and destiny and less an interpretation of the signs and times on the collective. Simultaneously, the orthodox interpretation of fires, wars

---

29 Ann Öhrberg, 'Den smala vägen till modernitet: Retorik och människosyn inom 1700-talets svenska herrnhutism', *Kyrkohistorisk årsskrift*, 107 (2007), 51–69 (66). Translation mine.

30 Anders Jarlert, 'Pietism and community in Magnus Friedrich Roos' dialogue books', in Jonathan Strom (ed.), *Pietism and Community in Europe and North America, 1650–1850* (Leiden: Brill, 2010), pp. 307–28.

and natural disasters as part of God's plan and harbingers of the Last Judgement was called in question. Such interpretations could also be altered by tragic events, such as the great earthquake in Lisbon on All Saints' Day 1755 in which around fifteen thousand people were killed and thirty-five out of forty churches destroyed. Prevailing views of Providence were shaken.

Voltaire used the earthquake in his *Poème sur le désastre de Lisbonne* (1756), and in *Candide* (1759) he attacked Gottfried Leibniz's (1646–1716) concept from 1710 of 'the best of all possible worlds', a world closely supervised by a rational and benevolent deity. Rousseau used the earthquake as an argument for a more naturalistic way of life. The traumatic event was commented on in the whole Western world and also interpreted in sermons. The Jesuits were eventually dispelled from Portugal by royal edict, largely as a result of their preaching on the earthquake as a consequence of the sins of Lisbon. The earthquake has been labelled a 'catalyst for reform'.[31] Portugal was secularized, and the power of the Church was circumscribed.

In the Nordic countries the earthquake was reported, with some delay, as the first modern media disaster. The first printed report in Sweden dates from 8 December 1755.[32] But the clergy, and not the press, were still the most important conveyors of news.[33] The religious interpretation was still associated with collective sin, punishment and repentance. The royal Intercession Day proclamation (*böndagsplakat*) of 1756, publicly read on New Year's Day in all churches, spoke about 'God's terrible judgments of wrath', and that 'the Highest' employed two ways of inducing human beings to repentance and conversion: kindness and punishment, with explicit mention of the earthquake. The Swedish realm had been graciously spared. The prescribed texts for the sermon on the general days of prayer were Nahum 3 on the Lord as an avenger, with the prophecy on the destruction of Nineveh, and Hosea 4 on the punishment of Israel, with accusations against priests and people.[34] However, in

---

31 Kathy Warnes, 'The 1755 Lisbon Earthquake: Marquis Pombal uses science to rebuild', Stories in Science [blog], https://storiesinscience.weebly.com/the-1755-lisbon-earthquake-marquis-pombal-uses-science-to-rebuild.html# [accessed 1 November 2021].
32 Gunnar Broberg, *Tsunamin i Lissabon: Jordbävningen den 1 november 1755, i epicentrum och i svensk periferi* (Stockholm: Atlantis, 2005), p. 33.
33 Broberg, *Tsunamin i Lissabon*, p. 38.
34 Broberg, *Tsunamin i Lissabon*, pp. 39, 151–4.

practice, this was interpreted within a new framework of individualism in respect of both divine wrath and grace. In Denmark, Hans Adolph Brorson (1694–1764) wrote a poem on *Lissabons ynkelige Undergang ved Jordskælv* (1756) with parallels to Babylon, Nineveh and contemporary times. Even a description of the natural causes of earthquakes, such as the Danish-Norwegian pietist bishop Erik Pontoppidan's *Afhandling om Werldenes Nyhet* (1755), suggests a coming judgement in smoke and fire. Linnaeus commented on the earthquake as an act of retribution in the traditional manner in his manuscript 'Nemesis divina'.[35]

A frequent and self-evident parallel was the destruction of Jerusalem in the year 70, or rather the story of Jerusalem's destruction after Josephus, which was commonly read or quoted in the churches on the tenth Sunday after Trinity. After the earthquake, references to Jerusalem's destruction were made even in the secular press.[36] A significant change in the interpretation of the destruction of Jerusalem was made by the Swedish poet Bengt Lidner (1757/1759–1807) in the oratorio *Jerusalems förstöring* (1787). God's wrath is limited, while the disasters themselves are simultaneously depicted as universal in such a way that the spectator is moved by the destiny of the prisoners and may identify with them. The collective expression 'the Jews of Jerusalem' is to a great extent replaced by named persons, which is new compared to traditional uses. The Jews are treated as individuals, the curse being limited to the High Priest and his contemporaries. Since the story is presented in a theatrical manner, all generalization is weakened. This is conveyed through a personal love story. The loving couple is pardoned by Titus, and their love embodies a future even for Jews.[37] Personalization thus changes both the balance between punishment and mercy and the final outcome of the story.

Pious Enlightenment and anti-Catholicism

At the end of the seventeenth century, polemical theology in the form of anti-Catholicism was still strong in the Nordic countries.

---

35 Broberg, *Tsunamin i Lissabon*, pp. 46–7.
36 Broberg, *Tsunamin i Lissabon*, p. 35.
37 Anders Jarlert, 'Lidners *Jerusalems förstöring* – och Wallins', in Anna Cullhed and others (eds), *Poetens monopolium: Bengt Lidner 250 år (1757/1759–2007/2009)* (Lund: Ellerströms, 2009), pp. 279–91 (pp. 285–6, 289).

Simultaneously, statues and images of the Holy Virgin, side altars, pilgrimages, holy wells and other popular pre-reformatory customs were kept almost without problems. Such practices could coexist with a Lutheran orthodox outlook in matters of faith, both on a collective and on an individual level. Not until the mid-eighteenth century did bishops strongly criticize such 'medieval' traces and customs. Images of the Holy Virgin were condemned and were to be removed from churches because they were considered to encourage 'superstition' among ordinary people.[38] Consequently, it would seem as if it was not Lutheran orthodoxy but the Enlightenment that tried to get rid of ancient and popular religiosity.

It may appear peculiar that these vigorous efforts were simultaneous with a weakening of dogmatic anti-Catholicism, and even a renewed interest in Roman Catholic splendour and ceremonies; but in practice, the transition was often smooth. The holy well became a health well, and the altar of the Virgin was used as a women's altar for offerings at churchings. The distance between sacrificing to the sacred and sacrificing time and money for one's health was not, after all, a very great one: there was but a small step from mysticism to rationalism, from sacred to healthy.

Conclusion

The Enlightenment entailed a change of emphasis: from the Creator and his Word of creation to the creation as such. The latter was often read as a Book of Nature, an equivalent of the Bible. Empiricism competed with rationalism. To the Pietists and the Moravians, spiritual experience was essential, and the Bible became a book of experience rather than a book of doctrinal teaching. Pious dialogue books supplemented traditional edifying literature.

Distinctness was a key concept in the Enlightenment. Each had his or her own responsibility and was not to mix this with the responsibilities of others. The Enlightenment may also be studied in terms of language, with reference to linguistic practices among Pietists and Moravians.

---

38 Terese Zachrisson, *Mellan fromhet och vidskepelse: Materialitet och religiositet i det efterreformatoriska Sverige* (Gothenburg: University of Gothenburg, Department of Historical Studies, 2017), pp. 301–13; Monika Weikert, *I sjukdom och nöd: Offerkyrkoseden i Sverige från 1600-tal till 1800-tal* (Gothenburg: University of Gothenburg, 2004), pp. 239–48.

Rationalism could be converted to rational mysticism in dreams or in rituals. To be initiated was to be 'enlightened' in a special way. An important result is that there were several Enlightenments that cannot be assigned to a single formula. In the Nordic countries, 'enlightened' was used in at least three senses: the enlightenment conveyed by the Holy Spirit in the Lutheran understanding; the Enlightenment of rational philosophy; and the special knowledge transmitted by secret rituals. In the liturgical blessing, the Lord even 'enlightened' his face upon the congregation.

Enlightened reforms could be practical and sensitive. Simultaneously, 'enlightened' bishops abolished popular medieval customs that had been left unassailed by the former, orthodox, ones.

Finally, the earthquake of Lisbon in 1755 questioned Providence and the enlightened belief in the best of worlds. That also brought a change in the interpretation of texts instrumental to the understanding of tragedies, such as the destruction of Jerusalem. Here, personalization might modify both the balance between punishment and mercy in God and the final outcome of the story. While deism without a mystery was easily punctured by radical Enlightenment, pious Enlightenment paved the way for Romanticism's restoration of mystery in individualized form. Consequently, the piety of the Enlightenment amounted to much more than mere rationalism.

Bibliography

Digital sources

Rohlf, Michael, 'Immanuel Kant', in Edward N. Zalta (ed.), *The Stanford Encyclopedia of Philosophy* (Stanford, CA: Stanford University, Metaphysics Research Lab, 2020), https://plato.stanford.edu/entries/kant/ [accessed 1 November 2021].

Warnes, Kathy, 'The 1755 Lisbon earthquake: Marquis Pombal uses science to rebuild', Stories in Science [blog], https://storiesinscience.weebly.com/the-1755-lisbon-earthquake-marquis-pombal-uses-science-to-rebuild.html# [accessed 1 November 2021].

Printed sources and literature

Bergquist, Lars, *Swedenborgs hemlighet: Om Ordets betydelse, änglarnas liv och tjänst hos Gud: En biografi* (Stockholm: Natur och Kultur, 1999).

Berry, Mark, 'Haydn's creation and Enlightenment theology', *Austrian History Yearbook*, 39 (2008), 25–44.

Epilogue: the piety of Enlightenment

Broberg, Gunnar, *Tsunamin i Lissabon: Jordbävningen den 1 november 1755, i epicentrum och i svensk periferi* (Stockholm: Atlantis, 2005).

Eneroth, Petrus, *Siälenes hwila och sötaste ro, Med tilflycht i sann och lefwande tro Til Frälsaren, fins i thess namn, blod och år, Then äger högst wisshet som nåden åtrår. Förestäldt i Enfaldig Lik-Predikan, Tå fordom Probsten för Kinds Härad, Samt Kyrckoherden för Giellstads Församlingar, Then Högährewyrdige och Höglärde Herren, Nu Salig hos Gud, Herr Daniel Ödman, Efter långsam och med beständigt tolamod öfwerwunnen siukdom, i Guds Sons tro den 4 Aug. Saligen afled ... den 15 Sept. Åhr 1747* (Gothenburg: Joh. Georg Lange junior, 1747).

Eriksson, Gunnar (ed.), *Svensk lärdomshistoria*, IV: *Gustavianska tiden* (Stockholm: Norstedts, 1981).

Frängsmyr, Tore, *Sökandet efter upplysningen: En essä om 1700-talets svenska kulturdebatt* (Höganäs: Wiken, 1993).

Hulthén, Tore, *Jesu regering: En studie i Henric Schartaus teologiska åskådning i jämförelse med ortodox, pietistisk och wolffiansk lärouppfattning* (Lund: Gleerup, 1969).

Jarlert, Anders, *Göteborgs stifts herdaminne 1620–1999*, III: *Fässbergs, Älvsyssels södra och norra kontrakt* (Gothenburg: Tre Böcker, 2016).

——, 'Hördes ljuset? Den kyrkliga receptionen av Esaias Tegnér', in Jerker Blomqvist (ed.), *Esaias Tegnér, Texter och läsningar* (Lund: Tegnérsamfundet, 2011), pp. 69–83.

——, 'Introduction', in Anders Jarlert (ed.), *Piety and Modernity*, The Dynamics of Religious Reform in Northern Europe 1780–1920, 3 (Leuven: Leuven University Press, 2012), pp. 7–24.

——, 'Kyrkohistoriens nu', *Svensk Teologisk Kvartalskrift*, 95:4 (2019), 237–53.

——, 'Lidners *Jerusalems förstöring* – och Wallins', in Anna Cullhed and others (eds), *Poetens monopolium: Bengt Lidner 250 år (1757/1759–2007/2009)* (Lund: Ellerströms, 2009), pp. 279–91.

——, 'Pietism and community in Magnus Friedrich Roos' dialogue books', in Jonathan Strom (ed.), *Pietism and Community in Europe and North America, 1650–1850* (Leiden: Brill, 2010), pp. 307–28.

Jonsson, Inge, 'Förord', in Martin Lamm, *Upplysningstidens romantik: Den mystiskt sentimentala strömningen i svensk litteratur*, 2 vols (Enskede: Hammarström & Åberg, 1981), I, pp. v–ix.

Koch, Sören and Kristian Mejrup, 'Introduction: the Enlightenment', in Kjell Å. Modéer and Helle Vogt (eds), *Law and the Christian Tradition in Scandinavia: The Writings of Great Nordic Jurists* (London: Routledge, 2021), pp. 153–61.

Lamm, Martin, *Upplysningstidens romantik: Den mystiskt sentimentala strömningen i svensk litteratur*, 2 vols (Stockholm: Geber, 1918–1920; repr. Enskede: Hammarström & Åberg, 1981), I.

Linderholm, Emanuel, *Sven Rosén och hans insats i frihetstidens radikala pietism* (Uppsala: Almqvist & Wiksell, 1911).

Lindmark, Daniel, *Uppfostran, undervisning, upplysning: Linjer i svensk folkundervisning före folkskolan* (Umeå: Umeå University, 1995).
Lindroth, Sten, *Svensk lärdomshistoria*, II: *Stormaktstiden* (Stockholm: Norstedts, 1975).
Lundström, Gösta, 'Johan Gothenius', in *Svenskt Biografiskt Lexikon* (Stockholm: Norstedts, 1918–), XVII (1967–1968).
Öhrberg, Ann, 'Den smala vägen till modernitet: Retorik och människosyn inom 1700-talets svenska herrnhutism', *Kyrkohistorisk årsskrift*, 107 (2007), 51–69.
Osselaer, Tine van, 'Reform of piety in the southern Netherlands/Belgium', in Anders Jarlert (ed.), *Piety and Modernity*, The Dynamics of Religious Reform in Northern Europe 1780–1920, 3 (Leuven: Leuven University Press, 2012), pp. 101–24.
Rosenstein, Nils von, *Försök til en afhandling om uplysningen, til dess beskaffenhet, nytta och nödvändighet för samhället, understäldt kongl. vetenskaps-academien vid præsidii nedläggande den 26 augusti 1789 ...* (Stockholm: Johan A. Carlbom, 1793).
Schmidt, Wolfgang, *Lars Lefrén – en herrnhutisk upplysningsteolog vid Åbo Akademi* (Åbo: Åbo Akademi, 1940).
Stålmarck, Torkel, 'Nils von Rosenstein', in *Svenskt Biografiskt Lexikon* (Stockholm: Norstedts, 1918–), XXX (1998–2000), p. 439.
Steuchius, Mattias, *'I dag Konung, i morgon död': Matthias Steuchius likpredikan över Riksänkedrottningen Hedvig Eleonora och Änkehertiginnan Hedvig Sofia. Utg. med inledning och kommentar av Anders Jarlert*, Meddelanden från Kyrkohistoriska arkivet i Lund, 11 (Lund: Lunds universitets kyrkohistoriska arkiv, 2015).
Trägård, Elias and Johannes Boström resp., *Dissertatio academica de quiete solis ac lunæ, Jos. Cap. X.12–14* (Greifswald, 1788).
Valentin, Hugo, *Urkunder till judarnas historia i Sverige* (Stockholm: Bonniers, 1924).
Weikert, Monica, *I sjukdom och nöd: Offerkyrkoseden i Sverige från 1600-tal till 1800-tal* (Gothenburg: University of Gothenburg, 2004).
Whitmer, Kelly Joan, *The Halle Orphanage as Scientific Community: Observation, Eclecticism, and Pietism in the Early Enlightenment* (Chicago, IL: University of Chicago Press, 2005).
Zachrisson, Terese, *Mellan fromhet och vidskepelse: Materialitet och religiositet i det efterreformatoriska Sverige* (Gothenburg: University of Gothenburg, Department of Historical Studies, 2017).

Index

Whenever names occur both in the running text and in footnotes on the same pages, references to the latter have been omitted. Editors of edited volumes who are quoted in that capacity are indexed with reference to the first mention of the book in question. Italicized figures refer to chapters by the contributors to this book.

Åbo, *see* Turku
absolutism 211n1, 212, 217, 267
adiaphora (res indifferentes)
   133–5, 159
Adler, Simon 345n16
Adlerbeth, Gudmund Jöran 233,
   247, 250
Adolfsson, Maria 62n18
Adserballe, Hans 279n33
Age of Liberty 16, 17
Age of Revolution 99, 102, 105–6,
   108, 120–2
Ågren, Henrik 20, 136n18,
   151–210
Agricola, Mikael 87
agriculture 11, 43–4, 109, 111–12,
   348–50
Ahlberger, Christer (ed.) 103n13
Ahnert, Thomas 7n5 and 7
Ahokas, Minna 80n3
Alanen, Aulis J. 378n45
Alenius, Kari (ed.) 369n14
Allardt, Anders 368n12
Alleine, Joseph 297n24
Alm, Mikael 241
alms 162, 196–7, 205, 207, 273
Alstrup, Erik (ed.) 37n9

Altona 12, 21, 288n3, 311–35
   passim, 355–6; *see also* free
   town; toleration
Amundsen, Arne Bugge 18, *33–53*
Ancher, Peder Kofod 275–7, 279
Anderberg, Göran 243n38
Andersson, Bertil 116n57
Angel, Ivert (ed.) 181n48
Angell, Karen 220
angels 89–90, 173–4
Ångström, Inga Lena 149n60
Anners, Erik 282n38
anthropology 20, 263
anti-Catholicism 148, 202n45,
   206–7, 228, 406–7; *see also*
   priestcraft
anti-clericalism 136
antiquarians 132, 144, 169,
   170n23, 184, 196, 233; *see*
   also collectors
Antonelli, Leonardo 236, 248
Antonsson, Niklas 104n20
Apelseth, Arne 45n32
apostolic succession 247, 254
Appel, Charlotte 14n43 and 45,
   34n2, 161n8, 288n2–3,
   358n55

Appold, Kenneth G. 302n42
architecture 184
Arentz, Frederik 306
Armfelt, Gustaf Mauritz 233, 247
Árnason, Jóhann Páll (ed.) 192n4
Aronsson, Peter 70n44, 103n13, 106
Asplund, Anneli 94n33
Assembly of Estates 212, 228
Aston, Nigel 3n5
autobiographical texts 82–3, 91, 93–4 ; see also ego documents; Lebensläufe

Bach, Johann Sebastian 395
Bachmann, Hans-Martin 11n29, 314n11
Bagge, Povl and others (eds) 265n8
Baggerman, Arianne 83n10
Bak, Sofie Lene and others (eds) 303n49
Bakke, Harald 42n28
ballads 303
Balle, Nicolai Edinger 163, 179–80
Balling, Emanuel 307
Bang, Hans Otto 294
Banning, Knud 295n19, 297n26
Barlow, Richard Burgess 54n1
Barnes, Harry Elmer 193n7
Barnett, S. J. 3n5, 5n11, 148n57
Barnhart, Robert K. 366n8
Bartholin, Thomas 371n25
Basedow, Johann Bernard 12, 318
Bastholm, Christian 8, 39, 46, 241, 253
Bauckham, R. J. 322n25
Bebbington, David 4n10
Beccaria, Cesare 282
Beck, Catherine 264n1
Beckus, Paul 346n18
Bell, David A. 3n5
Bellisomi, Carlo 247
Bellman, Carl Michael 400
Beneke, Chris (ed.) 322n27

Benzelius the younger, Erik 195
Bergen 18, 35–6, 41, 178, 296n21, 306, 317
Bergh, Karl Fredrik 104, 107, 109, 113, 368, 382
Berg, Johannes van den (ed.) 3n5
Bergin, John (ed.) 55n2
Bergquist, Lars 399n16
Bergstrand, Carl-Martin 146n50
Bergström, Carin 70n44
Berling, Ernst Heinrich 301
Bernis, François-Joachim de Pierre de 235, 240, 248, 250
Berntson, Martin 134n11
Beronius, Magnus 242–3
Berrios, German E. 264n1
Berry, Mark 395
Beutel, Albrecht 8n21; (ed.) 3n5
biblical exegesis 300, 401
Birn, Raymond 303n47
Bivins, Roberta (ed.) 263n1
Bjurling, Oscar (ed.) 113n50
blasphemous adoration 161
Blécourt, Willem de (ed.) 133n7
Bloch, Coppel Samson 305
Bloch, Søren 294
Blomqvist, Jerker (ed.) 401n21
Blomstedt, Yrjo (ed.) 16n51
Bobé, Louise 235n13; (ed.) 235n13
Bodensten, Erik 7n17
Bohnen, Klaus (ed.) 346n21
Bökman, Otto 373n9
Bönig, Holger 288n3
Bonsdorff, Bertel 365n5
book market 14, 290, 298, 304
Boström, Johannes 397n12
Boström, Johan Peter 397
Botin, Anders af 195, 200, 203–6
Bourdieu, Pierre 82
Boxström, Anders 366
Boye, Per 351n31
Bradley, James E. (ed.) 4n10
Bredsdorff, Thomas 50; (ed.) 358n52

Bregnsbo, Michael 7n17, 15n47, 17n55, 42n27, 66n32, 102n9, 106n26, 108n33, 110n40, 118n64, 120n70, 358n56
Breul, W. (ed) 267n15
Bricka, Carl Frederik (ed.) 295n19
Brilkman [Weber], Kajsa, *see* Weber [Brilkman]
Bringéus, Nils-Arvid (ed.) 144n43
broadsheets 83, 85, 91–4
Broberg, Gunnar 11n30, 405n32
Brodd, Sven-Erik (ed.) 149n60
Brodkorb, Clemens (ed.) 246n46
Brohed, Ingmar 69n21
Broman, Fredrik Conrad 199n33, 206n60
Broman, Olof Johansson 132, 136–8
Broocman, Carl Fredric 137
Brorson, Hans Adolph 406
Brown, Michael 3n5
Brummer-Korvenkontio, Markus 364n1, 372n28
Brun, John Nordahl, *see* Nordahl Brun
Bruun, Mette Birkedal (ed.) 319n23
Bugge, Ragne 171n24
Bulman, William J. (ed.) 3n5
bureaucracy 18, 34, 40–1, 49, 62–3, 70n42, 230, 335; *see also* central government; local government
Burgess, J. Peter (ed.) 38n13
Burson, Jefferey D. 3n5
Butterwick, Richard (ed.) 2n3
Bynum, Caroline 157n3

Calvinism 134; *see also* Reformed tradition
cameralism 304, 347, 348n25, 357; *see also* economic theory
Canon law 54, 264–5
Caradonna, Jeremy L. 10n27
Carlsson, Ingemar 13n41
Carlsson, Sten 101n8

Carlsson, Ulla (ed.) 15n46
Caroline Mathilde (Queen) 47
Carson, D. A. (ed.) 322n25
Castro, Raquel Poy 55n3
catechetical instruction 38, 63–4, 403
catechism 17, 79, 100–2, 179, 297, 323, 330, 334, 401
cathedrals 145–6, 148, 238, 245, 399
Catholicism, *see* Roman Catholicism
Celsius, Anders 10
censorship 15, 20–1, 41, 222–6, 252, 287–308 passim, 358, 398; *see also* book market; publishing
central government 11, 15, 36, 40–1, 62, 106, 192, 196, 233, 289n6, 341–2, 345–6; *see also* Chancellery; Clerical Estate; Copenhagen; courts of law; Estates, Political; *Riksdag*; Royal Chancery; Stockholm
Champion, J. A. I. 5n11
Chancellery 34, 40–1, 48, 233, 306, 313n5, 316, 325, 327, 355
Charles IX 19
Charles XI 58, 397
Charles XII 398
Charles XIII 236
Chartier, Roger 27n10
cheap print 303
Christensen, Hjalmar 45n32
Christensen, Palle Ove 16n50, 178n37
Christensen, Sigrid Nielsby 268n18, 269n20
Christensson, Jakob 8n23, 102n9, 112n44, 192n4; (ed.) 62n18
Christian V 214
Christian VI 216, 274
Christian VII 15, 47, 222, 224, 288, 347, 352n33

Christiania (Oslo) 348
Christiansfeld 12, 21, 341, 342n3, 356–8; *see also* Moravianism
Christina (Queen) 234, 249
church buildings 38, 138, 139n28, 145–6, 148–9, 155–187 passim, 238, 245–7, 251, 255, 399
Church Law (1686) 14, 54, 57–60, 60n13, 63, 65, 71, 73, 79, 87, 376n39
Church Ordinance
 (1537–39) 54, 286
 (1571) 54, 58
 (1629) 312
churchwardens 157, 167; *see also* sextons
Chydenius, Anders 15, 120n71, 250, 372
circular letters 60, 386
civil liberties 15, 17, 100
civil servants 40, 42, 47, 195, 369
Claesson, Urban 60n13, 313n4
Clark, J. C. D. 6n15
Classicism 184
clergy conference 37, 57
clergymen 15, 39, 43–5, 72, 92, 107, 113, 117, 121, 250, 254, 312; *see also* pastors
Clerical Estate 64, 245, 250–3, 322
Cochanski, Dagmar 288n3
Colbert, Jean-Baptiste 345
Cole, Charles Woolsey 345n15
collectors 131, 147, 219; *see also* antiquarians; topographers
Collegium Medicum 372–3, 379, 384
Collett, John Peter 222n31
Colloquy of Montbéliard 159
Commission of Statistics (*Tabellkommissionen*) 364
common sense 20; *see also* rationality

conduct 38–9, 48, 60, 74, 110, 115, 117, 139, 263, 265, 279, 355, 380
confessional culture 6, 8–9, 14, 18, 20–1, 47, 50, 74, 100, 322, 335, 395
confessionalization 5, 7, 54, 58, 171, 312
confirmation 14, 63–4, 68–9, 245, 314, 402
conscience 251–2, 278, 300
Conventicle Act 17, 134, 252
conversion 13, 89, 94, 206, 267, 405; *see also* Pietism; Moravianism
Copenhagen 10n28, 11–12, 18–19, 34–5, 39, 41, 43–4, 47, 49–50, 79, 180, 211, 219–23, 266, 270–2, 275, 281, 289, 290n7, 297, 301, 304–7, 314, 317, 325, 327, 330, 332–3, 343n9, 347, 351–5
coronation 242, 247
coup d'état of Gustav III 17, 229
courts of law 263–4, 266–7, 270–8 passim, 282–3
Cramer, Jens (ed.) 41n23
Cramer, Johan Andreas 294
Creutz, Gustaf Philip 233, 249
Cronholm, Christopher 147
Cronstedt, Fredrik Adolf Ulric 144–5, 149
Cullhed, Anna and others (eds) 406n37

d'Alembert, Jean le Rond 9
Dahl, Gina 298n29, 347n22
Dalin, Olof von 13, 195
Damsholt, Tine 358n53
Danish Code (1683) 54, 265–6, 272, 278, 281, 288, 323, 344
Danish colonies 355n41; *see also* West Indies
Danstrup, John (ed.) 322n26
Darnton, Robert 303n47, 305n54

Davies, Owen (ed.) 133n7
Davies, Simon (ed.) 2n3
Daxelmüller, Christoph 161n10
Dekker, Rudolf 83
Dekker, Ton (ed.) 358n53
Del Colle, Ralph 199n32
Derham, William 84
Desprez, Louis Jean 235, 238, 250
Diderot, Denis 9, 268
Dieleman, Kyle J. 312n1, 315n14–15, 322n27, 327n49, 333n73
Dijkman, Petter 138
diocesan chapters 58–60, 139, 144, 253, 366
Dippel, Johann Conrad 318, 343
disability 79–95 passim
dissenters 233, 326
Dorfner, Thomas 351n30, 357n49
Driedger, Michael D. 318n19
Dyrvik, Ståle 211n1

ecclesiastical administration 39, 62–3, 145
ecclesiastical law 54, 61; *see also* Danish Code (1683); canon law; Church Law (1686)
Échallard, Olivier 300n36
economic reforms 229, 345; *see also* economic theory; manufacture; mercantilism
economic theory 289n6, 291, 345; *see also* manufacture; mercantilism
Edelstein, Dan (ed.) 5n12
Edgren, Henrik 99n3
Edgren, Lars 113n50, 115n53
Edict of Toleration (1781) 230–2, 251
education, *see* catechism; parents; teaching
egalitarianism 358, 359n59
ego documents 83, 85, 87, 90, 93; *see also* autobiographical texts; *Lebensläufe*

Eijnatten, Joris van 54n1; (ed.) 6n17
Ekeblad de la Gardie, Eva 10
Ekman, Emanuel 131–2
Elf, Mads Julis (ed.) 264n1
Eliassen, Knut Ove (ed.) 213n3
Ellehøj, Svend (ed.) 295n19
Elstad, Hallgeir (ed.) 181n48
empiricism, empirical knowledge 1, 9, 62, 193, 395–6, 399, 407
Eneroth, Petrus 398n14
Engelhardt, Juliane 343
Engelsing, Rolf 290n8
England 243, 304, 322
enlightened government 317, 328; *see also* Gustav III; Struensee, Johann Friedrich
enlightened orthodoxy 129, 149, 231
Enlightenment
  Catholic 403
  French 2, 3n5, 13, 129, 136, 329, 402
  German 8, 9n25, 84; *see also* Wolff, Christian
  moderate 9, 401
  pastoral 18, 33, 38, 49, 56
  pious 395, 402–3, 406–8
  radical 9, 408
  symbolic world of 8, 330
  theology 8, 253
Enochsson, Ernst 65n28, 66n30
Erichsen, John (ed.) 184n52
Eriksen, Anne 219n21, 221n27
Eriksen, Trond Berg (ed.) 225n34
Eriksson, Gunnar (ed.) 397n10
Eriksson, Nils 192n3, 195n15–16, 206n63, 207n65
esotericism 21, 400, 408; *see also* mysticism; Freemasonry
Espinosa, Gabriel Sánchez (ed.) 2n3
Estates, Political 99, 101, 120, 122; *see also* central government
Eucharist 63–5, 68, 79, 88, 182–3

Europaeus, Mikko 385n70
Evertsson, Jakob 191n2
Ewald, Martin (ed.) 318n19

Fæhn, Helge (ed.) 40n22
Fahl, Laurids Kristian (ed.) 219n20
Faitini, Tiziana 322n25
family of the pastor 36, 39–40, 44, 50
Fant, Eric Michael 198n28
fasting 196–7, 200, 207
Fastrup, Anne (ed.) 220n23
Favreau, Marc and others (eds) 220n23
Feldbæk, Ole 291n10, 352n34
Fenn, Elizabeth A. 366n8, 371n24
Ferngren, Gary B. 385
Fernow, Erik 132
Fersen, Axel von 233, 249, 250
Finch, Jonathan and others (eds) 36n7
Fine, Jonathan B. 254n77
Fink-Jensen, Morten (ed.) 14n43, 191n2
Finnish Economic Society (*Finska hushållningssällskapet*) 373
Fischer, Ole 354
Flæten, Jon Øygarden (ed.) 276n30
Florutau, M. I. 55n3
folk magic 179; see also magic; superstition
folk medicine 385–6; see also healers
folklore 43, 85, 144, 281n36
forensic psychiatry 263, 268, 279n33, 280–3; see also melancholy
Forselius, Tilda Maria 13n41
Forsius, Arno 371n24, 372n26, 374n34
Forssander, M. E. 61n15
Forssenius, Anders 148
Forsskål, Peter 15
Foss, Gunnar (ed.) 220n23
Foucault, Michel 348n24

France 129, 302, 303n47, 305; see also Enlightenment, French
Francis, Keith A. (ed.) 103n15
Francke, August Hermann 291, 342; see also Pietism; Hallensian Pietism
Frängsmyr, Tore 401
Franzén, Frans Michael 401
Fredrik Adolf (Duke) 235
Frederik I 244
Frederik III 214
Frederik IV 214, 234, 318
Frederiksen, Hans Jørgen 161n10
Fredrikshald 36
free town 12, 19, 21, 316–18, 322, 324, 330, 333, 356; see also Altona
freedom of print 287–9, 307–8
freedom of religion 12, 17, 192, 327
Freemasonry 243–4
free port 351
Freytag, Erwin 318n19
Friedl, Hans 348n24
Friedrich II 347
Friis, Ib 348n24
Frijhoff, Willem 319n23
Fritz, Johan Michael 155
Frydenlund, Bård 12n33

Gadd, Pehr 372–3
Gad, Finn 355n41
Gagneraux, Bénigne 235, 237
Gascoigne, John 2
Gatz, Erwin (ed.) 246n46
Gawthrop, Richard 4n10
Gay, Peter 1
Geijer, Erik Gustaf 198n28
generations 20, 42, 67, 330, 379
geography 11, 34, 56, 67, 327
Gersdorff, Henrietta von 342
Gezelius the elder, Johannes 79
giants 214n4, 216–17, 219, 221–2, 225, 227; see also Icelandic sagas

Gibbon, Edward 194
Gibson, William (ed.) 103n15
Gjörwell, Carl Christopher 195, 204
Glebe-Møller, Jens 318n19, 356n47
Goldie, Mark (ed.) 349n25
Gothenburg 104, 113, 116–18, 121, 232, 245, 251, 399
Gothenius, Johan 401
Gothus, Laurentius Paulinus 134
grace 69, 89, 269–70, 277, 302, 395, 406
Gram, Hans 219
Granberg, Gunnar 241
Grandt-Nielsen, Finn 171n27
Grane, Leif (ed.) 295n19
Greenland 355n41
Green, Michaël (ed.) 322n27
Gregory, Brad S. 185n56
Gregory, Jeremy 55
Grell, Ole Peter 191n2
Grenda, Christopher S. (ed.) 322n27
Grongstad, Siv Bente and others (eds) 44n31
Gross, Hanns 231n3
Grundtvig, N. F. S. 181
Grunewald, Thomas 342n5
Guiffrey, Jules (ed.) 240n29
Gunnerus, Johan Ernst 213, 220–3
Gustav III 17, 20, 55, 224, 230–56 passim
Gustav IV Adolf 374
Gustav Vasa 244
Gyldensteen, Constance Frederikke Henriette 184

Haakonssen, Knud (ed.) 2n4, 7n19, 17n55
Haartman, Joh[an] Joh[ans]son 372n28, 373n29
Haartman, Johan 84, 371–3, 377
Hagberg, Lars 62n17
Hagesæther, Olav 38n14, 46n40
Hakkarainen, Susanna 364n1, 366n8, 367n9, 371n24, 383n66

Håkon Hårfagre 214
Halenius, Engelbert 65
Hallberg, Peter 192n4, 195n17
Halle 10, 47, 220, 268, 314, 328, 342, 356, 403n26; *see also* Pietism, Hallensian
Haltia, Matti 372n26
Hämäläinen, Pekka (ed.) 341n2
Hamburg 250n62, 317, 325, 327, 331, 333
Hamm, Berndt 185
Hansen, Anita 158n6
Hansen, Holger 342n3, 352n33, 353n36 and 38; (ed.) 341n2
Hansen, Lars Ivar and others (eds) 316n17
Hansen, Peder 42, 47–9
Hansen, Søren Peter (ed.) 6n16, 358n52
Hanska, Jussi (ed.) 79n1
Hansson, Klas 255n78
Hansson, Stina 91n26, 92n30
Härdelin, Alf (ed.) 149n60
Harnesk, Börje (ed.) 55n3
Härter, Karl (ed.) 315n12; and others (eds) 314n9
Hartlapp, Johannes 322n27
Harvey J. Graff and others (eds) 14n44
Hasselgren, Anders 104, 109–10
Havsteen, Sven Rune 158n6
Haydn, Josef 394–5
Hayton, D. W. 55n2; (ed.) 55n2
Heal, Bridget 155n2
healers 85, 385; *see also* folk medicine
health 84, 113, 221, 247, 263–4, 275, 282–3, 292, 367, 378, 385, 407; *see also* midwives; vaccinations
Hedvig Eleonora (Queen Dowager) 398
Heffermehl, A. V. 37n8
Heiberg, Knud 343

Hein, Lorenz 318n21
Helander, Dick 253n75
Helander, Olle 113n50
Hellemaa, Lahja-Irene (ed.) 87n18
Helslot, John (ed.) 358n53
Hemmingsen, Ralf 20, *263–86*, 300n34
Hennings, Beth 240
Henningsen, Peter 67n33, 178n37
Hermansen, Karsten 37n12
Herrnhut 341–2, 351n35, 353n38, 355–6; *see also* Christiansfeld; Moravianism
Hersleb, Peder 277n31, 292
Hessler, Carl Arvid 195n17
Hill, Christopher 315n13
Hindmarsh, D. Bruce 4n10
Hinners, Linda 12n34
Hirschfeldt, Johan 15n46
historiography 191–228 passim
  historical criticism 7
  historical narratives 19, 144
Hjerton, Sven Johansson 398
Hjort, Frederik Christian 177
Hobbes, Thomas 211n1, 217
Hodacs, Hanna (ed.) 11n30
Høiris, Ole (ed.) 168n18
Højer, Andreas 299
Holberg, Ludvig 12, 43, 211, 213, 217–28 passim, 356
Holenstein, André 315n12
Holm, Anders 181n47
Holm, Bo Kristian (ed.) 5n12
Holm, Peder Jakobsen 294
Holmboe, Tage 265n8
Holy Roman Empire 317
holy wells 147, 407
Hornborg, A. J. 366n7, 368n11, 369n14 and 16
Horstbøll, Henrik 15n47, 289n5; (ed.) 17n55
households 17, 39, 61, 65–6, 68–71, 107, 108n31, 109, 117, 121, 273, 333

Household Code 100–1, 107, 114, 120; *see also* listeners; patriarchal relations; Three Estates, doctrine of
Hovi, Tuija (ed.) 6n16
Huguenot 317, 331, 335
Hülphers, Abraham 137–8
Hulthén, Tore 403n28
Hume, David 193
hymns 41, 48, 81–3, 87–94 passim, 225, 401; *see also* music

Icelandic sagas 211, 213–14, 220; *see also* giants; Snorri (Sturluson)
Idum, A. R. (ed.) 158n5
Ihalainen, Pasi 6n17, 99n1, 100n4, 103n16–17, 105n25, 106n26, 108n33, 110n40, 112n43, 118n64, 119n66, 120n69 and 70, 121n72, 202n45, 241n32; (ed.) 12n33
Ihre, Thomas 365n3
Ilsøe, Harald 303n49
Imsen, Steinar 16n52
indifferentism 84, 133, 356
individualism 9, 54, 120, 358, 406
  individualizing practices 56
infanticide 93–4, 263–83 passim
Inger, Göran 58n10
Ingesman, Per 316n17, 358n51
Ingram, Robert G. (ed.) 3n5
inner person 273, 270, 279–82
Innocent XII 234
Intercession Days 104, 107, 119, 239, 405
introspection 263, 267–9, 279
Israel, Jonathan 9, 15, 346n21

Jacobsen, Gunnar 41n26
Jacobsen, Lis (ed.) 157n4
Jägervall, Martin 370n20, 372n28
Jakobsen, Jesper 20, *287–311*

Jakobsen, Rolv Nøtvik 20, *211–29*; (ed.) 220n23
Jakobstad 104, 111, 121
Jalkanen, Kaarlo 370n22, 374n33–6, 381n57, 382n60, 383n64
Jantzen, Albert Thorvald 295n19, 297n26
Jarlert, Anders 21, *394–410*; (ed.) 4n10
Jena 47, 220, 297
Jenner, Edward 366
Jensen, Chr. Axel 161n9
Jensen, Jens Toftgaard 315n13
Jensen, M. Langballe 300n33
Jensen, Mette Kristine, 173n30
Jesuits 232, 300, 405
Jews 17, 178, 230–3, 305–6, 318, 326–32, 334–5, 398, 406
Johannisson, Karin 11n31
Johannsen, Birgitte Bøggild 158n6, 184n52
Johansen, Anfinnur (ed.) 41n23
Johansen, Hans Christian 346n19
Johansen, Hugo (ed.) 184n54
Johansson, Egil 14n44, 100n7
Johansson, Karl Herbert 65n28, 70n44
John (Johan) III 134
Johnsen, Egil Børre (ed.) 225n34
Jokipii, Mauno (ed.) 100n7
Jonsson, Inge 400n17
Jönsson, Nils Quiding 104, 114
Jordheim, Helge (ed.) 213n3
Jørgensen, Eva Krause 6n16, 17n55
Jørgensen, Harald 288n5
Jørgensen, Jens Ulf 266n11, 267n14
Jørgensen, Sven-Aage (ed.) 346n21
Jørgensen, Troels G. 265n8, 279n33
Joseph II 233–4, 239, 242, 250
Julku, Maria 369n14

Jürgensen, Martin Wangsgaard 19, 135n15, 139n28, *155–90*
jurisprudence 20, 263–83 passim; *see also* courts of law
jus talionis 265
Juslenius, Daniel 139–42
Jussila, Anja (ed.) 87n18
Jussila, Raimo and others (eds) 377n44
Juster, Susan 322n27

Kaiser, Jürgen 312n1
Kallinen, Maija (ed.) 369n14
Kalm, Pehr 81n5, 85n14
Kaplan, Benjamin J. 317n18, 319n22, 326n46
Karlsson, Mattias (ed.) 137n22
Karonen, Petri 57n5 and 7; (ed.) 192n3
Kaschuba, Wolfgang 70n42
Kaufmann, Thomas 177n34
Kelley, Donald R. 194n11 and 13
Kelly, James (ed.) 55n2
Keravuori, Kirsi 82n2, 83n10
Kessler, E. 215n7
Ketola, Hanna-Maija and others (eds) 92n30
Kjældgaard, Lasse Horne (ed.) 264n1
Kjær, Morten (ed.) 280n34
Kjöllerström, Sven 58n10, 245n44
Klinckowström, R. M. (ed.) 249n61
Klinge, Matti 86n15; (ed.) 375n37
Klueting, Harm 233n6, 242n34
Knudsen, Henning 348n24
Knudsen, P. U. 266n9, 267n19
Knudsen, Tim (ed.) 358n51
Koch, Carl Henrik 13n38
Koch, Ludvig 180n45, 181n49, 287n2, 290n9, 294n17
Koch, Sören 7n18, 313n3, 397n11
Kodzik, Joanna 341n1
Koefoed, Nina Javette 14n43, 67n32, 316n17; (ed.) 5n12, 316n17, 358n57

Kontturi, Saara-Maija 384n69
Kopitzsch, Franklin 318n19
Korkman, Petter (ed.) 7n18
Korpiola, Mia (ed.) 276n30
Koski, Kaarina 88n21, 89n26
Koskinen, Seppo (and others) 365n5
Koskinen, Ulla and others (eds) 111n42
Kouri, E. I. (ed.) 191n2
Kraack, Detlev (ed.) 354n40
Krause, Peter 346n19
Krefting, Ellen (ed.) 288n4
Kristiansand 12, 35–6, 47–50, 318
Kroesen, Justin 155n2
Kröger, Rüdiger (ed.) 7n18
Krogh, Tyge 266n12–13, 276n30, 281n36
Krohn, Julius 92n31
Krüger, Kersten 346n21
Kuhn, H. C. 215n7
Kvideland, Reimund 39n20

Labadie, Jean de 318
Lagerbring, Sven 195, 200
Lahde, G. L. 223n32
Lahtinen, Anu (ed.) 276n30
Laine, Esko M. 21, 79n1, 80n3, 81n4, 82n5 and 8, 91n29, 92n30, 100n7, 102n10, 106n28, 109n34, *364–93*; (ed.) 80n3
Laine, Tuija 18, *79–98*, 100n7, 101n17, 102n10, 106n28, 377n44; (ed.) 87n18
Laitenberger, Henrique 8n21
Lamm, Martin 400n17, 401n23
Lancaster, James A. T. 137n19
Landen, Leif 240
Landwehr, Achim 316n16
Langebek, Jakob 219
Langen, Ulrik 15n47, 289n5, 346n21, 358n57
Larre, Virginie 235n15
Larsen, Christian (ed.) 180n44

Larsson, Olle 66n31
Laugerud, Henning 139n28
Laurentius Petri 148; *see also* Church Ordinance (1571)
Lauridsen, John T. (ed.) 303n49
Laursen, John Christian 15n46, 288n5
Lebensläufe 91; *see also* Moravianism
Ledet, Thomas (ed.) 168n18
Legnér, Mattias 62n18
Lehner, Ulrich L. 4n8, 54n1, 55n3, 148n58, 242n32; (ed.) 4n8
Leibniz, Gottfried 84, 405
Leikola, Anto 375n37
Lenhammar, Harry 230n1, 233n7, 243n38, 250n66, 251n32
Lennersand, Marie 133n7
Leppin, Volker 276n30
Leufvén, Edvard 104n18
Levan, Erik 104
Levitin, Demitri 5
Lext, Gösta 366n6
Lidner, Bengt 406
Lieburg, Fred van (ed.) 4n10
Lilja, Einar 63n20
Lillie, Eva Louise (ed.) 173n30
Lindblom, Jacob Axelsson 8, 61
Linde, Martin 106n27
Lindemann, Mary 263n1, 276n30
Linder, Tage 61n14
Linderholm, Emanuel 396n9
Lindhardt, Poul Georg 69n21; (ed.) 277n31
Lindmark, Daniel 102, 108, 121
Lindroth, Sten 192n3 and 6, 396n7
Linnaeus, Carl 10–11, 129–30, 348n24, 395, 399, 406
Lisbon 405, 408
listeners 47, 73, 100, 107–19 passim, 121–2; *see also* Household Code
liturgy 14, 37, 40, 58, 64, 68, 156, 181, 231, 240, 242–6, 255–6, 395, 401; *see also* Sunday service

Index

liturgical revision 40–1, 48, 64, 67, 157, 182, 241–4, 252–5
liturgical texts 46, 104
liturgical objects 129–87 passim, 243–6
liturgical year 48, 104
Ljungberg, Johannes *1–29*, *312–40*, 134n13
local community 39, 48, 72, 108–11, 117
local government 70, 106; *see also* courts of law; diocesan chapter
city council 316, 325
Loenbom, Samuel 202n44, 203n51
Løgstrup, Birgit 358n58
Lönnroth, Erik 240
Louise (Queen) 44
Lovisa Ulrika (Queen) 403
Løyland, Margit (ed.) 11n32
Lundby, Jørgen 343
Lundh, Carl 69
Lundhem, Stefan (ed.) 64n24
Lundström, Gösta 401n22
Lundström, Nils Erik 202n43
Luther, Martin 46, 85, 158, 167–8, 178–9, 302, 400
Small Catechism 179
Lutheran confessional cultures 6, 14, 20
Lutheran confessionalization 7
Lutheran orthodoxy 18, 55, 58, 60–1, 66, 85, 88, 94, 131, 134–5, 159, 164, 250, 287, 407
Lutheran Reformation, *see* Agricola, Mikael; Olaus Petri; Laurentius Petri

Maaniitty, Elina 365n3
McClellan, James E. III 62n18
McCullough, Peter and others (eds) 103n15
MacIntyre, Alasdair 8
Mackelprang, Romel W. 86n15

McKenzie-McHarg, Andrew 137n19
magic 44, 50, 385; *see also* folk magic; superstition
Magnusson, Lars 10n29, 11n33, 314n10, 328n50
Mai, Claudia (ed.) 341n1
Mäkinen, Virpi (ed.) 7n18
Maliks, Jakob 293
Malmö 113–14, 121
Malmstedt, Göran 12n36, 65n28, 242n35, 315n13, 323n28; (ed.) 103n13
Malmström, Carl 117n61
manufactories 350–1
Margrete (Queen) 215
Markussen, Ingrid 14n43, 314n7, 350n27
Marnersdóttir, Malan (ed.) 41n23
mathematical methods 396
Mathesius, Lars 104, 108, 111–13, 120
Matheus, Ricarda 232n4
Mathieu, Richard 244n40
Matthiessen, Christian Wichmann 35n4
Mattias, Markus 267n15, 269n19
Mattias, Markus (ed.) 269n19
Matytsin, Anton M. (ed.) 5n12
Matzen, Henning 287n2
Mauzi, Robert 3n5
Mayes, Benjamin T. G. 299n32
Mazur, Peter A. 231n3
Medelius, Hans (ed.) 230n1
medicine 39, 42–4, 84, 94, 267–8, 370–1, 374; *see also* folk medicine; health; surgeons; surgery; vaccinations
Mejrup, Kristian 300n33, 313n3, 397n11
melancholy 263–86 passim; *see also* forensic psychiatry; mental suffering
Melanchthon, Philipp 302
Melkersson, Martin 99n2

Melton, James Van Horn 290n8
Mennander, Carl Fredrik 245
Mennander, Jacob 90
Mennonites 317
mental suffering 281; *see also* melancholy
mercantilism 12, 304; *see also* economic theory
Meyer, Dietrich (ed.) 341n1
Michalski, Sergiusz 155n2
Middle Ages 19–20, 57, 59, 129–54 passim, 155–90 passim, 192–210 passim, 212, 242, 244, 315, 407–8; *see also* traditional religion
Midelfort, Hans Christian Erik 276n30
midwifery 318
midwives 271–2, 368
Miettinen, Riikka 266n12, 276n30, 281n36
Miller, Nicholas B. (ed.) 10n29
Miller, Stephen 315n14, 332n68
missionaries 137; *see also* Moravianism
Modéer, Kjell Å. (ed.) 7n18
modern society/modernity 1, 81, 282, 402
Molbech, Christian 184
monks 136–7, 147, 164, 198, 202–3, 205
monasteries 201
monasticism 136
Montaiglon, Anatole de (ed.) 240n29
Montègre, Gilles 235n15
Montesquieu, Charles-Louis de Secondat 12, 396
Montgomery, Ingun (ed.) 58n10
Moravianism 74, 398, 404; *see also* Christiansfeld; *Lebensläufe*; Zinzendorf, Nikolaus Ludwig von
Mordt, Gerd (ed.) 11n32
Moretti, Paulo 233

Mortensen Kirketerp, Ditlev 168
Morton, C. (ed.) 148n59
Mosheim, Johann Lorenz von 194
Mossin, Hans 306–7
Mühleisen, Horst 346n19
Mührmann-Lund, Jørgen 333
Mullaney, Steven 319n22
Müller-Bahlke, Thomas (ed.) 356n48
Mulson, Martin (ed.) 9n26
Munck, Thomas 10n27, 17n55
Münster-Swendsen, Mia and others (eds) 7n20
music 82, 245, 325, 374, 376, 394–5; *see also* hymns
Myllyniemi, Seppo 368n11, 369n14 and 16
mysticism 240, 243, 256, 403, 407; *see also* esotericism
mystical bonds 185
mystical dimensions 243
mystical experiences 300
rational mysticism 399–400, 408

Naakka-Korhonen, Mervi 373n32, 385n70
Napoleonic wars 225
Nativité, Jeanne de la 300n35
natural law 7, 12, 20, 101, 217, 220, 226–7
natural resources 11, 41; *see also* topography
Neiiendam, Michael 8n21
Netherlands 305, 315
newspapers 94, 99
Nexø, Tue Andersen (ed.) 213n3
Nicolas, Armelle 300–2
Nilsson, Anna 92n30
Nilsson, Sara Ellis 196n23
Nøding, Aina (ed.) 288n4
Nohrborg, Anders 399
Nokkala, Ere 15n46
Nokkala, Ere (ed.) 10n29
Nooke, Martha (ed.) 3n5
Norberg, Anders 246

Nordahl Brun, Johan 213, 223, 227
Nordbäck, Carola 101n8, 103n17, 105n21, 106n26, 110n40, 118n65, 120n71, 192n6
Nordin, Carl Gustaf, 254
Nordin, Jonas 15n46, 16n49
Nordstrandh, Ove 13n42
Nordström, Peter 56n3
Noricus Philadelphus [Willibald Pirckheimer] 302n43
Normann, Carl-E. (ed.) 62n23, 101n8
Nørgaard, Lars Cyril 20, *287–311*; (ed.) 319n23
North Sea trade 317; *see also* Altona; Moravianism
novels 404
Nummela, Ilkka (ed.) 100n7
Nurmiainen, Jouko 192n3
Nurminen, Raili 383n66
Nyberg, Kenneth (ed.) 11n30
Nyborg, Ebbe 184n52
Nyholm, Bertel 376n39
Nyman, Magnus 231n2, 236n21

Odenadt, Gerhard 85
Odhner, Claes Theodor 240
Oeder, Georg Christian 348
Oertel, Christian 197n23
Oftestad, Eivor Andersen (ed.) 181n48
Öhrberg, Ann 404
Öhrströmer, Fredric (ed.) 62n17
Oja, Linda 133n7
Olaf Trygvason 215
Olaus Petri 148
Olaf Engelbrektsson 212
Olden-Jørgensen, Sebastian (ed.) 7n19, 218n19
Olesen, Brian Kjær 7n19, 12n37
Olesen, Jens E. (ed.) 191n2
Olofsson, Sven 109n37, 110n39
Olsen, Olaf (ed.) 291n10
Olsen, Poul Erik (ed.) 37n9

Olsson, Claes G. 85n14, 86n15
ordination 232, 245, 247
Örnhjelm, Claudius 196–8, 200, 203
Osander, Olof 61
Östlund, Joachim 102, 108
Ottesen, Christian 273n27
Overhoff, Jürgen and Andreas Oberdorf (eds) 4n8
Oxenbøll, Erik 304n51

Pabel, Hilmar M. 5n13
Palladius, Peder 157, 167
Palmqvist, Arne 231n2, 232n5, 233n8, 236n18, 239n22, 249n58, 250n62
pamphlets 15, 182, 268–70, 348n24
papacy 146, 249; *see also* Roman Catholicism
parents 65, 68, 70, 79, 81, 83, 85, 107–9, 117, 330, 369, 371, 380, 383–5; *see also* Household Code; patriarchal relations (obedience)
Parish, Helen L. 129n9
Parker, Kenneth L. 312n1, 315n14, 322n27
Parvio, Martti (ed.) 87n18
passions 396
Pastor, Ludwig Freiherr von 235n16
pastors 15, 17, 18, 21, 33–53 passim, 58, 64, 73, 109, 112, 114, 117, 132, 135, 137, 140, 142, 144, 147, 161n8, 163, 171, 177, 179, 180, 182, 232, 239, 273, 279, 297n24, 364–93 passim, 401; *see also* clergymen; Enlightenment
pastoral assessments 277–8
pastoral care 232, 402
pastoral certificates 277
pastoral duties 377
pastoral practices 18, 42, 44–6

pastors (cont.)
  pastoral purposes 242
  pastoral dignity 47
patriarchal relations (obedience)
    101–2, 109, 112, 116, 121; see
    also Household Code; parents
patriotism 99, 225, 358
Pedersen, Johannes 300n33
Pedersen, Mikkel Venborg 304n51
Peringskiöld, Johan 196
Petersen, Carl S. 216n11
Petrejus, Joel Jacob 253
Petterson, Christina 21, *341–63*,
    304n51
Peucker, Paul 344n13
Pfanner, Josef (ed.) 301n41
Philibert, Claude 305n54
Philip, Guntram 356
philology 5
philosophers 19, 84, 401
physico-theology 10, 84–5
Pickstone, John V. (ed.) 263n1
Pietism 7, 13, 60, 74, 85, 88, 94,
    134–5, 140, 266, 268, 279,
    282, 343–4, 396, 402–3; see
    also Francke, August Hermann;
    Spener, Philipp Jakob
  conservative 399
  Hallensian 268, 291, 343
  state 7, 16, 64
  Württemberg 404
pietist [dimensions, non-specific] 4,
    17, 19, 49, 228, 242, 282, 295,
    300, 313, 342, 358, 402, 404,
    407
  anthropology 20, 263
  bishop 406
  clinic 280
  diagnostics 281
  ethos 313
  ideas 13, 17, 39, 67, 253
  introspection 267
  leanings 304
  literature 13, 252, 263, 267,
    279, 292
  milieus 270
  practices 13, 283
  preachers 251
  sentiments 64, 66, 82, 280, 293,
    304
  theology 268
Pilo, Carl Gustav 242
Pipping, Josef 369, 374
Pirckheimer, Caritas 301
Pirckheimer, Willibald 302
Pius VI 233–5, 237, 248, 255
Pleijel, Hilding 323
Plummer, Marjorie E. (ed.)
    281n36
pluralism, *see* religious pluralism
Pocock, J. G. A. 1, 191n1
poetry 81, 82, 91–2
police regulation 21, 312–40
    passim
political culture 67, 103, 106, 120,
    122
Pontoppidan, Erik 39, 43–4, 55,
    162, 178, 183, 186–7, 222,
    228, 294, 303–6, 406; *see also*
    catechism
popular religion
  popular piety 144
  popular religious culture 44
  popular religious practices 242
  popular religiosity 407
  popular traditions 43
Porter, Roy 1, 191n1
Poscharsky, Peter 155n2
poverty
  poor laws 13
  poor people 111–12, 115, 118,
    129, 205, 272–3, 297
  poor region 164
  poor relief 62, 81, 302
poorhouse 104, 116–17, 121
Praetorius, Lorenz 355
Presbyterianism 3
Press Act (1766) 14–15
Press Act (1770) 14–15, 20, 287
Presser, Jacques 83

priestcraft 136; *see also* anti-Catholicism
print shops 289
Printy, Michael (ed.) 4n8
private [terminology]
  private affiliation 307
  private arrangements 319
  private concern 307
  private devotion 156, 328
  private houses 319
  private matters 113
privileges 36, 56, 100–1, 114, 202, 230, 325, 341, 357
Pro Fide et Christianismo 80
Proschwitz, Gunnar von 230n1
providence 112, 386, 398, 405, 408
Prussia 346–7, 352
public [terminology]
  public secrets 319
  public space 319
  public sphere 40–2, 49, 290, 308, 358–9
  public surveillance 319, 335
publishing 40, 59, 91, 301
Pufendorf, Samuel 197, 217
Pulma, Panu (ed.) 370n22
Puuronen, Anne (ed.) 6n16

Qualen, Henning von 324, 327
Quantin, Jean-Louis 5n13

Räisänen-Schröder, Päivi 80n3, 84n12
Raitt, Jill 159n7
Raittila, Pekka 82n4
Rantanen, Arja 80n2
Rasmussen, Carsten Porskrog 36n7, 70n44
Rasmussen, Jens 181n47
Rasmussen, Tarald (ed.) 276n30
rationalism 63, 85, 156, 159, 187, 394, 396, 402–3, 407–8
rationality 8, 20, 131, 135, 148, 300, 400; *see also* reason

Raunio, Anu 232n4
reading public 14, 36, 44, 49, 72, 214, 227
reading skills 14, 79
reason 1–2, 7, 9, 21–2, 49, 84, 94, 129, 131–2, 140, 397, 400, 402; *see also* rationality
re-Catholization 239; *see also* Pius VI
reciprocal duties 117
rectory 38–40, 65, 70
Reeh, Niels 64n21
Reeh, Tine 6n16, 20, 263–86, 300n34, 316n17, 358n52; (ed.) 16n53
Reformed tradition 19, 133–4, 230–1, 318, 322, 327, 331; *see also* Calvinism
Regourd, Francois 62n18
Rehnberg, Bertil 240
Reinalter, Helmuth 243n38
Reinhard, Wolfgang (ed.) 276n30
Reitzel-Nielsen, Erik 293n14
religious images 19, 129–54 passim, 155–90 passim, 407; *see also* liturgical objects
  devotional art 156, 158
  images of saints 135, 139–44, 157, 161–3, 167–8, 186
  mural paintings 133, 142, 173
religious pluralism 19, 21, 316–17, 322, 326n43, 329–30, 334
Renaissance 345, 395
Reuss, Jeremias Friedrich 294
Rheinheimer, Martin (ed.) 354n40
Rhyzelius, Andreas 131, 136, 145–6
Rian, Øystein 41n25, 288n2
Riksdag 15–16, 56, 64, 66, 100, 103, 230, 250–3, 322
Ringvej, Mona (ed.) 288n4
Robertson, John 1n1; (ed.) 82n5
Robertson, Ritchie 3n6
Robertson, William 194
Rococo 174

Rogberg, Samuel 131, 142–3
Røgeberg, Kristin (ed) 11n32
Roling, Bernd (ed.) 170n23
Roman Catholicism 129, 131, 133–4, 140, 193, 195, 200, 204; see also Enlightenment, Catholic; papacy; priestcraft; Vatican
reform Catholicism 3
Roman law 264
Romanticism 13, 254, 256, 395, 401, 403, 408
Rome 202, 231, 233–6, 239, 240–1, 246–9, 255–6, 300
Roos, Magnus Friedrich 404
Ropponen, Jari 109n34, 379n50
Rørdam, Holger Frederik 269n19, 299n33
Rosén, Jerker and others (eds) 117n61
Rosenblad, Carl 69
Rosengren, Josef 61n14
Rosenstand-Goiske, Peder 294
Rothe, Tyge 13
Royal Chancery 306, 364; see also central government
Royal Society of Science and Letters (*Det Kongelige Norske Videnskapers Selskap*) 10n28, 221
Royal Swedish Academy of Science 10
Rudbeck the elder, Olof 216
Ruge, Herman 42–5, 50
rural societies 33–78 passim, 364–93 passim
  rural areas 112
  rural parish churches 161–87
  rural schools 14
Russia 56, 87, 99, 119, 232, 252, 341, 386
Rydén, Göran 11n30, 12n33

Saastamoinen, Kari 7n18
sabbath crimes/observance 12, 312–40 passim
sacrilege 322
Sahlstedt, Magnus 138
Salamnius, Matthias 87
Salatowsky, Sascha (ed.) 318n19
Salminen, Seppo J. 84n12
Salsgiver, Richard O. 86n15
Samson Bloch, Coppel 305
Sandal, Henrik Paulin 179
Sanders, Hanne (ed.) 191n2
Sarasti-Wilenius, Raija 89n24
Sarvas, Anja (ed.) 379n49
Satokangas, Reija 383n65
Sauter, Michael J. 54n1
scepticism 148, 193, 198–200, 387; see also rationalism
Schartau, Henric 403–4
Schaumburg, Ernst von 317
Scheel, Jørgen Erik 347
Schilling, Heinz 58n9; (ed.) 276n30
Schings, Hans-Jürgen 268n16
Schioppa, Antonio Padoa 54n1
Schmidt, Wolfgang 403n26
Schneider, Hans 342n4
Schomburg, Bernard Leopold Volkmar von 325
Schönberg the younger, Anders 195
Schøning, Gerard 213, 219–27
Schröder, Johan Henrik 198n28
Schrøder, Urban 301n39
Schröder, Winfried (ed.) 318n19
Schubert, Anselm 322n27; (ed) 322n27
Schütz, Heinrich 395
scientific enquiry 2, 58
scientists 10, 45, 129, 372–3, 395
Scribner, Robert W. 180
Sdzuj, R. B. 159n7
Secher, Vilhelm Adolf (ed.) 288n3
secularization 185, 287
Seidlitz, August 294
Sejersted, Jørgen Magnus (ed.) 218n19
self-examination 268
Selmer, Ludvig 42n28

Sepinwall, Alyssa 5n12
Seppel, Marten 351n33;
 (ed.) 11n33
Serenius, Jacob 66
Sergel, Johan Tobias 233
sermons 38, 43, 46–7, 65, 88,
 99–126 passim, 171, 182,
 200, 312, 314, 323, 325, 327,
 332, 334, 398–9, 405
 funeral sermons 40, 398
 sermon texts 48
servants 39, 112–13, 117; see also
 bureaucracy; civil servants;
 local government
Sevio, Martta 381n59
sextons 364–393 passim; see also
 churchwardens
sexuality 344
 sexual abstinence 196, 200, 203
 sexual relations 358
Shantz, Douglas H. (ed.) 269n19
Sheehan, Jonathan 3
shrines 135, 140–1, 146, 161, 212
Sidenvall, Erik *1–29*, *54–78*,
 199n32, 207n64, 244n43, 253
Sigismund Vasa 19
Sigurdsson, Ingi 11n32
simplicity 61, 315
Sinisalo, Henna 364n1, 366n8,
 367n9, 371n24, 383n66
Sinnemäki, Kaius and others (eds)
 5n12
Sjöberg, Marja Taussi (ed.) 55n3
Sjögren, Iréne 11n32
Sjögren, Åsa Karlsson (ed.) 358n57
Sjömar, Peter and others (eds)
 158n6
Skinner, Quentin 105n24
Sköld, Peter 11n31, 364n2,
 372n26
Skovgaard-Petersen, Karen 216
Slettebø, Thomas Ewen Daltveit
 104n18
Slottved, E. (ed.) 266n9
Smidt, Claus M. 184n54

Snorri (Sturluson) 212, 220; see
 also Icelandic sagas
Snowden, Frank M. 365n5, 367n9
Soboth, Christian (ed.) 356n48
Söderblom, Nathan 255
Söderhjelm, Alma 111n42
Soininen, Gunnar 369n15
Sommervogel, Carlos 248n56
Sørensen, Øystein (ed.) 4n19
Sorkin, David 3n5, 4n8, 241n32
Sorø academy 12–13, 221, 318
Sparre, Carl 233
Specht, Gerhard 318n19
Spegel, Haquin 198n29
Spener, Philipp Jakob 342; see also
 Pietism
Spicer, Andrew 158n6, 159n7;
 (ed.) 158n6
Spierenburg, Pieter 277n31
Spittler, Ludwig 194
St Dionysius 161–2, 164–7
St Erik 191–210 passim
St Martin 168
St Olaf 129–30, 143–5
Stålhane, Henning 233n9,
 234n11–12, 246n49
Stålmarck, Torkel 396n7
Starck, Eija and Laura Starck (eds)
 373n32
statistics 11, 364–5; see also
 Commission of Statistics
 (*Tabellkommissionen*); Table
 Office (*Tabellverket*)
Stavish, Mark 243n38
Steenbuch, Hans 292
Steenvinkel, Peter Christian 182–3
Steiger, Johann Anselm 86n15
Stenbæk, Jørgen 264n7
Stiernman, Anders Anton von
 144n42; (ed.) 135n14
Stjernfelt, Frederik 15n47, 289n5
Stockholm 18–19, 57–8, 232–3,
 236, 239, 243, 245–6, 249,
 251, 255, 399
Stockhorst, Stefanie (ed.) 6n16

Stolberg-Wernigerode, Ernst von 343–4, 353
Storm, Caspar Herman von 347
Strand, Karin 83n10, 86n15, 92n30
Sträter, Udo 269n19
Stråth, Bo (ed.) 4n19
Straubel, Rolf 345n16, 346n20
Strøm, Hans 42, 44–6, 50
Strom, Jonathan 267n15; (ed.) 404n30
Struensee, Adam 355
Struensee, Carl August, 341–63 passim
Struensee, Johann Friedrich 15, 222–4, 275, 287–8, 308, 318, 341
Stuart, Charles Edward 244
Stuart, Kathy 281n36
Stubberud, Tore 42n28
Suhm, Peter 213, 219–21, 224
Sunday 64, 68, 70–1, 103, 236, 252, 312–40 passim, 406; *see also* liturgy
    Sunday service 323, 325, 330, 368
Sundbärg, Gustaf 34n3
Sundholm, Olof 145, 147
Sundin, Anders 100n4
superstition 47–9, 129, 131, 133, 139–40, 142, 146–8, 156, 159, 164, 168, 172, 177–9, 181, 204, 241, 251, 328, 407; *see also* folk magic; magic
surgery and surgeons 85–6, 90, 93, 272, 274; *see also* medicine
surveys 11, 62–3, 145, 167; *see also* vaccination
Sutcliffe, Adam 5n12
Swedenborg, Emanuel 399–400
Sweet, Rosemary 170n23

Table Office (*Tabellverket*) 11, 364–5
Tamm, Ditlev 266n11, 267n14, 275n29, 312n2, 314n9; (ed.) 266n9, 280n34, 312n2

Tammela, Joonas 18, *99–126*
Tandefelt, Henrika 241
Taube, Carl Edvard 239, 245–6, 249
teaching 7, 12–3, 62, 81, 100–2, 109, 121–2, 129, 171, 232, 247, 250, 255, 275, 318, 330, 334, 341, 381, 396, 400, 404, 407; *see also* catechism; parents
    cathedral schools 58–9
    schoolteachers 48
Tegnér, Elof (ed.) 236n20
Tegnér, Esaias 401
Teich, Mikuláš 1
Teittinen, U. K. 385n70
Ten Commandments 7, 323
Tengström, Jacob 252, 386
Tharp, Daniel Smith 296n21
theatre 223–4, 227, 230, 252–3, 395
Thjulén, Lorenz Birger 232
Thomæus, Jöran Jakob 203n52
Thomas, Keith 179n41
Thompson, James Westfall 193n8, 194n13–14
Thomsen, Marie-Louise 161n10
Thordeman, Bengt (ed.) 196n22
Thorild, Thomas 13
Three Estates, doctrine of 100–1, 108, 111; *see also* Household Code
Titlestad, Torgrim (ed.) 214n5
Tjällén, Biörn 196n23
Tjønneland, Eivind (ed.) 289n6
toleration 17, 21, 230, 236, 239, 250, 252, 254–5, 358; *see also* Edict of Toleration
    tolerant [attitudes] 20, 67, 248, 329, 356
topography 43, 45, 49, 161
Torfæus, Tormod 212–27 passim
Totzeck, Markus M. 312n1

Index

trade 11, 35, 111–13, 116, 316–17, 325, 327, 351; *see also* North Sea trade
traditional religion 67, 164
Trägård, Elias 397n12
Trap, J. P. 174n33,
Tribe, Keith 345n14, 349n25; (ed.) 11n33
Troil, Uno von 62n17, 245, 251, 253
Trondheim 35–6, 41, 110, 212, 219–20, 222–3, 289
Tulle, Hans 299–300, 311
Tunefalk, Martin 116n56
Turku (Åbo) 57–8, 79, 83–5, 91, 94, 144, 252, 366, 371–2, 374–5, 382, 386
Turpeinen, Oiva 370n22, 372n26 and 28, 373n30, 387n74
Twelftree, Graham H. (ed.) 199n32

Union and Security Act 230, 252
University of Copenhagen 21, 266, 272, 275, 287, 291, 299
Uppsala 58, 61, 148, 196, 239, 243, 245, 314
Uppsala Synod (1593) 19, 251, 253
Urpilainen, Erkki 196n19
usefulness, utility 1, 9, 61, 71, 192, 218, 367, 376, 379, 400
utilitarianism 279, 282

Väärä, Seija 379n49
vaccinations 20, 21, 364–93 passim
Vaheri, Antti 372n26
Vainio, Kirsi (ed.) 79n1
Valentin, Hugo 398n13
Valkner, Kristen 43n29
Van Damme, Stéphane (ed.) 11n30
Van Kley, Dale K. (ed.) 4n10
Van Osselaer, Tine 402
Vanhaelen, Angela 319n22
Vatican 234–5, 237

Växjö 54–78 passim
Vehmas, Simo 81n4, 85n14
Vengeborg, Mikkel (ed.) 184n52
Vergennes, Charles Gravier de 240
Viitaniemi, Ella 106n27
Viken, Øystein Lydik Idsø 42n27, 103n16, 104n18, 106n26, 108n31, 112n45, 115n54, 118n64, 121n72
Vilkuna, Kustaa H. J. 386n72; (ed.) 369n15
Virgin Mary 140, 144, 163
Virrankoski, Pentti 11n42
visitations [parochial] 48, 57, 60, 63, 65, 66n31, 72, 131, 140–3, 145, 148, 157–8, 179
Visser, Arnoud 5n13
vocation 44, 109, 111, 114, 117, 121, 328
Vogt, Helle 13n38; (ed.) 7n18
Voltaire 1, 9, 15, 193, 230, 282, 329–30, 403, 405
Vuorinen, Heikki S. 366n7, 374n34

Waaben, Knud 264n4–5, 265n6–7
Wåhlin, Christian 204
Wakefield, Andre 346n17, 352n
Walker, Nigel 264n2–3
Wallquist, Olof 54–78 passim, 253
Wandel, Lee Palmer 163n14
Ward, Joseph 319n22
Ward, W. R. 4n10
Watt, Jeffrey R. 281n36
Weber [Brilkman], Kajsa 66n32; (ed.) 191n2
Weber, Hellmuth von 281n36
Weber, Max 187
Weikert, Monica 139n28, 407n38
Werner, Yvonne Maria 20, *230–59*
Wessel, Johan Herman 223
West Indies 355; *see also* Danish colonies
Whaley, Joachim 4n9, 9n25
Whitelocke, Bulstrode 148

Whitmer, Kelly Joan 403n26
Wichman, Holger 109n37, 110n39; (ed.) 109n37
Widberg, Anders 104, 107, 116–20, 122
Wijers, Carla (ed.) 358n53
Wiking-Faria, Pablo 117n61
Wilde, Jacob 196
Willebrand, Johann Peter 316–17, 328–35
Willis, Jonathan 312n1
Wilse, Jacob Nicolai 42
Wilskman, Sven 59, 131, 139
Wilson, Bronwen (ed.) 319n22
Winberg, Ola 231n3
Wingård, Johan 245, 251
Winton, Patrik 12n33
Wirilander, Kaarlo 101n8
Witoszek, Nina 4n9
Witte, Jr., John 299n32, 312n1
Wittrock, Björn (ed.) 192n4

Wokler, Robert (ed.) 349n25
Wøldike, Marcus 294, 297–8
Wolff, Christian 10, 43, 47, 84–5, 314, 328, 403; *see also* physico-theology
Wolffianism 45, 403
Worm, Christen 292
Wucher, Agathe 318n20

Yachnin, Paul (ed.) 319n22
Ylönen, Aulikki 376n39

Zachrisson, Terese 7n20, 19, 66n31, *129–54*, 157
Zedelmaier, Helmut (ed.) 9n26
Zeeberg, Peter (ed.) 219n20
Zetlitz, Jens 223n32, 224n33
Zinzendorf, Nikolaus Ludwig von 295, 322n27, 342–4, 353, 355, 396; *see also* Moravianism; Christiansfeld

EU authorised representative for GPSR:
Easy Access System Europe, Mustamäe tee 50,
10621 Tallinn, Estonia
gpsr.requests@easproject.com

www.ingramcontent.com/pod-product-compliance
Ingram Content Group UK Ltd.
Pitfield, Milton Keynes, MK11 3LW, UK
UKHW021824140426
5217IPUK00004B/84